LUDWIG PAULI

THE ALPS
Archaeology and Early History

with 166 illustrations

THAMES AND HUDSON

For Joachim Werner
on his seventieth birthday

(half-title) Pictures on Rock II at Cemmo near Capo di Ponte in the Valcamonica (Lombardy). 2000–1700 BC.

1 (frontispiece) The Gutenberg at Balzers (Liechtenstein)–since the fourth millennium BC safe settlement place, cult centre (Ill. 88) as well as observation post on the route from the Rhine valley (impassable a little farther on) across the Luzisteig pass and on into the mountains.

Translated from the German
Die Alpen in Frühzeit und Mittelalter
by Eric Peters

© 1980 C. H. Beck'sche Verlagsbuchhandlung (Oscar Beck) München.
Revised edition 1981.

First published in Great Britain in 1984
by Thames and Hudson Ltd, London.

English translation © 1984 Thames and Hudson Ltd, London

Printed in Hungary by Kossuth Printing House

Contents

Foreword to the English-language edition 7

Preface 9

I A Million Years of History in Review 10

Traces of the first men 10

Hunters and farmers after the end of the first Ice Age 13

Economic boom through copper 17

Cultural groups and transmitted tribal names 21

Iron and salt as sources of power 23

Brennus and Hannibal cross the Alps 28

Rome conquers northern Italy and southern France 30

A victory over forty-five Alpine tribes 32

Peaceful existence in the Roman Empire 38

Germanic peoples spill over the borders 41

Powerful emperors in the toils 45

Germanic kingdoms on Roman soil 50

The new power in the North 54

Teutons and the Roman people on the northern border of the Alps 57

Charlemagne – Frank and Roman emperor 58

The empire and the duchies 60

Savoy, Habsburg and the Swiss Confederacy 61

Napoleon and the consequences 63

Problems over the new frontiers 64

II From Wattle Hut to Palace – How the People Lived 64

Off on the chase 67

The question of pile-dwellings 71

Huts of the Late Stone Age at Salzburg 77

Hill settlements in Graubünden 78

The valleys looked different 82

Farms and villages between Salzach and Rhone 82

The first towns? 88

Roman life-styles 90

Towns in occupied lands 92

He who bathes much needs much water 93

Things to see at Roman sites 96

The manorial way of life 98

Want makes people undemanding 102

Invillino and the fortified settlements at the southern border of the Alps 104

Castles and villages in the early Middle Ages 106

III The Living and the Dead – The Individual and the Community 109

Forms of burial and conceptions of the after-life 109

Life was brief 111

The hunters of the Stone Age and the first miners 112

Only a heap of ashes remains 120

Professions, careers and genealogical trees 128

The Roman heritage and Christendom 137

Burial rites and the costume of the Teutons 142

IV Religion and Art 147

Bear cult and the first depictions of human beings 148

The house altar beneath a rock shelter 149

Animal sacrifice and votive offerings to unknown powers 151

The gods of the mountains 157

The great festival 164

The world of the rock engravings 165

Sun, bird, horse and other gods 172

Jupiter and his retinue 176

Popular belief and magic 179
Hope of redemption from the East 182
Bishops and churches, monasteries and missionaries 184

V Mule-tracks, Passes and Resthouses 193

Geology and its consequences: passes and defiles 193
The first mule-tracks 196
Greeks and Etruscans discover the North 197
Salt and amber routes of the Eastern Alps 201
Carriers and sumpters, artists and merchants 202
The Celts migrate to the South 204
Hannibal and his elephants 206
The first road-building engineers 208
Inscriptions disclose repairs 210
Masterpieces of Roman road-building 212
Resthouses, customs posts and temples 217
Road maps and guide books 221
Germanic peoples on Roman roads 227
Disintegration in the early Middle Ages 227
The monasteries and the road network 229
Pilgrims and hospices 232
From post-chaise to railway 235

The first transalpine flight and the prohibition of motor-cars in Graubünden 237

VI The Basics of Living – Husbandry, Mining, Trade 239

Little fear of large animals 239
Corn, cattle and pottery 239
Wealth from the earth 242
Metal-founders, smiths, turners and glaziers 248
Salt–the white gold 250
Precious money 259
Delicacies in luxury dishes, mash in stone pots 262
Poor farmers, well-filled treasuries 266

Notes 269

Sources of illustrations 300

Index 302

Foreword to the English-language edition

Not only are the Alps a region of scenic grandeur–an aspect which few had come to appreciate until the nineteenth century–but all who inhabit their valleys and mountain slopes are the inheritors of a history that reaches back a million years.

We have only to wander amid the mountains with our eyes open, and we shall find signs of the past on every hand. Among those who succumbed to the allure of the Alps was Edward Whymper of London: having gone there as a draughtsman at the age of twenty-five, he was the first to climb the Matterhorn with native guides in 1865. Thereafter he returned to the Valais time after time; and when in a hot summer thirty years later it was reported that a large quantity of coins had been found on the Matterhorn at the edge of the permanent snow, he promptly turned his attention to the scientific evaluation of such a sensational find some 3320 m up in the mountains. His subsequent report, 'A discovery of Roman Coins on the Summit of the Théodule Pass (Matterjoch)' appeared in the Numismatic Chronicle of London in 1897.

In 1881 a certain Clarence Bicknell, who had for reasons of health set up house in Bordighera on the Riviera, saw the rock-engravings of Mont Bégo for the first time. So fascinated was he by them, that for twelve successive summers he journeyed to this desolate region amid bare rocks, in order to record everything of importance and to try and unravel its coded secrets. At his death in 1918 he was found to have left a great many drawings and photographs as well as 3000 copies of his findings, which are today housed in the eponymous Bicknell Museum at Bordighera, centre of archaeological research on the Ligurian coast between the Pyrenees and the Apennines. Bicknell's *Guide to the Prehistoric Rock Engravings in the Italian Maritime Alps* appeared in 1913 and a French edition was newly published in 1971. Quite recently other publications have appeared, in which it has been possible to augment Bicknell's work by widening its range and interpretation.

Sir John Lubbock (later Lord Avebury), who in 1865 published his famous book *Prehistoric Times*, should also be mentioned. In it he devotes a whole chapter to the Swiss 'pilebuildings' (as he called them), the investigation and evaluation of which at that time arrested the attention of every scholar concerned with the beginnings of civilization. On his journeys he had of course seen the most important find-spots with his own eyes. A year later, scientific curiosity drew him to Hallstatt (Upper Austria), known throughout the world on account of the yields from its Iron Age cemetery. He himself was invited to take part in the excavations there, together with Sir Arthur Evans, father of the excavator of Knossos, and Sir Augustus Wollaston Franks. Franks later bought a copy of the comprehensive excavation report of Johann Georg Ramsauer, who from 1848 to 1863 had unearthed nearly a thousand graves. This valuable document containing fifty-seven watercolour plates is today in the Library of the Society of Antiquaries in London.

So we see that from the very outset archaeology relating to the Alps has been associated with many eminent British scholars. I am particularly pleased, therefore, that an English-language edition of this book is being published. Based on the second German edition, it has been brought further up to date and suitably adapted. Archaeology is a branch of science which discovers something new practically every day and knows no national boundaries.

L. P.
March 1982

Preface

This book describes the early history of a region in which six States and two duchies have a share. The Alps with their geological and climatic attributes encompass a territory stretching from Haute Provence to the Wienerwald, throughout which living conditions are clearly distinguishable from those in the surrounding areas. It is of great interest to observe whether and to what extent the political forces align themselves accordingly, and how they come to terms with the circumstances with which they are faced. This is what is usually termed *History*.

But it is only in the case of the Roman period that the tide of literary sources which from time to time allow us to perceive the motives of those who are in control of events flows strongly enough to matter. Prior to that, and subsequently in the medieval period, these sources dry up altogether or merely dribble here and there, without forming so much as a rill. He who wishes to write a history of those times must above all interpret excavations that bring to light settlements, fortifications, churches, burials and hidden objects. He must often have recourse to such sources for the Roman period too. This is what is usually termed *Archaeology*.

Of course, Archaeology is in fact History. Its literal meaning, namely 'Account of the beginnings', as used by Thucydides, has nothing to do with how one obtains the information: with spade and graph paper in the field, poring over books in the library, observing from the air an old fortification half concealed in a cornfield, on foot on a Roman road, or exposed to a biting wind on a mountain pass. That is why in this book I have treated all aspects on their merits; according to the nature of the source, either one aspect or another has received a greater share of attention. The specialists must make allowances if I have occasionally ventured upon a topic without adding my own critical assessment of every detail.

This book, then, has a double purpose. In the first place it seeks to provide a readable early history of the Alpine region, beginning with the first men of the Old Stone Age on the Côte d'Azur, and going up to the coronation of Charlemagne in Rome. It concludes with a short account of further developments up until today in those parts where it seems pertinent, by sharpening the focus on change or the maintenance of the status quo. Hence places that today still offer material evidence from those times receive rather more attention.

Secondly, the Notes are intended to provide the interested general reader, as well as those who are concerned with local history, with details of the widespread literature on the subject. Emphasis has been laid on recent works, because they offer ready access to older publications. Complete coverage has not been attempted, the selection is necessarily a subjective one and to a certain extent determined by what is available in the library in Munich; I much regret that, as a result, the French-language literature on the Western Alps is somewhat limited. Here and there I go into rather more detail, in order to make it easier for scholars to check some of the views expressed: I do not always accept current opinion.

I gratefully acknowledge the very considerable assistance I received everywhere during my travels: initiation into the interconnected problems of regional geography, economics and gastronomy, information on the latest finds and literature, introduction to excavations still in progress and provision of photographic matter. The much appreciated help I received from my friends and colleagues, in particular those in Munich, was invaluable. Lack of space prevents me from singling out others for mention: sources of information are given in the Notes. I was delighted and heartened to find that friendly co-operation across the frontiers is so forthcoming.

The dedication to Joachim Werner, a Berliner resident in Munich, a researcher who spends his vacations in the Alps, a member of the generation which is still able to embrace the early history of our world from Ireland to Japan, a stimulating teacher and unrivalled organizer, expresses a gratitude that, apart from my wife Sabine, he alone can appreciate.

Munich, September 1979   L. P.

I A Million Years of History in Review

The Alpine arc stretches from the Mediterranean coast of France and northern Italy eastwards to the Karawanken range of mountains, the frontier between Austria and Jugoslavia. Beyond this comes a less high hilly terrain, which then gives place to the Balkan mountains. Thus it takes in three regions that were at all times subject to differing climatic, geological and cultural influences.

At their southwestern end the Alps drop steeply down to the Mediterranean Sea; both as trading area and climatically this narrow coastal strip must therefore be counted as belonging to the Mediterranean zone. Bordering the eastern regions of the Alpine range from Vienna to Ljubljana lie the wide Hungarian plains and the valleyed countryside of the Balkans. Here influences from the East and Southeast jointly impinge on the mountain area; its continental climate is characterized by hot summers and cold winters. By far the greater part of the Alps, however, forms–and not just viewed from the present day–the border between Central and Southern Europe. Although the climatic and cultural differences are today still immediately apparent to anyone who crosses the Alps, they are not as clearly marked, particularly in the cultural field, as on entering the two aforementioned border regions of the Alpine range in the East and the West. This can be traced back to the first appearance of man.

Traces of the first men

Climatic fluctuations of long duration and extending over wide areas have accounted for the perpetual alternation between cold and warm periods, going as far back as it has been possible to ascertain the earth's climate. The 'Ice Ages' have become proverbial, and every cool summer gives rise to speculations in the newspapers as to whether we are not entering another ice age. But those of us who have set eyes–or even paid one-and-a-half Swiss francs to set foot–on the most accessible glacier in the Alps, the Rhône glacier below the Furka pass, return home with the comforting thought that they personally will not have to face such an eventuality.

For in the Ice Age things looked somewhat different. From the high altitude regions of the Alps the glaciers reached far down into the valleys, at their northern extremity even into the Alpine foreland. Only the highest mountain-tops rose above the many-hundred-metres-thick sheet of ice. Moving incredibly slowly (perhaps the present-day rate of flow of the Greenland glaciers, some 20 m in a day, offers the best comparison) the glaciers rolled great masses of earth and rock before and underneath them. This was then deposited as moraines at what had been their head and flanks when the ice had retreated during the warm periods, creating the ridged landscape of the foot-hills. Barriers of hills now dammed the streams, which had to find new routes; the thawed water from the glaciers filled channels and basins, resulting in the formation of countless lakes. These are among the principal tourist attractions of our day both north and south of the Alps.

However, the very fact that in the South these lakes scarcely extend beyond the fringe of the Alps, whereas in the North nearly all of them lie beyond the mountain area

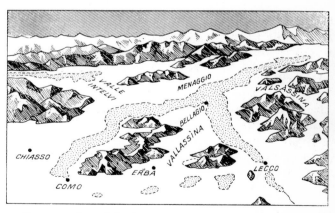

2 Reconstruction of the ice-age glaciation of the area round the Lake of Como. When the ice was at its thickest only the summits of the mountains were visible. Present-day lakes and places have been added for better orientation.

proper, shows that already in those early times contrasting climatic conditions were encountered. This can be seen even more clearly in the southern parts of the Western Alps, an area for the most part never covered by ice. It is not merely the more southerly latitude that is responsible for this but predominantly the proximity of the Mediterranean Sea with its compensatory effect on the temperature. It is hardly surprising, therefore, that the earliest traces of man in the Alpine zone are found in this region.[1] That in the whole of the rest of Europe Romania alone has produced an authenticated find of corresponding antiquity underlines their significance, though it is not possible to gauge what part chance has played in this strange distribution. For the chronological classification of the earliest human skeletal remains and tools rests on a geological and biological framework which enables us to arrive at the date of the deposits that contain the relevant finds. And a sufficiently accurate framework of this kind is not at present to be had outside the Mediterranean area.[2]

Nevertheless, it is certain that the finds from the 'Grotte du Vallonnet' on the Riviera at Roquebrune–Cap-Martin (Alpes-Maritimes), only a few kilometres east of Monaco, are about a million years old.[3] It was by determining the dates of the associated animal bones and plant remains, as well as calculating the Earth's magnetism, that this estimate was arrived at. The cave was sought out by its prehistoric inhabitants at a time when cold and dry conditions prevailed. In the course of time human refuse caused the strata to be covered with a layer of rubbish, which can likewise be dated. From all this it could be ascertained that human beings occupied the cave at some period during the third of the six Alpine ice ages.

These ice ages, taking the earliest first, are named–in alphabetical order for easy memorizing–after rivers in the Suebian and Bavarian foreland: Biber, Donau, Günz, Mindel, Riss and Würm. The first two, scarcely recognizable any longer geologically, have only recently been identified; during each of the six, moreover, fluctuations occurred which caused a number of substantial inroads of the ice. Applying the above nomenclature, the finds in the 'Grotte du Vallonnet' can be dated to the beginning of the Günz ice age.[4]

The archaeologist cannot deduce from the human remains themselves that prehistoric caves were occupied by man, only from the tools that he has left behind. These are quite simple implements consisting of segments chipped from large pebbles that were doubtless found on the nearby shore. The resulting edge, or point, will have served for cutting, scraping or hammering.

Such examples of the earliest tools occur not only in the Alpine region but all over Europe. What the people who used them looked like we do not as yet know. From the succeeding epoch comes a lower jaw-bone, found at Mauer near Heidelberg (in a stratum containing similarly primitive tools) which has been attributed to 'the first unquestionable human being',[5] *homo erectus (heidelbergensis)*, a type older still than the more familiar *homo neanderthalensis* and *homo sapiens*. Thus, the 'Grotte du Vallonnet' is in fact witness to the very first phase of 'man's' coming to settle in Europe, presumably from Africa. This makes us all the more anxious to know whether we shall one day find human bones from those ancient times in Europe, and whether they will prove to correspond to *Australopithecus*, so far discovered only in South and East Africa, or already to *homo erectus*.

The significance of this find may be judged by the fact that the next piece of evidence we have of human life in the Alpine area must be dated no less than 600,000 years later. It too, was found in the Côte d'Azur, within the purlieus of Nice (Nizza), about 26 m above today's sea-level, but then close to the shore.[6] The Günz ice age was over, a warmer interstadial had followed and the Mindel ice age set in. At that time, some 380,000 years ago, human beings had settled by a small spring. They lived in huts with supporting posts, and usually containing a hearth. The place served as a base for the elephant chase and was visited for many years in succession (p. 69). The hunters also produced their stone tools here, as the presence of countless chips shows. Many of these tools still resemble the primitive implements from the 'Grotte du Vallonnet', though more developed forms also occur, namely genuine handaxes, which are better finished.

So the handaxes–contrary to popular usage of the term– were by no means man's oldest tools, since they had undergone a lengthy evolutionary process. Once the selected pebble had been hammered out upon a larger stone (anvil technique), he learned–at about the time to which the Nice finds belong–to give it a finish with smaller stone

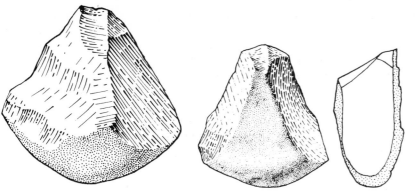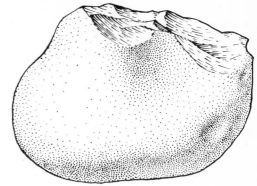

3 The stone implements from the Grotte du Vallonet in the Côte d'Azur are a million years old. Suitable pebbles were chipped so as to obtain points and cutting edges.

tools. Soon after, it was realized that better results could be obtained by using chisels made of wood or bone; in particular, this technique allowed thin blades and small points to be produced, which had till then played no part in the stock of implements, because they had only come about by accident in the production of larger tools.

Since the simple handaxes continued to be made over a long time-span, however, the single finds or find-complexes with only a few tools are often difficult to date with any accuracy. Here too, therefore, it helps to fit them into some sort of climatic or geological framework. This applies, for instance, to an early type of handaxe from the once open site known as 'Cava Vecchia' at Quinzano, in the province of Verona.[7] The stratification here points to the Riss ice age and the handaxe would appear to originate from a somewhat warmer, interstadial period. This find-spot likewise lies at the southern border of the Alps, not reached by the ice except perhaps in unusually cold phases. Man had not yet ventured into the mountains; not even during warmer intervals, when we may assume the climatic conditions to have been favourable.

The conquest of the Alpine region by man began, according to our present knowledge, in the Riss/Würm Interglacial, that is some 100,000 years ago. It is to this time that the finds from the 'Drachenloch' above Vättis in the Tamina valley (Canton St Gallen), a short distance west

of the bend of the Rhine at Chur, may be attributed. The 'Drachenloch' is 2445 m above sea-level, and its chief interest lies in the fact that, though no recognizable tools were found there, traces of hearths in geologically datable strata indicate the 'highly probable' presence of man.[8] Finds included also what could be stone implements or chips, but since the material is limestone these cannot be identified for certain as artefacts by applying the same criteria as to granite or flint.

The finds from other caves in Switzerland have yielded more positive evidence of stone tools.[9] They can be attributed to the warmer phase of the Würm ice age (roughly 40,000 to 70,000 years ago). Two of these caves are situated in the Simmental south of Bern, the 'Schnurenloch' and the 'Chilchli' respectively; though admittedly they yielded only a few stone chips. More significant and more numerous are the finds from the 'Wildkirchli' on the Säntis. Although made of quartzite, which is far from easy to work, these tools already betray a considerable deftness on the part of those who made them.

The Swiss picture shows particularly clearly that the lower Alpine approaches were also settled and, as was to be expected, a lot more densely. The sparseness of settlement in the central areas of Switzerland can be regarded as apparent only, owing to the fact that the final advance of the ice during the Würm ice age overlaid or wholly destroyed the dwelling-places of the preceding millennia in the lowlands. For in the adjacent region of the Jura to the west numerous find-spots occur, mainly caves in which traces of occupancy have been preserved. The caves in the Jura, like those in the Alps, should thus be regarded not as evidence of long-term high-altitude settlement but rather as temporary abodes of man at favourable times of the year when he was indulging in the coveted chase. This would also account for the paucity of finds as compared with the caves of western France and a few on the Riviera, which, having been more permanently occupied, yielded vast quantities of tools.

In the Western Alps north of the Côte d'Azur only few find-spots from this early period have come to light. The earliest is probably the settlement of Chanoz-Curson.[10] It may date back to the Mindel ice age and could be contemporary with the Nice finds. Maybe it should not be regarded as belonging to the Alpine region, however, lying as it does a short distance from the Rhône, barely 20 km north of Valence. Venturing rather closer to the edge of the Alps, a group of people established the settlement at Vinay;[11] from here they faced the first ridge of the Alps, where Vercors with its deep gulleys drops westward, but they had chosen an appreciably more favourable location on the edge of the Isère valley, barely 200 m up, and on the sunny side. The Vinay finds can be dated to the end of the Riss ice age. Also in the Western Alpine region around Grenoble once-occupied caves are found but they contain only leavings more recent than the Old Stone Age.

In the Eastern Alps nearly all the caves that show definite signs of having been occupied in the Old Stone Age are located in the Austrian province of Styria;[12] the occupants had worked their way up from the Hungarian plain. It is hardly surprising, then, that the environs of the two most important caves, the Repolust cave (named after its discoverer and having an altitude of 525 m) and the Drachenhöhle at Mixnitz (altitude 949 m), both situated between Graz and Bruck a.d. Mur,[13] presented no particular climatic problems. Whether these caves were occupied all the year round is open to doubt, even though during the warm intervals the winter snowfall will have been less than today's. We may assume that the Repolust cave was first visited during the Riss/Würm intermediate phase, some 100,000 years ago, whilst the finds from the Drachenhöhle belong in the Würm I/II Interstadial. Only the Salzofenhöhle in the eastern Toten Gebirge[14] is at an altitude (2005 m) that compares with those encountered in Switzerland; this renders all the more debatable its precise dating, which may still be in the Riss/Würm interme-

diate phase. All these caves–and there are one or two less important ones–were found to contain quite primitive stone tools. No recorded observations of a comparable nature relating to the northern edge of the Alps between Vienna and south Germany are as yet available.

To the finds dating from this time that relate to the Inner Alpine region the inclusive term 'Alpine Palaeolithic' has been applied; but this designation does not imply a cultural unity such as is ascribed to integrated areas of later date.[15] It is a question of a few adventurous folk who had only temporarily left the favourably situated Alpine fringes and made for the mountain area. Since for this period we have been unable to establish any convincing typological or even cultural differentiation between the individual settlement groups in the Rhône valley, the Po plain, in Hungary and Lower Austria, the 'Alpine Palaeolithic' can scarcely be expected to have earned a niche of its own.

This is best seen in the find situation along the Riviera; here, in the numerous caves centred around Grimaldi and the 'Balzi Rossi', all the various evolutionary stages of stone implements are represented.[16] Since many of the caves served as living quarters all the year round over long periods, the incidence of finds is correspondingly large. Occasionally they also contained human burials, enabling us to hazard guesses as to the build of these people.[17] *Homo erectus*, already referred to above, developed into *Homo neanderthalensis*, it would seem, during the Riss/Würm intermediate phase. His skull still differs substantially from that of *Homo sapiens*. It is characterized by a retreating forehead, pronounced cheek-bones, convex side walls and a strongly developed facial bone structure. Yet the capacity of the skull is not inferior to that of present-day peoples. *Homo sapiens*, on the other hand, known since the Würm I/II Interstadial (*c.* 35,000 years ago), resembles modern man so closely, that any further development may be disregarded. Nearly all known human types in Central Europe belong to the race that is named after the find-spot Crô Magnon in France. The two skulls of a negroid 'Grimaldi-race' on the Riviera were only combined in error. It is difficult at the present time to give in any detail the extent to which migrations from the Southeast, that is from the Eastern Mediterranean and Near Eastern region, contributed towards the emergence of *Homo sapiens*.

Hunters and farmers after the end of the Ice Age

When the last ice age finally came to an end, the people of that time did not celebrate the event, no date was imprinted on their minds. For climatic processes such as that take place so slowly as to be almost unnoticed, and in those days but few people lived long enough to enable them to gauge the changing climate over a few decades at the least from, say, the farthest extension of the glaciers. And did they, indeed, have so much as an inkling that many thousands of years earlier there had been warm periods during which their ancestors had ventured into the Inner Alpine region?

Around 10,000 BC the warm period in which we are still living began, and no one can tell how long it will last; for none of the hypotheses put forward to account for climatic fluctuations provides a reliable explanation. The glaciers receded, the large ones in the wide valleys, like those of the Adige, Inn, Rhine and Rhône, at the slowest rate. The inhospitable ground became exposed, either infertile rock scoured by the ice or great masses of rubble which the glaciers had carried along. The melt-waters channelled their way through the valleys, gnawed ever deeper into the detritus, were dammed up by barriers of rock to form lakes or gathered in hollowed-out valley basins. The Lake of Geneva and the Lake of Constance grew to about twice their present size, extending far into the upper reaches of the Rhône and the Rhine respectively. Large stretches of valley were still impassable, being filled by continuous chains of lakes. It took centuries, indeed millennia, for the masses of river-borne rubble to settle in many of the lakes, or for these to disappear; the final stage saw the formation of wide fenlands, many of which were only drained during recent centuries, so allowing proper communications between one region and another. Fresh lakes were, however, often formed by great rock falls—no rarity even in historical times—or when the debris pushed forward by the side-streams dammed up the water until it had dug a new outlet.[18]

The climate did not by any means change regularly in one direction only; the melting of the glaciers naturally meant higher temperatures but these only rose quite gradually. In the main, the millennia up until about 6000 BC were characterized by relatively moderate temperature and precipitation, more or less comparable with those of today. Gradually precipitation became heavier, initially with little change in temperature ('Boreal'); but from about 5500 BC this was accompanied by a substantial increase in the average warmth over the year. This latter period is known as 'Atlantic'; it set in shortly before the beginning of the Neolithic (or Late Stone Age) and ended approximately with its close. The ensuing period, the 'Sub-boreal', coincides with the Bronze Age. It then became somewhat colder and drier, until about 700 BC a swing to greater humidity followed, while the temperature appeared to change but little.

The climatic developments outlined above apply of course only in a broad sense to the Alpine region. Analysis of the strata in caves points to countless deviations within the main climatic phases, and naturally the climate in the French Maritime Alps was—as it is today still—so essentially different from that, say, in the Central Alps with their 3000 m-high summits, that a parallel development is scarcely to be expected.

The land that had been freed from the ice was first claimed by the plants—a process that was both difficult and protracted. There was, after all, a complete absence of humus, just barren stony ground. The plants could no doubt gain a foothold most rapidly on the lake shores, where small-grained deposits made soil production easier. From there they fought their way into the valleys and finally up on to the heights: first lichens and mosses, then grasses, bushes and shrubs, and ultimately the trees, which are so sensitive to climatic variations: first birch, pine and willow, then hazel and oak and lastly fir and larch. To take an example, during the 'Boreal' phase the tree-line climbed to 2400 m in the northern French Alps, which is about its present level.

The plants were succeeded by the animals: aurochs, bison, deer, wild boar, hare, ibex and chamois; but also of course the insects, birds and other creatures. The non-carnivores were stalked by beasts of prey: bear, wild cat, lynx, wolf and fox. Even so, man learned how to subsist: he gathered fruits and berries and killed game.

Small groups of people undoubtedly ventured anew into the wide valleys and more accessible heights.[19] Many places, it is true, they will have sought out only in the summer, with winter driving them back into the dales. Thus, in South Tyrol we know of a number of find-spots on passes, which, to judge from their meagre contents, could only have served as seasonal quarters: for example, a few flint tools attest the presence of man on the Sellajoch (2214 m), the Reiterjoch (1980 m) and the Jochgrimm (1993 m). The most important finds come from a camping place under an overhang in the Plan de Frea (1930 m), just below the Grödnerjoch.[20] Their nature points to a period known as the Epipalaeolithic (that is, end of the 'Old Stone Age') or Mesolithic ('Middle stone Age'). Attributable to the same cultural stage is a settlement site beneath a cliff overhang at Vatte di Zambana (Trento prov.) with several occupation levels and a burial of a woman aged about fifty;[21] radiocarbon tests gave a date between 6000 and 5300 BC. Of somewhat later date (4000 ± 100 BC) are stone tools and a hearth at Masocco (Graubünden).[22] These finds, then, relate to a period preceding the Neolithic—one of the most significant turning points in the prehistory of Europe.

In the Near East, in the 'Fertile Crescent', with Mesopotamia as its heartland, man had tamed animals, domesticated and bred them from as early as *c.* 6000 BC. He had also learnt, not only to gather certain grasses for their seed-grains, but to cultivate and develop them into what is known today as 'corn'. It was not long before he hit on the idea of firing vessels made out of moulded clay, and this he followed by not only making tools out of flint and obsidian but laboriously chipping and grinding natural rock into axes and clubs, and even boring holes through it.

These four skills spread gradually—though not all simultaneously—to the West; they led to a new way of life, namely farming, which was based on agriculture and cattle-breeding, and which with the introduction of new techniques helped man to get the better of his surroundings. This marked the beginning of the Neolithic, the 'New Stone Age', and it is evident that it set in at different times in different regions, depending on how quickly the new methods were adopted.

This 'neolithicizing' reached the Alpine region by two routes: from the South, that is from the Mediterranean, and from the Southeast overland diagonally across the Balkans. Here we see the spread of a culture which derived its name 'Bandkeramik' or Linear Pottery culture from the style of decoration on its pottery.

The way of life of the Bandkeramik folk was based on agriculture. They dwelt in large, long houses made of beams with wattle and daub in between, tended substantial herds of cattle, cultivated the land around the settlements comprising several farmsteads; but every few years they had to change the location of their settlements since the ground, through the use to which it was put (no fertilizers, no crop rotation to help the soil to recover), could no longer offer a sufficient yield. They selected ground that was easy to till but not too light, favouring loess in particular. So the spread of this culture—about which much has been written—was confined to fertile basins and loess terrain:[23] the wide Hungarian plains, Lower Austria, Lower Bavaria, central Germany and the Rhineland as far as Holland. Newly arrived and established settlers, who adopted the new agricultural life, took no interest in the mountain terrain of the Alps with its narrow valleys. They did not need to expend their energies on less fertile ground, for the land was then still so sparsely inhabited, that each could find a livelihood wherever he wished. Thus, distribution maps of settlements with Bandkeramik show very clearly how this culture by-passed the Alps in the North, while in the region between Basel and the Lake of Constance it virtually did not cross the Upper Rhine toward the South.[24]

At this time, say from 4500/4000 BC on, people were of course living in the Alpine valleys but they remained generally unaffected by the new developments introduced by the Bandkeramik folk. They adhered to the old way of life and style of husbandry, adopting only gradually the harvesting methods, the cattle-breeding, the pottery-making and the improved stone implements, with modifications their surroundings called for (p. 240f.).

On the southern fringe of the Alps the situation was somewhat different. True, neolithic find-complexes occur also in the Ligurian and Provençal littorals but these have little to do with the uniform Bandkeramik. Here, too, the people kept domestic animals (sheep, goats, cattle, pigs and the dog) and harvested corn, yet they would not appear to have led a 'farming' life. They still dwelt for the most part in caves or beneath cliff overhangs, seldom in round huts; on the coast they relied for their subsistence on catching fish and gathering shells. The shells came in useful, too, for decorating pottery; their serrated edges

Vorherrschaft/Einfluß

were pressed into the clay while still moist, several such impressions serving to make horizontal bands or clusters of lines. For this reason archaeologists have named this Mediterranean-oriented culture–corresponding to Bandkeramik–'cardial ware', after the shell *cardium edule* that was used, or 'Impressed pottery'. It penetrated only a short distance inland; a few find-spots occur in the Maritime Alps and in Haute Provence,[25] but the entire Po plain appears to have been outside its range, above all the South Alpine fringe.

During the Middle Neolithic the economy of the individual groups of inhabitants did not change materially. Agriculture and cattle-breeding gradually encroached on the chase, the technique of toolmaking was improved but there were no decisive advances. The greater potentialities for producing things and gaining ascendancy over the natural surroundings resulted in an increase in the population; this in turn led to an extension of the territories settled, so that the 'neolithicizing' process impinged more and more upon the Alpine region. The valleys, insofar as they were not marshy or endangered by flooding, were cultivated, as were the sunlit terraces above.[26] This was admittedly a slow process, for the warm and humid climate of the Atlantic phase had, particularly in the broader valleys with their low altitude and plentiful supply of water, caused an all but impenetrable forest to grow up; this had to be painstakingly cleared unless it was decided to resort to the margins of the valleys without further ado. Mühe / Aufhellung/ Traben Umstände.

The most important key to the identification of time-horizons is the pottery, the form and decoration of which underwent frequent stylistic changes; from these one can deduce, furthermore, from which parts the people moved farther up into the Alpine region. Particularly significant is the fact that from the middle Neolithic on, the pottery was decorated not only with incised or impressed designs, but also painted. This practice seems to have spread from the Eastern Mediterranean and Southeast Europe, but it did not quite reach the Alpine region: moving up from the South, it stopped at the Apennines, while in the Balkan area it did not get beyond Hungary, Lower Austria and Burgenland. North of the Alps styles of decoration were developed which perpetuated the old tradition of incising and punctating, whereas west of the Alps and in the Po

plain wholly undecorated pottery was favoured. Indeed, the Chassey culture (named after the find-spot near Chalons-sur-Saône) with its undecorated pottery spread across all southern and eastern France, as well as into the Western Alps.[27] Closely related to it is the Cortaillod culture in Switzerland,[28] and in northern Italy the long-lasting Lagozza culture likewise belongs in this category.[29] The last-named succeeded a brief phase featuring vessels with a square mouth,[30] an oddity that was not repeated for thousands of years thereafter.

These names, however, convey little to the layman, the important point being that the Alpine region participated in the developments taking place on all sides in the surrounding areas, but is not to be regarded as a unified cultural entity. The people who ventured into relatively inhospitable districts were all too fully occupied in coping with their arduous existence to find time to emancipate themselves from the milieu to which they were accustomed, in sufficient measure to work out for themselves an independent approach to living, handicrafts and art. Few of the basic attributes that characterized the Neolithic–complete adherence to the farming way of life and settlement in fairly large communities–were in evidence in the Alpine region at this time. Advantage was taken of the new achievements in the economic and technical fields but these did not lead to fresh impulses. The mountains still constituted a region where the people who were particularly venturesome, or who did not wish to live in settlements in the foreland, made do with the minimum requirements for survival.

In the Swiss foreland alone the 'Cortaillod culture' and its neighbouring peoples and successors introduced the characteristic lake-shore type of settlements which continued there for more than 2000 years. This led to the concept of the 'pile-dwelling' or 'lake-dwelling', now become almost proverbial and still the subject of debate in learned circles (p. 71f.). Yet the Cortaillod culture with its Western character was still predominantly orientated towards hunting, though corn was grown. By contrast, the cultures of eastern Switzerland with their more northeasterly orientation can be distinguished by the presence of a greater proportion of domestic animal bones in the settlements.[31]

This cultural and economic division in Switzerland was

arrested for a while at the transition to the late Neolithic, when the Horgen culture,[32] a new complex exerting in fact a rather primitive influence presumably coming from eastern France, was superimposed on the entire area. This may have been caused by the immigration of an unspecified number of people, though we do not know the manner in which they took possession of the land.

This, however, brings us to a time which has been labelled the late or even the final Neolithic, though in recent years a new terminology has been introduced which refers to this period already as the 'Copper Age'.[33] The reason for this was the occurrence of isolated copper objects in the related archaeological cultures, though these are confined to insignificant pieces, utility adornments (such as pins) or awls; and they are, at this early stage, merely hammered and not cast. For those who regard the universal use of copper and later of bronze (a superior alloy of copper and tin) and the mastery of the technical problems they present as the real break-through in the early history of Central Europe, the term 'Copper Age' has an artificial ring. For at this initial stage copper was nothing more than an intriguing new substance, much as was gold, which could be picked up here and there in its pure state and hammered into shape. It is to be assumed that at that time the people themselves were not aware of having made a discovery that would revolutionize crafting and technique in the space of two to three centuries. By the use of hindsight we now see how far back man's first hesitant confidence in copper can be traced. But by comparison with a similar situation of much later date, namely the discovery of iron, it is safe to say that it never occurred to anyone at the time that he or his village community were taking part in a technical revolution, just because they possessed an object made out of the new, ruddily gleaming and malleable material.

For a time life now proceeded along accustomed lines, both inside the Alpine region and beyond it. The technical

4 Finds of the 'Corded Ware' culture in Switzerland from the transition period from the Old Stone Age to the Bronze Age. Typical artefacts are vessels bearing designs made by punctating or impressing with cords (hence the name) as well as perforated axe-heads. Early 2nd millennium BC. Ht of beaker 11 cm. Historisches Museum, Bern.

potentialities remained as before, as did the settlement pattern and the commonplace nature of the objects of daily life, above all the pottery. Nevertheless, now for the first time we can detect direct contacts across the main Alpine ridge that do not pertain to general phenomena alone. Thus, in the Aosta valley and sporadically also in South Tyrol are to be found graves in the form of large cists made of stone slabs, which undoubtedly have affinities with corresponding phenomena in the Valais and southern Germany respectively (pp. 113ff.). On the other hand, the 'pile-dwellings' at the Mondsee and the Attersee in Upper Austria are certainly not attributable to direct influences from the Swiss midlands. They simply show how comparable settlements at the Lake of Constance or—somewhat later—at the Lago di Ledro or in Fiavè in northern Italy adopted a settlement pattern that was best suited to the geographical and economic conditions.

As was only to be expected, the Balkans exerted a cultural influence on the East Alpine region, whereas the eastern French cultures influenced the West. Whilst in the South the settlers ventured somewhat farther up the valleys, in the North the Alpine ridge constituted a scarcely penetrable barrier. Nothing lured the settlers into snow-bound valleys and inhospitable heights, even though the land, wherever it was at all fertile, would definitely have allowed folk to subsist.

Economic boom through copper

All this was changed as soon as it was realized that the Alps contained copper deposits and that these could be recovered. Copper—this was not only a new substance that could be used for ornaments, implements and weapons but one that possessed technical potentialities, particularly when alloyed with ten per cent or so of tin, to produce a resistant and more easily cast bronze: efficient methods of working it through casting replaced the laborious hammering and grinding of stone implements. It was now possible to produce entirely new forms—pins, for instance, could be given all manner of different heads—while the bone and shell adornments hitherto favoured all but disappeared. What is more, an object did not lose its intrinsic value, even when it got broken or went out of fashion, for the craftsman could reuse the bronze after smelting it. The

5 Copy in flint of a copper dagger. The grip is made of wood and attached to the blade with a wrapping. Found at the lakeside settlement of Vinelz (canton Bern). Early 2nd millennium BC. *L 19.6 cm. Historisches Museum, Bern.*

Bronze Age provided the Alpine region with an economic boom comparable only to the growth of lucrative tourism in our own century.

How to work copper was not a discovery of the inhabitants of the Alps. The art was known in the Near East for over 1000 years prior to reaching Central Europe shortly after 2000 BC. We can trace quite clearly how the related skills spread to the Balkans, groping their way so to speak up the Danube, until in Central Europe they encountered another diffusion-stream which followed the Mediterranean coast, using the Iberian peninsula as its base. Many decades, indeed centuries, were to pass, before Northern Europe, which has no appreciable copper deposits, had benefited from this advance.[34]

It was not, moreover, a question of the diffusion of a cut-and-dried method for the alloying process. Craftsmen, anxious to discover the best way to form an alloy of the rather soft raw copper (once it had been realized, indeed, that metal as such was a workable substance able to be transmuted), experimented widely so as to adapt it to their requirements. There is no need to go into details here (cf. pp. 250ff.), though it must already be evident how much the initiative and mobility of individual persons was responsible for disseminating knowledge of such phenomena. After all, somebody who had acquired a copper pin from an itinerant trader, or had been given one by a generous host, was far from being able on that account to make such an object himself, let alone master the whole production process from the reduction of the ore to the skilled finishing of the piece.

We are now able to understand why such progress was a slow one in prehistoric times; above all, it allows us to see clearly what an important part geographical consider-

ations played: physical distance from the point of departure usually indicates also a time factor. On the other hand we must beware of assuming that the technical (and likewise the economic, artistic, political and religious) advances obeyed quasi-natural laws and spread like ripples round a stone thrown into the water. It required also the willing acceptance of individuals and communities, a factor we should not underestimate.[35] It was in Central Europe in particular that there seems to have been opposition between the 'pro-copper' and the 'anti-copper' factions, but only for one or two centuries during the transition phase between the Late Stone Age and the Bronze Age.[36] Here archaeological behaviour patterns of regional communities come into play which did not immediately connect with each–theoretically available–fresh innovation. Naturally, economic considerations have also to be taken into account, for initially a bronze axe was many times more costly than a handmade one of stone, and the differences in the way they were used were not so great as to necessitate any additional investment.[37] It was not until copper was readily accessible and available in substantial amounts–was, in other words, to be obtained without difficulty at any time (tin, it should be mentioned here, had always to be imported from farther away–in fact mainly from Cornwall–since it is not native to the Alps)–that bronze became the obvious material for virtually all practical purposes, where stone, horn, bone and shells had previously been used.

There was doubtless a transition phase when the very existence of the metal had created demands which it could not fully satisfy, simply because there were insufficient quantities available. It was then that horn and bone came to fill the gap, and this to an extent previously unknown and never repeated.[38] That applies as much to implements as to articles of adornment. It accounts, too, for the presence of stone axes and bone needles that are copied from metal exemplars: the form itself was up-to-date, being designed to suit the new material, whereas unnecessary trouble–in the functional sense–was taken to copy this form in the traditional materials. From this we can deduce, furthermore, that the exploitation of the Alpine copper deposits proceeded only slowly, that a lengthy phase of prospecting and testing took place, much reliance being placed on the initiative and expertise of individuals.

In Central Europe at around this time a culture group made its appearance, to which the name 'Bell Beaker folk' has been applied because of the characteristic shape of their pottery vessels; they have been linked with the activities just described, in particular the search for the coveted copper. These people can also be singled out on anthropological grounds, by the shape of their skulls, which distinguishes them from the other inhabitants of Central Europe; they were, that is to say, aliens.[39] Their graves have yielded disproportionately large quantities of copper and bronze artefacts, and a distinctly warrior-like element (bows and arrows) is a feature of the male burials. Until a few years ago it was thought that they could have been expert 'prospectors' seeking copper, who might in this way have initiated the Central European Bronze Age. But of late this theory has been discounted since it seems unlikely that these people all migrated from one specific area.[40] A self-contained community of miners, smiths and traders (somewhat akin to the gypsies) seems less and less likely the more we think about it. We must bear in mind, too, that the area of distribution of the 'Bell Beaker' burials (there are virtually no proper settlements) ends for the most part before reaching the edge of the Alps and that the places that are associated with the earliest copper-mining yielded no 'Bell Beaker' material whatsoever. A significant exception are the graves at Sion-Petit-Chasseur (see pp. 113ff.) in which, too, some anthropologically 'alien' persons were buried.

So we still do not know who were the first people to discover copper in the Alps, or to understand how to take advantage of it. That the indigenous inhabitants soon played a big part in doing so and quickly learned the necessary skills is clear; and this is confirmed, moreover, by archaeological evidence, in that there is no sign of any alien element at the relevant find-spots.

Copper deposits are to be found above all in the Salzburg province; in the Mitterberg district around Mühlbach, near Bischofshofen, mining is still being carried on under the flanks of the Hochkönig. In addition, there are countless smaller deposits that are no longer worth working but which were attractive enough for early man, and in some instances for his medieval descendants, to treat them as a source of livelihood. Such sites occur more or less all over the Alpine region but only a few of them were sufficiently

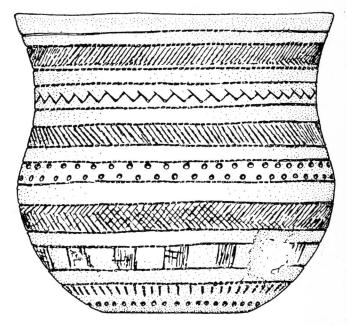

6 *Their shape, which underwent very little change, has given the Early Bronze Age 'Bell beakers' their name. They are restricted almost wholly to graves, and in the Inner Alpine region occur only at Sion in the Valais. 18th–17th century* BC. *Ht 11.4 cm. Musée Valère, Sion.*

productive to meet more than local requirements. Apart from Salzburg, they are to be found in East and North Tyrol, in fewer numbers in South Tyrol/Trentino, Lower Austria, Switzerland and the French Alps. It is difficult to determine which of the places where copper occurred were actually exploited, since the finding of associated galleries, waste dumps and smelting-places is all too frequently dependent on the chance observations of local people or on specific field research.

In the area beyond the borders of the Alps copper was recoverable only in central Germany (Thuringia, Erzgebirge) and central Italy.[41] This helps us to gauge how things now stood in the Alpine region; all at once it seems to have become the focal point of the economy of a large territory and had to provide many people with the new metal, and it profited accordingly.

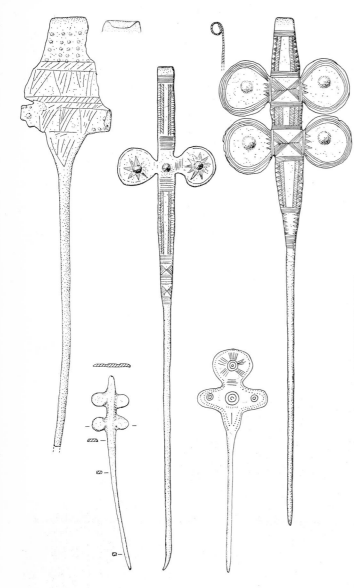

7 *Copper, the new material, encouraged people in many districts to parade their wealth in a showy manner. Long costume pins with broad hammered-out and ornamented heads were the height of fashion in the Valais and Graubünden in the Early Bronze Age. 17th–16th century* BC. *L of largest pin 30.9 cm.*

Nevertheless the number of cultural developments of a permanent nature that took place in the Alpine region at this time was limited. True, areas previously visited only intermittently became settlements and transalpine trading routes gained in importance; yet it is fairly evident that even during the Bronze Age events were determined by the cultures that lay outside the mountain area. Only in their life style did the peoples adapt themselves to the particular geographical conditions (hill settlements were favoured); articles of daily use (pottery, weapons, utensils, adornment) were modelled as before on prototypes of the surrounding regions. It is significant in this context that the Central European zone was the deciding factor; for the north Italian forms derive in large measure from the North, particularly where metal objects are concerned.[42] This means, among other things, that when working out the chronology of the Bronze Age for the South Alpine/north Italian zone one must always cast a side-glance at conditions north of the Alps. Only in the Valais was a local group able to establish itself which is recognizable by its characteristic metal forms, above all the large, richly decorated pins for garments. It is all the stranger, therefore, that this group lost its independence again in the Middle Bronze Age.[43] Maybe a brief (economic) boom during the earliest Bronze Age, which rapidly depleted the copper deposits, accounted for this.

During the Bronze Age a warm, fairly dry climate prevailed, and this encouraged people to move into places higher up. The results of this were manifold. Prospectors out to locate the coveted copper, not having to battle so hard against inclement weather conditions, could devote more time to searching out high-yielding sites. Moreover, with their bronze axes and knives the valley slopes and margins could be more thoroughly cleared, the cultivable ground grew in extent; more people found living-space and sustenance for a tolerable existence. The export of copper to areas beyond the mountains promoted communications with places outside and at the same time added to Inner Alpine traffic. All the important passes were crossed and in addition countless saddlebacks with whose names the local inhabitants alone are today familiar.[44] So a settlement such as the one on the 'Crestaulta' in the Lugnez (Graubünden), far back in a remote valley, must have served as a stopping-place on a pass route, if it is to make any sense (p. 198). Settlements of this period are mostly sited on little knolls at the margins of valleys or even higher up. There are virtually no associated graves since the way the dead were buried makes it extremely difficult for us to trace them today: they were cremated, leaving nothing more than a little heap of splintered bones and ash, which was deposited in a shallow hollow; the custom of making offerings was not generally observed. That such 'graves' can easily be overlooked or not recognized as such during earth-shifting in modern times, should occasion no surprise.

Cultural groups and transmitted tribal names

At the beginning of the later Bronze Age, around the thirteenth century BC, a change set in which brought fresh groups of peoples into the mountains and ultimately led for the first time to the formation of Inner Alpine com-

munities spread over a substantial area. In North Tyrol in particular a kind of colonization seems to have taken place, which saw small groups advancing from the Alpine foreland into the Inn valley.[45] The motive was the exploitation of the Tyrolese copper deposits, which now became intensified. Such migrations resulted in a denser settlement of the Alpine region but there was one instance at

8 Three of the 15 earthenware vessels from a cremation grave at Vuadens (canton Fribourg); they testify to supraregional links during the Late Bronze Age. The large vessel and the small bowl reflect local tradition, yet the latter bears, in addition to impressed roundels, traces of decoration consisting of pasted-on metal strips. Single examples of this fashion appeared all over the circumalpine area. The direction from which the influences came is indicated by the large bowl, for it is alien to the North whilst comparable pieces are found in the Po plain. 12th century BC. Ht of the large vessel 20 cm. Service archéologique cantonal, Fribourg.

least of a group of peoples from the North traversing the Alpine ridge.

Their target was the warm South, the region of Lago Maggiore and the Lake of Como down as far as the Milan area. Here it is possible to detect burial customs, pottery and metal forms (named 'Canegrate' after the group's largest known cemetery, northwest of Milan), which cannot be attributed to the local Bronze Age tradition. On the contrary, it seems highly probable that these peoples migrated southward from a region that is to be located somewhere between north Savoy and the northern part of Switzerland.[46] The scarcity of archaeological evidence precludes us from arriving at a more exact estimation of the place of origin. But it must have been these peoples who brought with them a dialect, closely related to the Celtic, which to a certain extent can be identified through inscriptions of several centuries later in this area, namely 'Lepontic', an Indo-European language and just as alien in the 'Ligurian' surroundings as the material objects of this culture group.[47] The archaeologically alien elements, it is true, vanished in the course of some two centuries, the local tradition gaining the upper hand as the aliens were assimilated. It appears that between the twelfth and the eighth century conditions grew stable once again, the transalpine contacts returned to normal.

It was at this time that cultural attributes of individual groups began to crystallize, a process better seen in the South than in the North. This was apparently accompanied by the formation of political structures that promoted a community feeling among larger groups, resulting in ethnic associations about which we learn from the earliest written sources. In the northwestern Po plain, in the aforementioned settlement area of the Canegrate group of Northwest Alpine provenance, it is possible to detect a continuous development up until the Roman conquest. The vehicle was the Golasecca culture, named after the cemetery close to where the Ticino flows out of Lago Maggiore.[48] Farther eastward concentrated and clearly defined cultural groups were first formed in the course of the tenth century BC.[49] One of them encompassed the Po plain, having its cultural and probably also its political centre at Este (near Padua). From Greek and Roman sources we learn that the Veneti occupied this region, enabling us to trace the origins of this people in northern

Italy as a united community back to the tenth century BC.[50] This so-called Este culture set its seal also on the Southeast Alpine region, in Venezia Giulia/Friuli, though relevant find-spots are not very numerous.[51]

Around Bologna are accumulated find-spots relating to the north Italian Villanovan culture (named after a cemetery in a suburb of Bologna). As a flourishing centre of commerce Bologna played an important role in establishing communications between northern Italy and Etruscan central Italy, as well as extending its manifold activities northwards, across the Alps to Central Europe.[52]

In the Inner Alpine region, after the somewhat more disturbed period marking the thirteenth century BC, a likewise fairly unified culture developed, recognizable in particular by its characteristic pottery (its jugs with pointed spouts and large handles, for example, are conspicuous). It is known as the Melaun or Laugen culture, after two find-spots in the Adige valley, and its distribution extended from the Alpine valley of the Rhine, across North and South Tyrol, to almost as far down as Villach in Carinthia.[53] By contrast, the Western Alps possessed, in the Late Bronze Age and as late as the Early Iron Age, no individual character of their own, remaining independent of the influences of the cultures beyond the mountains. The shores of the lakes in central Switzerland and Savoy were densely settled; the finds indicate a substantial population and a certain degree of wealth. Several of the artefacts, such as fibulae, razors and similar small objects, undoubtedly derive from Italy (Ill. 123) and testify to the importance of the transalpine routes.[54] And this points to another development that occurred towards the end of the Bronze Age in the Northwest Alpine region, namely a reversal of the direction taken by cultural influences.

For, from around the eighth century, Italy and the South in general assumed the leading role. In central Italy the Etruscans had established themselves as the dominant power, the Greeks had begun the great task of colonizing the northwest Mediterranean coasts, the Phoenicians actually fetched tin from Cornwall, while in the Balkans new centres arose that radiated stronger stimuli northeastwards. More advanced economic, political, religious ideas were able to spread more rapidly; Central Europe came under the influence of the technically and artistically superior Mediterranean culture.

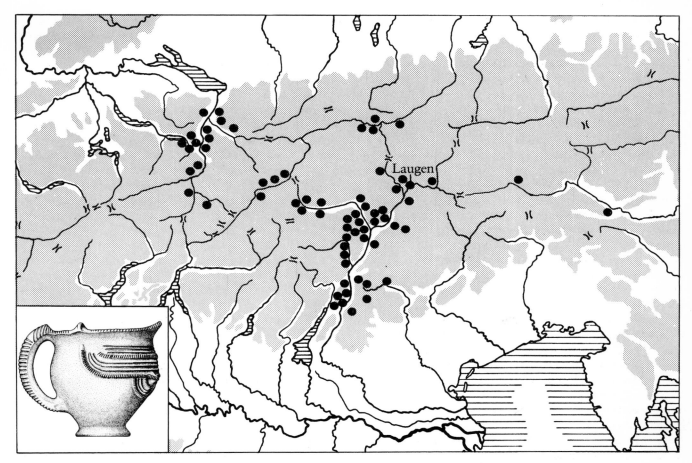

9   *Distribution map of pottery known as 'Laugener' Ware, after an important find-spot. The characteristic shapes of these earthenware vessels were very popular in the valleys of the Rhine, Inn, Adige and Isarco in the Late Bronze Age, here and there along the Rienz and Drau as well. The map points to active communication between the valley-dwellers across the passes, and more or less encompasses the territory where the Romans a thousand years later encountered tribes which they grouped together under the heading 'Raeti'.*

Iron and salt as sources of power

But there was something else that revolutionized conditions in the Alpine zone: iron. In the second half of the eighth century the Iron Age arrived in Italy and Central Europe. Just as in the case of copper-working, the know-how of iron-working came to the West from the Eastern Mediterranean, and that this occurred at the time of the Greek colonization was, we may be sure, not a matter of chance. The Etruscans had quickly recognized the significance of the rich ore deposits on Elba, and already in early Roman times the area around Populonia on the mainland opposite, where the ore was smelted on account of the amount of wood required, became the 'Pittsburgh of Italy'.[55] From here the new processes spread also to the North.

Iron brought with it certain basic changes in the economy. In the first place, iron ore deposits of varying size and geological provenance occur nearly everywhere.

For early man with his modest requirements by way of 'rentability', iron was appreciably easier and therefore cheaper to win, or to buy, than copper. Thus before long, where technical advantages existed, bronze could be replaced by iron. Since this applied above all to weapons and utensils, there was a corresponding increase in production in the fields of agriculture and handicrafts. This meant a further step towards coping more effectively with the environment and provided the necessary conditions for a population increase, much as at the transition from the Stone Age to the Bronze Age. Secondly, the readier availability of iron militated against the monopolistic activities of those communities and bosses who had hitherto controlled the mining and in particular the bartering of copper. Thereby, in the third place, certain political processes were no doubt set in train which sought to eliminate the crasser distinctions between the various strata of the population; at all events the trend towards 'democracy' in Greece and Rome was fostered by corresponding economic developments.

All this had important consequences for the Alpine region. There was, it is true, still naturally a demand for copper (chiefly for articles of personal adornment which because of their fine detail had still to be cast), but there was a marked falling-off in demand since weapons, utensils and other larger objects could be wrought in iron. Hence the importance of copper-mining diminished; the principal source of supply during the Bronze Age, the Mitterberg near Bischofshofen, has yielded scarcely any finds from the Iron Age. The same applies to the North Tyrolean deposits. At smaller sites, such as those at Uttendorf in the Pinzgau, at Welzelach and Zedlach in East Tyrol, work does however appear to have been carried on for rather longer (p. 248). Sketchy as is our knowledge of how long and how intensely individual sites may have been worked (as late as in Roman times, for instance, the land of the *Ceutrones* in the Western Alps supplied copper, though apparently for a few decades only until the deposits were exhausted),[56] one thing is certain: the advent of the Iron Age saw the economic and cultural rise of a region that had hitherto played a very subordinate role, namely the Southeast Alpine territory: Styria, Carinthia and Slovenia.

Here are found the most important iron deposits in the

Alps, and even early man found the ore so easy to extract and to smelt, that he could undertake to supply wide areas. In the West, it is true, smaller deposits were also worked, but they met local requirements only, as was earlier the case with copper.

That the district in the hinterland of Salzburg nevertheless did not sink into insignificance (as did, for instance, North Tyrol) is owing to another mineral which is just as important to man as metal, namely salt. Two localities are closely associated with it: Hallstatt in the Upper Austrian Salzkammergut and Hallein-Dürrnberg, a bare 20 km south of Salzburg. The very names point to the significance of this basic economic element, for the etymological root *hall* is intimately connected with the English word 'salt', in German 'Salz'.

In Hallstatt and Hallein-Dürrnberg the salt was obtained by mining, that is to say tunnels were used (pp. 251ff.), which suggests that this new industry took advantage of the skills and know-how of the copper-miners. That this coincided in time with the transition from the Bronze to the Iron Age, however, would appear to be fortuitous. The notion that jobless miners from the copper workings had been looking for alternative employment elsewhere and had thus discovered salt, does not fit the circumstances prevailing in early historical times. Rather, climatic changes had called for salt production in quantities unknown until then. For just at this time the climate– probably not only in Central Europe–deteriorated: it became appreciably colder and above all more humid.[57]

This directly influenced salt consumption in Central Europe. For not only was salt needed in small quantities to season food; its importance lay far more in the conservation of meat.[58] So, on account of the worsening of the climate, it was necessary to change from the mostly adequate air-drying to pickling in brine, the main features of which process were possibly likewise derived from the South, where sea salt was readily available in unlimited quantities. Since at the same time the introduction of iron, as we have seen, boosted agricultural output (through cheaper and more durable ploughs, mattocks, axes) and so also encouraged cattle-breeding where the land had been cleared, thereby allowing an increase in the population, while in Central Europe salt could be produced in only a few places,[59] it is hardly surprising that the salt-mining

10 Section of a sheet-metal belt ornament from Vače (Slovenia). Two warring horsemen face one another. The one on the right wears a bronze helmet and brandishes a battle-axe. One of his spears has a clearly depicted sling attached to its shaft in order to give it added momentum. The warrior on the left has long tresses and is armed with nothing more than a couple of spears. It is a moot point whether the artist actually sought to depict two dissimilarly attired and armed riders. He certainly knew how to introduce the element of contrast by way of differences in style: the long hair of the left-hand horseman matches the long mane of his opponents mount, the spherical helmet of the latter the shorn mane of the other's horse. 6th century BC. Ht 9.4 cm. Naturhistorisches Museum, Vienna.

works at Hallstatt and Hallein-Dürrnberg enjoyed a trade boom no less marked than that of the iron-producing centres of the Southeast Alpine regions.

As early as the middle of the nineteenth century the Royal Surveyor of Mines Johann Georg Ramsauer excavated the cemetery associated with the mine-workings and settlement at Hallstatt, since when the earlier part of the Iron Age in Central Europe has been called the 'Hallstatt period'. It ended in the fifth century BC and was followed by the 'La Tène period', named after the find-spot La Tène near Marin, where the Thièle/Zihl flows out of Lake Neuchâtel. Here, between 1906 and 1916, Paul Vouga discovered a large quantity of Late Iron Age material in the vicinity of an old bridge.

Not only a period but a 'culture' was named after Hallstatt. The Hallstatt culture incorporates numerous regional groups between eastern France, Bohemia and Slovenia, which have various features in common: style of ornamentation, religious symbols, burial customs, social structures.[60] The links with the surrounding cultures, particularly those to the south and east, are clearly of a flexible nature. To the north lies a region where the Teutons later made their presence felt; in the direction of the Atlantic lived peoples who were not strictly speaking part of the Hallstatt culture but who nevertheless ultimately belonged to the people known as Gallic, meaning the Celts. The Po plain, for its part, was far too much under Italic influence for it to be counted as directly appertaining to the Hallstatt culture. On the whole, these dividing lines that are arrived at through assessments of various phenomena of cultural life–and on what else can the archaeologist base his judgments?–are difficult to reconcile with the traditional ethnic conditions of more recent times. Or, to put it another way, whilst there are many contradictions, much becomes clearer through comparison. To illustrate this, let us take, for example, the division into a west and an east Hallstatt area, as envisaged by the archaeologists. What most clearly differentiates them are the weapons the well-to-do men bore: in the west, a sword and later a dagger,[61] in the east a battle-axe. There was a sharp line of demarcation between the two methods of fighting. This line runs more or less exactly from north to south: Bohemia and Moravia are still within the west Hallstatt area, the valleys of the Danube and the Inn forming the boundary to the northwest and west, while to the south the Isarco and Lower Adige valleys must be reckoned to belong to the eastern area. By way of confirmation, moreover, certain characteristic items of personal adornment are to be found, above all fibulae, which were worn mostly by women.[62]

Comparison with conditions in later times shows that the boundary between the west and the east Hallstatt area south of the Danube and in the Alpine region coincides with the frontier that in Roman times still separated the provinces of Raetia and Noricum in the North, and correspondingly the Italic regions of the Transpadana and Venetia et Histria in the South. Here, then, we can trace an historically transmitted and, as will be shown, a politically determined boundary-line at least as far back as around 700 BC.

The centres of the east Hallstatt area lay partly at the very edge of the Southeast Alpine region. Enormous burial mounds containing a great many graves and extensive forts with defensive ramparts and walls occur in great numbers between Ljubljana and Nove mesto in the hilly district of the Sava. In the mountain region itself only two outstanding finds have been made, neither of which is, however, likely to have been directly connected with ironworking but with the associated main communication routes: the extremely rich burial mounds of Kleinklein, southwest Graz (Ill. 69), and the cult-wagon of Strettweg near Judenburg (Ill. 102), so significant for the history of religion. That at this time lead, too, was being mined in Carinthia is evidenced by the well furnished graves at Frög, containing lead figurines.

But it is the cemetery at Hallstatt itself, in the border territory between the east and west Hallstatt areas, that puts all else in the shade. The graves, numbering more than a thousand, here laid bare yielded such a plethora of finds, that even today still researchers fight shy of undertaking a thorough scientific sorting of the material. The finds also make it difficult to determine the complex relationships of the Hallstatt miners with the surrounding districts, since east and west Hallstatt forms and weapon designs are found in various combinations.[63] Comparable wealth is to be deduced from the–so far only few–graves of the Hallstatt period in the Dürrnberg above Hallein. In the light of their geographical situation, they point to still closer relations with the West, that is with south Germany.[64]

The west Hallstatt area is to be associated with the Celts; certainly this is suggested by all the earliest accounts. It bears the stamp of a warlike people: characteristic are the long iron sword and a penchant for interring wealthy men in large burial chambers accompanied by horse-harness and chariot. The entire Swiss midlands still lay within this zone; even in the central Western Alps the graves at Chauvignières-Avançon (Hautes-Alpes) containing a classic Hallstatt sword testify to close links with the North.[65]

Though these graves and also one at La Côte-Saint-André (Dept Isère), in which were found a large bronze vessel and a ritual vehicle,[66] betray close ties with northern Italy, this only goes to show the flexible nature of cultural exchanges. This applies particularly to the upper class, which at all times adopted a more international stance than the rest of the populace. For this reason the simple graves of the Western Alps have a very local character.[67] We can count these people as being among the inhabitants of the northwestern Mediterranean littoral, the Ligurians.

11 The wealth of the salt-miners on the Dürrnberg above Hallein (Salzburg province) is most vividly brought home by Grave 44/2. It was not only his jewellery and weapons (including the pointed bronze helmet) that were placed in the grave with the warrior who was buried there but the symbols of a generous mode of living: a sheet-bronze bucket to hold nearly 190 litres of stew or meat soup, the Greek pottery dish which he used for helping himself to his share of its contents, and a rounded bronze bottle resting on human feet, which held almost 17 litres of wine from the South. Of a smaller wooden tankard only a few bronze fittings have survived. 400–350 BC. Ht of bucket 88 cm. Keltenmuseum, Hallein.

The northwestern Po plain formed part of the Golasecca culture, which has left its mark from the South northwards to the Upper Rhône and as far as the uppermost Rhine valley.[68] It enjoyed a degree of well-being, doubtless a consequence of its privileged situation in a climatically favourable area and at the foot of important passes. No corporate name has been applied to the people of the Golasecca culture, Roman sources naming several differ-

ent stems, which may reflect the heterogeneous composition of this folk.

In the Central Alpine region the Melaun or Laugen culture was still in evidence; in the La Tène period it spread somewhat farther into North Tyrol, being named the Fritzens-Sanzeno culture after two find-spots.[69] In the southern foreland of the Alps it bordered on the Este culture of the eastern Po plain. As we know from later written sources that the Raeti occupied the Inner Alpine area, we may roughly equate the Laugen culture and its offspring with this people, as we have related the Este culture with the Veneti. On closer examination such correspondences are admittedly not quite so clear-cut, particularly if we also take into consideration the language, but these are details which only the expert needs to go into.[70]

Little changed in regard to the economic, cultural and ethnic situation we have described, until the Romans conquered the Alps. True, the Greeks founded a colony in *Massilia*/Marseille around 600 BC, and from there daughter-colonies, such as *Nikaia*/Nice and *Antipolis*/Antibes sprang, but their political and trading activities were directed more specifically towards the North, up the Rhône valley into Burgundy and southwest Germany. An important entrepôt was the hill-fort of Le Pègue, some 135 km north of Marseille on the eastern edge of the Rhône valley, facing the Alps (p. 86).

About 500 BC the Etruscans[71] spilled across the Apennines into northern Italy and allegedly founded a league of twelve cities, which Parma, Piacenza, Modena and Mantua also joined. The centre-point was Bologna, called Felsina by the Etruscans, and in Spina on the north Adriatic coast they constructed a port for trading with Greece. So, in addition to the Rhône route, the transalpine connections with the North also gained in importance. Two of them seem to have been of outstanding importance in view of the distribution of finds: first, the eastern route from Venetia across the Tauern mountains into the valleys of the Salzach and the Inn, and on into Bohemia; secondly, a western route skirting the Golasecca cultural sphere, across the Great St Bernard into the Swiss midlands and up into Champagne and as far as the Middle Rhine. Yet this trading activity scarcely affected conditions in the Inner Alps; the mountain-dwellers gained some benefit from the important routes by acting as car-

12 *The Celtic princes received presents of costly bronze vessels from the Greeks on the Mediterranean coast. This three-handled flagon was found in a much disturbed burial mound at Grächwil (canton Bern); it originated in a south Italian workshop. The Oriental motif of the 'Mistress of the Animals', the winged goddess between wild cats, had its counterpart in the North; for the Celtic artists took it over and produced many variations of it. 580–570 BC. Ht 58 cm. Historisches Museum, Bern.*

riers, guides and innkeepers, but the really valuable goods did not remain in the Alpine region but were destined for the wealthy beyond the Alps.

Brennus and Hannibal cross the Alps

This turning towards the South on the part of Central Europe did have one consequence which presumably no one foresaw. In the fifth century BC, that is early in the La Tène period, Central Europe faced a crisis. In eastern France and southwest Germany the cultural framework of the Hallstatt period was radically disrupted; one can say, without exaggeration, that an event took place there which is comparable with the 'democratization' of Athens and Rome (though not, of course, to the present-day extent). This appears to have been accompanied by religious innovations, social upheavals and economic problems (one manifestation of which was an entirely new art depicting men and animals with distorted features).[72] All this set in train the historically attested Celtic migrations, which struck fear into the hearts of the peoples of the South.[73] For what could be more inviting than those lands where the sun was known to shine and all the luxuries that had hitherto been confined to the houses of the rich were easy to come by?

The eighteenth of July, 387 BC was imprinted on the history of Rome as *dies ater* ('black day').[74] The community on the Tiber, still in the process of expanding, suffered an annihilating defeat; the largely unfortified city itself had to be evacuated, the Capitol alone remaining occupied. The tell-tale cackling of geese thwarted an attempt by night on the part of the invaders to capture it; after a while they withdrew, not without first extorting a substantial ransom, as Livy ashamedly records: 'The price for the people who were shortly to rule the world was fixed at one thousand pounds in gold.' And in addition to the proverbial 'black day', this story gave birth to another household phrase, namely *Vae victis*–Pity the conquered!–coined by Brennus, the Celtic chieftain.

This event shows, firstly the violence with which the Celtic hordes invaded the South, in the second place it provides us with an approximate date for their crossing of the Alps; for written testimony from Etruscan, let alone Alpine, sources is lacking. Livy even mentions the exact routes, namely across the western passes between the Rhône valley and the territory of the *Taurini* (around Turin), and later on the *mons Poeninus*, the Great St Bernard pass. That lesser hordes also used other passes farther to the east, perhaps leading directly into Ticino, is quite possible.

The Celts arrived in whole tribes, whose names have come down to us, and occupied northern Italy so extensi-

13 *This clasp of a gold neck-ring from Erstfeld (canton Uri) is made up of a grotesque medley of fabulous creatures with grimacing heads and curiously distorted limbs. The seven rings of this offering to the mountain gods (Ill. 94) are particularly characteristic examples of the early Celtic art of Central Europe. Neither the composition as a whole nor the individual motifs have as yet been satisfactorily interpreted owing to the fact that such Celtic mythology as has come down to us is fragmentary. The Alpine people themselves probably found it no less strange. About 400 BC. Width of part illustrated 10.9 cm. Schweizerisches Landesmuseum, Zurich.*

vely, that the Romans were later to call the region between the Alps and the Apennines simply 'Gallia'. The Etruscans retreated southward, the northerly Picenum succumbed to the onslaught, but the Celts–like the Etruscans before them–did not penetrate the territory of the Veneti. This convinced the Romans that the South Alpine Raeti were none other than Etruscans who had fled northwards before the Celts, and hence Livy (V 33) provides the relevant environmental hypothesis: 'The Alpine peoples undoubtedly have the same origin (= Etruscan), particularly the Raeti. Surely the wildness of this region took possession of them, leaving behind nothing of what they inherited apart from the sound of the speech, and that not even pure.' The most that modern scholarship can contribute to this question is to establish that Raetian was no more an Indo-European language than Etruscan, and to point out that this is hardly surprising seeing that both have certain attributes in common with an old linguistic substratum, and that they were geographically adjacent. Nor do archaeologists believe that in the Iron

Age the Inner Alpine cultural sphere was noticeably affected by the Etruscans.

So the Celts became established in northern Italy, namely in the regions that hitherto had only been sparsely populated.[75] Yet the Etruscan *Felsina* was so thoroughly 'celticized' that it was given the Celtic name *Bononia*, perpetuated in the Bologna of today. The Golasecca culture, on the other hand, yielded only gradually to Celtic influences, and the farther they penetrated the Alpine valleys, the longer this took. The Celts found the mountains every bit as sinister as did the Etruscans and subsequently the Romans, and the country on both sides of the Adige they regarded as no less alien. Naturally, there will have been isolated incursions, but instances of typical Celtic placenames such as *Excingomagus*, present-day Exilles near Susa, are the exception.

Whilst at the western border of the Alps the cultural evolution went on, and Greek culture as well as Greek power continued to take over the Rhône valley, the northern border was more specifically affected by the new developments. The Swiss midlands participated in the change from the Hallstatt culture to the La Tène culture without evincing any noticeable discontinuity. In the south German Alpine foreland, on the other hand, a population decline occurred,[76] possibly a consequence of the Celtic migrations which must have carried along with them groups of peoples from eastern parts. The newly burgeoning La Tène culture spread so far afield as to affect even Lower Austria, and the Celtic migrations towards the Balkans, Greece and Asia Minor will have caused some upheavals there too; so far, though, they had not encroached on the Inner Alpine region.

Here the change did not come about until the third century BC, when Celtic tribes advanced into the Eastern Alps from Hungary and Slovenia.[77] They can be recognized by their characteristic weapons, jewellery and burial customs.[78] They merged with the 'Hallstatt' population already there, and provided the impetus for the establishment of a loose federation (with the previously mentioned precise orientation at the boundary between the east and the west Hallstatt area) between the rivers Adige, Inn, Danube and the edge of the Southeastern Alps. We know nothing of its exact political structure; it met the Romans in the second century BC under the leadership of the *Norici* tribe, in the guise of *regnum Noricum*, that is to say a 'kingdom'.[79]

For the Romans had meanwhile advanced into northern Italy. By the beginning of the third century BC they had made nearly the whole of Italy south of the Apennines part of their State. In the year 283 they thrust northwards, taking Picenum, the *ager Gallicus* roughly between Ravenna and Ascona, which had been settled by the Celts, and founded the colony of *Sena Gallica*/Senigallia, fifteen years later *Ariminum*/Rimini. Between 225 and 222, following a number of lesser skirmishes, came the decisive showdown between Celts and Romans in northern Italy. In 218 the colonies of *Placentia*/Piacenza and Cremona were established, able-bodied men being sent there for the defence of the land. Whether the territory was already organized as an actual province at that stage is open to question; for the Second Punic War interrupted everything that had been planned.

Horror and utter bewilderment spread like wildfire through Rome and Italy in the late summer of 218: Hannibal and his army had crossed the Alps and was now threatening to conquer the unprotected land and force Rome to its knees. The Celts, seeking revenge, scented their chance and joined the Carthaginians; Rome saw itself faced by two allied arch-enemies. Hannibal defeated the legions that had been rushed to the North in two battles, on the Ticino and the Trebbia respectively, pressed on southwards and on 2 August 216 at Cannae in Apulia destroyed practically the entire Roman army. It was some time before the Romans finally prevailed and the peace treaty of 201 BC was concluded; history tends to stand up for the victors, yet Hannibal lived on in men's minds as the warrior who–though a son of North Africa–with incredible daring planned and accomplished the crossing of the Alps (see pp. 206ff. for details). For the Alpine region and northern Italy, however, this deed was no more than an astounding episode which had no political aftermath.

Rome conquers northern Italy and southern France

Once the war was over, the Romans set about recapturing the Po plain. In 189 *Bononia*/Bologna became a colony, six years later *Mutina*/Modena and Parma. By 187 M. Aemi-

lianus Lepidus had extended the Adriatic coast road from *Ariminum* to *Placentia*, doubtless in order to facilitate rapid troop movements whenever danger threatened. From this *via Aemilia*, which was later carried still farther northwest, this region straddling the Apennines derives its present-day name Emilia-Romagna. The territory ruled or at any rate controlled by the Romans now stretched as far as the edge of the Alps, in accessible valleys perhaps even some kilometres into them. At this stage northern Italy appears to have been accorded the status of province, since there is testimony that for the year 183 BC a certain L. Iulius was *praetor*, i.e. governor.

The Romans now availed themselves peaceably of the mineral resources of the Alps. A decisive event was the founding of the colony of *Aquileia* between 183 and 181 as starting-point for relations with *regnum Noricum*. For here was to be found not only iron but also gold, a metal of which Italy itself is practically devoid. Moreover, it lay on an ancient route that ran from the Baltic through the Alps to the Adriatic, the 'amber route' known by this name already to the Greeks, and the shortest and most convenient link between the Baltic and the Mediterranean, a route with many forks and by-paths, which crossed the Danube near Vienna.

The focal point of the *regnum Noricum* was the large settlement on the Magdalensberg near Klagenfurt (Ill. 47), which Roman merchants and traders had already made their base early on (pp. 89ff.). It is recorded that, about 115 BC, a treaty of friendship between Noricum and Rome was drawn up, but this virtually only meant that Rome believed it could avoid having to take aggressive action, so long as its trading interests were safeguarded.

For Rome had meanwhile gained a foothold at the other end of the Alpine chain. When, following the Punic Wars, the Iberian peninsula (excepting the wild tribes of the Pyrenees) had been made into a Roman province, a land link between northern Italy and Spain became a matter of urgency. Traditional good relations had been maintained, it is true, with *Massilia*, which controlled the area round the Rhône delta and the coast as far as *Nikaia*/Nice, but this did not satisfy Rome. Successful wars having been waged against the *Volcae* in the later colony of *Narbo Martius*/Narbonne and the Alpine peoples, the *Salluvii* and the *Allobroges* (in this context it is worth mentioning the crossing of the Alps by the consul Fulvius Flaccus with his army), Cn. Domitius Ahenobarbus in 121 BC formed a new province, the *Gallia Narbonensis*. Thereby the Rhône valley from the Mediterranean to the Lake of Geneva, as well as the adjacent Western Alps to points far up into the valleys, were incorporated in the Roman empire; the Massiliote area remained independent rather longer. By this time at the very latest the name *Gallia Citerior* or *Cisalpina* ('the Gallic land this side of the Alps = Cisalpine Gaul) for northern Italy will have gained currency.

All the same, Rome was not to enjoy these successes for long. The Cimbrians and Teutons, Germanic tribes with Celtic groups that were swept along with them, poured over the Alps from the Northeast. In 113 the Roman army suffered its first defeat at *Noreia* (a place of uncertain location in either Carinthia or Styria).[80] The land-hungry foreigners retreated a little and turned towards Gaul. After some minor reverses, Rome was in 105 subjected to a catastrophic drubbing at *Arausio*/Orange on the Rhône. But Marius, elected consul four times running during this dire period, by reorganizing his army and using superior strategy, managed to destroy the disintegrating invaders at *Aquae Sextiae*/Aix-en-Provence and Ferrara in 102 and 101 BC. But from that time onward the *furor teutonicus* was the bugbear of the Romans. The tangled skein of this folk's activities has never been unravelled, but they must have crossed the Alps several times; the Cimbrians will have used the Brenner pass or the Pustertal as convenient transit routes for their final descent into Italy.[81]

After these drastic events the Romans had for the time being had enough of the North, besides being occupied with political affairs at home. The *regnum Noricum* between the Inn, Sava and Danube was a land of substance; its political independence brought benefits to both sides. The small Alpine communities between Gallia Narbonensis and Gallia Cisalpina as well as those in the Inner Alpine district between the Lake of Geneva and the river Isarco were not bent on expansion, but continued to live contentedly by cattle-breeding, a little agriculture and working small metal deposits. Maybe they sold their products at a modest profit to the Roman subjects in the Po plain.

In Central Europe north of the Alps the Celtic world had achieved a degree of consolidation following the upheavals of the fourth and third centuries BC. Friendly contact with the Mediterranean world was re-established, as evidenced in city-like settlements, specialized handicrafts and the striking of coins (Ill. 161); wine and oil were once again imported in earthenware amphorae.[82] *Oppida*, as the Romans called their well-fortified settlements, were also to be found at the northern border of the Alps (p. 88). The salt-mines in Hallein-Dürrnberg and Hallstatt continued to be worked, even though the Reichenhall brine-spring gained in importance. The Inner Alpine region, however, kept to its accustomed way of life; the hordes or armies that swept through left no lasting mark, at worst causing death and destruction along the main lines of communication.

But the surprise appearance of the Cimbri and Teutons had initiated a new era, during which the Germanic peoples from the North exerted considerable pressure. At the outset this affected the Celtic world. In the early decades of the first century BC the Suebian hordes of Ariovistus swept through south Germany, even harassing the Celtic Helvetii beyond the upper Rhine in present-day Switzerland. When these turned towards the West, in order to escape this pressure, they had to traverse the land of the Allobroges in Gallia Narbonensis.

This was the signal for the intervention in 58 BC of Rome, or rather of one man, Caesar, who saw here an opportunity to combine interests of State with personal aims. Judge as we may the manifold factors that lay behind his actions, the end result was the conquest by Rome of the whole of Gaul as far as the Rhine.[83] Yet once again the narrow Inner Alpine strip of the Côte d'Azur as far as the Adige valley, frontier of the *regnum Noricum*, escaped occupation. The attempt by Caesar's legate S. Sulpicius Galba in 57 BC to conquer the Valais and so to safeguard the route across the Great St Bernard, came to nothing.

Meanwhile the situation had changed for the inhabitants of the Po plain, in that their legal status was affected. Although the region remained a province, in 89 BC those inhabiting the area south of the Po (Gallia dispadana) were accorded Roman, those living north of the Po (Gallia transpadana) only Latin, citizenship. This meant differing legal status, but even so Latin citizenship represented a considerable improvement.[84] Nevertheless this northern region was still not a part of Italia. Thus Caesar could continue to treat as provinces both 'Gallia ulterior', that is southern France, and Gallia citerior or cisalpina, enabling him to keep his legions stationed there. For the stationing of troops in Italic civic territory had for long been forbidden. When on the night of 10 to 11 January Caesar and his legions crossed the *Rubico*/Rubicon, the river (running into the Adriatic) that constituted the frontier between the provinces of Gallia cisalpina and Italic territory, he broke this law, and that meant civil war. Caesar's fate is well known, but it is worth mentioning here that Brutus, Caesar's assassin, had, on his flight into the vicinity of *Lugdunum*/Lyon (probably across the Little, not the Great St Bernard), to pay the Salassi in the Aosta valley 'tribute' money of one drachma on every one of his soldiers.[85]

Caesar's 'avenger' Marc Antony, was awarded both Gauls in the shape of provinces; with his legions in northern Italy he was able to threaten the entire peninsula. These experiences led the Roman Senate to take a decisive step: Gallia cisalpina was added to 'Italia' in 42 BC, divided up into the regions Aemilia, Venetia, Liguria (extending as far as the coast) and Transpadana. From now on all stationing of troops in northern Italy was proscribed; the Alpine barrier, moreover, presented such an obstacle that whatever plans insurgent generals may have entertained will have lost their element of surprise. The inhabitants of Transpadana had to wait until Claudius occupied the imperial throne before being granted full citizenship.

A victory over forty-five Alpine tribes

From the upheavals of the civil war Augustus emerged as victor. On 11 January 29 BC he had the doors of the Temple of Janus closed–as a sign that peace reigned over all the Empire (it was only to last a few months!)–and had himself glorified as prince of peace and rebuilder of the Roman Empire.

To the Alpine peoples, though, this must have sounded like a mockery, for their 'pacification' was now included in the programme. Since the year 34 BC wars had been waged with the Salassi in the Aosta valley. These ended in 25 BC with a penal judgment of great severity. The two relevant sources available to us are not entirely in accordance, but we can at least deduce from them that all sur-

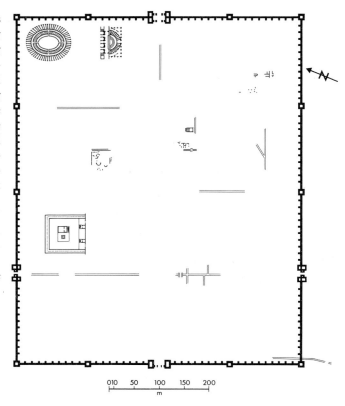

14 Town plan of Augusta Praetoria/*Aosta (Piedmont), founded after 25 BC at the fork of the important routes across the Great and the Little St Bernard in the territory of the subject Salassi. Because the present-day town grew up over it, with the exception of the walls, towers and gateways, only the large public buildings are visible or known through excavation: the forum (main square), the theatre and the amphitheatre. The town walls measure 572 × 724 m.*

viving young and able-bodied men were transported to *Eporedia*/Ivrea and there sold as slaves, with the proviso that they should not be freed before twenty years had elapsed.[86] The founding of a town for three thousand colonists, named *Augusta Praetoria* and strongly fortified with walls, made for peace in the land and the rapid Romanization of the remaining population.

Now the route across the Great St Bernard was open, and the Alpine people knew what they could expect. Among many lesser undertakings, the subjection of the *Camunni* (in the Valcamonica) north of Brescia and of the *Vennonetes* (in the Alpine Rhine valley or in the Venetic district in the East?) by P. Silius Nerva in 16 BC deserve mention;[87] these peoples had allegedly raided Empire territory from the North. That same year, it appears, Rome by unilateral action ended the sovereignty of the *regnum Noricum*. The inhabitants were wise enough to accommodate themselves to this inescapable decree, even gaining for a few decades a special status: relatively few Roman troops were stationed in the land, rigorous enlistment such as was enforced shortly afterwards in Raetia and Vindelicia does not appear to have been imposed, and authority was mainly vested in indigenous functionaries. Not until the year AD 45, under Emperor Claudius, was the province of Noricum created, its borders initially identical with those of the *regnum Noricum*; an imperial official from the ranks of the knights was appointed governor. *Virunum,* below the Magdalensberg, was built to serve as the new capital.

In the West, too, appeared a man who showed comparable skill in his handling of affairs. In *Segusio*/Susa, King Cottius ruled over his fourteen mountain tribes, and when he beheld the fate of the peoples all around, further opposition seemed to him to be futile; in 13 BC he made a treaty with Rome, under which his kingdom would be incorporated in the Empire. Augustus generously honoured this: he installed Cottius as *praefectus* (governor) of the Alpes Cottiae, accorded him Roman citizenship, and even allowed him on official occasions to mention his royal extraction. When visiting Gaul for the third time in 8 BC Augustus elected to go via Susa, not we may be sure without political interests in mind, and Cottius took the opportunity to honour Augustus by erecting a stone arch that spanned the Mont-Genèvre road. In large bronze characters he proudly referred to himself as *M. Iulius regis Donni filius Cottius praefectus ceivitatium*. His eldest son was even able to carry on the line as Cottius II, while a second son, Vestalis by name, made the Roman army his career. In AD 44 Emperor Claudius bestowed on an M. Iulius Cottius the lineal title of King. It was not until AD 63, when the last of the line of indigenous kings had died, that

15 The arch at Segusio/Susa *(Piedmont), erected in honour of Emperor Augustus by ex-king Cottius above the road leading to the Mont-Genèvre, has outlasted the centuries almost wholly intact; only the large bronze letters of the inscription were filched by medieval metal-thieves.*

with a stroke of the pen Emperor Nero converted this territory into the Roman province of Alpes Cottiae with all its administrative and political consequences.[88]

The other tribes did not fare so well when incorporated in the Roman Empire. In 15 BC Augustus's stepsons, Drusus and Tiberius, had conquered the entire Central Alpine region and the south German foreland in a pincer movement; relentless conscription of young men for military service in other parts of the Empire in the end crushed all resistance. The poet Horace (Quintus Horatius Flaccus d. 8 BC) glorified Augustus thus:[89]

16 *Marble gravestone from the Magdalensberg near Klagenfurt (Carinthia):* Ti(berius) Iulius Adsedi f(ilius) Taulus mil(es) coh(ortis) Mon(tanorum) pri(mae) stip(endiorum) XXXVI h(ic) s(itus) e(st) h(eres) f(ecit) = *Tiberius Julius Taulus, son of Adsedus, soldier in the mountain-infantry batallion with 36 years' service, lies buried here. His heir had (the gravestone) made.—The name betrays the indigenous origin of this man, who was granted Roman citizenship under Emperor Tiberius and thereafter was also entitled to bear the latter's family name 'Iulius'. First half of 1st century* AD. *Ht 1.36 m. Museum on the Magdalensberg.*

17 *This coin, struck in* Lugdunum/*Lyon shortly after* 15 BC, *commemorates in propagandist manner the subjection of the Alpine peoples: Emperor Augustus receives the victory laurels from Drusus and Tiberius. The sword and long robe show that they are victorious generals. Diam. 1.8 cm. Staatliche Münzsammlung, Munich.*

18 Emperor Augustus imposed upon the Alpine peoples a servitude to Rome that was to last for five centuries. Ruthless subjection, threats of war and brief treaties of friendship were the means he employed. The statue from Prima Porta outside Rome, a marble copy of what was probably a bronze original, produced about 19 BC, shows Gaius Octavianus, known from 27 BC as 'Augustus' (the exalted), as commander-in-chief addressing the army. His cuirass is covered with reliefs which proclaim the successes that attended his foreign policy. Ht 2.04 m. Museo Chiaramonti, Vatican Collections, Rome.

...thou whose power in war the Vindelici, free till now from Latin rule, have learned of late to know. For thine were the troops wherewith keen Drusus, with more than like requital, hurled the Genauni down, a clan implacable, the swift Breuni, and their strongholds set upon awful Alps. Soon too the elder Nero (= Tiberius) joined deadly battle and overcame the savage Rhaetians under happy auspices...

A few years later the securing of the North Alpine foreland began, with the establishment of military stations and a legionary camp (first in *Augusta Vindelicum*/Augsburg, then in *Vindonissa*/Windisch, near Brugg [Aargau]). Towns and market-places on the Roman pattern came into being, and Roman civilization was introduced. The Alps being now close behind Rome's front line, the land underwent steady development. The new administrative district, the province-to-be of Raetia, was bounded in the North by the Danube, later by the yet farther advanced *limes*, in the East by Noricum; the Alpine region between the Swiss midlands (belonging to the province of Belgica) and the Transpadana, which Augustus had conquered, was likewise annexed to Raetia, giving the province a somewhat strange shape: apart from the central area, approximating to southern Bavaria west of the Inn, it embraced the upper valleys of the Rhine, Inn, Adige and Isarco, and extended into the Valais as far as the Lake of Geneva. *Augusta Vindelicum*/Augsburg was made the capital, and we may imagine what a business it will have been to visit it for any reason. That was no doubt why Emperor Claudius separated the Valais from Raetia in the middle of the first century AD and set up an administrative district Vallis Poenina. It appears that this together with the adjacent Alpes Graiae formed a new province of Alpes Graiae et Poenina having two capitals *Octodurus* or *Forum Claudii Vallensium*/Martigny and *Axima* or *Forum Claudii Ceutronum*/Aime-en-Tarentaise.[90] Bordering it to the South were the Alpes Cottiae with its capital *Segusio*/Susa, and the Alpes Maritimae with its capital *Cemelenum*/Cimiez (today a suburb of Nice).[91] The western escarpment of the Alps continued to belong to Gallia Narbonensis. Not only in the mountain areas is it difficult to determine exactly where the boundaries ran; milestones beside the roads can help in that they normally give the distance from the capital (p. 211), but few of them any longer remain in their original position. This applies also to a boundary stone from

the year AD 74, which nowadays is to be seen outside the Hotel Panorama in Les Plagnes below Chamonix (Savoy), though we know that it was found in 1853 on the Col de la Forclaz du Prarion at the foot of Mont Blanc. The inscription tells us that here ran the frontier between the *Ceutrones* and the *Allobroges*, that is between the province of Alpes Graiae and Gallia Narbonensis.[92]

Augustus's conquests in the Alps were commemorated in an immense monument, the *Tropaeum Alpium*.[93] The Senate had it erected in 7 or 6 BC at the frontier between Italia and the new province of Alpes Maritimae, on the Via Iulia (leading from Italy to Spain), some 480 m above present-day Monaco but also clearly visible from the sea. On a square base with sides measuring 38 m rose a drum-shaped structure circled by columns and surmounted by a polygonal spire. At the very top, 50 m from the ground, stood a bronze statue of Augustus between two prisoners, which was to serve as a permanent memorial to the Emperor. Imposing as this edifice still looks–although it was used as a quarry in medieval times–and strongly as it expresses the Roman concept of might, it is more important for us as an historical document; for it bore an inscription which, though since lost, has fortunately been handed down to us through Pliny the Elder.[94] It was (measured in square metres!) the largest inscription of any kind bequeathed to us by the Romans. Here is a (supplemented) English version:

To the commander-in-chief and Caesar, son of the divine one (= C. Julius Caesar), to Augustus, high priest, general for the 14th time, possessor of tribune power for the 17th time, the Senate and people of Rome (dedicate this memorial), because he brought under the dominion of the Roman people through his leadership and strategy all Alpine peoples, stretching from the upper sea (= Tyrrhenian) to the lower (= Adriatic). The conquered Alpine tribes (are):

1 Trumpilini
Val Trompia north of Brescia

2 Camunni
Val Camonica north of Brescia

3 Venostes
Val Venosta

4 Vennonetes
Alpine Rhine valley

5–8 Isarci, Breuni, Genaunes, Focunates
Upper Inn valley

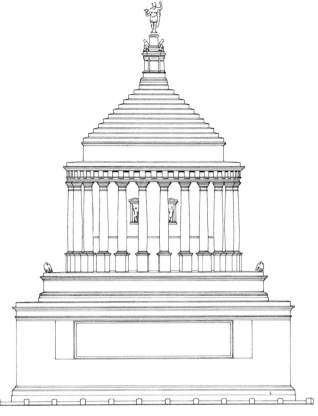

9–12 Cosuanetes, Rucinates, Licates, Catenates
Vindelician tribes in the Suebian-Bavarian
Alpine foreland

13 Ambisontes
Upper Salzach valley

14–17 Rugusci, Suanetes, Calucones, Brixenetes
Alpine Rhine valley with Engadin

18 Leponti
Ticino and Misox

19–22 Vberi, Nantuates, Seduni, Varagri
Valais

23 Salassi
Aosta valley

24 Acitavones
probably incorrectly instead of *Ceutrones*
(west of the Little St Bernard)

25–29 Medulli, Ucenni, Caturiges, Brigiani, Sogionti
Cottian tribes in the Western Alps

30–45 B(r)odionti, Nemaloni, Edenates, Vesubiani,
Veamini, Gallitae, Triullati, Ecdini, Vergunni, Egui, Turi,
Nematuri, Oratelli, Nerusi, Velauni, Suetri
Maritime Alps, counting roughly from north to south, still
partly belonging to the kingdom of the Cottians

The sequence, then, is broadly determined by the course
followed by the campaigns, the ethnic correlation and
geography, although certain details are still debated by
scholars. The names of those tribes that were peaceably incorporated into the Empire are in fact omitted from the
monument's inscription. Thus the sole Norican tribe to be
mentioned is that of the *Ambisontes*, who, as neighbours of
the upper Inn valley, perhaps took part in the battles.[95] Of
the Cottian tribes, six out of fourteen (the number on the
memorial arch at Susa) are mentioned, presumably those
who did not wish to associate themselves with Cottius's
prospective political activities.

19 Reconstruction drawing of the victory monument of La Turbie,
which rose to a height of 50 m.

20 At La Turbie, comparison with the church allows us to gauge
the great size of the monument–in process of restoration–commemor-
ating the subjection of the Alpine peoples. View from the West; on
the farther side of the hill the land falls steeply many hundreds of
metres to the coast at Monaco.

Peaceful existence in the Roman Empire

About the middle of the first century AD the incorporation of the entire Alpine region into the Roman Empire was concluded. The last existing special privileges of individual areas were abolished. The central imperial administration of the provinces extended across the whole territory, the Southern Alpine borderland alone, which belonged to Italia, enjoying the advantages this offered, such as full citizenship, exemption from land tax, etc.

The division of the Alpine region into a number of different provinces has already been briefly mentioned. At first, changes were confined to the Northwest through the splitting-up of the large province of Belgica in AD 85, where, with a view to newly organizing the frontier provinces along the Rhine, Germania inferior (west of the lower Rhine) and Germania superior were separated from it. Germania superior stretched from *Mogontiacum*/Mainz down to Geneva and from the Upper Seine as far as the western border of Raetia. So the whole of western Switzerland belonged to Germania superior, *Mogontiacum* being capital and headquarters of the legions stationed there.

Up until 212, the rights granted to the inhabitants of the provinces varied considerably. From the outset the Romans made a basic distinction between 'Roman citizenship' and the inferior 'Latin citizenship'. Since the inscriptions hardly ever take any notice of this differentiation, it is not usually recognizable or is open to doubt; as time went on, moreover, it seems to have acquired less and less importance.[96] The Romans called the indigenous population deprived of citizenship 'peregrini' (originally: those living on the land around the city of Rome, then simply 'the foreigners'), though it was really they themselves who were the foreigners. (But Rome, in a way that is unique in history, clung to the notion that the term 'full citizen' should only be applied to a citizen of the city of Rome, and not of a State of whatever size.) Of still lower standing were the freedmen, who could be glad they had escaped the wholly disfranchised existence of a slave. (It was not until AD 121 that Emperor Hadrian, through a ruling of the Senate, repealed the law permitting a citizen to have his own slaves put to death.)

Citizenship could be granted to individuals, groups (particularly brave army units, for example) or an entire town.

When Caesar in 50 BC or shortly after, with a view to securing the Helvetic territory, initiated the founding of *Colonia Iulia Equestris*/Nyon on the Lake of Geneva and *Colonia Augusta Raurica*, first of all perhaps Basel, then Augst, he settled there ex-legionaries, who were naturally already citizens. An instance of the subsequent granting of the status of *colonia* is *Aventicum*/Avenches, capital of the Helvetic *civitas*; in this way did Emperor Vespasian (who was also personally associated with the land of the Helvetii, his father having spent his declining years there, and he himself known it as a child) express his gratitude for their rebellion against the troops of his rival Vitellius. *Aventicum* was from then on officially allowed to call itself *Colonia Pia Flavia Constans Emerita Helvetiorum Foederata*: proclaimed by the (Emperor T. Flavius Vespasianus of the family of the) Flavians a confederate civic state of the Helvetii, loyal, steadfast, meritorious; and its citizens profited accordingly.

Individuals were granted citizenship in recognition of special services rendered. Instances like that of ex-King Cottius, already referred to, were of course the exception. Most significant, however, was the regulation under which men of the auxiliary troops acquired citizenship after serving twenty-five years. They could now officially marry, and their children ranked as Roman citizens.

On his discharge, the soldier received a small bronze tablet with a copy of the corresponding document kept in Rome, which applied to several units simultaneously. Such a 'military diploma', issued on 18 February AD 150 to a certain Publius Cornelius Crispinus, found in *Aguntum* and very well preserved,[97] is one of the most important Roman relics housed in the East Tyrolean Heimatmuseum in Schloss Bruck above Lienz.

On these lines the 'Romanization' of the provinces proceeded fairly rapidly. It was shortly after AD 200 that a fundamental change took place. The armies on the frontiers progressively assumed the character of a resident militia, and as a result the old strict rules were relaxed and the soldier's standing improved. An edict of Emperor Septimius Severus (193–211) has come down to us, permitting legionaries to live outside the barracks with their families and putting the hitherto merely tolerated soldier's marriage *(concubinatus)* on the same footing as civil matrimony, which had not previously been possible until he had served his full time. These developments were brought to a conclusion in 212, when Emperor Caracalla extended full Roman citizenship to all free provincials. This he did not do out of philanthropy, but mainly for the following two reasons: in the first place he needed for the fast-growing and ever more important army enormous sums of money, which he hoped to bring in by raising the death duty to 10 per cent. But it was only Roman citizens who were subject to death duty; by widening the circle of taxpayers, he therefore substantially increased the State's revenue. Secondly, by long-established tradition only

21 The 22 m-high wall of the Roman theatre at Aosta rears up dramatically against a background of mountains. It does not, however, represent the ancient stage's backing wall, of which only the foundations are preserved, but part of the south façade of the auditorium. Into it were set in a semicircle the tiers of seats, the first few rows of which are still to be seen. Wherever possible, the Romans made use of existing hills or mountainsides for the underpinning of the steeply raked auditorium. Nevertheless in Aosta, which lies in the middle of a flat valley bed, the theatre had for security reasons to be situated inside the town's fortifications and was therefore built entirely of walls and vaults. It held some 3500 spectators.

Roman citizens could serve in the legions; *peregrini* or mercenaries counted as auxiliaries. In this respect, too, the new dispensation operated more to the disadvantage than to the advantage of those promoted to citizenship, since they could now also be drafted into the legions. On the other hand, they were now eligible for public office, unless the class of knights and senators was given preference. The overall result was a certain equality on the part of the provinces with Italy, which Caracalla furthered by unifying the legislative procedure (Roman civic rights now became also imperial rights).

A Roman citizen, besides having to face the legal and political consequences of living within the Empire, was soon made aware of the advantages (and disadvantages!) of a superior culture. Roads criss-crossed the land; under Emperor Claudius, after whom it was named, the Via Claudia running through the Adige valley across the Reschen Pass to Augsburg, the capital of Raetia, was built; likewise a linking route through the Aosta valley to Gaul. There soon followed other roads that crossed the Alps: well constructed ones like that over the Julier Pass into the Alpine Rhine valley, or the one across the Brenner; others less easy to negotiate, such as those over the Mont-Genèvre, the Splügen or the Plöcken. Road-stations for overnight stays or changing horses made the presence of the State felt even in the more out-of-the-way districts (pp. 217ff.).

In the towns there was considerable activity, trade flourished; in the big centres like Milan, Augsburg or *Virunum* near Klagenfurt, one could buy everything that the Roman Empire–and its neighbours–had to offer. But the smaller towns up in the mountains, like Susa, Aosta, Martigny, *Aguntum* near Lienz, also benefited from the blessings of civilization: aqueducts (Ill. 49), public baths, theatres and amphitheatres (Ill. 52). Stone and bronze statues ornamented streets and squares, a temple or an entire temple complex formed the focal point of the religious cult and of Emperor-worship. Wealthy citizens dwelt in large town houses with floor heating and numerous rooms, usually grouped around a courtyard in Southern style; sometimes rooms were fitted with mosaic floors and glass windows. Those who were Roman citizens could hold an administrative office and so influence the city's future.

In fertile areas were to be found large agricultural undertakings incorporating extensive estates (for example, Sargans in the Alpine Rhine valley, Seeb north of Zurich [Ills 32 and 53] or Löffelbach in Styria [Ill. 54]), many having imposing mansions with appropriately appointed rooms. When situated close to forts or legionary barracks, they were frequently run by ex-soldiers.

The State administration was thoroughly organized. Assisting the governor, who was appointed by the Emperor and whose pay was commensurate with the importance of the province, were senior officials who looked after finance and the maintenance of roads. The governor was at the same time commanding officer in charge of the province's army, where this consisted of auxiliaries; the situation was reversed where an entire legion was stationed in the province, when the commander of the legion was also the governor, as was already the case in Germania superior.

Consequently a change took place in Raetia and Noricum as a result of the hostilities that interrupted the peaceful developments of the first and second centuries. In the year AD 121 the new Emperor Hadrian used the occasion of a visit of inspection to Noricum and Raetia to grant *Augusta Vindelicum*, Raetia's capital, the rank of *municipium*–civic rights of a kind. It may be that *Cambodunum*/Kempten and *Brigantium*/Bregenz were also *municipia*, but we have no inscriptions or literary sources to vouch for this. In Noricum, on the other hand, there were five *municipia* dating from the time of Emperor Claudius: *Virunum* near Klagenfurt, *Celeia*/Celje in Slovenia, *Teurnia*/St Peter in Holz in the Drau valley, *Aguntum* near Lienz and *Iuvavum*/Salzburg. *Flavia Solva* near Leibnitz south of Graz first became a *municipium* under Emperor Vespasian.

Hadrian's successor, Antoninus Pius (138–161), had the Upper Germanic-Raetian *limes* extended and reinforced. Along the Danube, which constituted the imperial frontier from Eining near Regensburg to the Black Sea (excluding the province of Dacia in Transylvania, from 107), watch was kept by means of a line of forts, each manned by 500, less often 1000 troops. Only in *Vindobona*/Vienna and in *Carnuntum*, a few kilometres to the east, which were both separated from Noricum at an early stage and joined to the province of Pannonia, was an entire legion of 6000 men stationed.

Germanic peoples spill over the borders

It was exactly opposite these fortresses that the settlement area of Germanic tribes began: Naristi, Quadi and above all, Marcomanni. The Northern world was on the move again; the southward pressure continued, soon resulting in congestion at the imperial frontier. As early as the year 167 the Marcomanni had determinedly demanded that they be allowed into the Empire and to have land for settlement made available to them[98]–a problem that was to exercise the Romans until the demise of the Empire. It had now come to isolated incursions, which the Romans dealt with to their own advantage. They had been warned, and from these activities grew a surer defence. Two new legions were conscripted in northern Italy, and a *praetentura Italiae et Alpium,* an organized frontier defence force in the East Alpine region was formed, to prevent any encroachment into Italy from the Pannonian lowland plain.

But all was of no avail. In the spring of 170 a combined force of Marcomanni and Quadi crossed the Danube, wiped out the Roman units drawn up against them (nearly 20,000 soldiers are said to have died), pillaged the East Alpine valleys, and finally broke through into Italy from the East. Aquileia was besieged, but did not give in; in reply, *Opitergium*/Oderzo was razed to the ground.

Now the whole of Italy was seized with panic: the way to Rome stood open, and had not the Celts a long while back swept down upon Rome? Had not the Cimbri and the Teutons reached northern Italy before being checked with the greatest difficulty? But the Marcomanni and the Quadi were content to plunder northern Italy. In 171 Marcus Aurelius had moved his headquarters to *Carnuntum,* and his generals Claudius Pompeianus and Pertinax successfully drove the Germanic forces back north. When these tried to escape across the Danube, their fate was sealed. The majority of them were killed, their booty taken from them and allegedly returned to the victims in Noricum and northern Italy (difficult as it is to picture this happening).

Like phantoms, the marauding hordes had disappeared again, the inhabitants of Noricum could breathe freely once more. But Rome had heeded the warning; at any time such a situation might recur, even though an offensive or two against the Marcomanni and Quadi between 172 and 180 restored a certain degree of calm. Of prime importance, it seems, was the better protection of the Danube frontier above *Vindobona,* since it was known that Marcomanni were located also in the Bohemian basin. These had spelt further trouble through having advanced as far as the Danube via the direct routes, namely the Cham-Furth depression (426 m) and the Kerschbaum saddle (685 m) above Freiberg, as the damage inflicted at a number of *limes* forts or associated Raetian civilian settlements and also in *Iuvavum*/Salzburg at this time shows.[99]

Rome took into account the geographical aspect, which had incidentally been crucial for the development of the trade routes for centuries past,[100] by ultimately stationing two newly constituted legions exactly facing the points where invaders would force an entry: the *Legio III italica* in *Castra Regina*/Regensburg (fortress finished 179) and the *Legio II italica* in *Lauriacum*/Enns-Lorch (from 174 in neighbouring Albing, but as this was subject to flooding, fortress in *Lauriacum* finished in 205). On account of the stationing of the legions, however, the status of the provinces of Raetia and Noricum changed, as already mentioned. In place of the imperial governor from the order of knights, with the title *procurator augusti*, there was now a legion commander from the higher senatorial ranks, with the title *legatus augusti pro praetore.* As the latter had for the most part to reside in the fortress, more and more office-holders and organizations of the old (and officially continuing) capital were moved to the legionary fortress fewer from *Augusta Vindelicum*/Augsburg to *Castra Regina* than from *Virunum* near Klagenfurt to *Lauriacum* or, alternatively, into neighbouring *Ovilava*/Wels, which was promoted to *colonia* by Emperor Caracalla. For, between *Augusta Vindelicum* and *Castra Regina* lay only 135 km of good road through uniform hilly terrain, whereas between *Virunum* and *Lauriacum* or *Ovilava* some 280 km as well as the 1227 m-high Präbichl had to be negotiated, which in winter would have necessitated a disproportionately complicated organization.

These measures had caused the main political and economic centre of gravity in Raetia and Noricum to shift to the border regions on the Danube; the Alpine region lost importance. The devastation in the East Alpine lands and the bubonic plague introduced from the Orient by the

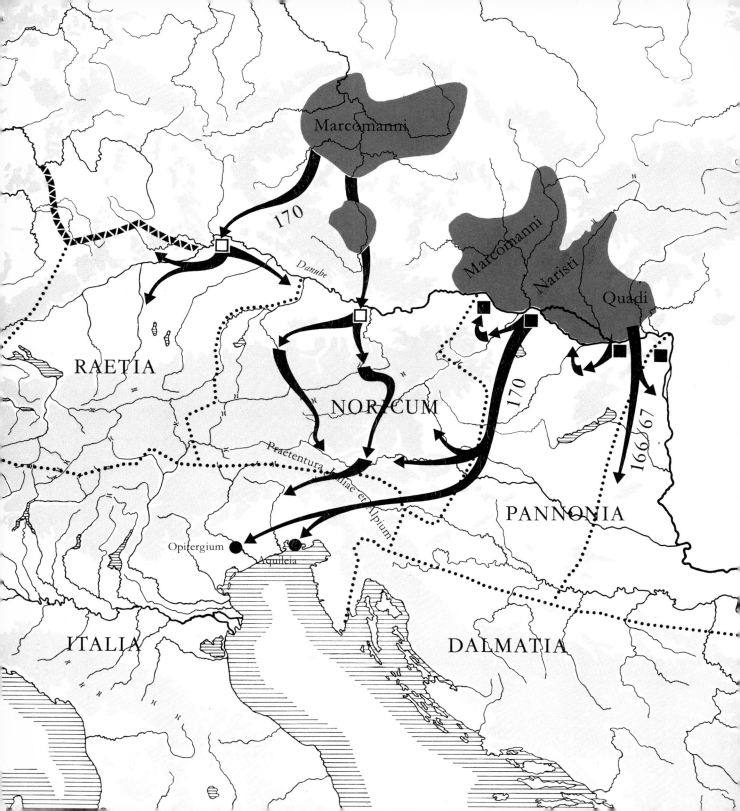

Marcomanni

Marcomanni

Naristi

Quadi

170

170

166/67

RAETIA

Danube

NORICUM

Praetentura Italiae et Alpium

PANNONIA

Opitergium

Aquileia

ITALIA

DALMATIA

troops shortly before, with its tally of countless victims, contributed to this overall trend.

There was something else, too, that had become clear to the Romans. The Germanic danger had grown to threatening proportions, and the *limes* plus the Danube forts could scarcely prevent a determined and fast-acting adversary from pressing on towards the South. Even if the Roman army's striking power sufficed by virtue of its superior tactics and technical know-how, to force the enemy back time and again, the latter caused so much damage on each occasion, that the population and the economy was made to suffer severely. And the Alps in general were no real obstacle on the way to Italy; for they were not provided with any military protection. The harshness of the unaccustomed alpine conditions was not enough to deter the Teutons, unless it happened to be the depth of winter. Besides, the Alpine settlements were not so well endowed as in themselves to constitute a target for pillaging expeditions. Hence it was, above all, the towns and villages situated on the main lines of communication that had to suffer, for invaders unfamiliar with the lie of the land will hardly have ventured into the side valleys whose approaches often took the form of narrow gorges.

At the *limes* and the upper Danube the foe was closest to the Italic heartland. Costly as were the wars in the East against the Parthians, and nerve-racking the skirmishes with the rebellious tribes of Scotland and Judaea, it was the Teutons between the Rhine and the Danube, driving southwards, who threatened the hub of power.

Initially it was the Alamanni who came to the attention of the Romans. The first incursions into Germania superior and Raetia are assigned to the year 213; a full-scale attack was directed against the North Alpine foreland, principally the Allgäu, in 233:[101] forts were stormed, settlements burnt to the ground—the inhabitants hastily hid their treasures. It is these treasures, most of which included coins, that have enabled us in some instances to discern invasions for which we have no direct historical

evidence. The Alamanni were not yet in a position to move into the Roman Empire, but it was only a matter of time before the *limes* would give way. A devastating invasion laid waste the whole of southwest Germany; the Alamanni forced their way past the Alps in the West, perhaps destroyed *Aventicum* in the Swiss midlands and suddenly appeared in northern Italy. They had reached Milan before the new Emperor Gallienus was able to halt them in 261. The *limes* between the Middle Rhine and the bend of the Danube at Regensburg could no longer be held, and Rome withdrew to behind the Hochrhein and the Danube. The parts of Germania superior and Raetia lying to the north of the Danube were immediately settled by the Alamanni–and there they remain to this day. In 270/71 an allied force of Alamanni and Iuthungi–likewise Teutons–broke through the military and topographical barrier by the Lake of Constance and poured into the Alpine Rhine valley; once again Switzerland and northern Italy were overrun. When the Romans actually suffered a defeat at *Placentia*/Piacenza, Emperor Aurelian hurriedly had a wall erected round the capital, Rome, a potent reminder of the Romans' deep-seated fear of the aggressor folk from the North; this monument, built under duress by the citizens, is still an imposing sight.

Nor were the Eastern Alps spared the menacing upheavals. By 254, the Marcomanni had forced their way down the familiar route into northern Italy and stood at the gates of Ravenna. In 275 *Aguntum* bore the brunt of the Alaman onslaught; burnt layers which can be dated, and a cache of hidden coins testify to arson and pillaging.[102] The hordes will, like those that Claudius II defeated at Lake Garda in 268, have swarmed across the Brenner, making a digression through the Pustertal.

Besides Alamanni and Iuthungi, other peoples were on the move, and these as well helped to determine the ultimate fate of the Empire. In 278, Emperor Probus drove Burgundians and Vandals out of Raetia; as early as 258, Franks had advanced right across Gaul to the east coast of northern Spain. The Visigoths began to settle in the province of Dacia (Transylvania), after Rome had surrendered it in 271; and far away in the North the Saxons plundered the coasts of northern France and the area round the Thames estuary.

22 *The invasions of the Marcomanni and other Germanic peoples around the year 170.* ■ *Already existing legionary fortresses;* □ *the legionary fortresses of* Lauriacum/*Enns-Lorch and* Castra Regina/*Regensburg set up thereafter.*

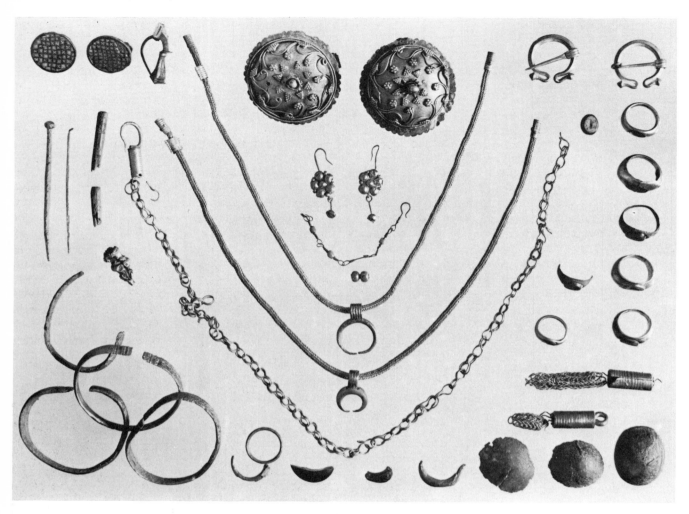

23   The onslaught of the Alamanni in 233 caused the well-to-do citizens of Cambodunum/Kempten (Allgäu) *to flee. One family, after only covering a few kilometres, hastily buried their treasure comprising 400-odd silver coins and valuable jewellery: gold ear-rings, silver brooches with flower and tendril decoration, bronze brooches with enamelled checkerboard patterns; also simpler brooches and necklaces of silver with pendants, finger-rings inset with glass or carnelian, arm-rings, hairpins and pieces of bronze.*

Diam. of large brooches 5.6 cm. Römische Sammlung Cambodunum Kempten.

24   In the wake of the invasions of the Germanic peoples the larger settlements in the Western Alps too were fortified. The wall of Dea Augusta/Die (Dép. Drôme) *dates from the end of the 3rd century* AD *and is for the most part still in excellent condition, because the medieval and modern town was conveniently accommodated in it.*

Powerful emperors in the toils

The external situation was not the only serious threat to Rome and its future; there were also the mounting inner tensions, inflation, crises relating to production, and ultimately also the conflict between paganism and a dawning Christendom. The period between 235 and 284 was the time of the 'soldier-emperors', and it has gone down in Rome's history as a terrible interlude, because personal intrigues, rivalries between army units and lust for power on the part of opposing factions frequently allowed emperors to rule for no more than a year or two, indeed sometimes only a few months. Scarcely a single one of these men, proclaimed Emperor by their troops, died from natural causes; even capable generals, faced with unaccustomed political problems, had to capitulate. To push the marauding Teutons back behind the frontiers was simply not enough.

C. Aurelius Valerius Diocles, the commanding officer of the body-guard of his predecessor Numerianus–having assumed the name Diocletian–was the first to take in hand the affairs of the Roman Empire, to endeavour by way of reforms to measure up to the changed circumstances. His long reign–284 to 305–enabled him to achieve the continuity needed for the planning and implementing of those targets which a consolidation of the *status quo* demanded. With him, we reckon late antiquity began.

Diocletian abandoned the idea of recapturing lost territories. The so-called *agri decumates* between the Upper Rhine, Hochrhein and Upper Danube thus remained in the hands of the Alamanni who–with a few exceptions, such as the 352/54 sally into northern Switzerland and the Alpine valleys[103]–rested content for the time being with the lands they had won. But then the frontier here was specially reinforced, a measure which Emperor Probus had probably initiated; the Rhine-Iller-Danube *limes* was created.[104] Unlike in former times when Rome, at the height of its power, set up forts wherever its wide-ranging activities called for them, the newly built forts of the late Roman period were on a much smaller scale, carefully tailored to the requirements of local topography. Elevated sites were favoured, whether on isolated hills or mountain spurs, with additional protection from streams or marshes. Most thoroughly researched of these is the *Vemania* fort at

Isny in the Allgäu (built before 277),[105] while for the fort of *Vitudurum*/Oberwinterthur we even have a foundation document, from the year 294,[106] namely an inscription carved into a large limestone block which once was fixed in the wall above the gateway.

Towards the end of the third century Diocletian had, furthermore, instituted a major reform of the administration: the Roman Empire was newly subdivided. At its head were to be two *augusti*, one responsible for the West, the other for the East, so as to make sure of the constant presence of the ruler and commander-in-chief. They were assisted by two *caesares,* who (in theory) were to succeed the *augusti* and in turn govern the territory assigned to them. That at this stage a name *(Caesar)* and a newly created title of honour (*Augustus* = the exalted) were adopted from the time of transition from Republic to Empire to represent a permanent badge of office ('Augustus', admittedly, was soon only understood and used as a title) says much for the tenacity of the Romans' conception of the State.

The old provinces were split up into smaller units, resulting in the creation of 101 new ones, which were grouped into twelve administrative districts (dioceses); their heads *(vicarii)* were subordinate to the competent emperor. Under this dispensation the Alpine region was naturally not treated as a unity but–regarded as an inaccessible block– allocated to the currently adjacent provinces and dioceses. Raetia and Noricum were each split in half, the former into Raetia I and II, the latter into *Noricum ripense* (riparian Noricum on the Danube in the north) and *Noricum mediterraneum* (south Norricum). Only the division into Raetia I and II with their capitals *Curia*/Chur and *Augusta Vindelicum* had further consequences, in that Raetia I, nearly identical with the subsequent Chur-Raetic region, managed to preserve the Romanic tradition unadulterated into the Middle Ages over a wide area. Raetia I and Noricum, and parts of the Western Alps as well, were later settled by Teutons and/or Slavs, who forced back the Romance element on an extensive scale.

But we are anticipating. The Roman Empire was still in existence, and the reign of Diocletian (294–305), who–as was stipulated–abdicated after twenty years and retired to his palace in *Spalatum*/Split (he came from Dalmatia), and of Constantine the Great (*caesar* from 307, *augustus* in the

West from 312, sole ruler, with *Byzantion*/*Constantinopolis* as his capital, from 325) did in fact bring about a certain degree of stabilization. Nevertheless, the decline of the Empire, less initially in the political than in the economic sphere, could not be checked.

The Alpine region, too, was affected. The barbarian invasions, the relentless recruitment of soldiers, and terrible plagues (in 250 a pestilence brought from the East had again taken hold) decimated the resident population, with the result that poverty became widespread. Safety was sought in hill settlements, most of which had a simple wall or palisade for protection, sometimes even in caves. In place of spacious houses built of stone, simple timber structures were put up (p. 104). Grave-stones and memorials grew scarce; since offerings in tombs implied a material outlay for the bereaved, they were increasingly dispensed with. Much of what had been accomplished by Roman civilization now proved too demanding, or too costly in terms of labour, and could no longer be used to advantage as a matter of course: public baths needed to be maintained and heated; the value of money decreased steadily the more people resorted to dealing in kind; imports from other parts of the Empire were often too expensive (though fortunately the prudent Emperor Probus had at least promoted viticulture in the provinces); the upkeep of militarily important roads became an increasing burden for neighbouring people.

After Galerius and Licinius, as *augusti*, had recognized the Christian religion in 311, and two years later Constantine the Great had with his edict of toleration decreed that there should be full religious freedom with equal rights for

25 No other monument conveys so vividly the idea of the tetrarchy, the 'four-emperor rulership', and at the same time the partition of the Empire as does the porphyry group of figures at the southwest corner of St Mark's cathedral in Venice. Each of the two bearded augusti *embraces his respective* caesar, *the subordinate ruler of a divisional domain and at the same time successor. All are represented as commanders-in-chief with weapons and general's cloak. Like the bronze horses above the main portal a symbol of Venice, this group was carried off from Constantinople (Istanbul) as booty in the heyday of the commercial republic (1204); it used to stand in the former imperial palace. About* AD *300/305. Ht 1.30 m.*

Christians, the way was open for the spread of Christianity, though with an essential bias towards the Roman administration. In at least every provincial capital, probably also in every *municipium*, there will by this time have been a bishop who (as the very name *episcopus* = overseer indicates) superintended his diocese.

Surprisingly, the Teutons, after their invasions of the third century, kept relatively quiet for quite a long time. The Romans busied themselves with strengthening their northern frontier. Emperor Flavius Valentinianus (364–375) had fortified watch-towers *(burgi)* built, to close the gaps between the forts on the Hochrhein, Iller and Danube; he foresaw, moreover, that the routes across the Alps could only be protected by means of cleverly located forts in the most important valleys, since thoroughgoing robber bands comprising intrusive Teutons and dispossessed townspeople or uprooted peasants were currently doing much damage. Dating from this time are the forts on the edge of and in the Alps, which were planned with such strategic brilliance that the maximum advantage was obtained from the balance between size and manning: examples of this are *Foetibus*/Füssen,[107] *Brigantium*/Bregenz Oberstadt,[108] Schaan in Liechtenstein,[109] *Curia*/Chur,[110] *Veldidena*/Innsbruck-Wilten,[111] *Teriolis*/Zirl near Innsbruck.[112] In the North Alpine foreland the distinction between the military and the civil population grew more and more indistinct. Most of the male population were under arms, once the local units of the militia had been drawn up. At the same time, there were many who, wishing and able to escape being conscripted, had repaired to Italy or at least to the Inner Alpine region. The civilians, for their part, were able to enjoy more security in the forts and fortified settlements. This explains the existence of places like the fortified road-station of *Abodiacum*/Epfach[113] situated in a bend of the river Lech south of Augsburg, the Wessling settlement near Munich[114] with its palisade, or Wimsbach near *Ovilava*/Wels with a simple encircling wall like the Mont-Musiège in France south of Genava,[115] the Moosberg stronghold near Murnau[116] with the additional protection of an extensive marsh. These places harboured a relatively large civilian population, at the same time carrying out important work, such as keeping watch on roads, storing grain supplies in *horrea* (large barns) and quartering troops in transit. Contact with army units, which continued to be moved from place to place, gave the occupants the feeling that they were still part of the great Roman Empire, even though between whiles they were largely left to their own devices. How conflicting must have been the emotions aroused by those Oriental or North African troops which unexpectedly, one day in the fourth century, passed through the Alpine foreland; they, too, suffered losses, for some of the accompanying pack and riding camels must have perished in *Abodiacum* and *Vemania*, as bones found there testify.[117]

Farther north, on the Danube line, the troops were to a large extent 'Roman' only by name. More and more Teutons had joined the Roman army, and many soon qualified as officers. Rome, in its time of need, had adopted a policy which admittedly could only put off the inevitable end for a few more decades: well-paid Teutonic mercenaries defended the northern frontier against repeated attacks by Germanic hordes.[118] But as late as 375, marriages between citizens of the provinces and 'barbarians' were proscribed, a clear sign that in certain areas these were already an everyday occurrence.

There was another people who, indirectly, hastened the end of the Roman Empire. In 376 the Huns,[119] mounted hordes from the steppes of Inner Asia, destroyed the kingdom of the Ostrogoths in the Ukraine. This started off a massive chain-reaction in a westward direction. The Ostrogoths, like the Visigoths, retreated, the Vandals went into action, as did the Quadi and the Suebians. All these stormed the Empire's frontiers, demanding land on which to settle; what was not handed over willingly, they took by force.[120]

The top generals were themselves by now Teutons, valued and urgently needed by the emperors by virtue of their proficiency. The most famous of them was Stilicho, a Vandal who in 392, as commander-in-chief to Theodosius the Great, drove back a combined force of Goths, Alans, Huns and Bastarnae on the Lower Danube. Following the Emperor's death in 395 the Empire was permanently divided into two independent halves. At the same time Illyricum was ceded to the Visigoths under Alaric, but they pressed farther westwards. In 401 Aquileia was besieged, and it must have been at this stage that some or even most of the troops were pulled out of Raetia in order to protect Italy. An incursion by the Ostrogoth Radagais,

26 In late Roman times people took refuge on barely accessible heights or behind strong walls. One such place is the Moosberg in the Murnauer Moos (Upper Bavaria). This photograph taken in the winter of 1927/28 shows the hill in the centre, surrounded by flooded marshland–an insuperable obstacle for Germanic hordes unacquainted with the locality.

who also struck at the Alpine region, finally sealed Raetia's fate in 405/6. In the ensuing years the Empire yielded up the province–even if not by formal agreement; the land lay open to the Teutons.

Immediately, the Alamanni began to extend their settlement area in a southerly and easterly direction, but it took several decades for the Raetian Alpine foreland to be reoccupied to any appreciable extent.[121] In the Alpine valleys the Teutons made even slower progress: they were for the

most part content to exercise political control of the passes, as future developments in what was Raetia I will show.

The Western Alps, too, were harassed by Germanic hordes on the move, but officially they still belonged to the Western Roman Empire. That this signified little is attested by a despatch sent by the priest Salvianus from Marseille about 440, which ended with the revealing statement that many Romans 'preferred to live as poor but free in the land of the barbarians than as slaves in their own'.[122] This was an allusion to the concentration of wealth and power in the hands of a few individuals and the arbitrariness of the officials. But at least the threat of invasion by alien peoples was not so great there in the West.

In Noricum the situation was more precarious. Here it was the Danube region in particular that had to cope with perpetual incursions by smaller bands of Teutons. No sooner had Flavius Aëtius won a major victory in Noricum (and once again driven the Alamanni out of Raetia) than the Huns burst into Central Europe; it was a joint victory of Romans and Teutons on the Catalaunian Fields at Châlons-sur-Marne in 451 that rid them of this plague. In the 'life' of St Severin, published at the beginning of the sixth century by his pupil Eugippius, we are given a graphic description of conditions in Noricum between about 460 and 482.[123]

The decimated populace dwelt in congested quarters in the forts along the Danube from *Quintanis*/Künzing (still in Raetia) to *Batavis* and *Boiotro*/Passau on either side of the Inn, as well as *Lauriacum* and from there down to the Vienna basin.[124] Severin tried to maintain a more less operational organization (he was probably a former high State official with experience to match), yet Noricum could in the end not be saved. About 473 Severin had to let the army and the civilian population be evacuated from the fort above *Lauriacum*/Enns-Lorch, and in the Inner Alpine settlements, such as for instance *Iuvavum*/Salzburg or *Cucullae*/Kuchl a few kilometres to the south, life must have been reduced to the bare minimum of subsistence. *Tiburnia-Teurnia*/St Peter in Holz near Spittal on the river Drau, Noricum's effective capital, was also repeatedly threatened. On one occasion, indeed, the occupants had to hand over to the Goths their stores of cloth and stuff destined for the North, in exchange for their lives. At this time the Church showed itself to be the only institution capable of taking over, at least in outline, the role of the 'State'. Yet in 488 the rest of riparian Noricum and parts of south Noricum had finally to be surrendered. Not that this meant the land was wholly depopulated, but those that remained, peasant and herdsman, were now left to fend for themselves.

Germanic kingdoms on Roman soil

For most of Italy had meanwhile fallen into Germanic hands. The general of a West Roman army division stationed in Liguria, Odovacar (a Scirian), had on 4 December 476 deposed the last nominal emperor, the youthful Romulus Augustus, mockingly dubbed 'Augustulus', and had himself appointed king by his Germanic followers. But even he, who regarded himself as legal adviser of Rome and sought East Rome's recognition, found himself in trouble when in 488/89 some 100,000 Ostrogoths from the Pannonian lowland plain marched into northern Italy, supported by East Rome which wished to bring down the usurper. Their leader Theodoric, who had at the early age of seven come to the East Roman court as hostage and there risen to high military rank, had Odovacar and his family murdered and himself proclaimed king in March 493. As his capital he chose Ravenna, which shortly after 400 (owing to the protection afforded by marshland and lagoon) had been made the seat of the West Roman court and was consequently sumptuously appointed. Theodoric, who owned ancillary residences in Verona and Milan, called himself 'Flavius Theodoricus rex', whereas East Rome seems to have called him semi-official 'King of the Goths and Romans,'[125] But the Goths remained aliens in Italy.

To their kingdom belonged not only Italy, but also the diocese of Illyricum (in so far as it could be controlled at all), so it had a frontier here with the East Roman Empire. How far north it spread is controversial. Certainly it still took in the South Alpine people within the confines of Italia, and probably also the former Raetia I; lowland Raetia, on the other hand, together with riparian Noricum up to the Danube, sparsely settled and its economy in poor shape, can best be described as an Ostrogothic 'sphere of interest',[126] for nobody had as yet formulated any political demands. Oddly enough, a fish played a significant role in this context. For Cassiodorus[127] lists among the native

27 Following the loss of the territory beyond the Rhine to the Alamanni the Romans from the late 3rd century AD strengthened the new frontier by means of forts. On a line that had been moved back lay the Irgenhausen fort, occupying a hillock by the Pfäffikersee (canton Zurich) and built upon the ruins of a farmstead demolished by the Alamanni, near an important road from the North to the Walensee and on into the Alpine Rhine valley. The air photo shows the regularity of the layout and the solidity of the walls, which were once at least 7 m high. Inside, the quarters of the officers and other ranks, the armouries and workshops abutted the outer walls (reconstructed to a small extent only). It is not known when the little building with two apses was put up nor what purpose it served. L of the sides including the towers about 61 m.

dishes at the Ostrogoth court ...*a Rheno veniat anchora-go*...–'from the Rhine comes the anchorago'. Since that presumably refers to the 'Rheinanke' *(coregonus wartmanni)*, the Ostrogoth realm must have extended across the main Alpine ridge and reached the valleys of the Vorderrhein and Hinterrhein beyond; in which case it will undoubtedly still have included Chur as administrative centre. None the less, Raetia I could still claim a special status: it was 'attached' to the kingdom, rather than 'incorporated' in it, and the military commander bore the title of *dux* (roughly translated, 'duke') and not *comes* (in the sense of 'nominal count', as royal official).[128]

We have a clearer picture of the political situation in the West. The Ostrogoths continued to occupy a coastal strip east of the Rhône, including the Maritime Alps, having probably chosen the provinces of Alpes Maritimae and Narbonensis II by way of orientation. To the west of the border with Italia and Raetia I, however, the Burgundians had established themselves. These had, until they were decimated and driven out by the Huns (ballad of the Nibelungs!) in 436, inhabited southwest Germany, in close proximity to the Alamanni; but in 443, as confederates of Rome ('allied' barbarians), they were settled between the Saône, the Rhône and the fringe of the Alps. There they were to serve as frontier defence against other Germanic peoples, and consequently regarded themselves as 'Romans'.

As, however, the West Roman Empire continued to break up, and the Huns were no longer on the rampage, the Burgundians in 457 founded their own kingdom,[129] which soon extended from the Upper Loire to the frontier with Italy; the fortified cities of *Genava*/Geneva and, soon after, *Lugdunum*/Lyon were the royal bases. By this means they commanded the important passes over the Western Alps and periodically harassed the Ostrogoths, who sought an understanding with the Franks, the new power in Central Europe. The Franks then proceeded to conquer the Burgundian kingdom in 532–34. As early as 496 they had subjugated the Alamanni, but not until they had beaten the Burgundians, a victory that enabled them to exert influence over the Western Alps, were they to lay hands on the former Raetia I.[130] The Ostrogoths were no longer in a position to maintain their mastery here, for after Theodoric's death in 526 East Rome went all out to

win Italy for itself. The attack was launched from the South, and by 552 the kingdom of the Ostrogoths came to an end. By the time the East Roman emperor Justinian died in 556, his commanders had not only taken the whole of Italy, Dalmatia, Corsica and Sardinia, but had in addition wrested North Africa from the Vandals.

Yet Italy soon came under Germanic rule once more. In 568 the Lombards, driven out of the Pannonian lowland plain by the Avars,[131] under their king Alboin conquered northern Italy and soon pressed farther south. Their capital was Pavia, but Cividale in Friuli also played a significant role.[132]

The boundaries in the Alpine area, however, remained for the time being the same as they had been under the Goths. Life in the mountains, moreover, was little affected by all that had been going on around. The Teutons took scant interest in the Inner Alpine region. They contented themselves with controlling the passes and roads from the military and political aspect. Because they have been so excellently researched, we are best able to assess conditions in what was formerly Raetia I. Chur evolved uninterruptedly to become the centre of medieval Chur-Raetia, as the name would imply. Despite the nominal sovereignty of the Franks, the region remained 'Romanic', regarded culturally and linguistically. The all-but-fully excavated cemetery of Bonáduz (p. 138f.) near the confluence of the Hinterrhein and Vorderrhein testifies to the continuity of the population from the fourth century well into the seventh or even the eighth (after which the cemetery was presumably transferred to the parish church); the same may be assumed to have happened in Chur itself, though the damage done by latter-day building activity has meant that comparable precise investigations could not be carried out here.[133] Alamannic influences diminish the farther one proceeds from the Lake of Constance into the Alpine Rhine valley.[134]

The kingdom of the Burgundians, to whom the Western Alps belonged, can be recognized by its characteristic cemeteries containing graves dating to as early as the fifth century. The people either settled in the Roman towns or used the Roman *villae* as living quarters. The rapidity with which they merged with the resident population makes it difficult to distinguish, from either the cemeteries or the settlements, between these two elements.[135]

The same applies to the East Alpine region, where we may safely assume larger population groups to have persisted from late Roman into medieval times.[136] Yet the struggle on the part of these people to survive and their utter poverty have so far allowed us to identify scarcely any material that can be dated with certainty to the fifth century. On this account the excavations at *Ibligo*/Invillino near Tolmezzo on the approach to the Plöcken pass (p. 104f.) are of special importance. Here, in addition to older settlements of the second-third centuries, fortifications, houses and finds from Ostrogothic and Lombardic times were discovered (Ill. 139), which effectively broaden our picture of the fifth to the seventh century in the frontier area of the Italic kingdoms of the Teutons. This settlement contained a richly endowed church on a nearby hill, surrounded by scattered graves. The early medieval *Teurnia* in the Drau valley, where there is likewise a large church dating to around 500 (Ill. 119), also has a cemetery (though in a different part of the town).[137]

All over the Alpine region researchers have paid particular attention to the earliest churches, many of which were built back in the fifth or, indeed, the fourth century. Their dating is, however, nearly always based on architectural or stratigraphic features, rather than on chronologically identifiable objects or graves in their vicinity, or actually inside the church. Uncertain as the dating may be in some instances, these do on the whole give us a very clear idea of what early Christianity meant to the Alpine people.[138] That there were monks we learn from the 'life' of Severin, who founded small monasteries by the churches belonging to Noricum's forts. It was, naturally, a question of providing modest quarters *(cellulae)* for those individuals who had dedicated their lives to the service of God and their fellow men.[139] By comparison, the monastery which the Burgundian King Sigismund had built in 515 at the vitally important road junction of St-Maurice d'Agaune, between Martigny and the Lake of Geneva, will have been far grander.[140]

Whereas in the Eastern and Central Alps information relating to these early churches is to be obtained from excavations alone, because they were later destroyed or replaced by new buildings, the evidence points to a somewhat different situation along the Mediterranean coast. There the people, the domestic economy and commerce were far less affected by the upheavals of the fifth and sixth centuries, allowing greater continuity. This applies in particular to the baptismal chapels that were additional to the parish church, since for liturgical reasons they played scarcely any further role in later times and so were spared when aging would otherwise have necessitated reconstruction or rebuilding. Particularly impressive examples are to be found in Fréjus and Albenga as well as in Novara and Riva S. Vitale in Ticino. Among the larger buildings, S. Lorenzo in Milan is the best preserved: this church was probably erected at the instigation of Empress Galla Placidia at the beginning of the fifth century. The ideals of monasticism, initially transmitted to Gaul from the East, were here put into practice at an early date. In 415 a monastery and a convent were founded in Marseille, and the convent on the island of St Honorat (Lérins off Cannes), older perhaps by a few years, served for long as nucleus of the spiritual life in southern Gaul and the Western Alps. His sojourn at Lérins even awakened in Saint Patrick emotions that would determine the future development of ecclesiastical life in Ireland and England. The international outlook and versatility of the Church at that time is particularly well exemplified by the fact that the Irish Saint Columban, having served successfully as a missionary in eastern Gaul (Luxeuil monastery in Burgundy, founded 595) and been expelled (609) for denouncing the immoral life led by Queen Brunechildis (Brunhilde), founded the monastery at Bobbio on the northern flank of the Apennines, after completing an adventurous march through Gaul, 'Alamannia' and across the Alps in 613. The literary sources convey the effectiveness of God-fearing, resolute individuals who preached the Gospel and backed up their faith with organized enterprises.[141]

All this could only take place in an evolving political climate that favoured wide-ranging contacts and consequent dissemination of ideas. After the victories of the sixth century the kingdom of the Franks acquired stability, a State with secure frontiers and a thriving economy. A Merovingian strain, named after Merowech, provided the kings, but individual ducal families enjoyed a far-reaching autonomy under an often weak central authority. For a long time the kingdom remained unmolested by outside enemies, having in the Southeast alone to contain the attacks of the Slavs as they pushed westwards. This people stemmed from the forest and marsh lands of central Russia and, by the time the Germanic tribes had retreated in a westerly direction, had themselves advanced to the borders of the Ostrogoth empire. Gradually they, in turn, fanned out westwards and took possession of the sparsely settled land of eastern Central Europe. In the sixth century the Slavs came under the domination of the Avars, who had earlier forced the Lombards to retreat from the western Hungarian lowland plain to Italy. At the end of that century the Avars and the Slavs, together with their subject peoples and allies, finally destroyed the thinly populated towns of old Noricum, namely *Virunum, Teurnia* and *Aguntum*. It took a hard-won victory on the part of the Bavarians in the Pustertal around 610 to bring the Avars and Slavs to a halt, not a few of whom settled down in the valleys of Carinthia and Styria (the heights, which they found uncanny, were not suited to their way of life which was based on agriculture); from this time on we can recognize the Slavic element there as a stable component of the population.[142] This is attested by the names of places and people all around, particularly towns and rivers ending in *-itz*; even the name of the Styrian capital (Graz) is Slavic, deriving from the word *gradec* = stronghold.

All this resulted in the distribution of the peoples, ethnic groups and also languages in the Alpine region being in the main the same as today. In the West and on the south side of the Alps lived, as they had long done, the 'romanized' indigenous peoples; the Germanic immigrants, such as the Burgundians and the Lombards, made only a slight impact on the culture, and none on the language (apart from a few loan-words and place-names). Latin remained the base, and it was only later historical developments with their different political alignments that led to its splitting-up into Italian and French; additionally, in the Inner Alpine region 'Raeto-romanic' (named Ladinic in the East), which stems still more directly from Latin and is spoken from Graubünden to Friuli, has persisted to this day.[143] From the northern border of the Alps the politically powerful Germanic element penetrated the Inner Alpine area. In this way the Eastern Alps once more became German-speaking, and the busy and influential Adige valley in South Tyrol separated the western Raeto-romanic from the eastern Ladinic sphere. In Switzerland the settling by German-speaking 'Walsers' in

a number of high-lying valleys caused a displacement of the linguistic boundary. This Alamannic people, who at the end of the first millennium had come from the North into the Valais above Sion, spread between the twelfth and the fifteenth century southward and eastward–to Piedmont, to Graubünden and even to Vorarlberg.[144] A special case, which only came to light in the last few years, is that of the Sette Comuni, seven communities in the mountains southeast of Trento with the little town of Asiago at its centre. The language that was spoken here until the beginning of the twentieth century was a south German-Bavarian dialect (attempts to revive which are currently being made), and a very early version at that, because, the villages there being isolated within a region where Italian was spoken, few subsequent changes in the German tongue reached them. These villages were probably settled by Germans in the eighth/ninth century, when Bavaria and some North Alpine bishoprics also owned many scattered estates farther to the south.

The new power in the North

But we have been anticipating events. For in the meantime the Frankish royal house of the Merovingians had been made to hand over power to the major-domo, the court administrator and leader of the belligerent retinue. The first to be encountered is Pepin the Elder in the kingdom's western sector. But the other sectors (the kingdom was usually divided into two or three parts on a hereditary basis) also had their major-domos, who did as they liked and took little notice of the kings of the older lines. Significantly, the office of major-domo itself became to a large extent hereditary, thus gradually giving rise to new dynasties. When Pepin II died in 714, his son Charles Martel assumed power, and he, for the first time, succeeded in uniting the kingdom under a single leader. And this, indeed, was urgently needed, for now a new danger threatened from the Southwest: Islam, under whose banner marched the 'Moors' or 'Saracens', as they were called in the North.

Islam, the religious faith founded by Mohammed between 610 and 632 and based on the monotheistic tenets of Judaism and Christianity, showed itself to be a force making for exceptional community-feeling among the

Arab peoples, and they now shattered the outposts of the East Roman Empire with a succession of victorious ons-laughts. Hordes of them fought their way westward along the North African coast, winning more and more adher-ents from among the native tribes, and finally crossed the Straits of Gibraltar. The Ostrogoth army could offer no resistance, and by the year 713 at the latest the Iberian Peninsula (with the exception of the extreme northwest) was firmly in Islamic hands. But not even this was enough: Gaul was the next target for raiding, pillaging and conquering. Not until Charles Martel with his disci-plined foot-soldiers and his new weapon, mail-clad horse-men bearing couched lances,[145] won victories at Tours and Poitiers, south of the Loire, was the Islamic flood halted. Nevertheless more than 700 years were to elapse before the Iberian Peninsula was again wholly Christian; for it was 1492 before Granada, the last Arab State on European soil, was captured.

Martel's victory, historically so significant, went far to-wards establishing his position as sole ruler. But he was not yet 'king', though he had every reason for regarding him-self as such. It remained for his son, Pepin III, proclaimed monarch in 747, to end the shadowy existence led by the Merovingian kings. The consequences of these events are of so much importance where the power politics and intel-lectual climate of this period are concerned, that it may also explain why the relationship of the medieval German emperors with the Pope and Italy proved to be of such im-mense significance.

For Pepin could not simply remove the nominal ruler, the Merovingian Childeric III, and have himself pro-claimed king. This would have gone against the still sur-viving Germanic interpretation of the hereditary nature of the royal sovereignty based on blood ties and the asso-ciated 'All hail' on the one hand, and the necessary con-senting voices of the kingdom's bigwigs on the other. Pepin would, notwithstanding his actual power, be counted as an illegal usurper, and that might result in a conflict among his own supporters. So he had to resort to a trick, one that, while showing considerable ingenuity, had far-reaching consequences. He entrenched himself behind an authority of a different order, the Bishop of Rome, the successor of Saint Peter, the Pope. The evolution of the West Roman papacy up to this point is somewhat con-fused and need not concern us here. At all events, what matters is that in the course of the progressive Christiani-zation and Church organization of the Frankish kingdom, a secular power was faced by an ecclesiastical one, each dependent on the other, and initially they co-operated outstandingly. Representing the Church was the Pope in Rome, and his authority in matters ecclesiastical, moral and spiritual was undisputed, in that at this time the rul-ing houses of Central Europe had long since embraced Christianity, initiated bishoprics, founded monasteries and themselves ultimately given active support to mission-ary undertakings among neighbouring peoples.

So in 751 Pepin put the question to Pope Zacharias whether it was a good thing that the King of the Franks no longer exercised any power. The Pope knew, of course, what Pepin was getting at, and replied–although the per-sonal issue had not been mooted–that that man should be king in whose hands the real power lay. This answer was no casual remark nor was it made out of kindness, it was dictated by necessity. For the Lombards were oppressing Rome. In 749 they overran Ravenna, then still a support base of the East Rome Empire, and encircled the city of Rome. The Pope, who laid claim to a 'Church State' extending from the upper Adriatic diagonally across the Apennines to Latium, the *patrimonium Petri*, saw his supre-macy imperilled and his role limited to that of a Lombar-dic regional bishop. He urgently needed assistance, and military assistance at that, so he had to cleave to the man who wielded the most power in Europe, namely Pepin. Since East Rome continued to assert its rule in southern Italy and Sicily, and even in the upper Adriatic, he could clearly not turn to that quarter, particularly as the Eas-tern Church contested the primacy of the Pope. Pepin conveyed the Pope's pronouncement to the bigwigs in the kingdom. They were glad to be given the opportunity to accept the actual situation without any pricks of con-science, and proclaimed Pepin their king. His anointing by Archbishop Boniface, the Papal Legate, signalled the end of the royal line; Childeric III, the last of the Merov-ingians, was relegated to a monastery.

It was high time for the Pope to provide himself with cover from the rear. The attacks of the Lombards were becoming so violent that Stephen II, Zacharias's succes-sor, decided upon a sensational sourse of action. In 754 he

journeyed through Lombard territory, crossed the Alps by the most direct route to the northeast, presumably via the Great St Bernard, and called upon King Pepin at one of his residences, Ponthion on the Marne. Casting himself down at the monarch's feet, he begged for his support against the Lombards. That he at the same time re-anointed Pepin and included his two sons in the ceremony made such an impression, that the Imperial Diet agreed to render assistance. Pepin indeed had his military successes, on several occasions compelling the Lombard king Aistulf to retreat, make concessions and pay tribute, but it took his son Charles–the great Charlemagne–to arrive at a final solution of the problem.

After Pepin's death in 768 the kingdom was divided between his sons Carloman and Charles. The former's early death (771) meant that the country's unity was preserved for several decades. When the new Lombard king Desiderius besieged Rome once again, Charles decided that the time had arrived to settle the matter once and for all. In 773 he marched into Italy with his army, relieved Rome, captured the capital Pavia and deposed Desiderius. Thereby the Lombard kingdom became Frankish a year later, and it was Frankish followers who faithfully governed the land as the king meant it to be. One of these noblemen is portrayed in his Frankish attire in the church of St Benedict in Mals (Vinschgau); he is dedicating a splendid sword on the occasion of the founding of the church.[146] For the first time a Central European power had reached across the Alps towards the South and, in the shape of the maturing Church State, taken protective charge of what remained of the West Roman empire. Nothing could better illustrate the fundamental shifting of the centres of political power in West and Central Europe.

If this is a clear case of the king's success in foreign politics, his control of home affairs was by no means as firm as it might seem to us today. The king was, as ever, depen-

28 Stucco statue of Charlemagne in the monastery church of Müstair (canton Graubünden). The emperor wears a crown and carries orb and sceptre; a riding-mantle covers the short coat. The brooch as well as the arm-rings will have been of gold set with precious stones. Opinions differ as to the age of the statue; it most likely dates from the beginning of the 12th century. Ht 1.9 m.

dent upon the goodwill of the dukes, counts and other members of the nobility; whenever he wanted to take steps that were contrary to the wishes of dissenting rulers, he had only his own vassals to fall back on, those who had pledged themselves to him because of the land he possessed and his means, plus, at best, maybe an ally or two who saw in it some advantage to themselves. There could be no question of an absolute hold on all his subjects; not until the seventeenth and eighteenth centuries did such a state of affairs come about in realms of any magnitude.

It is against this background that developments in the southeast of the kingdom must be viewed. As so often happens when the defence of border areas had in the main to be entrusted to local leaders and their vassals, there was in the decades around 700 a trend towards autonomy in such areas. This applied in the Southwest to Aquitania (against the Moors), in the South to the Alamanni (against the Lombards) and in the Southeast to Bavaria (against the Lombards and Slavs). Most threatening was the situation in the Southeast, because the Avars, having since 680 been relieved of Bulgar pressure, cast covetous eyes once again towards the West. By around that year, indeed, Lorch on the Enns was destroyed, the old *Lauriacum*, which then already belonged to the area settled by the Bavarians.

Teutons and the Romance people on the northern border of the Alps

The part played by the Bavarians down the centuries was largely governed by the fact that, as border people in the Southeast, they were accustomed to adopt a defensive attitude towards external forces or, when circumstances allowed, themselves ventured beyond the border. Thus, by around 600 at the latest, they had taken the Brenner and the upper Isarco valley; before 680 Bolzano, which had belonged to the Lombards, was firmly in Bavarian hands. Paulus Diaconus tells us that resident there was someone whom the Bavarians called *gravionem* (German *Graf* = count). At this time, indeed, the Bavarians had extended their sphere of influence so far southward, that they pushed the German language boundary, roughly identical with the southern border of latter-day Tyrol, to more or less where it is today, forming a kind of corridor where the inhabitants' way of life and speech was still Romance.[147]

It was just those parts of the Alpine region where the Germanic element exercised most power and influence– though the Romanic tradition lived on vigorously –that fostered the overbearing attitude which a writer at the end of the eighth century (probably from the vicinity of the Reichenau monastery on the Lake of Constance) refers to in the following terms: *stulti sunt romani, sapienti sunt Paioari*–stupid are the Romance-speakers (Welschen), clever are the Bavarians.[148] The Welschen, the old Romanized native mountain people, were in the first place only infiltrated by slow degrees by the Alamanni and *Bajuvarii*, as they spread southwards. Many names in the North Alpine foreland testify to the existence of these people, whom the new settlers regarded as aliens:[149] Walchensee in Upper Bavaria and Walensee between the Lake of Zurich and the Alpine Rhine valley, Strasswalchen east of Salzburg, Chur with its suburb of Welschdörfli, to mention only a few. We also owe it to the Romanic folk, moreover, that Roman place-names have come down to us, albeit in the modified form that the change in intonation and the passage of a thousand years has brought about. Here are a few examples:

Augusta Vindelicum	Augsburg
Augusta Raurica	Augst
Teriolae	Zirl near Innsbruck
Veldidena	Wilten (district of Innsbruck)
Cucullae	Kuchl (south of Salzburg)
Curia	Chur
Brigantium	Bregenz
Sabiona	Säben (high above Klausen)
Lentia	Linz
Foetes	Füssen
Parthanum	Garmisch-Partenkirchen
Cambodunum	Kempten
Sedunum	Sitten/Sion
Turicum	Zurich
Abodiacum	Epfach (on the river Lech)
Lauriacum	Lorch (district of Enns)
Vindobona	Vienna

These names, especially those of the Alpine foreland, are often of Celtic provenance *(-dunum, -iacum, -bona)*, but the Teutons will certainly not have been familiar with these original Celtic versions, rather with their modified Latin form. In this connection, Vipiteno, the Italian name for Sterzing, artificially adopted since South Tyrol became bilingual in 1919, clearly derives from the original *Vipitenum*. A little farther down the Isarco valley we find a somewhat different situation where the Latin *Claustra* corresponds to the German Klausen (= Ital. Chiusa); for Klausen is a loan-word from the Latin, which has always corresponded to the Italian.

Archaeologically, the best evidence of the progress made by the Bajuvarian folk is to be found in their planned cemeteries. The graves lie, as in the whole of Germanic Central Europe, in rows, the dead with their heads toward the West, adorned with jewellery and costume ornaments. The southernmost 'rowed' cemetery so far discovered in Bavaria is located between the old focal towns of Garmisch and Partenkirchen,[150] that is, close by the Roman road-station of Parthanum (Ill. 79). The oldest finds from there can be dated to a little before 650. This tallies with observations in North Tyrol, where about the same time, upstream along the Inn, Bajuvarian settlers established themselves among the Roman inhabitants.[151] That the Germanic people when settling in the mountain area chose locations on the trade routes is evidenced in the South by the rich warrior's grave at Civezzano (Ill. 81), a few kilometres east of Trento, a place associated with the control of the road in the Valsugana, the importance of which in the late Roman period lay in its military posts (and possibly abundant mineral wealth).

Seen against this background, the varying conditions in the Salzach valley, too, are easier to understand. When the Slavs and Avars settled in the Eastern Alps, the route across the Radstädter Tauern became of no account, virtually from the end of the fifth century. So the Bajuvarii saw no purpose in pressing farther into the mountains here. They occupied the open land north of Salzburg and also Reichenhall because of its salt-water spring,[152] but the extensive marshlands round and to the south of Salzburg[153] formed for centuries the natural boundary between the Bajuvarii and the Romanic peoples in the mountainous interior. This is evident not only from the distribution of Bajuvarian cemeteries but also from the abundance of Romanic place-names south of Salzburg and Romanic names of individuals in the earliest records of the bishopric.[154] In the Alamannic West the situation

developed differently, because in Raetia I and then in Chur-Raetia a well-organized State controlled the trade routes and a rapid advance by the Alamanni, say up the Rhine valley, was neither possible nor necessary.

But it was not only towards the South that the Bavarians deployed, but also eastwards. In the course of the seventh century the Bavarian settlers pushed on into present-day Upper Austria[155] and took over good arable land, guided by the old Roman roads with their adjoining formerly cultivated ground. There are, it is true, a few burials of the sixth century, but they are still the exception and should rather be attributed to scattered Lombards who had come up the Danube from Pannonia. The mountain valleys did not attract any Germanic settlers, and the river Enns may have constituted the frontier against the Slavs and Avars.

Charlemagne–Frankish and Roman emperor

By about 700 the Bavarian duke had attained such a degree of independence, that he could when necessary afford to oppose the royal command. For in actual fact the Merovingians were no longer in a position to ensure that their demands were met, and the Carolingian major-domos had first to consolidate their own position. Nevertheless, once Pepin III had had himself proclaimed king, one of his aims was to strengthen Frankish sovereignty. The Bavarian duke Tassilo III did in 757 swear allegiance, but soon he was scarcely bothering any longer about the far-off Frankish king. With Charlemagne, though, he could not take such liberties, and he and his country had in due course to pay for it. For when the Franks had conquered the Lombard kingdom in 774, the Bavarians suddenly found themselves without support; they were caught in a pincer movement. In 787 Charlemagne attacked the Bavarians; Tassilo hurriedly swore an oath of allegiance, but Charlemagne was vexed. At an Imperial Diet in Ingelheim between Mainz and Bingen a year later he had Tassilo apprehended and, after a mock trial, confined to monasteries, where he spent the rest of his days, first in distant Jumiège on the Seine, then in Lorsch north of Heidelberg. Bavaria became a Frankish province with a *praefectus* as governor.

Henceforward Bavaria's missionary role vis-à-vis the Slavs, ushered in by two ducally promoted monastic foundations (769 Innichen in the Pustertal, 777 Kremsmünster in Upper Austria), was taken over by the kingdom. In 795/96 Charlemagne's defeat of the Avars, with some ensuing skirmishes, eliminated this peril for good; but it took a few more years for him to accomplish his life-work, the creation of the great unified empire of the Franks. In 804 he was able to put a victorious end to the bloody war of conquest against the Saxons. Widespread resettlement operations dispersed rebellious opponents over the whole empire, including places at the Alpine border, such as Sachsenkam near Bad Tölz. Ultimately, in 806, Chur-Raetia, too, lost its special status: the bishop, and so also his line, lost their temporal power, which went to a Frankish count.[156]

The crowning of his life-work, literally, was vouchsafed Charlemagne at Christmastide in the year 800, when Pope Leo III placed the imperial crown on his head. The *patricius Romanorum*, the protector of the Romans (since Pepin III), became an *imperator Romanorum*. Thus did Pope and Emperor rebut the claim of East Rome to have inherited the Roman Empire. East Rome saw no way out of this, and in 812 Emperor Michael I recognized Charlemagne as *basileus*, as the East Roman emperors called themselves. Two years later Charlemagne died at the age of 71. With good reason, he lives on in the memory of the Central European peoples as a great ruler who laid the foundations of the Middle Ages. The Frankish empire was now the decisive power in the West, political unification having bestowed on it the ability to expand, whether southwestwards against the Moors, or eastwards against the Slavs.

29 This flagon constitutes a unique historical document. The technique and style indicate that the polychrome enamelled panels on the body and neck stem from the early Islamic Orient, in fact from a 'ball-sceptre' of the kind associated with the equestrian peoples of south Russia and Hungary. In all probability Charlemagne came by an object such as that as booty during his victorious battles against the Avars. It was divided up into its component parts and put together again in a totally different form and for quite a different purpose. The flagon, of embossed sheet-gold ornamented with sapphires, contained the consecrated wine at particularly important church ceremonies. Early 9th century AD. Ht 30.3 cm. Abbey of Saint-Maurice d'Agaune (Valais).

Through the incorporation of northern and central Italy, the Alpine massif no longer functioned as a frontier area, becoming once more, as previously under the Romans, merely an obstacle to trade and transport. Yet, since under the emperors regional and local forces were as strong as ever, and territorial control formed the basis of the State system, a struggle for possession of roads, passes and towns arose at the lower level. To go into this in any detail is beyond the scope of this book, but in order to give some idea of events that led to present-day political conditions in the Alpine region, a very cursory overview of the times that followed is appended.[157]

With Charlemagne, at all events, ends an era the history of which archaeology alone or in great measure allows us to reconstruct. At the same time, the coronation of the Emperor in 800 marks the point at which the political initiative passed for many centuries from the Mediterranean to the North.

The empire and the duchies

The Alpine region, as already mentioned, was virtually unaffected by what was happening in the empire as a whole. The determining factor was the development of local government, to be found everywhere under imperial sovereignty. For, ultimately, the emperor was nothing more than a land-owning nobleman who occupied a special post merely by virtue of his descent or, later, through having been elected by the aristocracy. An important point, too, was that in the next four hundred years the empire tended to be divided between sons in accordance with Germanic rights of succession, and to what extent it remained united both by law and in practice depended upon their insight.

As early as under Charlemagne's grandsons the final partition of France was effected. Initially, in 843, a division into three with boundaries running from North to South was decided upon, whereby the middle section, apportioned to Lothar I, extended from the eastern Friesian Islands to Marseille and Italy; then, after an intermediate period beginning 870, the Treaty of Ribemont (880) set conditions that were to determine developments for some time to come. Between the West Frankish kingdom (the hub of France), the East Frankish kingdom (the hub

of Germany) and the kingdom of Italy, a Burgundian kingdom incorporating the entire Western Alps in addition to the Rhône-Saône area had suddenly asserted its independence. Strictly speaking, Burgundy at that time comprised two kingdoms: Lower Burgundy (with Arles as capital) and Upper Burgundy, of which the Welf Rudolf I became king in 888. Both kingdoms put out feelers towards Italy and occasionally even provided its kings, but there was as yet no question of an expansionist policy.

The situation in the eastern part of the Alpine range was different. There the Carantanian kingdom, with a mainly Slav base, had established itself (for the archaeological documentation see p. 144). The name was once associated with the Ulrichsberg, the *mons Carantanus*, then with the Karnburg north of Klagenfurt, and is perpetuated in the Kärnten (Carinthia) of today; at that time, though, the Steiermark (Styria) and several adjoining areas belonged to it as well. But as early as 750 the Slavs had appealed to the Bavarians for help against the Avars, with the result that from this time on Bavaria maintained overall sovereignty. Then, at the beginning of the ninth century, Carantania was robbed of its autonomy, incorporated in the duchy of Bavaria and finally, after 876, handed over to the illegitimate Carolingian Arnulf, who later also became king of the East Frankish kingdom. In 936/37 Emperor Otto I, so as to protect the eastern frontiers, began to set up the so-called 'Marks', under the command of 'Markgrafen' (margraves). Thus the Ostmark south of the Danube, the Steiermark (Styria), the Mark Kärnten (Carinthia) and the Mark Krain (Carniola, in present-day Slovenia) were formed, after the victory over the Magyars in 955. But all this was subject to continual change: about the year 1000 the Steiermark was put under the command of Bavaria, while the new duchy of Kärnten (from 976) corresponded more or less with what is today Carinthia together with Carniola. Just at this time the Babenberg line came into possession of the Ostmark, and now it is possible to detect the beginnings of Austria.[158]

Faced with all this political manoeuvring, we must not overlook the fact that in the tenth century the Magyars terrorized Central Europe, as had the Huns earlier. Their hordes of mounted horsemen, pillaging and plundering, swept many times through the North Alpine foreland;

30 A mounted Saracen has captured a Lombard priest: rock drawing 1700 m above Villar Focchiardo in the Valsusa (Piedmont).

they even crossed the Western Alps and stormed through northern Italy to invade France. There is also convincing archaeological evidence confirming the Magyar onslaughts, as for example at Schäftlarn south of Munich, where are still to be seen large-scale systems of walls and ditches coupled with cleverly devised obstacles to keep horsemen from reaching the inhabitants' place of refuge.[159] This peril was not finally eliminated until Otto the Great's victory on the Lechfeld south of Augsburg in 955, after which the Magyars began to fit in with the Central European community of States.

No less terrifying were the Saracens; these hordes of Islamic folk, mainly from Spain, had since the end of the ninth century established themselves in Fréjus, the ancient *Forum Iulii* in the Côte d'Azur.[160] During their incursions they were not even deterred by the mountains, as is attested by the destruction in 940 of the wealthy monastery of Disentis high up in the Vorderrhein valley; at the same time Saint-Maurice in the Valais went up in flames. Not until 972, through concerted action, was Fréjus retaken, as a result of which West Mediterranean maritime commerce was given a great boost.

In the Central Alps meanwhile little had changed. The western part belonged to the duchy of Suebia, the eastern part to that of Bavaria which for a time was able to extend its influence as far as Trento. In pursuing its Italian policy, the German empire was keen to add the Western Alps to its territory. This aim was achieved when in 1033 the kingdom of Burgundy was united with the empire.

Germany–Burgundy–Italy now made up the foundation of the emperor's sovereignty. How important this was became clear in 1076, when the controversy over temporal versus spiritual authority during the investiture conflict reached its peak. Pope Gregory VII had declared King Henry IV deposed and excommunicated because the latter would not accede to the ecclesiastical demand that bishops be appointed by the Church alone. Since the Diet supported this move and called upon the King to give in, he had no option but to do so. In the early winter of that same year Henry and his loyal supporters crossed the Alps by the Mont-Cenis–at that time of the year a particularly hazardous undertaking even with native guides, and suggesting an act of desperation (p. 232f.). That he chose the Mont-Cenis rather than the far more convenient Reschen pass or one in eastern Switzerland was owing to the Suebians having blocked their roads and passes. So he had, also on his way back, to choose a route that circumvented this enemy power, namely across the Eastern Alps to Bavaria.

From 25 to 28 January 1077 Henry had stopped over at Canossa, a castle on the northern slope of the Apennines near Reggio Emilia. Having offered to do penance, his excommunication was revoked by the Pope, a humiliating acknowledgment of the Church's claim to have the right to regulate its own affairs–the beginnings of a split between Church and State, foreshadowing a dispute that continues to this day.

Savoy, Habsburg and the Swiss Confederacy

During the ensuing centuries it was primarily in the west of the Alpine region that new States were formed and new houses came to power, which led to the building-up of greater realms. Three names are prominent in this context: Savoy, Habsburg and the Swiss Confederacy.

The first of these to come to the fore were the Savoyards. When, on the death of the last of the Burgundian kings, Burgundy was united with the German empire in 1033, the sons of Duke Umberto managed to secure for themselves the erstwhile royal monastery of Saint-Maurice between the Lake of Geneva and the Great St Bernard, an important station for traffic thanks to its situation and one that was visited by pilgrims on their way to and from Rome. This place, together with the holdings that went with it, brought in a sizeable revenue and provided opportunities to take a hand in major political issues. Established as they were since the tenth century at the western edge of the Alps, the family had the foresight to take advantage of this when preparing for the struggle to control the most important passes.

By the thirteenth century, in the days of the German Hohenstaufen kings, the Savoyards (named, by the way, after the 'Sapaudia', the term the Romans applied to the northern part of the Western Alps) ruled over a large territory in the lower Valais including the Great St Bernard and–acquired through marriage–forward areas in northern Italy, extending beyond Turin. They had in fact created a small Alpine State belonging to the Burgundian kingdom of Arelat on the one hand, and on the other hand to the kingdom of Italy.

They had thereby gained control of the three most important Alpine passes between western Central Europe and Italy: the Great and the Little St Bernard and the Mont-Cenis. To the south, the duchy of Dauphiné had become autonomous in 1029, but the passes it controlled were far less important, its commerce on a small scale, its State organization undeveloped (even Grenoble could not count as the official 'capital'), so that this creation came to an inglorious end in 1349. Humbert II ('with the empty hands', as he was dubbed) sold his bankrupt State to the French king, who bestowed it on his son and heir (hence the name 'Dauphin' applied to the heir to the French throne). This was accompanied by a deliberate denial that the Dauphiné together with Savoy and the duchy of Provence with its Mediterranean coastline (1246 to the house of Anjou and not until 1481 to France) really belonged to the German empire. But these French-, or Provençal-speaking, districts were so alien to the German emperors, that–except in the case of Savoy–the latter did not feel inclined to press their demands. When Emperor Charles IV in 1378 acknowledged the Dauphin as his 'deputy' in the central Western Alps, this was, considering the current political situation, an empty gesture in order to save face. He was, moreover, the last German to be crowned king of Arelat–which has long since dwindled to a name on maps in the court chancellery. For, back in 1310, the house of

Savoy had come to an understanding with the Habsburgs and its members had princely rank bestowed upon them by Emperor Henry VII of Luxembourg.

From this time on Savoy and Habsburg went their own ways, and several centuries were to pass before they faced each other again in battle over the independence of Italy. The Habsburgs had their eponymous castle at Brugg on the Aare south of the Hochrhein, possessions in the vicinity as well as in the Alsatian Sundgau and in the Baden Breisgau. A decisive factor in their rapid rise was the acquisition of Austria (the old Ostmark) with the Steiermark (1282), Kärnten with Krain (1335) and Tyrol 1363. Rudolf von Habsburg (1273–1291) was the first king of that line, but he owed his position solely to the fact that Ottokar II of Bohemia, who after 1251 brought the lands from Austria to Krain under his command, lost the royal contest against him in 1273 and his life in the deciding battle of the Marchfield (beyond the Danube northeast of Vienna) in 1278.

Tyrol, then, a typical pass State, had held out longest against attacks from the outside. Following the Bavarian advance on the South Alpine flank and the acquisition of the bishopric of Trento, this area became a part of the duchy of Bavaria. But this leaves us little the wiser as to who actually wielded power in the individual territories at a time when the political structure was so stratified and decentralized. Thus it was the area between Innsbruck and the Verona defile with its tributary valleys divided up into several duchies, that at the beginning of the eleventh century went to the bishops of Brixen (Bressanone), Trento and Regensburg, mainly because the Emperor was determined to break up all monopolistic control and distribute power among various rulers. The bishops with the administrative apparatus available to them were not at that time in a position to cope with the temporal problems of such a State system, and handed over the ducal power to indigenous noble families. Since, however, the bishops themselves stemmed mainly from the very same houses, this did not lead to any fresh conflicts but underpinned the power and influence of the families resident there.

This being the case, the dukes of Tyrol–the name of their castle above Merano by which they identified themselves–for the first time play a major role. The Vinschgau around the Upper Adige valley (home of the *Venostes*, who were subject to the Romans, and the *pagus Venosta* and *pagus Finsgawe* of medieval times) together with their position of *advocatus* (German 'Vogt') in the Trento bishopric were the prime source of their power. By 1248 they ruled over the entire Upper Adige valley almost to Verona, as well as the Middle Inn valley in what is today North Tyrol. Subsequently they acquired still more estates, above all in the West and the East, which would determine the future extent of the province of Tyrol. In the political field, however, the relative independence of the dukes of Tyrol was short-lived, since in 1363 such authority as they had possessed passed to the Habsburgs, who regarded their gains in the Inner Alpine region as no more than a rounding-off of their far-flung territories. For their interests were those of a major power, which in 1516, through the acquisition of Spain with its Central and South American possessions under Charles V, could boast that 'the sun never sets' on their empire.

Whilst, on the far side of the Atlantic, the Spaniards and their Habsburg monarchs had no difficulty in prevailing over tribes and States whose way of life and thinking were altogether different from their own, and whose technology was far less advanced, it was precisely on their home ground that the Habsburgs had face the determined resistance of the mountain peasants of the northern Central Alps. Thus, after the dying out in 1218 of the Zähringen family line, which had held the most powerful position in the duchy of Suebia (and to whom we owe the founding of such beautiful towns as Freiburg im Breisgau, Fribourg and Bern, as well as the opening up of the St Gotthard pass), numerous smallish and very small political units had come into being in the mountain territories. Here lay the germ of the federal concept, in which partners with equal rights banded themselves together, refusing to be subject to a higher authority. When, in 1231 and 1240 respectively, the inhabitants of Schwyz and Uri acquired direct control, they were naturally still subject to the German emperor, but nobody else had a say in their affairs.

The Habsburgs were made aware of this when, towards the end of the thirteenth century, they tried to extend their authority to East and West. In 1315, at Morgarten on the Lake of Lucerne, the peasants of Schwyz, Uri and Unterwalden (incorporated 1291 into the 'eternal confederacy' as 'Ur-cantons') defeated the Habsburg knightly army, which was no match for the reckless courage of the country folk and quite unaccustomed to mountain conditions. More districts now joined the Confederacy, which was further strengthened by actually capturing some of the Habsburg possessions; finally, having warded off renewed attempts at annexation, its independence was guaranteed by the Habsburgs in 1388. There followed a phase of active expansion, which continued until 1536 when the Savoy-held districts of Geneva with the Vaud and Chablais were incorporated, thus–allowing for a few minor adjustments in more recent times–causing Switzerland to assume its present form.

The southward thrust was made easier by the political disruption of northern Italy. As it turned out, however, it was only possible to hold on to Ticino plus the Misox; the Veltlin between the Lake of Como and the Stilfser Joch, allotted to Graubünden in 1512, was in 1798 given to Italy by Napoleon, who for several years robbed Switzerland of its independence and made it an 'Helvetic Republic'. The Chablais south of the Lake of Geneva went to France in 1860, after Italy had surrendered the western parts of Savoy. From 1515 on, Switzerland pursued a policy of strict neutrality and full independence under international law, its final severance from the German empire being ratified by the Treaty of Westphalia in 1648.

Napoleon and the consequences

Although the great powers concentrated their attention increasingly on disunited Italy, the political and territorial situation in the Alpine region, including areas outside Switzerland, up until the end of the eighteenth century remained relatively stable. The Western Alps belonged to Savoy, which had Turin as capital; it was only in the far South that France held fairly large parts of them. The valleys to the south of Switzerland were now under the rule of Milan. In the East, power was shared between the Austria of the Habsburgs and the Venetian Republic; the archbishopric of Salzburg alone had preserved its independence. Savoy still remained a pass State, but in the War of the Spanish Succession, when Spain and its possessions were being carved up, Savoy's ruling house succeeded in getting hold of a piece: in 1713 it was awarded Sicily, which in 1720 it exchanged for Sardinia, at that time Austrian. In this way the dukes of Savoy suddenly became kings of Sardinia, as the kingdom as a whole was then called. At the same time Milan with its extensive territory came under Austrian rule.

The period of Napoleon's ascendancy wrought radical changes, though these were mostly revoked after his downfall. Savoy was annexed by France, and what remained of northern Italy wrested from Austria, to become part of a newly created kingdom of Italy. Switzerland was, as previously mentioned, subject to Napoleon as 'Helvetic Republic', and the Valais was for a short time actually incorporated with France, so as to ensure control of the Great St Bernard. For Napoleon, too, joined the ranks of those who made history by crossing the Alps. In May 1800–that is, at a somewhat unfavourable time of year–he led an army of 30,000 men together with his artillery over the Great St Bernard to Italy, in order to face the Austrians there. During those years even Bavaria, which was sympathetic towards Napoleon, tried to expand at the expense of Austria. In 1809 the archbishopric of Salzburg, North Tyrol, South Tyrol north of Bolzano and the Inn district went to Bavaria, Italy being awarded the rest of South Tyrol. The Tyrolese rose up against the Bavarians and the French, but a few military successes gained them nothing on the political front against superior power; in 1810 Andreas Hofer, instigator of the uprising, was executed in Mantua–a chapter of Bavarian history which did them little credit.

Once Europe was freed from the Napoleonic scourge, the Congress of Vienna of 1815 brought back some order to the political scene. Switzerland won back its independence and the Valais. Tyrol and Salzburg went to Austria, together with Venetia and most of Lombardy. The house of Savoy once more ruled over the kingdom of Sardinia, which now included the former Genoese coastal strip in Liguria. Thus the germ of a united Italy was planted, but the time was not yet ripe for it to sprout. It needed the aftermath of the events of 1848, when the call was for 'nation-states', for the unification and liberation of Italy to be realized. Sardinia-Piedmont allied itself with France and defeated Austria in 1859 at the battles of Magenta and Solferino. But the outcome was not quite the hoped-for one: Austria held on to Venetia, while France in return for its help laid claim to Lombardy. This last pro-

blem was solved in 1860 by Sardinia-Piedmont ceding to France its preponderantly French-speaking provinces round Nizza/Nice as well as the present-day départements of Savoie and Haute-Savoie, in exchange for Lombardy. This led–if we allow for certain slight adjustments after the second World War–to the present-day frontier on the passes between France and Italy.

That same year Garibaldi and his volunteer army succeeded in crushing the Bourbon kingdom in Sicily and southern Italy, and so, after annexing the central Italian duchies and large slices of the Papal States, laying the foundations of the new Italy. In 1861 they proclaimed Victor Emmanuel II of Sardinia King of Italy. Hence the capital was at first Turin, then Florence and finally, after the final occupation of the Papal States in 1871, Rome. In order to gain Venetia, Italy actually allied itself with Prussia, and the resulting military successes brought their reward: in 1866 Venetia became Italian, though south Tyrol remained in Austrian hands. The first World War and the dissolution of the Habsburg monarchy ultimately determined the–still existing–frontiers in the region of the Central and Eastern Alps. Under the terms of the peace treaty of 1919 South Tyrol as far as the Brenner as well as Istria went to Italy; Austria had, furthermore, to cede Carniola, parts of Carinthia and southern Styria to the newly-formed kingdom of the Serbs, Croats and Slovenes, later to become Jugoslavia. Istria however, did not become part of Jugoslavia until after the second World War.

Problems over the new frontiers

We have but to examine the frontiers that were decided upon in the nineteenth and twentieth centuries, to realize that they reflect an attempt to meet a changed geopolitical situation. The new Alpine frontiers are no longer made to run, as formerly, through defiles difficult to penetrate yet

31 Even the Great St Bernard pass (2469 m) lay within territories that belonged together culturally and politically; it offers the shortest route between Italy and western Central Europe. The photograph shows in the foreground the track hewn into the rock, used by the Romans up until modern times; above it stands the saints statue, and farther on is the hospice.

easy to defend, but follow mountain ridges and watersheds. Valley-areas on either side of passes, that once belonged together, are separated, while communities with a common tongue are regarded from the angle of 'nation-States' possessing a spurious cultural unity, and assessed on a percentage basis. This applies not only to South Tyrol, but also to the Western Alps, where the language spoken in the mountain district of Piedmont is predominantly French, and the Aosta valley at least possesses a certain degree of autonomy; it applies no less to the Eastern Alps, where the frontier on the ridge of the Karawanken cuts through a territory in which the German and Slovenian language and culture were intimately mixed.

Such a fixing of frontiers, though of course in itself an historical factor, can only be regarded as a flying in the face of history, a history that in the case of the Alpine region goes back thousands of years. It is self-evidently the handiwork of politicians, who as inhabitants of the plain see in mountain terrain only what is divisive, remote and uncanny. According to them, a mountain ridge must serve as a dividing line, the impassable state of the passes in winter will hamper communication between the valleys, whilst the problems presented by the narrowness of the passes can be overcome by building bridges and tunnels. But since administrative and territorial matters used to be ordered in a far more natural way (which even the rather less interested Romans widely respected), with due consideration for the language aspect, the modern nation-States with their newly-drawn frontiers have, particularly in the Alpine region, created more problems for intercommunal living than they set out to solve. These problems will not be solved until new types of State organization make it a matter of principle to guarantee co-existence, with equal rights, of peoples whose joint history has shown it to be justified. There is no reason why Europe should not one day succeed in achieving what Switzerland–though not without difficulties–has put into practice effectively for centuries.

A start has been made, for a few years ago a 'Working Group of Alpine Peoples' (Arbeitsgemeinschaft Alpenländer), which holds regular conferences at ministerial level, was formed. Were this, however, to confine its work to discussing tourism and the construction of motorways, little purpose would be served. Whether a knowledge of our own past leads us to devise the means of overcoming future problems remains to be seen.

II From Wattle Hut to Palace – How the People Lived

Nothing is more lasting than a post-hole. This fact, established during early excavations at north German ramparts and Roman forts, is as convincingly demonstrated there, as it is unrewarding for the Alpine region. It is of particular significance because every post, once it has been rammed or dug into the ground, tends to leave a permanent impression on the surrounding earth. The post itself will have rotted away, but what is left is a dark patch with a round or angled outline. In some instances the cavity itself is still identifiable. The archaeologist, having uncovered a largish area of an ancient settlement, can reconstruct the ground-plans of houses and huts from the way the post-holes are distributed (see Ill. 42). Even when neither hole nor post is any longer visible, reconstruction is still possible if stones have been used to wedge the posts. Such a clue is specially valuable where over many centuries generation after generation have built their houses on top of the rubbish of the preceding one; for in such instances the layers of refuse have become so dark and moist, that post-holes are no longer distinguishable.

In the Alpine region, however, this archaeological aid is seldom available–the wide valleys of large rivers, where the settlements were located on slopes or knolls above high-water level, being the most likely places. For in mountain terrain, rock lies directly beneath a thin layer of humus, so that no post could be made to hold. Even in moraines, consisting largely of pebbles and pieces of broken rock, a post-hole would be extremely difficult to dig. In such places man in due course solved the problem by turning to other methods of constructing his dwellings, as we shall see.

Off on the chase

When the earliest inhabitants of the Alpine region looked for protection from wind, rain and snow, they resorted in the first place to their natural surroundings. The most welcome were favourably sited caves, for in them it was comparatively easy to cope with fluctuations in temperature. If the sun shone, they could sit at the entrance and enjoy its warming rays; should a cold wind be blowing, they had but to retreat a few metres into the cave, where a fire would give out a pleasant warmth. In the Grotte du Vallonet at Roquebrune–Cap Martin (Alpes Maritimes),[1] the earliest known find-spot in the Alps, admittedly no traces of a fire were found. It is a moot point whether, at this stage a million years ago, man had yet learned how to make use of fire, or, indeed, whether–in view of the genial climate of the Côte d'Azur (though in winter it can be pretty cold even there)–he would have had any need of it. The Grotte du Vallonet was ostensibly occupied over a longish period, but we cannot tell whether it was used as a permanent base, or merely as a seasonal outpost for hunting forays. The stone tools and the fragments chipped off in the shaping process lay for the most part in the interior of the cave. The bones of the mammals the occupants had eaten were thrown against the rear wall; they were those of older animals, indicating that hunting was at a primitive stage, when the quarry was confined to creatures that were ailing or already dead. A number of deer antlers lay about, some of them apparently worked with a cutting tool in order to fashion them into implements. All this points to the very primitive nature of man's existence at this time. To what extent the cave was made habitable we do not know since no organic matter has been preserved. Perhaps a few handfuls of leaves or a layer of sea-grass from the sea nearby served as a pallet; possibly these people had already acquired an elementary knowledge of how to use hide and leather for making mats and clothing; maybe they possessed wooden implements, chopped into shape and carved with simple stone tools, for a variety of purposes.

The ensuing millennia saw little change in man's mode of existence. Caves and rock-shelters with overhangs were still used as resting- or dwelling-places, but it is now possible to identify and evaluate open-air settlements as well. None of this, of course, tells us much about the actual progress made in these early times since the growth in population presented the archaeologist with correspondingly more opportunities of finding such a dwelling-place.

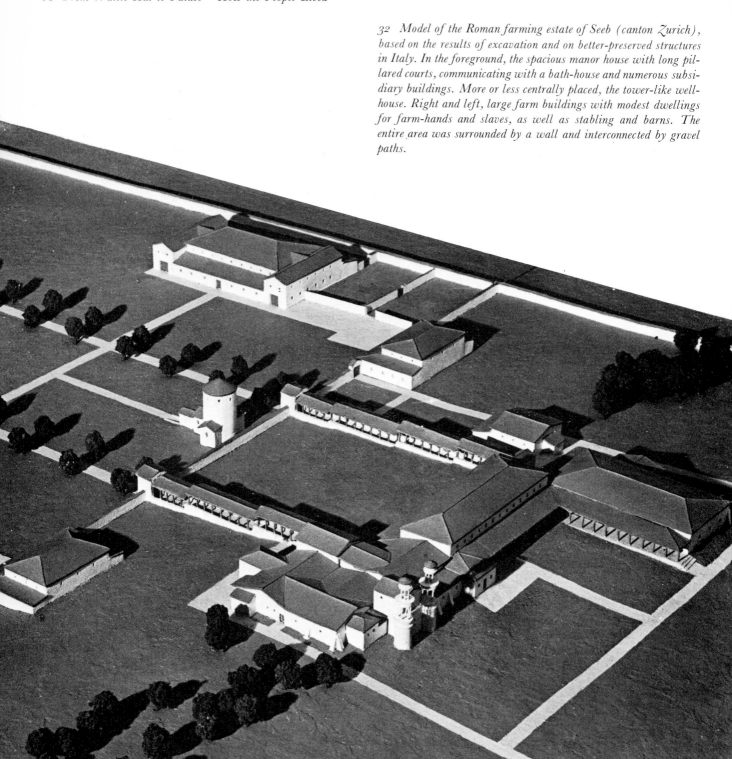

32 Model of the Roman farming estate of Seeb (canton Zurich), based on the results of excavation and on better-preserved structures in Italy. In the foreground, the spacious manor house with long pillared courts, communicating with a bath-house and numerous subsidiary buildings. More or less centrally placed, the tower-like wellhouse. Right and left, large farm buildings with modest dwellings for farm-hands and slaves, as well as stabling and barns. The entire area was surrounded by a wall and interconnected by gravel paths.

When man first appeared in the Alpine region, and not only there, he will doubtless have lived in open-air settlements consisting of little more than simple windbreaks made of branches cut from sheltering trees, or little huts. Only these, being–unlike the caves–liable to be destroyed or covered over later by the advancing ice, can very seldom be identified (p. 10f.).

It must therefore be regarded as an exceptional stroke of luck, that the campsite of 'Terra Amata' at Nice was still in a recognizable state, though some 400,000 years old, having on account of its location on the Riviera been spared the destructive inroads of the ice.[2] Thanks to the painstaking excavation work of Henry de Lumley and his team in 1966, it has been possible to discern more or less what this settlement looked like and what purpose it served. On the sea-shore, on or just behind a dune, were to be distinguished the ground-plans of a number of huts. The excavators were able to recognize in the sand the 'post-holes' of wigs and thicker branches (some of them had clearly been sharpened) and within the area thus demarcated lay food and tool-making residue. The huts were surprisingly large, being from 7 to 15 m long and 4 to 6 m wide, and they were oval instead of oblong in shape. They were made, it is to be assumed, of lopped-off branches with perhaps a few bigger supporting posts, which were rammed home close to each other and bound together. To give added support round the edges, a number of stones had been used. It is evident that this construction could not keep the wind out altogether, for the hearth in the middle of the huts (partly on a heap of gravel, partly in a hollow) was invariably shielded from the northwest by a little wall of layered stones. In some huts no trace of a hearth was to be seen, and the many pieces of charred wood and ash found were probably blown in by the wind.

In places pebbles had been strewn on the floor, and in some instances hides had actually left their imprint. Even so, the occupants had left all their refuse lying in the hut; this had been trodden into the floor, together with the chips left over from tool-making. From the excavation report, which meticulously recorded every object found, it is even possible to see where the individual who had fashioned a large stone implement had sat. For the precise spot he had chosen was entirely devoid of stone fragments, whereas these had accumulated all round him. So, on the accompanying plan which charts all these chippings, the man himself appears as an empty spot.

Such a record is only possible, however, when the huts have not been occupied for lengthy periods and the refuse has not grown into a thick, homogeneous layer. Actually, it looks as if the settlement by the sea had at no time been used for more than a few days at a time. For the excavation revealed as many as 21 'floors', one above the other, with the post-holes always conforming to the ground-plan of the prototype hut. Between each 'floor' was a layer of sand, several centimetres thick; so we get a pretty good picture of the sequence of occupation. In the spring or early summer a small group of people would come here and build huts of branches and twigs. In these they kept a fire going and hammered out their stone implements. Where the chase was concerned, elephants were the quarry, as the bones attest. (How this governed the existence of the hunters is well illustrated by the living conditions of the pygmies in Africa: 'When they kill an elephant, they do not drag it to the village but the village is moved to the place where the giant beast's corpse lies. No morsel of flesh remains unused'[3]). When they left the place again, the leaves withered, the wind roared through the branches, the winter storms created havoc among the structures and covered them over with a thin layer of sand. The following spring people returned, always the same group it would seem, for on the remains of the old huts they erected new ones, rebuilt the little protective walls for the hearth, and everything began all over again.

There is no need to conceal how we have come to know that this took place in spring or early summer. When the hunter wished to answer the call of nature, he did this simply by squatting beside the hut. The sun soon dried out the excrement, and so large numbers of little heaps are preserved in the sterile sand, which the scientists euphemistically call 'coprolites' (petrified balls of dung). Analysis of the plant remains in these showed that the people had, with actual food, also ingested pollen that was floating around–and this came specifically from trees and shrubs that flower in the spring or early summer.

Only a few hundred metres from the airy 'Terra Amata' camp-site at Nice there is a cave named 'Grotte du Lazaret'.[4] Here no less thorough excavations by Commandant Octoban and Henry de Lumley have exposed the winter quarters of early hunters. Admittedly, they date from 150,000 to 100,000 years later, but living conditions had changed so little in the interval, that we can confidently use the findings there to eke out our picture.

The cave is about 40 m long, at its widest some 20 m across, and has a relatively small entrance facing southwest. Just inside the entrance the hunters had built a hut, 11 m long and 3.5 m wide. They had made use of the natural rock for one side- and one end-wall. A system of posts had been used for the other two walls. There were seven post-holes, placed at regular intervals, into which wooden posts had been wedged with stones. Since these were vertical, they had presumably supported some sort of roof of cross-beams. As protection against wind and dripping water, this structure was then draped with skins, sewn together to form large pieces and weighted with a few stones at floor level. Further skins had been hung up to divide the interior area of some 35 m² into two different-sized rooms, each of which had its own entrance in the side-wall. In the larger room were two hearths in shallow depressions. The end-wall facing the entrance had no opening; on the contrary, it was augmented by a wall about half a metre high, made of piled-up stones, to keep out the wind and cold.

Around the hearths were grouped the 'beds' of the occupants; there was ample room to sleep ten people. The beds consisted of a scatter of sea-grass or seaweed, on which were laid the skins of wolf, fox, lynx or panther. Here, too, it is perhaps worth mentioning how the excavators arrived at their conclusions. What happened was that they found lying on the ground accumulations of little shells, which could scarcely have had any connection with food. There were similar accumulations of claws and small bones from the paws of the above-named animals, while large bones from joints of meat for their part corresponded to the distribution of implements and refuse. This implied that the little shells unintentionally found their way into the cave with the dried sea-grass (up to a few years ago we still regarded it as the most important filling for mattresses after horsehair) or seaweed, and that the skins, which were, to a certain extent at least, in a sense a hunter's trophy, were tanned with the paws attached, that is to say not first cut to shape or sewn. When such a skin became

worn or otherwise damaged, the departing owner would leave the whole of it lying, or cut away the damaged portions and leave those behind. This meant that a fair number of claws and little bones remained in the cave.

For the cave was occupied only during the winter. This is attested by the kinds of animals that had been chosen as prey. Five-months-old ibex indicate that the arrival time was November, and the marmots had already ended their hibernation when the hunters left. It is not possible to tell directly from the excavation whether they returned to the cave the following winter, or even oftener, to erect once again their hut structure, hang skins over the wooden framework and re-make their pallets. But since in a sheltered cave–unlike at the windswept huts of Terra Amata–a deposit thick enough to be visible is unlikely to form within a year, we may reasonably assume that the cave was revisited for several years running. Considering that the draughty wattle huts of Terra Amata, which were only used for a few days in the year, show such a continuity in the choice of location (near a spring!), it is surely highly probable that a small group would recognize the advantages offered by the Grotte du Lazaret with its durable interior wooden structure, and make repeated use of it. Since the occupants will have spent most of their time outside the cave in the light and sunshine, the interior of the hut is unlikely to have contained undue amounts of litter from food or toolmaking.

The above description of the nature of the settlements and of the life led by their inhabitants, the details of which we owe to recent excavations by the French, in particular Henry de Lumley, may be said to apply in a broad sense to the entire Alpine region up until the beginning of the Late Stone Age. Since investigation of the 'Epipalaeolithic' settlements in the districts of the Central Alps around the passes were only begun in recent years,[5] no precise information about the appearance of the shelters there is available. It can only have been a question of summer sites briefly sought-out by hunters, so nothing with durable structures is to be expected.

Not until the final Ice Age had ended was there sufficiently little change in the landscape of the Inner Alpine region to allow remains of settlements to be preserved even in the valleys. When in the Late Stone Age agriculture and cattle-breeding developed, this naturally had far-reaching consequences where the siting and layout of settlements were concerned. The restless life of the hunter, who was always on the look-out for new venues for the chase and had to follow his quarry on its seasonal changes of location, was superseded by the sedentary life of the farmer, who cultivated the land round his dwelling, sowing and harvesting his crop. Even if, after a number of years, the soil in the vicinity was exhausted, the farmer could always plan ahead and build and equip his home accordingly.

The classical examples of a farming life in villages with large wooden houses, which is a feature of the Bandkeramik (Linear Pottery) culture from the beginning of the Late Stone Age from the Balkans to the Rhine,[6] are–as previously mentioned (p. 14f.)–not encountered in the Alpine region. There the economic prerequisites for those accustomed to good soils and broad acres were lacking. Altogether, agriculture as a basic way of life seems to have featured in the Alps only very much later, though corn has been identified in assemblages which do not yet include earthenware vessels–do not, that is to say, relate to the fully mature Late Stone Age.[7] Be that as it may, if we want to acquaint ourselves with the Late Stone Age settlements, we have to turn to the very edge of the Alps, where the latest developments took place.

The question of pile-dwellings

The term 'pile-dwellings' or 'lake-dwellings' crops up not only in books on local history and topography but also in a far wider context, so that most people know what is meant by it. Not for nothing is the 'pile-built village' of Unteruhldingen in the Lake of Constance Europe's most lucrative archaeological enterprise. The way the settlement is perched above the surface of the lake, amid charming surroundings, and its homely wooden houses with their primitive appointments attract so many people, that on Sundays a large car park can barely accommodate the flood of visitors. But it was only at times of high-water, when the level of the lake had risen substantially, that such settlements bore any resemblance to present-day Unteruhldingen. The argument as to whether they were 'lake-dwellings' or 'lakeside-dwellings' has meanwhile itself become a part of history, following the publication in 1954

of a book in which a number of investigators expressed their differing views.[8] On the strength of that, it seemed as if all piledwellings were to be dismissed in favour of lakeside settlements, in which the buildings needed to be underpinned by wooden posts only where the swampy or marshy ground called for it. The latest excavations of Christian Strahm at Lake Neuchâtel (Auvernier and Yverdon) and Renato Perini at the lake of Fiavè, some 20 km north of Lake Garda, have finally shown that one has to take every possibility into consideration when trying to determine how man solved the problem of living on moist subsoil or by the shores of lakes.

Basically, a system of posts was used for the construction of the houses. The supporting posts for the roof, which served at the same time as a framework for the walls, were dug or rammed into the ground, particularly deep of course where the subsoil lacked stability. The structure was strengthened by means of cross-beams; the walls were made of poles, planks and wattling with perhaps some daub. But what distinguishes the 'pile-dwellings' from ordinary houses is the need for good insulation against rising damp. Sometimes a thick padding of branches and leaves, occasionally held firm with wooden poles, sufficed. Often, however, it proved necessary to raise the floor of the house clear of the ground. For this purpose supporting posts or planks had to be employed, which called for much technical ingenuity on the part of the builders. As this type of settlement is so well preserved–only because during the succeeding millennia marshland has grown up round it, or the level of the lake has risen permanently–it used to be taken for granted that the lake had washed around the house supports from the outset, as in the case of the reconstruction at Unteruhldingen. But careful investigations, as for example at Egolzwil in the Wauwilermoos (canton Lucerne), have shown that in most places there is no indication whatever that the houses have always stood in the water. At one of the settlements at Egolzwil the structure of such a village is clearly delineated.[9] The houses with floors of poles laid close together are rectangular, up to 6 m long and 4.5 m wide, and normally have a hearth in the middle. They are nearly all arranged in parallel and, together with two stables for cattle, separated on the landward side by fencing, to form a palisade. A reinforced path leads through the gateway. Settlements like this, then, are

33 Since archaeology in the Alpine region began scholars have argued about the 'pile-dwellings' on the shores of many lakes. Piles planted close together were at first interpreted as remains of 'pile-dwellers' villages' on the pattern of those in the South Seas. Subsequent excavations showed that the majority of these 'pile-built villages' had been located on firm ground and were only raised up to counter the danger of flooding or damp subsoil. From diggings most recently carried out at the Fiavè lake above Lake Garda, from which the water has receded, it has happily transpired that both views are right. Next to houses in the shore area that were only occasionally threatened by the water (Ill. 34) there is also a settlement place whose houses did in fact rest on tall posts. In several of the latter, notches for the cross-beams, some 4 m above the lake bottom, are still to be seen. When the excavators pulled up one of the piles it seemed to them as if it had almost no end: it was still embedded to a depth of 5.5 m in the ground and had total length of 9 m.

limited to those that were sited on the edge of a lake with marshy or swampy shores; at the very most, they would be standing in the water only a few days in the year after incessant rain had caused the level of the lake to rise unduly. The very existence of stables (attested by accumulations of fly larvae) would otherwise lead us to the unlikely conclusion that the cattle were conveyed to and from their pasture by barge.

On the other hand there are settlements which must have stood in the water over a long period. This has been proved beyond doubt by the excavations at Auvernier and Yverdon.[10] But even these were shore installations. They were, however, situated by lakes subject to substantial fluctuations of the water level. We know, for instance, that the lakes in the Swiss midlands, even after the first Jura water-regulating system had been installed (which was to have helped control lake levels), showed fluctuations of up to 2 m at times when the Aare as the sole outlet could no longer take the melt- and rainwater.[11] High-water carried with it all manner of flotsam, which then got lodged between the piles; it also deposited sediments which, on excavation, could be distinguished by their stratification. The periods of flood must therefore have lasted considerably longer than a few days. Yet the construction of the houses resembled that used at lake-shore settlements on insecure ground, so it will seem to have depended on the inhabitants' personal preference how close to the fish-yielding water they wanted to live and how often they were prepared to put up with flooding, which after all did them no harm provided they erected the platforms for the floors sufficiently high. (Today still, the Indians build in this manner along the great rivers and in the rain-forests of South America.) Those who preferred to keep their feet

34 The Bronze Age settlers on the island in the Fiavè lake used their ingenuity when they built their houses out into the shallow water by the shore. In order to strengthen the foundations and spread the weight evenly, they set up on the bed of the lake a rectangular horizontal framework of lateral bearers and double cross-bearers, and then rammed in vertical piles at the points where they intersected. Holes were bored into these at a uniform height. A piece of hard wood inserted into the holes transferred the pressure exerted by the supporting posts to the double cross-bearers and so in turn to the lateral bearers.

dry when stepping outside their hut settled a few hundred metres farther inland. What is more, there are signs that during periods of low-water workshops for minor activities were set up on the dried-out strips of the shore.

Whilst this explanation seems convincing where the large lakes of Switzerland with their fluctuating water levels are concerned, the findings at Fiavè are rather more equivocal.[12] Here, too, there are enough indications that water had washed round the piles. For during the Middle Bronze Age there had been a conflagration; the charred remains of the walls and roofs had fallen between the piles, but the piles themselves, the surviving height of which was more than a metre, showed no traces of burning. But even if they did stand in the water, this still does not tell us whether this was the case throughout the year. For they are part of a settlement on a former island in the lake (about 80 m long and 60 m wide), on which the remains of other houses not of comparable pile-construction were found. So the 'pile-dwellings' represent only the outermost line of houses of this island settlement, which may have encroached upon the lake for reasons of space. Here, moreover, the water was only 1 m deep at the most, to judge by the excavated material. Also, had it been deeper, the careful, well thought-out construction would scarcely have been feasible. This prevented the piles, which carried the whole weight of the superstructure, from subsiding. The entire lay-out of this Middle Bronze Age settlement (*c.* 1700–1400 BC) is fairly representative of the type found in Switzerland which we have been discussing.

A mere 20 m or so farther to the southeast, though, was found a second settlement, which was occupied from the Early Bronze Age until the Middle Bronze Age. It lies in a former inlet of the lake, and excavation revealed a dense jungle of piles (Ill. 33), as have a number of other findspots by Swiss lakes. Even allowing for the fact that the chalky substratum is a relatively soft sediment, what Bronze Age man achieved here is nevertheless astonishing. He handled huge tree trunks, propelling them with precision into the lake (probably with a twisting action), so that they could build their dwellings on them. In this case the houses do actually appear to have stood in the water, assuming the original bed of the lake to have consisted of genuine, undisturbed lake-chalk. But we cannot ignore the possibility that the level of the lake was likewise subject

to considerable fluctuations, either seasonal or due to geological changes at either the inflow or outflow points. The two settlements so far discovered in the Fiavè lake do not appear to have come into existence at the same time. At the settlement on the island it has so far been possible to identify three phases extending from the very end of the Stone Age to the beginning of the Late Bronze Age, with a definite interval between the first and second phases. And it is exactly into this interval that can be fitted the material found at the second settlement farther out in the lake, which may have been just as large. The way the houses are constructed points to a different type of base, but whether this settlement had stood in the water from the outset can only be determined by further excavation and analysis (in particular a comparison of the levels of the living quarters).

Pile-dwellings occur on the fringes of other lakes in the Alpine region as well. Prior to the discovery of Fiavè, the most important settlement in northern Italy was that by the Lago di Ledro.[13] This little lake lies west of the upper end of Lake Garda, and when the water level fell as the result of work on a hydro-electric installation, it revealed the remains of pile-dwellings with many artefacts. A selection of these is illustrated here (Ills 36–37), as they present a good cross-section of the inventory of a typical Bronze Age settlement: earthenware vessels of various shapes, utensils of stone, bone and bronze, bone and bronze ornaments, wooden implements and vessels. That artisans worked bronze on the site is evidenced by clay ladles for pouring the molten metal and clay nozzles for the bellows. They also made tools of stone, bone and wood, as was no doubt done at all but the smallest settlements. A little museum by the lake provides much useful information and contains many artefacts, giving the visitor a good idea of how Bronze Age man lived at the Lago di Ledro.[14] Where the Austrian lakes are concerned, the Mondsee, the Attersee and the Traunsee in the Salzkammergut had 'pile-dwellings' along their shores, as did, among others, the Lac du Bourget and the Lac de Paladru in the Western Alps.[15]

It may be assumed that most of the lakes in the Alps and Alpine foothills, to the extent that their altitude and shore conditions were favourable, attracted settlements from the Late Stone Age on, and that they lasted until the Iron Age

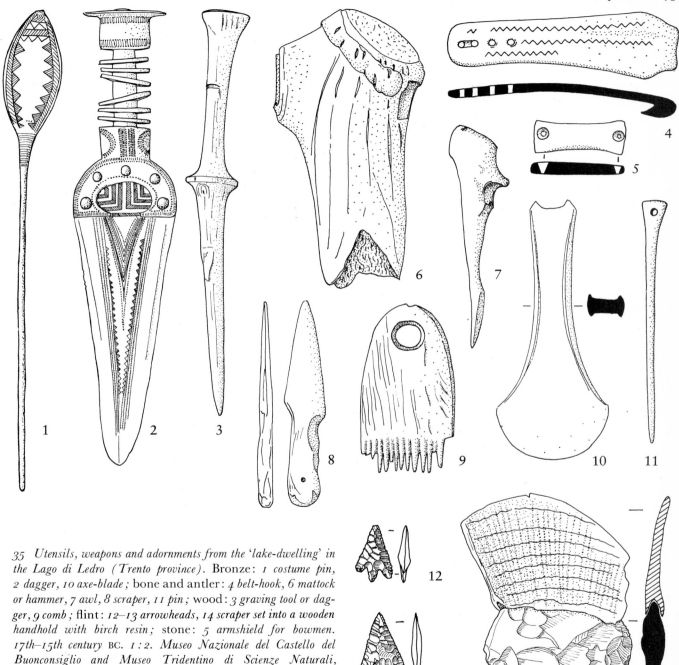

35 *Utensils, weapons and adornments from the 'lake-dwelling' in the Lago di Ledro (Trento province).* Bronze: *1 costume pin, 2 dagger, 10 axe-blade;* bone and antler: *4 belt-hook, 6 mattock or hammer, 7 awl, 8 scraper, 11 pin;* wood: *3 graving tool or dagger, 9 comb;* flint: *12–13 arrowheads, 14 scraper set into a wooden handhold with birch resin;* stone: *5 armshield for bowmen. 17th–15th century* BC. *1 : 2. Museo Nazionale del Castello del Buonconsiglio and Museo Tridentino di Scienze Naturali, Trento; Museo Civico, Riva.*

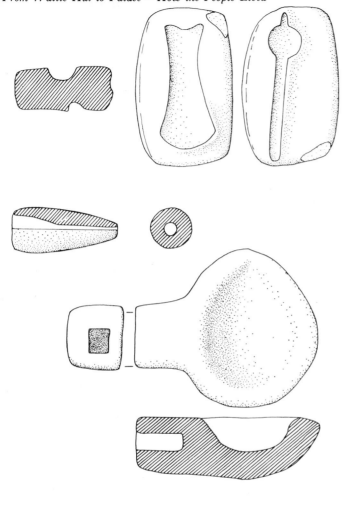

36 *Bronze-working at the 'lake-dwelling' in the Lago di Ledro (Trento province). Bellows with clay nozzles raised the temperature in the smelting oven. A clay ladle (wooden handle lost) was used to pour the molten bronze into the mould. The mould (top) shows the rough outlines of an axe blade and of a pin, which when cast would be carefully shaped by the smith. 17th–15th century* BC. *1 : 3.*

37 *Vessels of clay and wood found at the 'lake-dwelling' in the Lago di Ledro (Trento province). 17th–15th century* BC. *1 : 3.*

since this kind os settlement—once man had mastered the technicalities of working timber—remained viable down the centuries. From the ninth century BC, that is the very end of the Bronze Age, we have reliable evidence of 'pile-dwellings' in the Swiss midlands, where the most thorough research on lake settlements has been done. That more recent settlement sites are lacking may be due to changes in the water level of the lakes. For during deepening of the navigation channel of the Murtensee, a pile was dredged up a long way from the shore, which is dated in the Early Iron Age (C14 reading: 650 ± 100 BC).[16] At that time, it seems, the shores lay so much nearer the middle of the lake that the remnants of the settlements can now be located and investigated only with the help of divers. For in Lake Neuchâtel, too, piles have come to light which, on the strength of a common absolute altitude, a dendrochronological dating and a dagger concealed among them, must be assumed to belong in this or an even later period.[17] But here, too, it is advisable to wait for the results of further investigation.

Huts of the Late Stone Age at Salzburg

The Late Stone Age folk did not of course settle only the lake-shores. The terraces of the river valleys in the interior of the Alps offered equally good opportunities. At that time, too, projecting cliff-tops or spurs came to be chosen as dwelling-places. Such advantageous points may in fact have become important as places of refuge, though we can only guess at the prevailing political and social circumstances. We possess but few clues as to the appearance of the contemporary dwellings. Apart from the fact that—unlike at the lake-shore settlements—posts, planks and other organic material are scarcely ever preserved,[18] no major excavations have been carried out at these places, as might with modern methods of investigation bring to light further details of one kind or another.[19] As a rule, therefore, the archaeologist has to be satisfied with the occasional sherd or tool that he has accidentally come across, which does no more than indicate that a settlement was there.

Martin Hell has at least uncovered what appears to be the ground-plan of a Late Stone Age house in Salzburg-Maxglan.[20] It must have been about 12 m long and 3.3 m wide, with the narrow sides probably slightly rounded-off. Hell recognized the north-facing long wall of the house by the culture-layer which had built up into a kind of low step. The southern long side could only be traced by the distribution of finds, which formed a distinct borderline. Three post-holes running longways, which must have supported the ridge-piece, were the sole indication of the house's structure. Since their position was somewhat north of the central axis, the roof must have been asymmetrical. We frankly do not know how the walls were constructed. Since, apart from the said ridge supports, there were no signs of any other posts, the building must have done without further weight-carrying elements. This would only have worked if the roof sloped right down to the ground. Some kind of wattling may have been attached to thin poles which left no trace on the ground. Inside this narrow house was a hollow for a hearth. The entrance will have been on the south side, for here the culture-layer (admittedly containing only a very few finds) extended for a further 27 m. Perhaps there was a kind of forecourt here, where the occupants spent most of their time when the weather was favourable. Nearby, Hell came across two more dwelling-places with similar find-material, which seems to indicate a settlement of several houses. But these two were of even simpler construction. They had neither ridge-piece nor supporting posts, being recognizable only by a hollowed-out trough (House A: 6 m in diam. and originally 1 m deep; House C: 6.5 m in diam. and 0.9 m deep). The walls may have been made of the same material as those of the long house, but here they could only have been spread tent-like over the hollow. This arrangement had two advantages: firstly, it made the house somewhat warmer in winter and secondly, the walls could be set appreciably lower, thus offering a smaller area for the wind to beat against. Without supporting beams in the middle, the structure had to be very carefully bound together (nails had not yet been invented!); for, with an assumed height of more than 3 m above the floor, the length of the necessary transoms from the edge of the hollow to the middle must have been nearly 4 m. The framework and the wall covering thus provide an instructive example of a 'self-supporting' construction—always assuming that a centre-post was not in fact overlooked during excavation. About the way of life of the people who lived here, all we know is that they used earthenware vessels and stone implements; they were also familiar with copper, as a blob of the cast metal shows. To judge by the number of chips, they fashioned flint tools on the spot. Two sheep-bones indicate that they kept livestock, but where the animals were housed is not clear, since the excavation revealed no large free areas.

Hill settlements in Graubünden

Numerous Bronze Age houses using posts as the basis of their construction have come to light during the more recent excavations of Swiss archaeologists, above all in Graubünden.[21] This method calls for a supporting framework of wooden posts. Four corner posts are needed, usually augmented by at least two posts to carry the ridgepiece. Depending on the size, there are in addition side posts to increase the stability of the walls; these are often placed at irregular intervals. Which of several possible ways of constructing the walls has been used is only to be deduced indirectly. The first concerns the framework, in which horizontal or slanting shorter beams provide the ties between the supporting posts; the intervening spaces are filled-in with wattling and spread with daub. Or these spaces can be bridged with planks or poles. In that case, however, it would no doubt need some kind of slot for the posts, as nails were lacking. The chinks will have been stuffed with moss or filled-in with clay. Which of these two processes was used can only be established if the excavation reveals burnt, or at least dried-out, lumps of clay daub bearing on the back impressions of wattling, planks or poles. This also applies to logbuilt houses, the crevices between the logs of which have likewise to be stopped up.[22] The presence of such a building may be assumed if at a site which can unquestionably be interpreted as a settlement a rectangular outline is to be seen but no post-holes. A log-built house needs no vertical posts since the walls of dovetailed beams are sufficiently firm to bear the roof. We may be sure that the buildings were of a log-built or stilt type with a horizontal joist, if there is a kind of foundation or an entire plinth made of stones, which serves to protect the wood against rising damp, thereby indicating the exact ground-plan.

The floors used to consist either of pounded clay, sometimes on a layer of pebbles, or of boards. It is mostly difficult to decide; it seldom happens that clay floors have become permanently hardened by fire or that a layer of boards has been preserved because of the unusual condition of the ground, or charring. We know even less about the nature of the roofs. There was a choice of straw, reeds, boards, wooden tiles, stone slabs, even bark. Regarding the last-named, birch bark was preferred since its tar content of some 40% makes it singularly water-resistant. (It was the Romans who first introduced bricks into the Alpine region and farther north, as well as mortar.) The doors were fairly narrow. In the Stone Age 'pile-dwellings' of Robenhausen near Wetzikon in the canton of Zurich the wing of a door has actually survived.[23] It was made in one piece, perhaps from the shell of a hollow fir-tree, and was attached to the door-post with at least four cords. Whereas in the case of the doors we can sometimes at least reconstruct their width in the ground-plan of the house, we know absolutely nothing about the windows. In large houses a narrow door will scarcely have sufficed as a source of light. At night the fire in the hearth, the pine torch or the tallow lamp had to provide the illumination. Clay lamps, however, are also attested in the Late Stone Age:[24] a little dish would be filled with tallow and the impregnated wick lit with a flint. Hearths usually took the form of fire-places with a stone base, more or less carefully arranged.

It would be hard to exaggerate the meagreness of the rest of the interior appointments. The Alpine people may have adopted some things from the more civilized South: simple stools, long benches against the walls, which could be used as couches, crude chests. The luxurious bedstead with turned posts and springy mattress depicted on the fifth-century BC bucket from Sanzeno was surely quite exceptional.[25]

These general observations have been advanced, as they describe the basic features of house construction from the Late Stone Age to the spread of Roman civilization into the Alps. Clarification of certain details relating to individual examples follows.

A characteristic of the Inner Alpine settlements during the Bronze Age is their location on heights, whether hillocks of moraine or steep promontories. Such settlements

have been particularly well researched in Graubünden, where excavations have been carried out and are still in progress. The first to be investigated was on the 'Crestaulta' near Lumbrein in the Lugnez (Ill. 122).[26] Although several settlement phases could be distinguished, the excavator, Walo Burkart, was only able to identify the ground-plan of one house in any detail, a simple structure about 6.5 m long and 4.6 m wide, supported by three rows of five posts each. On the Hinterrhein ahead of the Via Mala, at the confluence of the Albula, is situated the 'Cresta' near Cazis, which was was investigated

38 The three scenes portrayed on the badly preserved bronze bucket from Sanzeno (Trento province) may have been intended to symbolize the life cycle in early times : man and woman united in love, farming, and the chase. 5th century BC. Ht of the upper register 7.6 cm. Tiroler Landesmuseum, Innsbruck.

by Emil Vogt over a period of many years.[27] The settlement there comprised 15 simultaneously occupied houses that held some 120 people, and which a broad cleft in the ridge of a hill screened in. They were ranged in rows one

39 *The approach to the Bernese Oberland with passes leading into the Valais was controlled in the Bronze Age by a settlement on the 'Bürg' at Spiez, the right-hand summit of the wooded ridge jutting into the lake beyond the inlet. Such a location was characteristic of many settlement centres at this time, when copper-mining and the commerce it gave rise to were an important source of profit in the Alpine region.*

40 *A number of rock-drawings in the Valcamonica (Lombardy) depict houses set on a tall substructure and only to be reached by ladder. It is more likely, however, that these were meant to represent granaries rather than actual 'lake-dwellings'. Such a method of construction is still to be found in the Alpine region, with stone slabs inserted between the posts and the floor in order to keep out rapacious mice.*

behind the other longways and measured 4–5 m in length and 3–4 m in width. Each of these unsectioned houses had a carefully built hearth in the middle. Some of the entrances were indentifiable by large doorsteps. The settlement was burnt down several times, with the result that rebuilding and the addition of new buildings over the years brought about an increase in height of 7 m. Here, too, the post-built type of house was clearly predominant.

Like Lumbrein 'Crestaulta' and Cazis 'Cresta', two further prominent hills with Bronze Age settlements are situated on important routes: the 'Padnal' at Savognin[28] between Tiefencastel and the Julier pass, and the 'Tummihügel' above Chur, right on the road leading into the

Schanfigg and on into the lower Engadin. At both places excavation work is still in progress and the reports issued to date (by Jürg Rageth and Arthur Gredig respectively) suggest that important results may be expected. Whilst the 'Padnal' resembles the 'Crestaulta' in its situation and form, the 'Tummihügel' is somewhat surprising.[29] When gravel-digging was about to begin on the jutting moraine hill, an experimental cut into the ridge and the south side did not produce any encouraging results. It was not until

41 High above Chur (in the background) the 'Tummihügel' guards the old route into the Schanfigg (to the right beyond the hill; left, the modern road). From the Bronze Age up until early medieval times it served again and again as settlement and observation post. In a few years' time gravel extraction will have caused it to disappear completely. Meanwhile archaeologists are excavating with a view to clarifying the checkered history of this important place. On the southern slope narrow trial trenches intended to show where more extensive excavation would be worthwhile are to be seen.

later that it was discovered that the Bronze Age settlers had, contrary to all expectations, selected the north side, facing away from the sun and extremely precipitous into the bargain, as their dwelling-place. Excavations at this somewhat dizzy site are now in progress. The rear of the houses was embedded in the gravel while the front end, supported on posts, rested on a layer of dumped earth. This naturally resticted their size, but they were set close together, and the rebuilt and newly built houses, as at Cazis, gradually caused a great culture-layer to accumulate, the location of which on the steep and slippery slope makes it particularly difficult to separate the individual building phases and structures from one another. Nevertheless, this place shows how adept the people of the Bronze Age were at adapting themselves to the natural surroundings.[30] They had probably chosen the north side, firstly because it was sheltered from the wind (there is another hillside opposite) and secondly, they could see right down into the Rhine valley to Chur. Besides, the old path to the Schanfigg runs close by on this side.

Apart from these four Bronze Age settlements there are of course a great many others in Switzerland, but they have been less well explored. Settlements from the same period, nearly all of them likewise on a height, have been identified by archaeologists in France, Italy and Austria. But they have been so inadequately researched, that they have yielded no information beyond that already set forth. Frequently, there is no indication of when the settlement began or when it ended. Many of the sites were occupied intermittently over a long period, some of them even in late Roman or early medieval times, as their sheltered situation was welcome in times of unrest, even if it meant no more than setting-up a little observation post from which to keep a weather-eye open: say at the 'Tummihügel' above Chur, or at the 'Rocca' high above the Adige at Rivoli (p. 229).

The valleys looked different

Whilst we can rest assured that the Bronze Age folk purposely chose high-altitude locations for their settlements, this does not mean that they did not live in the valleys at all. Narrow gorges naturally did not appeal to them, but wide river valleys with the favourable climatic conditions that prevailed on the upper terraces must have exercised a strong attraction. But it is precisely there that in later centuries changes took place that we can scarcely evaluate these days. True, one has always been aware of the possibility that through detritus carried down by tributaries, landslides and avalanches, settlements and burial places might be covered over to such a height that not even modern work on house foundations would reveal them. Yet the most recent research has shown that the valley bottoms and the river beds themselves have been subject to geological change.

Thus, for example, intensive research on the part of archaeologists, geologists, physicists and botanists[31] has established the surprising fact that in the Reichenhall basin, an extension of the Saalach valley shortly before it emerges from the mountains, the bottom of the valley must in Bronze Age times have lain some 15 m below its present level. Even as late as around the beginning of our era, the discrepancy was still about 4 m. It may be that increasing cultivation contributed to the large amount of alluvium being washed away and re-deposited.

Of course, these findings from the Reichenhall basin must not be applied without qualification to the Western, or even the Southern Alps. Nevertheless it does follow that, even during less remote centuries, profound changes in the earth's surface took place in the larger valleys which completely conceal whole periods from the probing eyes of the archaeologist and the chance destruction by dredger and bull-dozer. This problem has already been briefly treated where the Iron Age lake-shore settlements of the Swiss midlands are concerned. It may be for the same reasons that evidence is lacking for the Middle Bronze Age. It calls for more extensive research by archaeologists in conjunction with natural science, if this question is to be clarified.

Farms and villages between Salzach and Rhône

During the Iron Age from about 700 BC, as the population in the Alpine region increased, more and more settlements were founded or enlarged. Houses continued to be built in the same manner as in the Bronze Age. The coexistence of the various styles is best illustrated by two sites on the outskirts of Salzburg, both from the transition period from

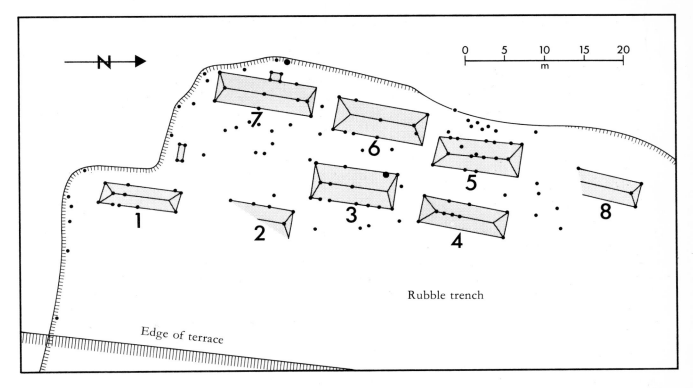

42 Only the dark stains of the post-holes of wooden houses were left to indicate the presence in Salzburg-Liefering of a settlement of the 6th–5th century BC. By joining those that lie in a straight line the ground-plans of the houses emerged. Single posts close to the lateral walls point to a hip-roof construction.

Hallstatt to La Tène, that is, around the fifth century BC, and both excavated by Martin Hell.[32]

The first of these he discovered at Schloss Klessheim in 1941, when work was being done in connection with the water supply; as a result of his thorough excavation of the site a clearly defined culture-layer was exposed. Burnt roughcast clay indicated a dwelling, of log-house type since there was no sign of posts. Its modest size–3.8 by 3.55 m–and the presence of numerous millstones and stone pounders led Hell to postulate a 'mill'. But since in addition some 300 potsherds, a fragment of a fibula and a spindle whorl were found, his interpretation is surely too res-tricted. At all events the building served as a dwelling-place, not just as a farm building used for a specific purpose. Yet the occupants may in fact have earned their living in part from some specialized trade, such as miller or baker. As the surrounding area could not be investigated, however, further speculation is useless.

The other, larger settlement of the same period was discovered in a gravel-pit. Seeing that it is more than 700 m away from the log-built house just described, the two are unlikely to be connected. Unfortunately the original culture layer was removed, probably during railway construction work in 1942, so that the only clues we have for the date of the settlement are items found in the 136 post-holes (still 60–80 m deep). Owing to prevailing war-time conditions, not everything was as carefully recorded as would have been possible during an unhurried, planned excavation; some post-holes may have been unwittingly destroyed. Even so, the surviving finds allow us to form a picture of the settlement's layout (Ill. 42). Since investiga-

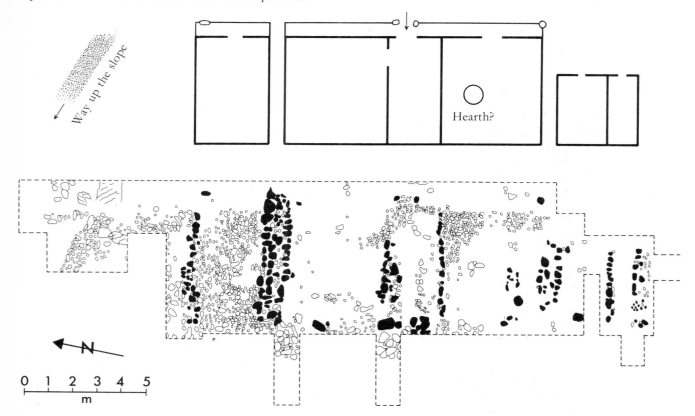

43 Of the farmstead of log-houses on the Dürrnberg above Hallein (Salzburg province) only the foundations of undressed stones are left. The results of excavation are shown in the lower part of the drawing; the larger-than-average stones of the partition walls are picked out in black. A tentative reconstruction of the ground-plan is shown at the top. 4th–2nd century BC.

tions had to be restricted to the gravel-pit itself, the original extent of the settlement cannot be ascertained.

The houses were of post-built type. Measuring 10–13 m in length by 3–5 m in width, they stood close to one another and were all similarly orientated. The actual or assumed interval between the posts was between 2.4 and 2 m. In the case of Houses 1 and 6, two of the posts were only 0.8 m apart, with a depression in between which will have taken a wooden doorstep. In the case of House 3 an identical gap in the east wall near the southeast corner points to a similar design, even though no step was to be seen there. The other houses lacked this feature, though in Houses 5 and 7 a doorway may have been placed slightly to the right of the centre of the west wall, where two posts stand equally close together; in the case of House 7 it may even have been protected by a small porch. There seem to have been no outbuildings, unless a tiny rectangular structure between Houses 1 and 7 served that purpose.

Here, then, we have a whole village which lasted for at least 200 years. There is no indication that the houses were not all built at the same time, though later alterations or additions cannot be ruled out. At all events there is nothing to suggest that the settlement was destroyed at any time, necessitating extensive rebuilding. The postholes beyond the reconstructed house-plans show no affinity with any older building phase.

Only a few kilometres south of the Salzburg-Liefering settlement lies Hallein with its mining settlement on the Dürrnberg. Although there–as opposed to the rich burials–the dwelling-places have scarcely been investigated, one housing complex shows up fairly clearly thanks to the excavations of Fritz Moosleitner and Ernst Penninger.[33] It was built on a partially levelled small terrace on a fairly steep slope. To start with, there was a log-built house barely 10 m long and 5.5 m wide. The logs had a diameter of 17–20 cm and were carefully cut to shape at the joints and perhaps also on the inside; the interstices were coated with clay. Since the logs rested directly on the ground, there is no way of telling how the large complex was divided up; it may have corresponded to the building that lay above it.

For the initial one did not last long. It was probably built about the middle of the fifth century, and burnt down in the first half of the fourth. The heat baked large sections of the clay floor (providing a clue to the area of the ground-plan) and of the clay roughcast from the walls. The rest was charred fragments and ash. But the occupants soon set about rebuilding. The layer of debris was removed, and a new log-built house arose. Since a partial foundation of stones was now used to support the beams, we know more about the layout of the interior. It appears to have comprised a large building complex made up of several individual units: on the north side a small, free-standing room adjoining but slightly separated from the main building, consisting of a narrow corridor with an entrance on the valley side, and a door to the right leading to a large room. Only a single hearth was found, and since this could not have functioned well in the open, the space south of the corridor must have been roofed over, particularly as the scattering of gravel conforms to the limits of the base. The approach may also have been on the valley side, and it looks as if the roof had been extended some 60 cm beyond the front wall and supported by posts, so that even in bad weather the various rooms could be reached more or less dry-footed. On the south side two tiny rooms, probably for storing implements or provisions, were attached. Because it was built on the slope, it was necessary to regulate drainage behind the house. In order to protect the back wall, therefore, a ditch was dug and filled with pebbles, several layers of which were also stacked against the wall.

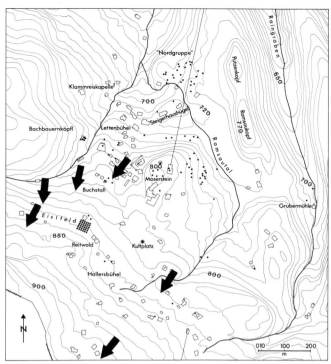

44 *Contour plan of the Dürrnberg above Hallein (Salzburg province) showing buildings put up in modern times. The distribution of Iron Age graves (as at 1975 and marked by small dots) indicates that each family had its own burial-place in the vicinity of the court-yard. The arrows on the higher land show approximately where the early miners tunnelled into the salt-mountain. Situated on the jutting Ramsaukopf is an as yet scarcely investigated fortification from the same period, which towers above the old approach route from the Salzach valley through the Raingraben.*

This building complex was not destroyed but simply abandoned in the second century BC, after which it was allowed to go to ruin. This is strange, considering that on the Dürrnberg intensive settlement was still going on. Generally speaking, individual homesteads of the miners were distributed over the wide area of the hilly plateau, even if there was a certain concentration within the area occupied by the present-day village centre and to a certain extent above it.

At all events the situation at the Dürrnberg clearly differed from those places where the inhabitants were crowded together within a limited area. But even there we know little about the actual function of fortified places within the political and social context. This applies, for example, to the recently discovered settlement of the sixth and fifth centuries BC at Châtillon-sur-Glâne,[34] south of Fribourg, the wealthy trading centre on a mountain spur above the confluence of the Sarine and Glâne (Ill. 124), protected from the hinterland by a mighty rampart. Or to the hill settlement of Le Pègue[35] near Valreas (Drôme) on the eastern edge of the Rhône valley, some 135 km north of Marseille. From the eighth or seventh century BC, large numbers of people lived here, but it was not until the arrival in the late sixth century of the Greeks, who settled on the coast, that it prospered. A granary testifies to the central function of the settlement, which presumably delivered corn and other commodities to the coast. Conversely, there was an outlet here for Greek pottery, wine and oil were imported, possibly even produced here, and the ceramic industry flourished. A great conflagration put an end to all this. It may have been the Celts who destroyed the settlement, probably about the middle of the fifth century. Thereafter Le Pègue never regained its erstwhile importance. About 30 BC its inhabitants deserted the place and withdrew into the valley. From Roman times, only a few sherds were found.

The burning of the granary has given us certain clues as to how it was constructed. It was at least 7 m, possibly more than 9 m, long and up to 5 m wide. The absence of any post-holes relating to it suggests that it was log-built; but since pieces of burnt clay (mixed with straw) bear imprints of wattling, the upper part at least must have been of this lighter construction. But it is still more likely that the building was supported on posts that were not sunk into the ground but firmly dovetailed into beams laid horizontally, and rested on a shallow stone base. What was used for roof-covering we do not know. In view of the considerable length of the building it will have been divided into two or three sections. In addition, it had a narrow porch (a good 1 m deep) running along its entire width, into which the entrance led via a door.

The corn was stored, in the customary Mediterranean manner, in huge jars which the potters made on the spot out of relatively porous clay. Since smaller and, above all, better quality earthenware vessels stood between the regular storage jars, it is to be assumed that the inhabitants of the settlement wanted to lay in as much corn as possible, so as to be able in case of need to survive a lengthy siege–in vain, as the great burnt layer shows.

The construction of the contemporary dwelling-houses in Le Pègue will not have differed materially from that of the granaries. In later times proper walls made of large, carefully layered stones were favoured, further strengthened with small pebbles and clay filling-up the crevices. But here, too, it was unlikely that house walls were built of stone all the way up; as in Roman times, a superstructure consisting of framework with wattle and daub will have been regarded as sufficient.

Deeper in the Western Alps, the settlement of Sainte-Colombe at Orpierre (Hautes-Alpes),[36] of which only a small part has been excavated, confirms the validity of the constructional principles already described. From the end of the eighth century BC people occupied a mountainside here, at an altitude of from 900 to 960 m, making terraces to take their houses. About 500 BC, on one such terrace a building with a framework of huge posts set 2.4 m apart was put up. The walls were of wattle and daub; the overall dimensions are not known, but if the building took in a hearth found at the same level, it must have been at least 7 m long. A particularly noteworthy feature is that on the hearth were several clay rings which the fire had hardened; these were probably used as holders for round-based vessels. Inside the house, close to the wall between two posts the excavators discovered the skeleton of a small child, some 20 cm beneath the floor of pounded clay, testifying to the widespread custom of occasionally burying children in the house.

Greek and Etruscan vessels under the sherds signify that this place was part of a widespread commercial network, even though to modern eyes it seems distinctly remote. People were most probably attracted there by the mineral wealth: silver-bearing lead, iron and perhaps copper. It must have been the middle of the fifth century BC when the unfortified settlement came to an end. Although there had been three earlier conflagrations, which led to the erection of new buildings, it is not possible to tell whether the final occupation layer was destroyed at a stroke. One

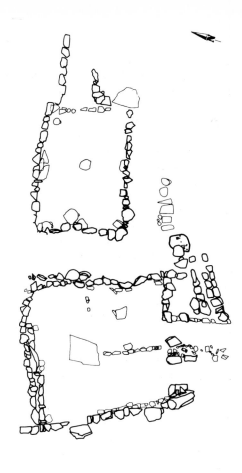

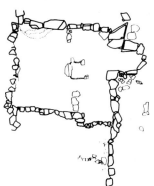

or two finds dating from the Late Iron Age may have come from dwelling-houses situated higher up on the slope.

As a final example of the architecture of the Early Iron Age, let us take the 'mansion' of the Mottata at Ramosch in the Engadin.[37] It is a square building with unmortared walls 2 m thick, the inner sides being nearly 12 m long. In the interior, four posts are also arranged in a square and these supported the roof. Since this substantial building, covering a good 140 m², exceeds in size all other known examples in the Alpine region, we must assume that it served a special purpose. Unfortunately, the finds within and around the structure provide no further clues. 'Mansion' is a convenient category in which to place it, though not so far corroborated by the archaeological material.

The large structures on high ground at Vill,[38] now a suburb of Innsbruck, present similar difficulties of interpretation. Helene Miltner, who excavated here, has designated one of these buildings a 'cult house', on account of a large block of stone standing in the interior, which cannot have had any constructional function. Close by stands a further 'hall-type' building, surrounded by smaller dwelling-houses. (Incidentally, the complex did not originate as late as the second century BC but at the latest between 400 and 350 BC; nor is the date of the fire by any means certain.)

To regard the large building, subdivided lengthways and with two entrances placed close together, which stands on the Montesei di Serso[39] near Trento, as a dwelling-house, on the other hand, would seem too secular an interpretation. For the numerous fibulae, the clay loomweights (?) found lying together, and the pebbles ornamented with scratched designs stand out amid the abundant pottery, and point rather to a cultic purpose.

At all events, a large variety of house types from the last three or four centuries BC is to be found in the Alpine region.[40] In addition to the simple post- and log-structures, we find an increase in the number of buildings in which the lower part of the walls takes the form of proper stone walling without mortar. At the same time, we know little about the actual nature of the settlements, the size of the hamlets or farms, the disposition of the individual buildings.[41]

45 *Ground-plans of three wooden houses with raised stone foundations on the Montesei di Serso at Trento. 5th–4th century* BC. *1 : 200.*

The first towns?

In the Celtic zone to the north and west of the Alps a propensity for large, townlike settlements had developed–doubtless owing to influences from the South.[42] Naturally, all the peoples did not suddenly gather together, but a certain concentration of settlement does appear to have occurred. On closer scrutiny, the towns–the Romans called them *oppida*, a term which the archaeologists took over–can be seen to have differed materially from one another, yet they had certain basic characteristics in common: they occupied a fair-sized area, in a situation that enabled them to be readily defended, enclosed by a rampart of stones, earth and timber framework; within, artisans would be engaged in a variety of occupations, perhaps in quarters assigned to their trade; sometimes the ruling families would reside in houses clearly set away from the rest; finally, there was the central tribal sanctuary. For it appears that such oppida constituted the political and commercial nucleus of smaller and larger tribes. When Caesar waged war in Gaul, he himself saw these oppida, it might be as the seat of a tribal ruler who was amenable or willing to negotiate, or as the target of a military campaign and a siege. In this, too, the archaeologists relied on his accounts; for investigations at such places have not so far met with much success, mainly on account of the vast areas that have to be uncovered. Even at the oppidum that has been most thoroughly investigated, namely Manching near Ingolstadt on the Danube, only a fraction of the interior has been examined to date, after twenty years of systematic excavation.[43] So it is difficult to find criteria for assessing such settlements, which, though comparatively large and fortified and having been occupied during the last two centuries BC, have at best received only tentative archaeological attention in the form of test soundings.

This problem becomes particularly acute when we approach the boundary of the Alps. In the West, French scientific opinion tends to refer to all hill settlements of this period as oppida. This covers the area from Entremont[44] near Aix-en-Provence, through Le Pègue and Aime,[45] the future Roman provincial capital, to Geneva.[46] Only a little more care is exercised in the German-speaking zone. The extensive ramparts on the more than 1000 m-high

46 The Celtic motif of the sacred stag combined with a Roman-influenced sense of form invests this bronze stag from the Biberg at Saalfelden (Salzburg province). It attests the close contact the kingdom of Noricum had established with the South, from which not only merchants but also artists in the principal tribal centres benefited. 1st century BC. Ht 10.8 cm. Museum Carolino Augusteum, Salzburg.

Auerberg in the Allgäu between Schongau and Füssen have led to the Celtic town referred to by Strabo as *Damasia* being sought there. But the protracted excavations of Günter Ulbert, which covered Roman settlement at this place, have since shown that the ramparts date from early Roman times and that there are no positive signs beneath the plentiful material of that period, of late Celtic forerunners (p. 92f.). To the west of the Irschenberg, on the motorway from Munich to Salzburg, lies the 'Fentbachschanze', a plateau high above the Mangfall protected by a mighty rampart.[47] Finds show that it was occupied towards the end of the Late Iron Age but it is uncertain how and when the rampart was constructed (it may have been added to in early medieval times); nor is the extent of the settlement known. As the surrounding territory was at this period practically without settlements, to interpret it as an oppidum, a tribal centre, is open to question.

In an area for which late Celtic occupation is well attested, lie two further important sites. The first is the Rainberg near Salzburg, repeatedly settled in the course of many centuries;[48] it is taken to be the main centre of the *Alauni*. Up the Saalach and farther into the mountains stands the Biberg at Saalfelden–or, more accurately, stood, since it is now almost wholly demolished by quarrying and only the finds collected by Martin Hell over many years convey any idea of its original significance.[49] It is believed that the Biberg was the location of the principal centre of the *Ambisontes*, the one Norican tribe that allowed itself to become involved in Augustus's wars of conquest. (p. 36f.). But so little excavation has been carried out at either the Rainberg or the Biberg, that nothing is known about the actual layout of these settlements. Their interpretation as tribal centres is, indeed, based solely on analogous Gallic circumstances, coupled with the fact that for some distance around these places no others are known that could have qualified as such. That the Romans in the mid-first century AD founded *Iuvavum* at the foot of the Rainberg may perhaps be regarded as a pointer. Yet even the Dürrnberg above Hallein, on account of its salt-works, still had some importance contemporaneously with the Rainberg–and so, presumably, did the not far distant settlement of Karlstein by the brine-springs of Reichenhall.[50]

The Magdalensberg at Klagenfurt, however, leaves no room for such doubts. From the very first excavations of last century it became clear that the capital of the kingdom of Noricum had been discovered.[51] The summit of the 1058 m-high mountain, on which a church now stands, was ringed by a rampart, parts of which are still to be seen in the area. The most recently unearthed entrance-way is largely preserved. Within this fortified place stood a temple, most likely the tribe's central shrine, and dwelling-houses. More of these were situated outside, on terraces lower down, particularly in the more sheltered south and west. Here Roman influence made itself felt early on. For the town acted as a magnet for Roman traders, who came up from Aquileia, the colony founded on the Adriatic in 183/181 BC, mainly to acquire Noricum's coveted iron. They set up proper offices with warehouses and accounts departments. Soon they were erecting stone buildings, using mortar, as was the Roman method by this time. In the ground-plans, too, Roman influence is evident: corridors, vestibules, inner courtyards for specially luxurious buildings. The steep slope was cleverly terraced with supporting walls. Many of the houses were of a considerable height on the side facing the valley, the upper end set into the hillside. Well laid-out paths, almost roads, stressed the urban character of this Celtic-Norican settlement.

With the peaceful incorporation of the kingdom of Noricum into the Roman Empire (c. 15 BC), the Roman government, in turn, established itself on the Magdalensberg, and this led to much reorganization. In accordance with Roman custom, a central square was assigned for meetings, the *forum*. It was bounded on one side by the great temple with its massive walls, on the other side by the *praetorium*, the official building of the chief Roman administrator, who from there addressed the populace. Many houses were renovated, more still adapted to suit Roman taste, not a few entirely rebuilt, for the administrative apparatus needed much room while indirectly improving the infrastructure of the settlement by its increased demands for comfort and luxury. An impressive example of this is the palace-like complex south of the *praetorium*, that is to say below the present-day (and Roman) road from the forum to the top of the mountain. Varying levels were evened out by substantial supporting walls, so that the buildings stood on one of only two levels. Here the basic elements of a grand household were to be seen: a large courtyard with a shady arcade, an enormous kitchen containing several stoves and a roasting oven, its own bakery and, finally, a heated private bathhouse with compartments for undressing and dressing, others for warm and cold baths and a steam bath. Inside, the bath itself had a mosaic floor.

47 *Air photo of the Magdalensberg at Klagenfurt (Carinthia) seen from the South. On the summit, the church of SS Helena and Magdalena above the old Norican tribal sanctuary. In the middle of the picture, the exposed houses of the town where merchants, artisans and municipal officials lived. Right, the ridge of the Lugbichl where the most important burial area is located.*

Since excavation at the Magdalensberg site is still far from complete, only a limited amount of information is as yet available where the areas farther away from the forum and the municipal buildings are concerned. It is mainly a question of artisans' workshops and shops; the proprietor and his family lived on the upper storey or next door. There will have been accommodation for the many travellers in the form of simple taverns. The public baths that were to be expected have not yet been traced. Nor is there any sign of the garrison of the *cohors montanorum prima*, the first battalion of Mountain Infantry. It is fairly certain that this unit was stationed here in the capital, as there are several gravestones of its members in the vicinity (Ill.

16).[52] One of the cemeteries was situated on the Lugbichl, the ridge that runs southwards from the summit; here the tombs can still be seen. Further burial-places along the roads leading to the town are attested by a second soldier's gravestone relating to the *cohors montanorum* found halfway up the Magdalensberg beside a small tomb.

Roman life-styles

The Roman phase of the town on the Magdalensberg lasted only two generations. For, when in Emperor Claudius's time, around AD 45, Noricum lost its special political standing and was organized as an official province on the customary pattern, the governor and his civil servants saw no reason why, in sunny Carinthia of all places, they should live high up on a mountain that was snowed-up for months on end. The imperial administration in Rome saw the point, and gave orders for a blue-print of a new town to be prepared, which was to be built in the Zollfeld at the foot of the Magdalensberg. It was given the name of *Virunum*[53] (possibly the earlier settlement on the height was similarly named[54]) and remained the provincial capital until the end of the second century, when the authorities were for the most part transferred to *Ovilava*/Wels close to the legion commander in *Lauriacum*/Lorch, who was also the governor. Only the finance department stayed in *Virunum*. About AD 300, when the province of Noricum was split up, *Virunum* became a capital once more, namely of Noricum mediterraneum. The large and impressive buildings were in keeping with a capital. Dwelling-houses and municipal buildings were now supplemented with temple, theatre, amphitheatre, public baths, paved streets with sidewalks, a water supply and other amenities.

People from the provinces, on visiting the capital, were amazed by such architectonic and decorative details as: baked bricks and tiles, stone arches and vaults, polished marble slabs, floors of artistically applied mosaic, as well as murals, life-size bronze and stone statues of emperors or high-ranking officials. What caused the greatest sensation, though, were the installations providing floor heating and a constant supply of hot water, not only in public baths but also in private houses.

Bricks were baked partly in State-run, partly in private factories; the military on the Danube frontier are known to have had their own brickworks, and they stamped their products. With the help of bricks and mortar it was possible, moreover, to construct arches and vaults. 'False' arches were known previously in the Mediterranean area, but they consisted of clumsily built vaulting made of flat corbelled slabs and held together by their own dead weight, which bore increasingly on the walls. It was the Romans who first succeeded in making the true arch and vault out of ashlar blocks and a keystone. (The most impressive examples are the subterranean vaults in Aosta and the amphitheatre in Verona.) Naturally, the Romans will hardly have obtained marble from Italy, but they tried to quarry it in the vicinity. Geology set certain limits to this, but the famous quarries at the Untersberg south of Salzburg were surely exploited as early as Roman times,[55] and laminated limestone was to be found in many parts of the Northern and the Southern Alps.

A floor with mosaics was the thing for well-to-do people to have. Little coloured stones had to be chipped into the desired shape, the abstract or figural design decided upon, and the pieces finally fitted into place. That is why mosaics are only found in wealthy townspeople's villas or large country estates, and even there only in particular rooms used for entertaining favourite guests or important persons. Less costly was the wall painting on smooth plaster, but because the walls of Roman houses are seldom preserved and, where they are, the colours have usually faded, it is only by a lucky chance that a fair-sized area can be reconstructed. The wall paintings of Pompeii, the prosperous little town near Naples, show how rich and polymorphic murals in the interior rooms could be. In the Alpine region, on the other hand, everything was rather simpler, though there are some beautiful examples, as for instance at the Baths of Schwangau in the Allgäu (restored on the spot and open for inspection beside the valley station of the Tegelberg cable railway).[56] Fairly large wall surfaces have also survived on the Magdalensberg[57] and in some Swiss villas.[58]

Floor heating is a Roman invention–even so, it was not until our own times that it was once more adopted. It was regarded as a necessity in public and private baths; in private houses it implied a certain affluence, though everyone was anxious to install it in at least one, or perhaps two rooms. The working principle on which it is based is as simple as can be. The bottom floor rested on a large number of supports, 40-100 cm high and usually built up of flat tiles, or on small stone pillars. This left a cavity under the floor, through which the warm air could circulate (in late antiquity they managed with one or two hot air canals under the floor). Heat was also conveyed into the walls themselves through hollow bricks. The heat was generated in a furnace outside the house or beyond the suite of rooms to be warmed. A slave attended to the fire itself several times a day, and saw to it that there was always a sufficient supply of logs and charcoal. The poorer citizen had to make do with a cooking stove (with or without a flue) which also served to heat the room. In the other rooms he had to resort to placing glowing logs on iron pans, but at best these only warmed those sitting close to them.

The Romans were also responsible for introducing the oil lamp. These were produced by the potteries in large series to all kinds of designs, but the basic form with a round oil container and a nozzle for the wick did not vary materially. The upper side is usually decorated, either

48 *Even the Romans enjoyed 'kitsch' in their day. This comically unambiguous bronze figure (an elderly silenus from the entourage of the wine-god Dionysus) served as an oil lamp. The olive oil was poured through the head into the body, and the aperture then closed with a cowl (since lost) attached to the shoulders by a hinge. The end of the enormous penis has an opening on top from which the wick protruded. 1st century* AD. *Ht 7.5 cm. Museum Carolino Augusteum, Salzburg.*

with an ornamental design or with scenes from everyday life or mythology. In the Landesmuseum Joanneum in Graz there is a clay lamp from *Flavia Solva*, Styria's Roman town, bearing on the underside the words:

Accendet facellam qui lucernam non habet
He who has no lamp must light a torch.

Whatever kind of torch was meant, it will no doubt have smoked and become rather sooty; but these people did not need to import olive oil from the South. All the same, no household that was committed to the Roman way of life was without an oil lamp.

Towns in occupied lands

The Roman town on the Magdalensberg is an exceptional case, as here a slow and systematic development took place, from a Celtic-Norican capital to a Celtic-Roman trading centre and right on to a well-ordered seat of government. Normally, the Romans did not establish themselves in existing settlements, or rather, Roman villages and towns were mostly too large for the pre-Roman nucleus–perhaps just a few peasants' houses–to play any further role, besides being for the most part hardly detectable archaeologically. In northern Italy alone, because it was Romanized early, is such continuity relatively frequent, but then principally owing to the favourable situation of the places. *Comum*/Como is a particularly good example of how evenly distributed settlements of pre-Roman times evolved into a well organized group community, which can justifiably be described as a town, even though exploration is still in its early stages.[59]

Even where a Roman town bears a Celtic name, this tells us nothing about the size and significance of the settlement out of which it grew. On the contrary, a remarkable discontinuity can be detected, if we except the cases where the occupation went ahead peacefully (Magdalensberg → *Virunum* and Salzburg–Rainberg → *Iuvavum* in the kingdom of Noricum; *Segusio*/Susa in the Alpes Cottiae). Thus, the Roman *Cambodunum*/Kempten bears a Celtic name, as do *Eburodunum*/Yverdon and *Octodurus*/Martigny, but we know next to nothing about their Celtic precursor-settlements since Roman rebuilding has rendered an older occupation phase difficult to recognize and even harder to reconstruct.

In this respect the previously mentioned Auerberg in the Allgäu is a problem place. Its system of ramparts encompasses several plateaux with springs, all suitable for settlement. Excavations carried out at the beginning of the present century had unearthed what was described as a 'wooden house' containing early Roman finds, so archaeologists and local historians equated it without hesitation with the Celtic town of *Damasia* mentioned by the classical writer Strabo. They assumed that–as at the Magdalensberg–the place was briefly occupied by the Romans and then deserted. But the excavation work of Günter Ulbert,[60] begun some ten years ago, has produced results to date that conflict with this assumption. In the first place, the ramparts proved to be not Celtic but Roman, as their relationship to the settlement strata has clearly demonstrated; secondly, among the finds there are none of which it can be said that they unquestionably derive from a Celtic settlement. Thirdly, whilst the Romans stayed on the hill for only a short time, this was not during the early phase when they conquered Raetia but in about AD 12/15 to AD 40, that is, when under Emperor Claudius the provinces were administratively reorganized and the frontier extended as far as the Danube. Fourthly, the excavations to date show that the Auerberg was a very large commercial centre with a great many workshops and factories. Long wooden buildings erected on pillars were ranged along one street; the 'wooden houses', it transpired from the most recent excavations, were in fact large reservoirs,[61] dug into the ground near the springs. Moreover, the settlement was not destroyed but evacuated according to plan. All this seems to add up to a clear picture of early Roman life on the Auerberg, but despite the presence of quantities of military finds, such an interpretation in no way tallies with what had hitherto been envisaged as Roman methods when occupying the Alpine foreland. Above all, it is hard to understand why, if no Celtic town had existed on the Auerberg, the Romans should suddenly have chosen to settle on this cold and often snow-covered height for close on thirty years. And what was the purpose of the rampart, not built of stone but consisting of earth and turves, and quite 'un-Roman' for a permanent settlement, thirty years after the victorious campaigns of Tiberius and Drusus? Since there are no worthwhile mineral deposits on the Auerberg, the raw material for numerous workshops (smithies, bronze-casting, glass-making) would have had to be brought up from the valley. Down below, it is true, ran the road to the North, the future Via Claudia, but since it was 4 km away, the security aspect hardly comes into question. One must just hope that future excavations will lead to a plausible explanation. The simplest would be the discovery of a late Celtic precursor, for then the situation would be comparable with that on the Magdalensberg, at least as far as topographical continuity is concerned.

By contrast, the situation in *Augusta Praetoria*/Aosta can be clearly visualized.[62] Following the bloody suppression of the Salassi in 25 BC, the Romans founded a town on the greensward to accommodate 3000 colonists–not by accident at the fork of the roads to the Great and the Little St Bernard. The town was conceived as a fortress in alien territory, surrounded by a mighty wall with four gateways along with a number of intermediate towers, and a rectangular ground-plan about 572 × 724 m (Ill. 14). The interior did not, however, conform to the usual camp layout with barracks and staff quarters, designed to meet military requirements; it had a *forum*, the main square with its subterranean vaults referred to earlier, an amphitheatre for animal-baiting and gladiatorial combats (only identifiable these days by the street alignments and one or two arches that have been preserved), a theatre for plays and spectacles with a large stage and a semicircular auditorium, and the customary public baths which were very elaborate.

He who bathes much needs much water

Every Roman settlement of appreciable size, and more particularly every town, had its controlled water supply. If villages and farms still managed with wells and wooden troughs or pipes,[63] the towns needed walled cisterns and conduits. Inside the blocks of houses or other buildings the water flowed along narrow channels to the kitchen and bath. In the large building on the *forum* of the Magdalensberg settlement there was a basin for regulating the water pressure, which was necessitated by the steep slope. The trades which required water (potters, dyers, fullers, tanners, brewers) also had to have a supply.

There is plenty of evidence in the Roman world for the attention town planners and engineers paid to the water

49 At a dizzy height of 52 m the aqueduct of Pondel (or Pont d'El) in the Aosta valley spans a deep ravine. In the masonry the holes for the scaffolding and the ventilation slits for the water conduit which runs along the narrow channel are still discernible. The less carefully made parapet, which converted the structure into a bridge for people, donkeys, cows and sheep, is of more recent date. How many persons, we may wonder, plunged into the depths below during the erection or this marvel of Roman building expertise. The brief inscription over the arch, which has a span of 15 m, records only the bare facts: the date of completion (the statutory year 3/2 BC), that it was subsidized by private individuals, and, finally, their names: Gaius Avillius son of Gaius, as well as Gaius Aimus of Padua. They belonged to those families in Aosta who owned, or had rented the mines in the side-valleys.

50 The main gateway of Aosta, the Porta Praetoria *on the road to Rome, is still in an excellent state of preservation. It is characterized by a large central archway for vehicular traffic and two small ones for pedestrians. The ancient street level, however, used to be 2.5 m below the present one. Above the entrances there was formerly at least one defensive passage, to either side of which rose a projecting rectangular tower. The archways enclose an inner precinct where the invader was liable to be shot at from all sides. In medieval times the town's nobility had the towers of the Roman wall enlarged and reconstructed, making them resemble small forts.*

supply. The latter showed particular aptitude in conveying running water from a spring, often some 10 to 20 km away, to the town, without the use of pumps. A measured down-gradient was necessary, which meant that valleys and ravines had where possible to be circumvented, or spanned by an aqueduct. When crossing ridges, on the other hand, where it was not possible to achieve a sufficient drop, diversions, cuttings and even tunnels[64] were resorted to.

The most thoroughly explored example of such a large-scale water conveyance scheme in Central Europe is the one at Cologne, which leads from the mountains of the Eifel fo the metropolis on the Rhine.[65] The most impressive monument of this kind, and the one most visited by tourists, is the Pont du Gard in Provence, a three-tiered structure of arches 49 m high, which carried spring water across the valley of the Gard, whence it flowed, via tunnels through the hills,[66] to the Roman Nîmes. Another rewarding sight is the bridge of Pondel (or Pont d'El)[67] at the foot of the snow-covered Gran Paradiso with its national park, west of Aosta. Here a single-arch stone bridge spans a formidable ravine. And this only to carry a water conduit to Aosta, along whose channel one can walk–marvelling and a little apprehensive perhaps–before pursuing it farther at the western slope of the valley.

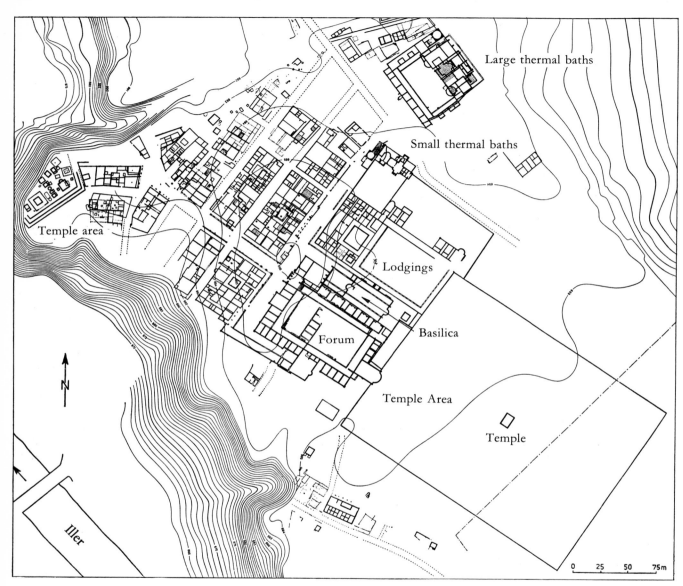

Large thermal baths

Small thermal baths

Temple area

Lodgings

Basilica

Forum

Temple Area

Temple

N

Iller

0   25   50   75m

51 Town plan of the Roman Cambodunum/Kempten, as revealed by excavation.

There is yet another place which conveys a good impression of how the Romans coped with the problem of water supply. If you travel inland from *Forum Iulii*/Fréjus,[68] a brick aqueduct accompanies the road on the right-hand side. Its height can be gauged by the fact that it crosses the town's defensive wall, before discharging the water into a distributor basin. The part of the aqueduct that runs beside the present-day road has been destroyed, but to the left there is a private park containing a well-preserved section of it. Higher up the slope the arches become progressively smaller, until finally a channel is cut into the rock. The course of the channel for many kilometres farther back is known, but the average tourist will have difficulty in following it back without the aid of a detailed map, on account of the way the land is currently parcelled out. A significant portion of the town wall has survived, the southwest gateway, which was discovered during excavation many metres below today's road surface. The paving of the Roman road at its point of entry, as well as the ruins of the great wall, can still be seen. Fréjus was withal a port, which accounts for its importance to the Romans, though virtually nothing remains by which we can recognize it as such. Only those who venture down to the former dock walls and the associated lighthouse, and scan the forest of reeds and the marshy rivulets, can visualize the scene in Roman times, when the sea came almost up to the fringes of the town.

Things to see at Roman sites

It was not only towns by the sea that had harbours; Bregenz, for example, which lies on the Lake of Constance, was a port. Here, too, the shore used to be farther inland than it is today, so that the quays came to light when a pedestrian subway was constructed in the present-day town centre. Exhibited there is a large show-case containing a documentary account, photos and finds. In the Notitia dignitatum, a record of troops and army units and thus one of the most valuable sources of information concerning the military history of late antiquity, there accordingly appears a *praefectus barcariorum*–i.e. naval commander–for the Lake of Constance.[69] For at that time the Lake of Constance once more constituted the frontier with the North and the Alamanni, so that a water-borne defence force was deemed expedient. More important still was the protection of commerce as a whole, since the transport of goods by water was appreciably cheaper than by land.

Whilst in Bregenz there is otherwise not much to be seen of the Roman town, several building complexes have been excavated in Vidy, a suburb of Lausanne. Their ground-plans can be seen between the arterial road to the west and the amusement park by the lake; there is a little associated museum near by.[70]

In relatively few towns are biggish areas with exposed ground-plans of houses or of whole blocks including public buildings open to inspection. For in most cases the modern town is superimposed on the Roman one, which may lie hidden under many layers of rubble or alluvial deposit. In this respect *Aguntum*, near Lienz,[71] was a lucky find, for the town was abandoned as early as late antiquity (the occupants moved across to Lavant, up on the opposite valley slope), and Lienz, these days the main centre of East Tyrol, grew up farther to the West. Excavations can thus proceed without hindrance, except that financial problems are handicapping the preservation or reconstruction of the remains. Nevertheless, the excavators have erected above the courtyard of a once luxurious house a fine museum, which should be visited before examining the ruins, so as to obtain an overall impression of the place. The remains of the public baths near by are particularly impressive. Great excitement was caused a few years ago by the discovery of a stone slab on which was incised a sort of town plan of *Aguntum*,[72] with the public buildings accentuated. It immediately started an argument as to whether the slab was in fact Roman, or just a clever forgery. For it struck a number of people that it shows for the most part only what was already known to archaeologists. What is more, such plans are extremely rare in the Roman Empire as a whole. Wilhelm Alzinger, the leader of the excavating team, swears that it is genuine and scientific examination of the incrustation seems to confirm this, though the doubters have not yet been silenced.

A surprise was also provided by the most recent excavations of François Wiblé in *Octodurus*/Martigny, the capital of Vallis Poenina.[73] True, it had been known for some time where, for instance, the amphitheatre lay, but only now were traces of the very first Roman settlement located, when a large temple with an ambulatory in the Gallic mode was discovered. Here the faithful had, since the time of Emperor Augustus, made offerings, principally of fibulae (brooches), to a deity–still unknown to us–,a custom going back to pre-Roman times (p. 156). With the ready co-operation of the proprietor of the land, it was possible to preserve the ground-plan of the temple and at the same time to build a museum above it, where the finds from *Octodurus* have at length found a suitable home.

Things are not quite so advanced at Chur. The excavations at the Markthallenplatz in Welschdörfli have brought to light such good, well-preserved remains of buildings, that here too plans are afoot to protect them and ultimately set up a museum. The show-piece will then be a house wall adorned with polychrome paintings. It had fallen all in one piece and lay flat on the ground. As soon as it was noticed that there was on the downward-facing side a thick coating of plaster with paintings on it, the excavators sought the assistance of the technician Alfons Defuns and the restorer Josmar Lengler from the museum, for the tricky task of salvaging the paintings.[74] They sprayed the exposed side of the wall with a thick coating of polyurethane, into which wooden beams were then inserted. When this material had hardened and adhered firmly to the wall, it was possible for the whole thing to be lifted up in five large sections and conveyed to the restorer's workshop for cleaning and touching-up.

We can gain a good impression of the appearance of a smaller town on the fringes of the Alps, and the kind of life the people led there, from the ruins and the up-to-date museum of *Vasio Vocontiorum*/Vaison-la-Romaine[75] in the northeast of Provence.

If we exclude what they erected at Arles, Nîmes and Orange, since these places cannot be reckoned as part of the Alpine region proper, then the most impressive monument the Romans have bequeathed to us is the amphitheatre in Verona. Not only did it escape serious damage but it has been refurbished so as to serve a new, and at the same time ancient purpose. Nowadays, every summer, it is the scene of a great spectacle, namely the presentation of grand opera on a lavish scale. When, during a performance of *Aida,* live elephants enter the arena and, to the sound of Verdi's rousing music, swing their trunks in front of the throngs of people packing the auditorium, it gives us some idea of what it was like in Roman times, when gladiators fought each other to the death, or battled frenziedly with wild animals, while the crowd yelled encouragement. *Panem et circenses*–'bread and games' was the cry of the people of second- and third-century Rome, and, no doubt, of other major cities within the Empire. The proletariat encountered a shortage of work and inadequate living standards in the towns. The State and the emperors had had to resort to welfare schemes and, to avoid arousing the discontent of the masses,–the wars on the long frontiers were making maximum demands–laid on great games and spectacles.

The manorial way of life

In the countryside, life went on rather more quietly and smoothly. In the Roman provinces rural settlement did not take the form of villages but, rather, individual farmsteads that were set amid their own fields and woods, and even had their own cemetery.[76] The size of such units in well researched areas can be put at about 2–5 km². This is arrived at by noting how far apart the traces of settlements lie,[77] though we cannot tell from the ground-plan of a simple farmhouse whether it was occupied by an independent smallholder, or by a tenant working for his master. The actual circumstances of tenancy therefore remain obscure, for we should not take the size and trappings of the archaeologically traceable remains as a reliable guide to the total extent of a property.

The case of *Sirmio* (p. 102), for example, shows us that well-to-do Romans who derived their wealth from widely distributed properties and other sources set their country houses amid attractive scenery, irrespective of whether the surrounding land could produce enough by way of agriculture, cattle-breeding and viticulture to make it self-supporting.

The larger agricultural installations along Italic lines only proved to be viable if situated at the fringes of the mountains or in the wider valleys. The Romans called such an installation a '*villa*'. It included a well-appointed

52 The Roman amphitheatre in Verona: '(The architect) begets a crater such as this by the application of the simplest possible art, so that the people themselves constitute its ornamentation . . . The simplicity of the oval engages every eye in the pleasantest way possible, every head becoming a measure of the vastness of the whole. Now, on seeing it empty, one has no idea of scale, one cannot tell whether it is large or small.' (Goethe, Italienische Reise: *16th of September 1786)*

main house having all the amenities of Roman cultured
life, with, naturally, floor-heating and bath (this might
also be accommodated in a separate building). Usually it
stood near the edge of a large plot of land that was surrounded by a wall. Scattered over this area were other,
smaller buildings: dwellings for slaves, barns, stables,
slaughter-house, curing-room, threshing floor, bakery, etc.
Structurally and in the materials used, the country houses
did not differ from those in the towns. The more significant the building, the more likely was it to be constructed
of stone and roofed with tiles. Ordinary houses still had
framework and roofs of straw or shingle, while for stables
and barns the old log construction was no doubt used to a
certain extent.

Only a few places have been excavated so completely
that the entire layout can be reconstructed. Aside from a
few *villae* in Switzerland,[78] Martin Hell has given his main

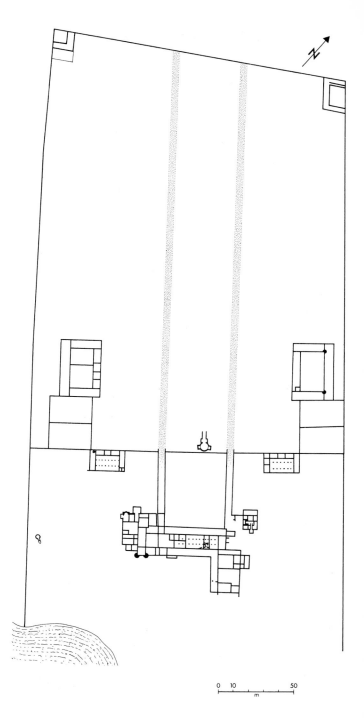

*53   Plan of the Roman farmstead of Seeb, parish of Winkel (can-
ton Zurich). It is likely that the original stone building was erected
shortly after AD 30; there were many subsequent additions and
modifications.*

54   Plans of two Roman villae, *illustrating the extent to which the
country estates varied. Left, a farmstead at Alpnach (canton
Obwalden) with a small dwelling-house, an adjoining courtyard, a
bath-house (bottom left) and several farm buildings. Second half
of the 1st century AD.–Right, the country house at Löffelbach
(Styria), suited to a stylish way of life. The first building phase
with the rooms ranged round the square pillared courtyard and the
bath-house (top) can be dated about AD 100; small additional
buildings were augmented in the 3rd century by an extension on the
northeast side comprising a large reception hall with adjoining
rooms.*

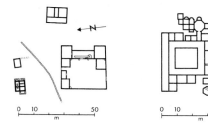

attention to the one at Liefering[79] near Salzburg. Even in the case of Katsch an der Mur, though, it is doubtful whether all the subsidiary buildings have been exposed, since the ground-plan[80] shows nothing more than an out-house beside the manor house with a single inner courtyard. Even so, it is wholly in accord with the Italic scheme of the *villa rustica*. Yet no bath has so far come to light, which casts further doubt on the completeness of the excavation.

Such smaller establishments were occasionally built on a hill rising above the cultivated land itself. This applies, for instance, to the groups of buildings of the second and third centuries on the island-like hill of Invillino (Ill. 56)[81] in the Tagliamento valley at Tolmezzo. The ground-plans here are not fully uncovered and seem to be somewhat irregular, perhaps on account of the unevenness of the ground, but there would seem to have been only two or three peasant holdings there and no *villae rusticae* to cultivate the valley soil which easily became flooded. The simple house construction suggests that the occupiers were not particularly well-off; here, too, a bath was lacking. Worthy of note are only the cisterns hewn into the rock-face and carefully lined with plaster; for there is no spring up on the hill. Since the way up from the valley is not too long and difficult (about a quarter of an hour by the old route), we may assume that the builders of these farm-houses were quite happy to choose this site. It offers a view of the entire valley, which will have appealed to the aes-thetic sense of the occupiers, as well as enabling them to supervise the work of cultivation.

That the Romans had an eye for scenic beauty when sit-ing their towns, villages and farmsteads (except where military, commerce-dictated geographical, or geological aspects were not of greater importance) is often over-looked. Thus, the *villa* of Löffelbach[82] near Hartberg enjoys a wide view across the quiet hills of east Styria. It is the most thoroughly researched *villa* of the East Alpine region, though it is only the domestic quarters that are known; it is to be assumed that the usual outhouses were near by. In a matter of two years Walter Modrijan exposed the complicated ground plan, which revealed a main building with a detached bath complex (from the second century) and a reception hall (probably from the end of the third century). The walls are still standing and may be inspected; a small museum on the fringes of Löffel-bach houses objects found during the excavation and a model of the *villa*.

Large as it is, the Löffelbach *villa* is not in the top flight of these country estates, which almost rank as castles and palaces in the modern sense. It contains no floor mosaics, for instance. Such a criterion, though, is somewhat arbit-rary, for mosaics are also to be found in smaller *villae*, as at Seeb or Orbe in Switzerland[83] and elsewhere. The largest and finest mosaics so far found in Austria came from the *villa* of Loig[84] on the outskirts of Salzburg. They were exa-mined at the beginning of the nineteenth century, when Salzburg belonged to Bavaria for a few years (p. 64), at the behest of the Bavarian Academy of Sciences, but the methods employed were of course governed by the times. Only the peripheral areas of the rooms containing the mosaics were taken in hand. Nor did Bavaria benefit, for the mosaics remained in Austria. They then mysteriously vanished, only to reappear by chance quite recently in a cellar. An archaeological team comprising Norbert Heger, Fritz Moosleitner and Werner Jobst has now undertaken to excavate the *villa* as far as is possible in the face of a threat to erect houses on top of it. As a result of prospect-ing the fields around, it appears that the area containing buildings must have been more extensive than was pre-viously thought. So the *villa* of Loig belongs to the major research projects concerning Roman times in the Alpine region, about which it is to be hoped we shall hear more in the next few years.

But the *villa* of Sirmione, the Roman *Sirmio* on a narrow peninsula at the southern end of Lake Garda, is likely to remain unchallenged. Here modern tourism vies with the Roman susceptibility to scenic beauty: a visit in the sum-mer season is not recommended. Those who wish to enjoy the attractions of this place must come in the late spring, when the air is already warm and snow still covers the mountain-tops, when the camping grounds resemble lonely parks, the pizzerias only open at will, the turn-of-the-century hotels have not set out chairs and tables on the forecourts and the proprietors of souvenir shops find it less easy to earn their livelihood. At such a time one can readily understand the feelings of Catullus, that most true-hearted poet of the Roman Republic:[85]

Sirmio, bright eye of peninsulas and islands, all that in liquid lakes or vast ocean either Neptune bears: how willingly and with what joy I revisit you, scarcely trusting myself that I have left Thynia and the Bithynian plains, and that I see you in safety. Ah, what is more blessed than to put cares away, when the mind lays by its burden, and tired with labour of far travel we have come to our own home and rest on the couch we longed for? This it is which alone is worth all these toils. Welcome, lovely Sirmio, and rejoice in your master, and rejoice ye too, waters of the Lydian lake, and laugh out loud all the laughter you have in your home.

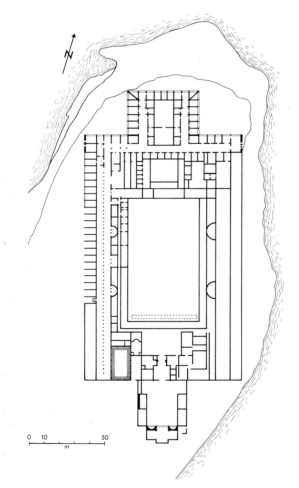

0   10   50
                m

55 Plan of the luxurious Roman villa *at Sirmione on Lake Garda (Lombardy). Built in the last third of the 1st century* BC.

Catullus's family dwelt in Verona and, it would seem, owned a country house at Sirmione.[86] But since the poet, as behoves unruly versifiers, died at the early age of thirty in 57 BC, it is to be doubted whether when composing his poem he beheld the *villa* that we see today. For the most recent research[87] dates the whole complex in the first decades of the Roman Empire, that is, later than 30 BC. At the same time it challenges the view–perhaps only a result of the impression conveyed by the poem–that the nucleus of the property was a small group of buildings lying to the south, which may well have existed as early as Catullus's day. Be that as it may, the Sirmione peninsula has found its way into Latin literature as the place where a *villa* was located (as is the case, incidentally, where Pliny the Younger describes two *villae* on the Lake of Como in his Letters).[88] Strolling among the extensive ruins these days, it is difficult to visualize the buildings that were ranged round an enormous inner courtyard. It was not the country house of an estate, but a pleasure mansion put up on a unique site at the top of a spit of land that drops steeply down to the lake. The terrain at the back of it would have been little suited to cultivation; it is narrow, rocky and surrounded by water, and would be uneconomic for either agriculture or cattle-breeding. The proprietor's farms would certainly have been located in more favourable districts of the nearby Po plain. We may safely assume that they were of a fair size.

Want makes people undemanding

By the fourth century AD this type of manorial luxury was a thing of the past. In the North Alpine foreland those who could had departed for the South when in the third century the Teutons devastated the land in a succession of pillaging raids. Although consolidation during the first half of the century had secured the Danube frontier, the decline in population could no longer be halted. At the same time many lesser settlements in the countryside were vacated; the people congregated at military bases and places up on the heights or on isolated hilltops that could be easily defended. The same applied to the Alpine region proper. The *villa* at Löffelbach was simply abandoned, the walls collapsed, the land was not cultivated and the forest again took over. The other *villae* suffered a similar fate;

there was no longer anybody around who could manage or take pleasure in such large properties. In the Alpine Rhine valley the ruins of some *villae* seem to have been restored for a few years or even decades in the fourth century, the people profiting by once cultivated land in the open valley, since it was easier to clear for small fields. But caves, too, were actually used as dwelling-places during times of trouble.[89]

The recession was reflected also in building techniques. Whilst the forts on the Danube front and along the main Alpine routes were provided with great, almost concrete-hard walls (Ill. 27), less important installations and, above all, private houses reverted to the age-old method of timber construction. (Experience with lime-burning and the works where this was carried on benefited only very important undertakings.)[90] A layer of stones on the subsoil served as insulation, and framework was presumably used for the walls, in conjunction with which, in contrast to pre-Roman technique, large quantities of iron nails were employed. A good example of this kind of structure is the fourth century fortified settlement on a rise at Wessling southwest of Munich. The palisade consisted of wooden beams, and even the largest building–most likely a granary and storehouse–was made of wood. The excavator, Helmut Bender, by determining where every iron nail belonged, has been able to reconstruct building complexes and interior partitions even where these are not indicated on the ground.[91] Used also for the houses inside the wall surrounding the settlement on the Moosberg in the Murnauer Moos was wood and wattling.[92]

In the Inner Alpine region there are only two examples of late Roman/early medieval settlements which it has as yet been possible to explore in any detail. The name Castiel, deriving from the Latin *castellum* (fortified place), of a little hamlet in the Schanfigg above Chur is the sole indication that its history goes back to Roman times. When it was decided to build a new school on the isolated hill known as 'Carschlingg', the Graubünden Archaeological Service under Christian Zindel and Jürg Rageth embarked on a major excavation that was to explore the whole flat top measuring some 75 × 15 m. The preliminary results ahead of a comprehensive evaluation[93] do at least throw some light on the 'dark ages' in the Alpine region.

The hill was occasionally sought out as early as prehistoric times (as, for example, a bronze helmet intentionally buried in the Late Iron Age, attests),[94] but it was not until the fourth century AD that it took on the character of a fortified place. Encircling the narrow plateau was a mortared wall, abutting the inner side of which were modest houses whose walls were made of pine slats with a roughcast. They were not very large, seldom more than 5 m long, and they did not all have a hearth. Because of the slope here, they were set in the ground at the rear end, while presumably resting on wooden substructures at the end nearest the wall, in order to achieve a level floor. Charred beams and planks suggest that a conflagration brought this settlement phase to an end.

The wall must have been destroyed at the same time, for the next settlement phase is only recognizable by indications of great wooden posts. The holes made to accommodate them were up to a metre deep and 0.8 m wide. They were aligned more or less with the late Roman wall and in places penetrate its foundations. It is difficult to say whether, apart from what was obviously a replacement of the fortifications, they served as supports for the structures inside the periphery. Strata that can confidently be ascribed to this late phase are now lacking in the inner area, probably because they were destroyed when the hill was given over to cultivation. The finds were numerous and instructive. There is much evidence of the late Roman and early medieval settlement phase (up until the second half of the seventh century) in the form of readily dateable metal objects (fibulae, belt accessories, ornaments). That the fifth century is practically unrepresented can be observed elsewhere as well, and is to be attributed to the poverty prevailing at the time. Of significance, however, was the discovery that in the early medieval period these people had no pottery, something they could be expected to have used concurrently with the metal objects that have been found. Since it is evident that during the late Roman period the greater part of the pottery took the form of imported luxury utensils, we must conclude that after the collapse of the Roman Empire and the extensive commerce associated with it, the supply of ceramic articles also dried up. The inhabitants of Castiel made do with those materials which in the Central Alps always had been, and up into medieval times continued to be the most important: wood and steatite, that is, soapstone. Wooden vessels survive very seldom in ordinary soil but can sometimes be identified by metal attachments, whilst steatite ones, owing to their being always made by the same simple method, were so alike and so stereotyped for centuries on end, that one can scarcely tell the difference between Roman and medieval exemplars (Ill. 164).

Invillino and the fortified settlements at the southern border of the Alps

An equally important object for research from early medieval times has in recent years been the Colle Santino at Invillino west of Tolmezzo in the Tagliamento valley. As mentioned earlier, there were on this island-like hill Roman peasant holdings in the second/third century (p. 98). But far more interesting and the real target of the systematic excavations of the Institute for Prehistory and Early History of the University of Munich were the early medieval buildings; for *Ibligo* is mentioned by the Lombardic historian Paulus Diaconus as one of a number of fortified places on the edge of the Southern Alps. The investigations, which covered a wide area of the plateau and are shortly to be the subject of a full report by Volker Bierbrauer,[95] produced some surprising information concerning the history and function of the settlement.

In the first half of the fifth century the hill was made to serve a completely new purpose. The Roman buildings with their mortared walls and cisterns were given up; they were allowed to go to ruin and were partially demolished, their stones being used for rebuilding. The new structures, however, looked entirely different. The interlocked box-like building complexes were replaced by simple long-houses, all more or less oriented West-East and varying in size between about 10×5 m and 15.8×8 m (Ill. 138). In one of them an entrance can be identified in one of its short sides. Some of the floors were paved with stone slabs, but most of them probably had boards laid on an insulating bed of pebble. Since nearly everywhere rock lay immediately below the thin layer of soil, no post-holes are visible and there is no way of ascertaining the interior partitioning of the houses. The outer walls were no doubt held by posts dovetailed into beams laid horizontally; as foundation, three layers of largish stone fragments without mortar were used. As the settlement escaped devastation

by fire, the excavators did not find any pieces of baked clay plaster such as would have allowed them to pronounce on the way the walls were made. The houses contained hearths, some of them carefully lined with, and surrounded by stone slabs. What material was used for the roof covering is likewise unknown; since neither bricks nor tiles were found, thatch or more likely shingle seem to be indicated.

The nature of the new settlement can also be fairly reliably determined. On the one hand the military aspect is well exemplified by the finds; on the other hand there can be no doubt that women and children were among the occupants. All this tallies with the historical tradition which has it that in the first third of the fifth century a frontier watch was established on the edge of the Alps, where the fortified places were guarded by a sort of militia. Thus Procopios,[96] writing of the Ostrogothic period, records that the Ostrogoths 'manned the frontier guard with their wives and children'. On the Colle Santino of Invillino, then, stood no late Roman, Gothic or Lombardic barracks, merely a defensive settlement comprising some ten houses, which in the event of a concerted enemy attack was dependent upon the support of larger military forces.

There were many more such militarily important defensive settlements. Paulus Diaconus[97] has recorded for Friuli, the border area which was to stem the Avar tide, some ten of these posts, of which Osoppo south of the Tagliamento bend is likewise situated on a hill that stands out like an island above the valley. On the Dos Trento above Trento–crowned today with a memorial for the politician Cesare Battisti, hanged by the Austrians in 1916–lay the fort of *Verruca*,[98] and at the western edge of the Po plain was recently discovered a fortified installation near the pilgrim church of Belmonte above Cuorgne on the Orco,[99] some 40 km north of Turin. Tools, weapons, a balance, a snaffle for a mule, a jewel and a clay spindle-whorl indicate a settlement from Lombardic times that was not confined to the military.

Invillino is, however, the only site of this kind that has been investigated fully enough for closer details to be available. The inhabitants of Colle Santino had, in late Roman times or earlier, established a cemetery on the Colle di Zuca, a few hundred metres farther up the valley, where there is today a bridge across the river. Though appreciably less high, this hill also rose above high-water level. In this burial place an imposing church with mosaic floor (Ill. 115) was erected in the first half of the fifth century, about 450 at the latest. It served as a place of worship for the little community up on the Colle Santino, who continued to bury their dead here, perhaps also for the peasants in the neighbourhood. This church was burnt down before the middle of the seventh century, whereupon a new building was put up near by. The settlement itself on the Colle Santino did not last much longer; in the second half of the seventh century, when the unrest in the borderland was over, it was systematically evacuated and probably transferred to the western foot of the hill, where the village of Invillino is still to be found. Only a few people went on living up in the dip between the main plateau and the present-day church dedicated to Mary Magdalene (Ill. 138), and they buried their dead on the now unoccupied plateau between the ruins of the deserted houses. The earliest church to be built up there dates from the eighth or ninth century; it was renovated five times and then entirely rebuilt in its present shape. But only when the church on the Colle di Zuca was abandoned (in the ninth century) did the inhabitants of *Ibligo*/Invillino remove their cemetery, too, to the Colle Santino. The function of regional centre which Invillino fulfilled in the early medieval period went on manifesting itself for many centuries, in that this church served as 'pieve' (assoc. Latin *plebs*), a place of worship for a large parish in the valley. Today it is no longer the parish church of Invillino (this is now located down below in the village), but at least the cemetery remains up above. Here in Invillino, thanks to the large-scale excavations and historical studies, an important slice of the history of the Alpine region is documented, a succession of settlement, church and cemetery that was brought about by changing circumstances down the centuries.

56 Villa Santina and Invillino (Udine province, Friuli), as seen when looking northwestwards up the Tagliamento valley. The Roman and early medieval settlement was situated on the steep-sided island-like hill on the right, the Colle di Santino; upon the little hillock on the left, the Colle di Zuca, stood the late Roman and early medieval church, surrounded by graves.

Castles and villages in the early Middle Ages

If at Invillino from the fifth to the seventh century it is the military character of the settlement on the Colle Santino that is unquestionably its salient feature, in the case of the other places it appears to be more a question of the local civilian population withdrawing to more secure heights. Even where a wall was built, it seems to have been rather less a matter of providing necessary strong points on central government orders than the taking of precautionary measures on the part of a community that felt itself threatened in troubled times. In the Eastern Alps some sites, whilst reasonably well researched, have been inadequately documented, among them the Ulrichsberg[100] in Carinthia (several longhouses, churches, but no walls), *Teurnia*/St Peter in Holz on the Drau,[101] the capital in late antiquity of Noricum mediterraneum (walls with abutting houses on the inside), the Kirchbichl of Lavant,[102] the successor settlement of *Aguntum* (houses, a large church complex and a wall, the dating of which is disputed).

In the Swiss Alpine region, too, a withdrawal on to the heights is evident. Apart from the aforementioned Castiel in the Schanfigg above Chur, there are numerous other places which since late Roman times were fortified so as to serve as refuges.[103] Most of them were probably not permanently occupied, but the houses were full of provisions and a little church catered for their spiritual needs when oppressed. Particularly impressive by virtue of their situation are St Georgsberg above Berschis (canton St Gallen), the Crap Sogn Parcazi at Trins, the Grepault hill overlooking the Vorderrhein at Trun, Hohenrätien at Thusis, all in either the Vorderrhein or the Hinterrhein valley, as well as the great valley barriers at Bellinzona and Mesocco at the edge of the Southern Alps. In the case of the last-named in particular it is easy to see how, during the centuries that followed, the fortified retreats for the entire populace became the castles of the feudal barons; for they, too, found such favourable, protected sites to their liking.

The most recent excavations on the Schiedberg at Sagens in Graubünden convey the full story of a fortified place from the fourth century to well into the Middle Ages.[104] Sagens was a particularly fortunate discovery since we even have a description of the early medieval buildings. When Bishop Tello of Chur, in his will of 15

December 735, bequeathed to the Disentis monastery his estates in the Oberland, he listed–so as to forestall later disputes–the properties with their houses, equipment, fields and other possessions. Focal point of the *curtis in Secanio* was a two-storey main house with partially heated living rooms, and store-rooms, cellar, kitchen and bath-chamber. In addition, there was a house (or several?) for guests with store-rooms, stables, granary and barns. There is no mention of either a mill or a bakery, but it is conceivable that they, not being in use all the time, were at the bottom of the hill; in which case they would be covered by the expression *et quidquid ad ipsam curtem pertinent, omnia ex integro*–and whatever belongs to the estate itself, all without exception. The larger buildings were of stone with wattling used for the upper storeys. We may assume that the outbuildings were simple structures supported on posts, or even log huts. Such a place would of course only belong to a larger establishment administered by the upper class. The peasant farmers had to make do with more modest buildings and smaller stables for their cattle; they will certainly not have owned a separate house for guests.

We can derive a lot of useful information about the area at the northern edge of the Alps from the Alamannic decrees,[105] coupled with the extensive excavations carried out at Berslingen[106] in the canton of Schaffhausen. Here, too, it seems to be a case of the properties of rather better-off people. According to the description, the manor comprised a large dwelling-house with a high roof, and a smaller house for the women, where the female members of the family and the maidservants did their work, principally spinning and weaving. There was also a *stuba* (bath-house) and among the ancillary farm buildings are mentioned pigsties and sheep pens, granaries, haylofts, cellars and barns. Of particular importance was the fencing that enclosed the property, for any unauthorized entry was severely punished. The houses were supported by posts, probably with straw or shingle as roofing. For the outbuildings simple huts with four corner posts, or sometimes only two ridge supports, sufficed. The walls will have been of wattle and daub. The sole stone building in Berslingen was a little church, some 30 m away from the nearest huts. More than 100 graves lay directly by it, showing how–unlike, for instance, at Invillino–the settlement itself and the burial ground of a small village community were both contained within the same area.

So Berslingen, too, was a lucky find, for the initial stages of Germanic settlement at a site on the fringe of the Alps nearly always lie beneath present-day village centres and are thus as a rule inaccessible for archaeological investigation. Only when for one reason or another a village was abandoned, and no resettlement took place there later, can the necessary extensive excavations be carried out.[107] This applies even more to those sites, above all in the Alpine interior, that have been occupied uninterruptedly since Roman times. Even where excavation on a small scale exposes Roman mortared walls, sometimes extending to somewhat larger complexes, it is hardly ever possible to extract archaeological evidence relating to the early medieval houses with their predominantly wooden structures, not to mention when more recent cellars have wholly destroyed the older strata.

For this reason it is generally only the churches and cemeteries that provide links between the Roman settlement phases of towns and villages and those of the high Middle Ages. Fréjus on the coast, Geneva in the West, Sion, Chur and Trento in the interior, Aosta, Como and Verona in the South exemplify the places that have retained their status from Roman times without interruption through the 'dark centuries' of the early Middle Ages up until today, documented by archaeological or indeed still visible structural evidence.

57 Plan of the extensively excavated early medieval hamlet at Berslingen (canton Schaffhausen), showing two groups of buildings each of which includes a four-aisled hall-type house and a smaller structure with side pillars (lightly shaded). Around them are ranged various little outbuildings. To the North, set somewhat apart, stands the simple church, the only stone building. Close by it are more than 200 graves which, on account of the absence of offerings, cannot date from before the eighth century AD. *There are signs of a division into two separate families in the graveyard as well.*

III The Living and the Dead –
The Individual and the Community

The archaeologist finds himself in a curious situation: he only really gets to know the object of his research, the human being of centuries long past, when the latter has crossed the frontier of death. For every human being was buried as an individual. The finds from a settlement, on the other hand, are little more than the jumbled leavings of a human community and very infrequently allow us to piece together particular events and happenings that are representative of social change. For this reason, in practically all prehistoric cultures, questions relating in a general way to such matters as the social structure, expectation of life and living standards of the people, provision for the dead and religious concepts can only be answered by studying the graves. Only when we come to Roman times does the situation change. Here we have an adequate literary tradition, pictorial depictions and inscriptions of various kinds, and these enable us to reconstruct tolerably well, or at least to come to certain conclusions regarding some areas of public life and the destiny of individuals.

Forms of burial and conceptions of the after-life

All the same, the graves have provided information not only about the individual and his place in the community, but also about the contemporary attitude towards the after-life. Funerary customs used to adhere to a very strict

pattern–something that in the twentieth century is virtually only to be met with in the countryside. The bereaved arranged the burial in what they considered to be the deceased's (and their own!) best interests. This means that everything that happened before and after the actual interment remains hidden from the archaeologist: the laying out, the mourning ceremonies, the choice of guests, the wake, and 'absolution' of the house of mourning or funerary chamber. Only what is actually present in the grave itself and has been preserved down the centuries can any longer be assessed.

The inferences we can make regarding early man's attitude towards the after-life must, even with the support of his burial customs, be limited. At certain periods the dead were buried in their finery, decked out with personal adornments and equipped with weapons, and provided with food and vessels filled with drink. This would seem to justify the assumption that a continuing corporeal existence after death was envisaged, an existence in which the deceased had need not only of food and drink but also of all the important status symbols that signified his personal or social rating. But even equipping the dead with weapons was sometimes subject to regulations, which makes it difficult to draw direct inferences–the Goths, who on principle buried even their warriors without weapons, are a case in point.

Where cremations are concerned, interpretation is even more difficult. Although the deceased is thereby deprived of his body, there were many different periods when a certain number, if not all of the offerings that were usual in the case of inhumations were placed in the grave. In that event, to decide what were his rightful personal possessions, what was treated as equipment for an after-life that was still thought of in 'concrete' terms, what was given to him because the living would find it 'unclean', is scarcely possible. At best, analyses of individual burial-grounds will provide models that can be interpreted within narrow geographical and chronological limits, but these should not be generalized. What images of the hereafter were

58 *Gravestones bearing the name of the deceased were set up even before Roman times within the mountain region, though nearly all were in the Ticino and the Misox. At the same time they provide the most important evidence of the Lepontic language, using an alphabet derived from north Etruscan. Left, from Daversco-Soragno (canton Ticino): slaniai uerkalai pala/tisiu piuotialui pala = tombstone for Slania, daughter of Verkos, tombstone for Tisios, son of Pivotios. Right, from Stabio (canton Ticino): minuku komoneos = Minuku (and?) Komoneos (son of Komonos?). 3rd–2nd century BC. Ht 1.87 and 1.32 m respectively. Schweizerisches Landesmuseum, Zurich and Rätisches Museum, Chur.*

conjured up by the introduction of cremation in the Bronze Age is less clear today than ever (p. 120ff.).

There were rare instances when the dead were disposed of in such a manner that archaeology has no means of tracing them–here fantasy, founded on ethnographical parallels, knows no limits. This phenomenon, applying as it does to a number of different periods, is a source of concern to researchers. There are, for example, no graves from the Early Bronze Age Polada culture[1] in northern Italy, notwithstanding the many settlements, nor from the Late Bronze Age 'pile-dwellings' of central Switzerland;[2] in southern Switzerland they are lacking between the eleventh and sixth centuries BC,[3] in the North Alpine foreland during the last century before the Roman conquest.[4] Every so often, but in widely separated regions, this custom emerges though there is no common ground or similarity in the prevailing social or religious climate.

With inhumations the corpse was initially buried in the crouched position, that is on its side with the legs drawn up. The shank is often pressed so tightly against the thigh as to suggest that they were bound together. But if the dead person's legs, and perhaps the hands as well, were shackled, then the body will automatically have been laid on its side. People used to refer to the 'sleeping'[5] or 'embryonic' posture, but there can no longer be any doubt that the underlying motive is far more likely to have been fear of the dead, fear lest they return and molest the living with nightmares, apparitions, sickness or cattle-pest.[6] On the other hand the careful preparation of the grave and the provision of ornaments and nourishment testify to a certain solicitude on the part of the bereaved, as does the uniting of the dead in common ground. They were, then, not rejected or forgotten persons; their graves in the burial-ground, cemetery or necropolis (the 'city of the dead', as the Greeks, the Romans and the romance-speaking peoples called it) constituted a part of the settlement area, usually a little apart (Ill. 57) but nevertheless in sight, and so a reminder of the transitoriness of human life. Where the custom grew up of building a mound of stones or earth over the graves, the burial-places often ran alongside the roads and paths, or occupied conspicuous sites. Since for the building of such a mound a certain work-force had to be available, the height of the mound reflected the relevant family's standing or power. In this respect the Egyp-

tian pyramids, the burial-mounds of the Bronze Age and the Iron Age in Central Europe, and the tombs of the Romans (the nearer the road, the more ostentatious) rate alike, even though they are, and always have been, totally dissimilar in appearance.

It is from the Late Stone Age that the earliest evidence is to be found in Central Europe of provision being made for the dead, the installation of a common burial-ground and the development of obligatory burial customs. Life after death, whatever form it might take, had now become an accepted principle. Burial in the crouched posture as a way of expressing fear of the dead is a logical first stage in the prescribed burial rites in Central Europe, and although during the Bronze Age it became customary to inter the dead lying flat on their back, or even more often to cremate them, memories of the meaning of the crouched posture persisted for a long time. Archaeologists are continually coming across single bodies that have been subjected to this treatment. Investigations over a long period of time show[7] that these without exception represent instances of 'dangerous dead'; that is to say, persons who, owing to the circumstances that surrounded their life or their death, were suspected of wanting to take revenge on those who outlived them, or to do them some harm. These fall into several categories:[8] suicides, the insane and epileptic, shamans and witches, those who had fatal accidents or were murdered, women who died in childbirth, non-integrated aliens, children, twins . . .

Being buried face-down also reflects a particular attitude towards the individual in question. In the post-Roman period the crouched type of burial as good as disappeared, but the adoption of the face-down position as a means of constraining a dangerous dead person continued into modern times.[9] Examples of bodies being turned over later are known: in such instances it was presumably not until after the burial took place that dangerous proclivities were attributed to the dead person. Coincidences may have played an important role here, but the underlying motive is evident: when a mishap, a fire, sickness, cattle-pest or drought were visited upon the people, somebody to pin it on had to be found. And if there was no one among the living who could be held responsible–which must frequently have been the case–then one of the deceased had to be made a scapegoat: his grave would be opened, the body turned on its front or even mutilated, perhaps a heavy stone rolled on top of it.

In only a few instances, admittedly, can the archaeologist discover the actual reason for the special treatment of any one dead person. The rare examples that allow of a general interpretation of exceptional burials, while not confined to any particular region or time, are nevertheless convincing when taken together. As a rule, anthropology, by tracing anomalies in the skeleton or the cranium, can help out.[10] In this way serious illnesses, unusual physical traits, alien racial attributes, injuries and attempts at therapy can be identified. Sometimes also offerings of amulet type provide a clue: for amulets can not only be worn during a person's life as protection against ill-fortune, but also be placed in the deceased's grave as a safeguard against the harm he might do posthumously.[11]

As all these phenomena continue through the ages, it seemed best to discuss them here in advance. In the Alpine region, though, they are less in evidence because there–some limited areas and specific periods excepted–cremation was customary. This means that anthropology can do but little to help interpret departures from the norm. During incineration on a simple funeral pyre the bones do indeed split and turn to cinder, but usually a lot of larger fragments remain, which were more or less carefully salvaged from the wood ash for burial in the ground. Hence the anthropologist can, with the aid of preserved cranial sutures, pelvic fragments and the ends of joints, find ways of determining the age and (less reliably) the sex of the deceased.

In the case of cremations, what is more, there are several ways in which the living may have dealt with the dead person and his personal possessions. The archaeologist is of course particularly interested in those instances where a great many articles of pottery or metal were placed in the grave with the deceased. But this was by no means a frequent occurrence. The dead person might, for example, be incinerated wearing nothing more than his shroud, the ash being then poured into a shallow ditch. It is very seldom that such graves are discovered by archaeologists–what bull-dozer operator is likely to take any notice of little black marks in the gravel? If the deceased was consigned to the flames complete with all his possessions, clothing and equipment for the hereafter, the objects usually

suffered so much from the heat, that their original appearance can be no more than partially reconstructed and used for an analysis of their shapes and combinations: pottery vessels shatter and the sherds become distorted, bronze ornaments melt into shapeless lumps, iron–though it keeps its shape to a certain extent thanks to its higher melting point–has its surface ruined. The archaeologist is best pleased when custom dictated that the deceased be burned clad only in a simple garment, and his entire outfit subsequently placed upon the ashes or next to the urn. Even then, it is less easy to draw conclusions about the individual in question, about age and sex, than in the case of inhumations; but at least the offerings reflect the intentions of the bereaved and thus to a certain extent also the status of the deceased.

Life was brief

There is a further problem which it seems reasonable to consider at this point, namely the treatment of children in connection with the burial customs. It is a well-known fact that in the Middle Ages child mortality was far higher than it is today. Since in antiquity hygienic conditions and medical knowledge were, if anything, even more rough and ready (apart perhaps from Roman times with their civilizing achievements), we must expect a very high child mortality rate in those early days as well.[12] Archaeological evidence should corroborate this by showing that about 50% of all the graves of a tolerably well excavated cemetery are those of children or adolescents. But such confirmation is only forthcoming in exceptional cases, such as the Late Bronze Age burial-ground of Canegrate north of Milan, for which we have an exact anthropological analysis.[13] Correspondingly valuable data are to hand only for the Iron Age graves at the Dürrnberg at Hallein, where, because inhumations far outnumber all others, they are particularly accurate.[14] Yet, among the more than a hundred distinguishable graves there, not a single one contained a child under four years of age. So we must conclude that children who died very young were treated in a manner which archaeology has been unable to discover. If they were buried in a separate cemetery, as according to tradition sometimes happened in Roman times, there is always the chance that some day one such will come to light fortuitously. It is more likely, however, that little children were not regarded as human beings in their own right, and that they were despatched in some way that made them disappear for good: hung up on trees, fed to the dogs, drowned in the Salzach... We just cannot tell. They may have been buried within the house or under the eaves (p. 86), in which case they could only be traced were extensive excavations to be carried out.

Dating from about the same time as the graves of the Dürrnberg is the cemetery of Tamins in Graubünden.[15] Of the identifiable cremated bodies, there are nineteen adults as against only five children.[16] Of the latter, two were definitely more than ten years of age, one under ten. The remaining two were infants, one possibly new-born, the other buried together with an adult. Here too, then, the proportion of little children is certainly too low; we cannot tell what were the reasons for the two exceptions.

It is worth mentioning here that Pliny[17] refers to the custom–actually claiming it to have been the rule–of burying without prior cremation infants whose milk-teeth have not yet come through, in contrast to the rest of the deceased. The latest excavations in the Roman cemetery at Kempten have wholly confirmed this,[18] even though here too there is some doubt whether all the children who died were buried there.

On this incomplete basis it is scarcely possible to assess the expectation of life in prehistoric times. In the case of infants it must always be a rough guess (at the Dürrnberg, for example, 26 years at most), since the graves do not normally give us a complete picture of child mortality.[19] Hence the calculations which arrive at a figure for the number of further years a person can expect to live once he has reached adulthood (say the age of twenty) are likely to be more reliable. At the Tamins cemetery the findings for this age-group show that the average life expectancy was 36.5 years (a little higher for men, a little lower for women). This corresponds almost exactly to the figures from Bonaduz (Graubünden).[20] The larger quantity of graves at the Dürrnberg means that the figures for there are more accurate. According to these, the men on average lived to be 41, the women 38. But this does not mean that there were not individual cases of people living to be 60–70.

Where larger series of skeletons or cremated bodies are

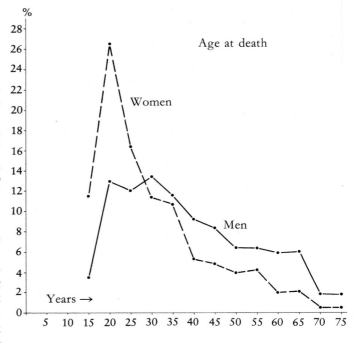

59 *Graph showing distribution of adults in the Iron Age graves on the Dürrnberg above Hallein (Salzburg province). The difference between the men and the women is manifest: more than a quarter of the latter died between the ages of 20 and 25.*

concerned, the differences between the men and the women can also be envisaged statistically. Nearly everywhere the women had a shorter expectation of life than the men. This can be traced back to the risk of death in childbed, which carried off not a few young women as late as the last century.[21] In Roman times–despite the longer expectation of life–the distinction was still manifest.[22]

The hunters of the Stone Age and the first miners

It was not until the Alpine people had adopted a sedentary way of life, that their dead, too, were allotted a fixed place of their own. Hence we owe our knowledge of the earliest phases of settlement on the Riviera and the other

Alpine fringe areas almost entirely to dwelling-places alone.[23] Stone implements lying around, or pieces chipped off when these were being shaped, and a few objects made of other materials, mainly bone and antler, show how modest were the means at the disposal of early man. When an animal was killed, it provided not only food but hide for clothing, bones for awls and needles, distinctive teeth as adornments or trophies of the chase.

Decorative articles of this kind are also found in the graves of the Late Stone Age. The earliest are a few graves in the Western Alps, which appear to derive from a middle phase of that era. A crouched burial in Fontaine (Isère) contained flint tools and the tusks of a wild boar; a multiple burial (at least ten bodies) at La Balme (Isère) has been dated in the same period on the strength of C14 tests alone.[24] It is characterized by the fact that all the dead had been decapitated–a custom that occurs very seldom in later times.

By the final phase of the Late Stone Age and at the time of transition into the Bronze Age, single burials became more or less standard. They frequently took the form of small groups of stone cists made up of large slabs sunk in the ground. Mostly they were just large enough to take a dead person in the crouched posture. If, exceptionally,

60 *In ancient times, too, accidents and war wounds were the order of the day. The man in Grave 248 in the early medieval cemetery of Bonaduz (Graubünden) had lost his right foot. He wore an artificial one, recognizable by the dark colouring, consisting of an iron plate and a plug, probably stuffed with hay or wool. It was attached to the shin-bone with tapes or straps.*

several bodies occupied the same cist, they were either packed close together in a row or even laid on top of one another. In order to make room for fresh burials the older skeletons were often thrown aside or pushed together, or they were covered with a layer of earth so as to provide a second level. Unfortunately, there are virtually no detailed analyses of group-graves of this kind, which might have given us an idea of what else those buried in one and the same grave had in common. It seems reasonable to assume, nevertheless, that they were members of a single family, perhaps of a generation, that had a right to communal interment and so remain together in the hereafter, be they parents and children, brothers and sisters, or man and wife.

The discovery of the burial-ground at Lenzburg (canton Aargau) with its multitude of multiple burials[25] provided a particularly impressive example of this kind. Its irregular lay-out would seem to accord with a population structure such as one associates with those early times. Of those buried there, 52.3% were children and adolescents, among the adults twice as many men as women–owing to the latter having borne children from an early age, and dying in giving birth to their first or second child? Standing out all the more therefore is a man aged about 35 who lay on his own in a fairly large stone cist, wore a necklace consisting of five perforated animal eye-teeth (with, in between, feathers, wooden beads, etc.?) and was provided with weapons (arrows–in a quiver?), implements, as well as a bone comb. Here, undoubtedly, was an important member of the community, perhaps the most senior of the tribe, who, not only because of his age but also by virtue of his skill as warrior and organizer controlled the tribe's destiny. Observations comparable to those for Lenzburg at the northern edge of the Alps are not to hand for the Inner Alpine area because no group of graves there has yet been investigated thoroughly enough or published. Even so, we can at least discern that the custom of burying the dead in a crouched posture in stone cists extends from the North-western Alps as far as the Aosta valley.[26]

Of exceptional interest in this context are the graves of Sion–'Petit-Chasseur'. Once building operations had brought to light the first stone cists in 1961, first Olivier-Jean Bocksberger, then Alain Gallay laid bare this group of graves, finishing the work in 1973.[27] What makes the cists of Sion so significant is that their builders took to using decorated slabs which had originally stood upright and bore depictions of men, heroes or gods. Their shape is roughly that of a human being; the Greek word 'stelae' is used to describe such free-standing slabs of stone or wood. On the front are incised in low relief the arms, weapons and attire. At first it was thought that the builders of the graves had dismantled a former shrine and used the stelae from it for a purpose not originally intended, but Gallay's latest interpretation, based on minute observation of the stratigraphical sequence, presents a different picture.

Gallay distinguishes between two types of stelae. The more ancient has a 'head' that is but indistinctly indicated, slightly bent arms with fairly naturalistic hands, only faint signs of clothing, and daggers as weapons. The later type places more emphasis on the human form, shows richly decorated attire, and the weapon is the bow and arrow. In one instance at least the bow has a double curve, thus anticipating the reflex bow that was to be widely used in later times, particularly by Eastern mounted tribes.[28] The stelae can be dated from the contents of the graves of which they were the main components. The results show that the older type can be brought into association with Stone Cist VI at Petit-Chasseur, and dated around the end of the Late Stone Age. Isolated examples of copper daggers and pendants of spiral wire of that period had already been found. On the other hand, the later type can probably be associated with those stone cists which were set up by the 'Bell Beaker folk' (p. 19) during the Early Bronze Age. Somewhat surprisingly, the excavations indicated that old stelae were used many times over in the building of the graves, whilst new stelae, some decorated, others just plain slabs, were put up near by. This would explain, among other things, why some of the stelae were decorated a second time, without the original design being first removed. This means that after a certain period of time, or following some particular event, the stelae lost their significance as cult objects and could be hewn into shape for reuse as material with which to build the stone cist. Whether their original function, expressed by the still recognizable decoration, any longer played a role, we do not know. At all events, a conspicuous feature of the process is that the 'head' of nearly every one of the stelae had been knocked off.

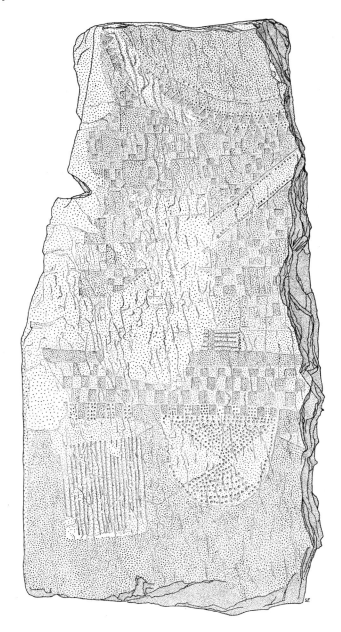

61 *Stone slab from Sion (Valais) portraying a woman in an elaborately patterned costume with two pockets attached to the belt. 18th–17th century* BC. *Ht 1.64 m. Musée Valère, Sion.*

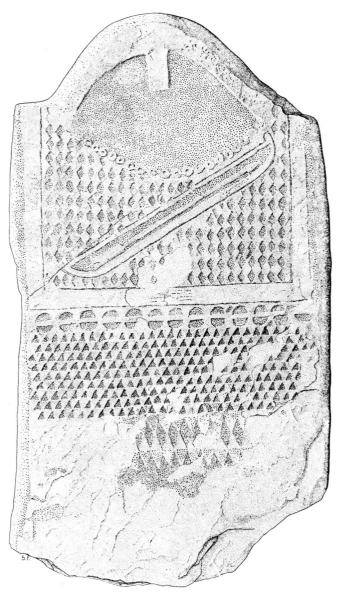

62 *Stone slab from Sion (Valais) portraying an archer. There is little more than a suggestion of the head and face, the hands are placed together on the belt, the costume elaborately patterned. 18th–17th century* BC. *Ht 1.7 m. Musée Valère, Sion.*

Anthropological examination of the skeletons from the stone cists shows that new groups, the 'Bell Beaker folk', spread into the upper Valais, as they did over half of Europe,[29] around 2000 BC. The bodies in the cists containing 'Bell Beaker' material were those of a larger, stronger type of human being, characterized moreover by their short skull. It is therefore all the stranger that these new arrivals, quite out of keeping with their other propensities, should have constructed their own graves along the lines of the already existing Stone Cist VI and even carried on the custom of using figurative stelae, more finely decorated especially where costume was concerned. This all suggests that the original inhabitants had gone on living much as before, passing on their ancient cults and burial rites to the newcomers, who were perhaps relatively few in number but politically in control.

The 28 stelae in various states of preservation, together with the offerings from the graves, provide us with a fairly detailed picture of contemporary man. No copper daggers were found in the graves (northern Italy was the nearest place for these from the corresponding period); instead, there were still flint daggers, wrapped around the upper end of which were cord or twigs (Ill. 5) to give a better grip and protect the palm of the hand. Since the spiral pendants of copper wire[30] have not yet been attested in Sion itself at this time, it is to be assumed that these articles either did not find their way into the graves at all, or were so rare that their abundance on the stelae does not reflect the true situation. It may be that at this early stage they were reserved for the use of high-ranking persons and were passed down over the years from one top tribal elder of the settlement community to the next. Bows and arrows, on the other hand, proclaim themselves in the graves of the later phase through carefully shaped arrowheads of flint or rock-crystal. These were the characteristic weapon of the Bell Beaker folk throughout Central and Western Europe, often accompanied by little plates of bone or horn intended to protect the forearm from the recoiling bowstring. Pieces of stone with grooves scored into them were probably for helping to produce arrow shafts that were as even and straight as possible. The Bell Beaker complex,[31] which, as mentioned earlier, derives its name from the typical vessel form associated with this folk, is further characterized by 'buttons' that have a V-shaped

63 The few depictions of weavers' looms, of which this rock-drawing from the Valcamonica is one, tell us how they worked. The threads were fastened to a vertical wooden frame and tautened by means of clay weights below. Such loomweights are more frequently found in settlements. The complicated woven patterns, in evidence since the Stone Age, presuppose a device for raising and lowering the warp.

incision on the underside, and decorated miniature bows which were worn as pendants, both carved in wood. Teeth of the wild boar were favoured both as adornments and trophies.

The multiplicity of designs on the clothing points to a highly developed weaving technique: lozenges, triangles, zigzag bands, diamonds and chequerboard patterns of various sizes. The belt is nearly always emphasized, as is the contrast between the upper garment and the apron. A characteristic feature is the round neckline, usually accentuated by a detached hem. One of the stelae without weapons apparently represents a woman wearing a kind of sash diagonally across the upper part of the body, with two pouches hanging from the belt. Irrespective of whether the stelae portray living persons, dead people or divine beings, the details of dress and weapons correspond to the daily life of the time, thus providing much-needed additional information with which to eke out the scanty clues the burial and settlement finds offer. The impact of these unique sculptures is fully conveyed by the display in the new Musée Valère in Sion.

The fate that befell some stone cists in South Tyrol was far less fortunate. Only a few fragments remain to show that the custom of the family grave, mostly confined to the area northwest of the Alps, had extended as far as this. Adequate evidence is provided by the large stone slabs, each with a round hole a good 20 cm in diameter (a 'spirit hole'), which had formerly served as gables of large tombs.[32] These were covered with a mound of earth and ringed by a circle of stones. As all the South Tyrolean examples had already been destroyed and the slabs hauled away (seemingly, in the case of Gratsch near Merano even built into a tomb of late antiquity), it is not possible to comment further on the construction, content and date of these graves. To judge by comparable examples at the Alpine fringe, they may be taken to belong in the final phase of the Late Stone Age.

At the southern edge of the Central Alps quite different burial customs prevailed at this time. The cemetery of Remedello di Sotto near Brescia, name-site of the 'Remedello culture', is the best known, and with at least 119 graves also the largest of its kind yet discovered.[33] The dead were still mostly buried in the crouched posture, practically all with head towards the West and lying on their left side, but the graves were no more than simple trenches, in nearly every case containing only a single body and relatively shallow, so that prior to the excavations in the nineteenth century much had already been destroyed by the plough. Unfortunately, not nearly as much care was then exercized as is called for today; for example, not even an accurate plan of the cemetery has been preserved and only about half of the graves can be even partially evaluated. Particularly well represented among the offerings are weapons and tools, that is articles pertaining to the male sphere of activity: arrows (and bow) in 24, flint daggers in 16, stone axes in nine graves, with in addition two copper awls, a silver pin and a copper ring. There were a few ornaments in the form of little perforated plaques of shell or soapstone (steatite) beads and a singular pendant of marble. The female sphere is thus sparsely represented, and such flint daggers as were given to children would presumably have gone to the boys. Only the few earthenware vessels belonging to the household inventory appear to have been placed in the women's graves. In view of the meagre information we have on the source itself, and also where preceding and ensuing centuries are concerned, there is little point in trying to draw from this distribution of offerings any direct conclusions about the social structure of the community whose dead were buried here. For only on the basis of a comparison with cemeteries that are both in close proximity and contemporary would further inferences be feasible and justifiable.[34]

So a very interesting group of graves at Romagnano-Loc in the province of Trento will be only briefly discussed here; it is reckoned to belong in the dawning Bronze Age. The excavations, begun in 1970, were actually intended to deal with a great accumulation of strata several metres thick at a cliff face, containing settlement horizons from the Middle Stone Age through into the Iron Age. Grabs and bulldozers had already removed large portions of it, so that only a narrow strip remained. To everybody's astonishment in transpired that this place had for a while served also as a burial-place,[35] for within a restricted space 15 graves lay close together, with a further three close by, though there was no longer any way of telling whether a single cemetery of substantial size had originally existed here. The first grave was uncovered as early as in 1969; it was that of a young woman and contained the most offerings. These were exclusively of bone or animal teeth: 28 bone beads in shape from flat to spherical, 22 little tubes made out of fossil snail-shells, three plaques carved from boars' teeth, two animal eye-teeth, a (human?) finger joint, two small club-shaped bone rods and a bone ring, all perforated and thus intended for neck or head adornment, as is indicated by the position they occupied when found.

Unfortunately the hopes raised by the grave excavated in 1969 were not entirely fulfilled, for the other 17 only yielded very scanty offerings, though useful observations were made concerning the burial custom. For adults the crouched posture was the rule, except when the skull alone was buried; the same applies to the children, only in one instance did a double grave contain a young woman and a six- or seven-year old child–that they were contemporary is not certain, however. New-born babies, on the other hand, were accorded a very special kind of burial; the parents put them in large earthenware vessels, usually it would appear head-downwards, and then deposited these in the communal burial-ground, where they were ringed by a few stones and covered over in the customary manner. It is a custom with a long tradition in the Near East

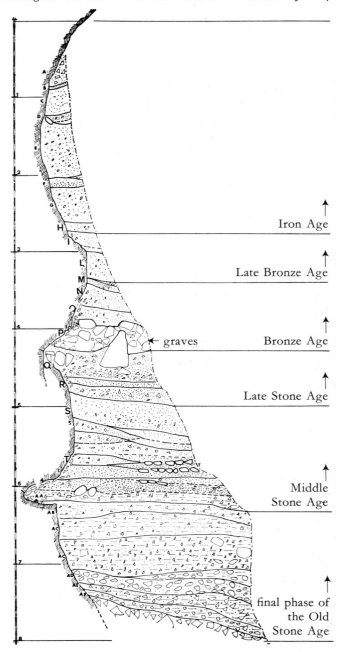

Iron Age

Late Bronze Age

← graves   Bronze Age

Late Stone Age

Middle Stone Age

final phase of the Old Stone Age

64 Stratification of the deposits under the rock shelter of Romagnano-Loc III (Trento province).

and the Balkans,[36] the idea ostensibly being that still-born babies and those who die shortly after birth are consigned to the earth in a kind of womb and in the relevant posture, so that perhaps they might soon be born again. This custom disappears almost completely in Central Europe during the Bronze Age.

At the cemetery of Romagno-Loc, what is more, it is evident that also the side facing the valley had soon proved a natural obstacle to further extension, because single graves were set one on top of the other, whilst large numbers of scattered remains of demolished burials indicate that the original total was appreciably greater. We have, in fact, to supplement the 19 identifiable individual bodies in the 17 preserved or accessible graves by a further 20 individuals who can be pieced together from additional bones or frag-

65 *Close-up photograph of a woman's grave with rich offerings in the Early Bronze Age cemetery of Raisting south of the Ammersee near Weilheim (Upper Bavaria). About the 17th century* BC.

ments of skull that were found. The anthropological distribution of the bodies should be noted, for it leads to the suspicion that the part of the burial-ground that has been uncovered does not necessarily provide a representative cross-section of the age-pattern of the dead as a whole. For there were only five women and three men to 16 children and 15 new-born babies. The way the few offerings are made up is instructive: eight rudimentary eye-teeth of stags, with perforations, a perforated eye-tooth of a fox, and seven flat beads of soapstone or mother of pearl. All of these almost certainly came from the graves of children or new-born babies, as the amuletic nature of in particular the stunted eye-teeth[37] of stags would suggest; for, seeing that for example in Grave 13–that of a new-born baby–a single stag's tooth was found, it is clearly not a case of 'adornment' but of a genuine 'offering', meant to protect the little being in the after-life–or else it was intended as an appeasement or exorcism of its spirit, so that the latter on account of its all too short life should not take revenge on the living.

How complicated the burial customs and the accompanying rites, insofar as we are able to reconstruct them, can be is evident from conditions at the northern fringe of the Alps. The settlements and cemeteries of the Early Bronze Age cultures of Central Europe made only tentative headway southwards against the inhospitable mountain barrier. One such advance post is the cemetery of Raisting south of the Ammersee, which was in fact excavated as early as 1964/65 but, regrettably, has so far only been published in provisional form.[38] Its 44 graves contained single crouched burials differentiated strictly according to the deceased's sex–children included: the men lay on their left side with head pointing towards the North, the women on their right side with head pointing towards the South–thus in all cases the face was turned towards the East. The difference between the offerings in the graves is less easily distinguishable, though it would appear that it was the men who had a greater abundance of ornaments and adornments comprising the usual bones, teeth, antlers and shells, whereas the women had more made of metal, which had newly come into fashion. The daggers of the men and older boys were of course also made of copper or bronze and these, coupled with an anthropological assessment of the skeletons, will one day

66 *The assemblage that was found at Arbedo-Castione (canton Ticino) comprised 67 costume pins, various pendants, wire spirals and hooking rings. It is indicative of the standardization of adornments at the southern edge of the Alps during the Early Bronze Age; it may be that the hooking rings functioned as money as well as adornments. 17th–16th century* BC. *L of largest pin 16.8 cm. Schweizerisches Landesmuseum, Zurich.*

allow us to deduce from his garb and equipment the age at which a youth was reckoned to have become an adult. It will perhaps be possible in due course to arrive at something similar in the case of girls and women. Associated with the burial rite or cult of the dead are two wooden houses, a bare 10 m long and each supported by six pots, at the eastern edge of the cemetery, but what rites were there performed we cannot tell.

Cemeteries of the Raisting type occur in all parts of the North Alpine foreland,[39] extending as far as Lower Austria and Hungary,[40] but they are, as previously stressed, not known in the mountain area proper. In the Western Alps the custom of using stone cists persisted until the end of the Early Bronze Age, partly as tombs for containing several dead persons, partly also for inhumations with the body fully stretched out on its back. As time went on, bronze adornments took increasing precedence over the materials previously used. The graves in the Valais and Graubünden in particular yielded many examples of pins (Ill. 7), which with their hammered, disc- and wing-shaped heads show off the new material to its best advantage.[41] Emil Vogt actually coined the term 'Blechstil' (metal-sheet style)[42] for them, since other ornamental objects were produced with the use of this technique: spectacle-shaped and crescentic or round pendants and armrings.

Only a heap of ashes remains

The Central European custom, introduced in the Middle Bronze Age, of covering the dead–now invariably buried lying fully stretched-out–with mounds of stones and earth did not catch on in the Alpine region. On the contrary, cremation was soon adopted, which appreciably reduces the chances of our coming to any decision about the way in which the deceased were fitted out, the grading of their possessions and how they were rated.

Archaeologists have from the outset attached great importance to the difference between inhumation and cremation. The antagonism of the Roman Catholic Church towards cremation up until 1964 seemed–heedless of the historical background–to justify the conviction that this was an expression of fundamental differences in the interpretation of life after death. But in antiquity the corresponding ideological and religious disparity will not have been nearly so marked. There are in fact burial-grounds where inhumation and cremation were practised in equal measure (in Hallstatt, for example); then, again, there were 'transitional' customs, such as that where the selected burnt bones were not deposited in little heaps or in an urn but strewn on the floor of the grave, to match the dead person's full length, with his adornments even arranged as if he were still actually wearing them.[43] More significant yet is the fact that offerings of food and drink, recognizable from earthenware vessels and animal bones, also sometimes accompanied cremation burials. In such cases it was not a mere shadowy future existence after death, making no demands on them, that was envisaged by the living; they considered it necessary to equip the deceased with the means of coping with what they saw as a tangible after-life, even after fire had consumed the physical body. Even in the case of cemeteries where inhumation and cremation were not both practised at the same time, but where one had superseded the other, it is difficult to discover what could have brought about the transition, since the burial customs do not appear to have altered in any other way. This applies above all to the valleys in the southern Swiss Alps. These were part of the territory of the Golasecca culture and its precursors, where cremation had been customary for many centuries.[44] Suddenly, towards 500 BC, the peoples in the South Alpine valleys of the Ticino and the Moësa went over to inhumation, without any discernible motive or encouragement from outside (from Bologna, say, or the North Alpine foreland), for the adjoining main area of the Golasecca culture to the South and the Inner Alpine valleys went on practising cremation. Nor can any influence have been exerted by the Celts who surged across the Alps around 400 BC, for the transition began earlier and the Celtic hordes scarcely penetrated these same South Alpine valleys. In such cases the archaeologist can do no more than record the facts.

The Romans, moreover, were quite unable to recall why their predecessors had at one time adopted cremation. The odd explanation provided by Pliny[45] in the first century AD betrays his lack of knowledge: 'The burning of corpses was not actually an ancient tradition among the Romans; the corpse was concealed in the earth. But when, after protracted wars, it was discovered that those who

67 *The custom of interment beneath burial-mounds was only adopted in the fringe areas of the Alps. The nature of the three visible mounds on the Seeweid at Plaffeien (canton Fribourg) is still uncertain, following the excavations of 1974 which showed that the small one in front of the wood is a natural hillock. Nevertheless the large mound in the foreground might contain graves of intrepid men who mined salt in difficult conditions under the Kaiseregg (2186 m, in the background left). Probably 7th–5th century* BC.

had been buried were grubbed up again, cremation was introduced. Nevertheless, many families followed the old usage, above all those of noble birth.' So perhaps we may conclude these assorted speculations with the assertion that when cremation was first introduced in any one region, this was probably associated with certain changes in current ideas regarding a continuance of life after death and a material existence in the after-life, but that later,

when recourse could be had to either method of burial, any one of a number of different reasons could have prevailed for preferring one rite to another–among them no doubt religious scruples.

It was in the eastern and central areas of the Alpine region that cremation was first practised. The cremation burials of Cresta Petschna near the settlement on the Crestaulta in the Lugnez[46] date back to the Middle Bronze Age. Here eleven graves were ranged against a boulder; only one of the hollowed-out graves had a lining of stones, in all the others ashes, burnt bones and scorched bronze offerings lay scattered. The dead, then, had been incinerated together with all their personal adornments, though some articles found their way into the graves later. The finds show that this small community had been a wealthy one: as many as 56 bronze pins, decorative discs of sheet-metal or coiled wire, as well as arm-rings. As there were no weapons, the burial-place may have been reserved for women; in that case, where the men and children found

68 The cemetery of Uttendorf in the Salzburg Pinzgau, excavated in the past few years, exemplifies the Early Iron Age burial custom in the Alpine region. The grave consisted of a hollowed-out cavity clad and covered over with stone slabs. The carefully selected pieces of burnt bone, as well as the offerings which had also been fed to the fire, were put into a small bag or wooden box by the bereaved; this was then placed on the floor of the stone cist upon a thin layer of ash from the funeral pyre.

their last resting-place is not known–one more instance of the incompleteness of our knowledge.

Whilst the Crestaulta settlement and cemetery did not persist into the Late Bronze Age, in North Tyrol the Middle Bronze Age cremations accompanied by few or no offerings sometimes proved to be the precursors of large urnfields. It is only because of this that we are able to attach so much as an approximate date to them and to order the cultural sequence. It would appear, however, that at the beginning of the Late Bronze Age, around the twelfth-thirteenth century BC, a considerable increase in the population occurred through the arrival of new settlers from the North Alpine foreland. These brought with them their own burial customs and modified the local tradition, just as they themselves were influenced in their turn. Lothar Sperber's[47] exhaustive evaluation of the cemetery

at Volders provides a number of pointers, even differentiating between single families (two or three), each of which initially had its own burial area, until in the course of time this segregation ceased of its own accord.

Still adhering to the Middle Bronze Age tradition were those racial groups which in the thirteenth century settled in and close to the South Alpine valleys north of Milan. People had lived there even earlier, but scarcely any graves belonging to their settlements have so far been found. Only a very few cremations can be assigned to this epoch.[48] It was the new settlers who brought with them the custom of burying all or most of a community's dead together in a common burial-place, the left-over charred bones and the offerings–often unburnt–being simply cast into a pit or placed in an urn, occasionally also covered over or mixed with ashes and the remains of the funeral pyre. Because lumps of stone were now placed round it, or even little cists made of stone slabs were built, it was easier to detect such graves and group-burials. The best known and largest cemetery is that of Canegrate[49] north of Milan, after which the whole culture group has been named. In the Alpine valleys, though, this movement did not make much headway: two centuries later the number of burials was already dwindling fast, though it must not be assumed that this signifies an actual shrinkage of the population. Not until the tenth century did large cemeteries appear once more in the South Alpine foreland, all now with urn burials, mostly in settings of stones and only shallowly embedded in the ground. In the valleys of the Southern Alps the interval lasted still longer, namely into the sixth century BC, when the inhabitants reverted to large cemeteries (many with more than 100 verifiable graves), which continued in use for many centuries.[50]

Whereas in North Tyrol in the ninth and eighth centuries BC climatic or economic factors led to a decline in the number of settlements and so to a thinning-out of the cemeteries, in other mountain areas a population increase occurred the effect of which was reflected in the burial-grounds, above all from the seventh century on, the beginning of the Iron Age. The customary cremations, mostly with stones set round the urn or the pile of burnt bones, dominated the scene. Cemeteries such as those at Uttendorf[51] in the Pinzgau (Salzburg), Welzelach[52] in East Tyrol, Niederrasen[53] in the Pustertal (South Tyrol), Pfat-

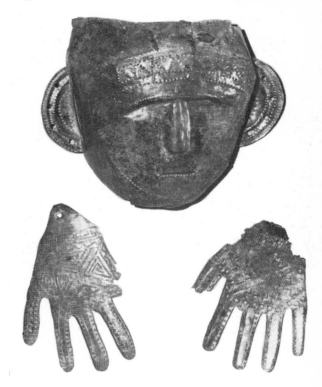

69 It must have been a powerful man who was interred in the 'Kröll-Schmied-Kogel', one of a number of large burial-mounds at Kleinklein in the Sulmtal (Styria). In addition to a sword, six spears, three battle-axes and numerous bronze vessels along with other articles, his possessions included a cuirass and a bronze helmet. Quite exceptional and only comparable with Greco-Balkan models is the offering of a face-mask and two hands in sheet-bronze. According to the confused reports relating to this burial-mound where, in all, three partial excavations were carried out (1860, 1905, 1917), the mask and probably also the hands had been nailed to a wooden coffin containing the dead man's ashes. At his laying-out the only parts of the body that were unclothed were covered with bronze masks which glittered like gold, sign of a regal, well-nigh superhuman dignity. As such, they had been removed from the body before it was cremated, and attached to an 'urn'—an instructive example of the adoption of Southern standards to suit altered circumstances. 6th century BC. Ht of cuirass 51.2 cm; width of facemask 23 cm. Steiermärkisches Landesmuseum Joanneum, Graz.

ten/Vadena[54] in South Tyrol, Tamins[55] in Graubünden, all testify to a uniformity in the burial customs, with only slight local variations. Weapons and ornamental rings allow us to distinguish the men's from women's graves, pins and fibulae as dress fastenings and adornments are often encountered, pendants and beads were popular (amber seems for the most part to have been consumed by the fire), bronze vessels point to a certain degree of affluence, and the clay vessels, used partly as urns, partly as additional offerings, provide evidence of the local tradition of the potters.

Since the beginning of the Bronze Age nothing much had changed where dress and fashion were concerned. Pins were used to fasten clothing and as embellishments– there were often so many in a single grave, that all of them could not possibly have been used for practical purposes. Over the centuries countless forms succeeded one another, and for this the archaeologist is grateful for he is able to work out individual time-horizons and follow them through supraregionally. Stylistic influences invaded the Alpine region from all sides, but quite a few forms were confined to valley areas, thus testifying to a craft with local associations. After all, costume and finery of every kind have at all times served as a means of setting-off one group of people against another, be it regionally (against neighbours), or socially (against poorer people or those of lesser standing). In the chapter dealing with commerce we shall see how, on account of this behaviour on the part of human beings, we can also occasionally identify alien persons should they have retained their traditional costume wholly or partially in their new environment (p. 206). At all events, an accurate analysis of the various types of adornment shows that what might appear to be unimportant details of the manufacturing process, style and decoration, are frequently confined to very limited areas, thus allowing exceptional articles to stand out all the more clearly. This applies not only to the pins and the fibulae (brooches) that appear from the thirteenth century BC, but equally to belt fittings, neck adornments (beads of bronze, bone, glass, amber, and pendants), ear adornments, hair adornments, as well as rings for the arms and legs; in the case of weapons and tools, being for practical use, local particularities are more diffi-

70 *The Iron Age cemetery of Arbedo-Cerinasca (canton Ticino) shows up particularly well the way a burial area develops in the course of time. In the border areas between individual time phases the archaeologists do indeed argue about the arrangement of one grave or another but that does not alter anything where the overall picture is concerned. It is not known why the cemetery was abandoned towards 300 BC.*

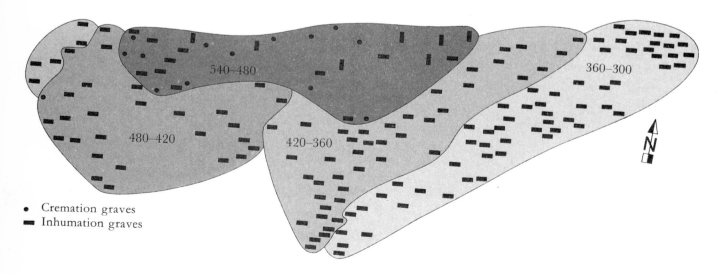

540–480

360–300

480–420

420–360

● Cremation graves
▬ Inhumation graves

cult to detect (also less to be expected). Even so, it is possible to work out the broader differences between East and West; these are most evident where weapons are concerned. Ever since bronze-casting was invented, slashing and thrusting weapons were used in equal measure: the

battle-axe and sword, or the dagger. In the Alpine region the sword never really found favour,[56] least of all in the East. There, from the Early Iron Age, the principal weapon, apart from spears (usually two in number), was the battle-axe. It is this combination that we meet with also in the situla-art of the Iron Age in the East Alpine area (Ill. 10). In the West Alpine area in general the dead were seldom furnished with weapons, so it is not possible to form any overall picture. Nevertheless, in the northern and western border areas of the Alps the warrior fought with sword and dagger, and in the adjacent Inner Alpine district, too, these, apart from the ubiquitous spears, are the few weapons to come down to us in graves and other find-complexes.

It was under the influence of the Celtic La Tène culture that the long sword gained the ascendancy nearly everywhere, not because it was basically superior to the battle-axe as a close-combat weapon, but because at all times and everywhere the less well equipped fighter adopted or tried to copy the tactics and weapons of his menacing or more commanding antagonist. So it is all the more remarkable that Horace, describing the conquest of the Central Alps by the Romans in 15 BC–that is, centuries later–should make a point of treating the battle-axe as a curiosity:[57]

...even such was Drusus as the Vindelici beheld him waging war beneath the Rhaetian Alps. Whence was derived the custom that through all recorded time arms their right hands with the Amazonian battle-axe, I have forborne to seek, nor is it vouchsafed to know all things...

How a man was armed in pre-Roman times can be almost wholly determined in cases where local custom

71 A recent find (1978) from a grave on the Dürrnberg above Hallein (Salzburg province) tells us something about what the men wore. This bronze brooch in the form a man (with behind the shoulders the spiral ending in buttons) shows many details: a not wholly identifiable head-dress, a jacket with long, rounded coat-tails, trousers that hang in folds and Etruscan-type pointed shoes. Though clearly similar to the representations on the Hallstatt scabbard (Ill. 74), the question remains whether such attire was in general use or merely confined to an unascertainable category of persons. 400–350 BC. L 4.4 cm. Keltenmuseum, Hallein.

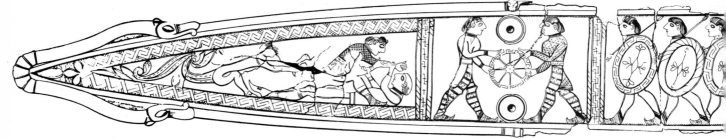

required that a deceased warrior's weapons should be buried with him. Even so, the reasons why not every male grave contained weapons will not have been the same everywhere. To start with, it is conceivable that poorer families just could not afford to surrender for good and all weapons that they had urgent need of. In such cases archaeologists tend to assume that the individual or the clan had an inferior social status, but one should not leave out of account altogether the material aspect. (It must be remembered that during the hard time of the decline of the Roman Empire the graves were conspicuously less well furnished: p. 138.) A further possible explanation, resting on recent anthropological analyses, is that those buried without weapons were in many instances no longer fit to fight, mainly through illness or stiffening of the joints caused by advancing years.[58]

Whilst weapons, then, were so much the man's province, that they determined and at the same time reflected his standing in the community, his occupation and other activities are only seldom to be deduced from the grave offerings. Quite clearly, tools and implements were not needed in the after-life, possibly because vocations and special aptitudes were not regarded, in a world that was as yet scarcely job-oriented, as key factors in a man's life. Only in the Early Iron Age cemetery of Hallstatt, the 'industrial settlement' close to a salt-mine,[59] have certain tools been found in appreciable quantities in the graves–which, after all, number more than a thousand. Where the axes and choppers are concerned, it is only possible to distinguish

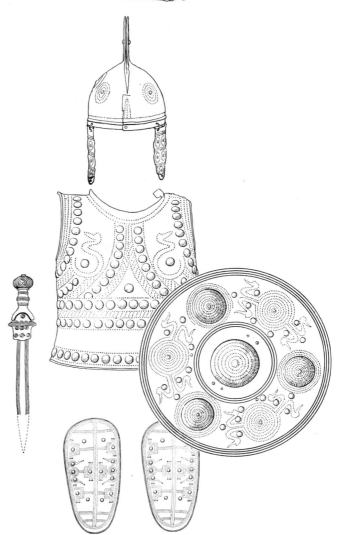

72 Composite drawing of Bronze Age armour comprising pieces from various find-spots: helmet from Pass Lueg (Salzburg province), cuirass from Fillinges (Dép. Haute-Savoie), shield from an unknown find-spot in Denmark, sword from Skocjan (Slovenia), greaves from Pergine (Trento province). About 1:9).

73 *In the Early Iron Age adornments that jingle were particularly popular. This fibula from Hallstatt (Upper Austria) secured the dress like a safety-pin (the pin is broken off at the spiral), will have caught the eye with its large sheet-metal crescent, and by its jingling and clinking protected the wearer from all manner of evil influences. 6th century BC. Width 13.1 cm. Naturhistorisches Museum, Vienna.*

74 *An outstanding artist, familiar with Southeast Alpine situla art, decorated the display side of this scabbard from Hallstatt (Upper Austria). His detailed depictions of the people, their attire and their weapons is based on his observations on the spot of the local populace. The long sword was a weapon of the Celts and testifies to early Celtic influence also in Hallstatt. 400–350 BC. L of scabbard 67 cm. Naturhistorisches Museum, Vienna.*

between weapons and implements in a few instances (Hallstatt with its manifold outside connections lies in the border zone between the sword/dagger and the battle-axe spheres), though sundry rasps and files occur which were used for woodworking. Everything else–a small anvil, say, or a few fish-hooks–may be disregarded. It is far from clear, therefore, why just the rasps should have found their way into the graves, when for example the bronze and iron picks of the miners (which we know from the finds in the mines themselves [Ill. 149]) are entirely lacking.

The smith alone seems to have enjoyed a certain privileged position since the invention of metalworking. His craft was so envied and admired, that–and this applies to primitive peoples of today as well, as observations during the past century have shown[60]–an aura of respectful awe surrounded him: either he occupied a high social position and was adviser to the king, or he remained outside the community and was only allowed into the village if he strictly observed the ritual rules. This being so, it is hardly surprising that it is the graves of the smiths that stand out individually from the general run of burials. In the Alpine region proper there would seem to be no authenticated examples of this kind, but mention might be made of two graves in Lower Austria which bear the stamp of Celtic cemeteries of the fourth to second centuries BC. These graves at Au am Leithagebirge and St Georgen am Steinfeld respectively[61] contained characteristic implements:

75 The impressed stamp of the originally orientalizing motif of ibexes by the Tree of Life on the sword from Port (canton Bern) points to its being the work of an accomplished and self-assured weaponsmith, who even incised his name Korisios in Greek characters on it. 2nd century BC. *L of sword 96 cm. Historisches Museum, Bern.*

hammers, tongs, files and a small anvil, plus what appear to be the results of experimental work on the part of the smiths: swords, spearheads, scissors, knives, fibulae.

More remarkable still is the grave at München-Obermenzing,[62] dated to between 320 and 150 BC, of a man whose medical expertise is indicated by two instruments for cranial surgery. We find a number of instances throughout prehistory of the trepanning operation for which these instruments were used, namely the cutting of a hole in the roof of the skull for therapeutic or magical purposes.[63] That not a few persons survived this treatment is attested by the healed edges of the roughly coin-sized apertures in many skulls. Whether the desired effect was

achieved (curing, say, mental disease, epilepsy or migraine) neither archaeologist nor doctor can say.

Professions, careers and genealogical trees

Once the Alpine region had been incorporated in the Roman Empire, it saw many changes. The knowledge of reading and writing, which soon spread over a wide area, caused many peoples to lose their anonymity in the eyes of the archaeologist. This invested the Roman period with an immediacy which the preceding and ensuing periods

76 Roman funerary monuments took very many forms. This splendid example at Donawitz, Stadt Leoben (Styria) copies Italic prototypes, in which it was customary to set up the urns or the sarcophagi and busts of the dead. At Donawitz nothing of this nature has survived, nor is there any inscription to indicate the name and status of the persons laid to rest here. They must have owed their wealth to the iron-mines in the vicinity. 3rd century AD. *Ht 3.15 m. Steiermärkisches Landesmuseum Joanneum, Graz.*

inevitably lacked. But concentration on this aspect also meant that departments of knowledge and problems which were to advantage brought to bear on other periods were neglected. In particular, not enough work has been done to date on Roman graves. Rudolf Noll's publication[64] of the cemetery of Salurn in the Adige valley, which was excavated back in the nineteenth century and then only partially, remained for long the sole assessment of its kind, if we exclude the summary by Christoph Simonett[65] of the Roman graves in the Ticino. It was the modern excavations, recently published, at the cemeteries of Solduno[66] near Locarno and above all at *Cambodunum/ Kempten*[67] that first established important facts concerning the burial customs of the peoples of the Alpine region in Roman times.[68]

There is one new development which calls particular attention to itself, namely the custom of putting one or more coins into the graves of some of the deceased. This is bound up with the proverbial obolus, with which the departed was to pay the ferryman who took him across the river Styx to the realm of the dead. It is a custom that originated in Greece, but the Romans took it over–as so much else–without originally having any comparable concept in the world as they themselves envisaged it. The coins are of little use for dating the graves since many were in a worn state and had been in circulation for decades. So it can easily happen that one and the same grave contains coins that were struck at intervals of up to a century or more; for, in calculating a coin's worth, what mattered was not the ruler's effigy on the obverse nor the coinage system, but its metal content.

In towns and larger settlements it was customary for the graves to be sited outside the inhabited area, running alongside the roads. Thus the cemetery did not occupy a remote position nor was it surrounded by a high wall, it was a natural part of everyday life. Scarcely had the traveller left the town than his attention was drawn to the resting-places of the dead: simple graves encircled by a little wall or hedge, tombstones of wood or stone painted or bearing a carved inscription, elaborate monuments or mausoleums adorned with reliefs and statues, erected by well-to-do families. Wealth, regional particularities and influences from the capital, Rome, accounted for the multiform picture, not two Roman cemeteries being alike. Lit-

tle villages and farmsteads had their own burial-places, usually a few hundred metres away from the habitations.[69] They exhibited as much variety as did those in the towns, ranging from the unadorned graves of poor tenants restricted to a little mound of earth, to the imposing funerary monuments of the big landowners.

Yet common to them all was the practice of cremation, which was only gradually superseded from the second half of the second century onwards by inhumation. The residual ashes from the funeral pyre of the deceased could be preserved in several different ways. Vessels of earthenware, glass or bronze served as urns, as did also wooden caskets and little cloth bags; quite frequently the bereaved appear to have simply emptied the ashes into a shallow cavity. The urns, too, were usually placed in a small hollow, occasionally protected by a ring of stones and covered over with stone slabs or tiles. Into the dead person's grave, as offerings, were put simple jars containing supplies of food, matching jugs and bowls, drinking-cups, glass bottles filled with drink. The vessels in particular were deployed in a number of different ways: they could, for example, be placed on the funeral pyre whole, thrown into the flames as a ritual gesture, or put into the grave later. The bereaved would also cast glass phials containing aromatic liquids on to the pyre–perfume played an important role now and subsequently in graveside ritual. Other articles of daily life are rare: knives as cutlery or tools, little boxes containing clothing or toilet articles, choppers, mattocks, shears and hunting-spears, things that point to a rural existence. The relatively frequent clay lamps, however, are more likely to have been associated with the after-life: they were to light the dead person's way through the underworld.[70]

Of the deceased's clothing only the metal parts were preserved, and then mostly so damaged by fire as to be unrecognizable. These were mainly fibulae used to fasten the costume or a cloak. Rather rarer are buckles and other belt fittings, used almost exclusively by soldiers as badges of rank, as well as bits of iron from nailed shoe soles. These go to show that the dead, both men and women, were indeed cremated fully clothed. The personal adornments were treated in various ways. Neck-rings and necklaces, finger- and arm-rings, beads and pendants were in part consigned to the flames, in part placed in the grave later.

It would therefore be difficult to reconstruct dress in Roman times had we to rely entirely on the finds from the graves.[71] Fortunately there are also large numbers of tombstones bearing likenesses of the deceased. They often enable us to recognize clothing and adornments, and they make another thing clear as well: Roman town attire, above all the men's *toga*, which was both uncomfortable and time-consuming to put on, played no part in the everyday life of the provinces. It was reserved for the upper class in the towns, who modelled themselves on the fashions of the capital, but only insofar as this festive garb was required on public occasions or at cult ceremonies. This applies even to Italy, as the second-century satirist Juvenal bears out: 'A large part of Italy it is, where nobody any longer wears the toga except on the bier.'[72]

The ordinary man wore a shirtlike garment, the *tunica*, or even, in accordance with Celtic custom, trousers with a little short jacket or a long cape over them, sometimes also a hood.[73] The long gowns of the women were cut in various ways and were worn with cloaks added. The regional distinctions in cut or where accessories were concerned have not as yet been thoroughly researched, the only available publication being a comprehensive work on the characteristic Norican-Pannonian women's costume of the Eastern Alps.[74] This even draws attention to the small differences between the Salzburg district, the vicinity of Vienna and the capital, *Virunum,* in Carinthia: an unusual belt here, a special head-dress there, exactly as folklore continues to teach us to this very day.

The funerary monuments provide not only pictorial representations but–which is still more important–often also inscriptions,[75] which give details of the origins, calling and career of the deceased. At the same time they occasionally disclose something about that person's attitude towards life and death, thus reflecting contemporary thought or indigenous ideas.

Despite the notion that life in the hereafter is but a shadowy one, a burial according to the rules was a necessity for the Romans, if the deceased was not to roam about as a restless spirit and terrorize the living. The paterfamilias attended in good time to the purchase of a suitable burial site in the cemetery. Poorer people could join funeral associations, while soldiers without families left substantial sums of money with comrades, who would conscientiously use it to buy the burial site and tombstone. Provision for the dead person and his prescribed burial is attested by a tombstone from *Axima*/Aime, capital of the Alpes Graiae; to judge by its inscription, it was originally set up in a neighbouring village named Brigantio:[76]

D(is) M(anibus) L(ucii) Exomni Macrini, Rustici fili, hic Brigantione geniti annorum XVI in studis Valle Poenina vita functi reliquis eius [huc] delatis Nigria Marca fili [o car] issimo et sibi viva faciendum curavit.

To the dead spirits of Lucius Exomnius Macrinus, son of Rusticus! Born here in Brigantio, he died aged 16 during his student days in the Valais. His mother Nigria Marca had his remains brought here and (this gravestone) erected for the beloved son and herself during her lifetime.

So it was possible to buy the tombstone and have it inscribed during one's lifetime; but it was often the heirs who paid for it (and then sometimes added a mention of the cost). A certain person from *Axima*/Aime also expressed his gratitude in writing:[77]

D(is) M(anibus). Laudio Montanio Cassiano Vireius Maximianus filius adoptatus (h)erens Cassiani supra scripti. Ago gratias tue (h)eredetati.

To the gods of the dead! To Claudius Montanius Cassianus from Vireius Maximianus, adopted son and heir of the above-named Cassianus. I give thanks for your heritage.

In memory of the deceased and by way of sacrifice to the gods of the dead, the living met together at the grave on festive days, and this was a truly convivial occasion. For death was not–as is the tendency nowadays–regarded as a disturbing or tabu topic, which could only be broached in 'dead earnest'. In their wills, people who were particularly considerate bequeathed a sum of money to defray the cost of such commemorations, as did for example Claudia Severa of Riva on Lake Garda, who had this recorded on her family tomb:[78]

...et in memoriam eor(um) et sui coll(egio) n(autarum) B(rixianorum) ad rosas et profusiones q(uot) a(nnis) fac(iendas) HS n(ummum) LX mil(ia) dedit.

...and in whose (her husband and her sons) and her own memory she bequeathed to the mariners' guild of Brescia for the annual rose-offering and libation expenses (at the grave) a sum of 60,000 sesterces.

This suggests that the family derived an income from water transport on Lake Garda–ostensibly a lucrative business (on account of the need to by-pass the frequently flooded Lower Adige valley?),[79] seeing that, by comparison, the annual salary of an imperial governor in Raetia and Noricum in the first and second centuries was 'only' 200,000 sesterces.

It is under the influence of Christianity that propositions leading to a new understanding of the hereafter were first formulated. It was conceived as the realm of eternal bliss. So, on a tombstone from *Lugdunum*/Lyon a father comforts his children with a couplet:[80]

Functus honorato senio plenusque dierum
evocor ad superos : pignora, quid gemitis?

After an old age full of honour and rich in earthly days
To the blessed I come: children, wherefore do you mourn?

In neighbouring *Vienna*/Vienne, the grieving parents let their dead child speak in the same verse form:[81]

Ne doleas genitor, genetrix quoque flere desiste.
Aeterna vitae gaudia proles habit.

Father, do not grieve, cease weeping, mother!
The joys of eternal life are bestowed on the child.

Public access to the graveyards alongside the roads and the protracted celebrations at burials or anniversaries nevertheless also aroused anger and vexation, to which some protesters gave vent with harsh words already in advance of their own demise. One famous tombstone in Rome bears this terse legend:[82]

Qui hic mixerit aut cacarit, habet deos superos et inferios iratos.
He who pisses or shits here, let him suffer the anger of the supernal and infernal gods!

Somewhat less crudely, but still not in the manner of today's churchyard injunctions, a citizen of Verona expressed the following sentiment:[83]

Stercus intra cippos qui fecerit aut violarit, nei luminibus fruator.

He who deposits litter between the gravestones or damages them, let him be deprived of the pleasure of seeing!

Normally, however, people were satisfied with recording on the gravestones the name of the deceased and his or her age, together sometimes with some characteristic traits

and a pious wish. Family graves being no rarity, far-reaching interrelationships can occasionally be reconstructed. A shattering record on a tombstone, destroyed in the second World War, which was built into a wall of the church at Eggstädt near the Salzburg-to-Augsburg Roman road west of the Chiemsee, reads:[84]

Dedicated to the dead!
Iulius Victor, son of Martialis, died aged 55;
Bessa, daughter of Iuvenis, his wife, died aged 45;
Novella, daughter of Essionus, died aged 18.
Victorinus erected (this tomb-stone for)
the parents and his wife and Victorina,
who were carried off by the plague under
the consuls Mamertinus and Rufus,
and for Aurelius Iustinus, his brother,
soldier of the II Italic legion, died
aged 30 after 10 years' service.

The unfortunate Victorinus had lost parents, wife and daughter in the year 182 through the plague introduced from the Orient in 166, and shortly afterwards also his brother, who had served with the II Legion at their first camp in Albing on the Danube near Enns (p. 43).

A monument unique of its kind in Gaul and the entire Roman Empire is the commemorative arch in Aix-les-Bains,[85] 9.15 m high and 6.7 m wide, on which a certain Lucius Pompeius Campanus had his genealogical tree inscribed, going back as far as his grandparents. What relationship each bore is accurately recorded: *avus* and *avia a patre* (grandparents on the father's side) and, correspondingly, *avus* and *avia a matre* as well as *amita* (aunt on the father's side). The niches above the archway no doubt contained busts of the deceased; where the actual graves were located or the urns installed we do not know.

Clearly, only a very few families could afford such elaborate funerary monuments, and it was precisely these who set such store by making their lineage and standing known. The less well-off citizen had to be satisfied with a plain memorial tablet which, besides the inscription, might portray members of his family (Ill. 163). Thought worth mentioning, with a view to informing posterity, were details of the calling, public offices held and corresponding career. Also occasionally encountered are tombstones which give more private details illustrating what befell an individual.

77 *The sides of many tombstones in the Eastern Alps bear portrayals of male and female servants who attended to the sacrifices for the dead. The female servants are mainly young girls, who hold in their hands the utensils needed for the ceremony, in this instance a little box and a mirror. The Norican costume is painstakingly reproduced: short hair, a pleated undergarment, a sleeveless dress of heavy material fastened at the shoulders with two large fibulae, a wide belt with tassels, felt socks. Found in Klagenfurt (Carinthia). 1st century* AD. *Ht 88 cm. Kärntner Landesmuseum, Klagenfurt.*

Thus the tombstones give us a fairly complete picture of people's occupations in Roman times, above all of course in the towns, and of the special abilities of individual persons. Since the larger colonies of settlers were nearly all located on the borders of the Alpine region proper, the undermentioned examples have for the most part had to be taken from those parts:[86] a wool-carder from Brescia, a doctor from Lyon, an actor from Vienne, a circus pugilist from Die, a boy actor from Antibes, a worker in an arrow-factory from Concordia, the commander of a cavalry unit from *Virunum*, a customs collector from Reisach in the Gail valley,[87] a shoe-merchant from Milan, traders of various kinds from Augsburg,[88] a path-finder in the service of a hunting establishment from Salzburg, who probably caught bears for animal baiting in the amphitheatres.[85] At many places soldiers, too, settled down; after completing their army service they either returned to their home town or invested their pay-off money in landed property or a small business undertaking, wherever suited them better.[90] The ultimate rank they attained is recorded on the gravestone.

We owe particulars of careers in the military and the civil fields less to the tombstones than to the nearly as many honorary inscriptions and above all to the Roman predilection for invariably recording on the latter an individual's entire official career. Inscriptions of honour were set up or inserted in the walls of buildings on every possible occasion; they relate principally to municipal officials or imperial governors who had served a community well.

As an example of the career of a municipal official, let us introduce Quintus Severinus Marcianus from *Colonia Iulia Equestris*/Nyon on the Lake of Genova.[91] In the first place there was his membership of the city council as *decurio*. His first post was that of *aedilis*, making him responsible for public order and the control of industry. Next he was made *praefectus pro duobusviris*, deputy to one of the two burgomasters, either owing to a vacancy or on the post going in an honorary capacity to a senior personage (from outside). The third appointment as *praefectus arcendis latrociniis* called for determined handling, in that he was required to combat the insidious effects of robbery throughout the whole of the territory belonging to the town.[92] Finally, he was elected *duumvir* and *flamen Augusti*, that is, burgomaster and high priest of the imperial cult. This meant that the highest rank within an urban community had been attained.

Even so, such a succession of appointments should not be compared with a present-day political career. In the first place, the period of office was restricted to a single year; secondly, officials were paid no retainer, being in fact called upon instead to take on the financing of public works: the paving of roads, the repair of baths,[93] temples and town walls,[94] the building of water conduits (Ill. 49) or theatres. For the Roman State imposed no taxes that went straight to the municipality, and when neither the governor nor the emperor dipped into their own coffers, everything was left to the initiative of the citizens themselves. Numerous inscriptions announce building undertakings of various kinds, for if a person actually had to pay for such, then he wanted to see his name inscribed in stone. The generosity of Pliny the Younger has become part of literary tradition through his letters. The son of a knightly family of landed gentry, he was advocate, officer and State official, rising to be imperial governor in Bithynia (Asia Minor).[95] In 102 he founded a public library in his home town of *Comum*/Como, and initiated two charitable endowments to meet the cost of tuition at a school and to support poor children.[96] The fact that it was the moral duty of well-to-do citizens to devote some of their wealth to social welfare may have irked quite a few niggardly persons, but it only became a genuine burden in the third and fourth centuries, when the general decline of the economy and compulsory State measures caused this indirect system of taxation to be carried to absurd lengths, because scarcely a soul was any longer prepared or able to take on, of his own free will, public office with its financial obligations.[97]

Hence, whilst every citizen was entitled to be elected to the district council as *decurio* (town councillor), it called for a considerable fortune. But in order to tap all possible sources of money, particularly in the smaller communities with few full citizens, special posts and departments for the newly rich, well-to-do traders or landowners without full citizenship who were capable of fulfilling less important tasks such as organizing public games or matters connected with the imperial cult, were initiated. Such people paid for the privilege of having their names perpetuated somewhere on a tablet, though they were denied political rights.

There are only a few known cases where a person was appointed city councillor strictly on merit. Even then, the honour was a superficial one; it did not involve official or influential posts. Apart from persons without full citizenship or freed slaves, such awards were also available to citizens living elsewhere who had deserved well of the relevant community. As an example we may cite the case of Claudius Decrianus,[98] a Roman citizen from the Chiemsee district, who is designated *decurio ornatus aput municipium Altinatium* (honorary member of the city council of *Altinum*) on his tombstone. *Altinum*, situated where the Piave flows into the Adriatic northeast of Venice, was the starting point of the Via Claudia, the transalpine main road connecting northern Italy with Raetia, which also had a branch running down the Inn valley into western Noricum. So Claudius was probably a merchant and trader with close and direct contacts with the nearest Mediterranean port, having there perhaps a small establishment and good business friends who, by virtue of his generosity–which is unlikely to have been altogether disinterested–accorded him the honour of acting as proconsul for outlying States–the sort of post which, for comparable reasons, has today fallen somewhat into disrepute, underlining as it does the extent to which worldly and intrinsic merit, initiative and self-aggrandisement are connected. A question that has still not been answered is whether such honours were bestowed as a pure formality or indeed not until after the death of the individual in question (in Claudius's case the title comes at the very end of the otherwise normally composed memorial inscription), or whether–analogous to a proconsul of today–this entailed certain duties and activities in the way of attendance upon bigwigs from the well-disposed town with which trade was being carried on. *Bedaium*/Seebruck on the north shore of the Chiemsee was an important staging post on the main road between *Augusta Vindelicum*/Augsburg and *Iuvavum*/Salzburg.[99] A great many funerary monuments and dedicatory inscriptions in stone attest the easy circumstances of the population; the provincial administration will have set up a control point here, to guard the nearby frontier on the Inn. It might well be, therefore, that Claudius Decrianus was appointed honorary town councillor of *Altinum* because he not only maintained personal and business contacts with this town, but in his home territory also did all in his power to further the interests of the merchants from the South.[100]

While the municipal officials spent their whole lives within their own borough, provided they did not, like some merchants, also install themselves elsewhere, the careers of the senior State officials are a useful guide to the particular features of Roman imperial government and the demands it made. To start with, it is characteristic that a citizen had to be a member either of the higher (senatorial) or of the lower (knightly) nobility if he wished to become an officer and government official. His means had to meet a prescribed minimum, although State officials–as opposed to municipal ones–received a good salary, graded according to what was required of them. Secondly, there was no strict line of demarcation between the military and the civil sphere; on the contrary, an official would normally make frequent switches, assuming that he did not possess any special aptitudes in one or the other field. Thirdly, everyone had to be prepared to do service in the most distant provinces of the Empire.[101]

The Alpine region provides us with two clear-cut examples of the careers of men from the order of knights who attained the rank of provincial governor in the first and second centuries respectively. Since they did not belong to the senator class, they were excluded from the very highest posts: governor and legionary commander in one of the wealthier or militarily more important provinces, consul and the other top jobs in the capital, Rome. The first stage of a knightly career, as more or less standardized from the first century onward,[102] was military service of about ten years' duration as an officer in several different units. This was followed by various civil and further military appointments, depending upon individual performance. The final stage of the career was governorship of a province that had no legion, a post with which went supreme command of the auxiliary troops stationed there[103] (cf. p. 158).

Gaius Baebius Atticus is known to us through two honorary inscriptions which were erected in his home town of *Iulium Carnicum*/Zuglio, the northernmost town of Italia at the foot of the Plöcken.[104] Here he had already served as one of the two municipal officials qualified to administer the law, before entering the army under Emperor Augustus. Immediately given the highest officer rank of the middle career phase, he served with the 5 Macedonian legion, which was then stationed in Moësia on the Lower Danube (present-day Romania). This position he most likely held for a year, as was customary, before being promoted–ostensibly by virtue of his particular organizing skill–to a sort of military governor in that same newly occupied area, where he participated in building-up the civil administration. Since, however, Moësia only became a province under Tiberius, Baebius Atticus will, as *praefectus*, have been subordinate to the regular legion commander, as appears to have been the case also in Raetia after the conquest.[105] He returned, as independent governor, though still only with the title *praefectus* and not *procurator*, to his Alpine homeland, namely the province of Alpes Maritimae. There he could devote himself almost exclusively to the civil administration, for in this small and peaceful province only a few auxiliary units on guard and police duty were stationed. His further advancement was once more via two military commands, the first in the imperial guard in Rome, the second in a capacity that is not entirely clear but may correspond to colonel on the general staff, whom the emperor detailed to assist a legion commander.[106] Baebius Atticus spent the closing stage of his career almost back in his homeland proper, that is to say as imperial governor of the province of Noricum, based in *Virunum*. We have every reason to think that he was even the first governor following the setting-up of the province under Emperor Claudius and owed the appointment to his wide-ranging experience of conditions in occupied areas in particular. We know nothing about how he performed in this capacity, or how satisfied his subjects were with him; for the erection of honorary inscriptions in his home town need not have been much more than a formality. On one of them the name of the donors is still legible, namely the tribal community of the *Saevates* and *Lianci* in the upper Pustertal and the Lienz basin.

The custom of setting-up in their home town inscriptions in honour of departing governors is well exemplified in *Celeia*/Celje on the border of the Eastern Alps. There they honour Titus Varius Clemens, who was governor in a number of provinces including, about 155/157, Raetia.[107] Three inscriptions give exact details of the donors:[108] in the first place, two *decuriones alarum* (leader of an cavalry

Gaius Baebius Atticus

primuspilus *legionis V Macedoniae*	Highest-ranking captain (commanding 800 soldiers) of a legion	Lower Danube
praefectus civitatium *Moesiae et Triballiae*	Military governor of an occupied area: civil administration and command of auxiliaries	Lower Danube
praefectus civitatium *in Alpibus maritumis*	Governor in a province that has no legion	Alpes Maritimae
tribunus militum *cohortis VIII praetoriae*	Commander of a cohort of the imperial guard	Rome
primuspilus iterum	Officer on the General Staff with special duties	Rome or detailed to a legion
procurator Augusti	Governor	Noricum

Claudius Paternus Clementianus

praefectus cohortis *I classicae*	Commander of a cohort of auxiliaries (500 or 1000 soldiers)	Germania inferior
tribunus militum *legionis XI Claudiae*	Staff officer (one of six) in a legion	Pannonia superior
praefectus alae *Silianae torquatae* *civium Romanorum*	Commander of a cavalry regiment consisting of Roman citizens (500 or 1000 soldiers)	Dacia
procurator Augusti	Chief fiscal officer	Judaea
procurator Augusti	Chief fiscal officer	Sardinia
procurator Augusti	Chief fiscal officer	Africa
procurator Augusti	Governor	Noricum

unit) from Mauritania in North Africa; secondly, the *cives Romani ex Italia et aliis provinciis in Raetia consistentes*, that is, citizens who moved into Raetia from Italia and other provinces; thirdly, the *civitas Treverorum*, the tribal community of the Treveri around Trier, which acclaimed the recipient of the honour as 'very best of governors'. This goes to show that individuals, groups and whole administrative districts wished to express their gratitude by bestowing this kind of honour. The inscriptions were of course accompanied by busts or statues of those thus honoured.

A marble bust from the shrine of Noreia in Hohenstein near the capital, *Virunum*, almost certainly represents Claudius Paternus Clementianus, the second person whose career we shall examine.[109] Of special significance are the two inscribed memorials from his native Raetian community *Abodiacum*/Epfach on the Lech, where he also had a tombstone for his mother set up. The family must have been among the most distinguished in the land–his maternal grandfather still bore the Celtic name of Indutus–for this man's parents already possessed civic rights (probably bestowed under Emperor Claudius after the formation of the province) and he himself could embark on a knightly career without further ado. It is to be assumed that he previously held municipal posts since he did not take on his compulsory military commands until relatively late, some time between 100 and 110. As he was born about the year 70 at the latest, he would have been over thirty at this point. After serving as cohort commander, staff officer in a legion and commanding officer of a cavalry regiment, he went over wholly to the civil administration. In Judaea, Sardinia and Africa (Libya), imperial and senatorial provinces respectively, he was, as fiscal officer, subordinated to the existing governor. About 125 came the culmination of his career, when he was made governor of Noricum. After that, he returned to the little Raetian town of *Abodiacum*, where he spent the evening of his life. It is to be assumed that he owned a fairly large country estate in the vicinity such as befitted a distinguished and wealthy citizen.

That so widely travelled a man should find stimulation in every sphere of activity is only natural. This mobility on the part of the upper class accounted in large measure for the rapid spread of new fashions, ideas and discoveries. Coupled with the continual switching of troops from one theatre of war to another and the wide-ranging trade contacts, it created the uniformity of imperial Roman culture that enables us to make comparisons between the results of excavation work in Scotland and in Mesopotamia. One is tempted to go more closely into the question as to which spheres of life were most influenced at this time by the nobility in the service of the State, soldiers and traders respectively. Experienced craftsmen and artists brought innovations to the far corners of the Empire whenever rich customers or substantial monetary rewards provided the necessary inducements. The building of costly villas and the standards they demanded concerned the upper class above all, whereas new religions and cults were mainly disseminated through soldiers and traders.

We should not overlook the personal inconvenience that could be occasioned by having at all times to be ready to go into action and by frequent moving from place to place. To this an inscription in *Axima*/Aime bears amusing witness.[110] Titus Pomponius Victor, in 165 governor of the province of Alpes Graiae et Poeninae, did not relish a stay in his little capital amid the snow-covered mountains. In well-phrased verse he addressed himself to Silvanus, god of the woods and hills:

O Silvanus, half-concealed amidst the sacred ash-trees,
prime protector of these mountain plains, to you
I dedicate these lines in gratitude.
For, whilst I administer justice and hold imperial
office, you watch over us all with your tutelary power:
over me, when I travel through the land and across
the mountains, over my people who in your sacred wood
delight in the sweetest scents.

May you lead us back to Rome, me and mine,
and to our estates in Italy, so we may cultivate them
under your protection; I, for my part, shall dedicate
1000 tall trees to you for that.
This is the solemn vow of Titus Pomponius Victor,
the imperial governor.

In *Brigantium*/Bregenz, too, somebody spoke to posterity by recording his yearning for the end of his stay in the inhospitable land. He was, to be sure, no imperial governor who could have his wish carved in stone, but one who had scribbled his message on a wall.[111] None the less he showed himself to be a cultured man, for he chose two lines from Vergil's *Aeneid* (XII, 59 f.), that great epic on the beginnings of Rome:

te penes, in te omnis domus inclita recumbit),
unum oro: desiste manum committere Teucris.

. . .,on you alone rests the entire subsiding house),
one thing alone I beg of you: cease warring with the Teucrians!

In this connection we need to know that Amata, legendary queen of the indigenous Italic peoples, addressed these remarks to her son when he challenged Aeneas, leader of the Trojans (= Teucrians) to single combat (thereby losing his life!). It is quite possible that the literary-minded Roman wrote these words down at the time of the protracted Alamannic invasions of the third century–he appears to have ignored the fact that Rome wanted to use her military might to conquer lands occupied in any case only by barbarians and which had now become unsafer than ever. Let us hope that he was indeed able to return to the South in good time!

The Roman heritage and Christendom

During the course of the Romanization of the Alpine region cremation did not become the general rule. In southern Switzerland, for example, where inhumation had been practised since the fifth century BC, the old ritual was to a large extent retained. In the Maritime Alps, too, it appears to have been quite common. In the other areas inhumations were used here and there from the second century AD, a practice which finally gained the ascendancy in the second half of the third century. Archaeologists have given much thought to the possible reasons for this change, but although plenty of written sources are available for the Roman period, that it reflects an altered attitude towards the after-life remains no more than surmise. The influence of Oriental religions, among them of course Christianity, is stressed because belief in a continuing physical existence after death was common to the majority of them. It meant that the body had to be conserved in its outward form.

In the light of what was said earlier (p. 132f.) about the manifold and after all but seldom explicable alternation in the two main kinds of burial through the millennia, there is no need for us to seek just a single reason for the transition in Roman times. It is worth bearing in mind, for example, that because of the quantity of wood required a cremation entailed a greater outlay than did digging a hole in the ground in which to lay the dead. This point seems worth bringing up for the reason that in large areas of the Alpine region and its foreland the ultimate change from cremation to inhumation coincided with a time when invasions by the Teutons from outside, and the resulting enforced measures imposed within the Empire in order to maintain its defences on the one hand and anything like a regulated economy on the other, lowered the living standard of the provincial populace, scarcely allowing more than a minimum level of subsistence. The incursions were those of the Alamanni and other Germanic tribes, which continued without cease from 213 and led, moreover, to the loss of much territory. The general poverty, the collapse of the economy which rested on safeguarded estates of smaller or larger compass, the abandonment of destroyed towns and settlements in favour of smaller but more easily defended fortifications in more sheltered or out-of-the-way locations, these are some of the possible explanations for the fact that only a few burial-places in the Alpine region show any continuity from the zenith of the Roman Empire in the first and second centuries to the third or even the fourth.[112] The most significant turning point seems in fact to have occurred in the late third or early fourth century, for it is the late Roman settlements and cemeteries that frequently carry on without a break into the early Middle Ages.

The best-researched example is provided by the cemetery of Bonaduz at the confluence of the Vorderrhein and the Hinterrhein in Graubünden.[113] Some 700 graves were laid bare–there may well have been about 1000 originally–which extend over the period from the fourth to seventh century. Opposite a small group of graves in which the dead were buried with head toward the East, lay a great many with head facing North and (the majority) West. Owing to the sparse offerings, the first group can be assigned to late Roman times, during which accompanying gifts of soapstone (steatite) vessels and of meat were still customary. Clearly distinguishable from these, the graves of the second group, while occasionally containing items of dress or a few ornamental accessories, are predominantly devoid of offerings. Since they belong in the sixth and seventh centuries but no interruption in the use of the cemetery is either observable or likely, the only possible explanation for the fifth-century gap would seem to be that the burials had not been furnished with offerings. At this time, too, the change in orientation of the dead (now with head to the West and facing East) appears to have taken place, probably in connection with the advance of Christianity. Likewise attributable to Christianity is the fact that henceforth offerings of vessels and meat for the after-life were discontinued. That the Germanic folk on the border of the Alps gave up the custom only gradually goes to show how tenacious were the old traditions, which were–as long as possible–coupled with the new faith. It accords with these archaeological findings that in 451 a bishop of Chur is mentioned for the first time, in other words that Christianity and the ecclesiastical establishment probably first prevailed in the fifth century. There had no doubt been individual or even larger groups of Christians before that but their influence upon the way in which the rest of the populace visualized the after-life and upon their burial rites was slight.

At the edge of the Bonaduz cemetery stood two rectangular walled structures in which a large number of dead had been gathered together. These are the so-called memorials, small funerary buildings to house the remains of one or more particularly notable persons around whom further burials were grouped. From Christian sources we know that this was often done in the case of martyrs, whose graves then formed the nucleus of new confines of a churchyard, especially when a little church was erected over the grave. Such memorials are a feature of many Alpine cemeteries or as forerunners of churches, but we do

not really know exactly what role they played in funerary practice or Christian ritual. As further examples may be mentioned Saint-Maurice d'Agaune,[114] La Madeleine in Geneva,[115] and Biel-Mett.[116] Three costly glass vessels and a gilt fibula, which can be dated in the first half of the fourth century, show the man who was buried in the Mett memorial to have been a dignitary of high rank.[117] Later, three more dead persons were housed in the memorial, after which the first church was built in the sixth century. Large numbers of early medieval graves were subsequently grouped around this church.

So, from the fifth century on, the burial-ground and the cemetery church normally formed a unified whole. Personal relations with the dead, which the Romans took for granted, were superseded by incorporation in a larger

78 The smaller of the two burial chambers at Bonaduz (Graubünden) as it looked during excavation. It was originally intended for a single dead person but later enlarged to take a second. Subsequently, over a long period, 34 further bodies were interred there in several layers, all of which archaeological analysis showed to be those of men and boys. Constructed about AD 400 and used up until the 7th century. Inside measurements 2.7 × 2 m.

community. Commemorations were no longer held at the grave-side but in the church, the rites were no longer performed by the family but by the priest, who regarded himself as intermediary between this world and the next. In this context it is apposite that also a simple church with sacred relics should serve as the crystallizing nucleus of Christian churchyards.

Even so, it remained the prerogative of the nobility to have themselves buried within the church precincts, that is, especially close to the martyr or relic, whereas the graves of ordinary people made up the cemetery outside. This can be corroborated archaeologically up until about 800; for the opulence of the graves within the church, often only a single one or perhaps two, set them clearly apart from the rest.[118] From literary sources we know that at this time churches (and pastoral appointments!) were instituted and maintained by the nobility, an economically independent Church organization being still lacking. Such 'donor graves' came to light during excavation work carried out in churches going back to the early Middle Ages. If they are especially plentiful in Switzerland, this is mainly owing to the present-day prosperity of this country, which allows floor heating to be installed even in small churches, and the previous archaeological investigations to be used to best advantage. Well-known examples are: a rich female grave from Bülach (canton Zurich),[119] three warrior's graves from Tuggen (Schwyz),[120] a horseman's grave close to the parish church of Spiez (canton Bern),[121] a male grave in the church of Spiez-Einigen (canton Bern),[122] a male grave from Schiers (Graubünden),[123] two graves with no offerings in the vestibule of the church at Rhäzüns on the Hinterrhein (Graubünden)[124] and a male grave in Stabio (canton Ticino).[125] In North Tyrol, at all events the church of Pfaffenhofen contains graves.[126]

The difference between, say, the opulent horseman's grave of Spiez (belt mountings, sword with decorated scabbard and one spur with fastening straps), and the two graves without offerings in Rhäzüns shows most clearly that there were reasons other than mere wealth where the fitting-out of a grave was concerned; for each of these families had sufficient means for the building and maintaining of a church. The Inner Alpine 'donor graves' certainly continued the late Roman tradition as far as burial custom and also certain externals of dress were concerned, whilst everywhere on the borders of the Alps–except in the extreme East, where since 600 the Slavs and the Avars were dug in–the Germanic influence made itself felt. Among the graves of the poorer inhabitants, too, these differences are for the most part clearly evident, so that–thanks to increasingly accurate means of dating by

archaeologists–the gradual advance of the Teutons and their culture into the Alpine region can be observed.

The early medieval inhabitants of the Inner Alpine region, whom we like to refer to as 'Romanic' peoples, continued to bury their dead fully clothed but it was no longer usual to provide them with weapons, implements and utensils. This is evident not only from the large cemetery of Bonaduz (where bone combs alone play a role that is difficult to explain in terms of burial custom) but also from the cemetery of *Teurnia*/St Peter in Holz in the Drau valley.[127] By 1975, 111 graves from the time between 540 and 600 had come to light there (a few more later).[128] Only 32 of them contained offerings, all manifestly female adornments: ear-rings, bead necklaces, pins for garments, fibulae, arm- and finger-rings. The combination was rather haphazard and did not show the uniformity that characterizes Germanic women's attire. What was selected from among the modest supply of styles available was probably determined mainly by the individual's means. Consequently metal ornaments are extremely rare and sometimes come from the Outer Alpine region. In this connection (partly from closer examination in the Graubünden area) it has been established that Frankish or Lombardic belt mountings were sometimes split up and their components worn by several women as single pieces. Among the fibulae, there is a not only an Inner Alpine but ultimately a unique Romanic form (a longish brooch symmetrically shaped), but imported or bartered pieces from the Alpine foreland or farther afield are not scarce.

That the small quantity of metal in the Romanic graves was not just due to a shortage of materials but also to peculiarities of dress is indicated by Grave 46 at St Stephan in Chur, in which a woman was buried with a gold-threaded veil,[129] though all other offerings were lacking. So her remaining attire, whose sumptuousness must be left to the imagination, did not include any metal components, for these would have been preserved in the grave. A chronological ordering of the few items of adornment from the settlement of Carschlingg at Castiel above Chur confirms the existence of this 'metal gap' (and also the absence of other valuable objects of everyday life: p. 104) during the fifth and to a large extent the sixth century. Not until the politically motivated Frankish influence made itself felt in the northwestern part of the Alpine

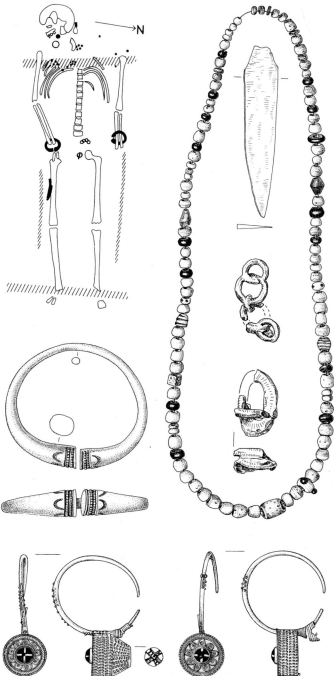

region from about 550 did single pieces of jewellery and costume accessories find their way back into the mountain interior, without however affecting local traditions. Consequently, in certain instances persons of foreign extraction can be readily identified, such as, say, the warrior wearing Frankish-Alamannic dress and arms in Tamins,[130] who had probably manned a Frankish sentry-post at the confluence of the Vorderrhein and the Hinterrhein at the foot of the Kunkels pass.

We can in a similar way trace the interplay between the Romanic people and the Lombards. Between 527 and 568, when the Lombards were established in Pannonia,[131] they influenced the East Alpine region, so that the cemeteries of Kranj[132] and Bled[133] in Slovenia, as well as that of *Teurnia*, reflect the difference in the situation and significance of the settlements. At the fringe of the Alpine region the influence of the Lombards progressively increased, and they themselves may well have inhabited Kranj, so as to keep control of this important place. After 568, when the Lombards had moved into Italy, the South Alpine fringe area was drawn into their cultural orbit. A rich warrior's grave at Civezzano[134] near Trento shows that a Lombardic group had penetrated deep into the mountain region. For many decades Bajuvarian influence was scarcely felt in the Inner Alpine area because–unlike in the South–settlement of the extensively depopulated Alpine foreland progressed but slowly. The salt-producing centre of Reichenhall alone, so vitally important economically, lured Bajuvarian settlers there as early as the sixth century, and their graves[135] accordingly show no recognizable signs of indigenous Alpine inhabitants having lived there. Should any such group have existed, as was the case in the neighbouring Salzach valley and even at Marzoll (named *Marciolae* towards the end of the eighth century)[136] only 4 km away to the north, which literary sources and place-names suggest (p. 56), then they may have buried their dead at some other place–and, assuming their graves con-

79 *Offerings from a Bajuvarian woman's grave between Garmisch and Partenkirchen (Upper Bavaria): two silver ear-rings, necklace of coloured glass beads, two heavy bronze arm-rings, iron belt-buckle, remnants of little iron chain, iron knife. AD 650–700. Various scales. Prähistorische Staatssammlung, Munich.*

tained scarcely any offerings, the chances of finding them are remote.[137]

Burial rites and the costume of the Teutons

In their dress, their arms and their burial customs the Franks, Alamanni, Bajuvarii and Lombards differed but little, at all events by comparison with the Romanic peoples. Naturally, there were regional traits, which were sometimes even confined within tribal borders. Thus the Lombardic men wore white puttees, which caused them to be compared with mares. In the North, leggings were only worn by women, mostly fastened with straps. Here the boundary between Alamanni and Bajuvarii is indicated by the fittings: silver ones of sheet-metal to the west of the Lech, iron ones with inlay in the east.[138] But for the most part it was the market outlets of the metalworkers[139] or potters and outside influences that determined the distribution centres for individual forms or combinations.

Essentially, Germanic attire for men and particularly for women was augmented with a liberal supply of metal and other archaeologically identifiable material.[140] Fibulae, often worn in pairs, were used to fasten garments; necklaces of beads, amber and semi-precious stones were popular, arm-rings less so; richly embellished mountings enhanced the magic power of the belt, women hung amulets and small utensils of everyday life from ribbons; shoe-straps, as well as leggings, had ornamental fittings of metal. The warrior was armed with sword, dagger, spear, shield, sometimes also a casting-axe or bow and arrow; riding equipment was reserved to the wealthy and is recognizable by snaffles, saddles, stirrups (an Eastern invention!) or spurs found in the graves. Whilst offerings of earthenware vessels in the different regions were treated in a variety of ways, valuable bronze and glass vases everywhere signal a higher social standing.[141] Thanks to the manifold gradations of combined offerings the archaeologist has a better chance of recognizing in the burials the social order with its three main groups–nobles, free men and those in bondage–as handed down by literary sources. But we have already seen, in the case of the 'donor graves' in the churches, how unreliable such an equating of the material furnishings of a grave with the social status of the individual is and must always remain.

The custom of interring the dead fully clothed together with all their possessions cannot be traced back very far in the case of the Germanic peoples either. In the late third century it emerges for the first time among the upper class in central Germany, which had close contacts with the Roman Empire.[142] Inhumations in the early-Alamannic area of southwest Germany facing the Roman frontier which had been pulled back to the Rhine, Iller and Danube, are of only slightly later date; but even here the custom was not adopted by the entire population.[143] From the late fourth century, inhumation (now with weapons) is traceable among Germanic groups to the west of the Lower Rhine.[144] That here 'newly arrived Teutons, who for the first time came into contact with the Romans and who were conscious of their prowess in battle and their raised status in Gaul',[145] had introduced the custom of allotting weapons to the dead and had in turn passed this on to related tribes in free Germania, is a hypothesis[146] the socio-psychological and religious background to which (inhumation–offerings of weapons–upper class) should be more thoroughly investigated. It is certainly conceivable that the example of the Frankish royal court in Belgium and northern France from the second half of the fifth century rapidly led to a widespread standardization of burial custom among the Germanic peoples of all social levels north of the Alps.[147]

Seen against this background, it is not difficult to understand why the ethnic situation in the Western Alps is particularly hard to judge and still debated. We know, it is true, that Germanic Burgundians had inhabited this region ever since, in 443, they were settled there on what was still Roman imperial soil. But this happened at a time when the Germanic garb and burial custom we have described were as yet barely developed. Which means that the most important criteria for differentiating the graves of the Germanic peoples and Burgundians on a strictly archaeological basis are lacking. And several decades later, when in the case of some types of article, in particular belt embellishments, certain features became crystallized in what was, politically regarded, Burgundian territory, this reflected above all Frankish and Alamannic influence. Yet it must not be assumed that only 'Germanic', but not 'Romanic' Burgundians participated in the new fashions;[148] for we know from the literary sources how

rapidly the fusion of indigenous and immigrant folk took place. The Burgundians may also have occupied this exceptional position with regard to dress and burial custom because they were one of the East Teuton tribes among whom—as in the case of the Goths in Italy and Spain—the placing of weapons in male graves was not normal practice. That, prior to their settling first on the Rhine and then on the borders of the Western Alps, the Burgundians had close contact with the Huns can be corroborated on anthropological grounds, some artificially deformed skulls having been found in Burgundian cemeteries.[149] If this is to be interpreted—as in individual instances among other tribes, East Germanic ones in particular—as a conscious pursuit of the Hunnish ideal of beauty, then at least some persons of Mongolian extraction must surely have married into the clan. They (and a

80 In accordance with Germanic custom the Lombards in Italy also put the weapons of deceased warriors in their graves with them. The gilt bronze fittings from a splendid round shield found at Stabio (canton Ticino) presumably came from the same grave as the beaten gold cross (Ill. 118). About AD 600. L of horse and rider 10 cm. Historisches Museum, Bern.

few of their descendants too?) can be identified by the fact that their dental enamel extends as far as the root of the tooth.[150] All this goes to show how intensely the old Roman legacy and the Germanic influences intermingled in the West in particular (as indeed the whole of Gaul west of the Rhine). Here, though in a more modest form, was perpetuated the custom of erecting inscribed gravestones for especially important persons;[151] here instances of early

Christian symbolism are encountered on articles of every-day life, above all belt-buckles[152] (Ills 110 and 151); here King Sigismund built the monastery of Saint-Maurice in the Valais in 515, and farther to the northwest, beyond the Jura in north Burgundy, those monasteries began to flourish whence at the beginning of the seventh century missionaries travelled along the fringe of the Northern Alps as far as Bajuvarian territory.

In the Western Alps to the south of the Burgundian kingdom Germanic influence was so far much less. In the cemetery of Beaulieu-sur-Mer[153] on the Côte d'Azur, which was in use from the second to the eighth century, there is no sign of it at all, even the Roman-Italic element in the burial rite being barely evident. The dead were practically all interred without offerings, though the custom of casting into the grave a sherd (not a whole vessel!), shells, snails or little pebbles indicates a modest form of burial custom. Clothing and articles of adornment are wholly absent, so that the graves can really only be dated on the strength of how they are constructed:[154] house-shaped graves made of brick slabs, limestone cists, a circle of stones round the grave pit, and–an old tradition–an infant in an amphora. Crosses scratched on several of the brick slabs testify to the Christian faith of the community whose dead were buried here, but from what point in time and to what proportion of the people this applied we cannot tell.

It goes without saying that here the archaeologist will find scarcely any further clues as to the way of life and the social structure of a community, assuming he has no literary sources to help him. In this connection, the Central and Western Alps and their border zones are fertile ground, particularly for those seeking to ascertain how the Roman inheritance in the milieu of the Romanic peoples adjusted itself to the new Germanic influences. Since we know something about the political circumstances, at least in broad outline, such observations also enable us to judge corresponding events in earlier days–at the time, say, of the migrations and conquests of the Celts in the circum-alpine zone. Besides the ethnic problems, those relating to social distinctions deserve attention, though in the Romanic milieu, owing to the minimal information that the graves yield, they can as a rule only be derived from literary sources. The evolution of a nobility with well-defined rights and obligations, with country estates and retainers was set in motion slowly after the dark, restless

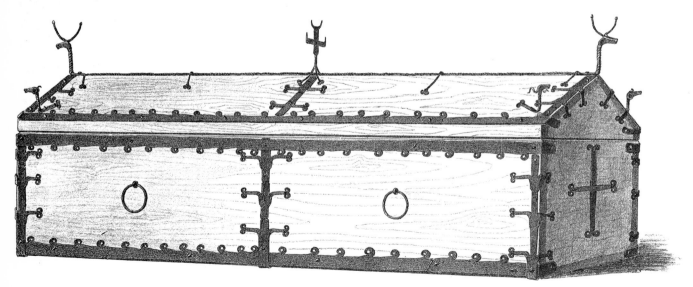

81 Reconstruction of a wooden sarcophagus based on the iron fittings preserved in a grave at Civezzano (Trento province). In it had been laid a mighty Lombard warrior. 7th century AD. L 2.36 m Tiroler Landesmuseum, Innsbruck.

and economically unstable fifth century, until in the course of the seventh century the great families crystallized out–some to determine the fate of many people and whole territories for centuries to come. Only the aforementioned 'donor graves' in the churches allow us to go into these developments archaeologically as well. For, towards the end of the seventh century the Romanic and Germanic peoples abandoned the custom of putting offerings in graves–the history of the ensuing centuries is based on written records and the life-stories of the saints.

But the situation was different on the border of the Eastern Alps. Towards the end of the sixth century the Avars and the Slavs had demolished the Roman inheritance as far in as the valleys, driving out or killing the inhabitants over a wide area. We know nothing of the burial-places of the new arrivals (the earliest Slav graves in the Balkans, Slovakia, Bohemia and Poland are in the main cremations); it was much later, in the course of the eighth century, that cemeteries containing inhumations, with offerings, were reverted to. Of these, the most thoroughly explored is Villach-Judendorf with several dozen graves dating from the period between the eighth and tenth centuries.[155] The finds indicate a certain degree of prosperity and are made up almost exclusively of women's adornments:[156] ear-rings of various kinds, rings of wire worn at the temples or on a bonnet, necklaces of beads made of glass, rock-crystal and carnelian, the occasional clasp, finger-rings (of gold in one instance), a necklace of silver wire, a disc-fibula with enamel inlay. Particularly striking are some bonnets or hair-nets the gold threads or ribbons and round pendants from which have been preserved. There are no ornaments by which the men can be identified, and weapons were not used as offerings. In just one grave a few remnants of iron could be interpreted as spurs. Thus the conditions closely resemble those in the Romanic area, though the forms of the objects point in quite different directions:[157] to the Balkans and Byzantium in the Southeast, to the Avar-Greater Moravian realm in the North, while some of them may have been Central European general wares from Carolingian-Ottonian times, although comparable items (because offerings in the graves had been discontinued) are seldom present. The research work being carried out by Jochen Giesler[158] should throw fresh light on these problems and also take

82 *'Beneath this tombstone rests in blessed memory Rusticus, the monk.'–Simple words in faulty Latin on one of the finest early medieval gravestones in the West, found as recently as 1974 during excavations at the abbey of Saint-Maurice d'Agaune (Valais), founded 515. The doves drinking from the chalice symbolize the human soul, which derives refreshment from everlasting bliss. 6th century* AD. *Ht 68 cm. Abbey of Saint-Maurice d'Agaune.*

into account the connections with the cemeteries of Slovenia not so far away, such as Bled.[159] At all events, it is worth noting that the immediately ensuing cemeteries of the Köttlach culture, so named after an important find-spot, are contemporary with the expansion of the Frankish kingdom in the East Alpine region and the Slavic mission of Innichen and Kremsmünster. Here, then, a people reacted to new political and religious circumstances in a manner which no longer manifested itself in the territory whence they came. For in the Frankish kingdom the dead had long since been buried according to Christian precept, without offerings, in the graveyard close by the church–providing the archaeologist with yet another example of the variety of ways in which the relationships between belief in an after-life and burial rite, political initiative and dissemination of culture are to be seen. Graves, notwithstanding all the testimony they can provide, grant us only a limited view of the living.

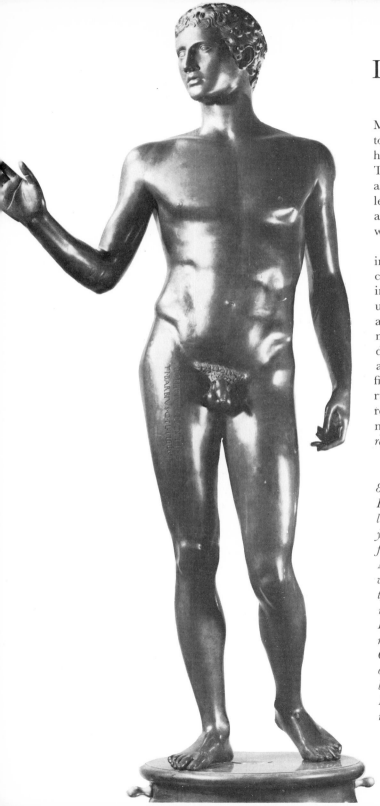

IV Religion and Art

Man's ability, developed in the course of millennia, to use tools and himself prepare them, to utilize fire and adapt to his surroundings put an end to his accord with nature. The human race underwent an experience which raised it above the animals. Every step forward, every awareness of learning, skill and mastery engendered at the same time and inevitably the realization that many spheres of life were beyond direct human influence.

To overcome this state of conflict needed action, not by individuals but by the group, excluded from which no one could live: the provision of housing for shelter, the bringing-up of children, the hunting of wild beasts–all this was undertaken jointly by the entire family or clan. Events and experiences were likewise common to all: the inclemency of the weather and the courses of the stars, life and death, the unpredictable nature of the chase. These were all integral parts of a world scene in which man had to find his place and in which he held in check by means of rules what was beyond his control, so as to mitigate its terrors. Thus religion came into being at the same time as man himself. Our word 'religion' derives from the Latin *religio*, and in its original sense the key element of some-

83 The most important ancient bronze sculpture found north of Italy was unearthed in 1502 by a farmer ploughing on the Magdalensberg at Klagenfurt (Carinthia): a Roman copy of a statue of a young man from the school of the Greek sculptor Polycletus. It found its way north as a votive offering to the Norican tribal god Mars Latobius from merchants of Aquileia. It would seem that it was there converted into a cult statue of the god himself by the addition of shield, sword and spear. The donors' names are etched on the right thigh: 'Aulus Poblicius Antiocus, freedman of Decius, and Barbius Tiberinus, freedman of Quintus and of Publius.' The round shield (now lost) gave further information: 'For Mars! Gallicinus, son of Vindilus, Lucius Barbius Philetaerus, freedman of Lucius, businessman, and Craxsantus, slave of Barbius Publius.' Early 1st century BC, after an original of the 5th century BC. Ht 1.83 m. Kunsthistorisches Museum, Vienna. Cast in the museum on the Magdalensberg.

thing controlled and binding still finds expression.[1] *Religio* possessed the 'objective meaning of a binding force, a tabu that attaches to particular places, days and activities, and has a restraining effect on people.' Only later did it acquire the subjective meaning of 'religious awe, piety', which finds expression in a scrupulous observance of the ritual precepts.

In the archaeologically tangible sense, religion can only be comprehended where individual acts and recurring rituals have left traces which allow us to arrive at conclusions concerning attitudes that lie beyond the realm of material progress. In this sense art, too, is intimately connected with religion. Up until recently art was only at given times, and then not wholly, pursued for the artist's own pleasure, an outlet for his unbounded creativity. When it was taken over by religion and the cults, these more or less determined the themes, motives and abstract ideas that were to be conveyed. There were many different ways of envisaging and depicting 'reality'. To saddle primitive man with the Western concept of art, which was valid from the late Middle Ages until the early twentieth century, would be to distort the appearance of what is vital and strange. Modern art of the past few decades, not a little influenced by contact with non-European 'primitive' art, has helped us to understand alternative ways of looking at things.[2]

Bear cult and the first depictions of human beings

Those who are acquainted with the impressive cave paintings of western France and Spain will look in vain for anything similar in the Alpine region. There the early hunter employed other means of attaining the same end, which was to ensure a lucky and successful chase. But we do not know how he set about this since there is no material evidence for us to go by. Only by observing primitive peoples of recent times can we begin to envisage the various possibilities. Dances and the retrospective–or better, prospective–enactment of hunting-scenes, the representation of the animal victim and the donning of its hide establish an inner bond between man and the animal as a creature coexisting in the natural world and at the same time the quarry. Whether in antiquity the shamans, who as priests

had access to the spirits and totem animals, set their seal on the religious life of the roving hunters is a much disputed topic, as is the question whether animal sacrifices were made to a higher being, a god.

The last question could only be answered, assuming carefully conducted and precisely recorded excavations were to provide unequivocal proof. This, however, is not forthcoming, for even the findings from the Drachenloch at Vättis (canton St Gallen)[3] do not satisfy the sceptics. Here, between 1917 and 1923, Emil Bächler had discovered in the inner recesses of the cave skulls and primary bones of cave bears, which in some cases gave rise to the idea of a deliberate deposition, particularly as they were reputedly surrounded or covered by stones. Since similar 'burials' of cave bear skulls have been confirmed at several places in palaeolithic Central Europe,[4] there is no sound reason to doubt a bear cult at the Drachenloch,[5] particularly as comparable observations were made in the Wildenmannlisloch in the Churfirsten mountains (canton St Gallen).[6] What sort of religious concepts were associated with this can admittedly not be determined with any certainty by studying primitive peoples of today, seeing that their own history goes back many thousands of years: whether it was worship of the bear as a life-supporting animal of the chase, or belief in a higher being on whom one bestowed some of one's wealth.[7]

Man first reached the point of depicting animals in the later stages of the Old Stone Age, that is to say when the final Ice Age was nearing its end. The hunter had become more skilled: bow and arrow, spears, harpoons and well-finished stone tools are among the artefacts he has bequeathed to the archaeologist. The chase must indeed have determined people's whole lives and thinking, their relationship with animals, their religious views, the social structure. So it is scarcely surprising that the animal soon came to govern the art they produced.[8] Cave paintings are, as mentioned above, entirely lacking, but a few instances of small-scale art using bone or antler as medium or in the form of incised stone tablets[9] make one thing clear: the sculptures and drawings are not 'primitive', they are not 'children's scribbles'. From the very beginning, man (admittedly, as today still, only specially gifted individuals) possessed the ability to seize on and render the quintessential physical and non-physical attributes of

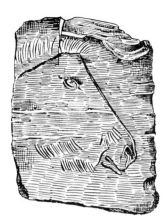

84 *Heads of horses engraved on a small panel of jet amber, found in the Kesslerloch at Thayngen (canton Schaffhausen). Approx. 10,000–8000 BC. L 5.9 cm. Museum Allerheiligen, Schaffhausen.*

The house altar beneath a rock shelter

Finds that tell us anything about the religion and mentality of Late Stone Age man are very scarce in the Alpine region. Since settlement proceeded only tentatively after the end of the Ice Age and in any case the first farmers did not push on into the mountains, clues concerning the fertility cults that are elsewhere associated with this process are scarcely to be expected. A few clay figurines of animals from a settlement at Seeberg-Burgäschli (canton Bern)[12] are isolated instances and it is difficult to determine which animals they represent (ram, dog, aurochs?). For such art as was produced at this time is of poor quality. The drawings and sculptures of the Early Stone Age cease, nowhere is there any positive indication of a continuance. What this was due to and what changes in the religious, economic or social spheres were associated with it we have no means of telling.

Against this background a recent discovery in the Trento district is of particular significance. At Martignano in the Val Sugana excavations beneath a rock shelter named Riparo Gaban revealed a thick band of strata, showing

an animal. He portrayed reindeer, wild horses, wild asses, musk-oxen and larger beasts that called for considerable courage, agility and accuracy of aim on the part of the hunters. These animals barely penetrated the Alpine region proper but stopped at the borders: at the Rhône in the West, at the Upper Rhine and in the plains of Lower Austria in the North, in the Po plain in the South. The second art form, too, the female figurines made of ivory or easily worked stone, the best-known of which is the 'Venus of Willendorf'[10] from Lower Austria, is restricted to this circumalpine zone. A few finds from the Balzi Rossi[11] at Ventimiglia on the Riviera testify to the exceptional nature of this area with its congenial climate. If the artist exaggerated the characteristic female attributes, this was to emphasize the sex, the function as mother, even when–as may occasionally have been the case–he had a particular person in mind. These works of art from the Upper Palaeolithic (later Old Stone Age) provide evidence of a fresh step in the mental development of man, the ability to observe his fellows and ultimately himself from the outside, and to convert this into a depiction that could be recognized and understood by those who looked at it.

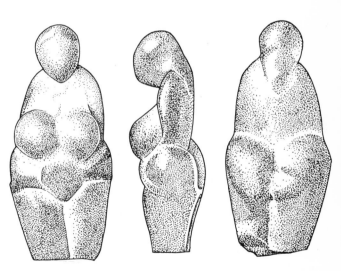

85 *Female figure in soapstone (steatite), found together with five similar ones in the 'Barma Grande', a cave by the sea at Ventimiglia (Liguria), or possibly in the neighbouring 'Grotta del Principe'. 30,000–20,000 BC. Ht 4.8 cm.*

that this place was settled from the transition period Early/Late Stone Age up until the Bronze Age. The findings have so far been only provisionally published,[13] but a rough picture does emerge. There was, it appears, a little niche dating from the Late Stone Age in the rock-face, largely covered and sealed (probably secondarily) by a stone block. In the niche itself and within a range of not more than 1 m the excavators found four objects whose form and ornamentation suggests a religious connotation: a bone tablet in the shape of a woman whose pudenda are stressed; a rectangular wooden dish with simple incised decoration and two perforations; a broken-off bone (probably the humerus of a pig) on which a variety of designs and possibly a stylized human figure were carved; finally, an elongated, roughly oval pebble made to resemble a human head by means of incised lines. Later on they found a whistle with incised decoration, and other strange objects. If the female figure still recalls the Early Stone Age sculptures with their small heads, prominent sexual attributes and legs that are merely hinted at, the stone head represents something alien and novel. The staring eyes, long nose and open mouth immediately put one in mind of the heads found at Lepenski Vir by the Iron Gates in Jugoslavia.[14] But any direct connection with the Southeast is not feasible. In the first place, the Lepenski Vir heads are properly sculpted, not produced by just incising lines; secondly, they are much larger (mostly 20–60 cm); thirdly and conclusively, C14 tests have shown them to be at least 1500 years older than the pebble from Riparo Gaban, which must date from the middle phase of the Late Stone Age in northern Italy, to judge by the stone tools and pottery sherds. The Lepenski Vir heads, on the other hand, stem from the two earliest settlement phases there, which had no pottery vessels of any kind, and consequently were made before the beginning of what is, properly speaking, the Late Stone Age.

At all events, in comparison with the Old Stone Age sculptures, the small work of art conveys something new. The body no longer plays any role, being merely suggested by a few lines. It is the face with its clear contours that is dominant, and into it the modern observer can readily read a look of terror. A notable feature is the beard with its two pointed ends (there is nothing that corresponds to this in Lepenski Vir).

From the careful excavations carried out at Lepenski Vir we know that the heads and the ornamented or plain stones of the same shape found there had their appointed place inside the houses: behind the hearth on the floor, exactly in the centre of the room and slightly inset in order to hold them in place. Only a detailed evaluation of the excavation work done at Riparo Gaban will tell us whether similar conditions prevailed here, whether the very disparate objects belong to a single settlement phase, or perhaps represent different time spans during which the dwelling-place beneath the rock shelter was modified several times. With our present very limited knowledge of early art it would be imprudent to conclude merely from the stylistic variations between the objects that a time factor is involved. For it is no less possible that, while the

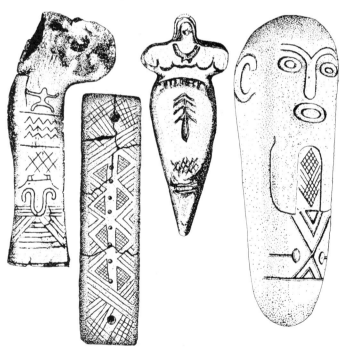

86 *Devotional objects of stone and bone, found in the rock-shelter of 'Riparo Gaban' at Martignano (Trento province), which was inhabited for several thousands of years. 4500–3500 BC. Various scales. Museo di Scienze Naturali, Trento.*

87 Unquestionably this find from Spiez-Obergut (canton Bern) must be regarded as a votive offering to an unidentified god. Five arm-rings–originally there were also three smaller rings–are strung on a bent-together costume pin. They were found at the base of a granite boulder together with ashes and charred wood. Here, then, a sacrificial cremation had taken place, to which the bronze objects were later added. 14th century BC. L of pin 60 cm. Historisches Museum, Bern.

form and ornamentation in each case reflect a different outlook on life and religious purpose, they may nevertheless have been contemporaneous. The small size and nature of the objects suggests that they were not just placed on the floor, but stood at a higher level, perhaps in a niche in the back wall of the house, whose hearths were renewed from time to time.

Animal sacrifice and votive offerings to unknown powers

From the Bronze Age on, it is possible to discern the various categories of sacrifices that were suppressed and proscribed (but not eliminated) by Christianity during the early Middle Ages. The large number of examples enables us to investigate what kind of sacrifices they were, what places were favoured and what objects chosen for the purpose. To discover to whom the sacrifices applied, what names the gods bore, is seldom possible before Roman times with their literary sources.

From the Early Bronze Age onward it was the custom to go to the same places time after time, often over a period of centuries, in order to make sacrifices. These places are recognizable from the great quantities of burnt animal bones, ashes and broken pottery.[15] The 'bone mound' in the Langackertal at Reichenhall is said to have been still as much as 4 m high immediately prior to the excavation

(which ultimately removed it entirely!); the sherds from it fill dozens of large packing-cases.[16] For, owing to the sanctity of the spot, it was forbidden to dispose of the ashes and other remains from the sacrifice once the ceremony was over. Thus the mounds grew ever higher, until such time as the cult was discontinued or the ceremony was transferred to some other place.[17]

There are quite a lot of such burnt-offering places in the Alpine region between the Lake of Thun and the Salzach, and new ones are continually being discovered, which ploughing alone had wholly flattened.[18] Where dating and type of location are concerned, they vary appreciably. There is, for example, a cult centre at the Burgstall (2510 m) on the Schlern massif above Bolzano (Bozen), dated in the Late Bronze Age and Early Iron Age.[19] Whoever wanted to sacrifice here had to make a laborious ascent, but he was then particularly near the mountain god who was perhaps involved in the sacrifice. The siting of these cult places immediately below the summit is not unusual, and La Chalp below Monte Genevris (2536 m) in the Piedmontese Alps is one instance.[20] The finds from there (above all, sherds and coins) belong in the Celtic and Roman period; a few ruins hint at buildings belonging to the sanctuary, possibly small temples or shelters for the pilgrims. The inscriptions incised on many of the sherds show that primarily a god Albiorix was worshipped here, a mountain god with a Celtic name which in other inscriptions from the Western Alps is identified with the Roman Mars, the god of war. This is confirmed by the Roman name of the little town of Oulx at the foot of the mountain, which on maps of late antiquity is designated 'ad Martis'. The second god to be worshipped was Apollo, whom the Celts did not distinguish from their native gods of healing. The absence of ashes and burnt animal bones associates this place with other, older ones where likewise a pit filled only with broken vessels was found.[21]

Burnt-offering places were, however, located not only on lonely mountain heights but also in the middle of settlement areas, such as the Dürrnberg at Hallein (Ill. 44: 'cult area') in the Late Iron Age[22] and on the Auerberg at Schongau in early Roman times.[23] Finally, there appear to have been burnt-offering places at and above graves, as the findings from Reichenhall in conjunction with those from Pula in Istria would suggest.[24] That the cemetery was still in use, though, seems unlikely from the not very clear reports.

Whilst it was principally animals, drink, food and the relevant pottery vessels that were sacrificed at these places, there is a second category showing a preponderance of metal objects. From as early as the Late Stone Age man worshipped gods or higher beings by dedicating valuable articles to them at places that were regarded as sacred by virtue of some particular feature. He might ram a spear into the ground, shoot an arrow into the sky, thrust an axe into a tree-trunk, hang rings on branches or place them beside a stone, conceal a sword in a rocky cleft, wedge coins into a split in some wooden statue,[25] cast pins into a swamp and submerge weapons in running water. With submergence in a bog or in water, the purpose is quite clear, namely to cast away the votive object for good, but in the case of finds on dry land the archaeologist often

hesitates to attribute this to an intentional deposition, preferring to believe in an accidental loss or concealment in a dangerous situation. Yet the idea of a hunter who throws his spear at a fleeing animal and does not retrieve it is not in accord with most of the other finds. Moreover, we even have literary evidence to the effect that every passer-by, coming across such a sacred place, would recognize it as such, and that for early man an exposed offering was every bit as inviolable as one that had been cast into the water. Thus, Diodorus[26] says of the Celts in the first century BC: 'In the temples and at the sacred places which one comes upon now and then, much gold lies about which is dedicated to the gods. Fear of these is however so great, that no one touches this gold, even though the Celts are in other respects most avaricious.' Who would have wanted to risk bringing down on himself the wrath and revenge of the gods, by purloining votive weapons? We must not forget that we only possess the metal parts of these objects and have no idea of the many possible ways in which the venerated place may have been distinguishable.

By way of further explanation, let us first consider what part the finds in the waters played. For many early peoples water[27] gave access to the Underworld, to the spirits of the dead. Moreover, the spring seems to have represented the beginning of existence, the ever-flowing source of all things, particularly the necessities of life. If in addition the spring possessed healing properties, of which early man was aware even without the benefit of chemical analyses (smell, taste, temperature, its attraction for animals), this caused it to be even more venerated. One of the best known examples of such a place is the mineral spring at St Moritz in the Engadin, where, when it was being converted in 1907, an old framework containing votive offerings of the Bronze Age[28] was discovered. An axe found in the vicinity of the saline springs of Bad Reichenhall[29] has proved to be of Early Bronze Age date. Its wooden haft is still in superb condition, having been protected–as was the case with the mines of Hallein and Hallstatt–by the salt.

In later times, sanctuaries were inaugurated at springs without any offerings being cast into the waters. Little known outside Italy is Calalzo 'Làgole' in the uppermost part of the Piave valley, where a succession of chance finds and ultimately small-scale excavations carried out by Giu-

88 *Votive offerings from a sanctuary on the Gutenberg at Balzers (Liechtenstein). Stag and boar as sacred animals of the Celts, the sheet-metal jingle-segments in the native Hallstatt tradition, and the large warrior with his Italic-style leather jerkin attest the various cultural influences in this transit area. The small figures were originally attached to a base (now lost). Names and functions of the gods who were venerated here are unidentified. 3rd–1st century* BC. *Ht of large warrior (excluding peg) 12.8 cm. Liechtensteinisches Landesmuseum, Vaduz.*

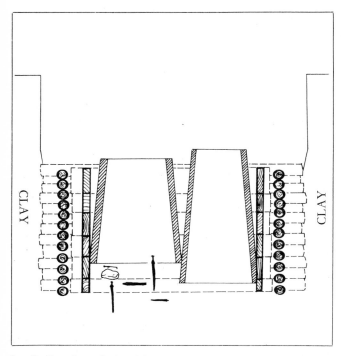

CLAY

CLAY

89 Section through the old wooden structure of the spring at St Moritz (Graubünden) with votive offerings of the Bronze Age: one fragmented and two whole swords, a dagger, a costume pin. 13th century BC. Diam. of the frame of tree-trunks approx. 4.3 m.

lia de' Fogolari in the 'fifties established the existence of a sanctuary close by sulphur springs.[30] A vast quantity of objects with nearly 100 inscriptions, together with recordings made during the excavation, meant that the essential features of the rites observed there could be reconstructed. In the first place, what is remarkable is that according to the deciphered names in the Venetic and Latin inscriptions[31] only men took part in the rites. Secondly, these cult practices were continued over a period of many centuries, from about the third/second century BC until towards the middle of the fourth century AD, when presumably Christianity put an end to them. It is not clear whether, and if so to what extent, the rites underwent any changes during this long period.

They all centred, however, around the worship of a god

of healing, to whom a suitable selection of objects was dedicated: bronze tablets with and without pictorial matter, little bronze figurines, mostly of warriors but also gods associated with the male sphere (Herakles, Jupiter, Victoria, Mercury) and 'Apollo', the god of healing himself, large vessels, ladles, belt-hooks, fibulae and votive images in bronze of those parts of the anatomy for which a remedy was sought, wrought iron swords, knives, daggers and even a scythe; in Roman times (about 80 BC to AD 340) coins as well. The inscriptions are mostly confined to the bronze tablets, figurines and ladles. The last-named were for scooping up and drinking the healing water, mostly bore a votive inscription on the handle and, after use, were broken and deposited in the sanctuary as offerings, in the same way as the other objects. Large bonfires featured in the cult, around which possibly feasting and drinking, certainly sacrificing, took place; with their piles of burnt animal bones and smashed pottery, these places are comparable with the burnt-offering sites mentioned earlier.

The particular god who was venerated can be inferred from the votive inscriptions. The Venetic ones follow a pretty regular pattern:

Eskaiva libertos Arsletijakos donasto Śainatei Trumusijatei.
[Scaeva Arsleti libertus donavit Sainati Trumusiati.]

The transliteration of the Venetic into Latin makes the lexical and grammatical correlations clearer, and is verifiable because such votive formulas were very similarly constructed in the old Italic languages–and even in non-Indo-European Etruscan. In English, it would read somewhat as follows: Scaeva Arsleti, freed slave, has given (this to the deity) Sainat(is) Trumusiat(is).

The principal name or surname of the deity was–to judge by the frequency of its use–*Trumusijat(is)*, whilst *Sainat(is)* may be a further surname (perhaps meaning 'the healer'; cf. Lat. *sanare*) or a second deity.

Simpler versions of the votive formula would run as follows:

On a small bronze jug

Kśutavikos doto donom Śainatei.
[C(o)ssutavicus (?) dedit donum Sainati.]
C(o)ssutavicus has given (this) gift (to the deity) Sainat(is).

On the handle of a ladle

Suros Resunkos tonasto Trumusiatin.
[Surus Resun(i)cus donavit Trumusiatem.]

That it was not only individuals who dedicated offerings is shown by a votive plaque depicting a horse (cf. Ill. 90), and the short legend:

teuta toler.
[Civitas obtulit.]
The community has given this.

And the man who had etched the word *Trumu*, the abbreviated version of the deity's name, twice over on the handle of his ladle clearly wanted to be on the safe side.

As Roman culture and language took over the Venetic Alpine region, the votive inscriptions soon adapted them-

90 Votive plaque of sheet-bronze from the sacred spring at Làgole, Calalzo municipality (Belluno province, Veneto). The inscription reads: Kellos Pittammnikos toler Trumusijatei donum d(onasto) a(isum)–*Cellus Pittamnicus has presented this gift to (the god)* Trumusiati(s). *2nd-1st century* BC. *19 × 17 cm. Museo della Communità Pieve di Cadore.*

selves accordingly. Initially, the old name of the deity was retained, even though the Latin votive formula was used:

L(ucius) Apinius L(ucii) f(ilius) Trum[sia]tei v(otum) s(olvit) l(ibens) m(erito).
Lucius Apinius, son of Lucius, has fulfilled his vow to (the deity), Trumsiat(is) willingly and according to merit.

Ultimately the Greco-Roman Apollo, revered in many parts of the Empire as god of healing, supplanted the native deity:

Firmus Vettius Apolini v(otum) s(olvit) l(ibens) m(erito).

The two last inscriptions, too, were etched into the handles of ladles, which was in keeping with the prevailing style, thus most clearly showing that, despite the Latinizing and Romanizing of the Alps, the basic structure of ancient customs and conduct persisted, as did also the belief on the part of the inhabitants in the sanctity of a place and the benefits bestowed by a god who was worshipped there. The god's name was officially adapted to the new world, nothing more.

North of the main Alpine ridge there is a spring which in the Late Iron Age was likewise regarded as being particularly sacred; at all events, there at Steinberg on the Achensee, at an altitude of some 1400 m, are the only pre-Roman inscriptions so far found in the North.[32] They are scored into the rock face of a cleft from which issues a small spring. In contrast to Làgole, it is mostly the names of women that are here perpetuated:

Water is there
To Castor Mistress Etuni has here sacrificed
Here Mistress Mnesi has sacrificed to Castor
Usipe the prisoner has sacrificed
Here Elvas has drawn water
Estas has donated the votive image

There are plenty of springs and wet places in the neighbourhood but we have no confirmation of the water's mineral content, and therefore do not know why this spring was especially sacred. Quite recently, though, a cleft in the rock was discovered at Telfes in the Stubai valley; here water with a high mineral content collected after issuing in a thin stream.[33] Quantities of dishes and also earthenware jugs show that this spring was likewise used and venerated in the Late Iron Age. The custom of dedicating the used ladles and drinking vessels to the deity corresponds–though on a more modest scale–with that observed in Làgole.

We know very little about the sacrificing at streams and rivers. For the chances of finding the relevant offerings are slight. Dredging of rivers and gravel pits which bisect old river channels offer the best opportunities, but now that mechanization has almost completely taken over, the quota of finds is diminishing here as well. It may be safely assumed, though, that particularly conspicuous places were favoured, not just the springs but also narrows, rapids and the outflow points of tributaries, even of rivulets, which are distinguishable by the colour of the water. The extensive work carried out by Walter Torbrügge[34] on the river finds has gone a long way towards solving the associated problems. The examples that follow may serve to show, among other things, that weapons preponderated, and this not only because their size makes them easier to find. For at specific times and in certain regions it was the custom to offer up pins[35] (also an article characterized by a sharp point which is able to penetrate; rings are scarcely ever present) instead, and these are nearly all smaller than swords, axes and spearheads.

The custom of river-sacrificing extends from the Late Stone Age to the early Middle Ages and beyond: stone axes from the Salzach and its tributaries;[36] early bronze axes from the Salzach and Saarlach;[37] bronze ceremonial axes of the Iron Age from where the Alm (= Königsee-Ache) flows into the Salzach, and from the Ache at Dornbirn in Vorarlberg;[38] Iron Age helmets from the Po;[39] even two breast-plates of Early Iron Age date from a rivulet near Véria in the French Jura.[40] In Roman times the practice apparently declined because new standard forms of religious observance gained the upper hand. But where large quantities of finds occur within a small area, the Roman period is also definitely represented; for example in the marshy Alpine Rhine valley round Lustenau just above the river's point of entry into the Lake of Constance.[41] Since the Germanic peoples brought with them a wholly similar tradition, the offerings consigned to the waters in the Alpine and circumalpine regions increase in numbers once more in the early Middle Ages. Splendid helmets from the sixth century were found where the Rhône flows into the Lake of Geneva and in a bog at Vézeronce (Dep. Isère).[43] Still more recent are spearheads

from the eighth/ninth century, whose frequency in the Swiss midlands is affected by the extensive dredging work connected with the Jura water control undertaking.[43] The Danube rapids at Grein in Upper Austria have yielded finds from all periods;[44] among other objects, an Etruscan bronze bucket–so far singular in the North–from the Salzach at Laufen,[45] where, prior to the blasting of the rocks in 1773, rapids hindered navigation, shows the exceptional situation of such places.

The numerical decline during the Roman period is presumably to be attributed to the different circumstances that prevailed when the finds were made. For if, as in the case of, say, sacrifices on heights or passes, the objects most often thrown into the water at that time were coins, the chances are that those working with mechanical scoops, however observant they might be, are less likely to notice these than weapons or other larger objects. Whilst offerings of coins at springs are fairly frequent,[46] river offerings of 'money' dating from as early as the Late Iron Age are occasionally found.[47] Here it is a question of iron ingots shaped like a double pyramid or sword, such as those from the Bregenz Ache or the Limmat in Zurich.[48] A bronze ring ingot, dating back to the Early Bronze Age when north of the Eastern Alps something in the nature of standardized money circulated for a short while (p. 259), was found in a brook at Rosenheim.[49]

A puzzle for which a great many possible explanations have been put forward concerns a find at La Tène, at the point where the river Zihl flows out of Lake Neuchâtel. Here thousands of objects, above all from the last two centuries BC, were discovered. The number of weapons and fibulae was disproportionately large. At the same time the remains of a wooden bridge were identified and traces of buildings on the shore. During the past century this place has been variously interpreted as anything from a 'trading centre' to a 'place of sacrifice'.[50] Recently, the collapse of a bridge–by way of analogy with a discovery at nearby Cornans–during floods was brought into the argument.[51] This diversity of opinion does not in itself mean that the explanations offered are mutually exclusive. If, as at La Tène, an important trade route leads across the river to a place that is also of cultic significance (outflow from the lake),[52] then all three factors could have played a part. But in that event there is no way of determining in each case whether an object was inadvertently lost, washed out of a house or storage place by the flood water that caused the bridge to be carried away, fell with a loaded wagon from the collapsing bridge, or was cast into the waters as an offering to the god who was venerated here beside the ford and bridge.[53] In France, there are many instances of river finds having accumulated at fords, but this cannot be explained solely by assuming that particularly many people or transports came to grief there: for a mundane interpretation of this kind by no means allows for all the possibilities inherent in such a situation.[54]

The gods of the mountains

In the life and thought of the Alpine peoples the powers which they believed ruled the mountains played a major role. Notwithstanding their familiarity with their surroundings, they nevertheless felt there was ultimately something uncanny about the unpredictable mountain realm. They believed the peaks to be personifications of gods, that the weather was controlled by the gods, and they gave thanks to the gods for safe journeys through the passes and when men and cattle remained unharmed on the mountain pastures. We know from the Greek and Roman worlds that there were a great many gods of this nature, who in the course of time merged with the limited number of members of the canonized pantheon and lived on under the many appellations of the chief gods.

This accounts for Poeninus, the native tutelary god of the Great St Bernard, being equated with the highest Roman god, Jupiter. The Valais retained his name in Roman times in the form of Vallis Poenina–'valley of Poeninus'; the pagan god was later made tabu, but that part of the name which ultimately became meaningless in the Alpine region, the 'valley', endures in the present-day name. Close by the Italian customs post on the Great St Bernard the most important pass-sanctuary in the Alps, possibly of the entire Roman world, came into existence. Excavations carried out at the end of last century[55] revealed the ground-plans of temples and countless offerings left by travellers. The earliest objects belong in the Early Iron Age, and from then on the sanctuary was in continuous use up until late Roman times. Unfortunately these finds have never been systematically published, and

since the little museum in the hospice also houses others from Martigny and its environs, it is not possible to tell by examining the exhibited objects what is actually a votive offering and what is not. There can, however, be no doubt about the many Roman coins and inscriptions having been deposited in the sanctuary. The inscriptions,[56]

91 This fragment of a unique stone relief provides archaeological evidence of a cult centre at the hot springs of Bormio (Lombardy) at the foot of the Stilfser Joch pass. It shows the statue of a god, relatively greater than life-size, wearing a horned helmet, who carries a shield in the form of an animal hide and holds a kind of standard. A man in a short skirt with a knife at his belt advances towards him; he is blowing a large U-shaped horn. Between him and the statue is a spear on which hangs a round shield, perhaps a votive offering to the god. Above the horn can be discerned a slim sabre which a man (left, broken off) is wielding. Of a second frieze below, all that is identifiable is a bit of a helmet. 5th–4th century BC. *Ht 34 cm. Museo Civico, Como.*

apparently executed to order (several even containing errors) by a bronze-smith and engraver domiciled up on the pass give us a very good idea of the type of people who used the pass when en route from Italy to Gaul. It is evident from the formula *v(otum) s(olvit) l(ibens) m(erito)*, with which we are already familiar, how fervently the plainspeople from all civilized countries prayed when embarking on the journey over the pass which may already have been snowbound or subject to avalanches, venting their relief and hopes by means of offerings to the god. The wealthy were able to afford sheet gold or silver, ordinary citizens sheet bronze in the form of the customary little tablets with two 'handles'; those who had not

92 Votive plaque of sheet-bronze from the Great St Bernard: Iovi op(timo) m(aximo) Poenino T(iberius) Cl(audius) Severus fr(umentarius) leg(ionis) III italic(ae) v(otum) s(olvit) l(ibens) m(erito)—*For Jupiter, the best and greatest, with the cognomen Peoninus. Tiberius Claudius Severus, frumentarius of the 3rd Italic legion, has fulfilled his vow gladly and according to merit.—The legion in question was stationed in* Castra Regina/Regensburg, *and seeing that Claudius Severus crossed this pass so far to the West, he is likely to have been on an official mission. The* frumentarii *were originally responsible for provisioning the troops with grain but were later required to perform more and more duties, among them that of courier. About* AD *200. Width 20.3 cm. Hospice on the Great St Bernard.*

much money to spare donated at least a miniature tablet bearing a short inscriptions, or a coin.

The following examples, selected from some fifty, will serve to show both the uniformity and the individuality of the votive inscriptions:

1. *T(itus) Annius Cissus.*
2. *M(arcus) Papirius Eunus ex voto.*
   Marcus Papirius Eunus in accordance with a vow.
3. *Poenina sacrum P(ublius) Blattius Creticus.*
   To Poeninus as sacred offering, Publius Blattius Creticus.
4. *Poenino pro itu et reditu G(aius) Iulius Primus v(otum) s(olvit) l(ibens) m(erito).*
   To Poeninus for an auspicious outward and return journey. Gaius Iulius Primus has fulfilled his vow gladly and according to merit.
5. *I(ovi) O(ptimo) M(aximo) Poenino G(aius) Domitius Carassounus Hel(vetius) Mango v(otum) s(olvit) l(ibens) m(erito).*
   For Jupiter, the best and greatest, known as Poeninus. Gaius Domitius Carassounus, Helvetian, slave-trader, has fulfilled his vow gladly and according to merit.
6. *Numinib(us) Augg(ustorum) Iovi Poenino Sabineiius Censor Ambianus v(otum) s(olvit) l(ibens) m(erito).*
   To their divine majesties the Emperor and Jupiter Poeninus! Sabineiius Censor from Amiens has fulfilled his vow gladly and according to merit.

Those who had a high opinion of themselves would add their profession or military rank. Here is a charming poem by one Gaius Iulius Rufus:[57]

At your temples I have willingly
fulfilled the vows I made.
I supplicate your divinity
that you may find them agreeable.
The cost was not high, to be sure;
We beg of you, divine one,
to rate our loyalty higher
than our purse.

Whereas on the Great St Bernard the votive tablets dominated the scene, the excavations and other investigations on the Julier pass have yielded little else but coins, plus the ground-plan of a little temple some 5 m square.[58] The clearly visible column stumps, one on either side of the road, are parts of the same column, which, seeing it was at least 4 m high, may be interpreted as a free-standing monument. (A gneiss column, 4.03 m high, still stands on the Little St Bernard pass; today it is graced with a statue of the eponymous saint.) To judge by the extensive sequence of coins, worship of the relevant deity, whose name we do not know, began in the middle of the first century AD and went on uninterruptedly until the time of Emperor Valentinian shortly after the middle of the fourth century. A coin of the Vandal king Geiseric, struck between 439 and 477, testifies to the significance of the place in early medieval times and confirms that the possibly already ruined sanctuary and the nature of the rites performed there were known.

There is no evidence of so clear a concentration of offerings in pre-Roman times on the actual summit of the pass. Most of the finds come from places below the pass itself, from upland pastures at an altitude of between 1500 and 2000 m, sometimes near a spring, or from quite inconspicuous places which might have been on short cuts or linking routes that no longer serve any useful purpose today. Attempts to discover the precise reason why any one find came to be deposited are doomed to failure from the start. We can do no more than hazard a guess, while taking into account the geographical conditions. In those days, it would seem, less importance was attached to making an offering at a particular place than in Roman times, when everything was strictly regulated. But since single coins are far less likely to be accidentally encountered than spearheads or axes, this conclusion—as in the case of the river-offerings—might well be a mistaken one that does not take into account the varying circumstances in which the objects were found.[59]

In Austria, Italy and Switzerland nearly every important pass and its approach routes have yielded finds which can be interpreted as offerings to the gods of the roads, the mountains and perhaps the flocks as well. No comprehensive work on the subject exists, though it would be quite as important as the one on river-finds. The examples that follow are little more than pointers to the categories that are represented. An early bronze dagger was discovered during the building of the Glocknerstrasse.[60] The Late Bronze Age is represented by a find from the Lueg pass on the Salzach south of Golling (helmet, together with pieces of a socketed axe and chopper and two fragments of a copper casting)[61] and one from the Luftenstein pass on the Saalach (spearhead, knife and meat-fork),[62] both narrow defiles difficult to negotiate, just above where the respective valleys emerge from the mountains. Individual finds of this period from high-altitude pastures and tracks have been assembled by René Wyss for Switzerland and Elmar Vonbank for Vorarlberg.[63] Important supplementary information relating to the Bronze Age in a wider context has recently been published.[64] From the higher parts of the Splügen pass came a Late Bronze Age knife and an iron ingot (Ill. 160) and, lower down, a sword of the Late Iron Age.[65] These only go to show how full of gaps our knowledge of the actual votive offerings is, for also at the Splügen offerings will have been made to the mountain god–in accordance with the custom of the day–during the intervening 1000 years.

In the Late Iron Age, after about 450 BC, in addition to the traditional weapons[66] and primitive currency tokens (ingots), rings[67] came into prominence. A gold neckring from the Maschlalm[68] on the path from the Rauris valley to the Hochtor near the Grossglockner should certainly be treated as a votive offering, as should a silver neck-ring from Pallon (Hautes-Alpes)[69] and probably also a gold arm-ring from Schalunen[70] between Bern and Solothurn. That these 'torcs' were made of such rare material suggests that it was a case of dedicating exceptionally valuable single objects, perhaps even ones specially produced for the purpose.

It is in this context that the sensational find from Erstfeld[71] in the canton of Uri must be considered. On 20 August 1962, while removing a great rock from the hillside above the Reuss valley, workmen came across four neck-rings and three arm-rings, all made of gold. The find-spot was covered by more than 9 m of detritus which had subsequently slid or been washed down–proof of how little the present-day valley slopes conform to their former states and of the large part chance plays where our knowledge of settlement, burial and offering customs and the finds associated with them is concerned. There can be no doubt that the Erstfeld torcs were made north of the Alps, presumably in the Rhineland, and that somebody carried them in his luggage when travelling to the South. In view of what we know about the relationship of ruler to artisan, of material possessions to artistic skill up until medieval times (p. 266), it is surely out of the question that a journeying trader, when threatened with danger, should have buried his bag of samples–it was his expertise, not a collection of finished articles, that a famous goldsmith would offer for sale. So the costly torcs were consigned to the earth by someone who either himself numbered among the rich and powerful, or who was taking them southwards as an official gift at the behest of such a person. The most likely explanation would seem to be that, in the course of the great Celtic migrations which began in the late fifth century, one of their leaders dedicated these torcs

93 Among the sacrificial offerings swords are well represented, though they are seldom found in graves. These four swords from Graubünden illustrate the changing form of this weapon. From the bottom: *Felsberg on the Vorderrhein (probably 13th century* BC; *isolated find)–Davos (13th century* BC; *from the lake)–Castaneda in the Misox (4th–3rd century* BC; *from a grave; blade still in its sheet-iron scabbard)–Splügen, at the foot of the pass (2nd–1st century* BC; *isolated find). L of last-named sword 97.6 cm. Rätisches Museum, Chur.*

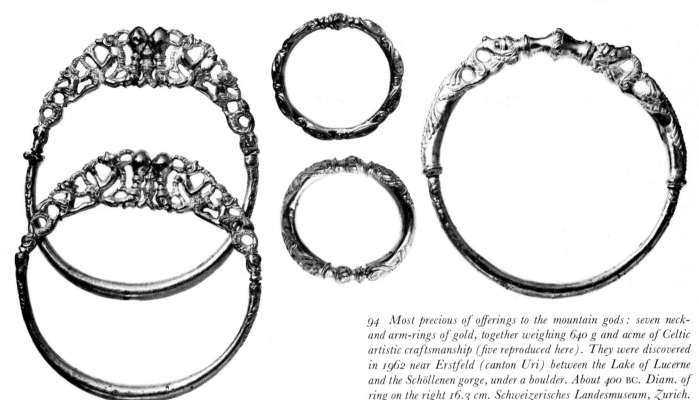

94 *Most precious of offerings to the mountain gods: seven neck-and arm-rings of gold, together weighing 640 g and acme of Celtic artistic craftsmanship (five reproduced here). They were discovered in 1962 near Erstfeld (canton Uri) between the Lake of Lucerne and the Schöllenen gorge, under a boulder. About 400 BC. Diam. of ring on the right 16.3 cm. Schweizerisches Landesmuseum, Zurich.*

as votive offerings to the unknown and wayward mountain gods, in order to secure a propitious crossing of the Alps. The find-spot in the valley of the Reuss between the Lake of Lucerne and the St Gotthard, which could be traversed only by means of narrow and dangerous tracks (p. 194), is well suited to this purpose. The situation in the upper valley of the Durance is very similar. Pallon, the place where the silver neck-ring–also unique of its kind–came to light, is situated just below the treacherous ravine outside Briançon and some 30 km–i.e. a day's march–from the Mont-Genèvre, on what is possibly even the route that Hannibal took.[72]

Still more remarkable and out of keeping with its surroundings is an Egyptian scarab amulet of clay, found in 1954 near the Rojach hut in the Rauris valley.[73] It stems from Ptolemaic times (third century BC on) or even the very early Roman period. It is not possible to say, there-

fore, when precisely it was lost, or consigned to the earth as a votive offering. Since gold was not extracted in the Rauris valley even in Roman times (pp. 248f.), it is likely that the find has to do with a route over the Tauern mountains.

A far more valuable offering to the mountain gods was a pair of gold fibulae picked up by a shepherd on the Kranjski Rak, on an upland pasture near a track through the Stein Alps between Styria and Slovenia. Apart from this pair of fibulae–belonging, incidentally, to women's costume–there is only one other known gold fibula of comparable worth; it is housed in the Metropolitan Museum, New York,[74] but its provenance is not indicated. All other fibulae of this Norican-Pannonian type, some 1600 in all, are made of bronze.

In post-Roman times the old custom of making votive offerings on heights and passes was to a certain extent

95 *The most important themes of the 'great festival' are depicted on the bronze bucket from Vače (Slovenia). This exploded section of the design on the vessel's wall shows vehicles and horsemen processing, contests, scenes of drinking to the accompaniment of music on the pan-pipes, as well as an animal frieze conforming to Mediterranean custom; extreme left, a predator devouring a human leg. 6th century* BC. *Ht 23.8 cm. Narodni muzej, Ljubljana.*

revived. At all events, a conspectus by Gudrun Schneken-burger[75] has identified for eastern and southern Switzer-land a dozen independent iron spearheads that can be dated in the sixth to the eighth century. There can be no question here of hunting weapons which were accidentally dropped or casually discarded, even if it is unclear why this particular region should have reverted to the old cus-tom. Perhaps it has something to do with the fact that here –in contrast to other districts–the indigenous Romanic inhabitants had weathered the upheavals of late antiquity without incurring heavy losses and were subjected to no more than slight Germanic influences. They were still clo-sely bound up with the Alpine world and its way of life, and even if, in accordance with Roman tradition, the men did not have weapons placed in their graves, they natur-ally possessed them while still alive and could dedicate spears (and arrows?) to the native gods of the mountains. That since the fifth century Christianity was the dominant religion does not for the time being appear to have affected the old mountain cult to any appreciable extent. Similar circumstances are likely to have prevailed in the Western Alps, but not nearly enough research has been done there, particularly for early medieval times. Nevertheless there is evidence that, specifically in the Bur-gundian empire, precious sixth-century helmets, instead of being placed in the graves, were cast into rivers and swamps as votive offerings.[76]

The great festival

Whilst the customs so far described can only be indirectly deduced from the remnants of the sacrificial rite or the offerings themselves, a particular type of object from the sixth and fifth centuries BC gives us an insight into a vari-ety of ceremonies which, together, point to a great festival. Large buckets of sheet bronze, called situlae (from the Latin), though rarely other objects,[77] have embossed on them scenes of a festive masculine world, in which women only participate as servants. Pertinent to the festival are ceremonial processions of warriors or men in long gar-ments, horse-racing, races with two-wheeled chariots and boxing contests, for which the men wear hand guards(?) and the prize (a helmet or a bronze vessel) is set between them. Judges ensure that the rules are obeyed. A situla

from Bologna depicts a long procession of men and women marching to the place of sacrifice. They lead an ox and a sheep, carry a bucket and other vessels in their hands or on their heads, and bring with them further objects which are needed for the sacrifice: spits, a chest, bundles of wood. Drinking played an important part at these ceremonies. Servants ladle the drink out of large buckets with handled scoops and hand it to men seated in statuesque attitudes on settees, and musicians play the pan-pipes or harp. We do not know which sections of the populace were allowed to take part in the festivities, but one thing seems certain: what is depicted is not some sort of carousal laid on by a prince for his circle of wealthy neighbours and favourites, but a festival that had the official stamp of a communal event and may even have had a religious connotation.[78] It would be difficult to account in any other way for the fact that, among what is after all a fairly limited number of motifs, the coupling of man and woman appears in a detailed yet sympathetic rendering (Ill. 38).[79] That it found its way into the framework of the festival suggests that perhaps a kind of fertility cult formed part of the cere-monial procedure. A number of depictions of farmers ploughing and men hunting would fit into this context since such activities–and they are the only 'everyday' ones included in the scene–could likewise be regarded as necessary to the continuing existence of a community.[80]

The 'situla art' that characterizes the East Alpine and Venetic region is, despite the originality of its scenes, details and artistic style, not an independent creation. Etruscan and, ultimately, orientalizing influences[81] of the seventh and sixth centuries BC are most clearly evident in the many animal friezes, which show a combination of realistically rendered animals and fabulous beasts. It is these friezes, too, that preponderate on the earliest works of situla art, even though the vessels of Kleinklein in Styria with their primitive repoussée dot-outlined technique already depict battle and hunting scenes.[82] A group of metalworkers centred on the Venetic Este stuck to their preference for animal friezes, whilst on the products of 'sit-ula art' in the narrow sense friezes showing human figures and ceremonial scenes are in a majority. They came mainly from the Inner and Southeast Alpine region, and the artists took great pains to make details of clothing, equipment and other items agree as precisely as possible this more clearly than the sword scabbard from Grave 994 at Hallstatt (Ill. 74), fashioned on the northern border of the Alps in the late fifth century BC by an artist who was familiar with the situla art. The ceremonial procession of warriors has turned to bitter conflict: one of the horsemen is killing an already downed foe, while two men struggle with one another on the ground, in marked contrast to the boxers who, in accordance with strict rules, solemnly compete for a valuable prize.

The world of the rock engravings

Two districts in the Alps are of great archaeological interest on account of the rock engravings there, and in order to see them it is well worth while wandering around the area on foot. The tourist industry has not yet discovered them, and long may it remain thus. For nothing is less well suited to taking in the simple, unassuming naturalness of this art than coach-loads of sightseers crowding round the best-known pictures like bees round a honey-pot.

Near the Italian frontier and the Col de Tende in the Alpes Maritimes rises Mont Bégo; with an altitude of 2873 m, it dominates a high-level Alpine countryside dotted with many lakes and some 40,000 rock engravings.[83] They are to be found at an altitude of 2100–2500 m on rocky declivities and isolated boulders, not incised but punched with stone or metal implements into surfaces ground smooth by the glaciers of the Ice Age.

A visit to this area calls for a certain amount of exertion. The starting point is the village of Saint-Dalmas-de-Tende, south of the pass. From there a road runs to the Lac de Mesce, lying at 1375 m. A track, which is only suitable for land-rovers (walking time about 2½ hours), after making its way through the Val de l'Enfer, finishes at a little refuge hut at the entrance to the Vallée des Merveilles. During the short summer months this hut, at an altitude of some 2100 m, provides camp-beds which–apart from a tent–are the only facilities enabling the visitor to spend a few days in this inhospitable yet fascinating environment. The rock engravings mainly occupy two zones: in the Vallée des Merveilles itself and in the northwest part of Mont Bégo in a depression that opens out from the Fontanalba, between 5 and 8 km from the hut. They vary considerably in size–from a few centimetres to about 3 m in any one dir-

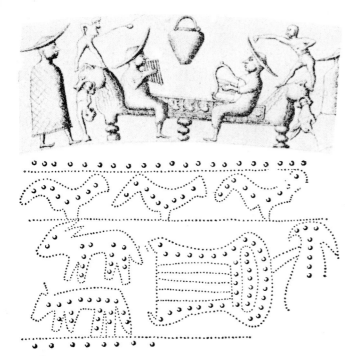

96 The scenes appearing on the works of 'situla art' inform us about early musical instruments, which, being made of organic materials, rotted away in the ground. Most frequently encountered are the pan-pipes and a small harp which the Greeks called a 'kithara'–a word that survives in the Alpine 'zither'.

with those of their daily surroundings. Thus they did not cling to the southern models but freely adapted these to suit their own idiom. To this extend, situla art must count as an original achievement of the East Alpine region, as a product of the intimate southern contact with the expanding world of the Etruscans and Greeks from the sixth century BC.

Towards 400 BC the last of these works were produced. True, they repeat the old motifs, but in style and artistic content they are inferior to the earlier masterpieces. The time of festivals was over, and even in the East Alpine and Venetic region which at first was not directly affected, the unrest caused by the Celtic migrations put an end to the safe world and the self-indulgent festivals. Nothing shows

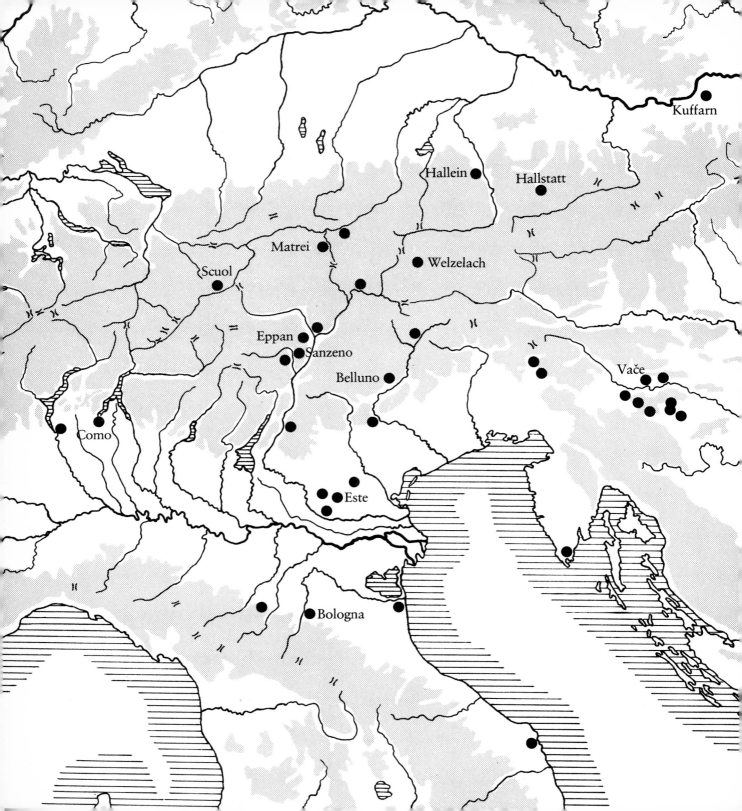

Kuffarn

Hallein

Hallstatt

Matrei

Welzelach

Scuol

Eppan

Sanzeno

Belluno

Vače

Como

Este

Bologna

ection–and are many of them composite pictures: geometric forms, weapons and implements, as well as human figures. Identifiable are oxen drawing a plough, daggers and halberds, spears and axes, heads of cattle and stags, intermingled with human beings shown in different postures and varying degrees of stylization.

The remoteness of this region, away from the agriculturally exploitable valleys and with little attraction for herdsmen, leads us to the conclusion that this was a sacred area which was only visited for the purpose of worshipping a god. Seeing how frequently the different motifs are represented, the god and the bull would seem to have had a close relationship.[84] It may be that the unpredictability of the Alpine weather, the conspicuous mountain round which storms rage, or which is shrouded in mist or cloud, was compounded with the bull's savage nature, to form an image which found expression in the rock carvings. If the bull (or, more usually, the ox) was often depicted as a draught animal for the plough, it was probably less as a simple representation of a life-sustaining activity,[85] than an attempt to harness the ancient powers symbolically and put them at the service of man. The god of Mont Bégo was thus the lord of the weather and of the storm, a god whom the Bronze Age inhabitants of the Maritime Alps worshipped with fear in their hearts and for whom they permanently recorded their wishes and prayers in stone. It may be that they–like the Romans after them and the faithful in the pilgrim churches–carved much of this only after their petitions had been granted, but this is something we can no longer tell.

A chronological classification of the weapons depicted shows that the cult was restricted to the Early and Middle Bronze Age (about 1800–1400 BC). There are no indications whatever that it continued into the Iron Age. Yet the

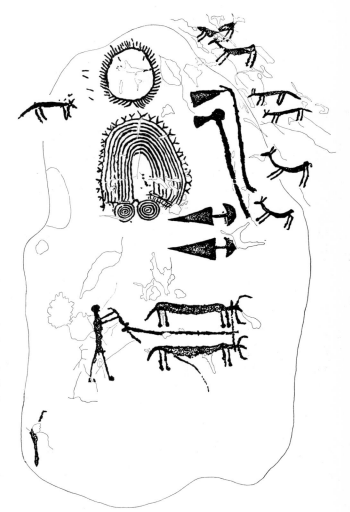

97 The distribution map of the works of 'situla art' in the 6th and 5th centuries BC encompasses a territory in which specific ceremonies took place that are rendered archaeologically intelligible through pictorial representations. The creation of an independent art form presupposes a certain solidarity on the part of the peoples and tribes concerned, a concordant world of the imagination, a shared need for artistic expression. To what extent a loose political organization was linked with this cannot be ascertained with any certainty where those early times were concerned.

98 Drawings on a rock at Bagnolo near Malegno in the Valcamonica (Lombardy): a sun-symbol, a kind of pectoral ending in a double spiral, two hatchets, two daggers, a farmer ploughing with a team of oxen, and seven further animals. Whilst motifs such as these are encountered on many rock-drawings, it is not possible to determine the true significance either of the individual representations or of the composition as a whole; besides which not all of it seems to have been incised at the same time. 2500–1500 BC. Ht 1.2 m.

Roman period is again represented, in the shape of a clearly legible inscription:

Hoc qui scripsit patri(s) mei filium pedicavit
He who wrote this engaged in unchaste behaviour with my father's son.

Faced with the unequivocal nature of the message (at Pompeii are to be found several inscriptions with similar homosexual implications[86]), archaeologists are at a loss to explain why the writer should have chosen this particular place to perpetuate his name. At all events, it is in keeping with the Romans' addiction to scribbling and their candour, that this period should be represented here by that kind of inscription.

Of more recent date are incised designs made with thin strokes: tree-like and geometric figures, zigzag lines, men and birds make up the picture. These, too, most likely pertain to Roman times, and still more recent inscriptions and scenes of various kinds (some of them bearing a date) seem to hint at what the earlier pictures put into the minds of herdsmen, deserters and robbers after living up there for a time. Oddly enough, there are several depictions of sailing ships among them, obviously incised by people who were able to reproduce details that were true to the originals.

If the high-altitude valleys round Mont Bégo can on account of their situation lay claim to be regarded as sacred areas which were visited at particular times, such an interpretation seems at first sight less applicable to the Valcamonica. For in the Oglio valley, which terminates at the Lago d'Iseo north of Brescia and opens out into the Po plain, quite different climatic and economic conditions prevail. A sequence of settlement finds, as well as graves, attest the continuous presence of people in the valley.[87] At the same time, what with the scanty building activity there and the inadequate archaeological attention paid over a long period, they provide us with no more than a limited view of what the actual conditions were like. Yet there are no grounds for assuming that the more than 100,000 rock engravings owe their existence merely to the art-loving proclivity of the valley dwellers who wished to record their daily life for posterity on the smooth surface of the rocks. Nor, on the other hand, is there any obvious reason why the Valcamonica–as opposed to neighbouring

valleys–should have had such an attraction for the people in the immediate and more distant sourroundings, that they expressed their devotion to one or more deities there in the form of votive pictures–for that is virtually what these rock engravings were.[88]

The investigations in this area were carried out by Emmanuel Anati, who worked there from 1956 on; he has meanwhile founded his own internationally renowned Institute[89] and has initiated countless students in the problems posed by the rock engravings. Individual examples, it is true, had been noticed as early as 1929 but it was not until thirty years later that planned investigation and recording were instituted; today a National Park at Capo di Ponte encompasses the most readily accessible rock engravings. Visitors are advised to leave their car down by the main road or by the cemetery just to the east of it, and then to proceed on foot up the narrow road (at the top of which there is only a tiny car park) or along the more direct footpath to the Park enclosure above. On the opposite side of the valley above Capo di Ponte lies the village of Cemmo, near which two boulders bearing a multitude of engravings have been laid bare[90] (half-title); fenced in; to obtain the key it is best to apply at the Centro Camuno di Studi Preistorici, to the left of the road between Capo di Ponte and Cemmo). Around Capo di Ponte anybody who wishes can go looking for rock engravings. The boulders, their surfaces ground smooth, lie all over the place and thanks to the attention of the Centro Camuno many of the pictures have been cleared of moss and other growths. Some still bear traces of white paint applied during cataloguing in order to make the outlines clearer.

Unlike at Mont Bégo, the rock engravings of the Valcamonica were executed over a period of many centuries–actually, it would seem, from the Late Stone Age up until the Roman invasion. By taking overlapping into consideration and analysing the objects depicted, archaeologists have been able to divide up the engravings into stylistic

99   For precise documentation students from many countries are put to work on reproducing the rock-pictures of the Valcamonica (Lombardy). The figures, after cleaning, are traced with a felt pen on a transparent sheet. These sheets then go to the Centro di studi preistorici in Capo di Ponte (Brescia province, Lombardy) to be expertly evaluated and housed.

groups, which for the most part succeeded one another. Further subdivision into 'phases', such as Anati claims to have recognized, is however carrying categorization too far, in that it does not take into account the fact that most forms of artistic expression are enduring.

The earliest rock engravings are elementary compositions, depicting only markedly schematized human figures, heads of bulls and primitive ploughs. The Bronze Age saw the advent of more comprehensive scenes, groups of animals and above all illustrations of weapons, implements, vehicles and houses (Ill. 40). During the first millennium BC the number of battle scenes increased; men out hunting with a dog and women at the loom are also identifiable (Ill. 63).

While on the one hand certain similarities to situla art[91] can be attributed to synchronism, they are so much the more noticeable because the number of pictorial motifs is in both instances very limited. Yet the extent to which they correspond is not so large, nor are they so near to one another in what they convey, as to enable one to conclude that in the Valcamonica the people had no bronze buckets but used the natural rock surfaces for depicting a combination of themes based on the 'great festival'. What we do notice is that battle scenes are much more numerous, while the ceremonial procession of warriors, unequivocally portrayed, is lacking. In this connection, quantitative analyses of whole zones of rock engravings which appear to possess a certain identity of intention and composition might perhaps come in useful. Even so, this is scarcely likely to help solve the basic problem as to why the Valcamonica in particular was for many centuries the most important nucleus of Alpine rock art.[92] But that, if anything, adds to the attraction of this valley.

In the case of the rock engravings in Austria, researched by Ernst Burgstaller,[93] it is once again the eeriness and remoteness of the locality that is paramount. The name 'Höll' (Hölle = Hell) in the Totes Gebirge, the all but inaccessible Kienbachklamm (= Kienbach ravine) at Bad Ischl and even the 'Hexenwand' (= witches' wall) on the Dürrnberg at Hallein (Salzburg) speak for themselves. The many incised pictures from medieval and still later times make it difficult to certify the prehistoric character of each individual representation. For much of what appears on the rock faces comprises merely geometric and other undateable forms. Only a few of the drawings are of human beings, animals or identifiable objects. They accord quite well with the world of Alpine rock art and most of them appear to have originated in the first millennium BC. Worth noting are a few inscriptions in the Kienbachklamm, of which one in Latin could be deciphered:

Dedicated to Mars Latobius!
Latobius has fulfilled his vow, willingly and according to merit Sextus Flavius.

Mars Latobius was the tribal god of the Noricans and his principal sanctuary was on the Magdalensberg in Carinthia (Ill. 83). This inscription, in association with the Christian-inspired engravings of later centuries, strengthens the suspicion that pre-Roman rock art was not intended to represent general concepts or scenes of daily life, but should be seen rather as being associated with the invocation and worship of a god. The pictures can in this way render visible the deity in his 'pictorial manifestation' as warrior, as animal, as symbol–for instance as the 'Bull God' of Mont Bégo–or depict activities and events which had a direct bearing on the deity or the worship accorded him, as most likely did the situla art too. With the intrusion of Roman culture and thinking, respect for and worship of the native gods did not cease but took a different form. The ability to express oneself in writing acted as a considerable curb on pictorial and material offerings. It will be remembered that the same thing happened in the case of the cults centred around the heights and the springs, where all of a sudden the small bronze tablet and the convenient coins replaced the weapons and other objects previously used as votive offerings.

For the sake of completeness, reference should be made to the rocks of Carschenna at Sils in the Domleschg (Graubünden), which bear abstract designs and a few figural drawings.[94] There are some rock engravings in the Valais as well.[95] The stelae and menhirs with figural art from Sion and the rest of the Valais, the French Alps[96] and South Tyrol[97] mostly fall into the burial customs category and were discussed above (pp. 113ff.). On the other hand, the decorated boulders in the Veltlin[98] are closely allied to the early rock drawings of the Valcamonica.

Rocks or boulders in which so-called cup-marks, little hollows nearly always haphazardly distributed, have been scooped out almost merit a chapter of their own.[99] As these

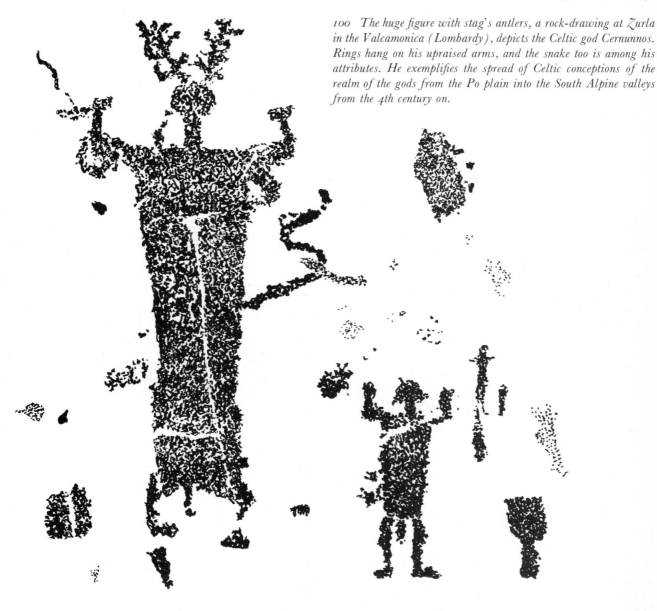

100 The huge figure with stag's antlers, a rock-drawing at Zurla in the Valcamonica (Lombardy), depicts the Celtic god Cernunnos. Rings hang on his upraised arms, and the snake too is among his attributes. He exemplifies the spread of Celtic conceptions of the realm of the gods from the Po plain into the South Alpine valleys from the 4th century on.

hollows themselves provide no clue as to their age, estimates of when they originated vary between the Late Stone Age and medieval times; this is understandable since these rocks are known to have attracted the attention of and been venerated by the people in the vicinity from time to time down the centuries, on account of this remarkable feature. How these little bowl-shaped hollows should be interpreted is also disputed,[100] chiefly because the traditional uses to which they were put in the Middle Ages and in more recent times (for candles, for holding milk, etc.)[101] do not throw any light on their original purpose. Attempts to read some sort of system into the arrangement of the cup-marks on certain rocks and to find a connection with points of the heavens[102] which, from astronomical observation, have a special significance at certain times of the year, fail to convince.

Sun, bird, horse and other gods

The need to reckon with the possibility that what at first sight appear to be random figures and symbols in the rock engravings constitute a thematic unity is brought out with great clarity by the cult wagon of Strettweg in Styria.[103] The concept of a 'cult wagon' originated with the

101 It was not until 1965 that the rock-drawings of Carschenna above Sils in the Domleschg (Graubünden) were discovered. They are punched into surfaces ground smooth by the glacier. Little dish-like hollows, circles, spirals and plain lines predominate, with just a few figures of animals and one highly stylized rider. Thus it is impossible to give an exact date for these drawings. Casts in the Rätische Museum, Chur and in the Schweizerische Landesmuseum, Zurich.

102 *Bronze cult-wagon from Strettweg, municipality of Juden-burg (Styria). In the centre stands a large female figure with upraised arms, wearing a small toque and a broad waistband. Above her head, supported by cable-like bars, is a shallow bowl. Arranged symmetrically in front and behind her are two similar groups of figures: a human couple (the man brandishes a battle-axe, the woman, who wears ear-rings, has her right arm slightly* *raised in a sort of welcoming gesture), and two persons of indeterminate sex who are leading an ill-proportioned stag with a small body and a large head by its enormous antlers. At the outside edge are helmeted horsemen with spear and shield. The base-plate has an open-work radial pattern; heads of cattle are affixed to the axles. Ht of central female figure 22.6 cm. Steiermärkisches Landesmuseum Joanneum, Graz.*

archaeologists, who today still, nearly 130 years after its discovery, argue among themselves about the meaning and purpose of this remarkable object. They are, however, agreed on some points: first, the 'cult wagon' comes from the grave of a wealthy man, buried in the sixth century BC. Secondly, little vehicles with bowls or buckets on top are to be found in comparably rich graves of this period elsewhere;[104] hence the added figural decoration does not necessarily explain the main purpose of the artefact. Thirdly, the base plate with its ray-like slots suggests a connection with sun worship. In the fourth place, there is no compelling argument against the Strettweg wagon having in fact been conceived and executed in the East Alpine region (unspecified doubts about the artistic capabilities of the craftsmen there can be discounted). But there is no way of determining what lies behind the combination of central female figure, mounted warrior, man and woman, androgynous being, stags, heads of cattle and sun emblem. To interpret it in terms of a fertility cult would be mere guesswork and essentially unsatisfying since we just don't know anything about what was in the minds of the maker and user of the wagon. We can, however, dismiss the idea that it was just an exceptionally ornamental piece of table decoration, as folklorists with half an eye on trivial present-day replicas would have us believe.[105]

The people of ancient times were well aware of the meaning of the symbols with which they surrounded their lives. Over the centuries much may have become diminished or changed, but it is only in the far-off fringe areas of a culture that alien symbols might conceivably have been adopted without retaining their inherent significance. The force of this argument is clearly demonstrated

103 The 'cauldron-wagon', of which the Strettweg 'cult-wagon' is an actual ornate version, is also to be found among the rock-drawings of the Valcamonica (Lombardy). The miniature 'cauldron-wagons' were ostensibly only symbols though at the same time they conveyed the quintessence of a ceremony in which large bronze cauldrons mounted on proper vehicles with draught-animals were paraded around. 8th–5th century BC.

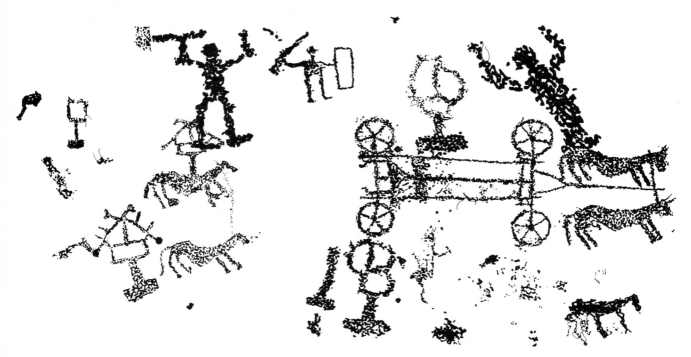

by the symbolism in Central Europe during the Late Bronze/Early Iron Age.[106] Here the 'bird barque', a vessel with a bird's head at either end, plays an important role. The birds are nearly always clearly identifiable as water-fowl. In its augmented form the 'barque' carries a sun-disc, and when this comes to the fore the vessel assumes a corresponding rounded shape, though naturally it is still meant to be a 'bird barque'. In a variant of this the sun was replaced by a human figure, the personification of a god.

In the Apollo cult of the early Greeks the same symbols appear: the sun and the swans which draw the carriage. Here echoes of the Central European-Balkan representational pattern of a sun-god are still perceptible.[107] A little later the horse appears on the scene as a new and at once important symbol; any mingling with the 'bird/sun barque' is, however, rare and limited to a later period. How much this religious world of the 'bird/sun barque' and the horse image was an integral part of an associated image of 'God and the world' is shown by its disappearance at a stroke in the fifth century. At that time a new religious movement was launched to the north of the Alps, which expressed itself artistically in the La Tène style so characteristic of the Celts.[108] This made but few inroads into the Alpine region (apart from the Salzburg urban centres in the North with their widespread connections), so that here the waterfowl of earlier times still numbered among the individual objects represented at this late stage (Ills 104–105).

We have already encountered some native deities whose names we know from Latin inscriptions in which they are partly equated with Roman gods. At the sacred spring of Steinberg on the Achensee a god named Castor was wor-

104 Orientalizing patterns deriving from northern Italy and indigenous motifs are combined on this bronze belt-buckle from Hölzelsau near Kufstein (Tyrol): the traditional water-fowl and the 'Master of the Animals' reduced to a manikin between two S-shaped bodies of animals with double horse-heads. In order to fasten the two-ply belt, the narrow tongue was inserted, its front edge pressed home against the grooved fitting and finally held in place by means of the circular projecting knob at the end. About 400 BC. L 16 cm. Prähistorische Staatssammlung, Munich.

shipped, in Este a goddess of healing, Reitia, after whom
the entire tribal group of the Raeti may have been
named,[109] on the Magdalensberg in Carinthia, Latobius.
A votive inscription on a bronze bucket from the Piave
valley refers to a goddess Loudera,[110] who appears in a
Latinized form as Libera and is the female counterpart of
Dionysus, the god of wine. On bronze discs from Montebelluna, likewise in the Piave valley, a goddess(?) in a long
robe is depicted, whose attribute is a large key.[111] The
numerous Venetic inscriptions and the ability, here too, of
their originators to express themselves pictorially provide,
at least for the East Alpine area, some information about
the native gods, their attributes, their 'field of duties' and
sometimes even about their names.[112] In the West, on the
other hand, the fund of sources is far scantier; apart from
the Celtic or Ligurian surnames of Roman gods, nothing
has come down to us.

Jupiter and his retinue

When the Romans advanced into the Alps they brought
their gods with them. Since the old Italic deities were subjected to strong Greek influences in Rome, there was assi-
milation of various sorts. But, in contrast to the Greeks,
the Romans had retained virtually no mythology, no
stories of the creation of the world and the doings of the
gods. Of more importance was a god's function, his sphere
of responsibility. One had to know to whom one should
address oneself for any specific purpose and what sacrifices
or rites were prescribed. This meant that the relationship

*105 In the South Alpine valleys of Switzerland the native bronze-
workers already treated Etruscan models in a somewhat arbitrary
manner. In the case of certain flagons, on the hinge between the handle and the fastening-plate, the Southern motifs are replaced by
water-fowl, which theme can be ultimately traced back to the Central European 'bird/sun barque' of the Late Bronze Age. The
Lepontic inscriptions on the flagon from Giubiasco (canton
Ticino), while legible, cannot be deciphered with any certainty.
That the flagon was made in the Ticino can be deduced from the
fact that its body was made up of several separate parts and not
fashioned in one piece, as the Etruscans knew how to do. 470–430
BC. Ht 38 cm. Schweizerisches Landesmuseum, Zurich.*

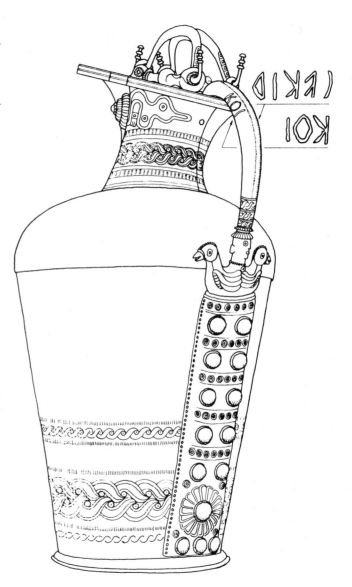

of the Romans to their gods resembled a legal transaction; it was an impersonal one quite unlike that of the Greeks, whose gods dwelt on Mount Olympus like a big family with all their 'human' failings, and occupied much of their time playing practical jokes.

The Roman gods were all very earnest, headed by Jupiter (originally a weather god), his consort Juno (representing women and the family) and Minerva (tutelary goddess of Rome and later, like Athene, protectress of the arts and crafts), and continuing with the god of war Mars, Ceres the goddess of corn-bearing earth, and the huntress Diana. Bacchus, the god of fertility and wine, was by virtue of his stimulating sphere of operations accorded somewhat more personal veneration, but ostensibly the

most popular was Mercury, counterpart of the Greek messenger god Hermes. He was patron of travellers, and in early times these were mainly merchants. Thus he became protector of money-making in general, shown not only with winged shoes but also with a purse in his hand. It was

106 The narrow frieze of the commemorative arch at Susa (Ill. 15) shows a Roman-style sacrificial procession: horsemen, trumpeters, servants carrying the cauldrons and leading to the altar the animals to be sacrificed: two bulls, a ram and a pig. The difference between it and the many 'triumphal arches' of later times is unmistakable, for the scenes depicted on the latter glorify above all the achievements in battle of the emperor.

in keeping with the mentality of the Romans, that thieves also invoked him, for in the long run robbery also counted as a way of making money (or, to put it another way, many a citizen regarded the difference between grasping traders and thieves only as a question of degree).

Jupiter, Juno and Minerva as principal deities constituted the 'Capitoline Triad', and every town had a temple or tripartite temple complex dedicated to them.[113] This underlined the omnipresence of the city gods of Rome and so of the State itself. These temples therefore stood for the most part on the *forum*, the main square, and were the focal point of the official cults. They did not serve as meeting places for the faithful, but only to house the statue of the god. The sacrifices were made at altars in front of the building, which itself sometimes stood in a walled sacred precinct, as for example at *Cambodunum*/Kempten (Ill. 51). As a rule the gods received only a part of the meat (if not merely the entrails), the remainder being eaten by the celebrants or distributed to the poor. Among the sacrificial offerings were also bread, fruit, corn, milk, oil, wine and incense, all things which in the ordinary way leave no archaeological evidence. The citizen was expected to follow the same procedure at home, though on a lesser scale. A domestic altar housed bronze or clay statues of gods, and here on important occasions the head of the family offered-up prayers and sacrificed a small object. Every house possessed in addition its own lar, a benign house spirit; hence the name *lararium* applied to the altar.

Besides the above-named gods there were many more, less important ones, whose popularity varied from place to place, from region to region and in relation to occupation: Vulcan, god of smiths and of fire and the furnace; Sylvanus, god of flocks and the woods; Neptune, god of the waters. They frequently appear in inscriptions on altars, memorial slabs, votive tablets and sundry articles. For when a god had fulfilled a petition, the pledged offering became his, as the formula *v(otum) s(olvit) l(ibens) m(erito)* referred to earlier repeatedly stresses: the devotee 'fulfilled his vow willingly and according to merit'.

The official religion of Rome was decisively revolutionized under Emperor Augustus by his pronouncement that the *genius* of Caesar, the immortal soul of his great predecessor, was imbued with divine attributes and that he should thenceforth be revered as a god. That was the beginning of the emperor cult in Rome, which ultimately led to the emperor acquiring the status of a god already in his lifetime. The forms taken by the cult were the customary ones, and its own priesthood, the *flamines Augustae*, was inaugurated. As posts of honour, which were not difficult for rich people to come by, they feature in large numbers of grave and memorial inscriptions in the Alpine region.

Yet with the emperor cult the Roman religion was extended in one respect only, one in which the citizen put little trust because of its blinkered ideological viewpoint, its rigidity, and ultimately its pointlessness and lack of substance. In the provinces, as in Rome, the official oracles and soothsayers partially met the irrational aspects of contemporary life and thought, while at the same time every conceivable form of superstition flourished everywhere.

107 It is not until Roman times that many of the native gods, Celtic and Inner Alpine, assume concrete form for us, because prior to that standardized portrayals are largely lacking and it is not possible to link them with names appearing in inscriptions. The Celtic goddess Epona was very popular in the area between the Loire and the Neckar; she is generally shown on horseback. One of the rare depictions found farther to the East is this limestone relief from Bregenz. 2nd–3rd century AD. L 1.03 m. Vorarlberger Landesmuseum, Bregenz.

Popular belief and magic

There has been operative through the ages a world of the imagination which could be called, if not exactly 'superstition', then at least 'popular belief'.[114] Even this term naturally met with the disapproval of those superior and cultured members of society who felt obliged to conform to the standard religion or philosophy of their day and considered themselves above bothering with the magic practices of simple people. All the same, many members of the upper class adhered to the popular beliefs and associated practices.

In particular the belief in demons, beings that stand between gods and men, was common ground in antiquity and was adopted by Christianity in the form of the Devil and his accomplices–to this very day in the Catholic Church. The world of demons stemmed from man's tendency to personify everything that affected him and to see it as a living being: the sun, the rain, which made the corn grow (or failed to do so), the hail which devastated it, the ailments which tormented and cast men down, the will-o'-the-wisps of the fens, the hallucinations brought on by a day's march across snow-bound mountain passes, the wind howling round the house. But there were also good demons who dwelt in curative plants, who prevented the house from being struck by lightning, and who watched over the cattle on the upland pastures.

A special group of demons was made up of persons who had died. In ancient Greece in particular it was widely believed that every human being was allotted a certain life span,[115] and that anybody who died in an unforeseen manner, owing to an accident, through being murdered or while still a child (even single or childless individuals were regarded as 'unfulfilled'), had to roam about as a restless spirit for the time that was still owed him. Also dead persons who had not been buried or whose burial had not been according to the rules, molested the living if these did not make good the omission in the appropriate manner.

People did not merely believe in demons but also in the ability of certain materials or forms to influence events by giving aid or protection. In many instances a direct analogy lay behind such notions, as for example when teeth were hung round little children's necks in order to promote easier teething; prehistoric stone axes, which were held to have descended from the heavens, were looked upon as a protection against thunderbolts, a red stone to be able to staunch bleeding. At the same time people were convinced that imprecations could do literal harm to others, provided they were uttered in a particularly telling manner. Everyone was conversant with magic incantations, whether intelligible or not, and in general each individual felt himself perpetually exposed to influences of one kind or another which needed to be curbed.

All this can be verified by reference to countless Greek and Roman sources. Concerning those periods for which literary testimony is lacking we may draw certain conclusions, but the findings offer far less choice since it is the graves alone that can provide any useful information. In them we often find objects that have served as amulets up until recent times,[116] and occasionally we can actually discover why the person in question needed them for protection.

Thus on the Dürrnberg at Hallein, the wealthy salt-metropolis, a child's grave was found which, because of the large quantities of amulets it contained, departs from the norm for Central Europe at the time in question.[117] Two of the three neck-rings are ornamented with threaded beads and fragments of bronze rings. Two large necklaces had been placed on the child's body. As well as standard and costly beads (some displaying the primeval 'eye' motif, one of the most important symbols for warding-off evil), they are made up of two big amber rings and five bronze pendants, whose design clearly has a magic significance: a wheel, two triangles, an axe, a pointed shoe. Beside the head there lay yet another long string of amber beads; for amber and glass too possessed magic properties which set them far above mere 'decoration'–and so, incidentally, did coral. But what was it that called for this child's need of protection? Analysis of the teeth provided the necessary anthropological clue (all the rest of the bones had virtually rotted away). Although the little girl was between seven and ten years old, she cannot have been taller than 80 cm, to judge by the position of the neck-, arm- and leg-rings. That is to say her body was stunted, and it is to be assumed that she had worn most of the amulets while still alive, because she needed protection. That the parents made provision also for the time succeeding her death, by laying the string of amber beads

beside her and possibly adding further ornaments to the necklaces, betokens their loving care, but perhaps also a cautious attitude towards this human being who could seek revenge for its sad fate and its premature death.[118]

Over long periods of time the categories into which amulets fall remained unchanged. In some cases it was the form they took that counted: shoe, axe, human and animal figurines, pendants like little baskets, triple rings. The uninhibited use of sexual symbols is particularly noticeable among the Romans. In other cases it was to the material that special properties were ascribed: iron was regarded as highly effective against demons; it was on lead that the Romans wrote down their imprecations;[119] to glass, amber and coral, which have already been mentioned, must be added rare minerals (jasper, meteoric stone, marble). Significant form and arresting material are most often combined in objects from the animal realm: teeth of bear and stag, boar's tusks, shells, burrs of stag's antler; but there were also pebbles with holes in them. Another point to note is that arresting features stand out all the more for the reason that collections of amulets often contain articles which had come from a different district, and these, whole or fragmented, had now become exotic objects which were invested with magic properties. The same applies to artefacts from earlier periods, which somebody happened to have come across and instinctively recognized as the handiwork of men in bygone days: flint spearheads, stone axes, bronze rings, pendants, fragments of glass arm-rings, coins.

In Roman times, too, people openly confessed to their faith in preventive magic. Countless amulets from their settlements and graves[120] go to show this, as does their fondness for masks, caricatures, animal heads affixed to the doors of houses,[121] wagons, furniture and implements. Later, in early medieval times, it was long the custom for

108 Since the finds in Grave 71/2 from the Dürrnberg above Hallein (Salzburg province) were still exactly in place, it has been possible to arrive at the approximate size of the child's interred body, even though the bones with the exception of a few teeth had decayed. In addition to a variety of rings there were two necklaces of glass beads and amulets as well as an amber chain placed by the head. 430–400 BC. Keltenmuseum, Hallein.

Teuton women to carry a pouch attached to the belt by a ribbon, in which they kept little utensils of everyday use and a few amulets.[122] For these, too, the women needed in their daily life and wished to have always by them, often visibly hung on the ribbon or sewn to a leather strap. The incursion of Christianity in the area north of the Alps during the sixth and seventh centuries had but little effect on this; the 'pagan' amulets were simply replaced as time went on by Christian tokens.[123] In the Romanic zone, especially among the Burgundians, who were soon converted to Christianity, the visible belt became the chosen vehicle for the guardian concept; by preference it was adorned with Christian scenes and symbols. On the other hand hanging amulets from the belts was all but discontinued.[124] In this connection we eagerly await the evaluation of the many cemeteries recently laid bare in the Burgundian zone, to see whether there is any distinction between the symbolism attaching to the men's and the women's belts respectively. What has already been ascertained is that at least the wide bronze buckles on which the Christian scenes are particularly well represented seem to be a component of the women's attire.[125]

Since most Romans were able to write, we find them indulging in other magical practices too. During excavations at the city of *Cambodunum*/Kempten a lead tablet[126] was found which, in view of the traces of mortar adhering to it, must have been built into a wall. In clearly legible italic writing an unknown person wills a man named Quartus to be struck dumb, better still to die at once. Here we have a document that has ostensibly a bearing on a lawsuit: he who is dumb cannot defend himself in a court of law, but must lose the case. As apposite demons the *Mutae Tacitae*, the dumb ones, the silent ones, are invoked:

109 Phallic amulets were very popular with the Romans. The effectiveness of this talisman from the Auerberg near Schongau (Allgäu) is enhanced by the symbol of the crescent moon and above all by the obscene 'fig' gesture, which is still much in evidence in Mediterranean countries. First half of the 1st century AD. Bronze; Ht 5.8 cm. Prähistorische Staatssammlung, Munich.

Mutae Tacitae!
ut mutus sit Quartus,
agitatus erret ut mus fugiens aut avis adversus basyliscum
ut eius os mutum sit, Mutae!
Mutae (d)irae sint.
Mutae! Quartus ut insaniat,
ut Eriniis rutus sit Quartus et Orco.
ut Mutae tacitae
ut mutae sint ad portas aureas.

O Mutae Tacitae!
May Quartus be dumb,
may he stumble around despairingly like a fugitive mouse or
  a bird face to face with the Basilisk.
May his mouth be silent, O Mutae!
May the Mutae be terrible,
may the Mutae be silent.
O Mutae! May Quartus go out of his mind,
May Quartus be banished to the Erinnyes and to the Orcus.
May the Mutae be silent,
may they be dumb by the golden gates.

This document, not unlike a litany, speaks for itself, even if some details, as for instance the 'golden gates' (of Elysium, of Paradise?), are not clear to us. Probably it was not enough merely to write down the text and conceal it in some suitable place, but an accompanying rite, such as a sacrificial offering, was called for. Indeed, we have a maledictory tablet from Carthage, which records what else the prompter or the sorcerer has done.[127] It deals with much the same problem as does the tablet from Kempten, namely the striking dumb of an adversary. In addition, the ancestor spirits were invoked: 'Just as I have torn out the tongue of the living cock and firmly nailed it down, so may they silence the tongues of my adversaries, should these wish to say anything against me. A find in a little sanctuary in Mautern (Lower Austria) establishes the connection between imprecation and sacrifice, for the lead tablet shut in a small jar in which the ashes of the burial offering were preserved.[128]

Such tablets were employed, not only to lay a curse on someone but also, conversely, to win someone for yourself.[129] This is attested by a slim tablet found in a *villa* at Peiting near Schongau,[130] in the foundations at one corner of the building. Since the text cannot be interpreted as certainly[131] as that of the Kempten maledictory tablet, there is no need to reproduce it here. In point of fact it refers to a love-spell by which a man named Clemens sought to establish a binding relationship with a certain Gemella. In particular he exhorts her to love him even when he is out of her sight, and the wording as a whole makes it clear that he had more than mere platonic love in mind. Its author tried to heighten the magic effect by writing from bottom left to top right and distorted the characters just as it entered his head.

Hope of redemption from the East

The difficulty the citizen had in identifying with the official Roman religion, the growing political and social tensions within the Empire and the resulting anxiety over his existence experienced by the individual prepared the way for the new religions from the East.[132] These were 'religions of deliverance', promising the faithful a joyous life and physical resurrection after death, instead of a shadowy existence. This led to the formation of closed socie-

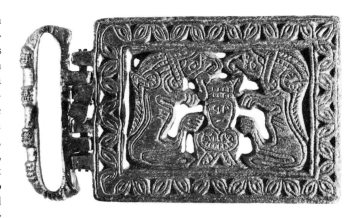

110 Christian motifs abound on belt-buckles of the Burgundian kingdom. The story of Daniel in the lions' den was particularly popular, for it was seen as symbolizing the victory of the faithful over the powers of evil. Thus the wearer of this buckle from Riaz (canton Fribourg) depicting two mighty lions which seem to be menacing a somewhat hapless Daniel instead of licking his feet – as they should be doing – will have expected it to afford him active protection from the perils of daily life. Middle of the 6th century AD. *Bronze; L 10 cm. Service archéologique cantonal, Fribourg.*

ties, to qualify for which involved detailed instruction and many ceremonies, and this greatly strengthened the sense of solidarity. Its spread was expedited above all by traders, soldiers and slaves, who – each in their own capacity – were often called upon to go to the farthest reaches of the Empire.[133]

Initially, the most important among the new gods was Mithras[134] from Persia, who fought all things evil. Cult pictures show him leaping on to the back of a bull and stabbing it with a dagger. How widely the cult was disseminated in the second and third centuries is indicated by the presence of a little Mithraeum even at the high-altitude stopping-place of *Immurium* on the Tauern road (Ill. 135). From Egypt came the Apis bull, symbol of fertility, of life, death and resurrection, besides Osiris, Isis and Serapis. A Phrygian-Near Eastern version of the Greco-Roman Dionysos cult was that of Sabasios. He can be inferred from bronze votive hands with all manner of symbols and animals, among which reptiles such as the snake, the toad and the lizard represent the powers of the Underworld. *Aventicum*/Avenche and the Great St Bernard are two places where examples have been found.[135] Soldiers brought from Syria the cult of Dolichenus,[136] the Baal of Dolichene who was equated with Jupiter. The most important find came from Mauer on the Url (Lower Austria),[137] where during a Teuton invasion of the third century the Dolichenus priests concealed the entire contents of a sanctuary near the fort: votive plaques of bronze and silver, bronze figurines of Jupiter Dolichenus and of Victoria, lamps, cauldrons, sieves, jugs, even a little ink-pot and, oddly enough, several steelyards (traders' offerings?), plus sundry iron utensils (from the priests' household?); 88 objects all-told, which remained in the ground for 1600 years because nobody any longer knew where they had been hidden.

All these religions were tolerated by the Roman State, some actually promoted by certain emperors, since they did not conflict with the emperor cult. But Christianity was a different matter, though it–like Judaism–is also one of the oriental 'religions of deliverance'. According to Christian teaching, the deification of a deceased person rather than God could not be accepted. This led, as early as the year 64, to the first persecutions of Christians under Emperor Nero. They recurred with varying degrees of intensity, reaching their peak with the rigorous measures taken by Emperor Diocletian around and after 300. Initially, every soldier in the army who refused to engage in sacrificial rites was discharged. Then gatherings of the faithful and holy writings were proscribed, Christians lost their citizenship, clerics faced imprisonment. It is estimated that of the fifty million or so citizens one in every ten was affected by these measures–a figure that indicates how strong Christianity had already grown despite all the suppression. As a result of this, Emperor Constantine I decreed in 313 that Christianity should have equal rights with the other religions, two years after Galerius had removed the obligation to sacrifice for the emperor cult. After many fluctuations, Emperor Theodosius I ultimately proclaimed Christianity the new State religion in 391, forbad all other cults and confiscated the temple treasures. Christians, now become intolerant in their turn, set the temples alight, dashed the pagan statues to pieces and cast them into pits.[138]

It is hardly to be expected that, against this background, there would be any appreciable archaeological evidence of Christianity in the Alpine region prior to the fourth century. Symbols such as A and Ω or ✳ only came into use gradually, and the small communities could not afford to build their own churches. Pictorial representations of the Christian God or of Biblical events were, still conforming as they did to earlier Jewish tradition, out of the question. So it is solely the legends of the saints, often tied to local tradition, that enable us to go back at least to the time around 300, when many of the faithful met a martyr's death: Maurice and his companions at *Agaunum* in the Valais, Victor and Urs in Solothurn, Afra in Augsburg, Florian and his companions in *Lauriacum*/Lorch, Cassianus–who is reputed to have previously journeyed to the Alps as a missionary–in Imola, Victorinus in *Poetovio*/Ptuj (Slovenia). The graves of these and other martyrs became focal points of special veneration: through them, the continuity of circumalpine Christianity in early medieval times is most easily traced.

The earliest concrete testimony of Christianity, then,

111 Magic inscription on a small lead tablet from Cambodunum/Kempten (Allgäu). The scurrying italic Roman script is much harder to decipher than the large capital letters on the stone monuments. About 3:4.

112 Mithras-worship was closely linked to a firmly implanted mythology that continually recurs on the altar-stones, including this one found in 1559 at Mauls, which is now set up in the town hall in Sterzing (South Tyrol). Mithras, the sun-god from the Orient, is killing a white bull in a grotto. Out of its blood, which the dog and the snake avidly lick up, springs new life. The two torch-bearing figures on either side symbolize East and West, Morning and Evening, Spring and Autumn. Above, Sun and Moon appear as heavenly bodies; little scenes frame the principal theme and recount further events from the life of the god. 2nd–3rd century AD. Ht 1.2 m.

stems from the fourth century: glass beakers with the inscription *vivas in deo*–may you live in God;[139] a sarcophagus with a representation of the Good Shepherd;[140] even such mundane objects as clay lamps and toothpicks[141] bore the Chi-rho sign ☧ .[142] The silver toothpick from the treasure found in the fort at Kaiseraugst (Aargau), presumably consigned to the earth shortly after 350, testifies to the adoption of the new religion and its symbols even in the highest social circles of the Empire. For this costly treasure[143] could only have belonged to the fort

commander or to the emperor himself (though this would scarcely have been Julian the Apostate, who in 361 sanctioned the pagan cults once more and reopened the temples or in some instances had them rebuilt).

Bishops and churches, monasteries and missionaries

The growing association of the Christian Church with the Roman State also affected its internal organization. A hierarchical system of clergy with the bishops at its head came into being. It may be assumed that in the Alpine region, too, from the fourth century every *municipium*, every town, had its resident bishop, whose diocese corresponded to the town area.[144] We have literary evidence for only a few, as for example the above-mentioned Victorinus from *Poetovio*/Ptuj, one in *Iulium Carnicum*/Zuglio on the Plöcken pass, Iustinianus in *Castrum Rauracense*/Kaiseraugst near Basel, Theodorus in *Octodurus*/Martigny in the Valais, and several others on the southern and western borders of the Alps, where towns with municipal rights were commoner. (This tradition has, incidentally, persisted up until the present day; in Italy far fewer believers are subordinated to one bishop than is the case north of the Alps.)

In this connection, it should be borne in mind that Christianity was at the outset mainly confined to the towns and large settlements and had but few adherents in the open country, insofar as any people at all lived there in those troubled times. Indeed, as late as 397 three clerics sent to the Val di Non by the bishop of Trento, Vigilius, lost their lives when they attempted to keep the newly baptised from taking part in the old pagan processions. And in 405 the bishop himself died for his faith, when he toppled an idol in the Rendena valley. He breathed his last amid a hail of clogs hurled at him by the enraged peasants.[145] In the Alps, then, at the beginning of the fifth century an internal mission was still in progress, carrying the Christian faith into the remote valleys. Even in Severin's day, after 460, there were still people in Noricum who clung to the old pagan sacrificial rites and whom the saint did his best to convert by way of miracles.[146]

The larger the Christian communities grew, the greater was the need for a meeting place of their own, a church.

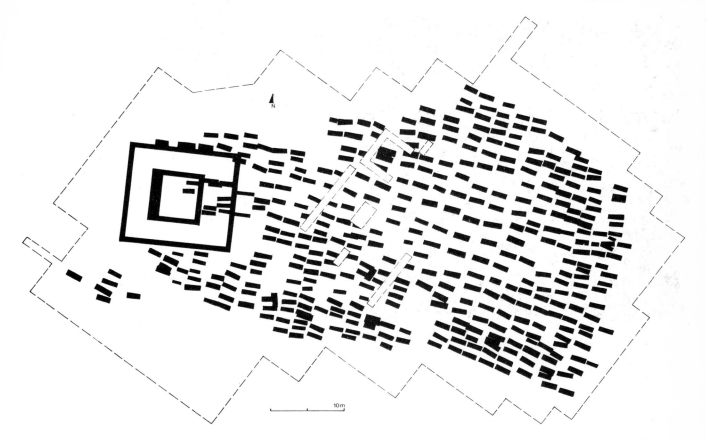

113 The cemetery of Tronche-Bélon in Riaz (canton Fribourg) is an example of the early medieval 'rowed' type of burial-ground in which the dead all face in the same direction. The 400-odd graves encroach directly on a Roman temple. During the excavations of 1973/76 no traces of any church were found even in the temple precinct. So it may be assumed that the site was chosen because the ruin-strewn terrain was unsuitable for cultivation.

Whereas during the first centuries of oppression a room in a private house sufficed–also on the grounds of safety–the custom arose in the fourth century of erecting independent buildings which from the start met liturgical needs. A distinction was drawn between parish churches inside the residential area and cemetery churches, which usually lay outside the fortifications of late antiquity. In some cases the latter can be seen to have incorporated one or more late Roman graves that lay in or close to small cemetery chapels, and so were already venerated before the church was built. Those who were interred in them did not necessarily have to be martyrs, it could have been a particularly kindly and charitable cleric or official. This sequence of late Roman burials, via a cemetery chapel *(memoria)* of the fourth or fifth century, to a sixth- or seventh-century church around which graves were again ranged in early medieval times, is of course to be expected only in the Central and Western Alpine region, where there was a continuity of inhabitants and of the faith. As examples the following may be mentioned: La Madeleine in Geneva,[147] the Reformed church in Biel-Mett,[148] St Jean-Baptiste in Ardon (Valais)[149] and Saint-Laurent in Grenoble.[150] On the other hand the situation at *Teurnia*/St Peter in Holz (Carinthia) is confusing; here, whilst the church with its unique mosaic floor in a side chapel was erected about 500 in a cemetery dating from late antiquity, the sixth-century graves came to light in a different place altogether at the foot of the hill, actually among the ruins of Roman houses.[151] In view of the new findings at Invillino Ill. 116), the whole problem of 'parish church' or 'cemetery church' urgently needs reconsideration.

The custom in late and post-Roman times of requisitioning for burials uncultivable land dotted with ruins has meant that many churches–particularly well researched in Switzerland–rest on former Roman villas,[152] without any continuity in construction being either perceptible or likely.[153] There have, naturally, been instances of the latter, however, as in the case of St Peter's in Chur-Welschdörfli, where a church was built into an existing or reconstructed private building.[154] This constructional continuity is even more evident in the church at Ursins (Vaud),[155] for which the *cella* of a temple was simply extended by adding a chancel. And if in *Axima*/Aime the church of Saint-Sigismond is set directly above a Roman temple,[156] this too is clearly to be seen as a conscious choice of location, not merely to be attributed to the convenient use of the existing hewn stones.

The early churches in the Alpine region show little uniformity of design and in their fitting-out, allowing us at the very best to recognize regional groups.[157] A characteristic feature of the churches of the fifth and possibly also of the sixth century is the priests' bench behind the altar, on which the clergymen sat during divine service, whilst the congregation had to stand. Often one seat is given prominence and is ostensibly for the bishop's use. Yet this does not in itself prove that the church was an episcopal one–as used to be all too readily assumed–because such a special seat was at the bishop's disposal when he visited his parishes for an inspection, a baptism or a confirmation.[158] Baptism was effected by immersion or at least by sprinkling water on the adult candidate. That is why the fonts are let into the floor with a few steps leading down to them. They are housed in independent or connected buildings, among which the still extant baptisteries of Fréjus and Albenga on the Mediterranean coast, as well as Riva S. Vitale in the Ticino, are impressive architectural exem-

plars from this period. Excavation has brought to light such baptisteries at a number of other places, as for example that on the Hemmaberg in Carinthia, a hexagonal building 15 m away from the frontages of two parallel churches; and recently another at Invillino (Friuli), taking the form of an extension with three apses and an altar of its own. Double churches are frequently found in the Eastern Alps and adjoining areas. One of them was probably used for divine service, the other for initiating candidates for baptism–who were particularly numerous in the fourth and fifth centuries–and for confirmations. At Lavant in East Tyrol the two stand on a hill, one behind the other (their ground plans can still be inspected), no doubt for lack of space on account of the steepness of the slope.

Should a church not have been built over or beside a martyr's grave, then at least a holy relic was indispensable. Since there was soon a dearth of genuine relics of

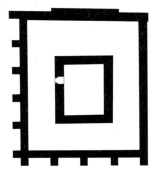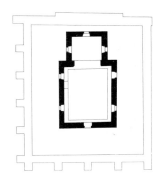

114 Occasionally ancient sources record that Roman temples were transformed into Christian churches. One of the clearest examples was laid bare by archaeologists at Ursins (canton Vaud). In conformity with the late Celtic tradition the temple had an almost square ground-plan (left) with a cella *(the inner enclosed chamber, about 10 × 8.4 m, as the sanctum of the god) and an ambulatory with columns. The* cella *was then converted into a church (right) by retaining the walls, piercing windows up above and adding a rectangular apse for the altar. Through the retention of the Roman foundation walls round the little church the visitor is afforded a clear picture of the continuity between late antiquity and medieval times in the West.*

martyrs or saints, 'touch relics' sprang up, objects of various kinds, often pieces of cloth which through contact with a genuine relic and a blessing had themselves taken on the character of a sacred article.[159] They were placed in a receptacle and let into the ground beneath the altar table. For this purpose plain boxes of stone or wood were used, but also–where resources allowed–costly and richly decorated chests or miniature caskets of ivory, bronze or even gold.[160] When the Avars conquered the East Alpine region, they soon discovered this. Before destroying the churches, they rummaged in the area of the altar, searching for valuable reliquary articles. Consequently in these

115 It was only during excavation work on the Colle Santino at Invillino (Friuli) that ruins, overgrown and barely visible, were discovered on the neighbouring Colle di Zuca. On investigation, greatly to everyone's surprise the foundations of two churches came to light, the older dating back to around AD *400. It was adorned with mosaic floors which, just beneath the soil, were in quite a good state of preservation.*

parts–unlike in the West with its uninterrupted church tradition[161]–the earliest examples of this kind have practically all vanished.

The archaeologist is therefore all the more grateful for
the mosaic in the cemetery church of *Teurnia* in Upper
Carinthia.[162] It adorns the floor of the southern side chapel, which has been reconstructed in its original form and
today constitutes the most arresting item in the museum
for *Teurnia* in St Peter in Holz, of which it forms a part.
According to the inscription, it was donated by the governor of the day, Ursus by name, somewhere around 500,
that is during Gothic rule: *Urs(us) v(ir) s(pectabilis) cum
coni(u)g(e) s(u)a (U)rsina pro(v)oto sus(cepto) fecer(unt)
h(a)ec*–Ursus and his wife Ursina have had this mosaic
made in accordance with a vow they took on. Murals are
still more rarely preserved; the remains in the funeral chapel of St Stephen in Chur allow at least an approximate
reconstruction of the paintings.

In the early fifth century a new religious movement
reached the Alpine region from the East: the ascetic
monastic ideal.[163] The first monasteries were established in
Marseille (415) and on the rock-island of St Honorat
(Lérins, the ancient *Lerinum*) off Cannes. When Severin
journeyed through Noricum in the sixties and seventies of
the fifth century, he founded little monastic communities[164] at various places, and the royal-Burgundian monastery in Saint-Maurice d'Agaune (Valais) near the saint's
grave[165] was a forerunner of the early medieval monasteries on the northern edge of the Alps.

But those are all areas where the Christian tradition continued without interruption into the Middle Ages.

On the other hand, at the northern edge of the Alps and
the adjoining foreland, where the newly arrived Germanic
settlers had established themselves, Christianity regained
general access only through determined missionary work.
The point of departure was the monastery at Luxeuil west
of the Vosges, founded about 590. The monk Eustace and
his companions journeyed eastward from here about the

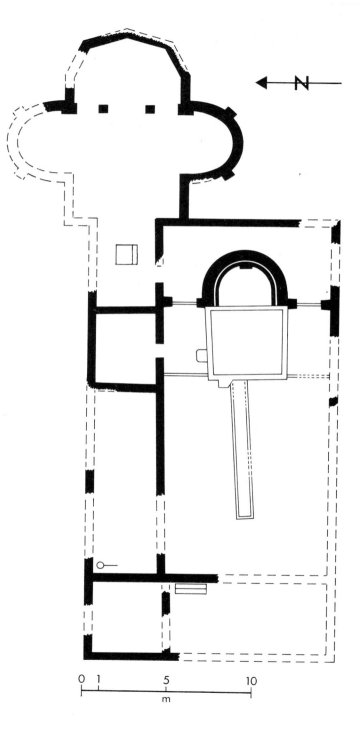

*116 The older of the two churches on the Colle di Zuca at Invillino
(Friuli) has a ground-plan that fits in well with the late Roman
traditions of the diocese of Aquileia on the Adriatic. The area
assigned to the congregation, with its narrow corridor, was separated from that of the priests by wooden partitions. The priests offi-
ciated at a semicircular stone bench round the altar. A doorway led
into a clover-leaf baptistery, in which stood another altar with a
reliquary, and a font set into the floor.*

beginning of the seventh century, in order to convert the Alamanni and above all the Bavarians. They did not meet with much success: it was the monks of the early Frankish mission of Irish-Scottish stamp (like Emmeram, Corbinian, Rupert and Boniface) who in the late seventh century helped to bring about an ultimate break-through for Christianity. Many of the leading families had, it is true, already embraced the new faith earlier. Among the first to do so was Clovis, the Frankish king who–probably in 486–had himself baptised together with some 3000 of his warriors. Towards the end of the sixth century there were mounting outward signs that Christianity was also making headway among the Alamanni,[166] whether in the shape of symbols on pieces of jewellery or the first little churches of wood or stone. During the eighth century, on the fringes of the Alps, the first monasteries were founded in the zone of mixed Romanic and Germanic peoples: St Gallen, Reichenau, Pfäfers. Farther east, Salzburg, where Rupert began to operate shortly after 700, acted as ecclesiastical centre.[167] Still farther afield were the monasteries of Innichen in the Pustertal (founded 769)[168] and Kremsmünster in Upper Austria (founded 778),[169] which served as bases for the Slav missionary movement.

To what extent the old Christian tradition remained alive in the larger settlements of the Central Alps and was absorbed into the missionary activities from the Northwest cannot be gathered either from the literary or the archaeological sources. Even though, when a synod was held in Grado between 572 and 577, there is mention for the first time of a bishop of Säben, it is still uncertain how long this bishopric had been in existence at the time and who had established it. There is no evidence to support the once-fashionable hypothesis that the bishops of Augsburg, the former provincial capital of Raetia, had retired thither.[170] At all events it would seem that after the late Roman period the episcopal see in Augsburg was no longer occupied, being only refounded around 650/660 even though the uninterrupted veneration of Saint Afra presupposes the existence of Christians in this town also in the fifth and sixth centuries.

In those early days of Christianity there was still much argument as to the system of teaching that should finally be adopted. The priority of Rome by no means went unchallenged, and the Metropolitan of Aquileia in particu-

117 Carved ivory jar with a design representing the Resurrection of Christ. On the left can be seen the two Marys and a disciple, on the right three of the soldiers who kept watch over the tomb and who fell to the ground at the appearance of the angel. The motif suggests that this receptacle was intended as a reliquary from the outset. 6th century AD. Diam. 11 cm. Musée Valère, Sion.

lar set much store by his independence, right up to the temporary break-away from the rest of the Church. Furthermore, there was, conflicting with the 'Catholic' faith, the Arian doctrine, which denied that Christ was consubstantial with God. It had found favour mainly in the east of the Roman Empire and was also adopted by the Goths, Burgundians and Lombards. It was the Bavarian ducal daughter Theudelinda, wife of two Lombard kings, who succeeded in converting the Lombards to the Catholic faith in the seventh century. Incidentally, she was not the only woman to play a part in moulding the destiny of a realm in this way. The Catholic wife of the Burgundian king Gundobad, an Arian, persuaded him to parley with the Catholic bishops; her son Sigismund, who in 515 founded the monastery of Saint-Maurice d'Agaune in the

118 In the Italy of the Lombards and later also in Alamannic territory there was a widespread custom of sewing a cross to the winding-sheet of someone who had died. It would be cut from thin sheetgold and was sometimes ornamented with the aid of such dies as were to hand and actually meant for other uses. The sheet-gold cross from Stabio (canton Ticino) with its regular ornamentation, its scrolls, birds and a quadruped in the middle, points to the sure hand of a gold- and bronzesmith who had the required models at his disposal. Since virtually no crosses in the cheaper sheet-silver or sheet-bronze are known, this custom must have been confined to the upper class. It reflects most tellingly the advance of the Christian faith among the Germanic peoples at the southern and northern fringes of the Alps.

119 Ever since it was uncovered in 1910/11 the floor-mosaic in the early Christian church in Teurnia/St Peter in Holz *(Carinthia) has aroused the curiosity of scholars. All are agreed that the various motifs were chosen with a purpose but how they are to be individually interpreted and whether their arrangement holds some secret meaning cannot be ascertained with any degree of certainty. The suckling hind and the duck with its ducklings may be symbols of 'Mother Church'. Eagle and heron with a snake stand for Christ as patron of the Church. The tree with birds points to the parable of the grain of mustard seed: '. . . and becometh a tree, so that the birds of the air come and lodge in the branches thereof'. Above it, in the centre of the axial cross, is a scene that also has a central meaning: the soul of the Christian believer, in the form of a dove, finds protection from the powers of evil (the snakes) in baptism and Holy Communion (goblet and plate). The stag in the adjoining square is a reminder to the faithful of Psalm 42: 'As the hart panteth after the water brooks, so panteth my soul after thee, O God.' About* AD *500. Approx. 5.6 × 4.2 m.*

Valais, then completed the process of conversion, thereby facilitating the fusion of the Burgundians with the Romanic peoples. And the baptism of the Frankish king Clovis is difficult to understand unless the influence of his wife Crotechilda is taken into account (a comparable case was that of King Ethelbert of Kent, whose wife had long been a Christian when in 597 he was converted by the missionary archbishop Augustine). In all three instances the rulers and the upper class adapted themselves to the faith of their resident subjects, the Romanic peoples, for they wished to avoid a confrontation with the influential Church. (It is perhaps worth mentioning here that with the entry of the various Germanic folk into Roman imperial territory its clan structure changed, moving in the direction of a territorial State system. This accorded, in the religious sphere, with the rapid renunciation of the old clan cults in favour of Christianity with its more comprehensive ordering of the divine, making intensive missionary activity here scarcely necessary.[171]) This resulted in an intermingling of secular and ecclesiastical power also in

the Romanic kingdoms, as well as an improving relationship between the Franks and the Pope in Rome (pp. 56 ff.). The coronation of Charlemagne by Pope Leo III in 800 constituted the climax and, for the time being, the conclusion of a development that ultimately led to the Holy Roman Empire.

120 High above Klausen in South Tyrol lies the convent of Säben, which carries on the tradition of the early medieval bishopric, in 992 transferred to Bressanone, 10 km to the North. Its well-nigh impregnable situation on a mountain spur between the Isarco and the gorge of a small tributary often proved to be a life-saving factor during the troubled times of the early Middle Ages.

V Mule-tracks, Passes and Resthouses

Geology and its consequences: passes and defiles

The Alps are folded mountains. Before they formed this was a wide stretch of ocean (named by geologists Tethys, both sister and spouse of the primitive Greek god Okeanos), into which over many thousands of years deposits of every kind settled in layers. When enormous forces from North and South came into conflict this sedimentary sea-bed gave way, rearing up like a giant folded cloth. In the process, the folds naturally aligned themselves mainly at right angles to the line of thrust. Long mountain ranges were formed, which run from East to West and then branch off southwards to the Mediterranean Sea. The intervening valleys were further scooped out by glaciers and deepened by rivers.

Those who wish to cross the Alps by the most direct route must cope with these conditions which Nature has created, and the degree of difficulty encountered will vary according to individual circumstances.

There is a route that runs up the broad Inn valley from Kufstein, with a barely perceptible gradient, and only really presents a problem in the Finstermünz defile close to the present-day frontier between Austria and Switzerland. The valley is aligned NE/SW, like most of the large drawn-out dales in the Alps. A last short climb takes the traveller up to St Moritz, where the valley opens out again into a plain with green lakes reflecting the wooded lower slopes of the encircling mountains. Only the clear air and the appreciably lower temperature give away the fact that here one is 1800 m above sea-level. However, beyond the last lake, Lake Sils, a unique sight meets the eye. The valley does in fact continue in the same direction, but it drops down, almost sheer, for some 250 m: this is the Maloja pass. Nowadays thirteen hairpin bends lead down into the valley basin of Casaccia, from which the Mera flows almost due West. Its valley is much narrower than that of the Inn, for the glaciers here in the South have not delved so severely, though the erosion caused by the fast-flowing water has been all the greater. (It was this that gave rise to the amazing prospect, by pushing the valley of the Mera

ever farther back eastwards into the Trog valley of the former Inn glacier, with the result that the original 'Inn' glacier is no longer connected in any way with the Inn valley, but lies above the Mera.) A few kilometers farther on, the defile of La Porta forms a natural barrier in the valley, which was fortified already by the Romans, who set up a road-station there.[1] Moreover, the frontier between Switzerland and Italy lies just beyond this point. From here it is not far to Chiavenna, where the road is joined by the one from the Splügen pass and turns southwards. The valley then widens somewhat, until the Lake of Como is reached. Prior to the building of the lakeside roads it was more convenient to proceed by water to Como, situated where the mountains no longer exceed 1500 m.

But this most accessible of all the routes across the Alps with its almost abrupt transition from the Alpine region of the Engadin to the almost Mediterranean countryside of Val Bregaglia has never played an appreciable role in history. Ease of travel was more than offset by the length of the route and the direction in which it runs. In order to save one or even two days en route, the traveller was prepared to face greater hardships and, above all, higher passes. For the passes were not the real obstacle to crossing the Alps, even if they were snowed-up in the cold season and then little used. Far more difficult to negotiate were the ravines which the rivers had gouged out as they cut their way through one longitudinal ridge after another before finally emerging into the Alpine foreland. In German, originally the word 'Pass' referred to these narrow gorges, there being no separate word for the way through on the heights. In Salzburg the saddlebacks were called 'Tauern', a name that was ultimately applied to an entire mountain range. And in Austria in particular it is used to describe ravines which, in the modern sense of the word, are not 'passes' at all. No one who drives southward along the Salzach valley road will readily forget the 'Pass Lueg'; here the Salzach has carved out a gorge deep down between the Hagengebirge and the Tennengebirge, which as early as pre-Roman times was circumvented by means of a diversionary route halfway up the mountainside. It needed the modern motorway, with its tunnel, to solve the problem in a radical manner. In South Tyrol they use the word 'Klause' for these gorges (from Lat. claudere–to close); the village of Klausen in the Adige valley lies at the northern entrance to one of the most difficult defiles in the entire Alpine region.

The usefulness of an Alpine crossing depended upon the ability to cope with these gorges, however low-lying and convenient the pass itself might be. This is most suitably illustrated by the Brenner and St Gotthard passes. North of Bolzano a gorge for long presented the traveller on his way to the Brenner pass with an insuperable obstacle. It entailed making a detour over the Ritten above Bolzano, which almost amounted to a second pass, or even through the Passeier valley across the Jaufen (2094 m). In the second century AD at the earliest, the Romans managed to forge a road through the gorge,[2] but when Roman rule came to an end this soon went to ruin; from then on until well into the Middle Ages all travellers–not excepting the Emperor and his retinue–had again to put up with the old detours.[3] Not until the fourteenth century was it technically possible to deal with the ravine once more. On 24 September 1314 Emperor Henry VII gave Heinrich Kunter, a trader and contractor from Bolzano, permission to reconstruct the road at his own expense and levy a toll. From this time on, the Brenner route came to rank anew as the most important Alpine crossing from the cosmopolitan point of view.

A more difficult problem still was posed by the Schöllenen gorge north of the St Gotthard pass. In pre-Roman and Roman times the only way of getting across will have been by following isolated paths over the Bätzberg in the West or the Fellilücke in the East, most likely by travellers trusting to luck or by locals who wished to reach the neighbouring valley by the most direct route. In spite of its central situation in the Alpine region and its relatively short approach routes from South and North, the opening-up of the pass was not undertaken until late in the twelfth century. Added to the fact that the necessary new techniques were now available, political considerations naturally made it desirable or even imperative to open up such difficult passages; in the case of the St Gotthard it was the Zähringers in central Switzerland who wanted to establish for themselves a direct route to Italy.[4] The con-

struction of daring bridges, among them the 'Teufels-brücke' (Devil's bridge)–only later rebuilt in stone–enabled the long Schöllenen gorge connecting the valley with its Andermatt and Göschenen extension to be spanned. All those who recorded their impressions of this part of the route have described their experience as 'terrifying'.

Equally impressive is the gorge above Gondo (another frontier post between Italy and Switzerland) south of the Simplon pass, though before the modern road was blasted through by Napoleonic troops it was not unduly inconvenient to by-pass it by crossing over the adjacent mountains. Better known still is the Via Mala, the 'bad way' as it is justifiably called, the gorge carved out by the Hinterrhein, which all who wanted to travel to the South from Chur across the Splügen or the San Bernadino pass had to face.[5] It is significant, too, that for example the Schnalstal, a narrow subsidiary valley of the Adige west of Merano, was not settled from the Vinschgau but via distinctly high passes in the North from the Ötztal, because the defile at the exit from the valley was virtually impassable. The still operative grazing rights of the Schnalstal herdsmen in the Ötztal and the annual droving of sheep over the snowbound passes in early summer and autumn testify to the old communications that extended beyond today's State frontiers.[6]

Then again–to conclude this general introduction to the geographical problems relating to communications–early man did not shrink from crossing an additional pass if the valley road became unusable or difficult to maintain because the meadows had become too swampy or there was a likelihood of flooding or landslides. If this should also entail a short-cut, he would not have needed long to make up his mind which route was best at any particular time of year. A case in point is the Kunkels pass (1361 m), by means of which the sharp bend of the Rhine at Chur can be by-passed by following a direct line between Bad Ragaz and Tamins at the confluence of the Vorderrhein and the Hinterrhein. More important was the Col des Mosses, to the West, since the road beside the Lake of Geneva, there where the castle of Chillon blocks the way, was first hewn into the cliff face in Roman times and the Rhône delta was still probably rather marshy. The pre-Roman line of communication, insofar as it was directed towards the North, parted from the Rhône valley at Aigle, branching off towards the east over the Col des Mosses (1445 m).

Yet it is only by indirect means that such routes, which play no more than a subordinate role these days, can be revealed; for no one is able to tell from its appearance the age of an overgrown rocky path. At a pinch, blast-holes may be a guide to more recent dating. Least speculative are those instances where the wealth and significance of a

121 Many routes crossed the Alps that form the boundary between Southern and Central Europe. Several of them were built by the Romans for vehicular use. Where abrupt slopes and above all gorges were encountered they had to resort to daring supporting structures which called for expert handling of vaulting and the application of mortar. The stretch of road above the gorge of the Bouthier between Aosta and the Little St Bernard is particularly impressive (see also Ill. 130).

settlement can only be explained by its having been situated on an important trade route and not in some out-of-way side valley. The early medieval monastery of Pfäfers, for example, high above where the Vättis valley enters that of the Rhine,[7] and the Iron Age fortification of Châtillon-sur-Glâne[8] near Fribourg (Ill. 124) are in this respect to be regarded as providing important evidence of communications of this kind.

Periods from which literary evidence has come down to us show that political circumstances also played a significant role in the choice of specific routes and passes. Thus in late antiquity the Vinschgau in present-day South Tyrol belonged to the bishopric of Chur and for long to Chur-Raetia politically. If the bishop journeyed thence for an inspection, he chose a route which, while it led over three passes, was in the first place the shortest and secondly took him through large tracts of episcopal land: from Chur (587 m) through the Schanfigg across the Strela pass (2353 m) to Davos (about 1500 m), then over the Flüela pass (2383 m) into the Lower Engadin to Zernez (1472 m) and finally over the Ofen pass (2149 m) into the Münster valley and on to the Vinschgau. Today still, even after the loss of the Vinschgau, the Graubünden frontier, which is likewise the Swiss one with Italy, runs in characteristic fashion not over the pass but in the first place below the Carolingian monastery of Müstair at an altitude of some 1200 m. Only when viewed against this background does it become clear why two fortified settlements from late Roman and early medieval times were situated behind the gorge that could only be by-passed high up the hill-side at the approach to the Schanfigg; for these must be regarded as an organized strong-point on an important route rather than hastily constructed emergency quarters in a remote valley for the inhabitants of Chur (pp. 103 and 196).

The first mule-tracks

Before the Romans arrived there were no roads over the Alps. People were thankful if they knew of paths which enabled them to contend with the passes either on foot or a bridled mule. Building wooden bridges across cascading streams, laying down brushwood or scatterings of broken stones on stretches of swampy ground, and making tracks up steep slopes more secure—all this constituted the beginnings of a network of routes that was intended for permanent use. This called for organized groups, village communities or federations which attended to the maintenance of the routes and naturally also profited thereby. Initially, though, people wanted to find out what lay beyond their own valley, who lived there. In the beginning it was the herdsmen, who met on the upland pastures and exchanged news. It was not until the inhabitants of the Inner Alpine area encountered their neighbours and learned where the paths led and about their state at various times of the year, that they were able to use this information in order to supplement their income, while at the same time encouraging fresh initiatives.

As early as 1758 the Swiss politician and historian Aegidius Tschudi went into these matters in his comprehensive work entitled 'Haupt-Schlüssel zu zerschidenen Altherthumen...' Not able to believe that, prior to the southward migrations of the Celts, no one had crossed the Alps, he discussed the whole question in considerable detail.[9] Nor do we possess any more direct sources than Tschudi today: the legendary crossing of the Alps by Herakles, the Celtic craftsman Helico who is said to have worked in Rome and on his return to have initiated the Celtic migration to the South, finally a description of this great movement itself, as well as Hannibal's astounding achievement. As for the rest, archaeology is only able to make indirect inferences; nevertheless we can fortunately see how different its conclusions are from those of Tschudi.

Although seasonal upland settlements were located at considerable altitudes as early as the Middle Stone Age, as round the Sella mountain group for instance,[10] it must not be assumed that there was any planned and regulated commerce across the Alps. Even in the Late Stone Age contacts between the territories to the South and North of the Alps were so little developed, that direct encounters will at best have been few and far between.

Active trading in the Alpine region first occurred in the Bronze Age. That coveted metal, copper, was extracted in many places. The most important depots, those in the Salzburg district, supplied large tracts in the Alpine foreland. Experienced men had ventured into the mountain regions in search of copper. What they gained there they traded along routes the choice of which depended on their state at the time, primarily on the purchasers' require-ments. At this time, too, smaller settlements were estab-lished, such as the one on the 'Crestaulta' opposite Vrin[11] in the Lugnez (Graubünden). What would appear to be its out-of-the-way situation is to be explained by the fact that the passes at the top of the valley and wholly un-known today, were then regularly used. In fact, it was the shortest way from the Vorderrhein valley to the Ticino, assuming one was unwilling or unable to use either the Splügen or the San Bernardino pass on account of the pro-blems presented by the Via Mala and the Rofla gorge. The high-altitude Diesrut (2424 m) and Greina (2360 m) passes are not so difficult as to prevent an experienced tra-veller from negotiating them at any reasonably favourable time of the year.

The votive offerings found on passes or upland pastures, serving as evidence that these had been used, date as far back as the Late Stone Age though it is not until the Bronze Age that they become abundant (pp. 157 ff.); yet they only reflect conditions in general at the settle-ments. Since we can do no more than hazard a guess as to the reasons for their deposition and individual motives cannot be divined, it would be unwise to draw any direct conclusions from the quantity of such finds on specific mountain crossings.

Greeks and Etruscans discover the North

In the Iron Age an economic decline in the former centres of the copper-mining industry set in, and the Alps became a transit area. The rise of powerful families of the nobility from eastern France to Bohemia and wealthy city-states in the South built up by the Greeks and Etruscans led to in-tensive trading from the sixth century on. Valuable objects such as bronze vessels (Ill. 12) and Greco-Attic pottery having been among the goods reaching Central Europe in this way, research has tended to concentrate upon this aspect of the problem–rather too intently and dogmatically, as is invariably the case when archaeologists become fascinated by what is alien and costly.

The argument was that in the first place the Greek col-ony of *Massilia*/Marseille, founded about 600 BC, had traded with the North, using the exceptionally convenient route up the valleys of the Rhône and Saône. That in the fifth century the political changes in the Western Mediter-ranean had led to the Etruscans–who had meanwhile set-tled in the Po plain and had built up a controlled trade across the Alps–becoming pre-eminent, until towards 400 BC the Celtic onslaughts had destroyed the well-organized trading system in goods from the South.

Recent investigations have caused this picture of two competing and alternating 'trading channels' to be modi-fied.[12] They show that the transalpine routes have always been used at the same time as the Rhône route, giving the Great St Bernard pass its exceptional importance. For, for anybody who wished to go from the Po plain northwest-wards into the Swiss midlands and from there across the Jura to France or on into the the Upper Rhine valley, this pass, despite its height (2469 m), was far and away the most advantageous route. Here one can cross the Alpine ridge most quickly nowadays along a stretch of road only 84 km long from Aosta (583 m) to Martigny at the bend of the Rhône in the Valais (417 m), soon reaching broad, peril-free valleys with a pleasant climate, leading into the plain. Of the finds from the sanctuary on the pass, where votive offerings continued to be made well into Roman times, some had been deposited in the Early Iron Age.[13]

Offering a direct route to southern Germany were the passes approached from the Lago Maggiore or from the Lake of Como, the most important being San Bernardino (2065 m), Splügen (2113 m), Septimer (2300 m) and Maloja with Julier (2284 m). Since the lake district was densely settled during the Iron Age and the Vorderrhein valley, too, has produced not a few find-spots, especially at the Rhine dog-leg round Chur, we can be sure that these passes were used at least for Inner Alpine commerce. But whether long-distance trade availed itself of them to any great extent is extremely doubtful. To assume merely from the density of settlement in the South and the relative pro-sperity of the people there that this area participated in in-termediary commerce is liable to lead to over-hasty con-clusions.

For we have to keep in view the factors in historical research that determine the settlement pattern in the Aosta valley on the one hand, and in the South Alpine val-leys round the Lago Maggiore and the Lake of Como on the other. It is common knowledge that modern building activity is in the main responsible for the discovery of

122 *Close to the little village of Surin, far back in the Lugnez, a side valley of the Vorderrhein, lay a Bronze Age settlement on the hill called 'Crestaulta' (in the centre of the photograph), which dominates the deep cleft of the river valley. On its flat top dwelt people who lived by cattle-breeding and occasional trade with the South across the high passes.*

graves and settlement sites. When the Gotthard railway was being built, the largest cemeteries so far found in the Ticino were brought to light; the gravel-pits in the moraines round Como yield rich finds, and the rush to build everywhere in this region with its genial climate has led to the unearthing of a great many sites. This plethora of finds in due course aroused greater interest on the part of the local community, which resulted as early as 1872 in the founding of a–still very energetic–archaeological society in Como, and this in its turn led to more careful supervision of earth removals and systematic digging by experienced assistants. All this applies to a far lesser extent to the Aosta valley. What is more, local research concentrated so much on Roman Aosta, that very little attention was paid to the pre-Roman periods. It is only in quite recent years that things have changed, and the results have been encouraging.[14] So the essential cultural relationship of the pre-Roman Aosta valley with the Valais becomes increasingly evident, and this is wholly in keeping with the general conclusion that passes–even very high ones–are an aid to communications, rather than a hindrance.

(An exceptional find showing that people passed through the Aosta valley and so over the Great St Bernard in the Late Bronze Age is a stone casting-mould for a bronze sword found by the Lago di Viverone between Ivrea and Santhià. For the sword type is only known from north of the Alps; not a single example of it exists in northern Italy.[15] Since other types of sword are definitely associated with this area at that time, there can be no question of a break in supplies. Thus in this instance a trader or even a craftsman must have travelled to the South with the mould in his baggage, with a view to producing his wares there–only to get stuck when barely out of the Aosta valley. Maybe the mould itself was manufactured south of the Alps, but in any case the man came from the North and he must have seen what the sword looked like. Transported in the reverse direction–likewise in the Late Bronze Age– were fibulae of Italian type, a fair number of which have been found in the lake-shore settlements in Switzerland.) For hitherto these people had no fibulae resembling present-day safety-pins and brooches since men as well as women adorned their garments with bronze pins. Now a new fashion had found access, and on such a large scale that individual fibulae of this kind were imitated in a somewhat crude manner.[16] As a means of establishing this contact, too, the Great St Bernard pass alone comes into consideration. Moreover, they imply fairly intensive and regular connections, for the adoption of what was after all a pretty arresting technical innovation will scarcely have resulted from someone having by chance brought home with him a fibula from Italy.

After reaching the Rhône valley at Martigny, the Great St Bernard route at first follows it in a northwesterly direction, although the way along the east end of the Lake of Geneva, as previously mentioned, was extremely unpleasant and dangerous in pre-Roman times. The great significance of the diversionary route over the Col des Mosses into the Üechtland and farther north is indicated by the

quite recently discovered settlement of Châtillon-sur-Glâne[17] southwest of Fribourg, so to speak the forerunner of today's cantonal capital. Here, on a steep spur of rock above the confluence of the Sarine (Saane) and the Glâne (Glaane) people settled from the Late Stone Age up until the early Middle Ages; a fortification in the form of a rampart and ditch on the more accessible 'landward' side provided good protection. According to our present knowledge, the settlement's most prosperous period was in the Iron Age prior to the Celtic migration, that is in the sixth and above all the fifth century BC, when the route across the Great St Bernard was the main artery between northern Italy and western Central Europe. Although only small areas have been systematically explored so far, the wealth of the people who formerly inhabited this exposed place must have been boundless. The pottery in particular testifies to its long-distance connections: black-figure ware from Athens, grey ware with wavy band decoration from Marseille, fragments of a vessel and a fibula from northern Italy, also vases fashioned on the newly introduced potter's wheel, which at this time are found only north of the Alps at 'princely' residences, and even a glass phial from Egypt. In short, Châtillon, despite the relatively meagre excavation work so far carried out there–the place is no longer threatened by the gravel-pit–has already shown itself to have been an extremely important station in those days on the route across the Western Alps.

It is not only its easily defended situation on a rocky spur that led to Châtillon's importance, but even more the fact that from this point onward the Sarine is navigable for flat-bottomed boats. The Sarine flows into the Aare, this in its turn into the Rhine. If one considers what an important role even the smallest of waterways played in travel and the conveyance of goods as late as medieval times (we may recall that Charlemagne planned to build a canal between Rezat and Altmühl in central Franconia, thus anticipating the Rhine-Main-Danube canal–still under construction today!),[18] there seems good reason to assume that it was as a re-loading point from land to water transport that Châtillon came to attain its overriding importance. The boatmen who conveyed the goods with which they were entrusted in undamaged condition to their destination along what were still fairly small and unregulated waterways[19] no doubt earned every bit as much respect as

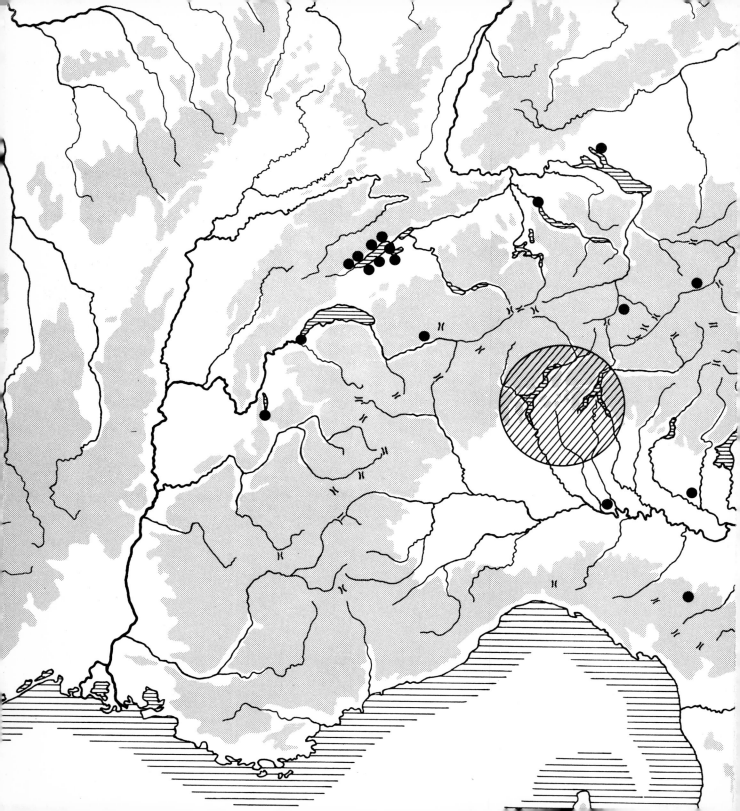

the Alpine guides who had brought the traders and other travellers safely over the mountains from the South. Indeed, the boatmen actually took more on, since towing a barge upstream–even over short distances–was more laborious than leading back a laden pack-animal. Admittedly, navigation was limited, even in later times, to rivers outside the actual mountain area and to the lakes on their fringes, for in the interior the unpredictable problems presented by rocks, rapids, sandbanks and alluvial deposits were too great to allow anything more than the transporting of timber in the form of rafts (cf. description of the *Druentia*, p. 206).[20]

The difficulties we are faced with when attempting to assess the significance of a route across the Alps merely by the settlement conditions in the valleys are greater in the case of the Central and Eastern Alps. Investigations in the South Tyrol have resulted in the discovery of vast numbers of pre-Roman find-spots, mainly from the Bronze and Iron Ages,[21] but the passes that emerged there played scarcely any role before the Romans. For the Bavarian Alpine foreland was by comparison sparsely settled and not well endowed, and so did not attract long-distance trade from the South.[22] Contacts were of course made here and there, and some foreign articles will have found their way across the mountains, but none of this can be compared with the brisk traffic over the Great St Bernard pass, even though the geographical conditions give the appearance of being more favourable (one must remember, nevertheless, the impassable Kunter gorge on the way to the Brenner pass).

124 At Châtillon-sur-Glâne (canton Fribourg), above the confluence of the Glâne and the Sarine was situated the important reloading station where goods were transferred from land to water transport. Steep cliffs together with a high rampart gave protection to the well-to-do inhabitants during the 6th and 5th centuries BC.

123 Fashion in clothes was from the very beginning one of the prime aspects of living to be subject to outside influences. Whereas in the Late Bronze Age north of the Alps men and women fastened their clothing with pins, there were some who in the Italic manner used simple fibulae that closely resembled the present-day safety-pin. Except in the Valais, these were all found inside the settlements, never in graves; for this personal preference had no place in the strictly controlled burial custom. The distribution of these early Italian fibulae and their local imitations is an indication of how the cultural influence of northern Italy spread across many of the passes to the North. The hatched circle represents the densely settled area of the 'Protogolasecca Culture', the source of large quantities of fibulae.

Salt and amber routes of the Eastern Alps

The situation in the Eastern Alps is just the reverse. In the Italian part in particular archaeological research has been meagre. The clearest evidence of this is the fact that in 1976 a book was published under the title *I Paleoveneti alpini*, which was nothing more than a reprint of old reports of finds from the years 1871 to 1899. It is therefore very questionable whether the small number of reported pre-Roman find-spots on the borders of the Eastern Alps[23] reflects the true position regarding settlement there. At all events the crossings which led thence to the North must have had a significant part to play, as is shown by conditions at the northern edge of the Alps. In the cemeteries of the salt metropolises of Hallstatt and Hallein-Dürrnberg we find evidence of so many connections with northern Italy, that close contacts must have been established not merely in the fields of commerce and imports but also in the religious and artistic spheres.[24] In particular the route running from the Salzach and Inn right across into Bohemia can be figured out from the spread of Etruscan bronze vessels and even the Etruscan fashion of pointed shoes.[25]

Where exactly the travellers and traders crossed the Eastern Alps is less easily determined. Those who journeyed from Este, the capital of the Veneti near Padua (Padova), to the North had to cross at least two passes if they wished to avoid a long detour via Villach and the Drau valley. There is, in the first place, the way through the Piave valley up to the Misurina lake (Col S. Angelo, 1756 m), down again into the Pustertal and over the Kreuzbergsattel (1336 m) eastward into the Lienz basin and from there across the Felber Tauern (2545 m) into the broad valley of the Salzach. The alternative farther to the East, namely from Lienz across the Iselsberg (1204 m) and the Hochtor (2575 m) by the Grossglockner, has no advantage over this. A second choice is to go northeastwards along the foot of the mountains in the direction of Udine and then follow the Tagliamento, branching off northwards over the Plöcken pass (1362 m) into the Lesach valley and across the Gailbergsattel (982 m), to reach the Drau valley below Lienz. From here the two aforementioned Tauern passes again offered a choice. Owing to the moderate height of the Plöcken pass, this route was preferable to the Piave valley in spring and autumn, seeing that it is also no longer.

For commerce between Slovenia and the border of the Northern Alps recourse could be had to the passes over the eastern Tauern: the Mallnitz Tauern (2446 m), under which a railway tunnel now runs, and the Radstädter Tauern (1739 m), which can only be reached from the Drau valley by crossing the Katschberg (1641 m) or the Turracher Höhe (1763 m). Apart from these Tauern, which today are opened up by roads or tunnels, there were no doubt sundry smaller ways across (still used until quite recently), such as the Rauris Tauern and even the Hochtor by the Grossglockner; this is borne out by the Late Iron Age neck-ring found on the Maschlalm in the Seidlwinkl valley leading up from Rauris to the Hochtor, and a scarab dating from the Late Iron Age or the Roman period near the Rojacher Hütte (2718 m).[26] The passes farther to the East, from which Hallstatt could be directly approached, are all lower and so presented fewer difficulties. The valley basin of the Mur at Judenburg in Styria occupies a central position, for here many valleys and routes converge. This would seem to explain why the famous Early Iron Age cult wagon was found at Strettweg.[27] Likewise the rich graves from the seemingly remote Kleinklein in the Sulm valley (Ill. 69) are–since it lacks any mineral resources worth mentioning–best understood from its situation on an important trade route from the Hungarian plain through the hilly south Styrian countryside, across the Radl pass (670 m) into the Drau valley, on into the Klagenfurt basin and thence to Friuli.[28] The approach to the Sulm valley was blocked by a prehistoric fortification on the Frauenberg above Leibnitz,[29] and possibly the nearby Roman town of *Flavia Solva* owes its importance to a similar advantageous geographical situation. For here along the eastern edge of the Alps ran those ways which, ever since antiquity, have been grouped together under the title of 'amber routes'. There is a tendency to regard them as having been more important than they actually were, but there was unquestionably a wide-ranging long-distance trade connection between the Baltic and the northern end of the Adriatic.[30]

Carriers and sumpters, artists and merchants

All traffic across the passes in pre-Roman times proceeded on foot or with pack-animals. Wagons were of course known, but in the mountains it would have needed well built roads if two- or four-wheeled vehicles were to be used away from the flat valley bottoms. The loads to be transported in this manner had not to be too large, too heavy or too awkwardly shaped. A powerfully built carrier could haul up to 50 kg, a pack-horse about three times as much. Whether donkeys or mules from the South were used for the purpose cannot be archaeologically ascertained, as so far no asses' bones have been found in settlements north of the Alps. As is ever the case where such technical limitations exist and the economy is at an elementary stage, there was no question of trading in mass-produced goods, the transportation of profit-earning luxury articles or important utility goods alone being worthwhile. The freight conveyed from the South to the North was mainly wine and perhaps also olive oil, filled for convenience into earthenware amphoras, leather skins or

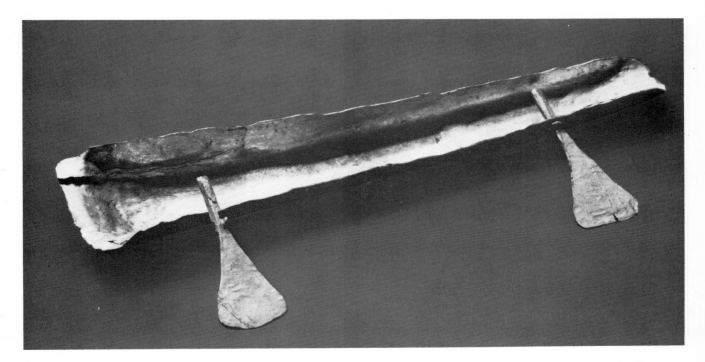

small wooden containers. The south German potentate was further provided with the appropriate pottery table-ware from Greece or bronze table-ware from Etruria. An enormous bronze wine-mixing bowl found in the elaborately furnished grave of Vix[31] near Châtillon on the Upper Seine and manufactured in southern Italy was presumably not conveyed across the Alps. As it was 1.64 m high and weighed 208.6 kg–a weight which, even had the massive cast handles and other embellishments been soldered on subsequently, would not have been appreciably reduced–it could not have been loaded on an animal, and wheeled transportation through the mountains was out of the question. So there can be no doubt that this huge vessel was conveyed by water up the Rhône and Saône to a point where it could be carried by cart along the upper course of the Seine.

How the inhabitants of the Northern Alps paid for the luxury articles we can only surmise, since it was for the most part with perishable material which cannot be identified by archaeological means. In a few passages, frequently cited, the geographer Strabo lists what the bar-

125 This little model boat made of sheet-gold, found in a grave on the Dürrnberg above Hallein (Salzburg province), conforms in every detail to a type which up until quite recent times was in use on the lakes and rivers on the northern edge of the Alps. Men accustomed to the perils of the Alpine rivers used them to transport goods of all kinds down the valleys. 400–350 BC. L 6.6 cm. Keltenmuseum, Hallein.

barians in the Roman colony of Aquileia at the northern end of the Adriatic proffered:[32] skins, hides, honey, amber and slaves. In the Eastern Alps, however, iron, gold and salt played a bigger role.

But the traffic was not confined to goods, for there was a constant coming and going of people along the routes. This applied not only to local traffic between valley communities in the Inner Alpine area but to activities that can be deduced indirectly from works of art beyond the Alps. There can be no doubt, for example, that the sculptor who about 500 BC carved the life-size stone statue of a warrior found in Hirschlanden[33] near Stuttgart had himself been in the South and seen the Greek or Etruscan originals. Equally revealing are small articles of jewellery or costume adornments when these are found outside the area where they originated. Here we should not really think in terms of 'trade', these articles having probably been carried abroad by people who wore them and then lost them or gave them away while there. They thus register the mobility of individual people, be they itinerant craftsmen, tinkers and hawkers, mercenaries, herdsmen and drovers, or venturesome men and women who married away from home. So two 'Certosa fibulae', dress fasteners of the fifth century BC from northern Italy, found in Martigny and Châtillon-sur-Glâne respectively, mark the route over the Great St Bernard pass into central Switzerland.[34] A belt buckle from Illnau[35] near Zurich derives from the district round the Lago Maggiore and the Lake of Como; a bronze pin of the seventh/sixth century BC managed to find its way from the Eastern Alps to Tamins[36] in Graubünden. In the Celtic town of Manching near Ingolstadt on the Danube was found jewellery that was native to the Inner Alpine region.[87] Even fragile pottery occasionally allows one to tell with certainty its alien origin. Since, for instance, on the Dürrnberg above Hallein in the region of the northern limestone Alps there are to be found a number of vessels in which the clay is contaminated with crystalline particles of primeval rock and silica, either the raw materials must have been obtained from more than 50 km away, that is from the Central Alps, or the finished vessels were imported,[38] most likely from North Tyrol. In the same way it is possible to establish that pottery from the vicinity of Bolzano reached the Engadin; for mixed with the clay are particles of volcanic rock which only occurs round Bolzano.[39]

Such observations should really come as no surprise, being more or less self-evident; for every dissemination of forms, fashions, techniques and so forth depends upon personal contact of individuals and groups. And the essential trade in scarce raw materials has at all times created and promoted such contacts. If, for preliterate times, we choose the somewhat cumbersome way of interpretation via individual finds, this serves only to put the scholar's mind at rest when he finds that the theoretical contacts and long-distance connections that had been put forward are refuted by the archaeological material.

The Celts migrate to the South

Coming over the passes and through the valleys were, however, not just good neighbours, garrulous pedlars and commercial travellers, but also armed multitudes intent on plunder or simply making for the enticing South. This sort of thing will have been going on at all times, but the archaeological sources are for the most part so difficult to interpret, that it is unwise, prior to the incidence of literary evidence, to make anything like a firm statement. Who is to decide whether a settlement was burnt to the ground because a child played with fire, or because an enemy set it alight? How is one to determine whether it took fifty years or ten days for three neighbouring settlements to be destroyed or deserted? The potentialities and methods of archaeology do not suffice to answer such questions.

Periods for which literary sources are available–even the second World War–have shown us that people hide valuable objects when danger threatens, in order to avoid their falling into the hands of marauding enemies. When those who know of the hiding-place are killed, driven out or carted away, the treasure remains in the ground. As a result, the archaeologist comes into the possession of 'caches' which, always allowing for the degree of accuracy in dating possible for the time in question, can sometimes be closely associated chronologically and so point to a decisive threat to the relevant territory.

One way of putting this to the test is to consider the Celtic incursions into northern Italy towards the end of the fifth century BC. The Celts must have come over the Alps, or so the geographical situation would suggest and the Roman writers tell us (p. 28). In the area of the western Central Alps, it is true, we know of only three caches that are believed to belong in this period. Two of them came to light on the south side of the mountains and apparently represent collections of scrap metal–in times when there were no coins, the only way of stowing away things of value in a small space. This certainly applies to the find from Arbedo[40] north of Bellinzona, at the confluence of the Ticino and the Moësa, where the routes leading over the passes meet. The other hoard, which contains conspicuously many amulets in addition to broken bronze objects, was found at Menaggio-Plesio,[41] that is to say there where, going eastwards from the Lake of Lugano, one strikes the Lake of Como, a place not actually situated on a through route. The third of the caches is that from Erstfeld in the canton of Uri, on the way to the St Gotthard pass between the Lake of Lucerne and the then impassable Schöllenen gorge north of Andermatt. Here we are faced with a set of circumstances that are again different. There is certainly no question of a hasty concealment by a trader suddenly taken unawares by some danger or other; it concerns a reverential offering to a deity whom we have no means of identifying (Ill. 94). Its sumptuousness, which is unique for the whole Alpine region (seven richly ornamented neck- and arm-rings of gold), coupled with its unfamiliar nature is only to be explained by assuming it had some special purpose. There is a strong temptation to think in terms of a votive offering on the part of the Celts from the North who were unfamiliar with the mountains, seeing that the find-spot faces the most difficult way across them. The disparity between them makes it hard at first to connect the three 'caches' with one another and with the discontinuance of the large cemeteries at the southern end of the Lago Maggiore (not, on the other hand, in the Swiss southern Alpine valleys).[42] Besides, there were also 'caches' from this time in South Tyrol, such as that from Obervintl[43] in the Pustertal, which hardly lay on an invasion route of the Celts.

How sinister the Celts felt the mountains to be is recorded by the Roman historian Livy,[44] legendary as parts of his account may be. Under the leadership of Bellovesus, those swarms who had chosen the South as their goal set out 'on foot and on horse-back', he writes.

There the Alps stood over against them; and I for one do not wonder that they seemed insuperable, for as yet no road had led across them—as far back at all events as tradition reaches—unless one chooses to believe the stories about Hercules. While they were then fenced in as it were by the lofty mountains, and were looking about to discover where they might cross, over heights that reached the sky, into another world... (The Gauls) themselves crossed the Alps through the Taurine passes and... routed the Etruscans in battle not far from the river Ticinus...

The Taurini, incidentally, inhabited what is present-day Piedmont—Turin/*Augusta Taurinorum* derives its name from them—and the Ticinus is the Ticino, whose upper course has given the Swiss canton its present name; this localiza-

126 Reconstruction of a Celtic harness based on finds from La Tène at Marin-Epagnier (canton Neuchâtel). 2nd-1st century BC. *Schweizerisches Landesmuseum, Zurich.*

tion of the route fits in with the fact that for tribes arriving somewhat later the P(o)eninus crossing, that is the Great St Bernard pass, is mentioned. Naturally, Livy embroidered his account—some 400 years later—for the educated classes of the city of Rome, but he himself hailed from Padua and must have known the Alps at first hand. The Alps were as foreign to the Romans of the Apennine peninsula as to the Celts, and Polybius, initially a Greek hostage in Rome and later the author of a history of the Romans (in the second century BC), journeyed to northern Italy expressly to inspect the area where Hannibal had crossed the Alps with his army in the year 218 BC.

Hannibal and his elephants

For Hannibal, the Carthaginian army commander, was the second danger to threaten the Romans from the North. How the crossing of the Alps was accomplished we learn not only from Polybius,[45] but once again from Livy.[46]

Hannibal had been warring with the Romans in Spain and had then pressed on across the Pyrenees into southern France. The behaviour of the Gallic tribes there was partly amicable, partly resigned, partly antagonistic, but Hannibal knew how to deal with all of them. Faced with a Roman army that wanted to bar his way along the coast, he dodged northwards. After a dramatic crossing of the Rhône, during which he was impeded by hostile Gauls, he proceeded farther up the valley and then followed the Isère, where the resident Allobroges gave him able assistance 'with provisions and all other supplies, principally clothing; the cold in the Alps was notorious, and one had to take precautions.'

Since no more detailed and vivid account of an Alpine crossing has come down to us from the centuries that followed, let us give here an English rendering of Livy's own Latin. He, as a Roman, saw no reason to play down what Hannibal had accomplished; quite the contrary, for the greater the achievement of Hannibal and his army, the greater ultimately was the credit that should go to the Romans for their final victory–years later, it is true. So Livy has, if anything, embellished his story, and it is above all the stirring speech which Hannibal addressed to his faint-hearted troops at the foot of the mountains that reveals the rhetorical art and historical knowledge of the narrator:

...what else did they think that the Alps were but high mountains? They might fancy them higher than the ranges of the Pyrenees; but surely no lands touched the skies or were impassable to man. The Alps were indeed inhabited, were tilled, produced and supported living beings; their defiles were practicable for armies. Those very ambassadors whom they beheld had not

crossed the Alps in the air on wings. Even the ancestors of these men had not been natives of Italy, but had lived there as foreign settlers, and had often crossed these very Alps in great companies, with their children and their wives, in the manner of emigrants. For armed soldiers, taking nothing with them but the instruments of war, what could be impassable or insurmountable?

Thus Hannibal had Celtic guides from northen Italy, who had come forward to help him. On the other hand, native mountain tribes harassed him with lightning attacks when his way was blocked; it was the elephants alone that terrified them. But, as well as the mountains themselves, the river valleys prevented a steady advance, an example being the valley of the *Druentia*/Durance, which Hannibal presumably did not follow:

This, too, is an Alpine river and by far the most difficult of all the rivers of Gaul to cross; for, though it brings down a vast volume of water, it does not admit of navigation, since, not being confined within any banks, but flowing at once in many channels, not always the same, it is ever forming new shallows and new pools–a fact which makes it dangerous for foot passengers as well–besides which it rolls down jagged stones and affords no sure or stable footing to one who enters it. And at that time, as it happened, it was swollen with rains, and the crossing took place among the wildest tumult, for the men–besides their other difficulties–were confused by their own excitement and bewildered outcries.

All in all, the Carthaginians and their levies from North Africa and Spain regarded with alarm and abhorrence the unfamiliar sight that met their gaze. Reality outvied all the advance rumours:

...the near view of the lofty mountains, with their snows almost merging into the sky; the shapeless hovels perched on crags; the frost-bitten flocks and beasts of burden; the shaggy, unkempt men; animals and inanimate objects alike stiff with cold, and all more dreadful to look upon than words can tell, renewed their consternation.

Here, in all its detail, is Livy's account of the final phase of the ascent and of the particularly difficult descent:

On the ninth day they arrived at the summit of the Alps, having come for the most part over trackless wastes and by roundabout routes, owing either to the dishonesty of their guides, or–when they would not trust their guides–to their blindly entering some valley, guessing at the way. For two days they lay encamped on the summit. The soldiers, worn with toil and fighting, were permitted to rest; and a number of baggage animals which had fallen among the rocks made their way to the camp by following the tracks of the army. Exhausted and discouraged as the soldiers were by many hardships, a snow-storm–for the constellation of the Pleiades was now setting–threw them into a great fear. The ground was everywhere covered deep with snow when at dawn they began to march, and as the column moved slowly on, dejection and despair were to be read in every countenance. Then Hannibal, who had gone on before the standards, made the army halt on a certain promontory which commanded an extensive prospect, and pointing out Italy to them, and just under the Alps the plains about the Po, he told them that they were now scaling the ramparts not only of Italy, but of Rome itself; and after one, or, at the most, two battles, they would have in their hands and in their power the citadel and capital of Italy.

The column now began to make some progress, and even the enemy had ceased to annoy them, except to make a stealthy raid, as occasion offered. But the way was much more difficult than the ascent had been, as indeed the slope of the Alps on the Italian side is in general more precipitous in proportion as it is shorter. For practically every road was steep, narrow, and treacherous, so that neither could they keep from slipping, nor could those who had been thrown a little off their balance retain their footing, but came down, one on top of the other, and the beasts on top of the men.

They then came to a much narrower cliff, and with rocks so perpendicular that it was difficult for an unencumbered soldier to manage the descent, though he felt his way and clung with his hands to the bushes and roots that projected here and there. The place had been precipitous before, and a recent landslip had carried it away to the depth of a good thousand feet. There the cavalry came to a halt, as though they had reached the end of the road, and as Hannibal was wondering what it could be that held the column back, word was brought to him that the cliff was impassable. Going then to inspect the place himself, he thought that there was nothing for it but to lead the army round, over trackless and untrodden steeps, however circuitous the detour might be. But that way proved to be insuperable; for above the old, untouched snow lay a fresh deposit of moderate depth, through which, as it was soft and not very deep, the men in front found it easy to advance; but when it had been trampled down by the feet of so many men and beasts, the rest had to make their way over the bare ice beneath and the slush of the melting snow. Then came a terrible struggle on the slippery surface, for it afforded them no foothold, while the downward slope made their feet the more quickly slide from under them; so that when they tried to pull themselves up with their hands, or used their knees, these supports themselves would slip, and down they

would come again! Neither were there any stems or roots about, by which a man could pull himself up with foot or hand–only smooth ice and thawing snow, on which they were continually rolling. But the baggage animals, as they went over the snow, would sometimes even cut into the lowest crust, and pitching forward and striking out with their hoofs, as they struggled to rise, would break clean through it, so that numbers of them were caught fast, as if entrapped, in the hard, deep-frozen snow.

At last, when men and beasts had been worn out to no avail, they encamped upon a ridge, after having, with the utmost difficulty, cleared enough ground even for this purpose, so much snow were they obliged to dig out and remove. The soldiers were then set to construct a road across the cliff–their only possible way. Since they had to cut through the rock, they felled some huge trees that grew near at hand, and lopping off their branches, made an enormous pile of logs. This they set on fire, as soon as the wind blew fresh enough to make it burn, and pouring vinegar over the glowing rocks, caused them to crumble. After thus heating the crag with fire, they opened the way in it with iron tools, and relieved the steepness of the slope with zigzags of an easy gradient, so that not only the baggage animals but even the elephants could be led down. Four days were consumed at the cliff, and the animals nearly perished of starvation; for the mountain tops are all practically bare, and such grass as does grow is buried under snow. Lower down one comes to valleys and sunny slopes and rivulets, and near them woods, and places that begin to be fitter for man's habitation. There the beasts were turned out to graze, and the men, exhausted with toiling at the road, were allowed to rest. Thence they descended in three days' time into the plain, through a region now that was less forbidding, as was the character of its inhabitants.

The losses must–at least according to the ancient sources–have been huge. Hannibal had set out from Spain with 50,000 foot-soldiers, 9000 horsemen, 37 elephants and a large baggage train. Some 20,000 foot-soldiers, 6000 horsemen and an unspecified number of elephants reached northern Italy. Of these, the Alps are said to have claimed 18,000 foot-soldiers and 2000 horsemen, as well as a substantial amount of baggage. Many people have since cudgelled their brains over which route Hannibal decided to take on the advice of the native guides.[47] It is clear that, in the first instance, he marched up the Isère valley. Opinions differ as to whether he followed the Arc farther and crossed the main ridge of the Alps via a small pass south of the Mont-Cenis (probably across the Col du Clapier at 2482 m)[48] or whether–far less likely–in the Grenoble basin he branched off southward over the Col Bayard (1248 m) or the neighbouring Col de Manse at Gap, in an effort to reach the Durance valley.[49] This would have brought him to the Mont-Genèvre pass (1854 m) with the crossing to Susa, where–in the land of the Taurini–he was in the plain.

Livy's account already tells us about the countless difficulties all commanders who wanted to cross the Alps with an entire army had to contend with. Hannibal's elephants posed just as many problems when it came to getting through as did, nearly 2000 years later, Napoleon's cannon, which were dismantled before being transported across the snow-bound Great St Bernard pass.[50] But Hannibal was faced with narrow mountain tracks, which had to be widened, whereas Napoleon was able to use existing pathways that had been kept in good repair.

The first road-building engineers

It was some time before the Romans themselves crossed the Alps with an army. In 125 BC, during the conquest of southern Gaul, M. Fulvius Flaccus chose the Mont-Genèvre pass for the purpose of launching a surprise attack from an unsuspected quarter. But Italy continued to be threatened from the North. Towards the end of the second century BC Teutons, apparently Germanic tribes with Celtic elements, broke into the South across the Alps. Their route is, like all others, not mentioned or only vaguely indicated in the literary sources, a matter of contention to this day. Moreover, these invaders were constantly on the move and, in their search for lands to settle, changed their course several times. What is certain is that they roamed about in the Central and Eastern Alps.[51]

After that the literary sources are silent for a time. In the first century BC the Celts were in fact too much occupied with coming to terms with the Germanic tribes that were pressing southwards, and the Romans for their part were only interested for the time being in safeguarding connections with the new province of Gallia Narbonensis in southern France. Except for the sea, only the rather inconvenient route through the southern Maritime Alps was at their disposal for this purpose, a route that Augustus ultimately had newly constructed as the Via Iulia. As all the valleys open out in the direction of the sea, the road had to

be sited as high up on the mountain-side as possible and the many ravines had to be spanned by bridges. Where it crosses the frontier between Italia and the province of Alpes Maritimae stands the monument commemorating the subjection of the Alpine peoples (Ills 19–20).

This event, which reduced the Alps from a forbidding mountain barrier to a troublesome obstacle to the commercial aspirations of an expansionist imperial policy, ushered in a new epoch. The Romans, a people proud of their roads, were anxious to introduce a regulated traffic across the Alps as well. In this, the requirements of the military and the subsequent administration were the determining factors. From the outset the long-distance roads of the Romans were conceived as lines of deployment and support routes for the army, their construction was preliminary to taking over and infiltrating a newly won territory.

Hence the history of Roman road construction northward across the Alps begins with the campaigns of Drusus and Tiberius, the generals from Augustus's family. Following the subjection of the Alpine peoples and the conquest of the North Alpine foreland in 15 BC, roads that as far as possible allowed traffic over the Alps also in winter had to be built. Two routes were already begun at that time. The first went up the Adige valley across the Reschen pass into the Inn valley and on over the Fern pass to the Lech as far as the legionary camp and future provincial capital of Raetia, *Augusta Vindelicum*/Augsburg; the second was the route from *Augusta Praetoria*/Aosta over the Great St Bernard in the Valais and on into Switzerland as far as *Augusta Raurica*/Augst at Basel. All this could not of course be accomplished in a few weeks, and it was several decades before the work was completed. This was under Emperor Claudius, and the inscriptions on the milestones proudly announce the fact:

Ti(berius) Claudius Drusi f(ilius) Caesar Aug(ustus)
Germanicus pontifex maximus, tribunicia potestate VI,
cons(ul) IV, imp(erator) XI, p(ater) p(atriae), censor,
viam Claudiam Augustam,
quam Drusus pater Alpibus bello
patefactis derex[e]rat, munit ab Altino usque ad flumen
Danuvium. M(ilia) p(assuum) CCCL.

Tiberius Claudius, son of Drusus, known as Caesar Augustus, Conqueror of Teutons and High Priest, in the 6th year of office as tribune, in the 4th year as Consul, proclaimed Imperator for the 11th time, Father of the Fatherland, Censor, built this road named for Claudius Augustus, which his father Drusus had already prepared after the warlike opening-up of the Alpine routes, from Altinum to the Danube. It is 350 miles long.

This Via Claudia is one of the last of the long-distance roads that, in accordance with ancient tradition, was named after its builder. The recorded titles enable us to date it in the administrative year AD 46/47. The above inscription comes from a milestone north of Feltre in the Piave valley; a very similar one is known from Rabland near Merano.[52] Latest research on roads[53] has shown that the Via Claudia actually comprised two routes, owing to the Isarco gorge above Bolzano being impassable. The first and probably more important of the two ran from Verona out of the Adige valley as far as the Reschen pass and on to Augsburg and the Danube. The second kept to the Piave valley, then curved westward in the Pustertal and, via the Brenner, reached the Inn valley, which it left to go north across the Seefeld saddle; a branch followed the Inn valley downwards. It would appear that initially the provincial boundaries between Raetia and Noricum were made to conform with these lines of communication;[54] for when, in the second century, a road opened-up the Kunter gorge, and the Brenner pass as the most direct route gained in importance, the frontier was moved farther to the East; though the Isarco and the Wipptal as far as Innsbruck formerly belonged to Noricum, they were later added to Raetia. Behind this lay the fixed determination to prevent such roads from unnecessarily crossing provincial boundaries, since these were often customs frontiers and the road administration was subordinate to the provincial governors. In the mountains the provincial frontier had to follow the course taken by the roads, not the other way round.

We know rather less about the arrangement of the early roads in the West. The Little St Bernard pass could be used by carts, whereas there was only a mule track across the Great St Bernard.[55] As early as in the reign of Augustus a Via Iulia Augusta had been built across the Plöcken pass and on into allied Noricum. The extension of this road across the Tauern was apparently not undertaken until later, Altogether, there was much uncertainty about when many of the roads were built, also whether or

to what extent they were improved to take through vehicular traffic and exactly where each of them led. In the course of time, what is more, new routes or road links were added. Since road gazetteers and maps date from no earlier than late antiquity, they present a picture that does not necessarily tally with the first two centuries of Roman rule in the Alps. So it was not until later that the road link from the Piave valley through the Val Sugana to Trento was built,[56] likewise the short-cut from the Radstädter Tauern across the Lausnitzhöhe (just east of the present-day road across the Katschberg pass)[57] into the Liesertal and on to *Teurnia* in the Drau valley and *Virunum* north of Klagenfurt.

In the Alps the Romans had to depart from their principle, to build firmly based highways for long-distance communications; the difficulties the terrain normally presented were just too great. So in Roman times there were relatively few genuine highways across the passes (and the Middle Ages still profited from these): they were, it would seem, the Reschen and Brenner, Radstädter Tauern, Septimer and Maloja with Julier, and in the Western Alps the Mont-Genèvre and the Little St Bernard. Across the other passes led tracks that had been widened to a greater or lesser degree, and these, too, of course called for careful surveying and the construction of bridges. And because roads in the High Middle Ages and even later often followed the old mule-tracks, it is sometimes difficult to decide what kind of path was originally there, especially since simple arched bridges made of stone were built in the same way for centuries. So by no means all 'Roman bridges' in the Alpine region in fact date from this period. The argument about the age of the road across the San Bernardino pass[58] clearly shows up this problem.

In the lowlands and in the wide valleys the Roman engineers built metalled roads. On a foundation of fairly large stones, several decimetres deep, was laid a layer of rubble or gravel. If the subsoil was suitable the base could be dispensed with; in traversing swampy or moist ground it was necessary to use planks. Only in towns and larger villages was an additional paving of flagstones applied to the roads–as every visitor to Pompeii will remember seeing.

The recorded observations of Wolfgang Titze on the Via Claudia north of Füssen (now vanished into the dam-

med-up Forggensee) give a good idea of its construction and utilization:[59]

'The investigation showed that the core of the road, by using a raised natural subsoil without removing the thin covering of humus, had been heaped up in two to three stages to a height of 50–60 cm. After this loose deposit had, possibly by pounding, become sufficiently firm, a muddy, internally consolidated road-way had been produced, every phase of which was clearly recognizable from the excavation. In due course the tracks of vehicles caused deep ruts, so that a fresh layer was needed. Yet the old road surface was not first torn up, so each additional layer could still be distinguished from the underlying road surface... The road, which was still in use in the early and High Middle Ages, was then no longer maintained but turned into a sunken track through wear. On account of its ever-worsening condition, it

127 Since Roman times the bed of the river Bouthier (Ital. Dora Baltea) has moved a good 200 m westward. As a result the bridge across which the high road to Augusta Praetoria/Aosta *formerly ran now stands on dry land. It was recently exposed down to the ancient ground-level. It has a span of 17 m and is 6 m wide. The breastworks have been repaired and renewed many times.*

became necessary for traffic to leave the roadway at particularly bad places. Thus there are today still sections of the banking that are marked by numerous tracks of varying width.'

Inscriptions disclose repairs

What is especially interesting about this account is that, in spite of 350 years of Roman traffic on the Via Claudia, it would appear that major repairs were only undertaken on two occasions at the most. Thus what seems to be such a simple method of road construction proved to be exceptionally effective, at all events where the amount of traffic and the loads carried in Roman times were concerned. Viewed against this background, we can readily see why those emperors who authorized and financed the general overhaul of a road should wish to commemorate themselves as proudly on the new milestones as was the original builder of the road. This could lead to the setting-up of several milestones from different periods at the same point beside a road. The eastern border of the Alps offers three examples of this (see accompanying table).[60]

From a comparison with the findings at the Via Claudia, moreover, it can be seen that–even where the emperor prides himself on the repair of a road and its bridges *(vias et pontes restituit)*–this did not necessarily apply to the entire length of the road. In late antiquity milestones were actually set up with the sole purpose of testifying to the devotion of one or other of the short-lived emperors (cf. Valerian on two milestones at Wien-Inzersdorf). But Antoninus Pius and Septimius Severus in fact made a name for themselves as road-builders at the peak period of the Roman Empire, and even under Decius a new link-road, the Via Decia, from the Brenner route along the northern edge of the Alps to Bregenz was built.[61] At Seefeld it branched in a westerly direction off the road lead-ing towards *Parthanum*/Partenkirchen, joined the Via Claudia between Ehrwald and Reutte and then, continuing its northwesterly course to Immenstadt via Sonthofen, reached Bregenz after running just south of Isny. Two milestones are known from this new road, one from *Veldidena*/Innsbruck-Wilten (initially a road-station, then an actual fort) and the other from *Teriolis*/Zirl, which in late Roman times was likewise converted into a fortified checkpoint. From Wilten to Bregenz was, the milestone recorded, a distance of 112 miles. In late Roman times this connection fulfilled the function of the subsequent Arlberg route, which the Romans never developed. The Romans met new military and economic requirements by building further roads; but by late antiquity the State could not afford a new road unless it was absolutely essential.

For the construction and maintenance of such a long-distance road must have swallowed up vast sums of money. Even if the emperors, according to tradition, occasionally made contributions from their privy purse, it was principally the people living near the roads who had to spend their time and energy on them.[62] In a town wealthy citizens might still be called upon to improve the roads and make them more attractive. From Treviso, for example, comes an inscription[63] in which a group of municipal officials boastfully announce that they 'paved the way with its side-walks from the crossing to the town wall' *(viam cum crepidinibus a quadruvio ad murum straverunt), ob*

Ivenca	Vienna–Inzersdorf	Schwechat near Vienna
6 miles from *Celeia*/Celje on the road to *Virunum* near Klagenfurt	4 miles from *Vindobona*/Vienna on the road to *Scarbantia*/Sopron	21 miles from *Carnuntum*/Deutsch-Altenburg on the road to *Vindobona*/Vienna
1 Trajan 101/102		
2 Hadrian 131/132		
3 Antoninus Pius 142/143	1 Antoninus Pius 142/143	1 Antoninus Pius 142/143
4 Septimius Severus 199/200 renovated 213/214	2 Septimius Severus 200/201	2 Septimius Severus 198
5 Macrinus 217/218		
		3 Maximinus Thrax 235/238
		4 Gordianus III 239/240
	3 Decius 249	5 Decius 249
	4 Valerianus 253	
	5 Valerianus 256/258	6 Valerianus 256/258

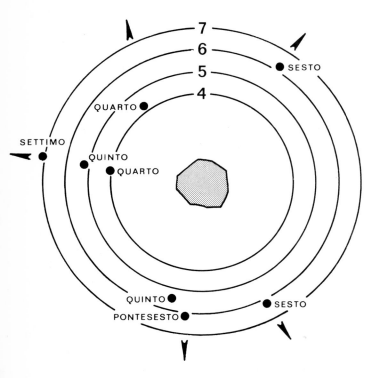

128 All round **Mediolanum**/*Milan, in later times the principal town of northern Italy, unusually many place-names point to the fact that small settlements along the roads were known simply by the distances from Milan recorded on the milestones in the vicinity, a mile being 1480 m (the tinted area represents the town nucleus). Nowadays, in order to distinguish them from many others in Italy, the names of such places are amplified for purposes of identification–for example on the main route to the West we find Quatro Cagnino, Quinto Romano and Settimo Milanese. At the same time the little diagram shows where the routes led: via* **Novaria**/*Novara and* **Vercellae**/*Vercelli to the Alpine passes in the West, via* **Comum**/*Como to those in the North, via* **Laus Pompaea**/*Lodi to* **Placentia**/*Piacenza and* **Cremona** *in the Southeast, as well as to* **Ticinum**/*Pavia in the South. Such indicative place-names are to be found in the vicinity of practically all the large Roman towns in northern Italy. In the dialect of the Aosta valley, though, they are difficult to recognize:* Quart *(ad quartum),* Chettoz *(ad sextum),* Nus *(ad nonum),* Diémoz *(ad decimum).*

honorem–in their own honour, in honour of the emperor, or in honour of the town? They had it done, then, at their own expense.

Nevertheless the rural population had to give their services by way of manual labour and providing draught-cattle, and were thereafter to a certain extent responsible for the upkeep of the road. For it was precisely the Alpine region that was subject to flooding and landslides. This is borne out by an inscription[64] of the year 163 from *Bergintrum*/Bourg-St-Maurice between the provincial capital of *Axima*/Aime and the Little St Bernard pass. As it happens, the people were lucky in adversity, for the emperor met the costs of the repairs:

The Imperator and Caesar Lucius Aurelius Verus, Augustus, for the 3rd time invested with tribunitian authority, for the 2nd time Consul, has in the territory of the *Ceutrones* had the roads that were carried away by the force of the torrents, by regulating the rivers and rebuilding the banks at many places, likewise the bridges (?), temples and baths, made good at his own expense.

On the way up to the Plöcken pass from the South three inscriptions that had been carved into the rock in late antiquity were found, veritable eulogies of the emperors Valentinian and Valens as well as the appropriate officials from *Iulium Carnicum*/Zuglio, for having had the dangerous passages rendered safe or repaired.[65] If, by contrast, on the milestone marking the height of the pass over the Radstädler Tauern, Emperor Septimius Severus merely records that he and his two sons Caracalla and Geta had in the year 201 'set up anew the milestones fallen into decay through age' (*miliaria v[etustate c]onlapsa restituer [unt]*),[66] this was doubtless an understatement, particularly as it was the provincial governor's personal responsibility. Not only had Septimius Severus, as mentioned earlier, attended to the thorough-going maintenance of the roads in the Alpine area; he was one of the last emperors in Rome to show such modesty.

Masterpieces of Roman road-building

But let us return to the Roman road-building engineers, for the setting-up of milestones, columns up to 3 m high (Ill. 139), represented only the propagandist final stage. To begin with, the actual course had to be decided upon. The Romans, just as their way of thinking was direct and

129 Roman milestone from the route, not fully developed as a road for vehicles, over the Great St Bernard, set up beside the church of Bourg-Saint-Pierre (Valais). The rectangular base was originally meant to be set into the ground; the brass plate with the restored inscription is a more recent addition.

practical, did not hold with curving roads either. On level ground or in slightly hilly country, this aim was readily achieved. The dead-straight Roman road linking Salzburg with Augsburg through the wooded gravel plain south of Munich is the best example of a route that can also be covered on foot; the banked-up section in the timber forest should not be overlooked.

In the mountains the engineers had to adapt themselves to the terrain. It was necessary to pass through valleys liable to flooding, triumph over defiles, span deep gorges and climb up steep slopes. This meant the fulfilling of four requirements. Firstly, the road had to be wide enough to take a vehicle having what seems to have been the customary width of 107–110 cm, allowing for sufficient passing-places for opposing traffic. Secondly, the gradient should not exceed that which would allow a draught animal to pull a loaded vehicle. Thirdly, sharp bends had to be avoided, since the large four-wheeled wagons, despite their adaptable front axles, required a fairly large turning circle. Fourthly, tunnels–though there are three examples in central Italy[67]–if they needed to be more than a few metres long were out of the question.

Taking all this into consideration in reviewing Roman road construction in the Alps, it can be quite fascinating to compare the achievements of the Romans with those of later and present-day road-builders. We must marvel at a remarkable example in the Western Alps between Aosta and the Little St Bernard pass, marked on maps as 'Défilé de Pierre-Taillée'. Between the villages of Runaz and Derby the Dora Baltea has carved a deep gorge; the road link between the somewhat wider sections of the valley in which the villages lie had of necessity to traverse the slope. The Romans solved the problem by siting the road as high up as possible, taking subsidiary slopes into consideration. In place of a tunnel, they used bold arched structures for shoring up the hill-side, cutting into the cliff face for several metres above the road, so that it there runs beneath an artificial roof of rock. By contrast, the latter-day road runs round the awkward mountain spur at a fixed height, necessitating only a relatively short tunnel which is not even lined on the inside, thus eliminating elaborate supporting structures on the side facing the valley. In recent years, in the course of building the road tunnel under Mont Blanc, a third system of alignment is being used: a

130 *Three sections of road spanning two millennia in the Aosta valley above a gorge on the route to the Little St Bernard: at the top, the Roman road built on a structure of arches beneath the hollowed-out rock (Ill. 121) with a supporting pillar (right, a super-* *posed strong-point from the second World War); below, the more recent road with a short tunnel, and on the right the concrete wall of the present-day tubular tunnel which cuts straight through the mountain spur.*

large, well-lit tunnel carries the wide motorway through the mountain spur, the concrete tubular structure being carried well out into the open as a protection against rock-falls. That this has caused one of the outstanding monuments of Roman road-building art to be largely destroyed (the remains can only be reached by clambering around) seems to have caused nobody any concern–a sad example of brutal route-planning and the negligence of the official bodies responsible for the preservation of ancient monuments. By comparison, the damage suffered by the Roman road during the second World War when it was a battle-station–evidence of the strategic importance of the defile–was minimal.

At Donnaz, on the same road but some kilometres below Aosta, a further masterly example of Roman[68] engineering skill is preserved; a stretch of road, 220 m long, has been hewn out of the rock, necessitating the under-cutting of a substantial part of the hill-side. The engineers and construction workers set up a monument to themselves by leaving a kind of rock-arch standing, which would not have been needed for structural purposes.

The Maloja–Julier route has of late been the object of a particularly full investigation by Armon Planta.[69] This underlined the fact that road research calls for someone who is capable of assessing the given circumstances and exigencies of the terrain while covering it on foot; for often stretches of road several kilometres long must be visualized and reconstructed intuitively on account of their having been blotted out by landslides and rock-falls. The Maloja pass, as already mentioned, is really nothing more than a high-lying step in the valley. The present-day road (since 1839) runs down from the village of Maloja in 22 curves, half of which are hairpin bends, to Casaccia. Prior to the rebuilding there were only nine bends, while the medieval track needed only three. The connection between the number of curves and the gradient is evident. So it need not surprise us that the Roman road was seen to have only two, or at most three curves; for it aimed at the shortest and all but straight way up from Casaccia on the north-west side of the valley. A pathway, today still the shortest route, more or less follows that course. A unique feature is an 8 metre-long stretch which surmounts a slab of rock with a 30° gradient. The grooves in the track are relatively shallow, but for the draught animals and wagoners steps

to provide a foothold had to be hacked out in between, to prevent their slipping, especially in rain or snow. In addition, there are four deep holes at intervals of 1.5 m in the rocky side wall for inserting levering bars which the wagoners could use to ease the work of the draught animals.

Track grooves are found in many places on the Alpine roads of the Romans.[70] Besides those at the Julier pass, notable examples are to be found in the sunken roads above Warmbad Villach, on the Pass Lueg and at Klais near Mittenwald. They occur almost exclusively at steep sections, where the road traverses naked rock and a topping of gravel would not have remained in place. It is noticeable, moreover, that they keep to the same gauge of about 107–110 cm. We may assume, therefore, that the grooves were already cut to a depth of a few centimetres when the steep sections of the road were put in hand; for they also offered a certain protection against the vehicles side-slipping.[71] It took decades or centuries after that for the grooves to be ground down to their often considerable depth (up to 45 cm). On steep descents, where the draught animals could not hold back a laden vehicle, the wagoners would block the wheels by inserting thick staves between the spokes. The added friction generated by the locked wheels seems likely to have accounted for the depth of the grooves. No doubt they then tended to be more of a handicap to those in charge; any gravel possibly used as a filling would of course have been washed away long ago.

The Romans were familiar with many different types of vehicle; among them were the ordinary creaking cart, the fast two-wheeled van of the imperial post and the ponderous luxury conveyance, a form of four-wheeler of the kind so well depicted in the relief from Maria Saal. Seated in this, one could–provided it did not jolt too much–take a rest, hold a conversation, dictate letters or write philosophical works, as Caesar is said to have done on the occasion of a journey across the Alps.[72]

By Roman times at the latest, as the demands made upon draught and riding animals required to traverse the often rocky roads of the Alps grew greater, iron horseshoes came into use. If doubts have been expressed until quite recently about dating their introduction in Roman times, these have now been dispelled by the discovery of horseshoes in Roman forts north of the Alps as well. Indeed,

131 The Roman road from the Brenner to Augusta Vindelicum/Augsburg at Klais near Mittenwald (Upper Bavaria), where it runs through a hollow. In 763 the 'in der Scharnitz' monastery was built hereabouts.

132 Roman traveller's coach: relief on a tombstone from Virunum, the capital of Noricum, built into the outside wall of the church of Maria Saal near Klagenfurt (Carinthia).

Martin Hell's hypothesis that they were known in the East Alpine region prior to the Romans is gaining more and more acceptance. The distribution of Roman and possibly also pre-Roman horseshoes is there confined to the mule-tracks known of old and still used until early in our own era.[73]

Resthouses, customs posts and temples

For the benefit of travellers on official or private business resthouses were set up along the roads at appropriate intervals.[74] They normally comprised a bathing-establishment, a bureau of the imperial post and a highways department for traffic control. A complex of this kind has lately been extensively excavated (Ill. 133), its name having been ascertained from road-maps of late antiquity: *Immurium*[75] at Moosham in the district of Salzburg, at the road fork leading southeastward below the Radstädter Tauern, mentioned earlier. But the road-station already existed before the short-cut to the South across the Lausnitzhöhe was built in 201, for the earliest finds date back to the first half of the first century AD, that is to say to a

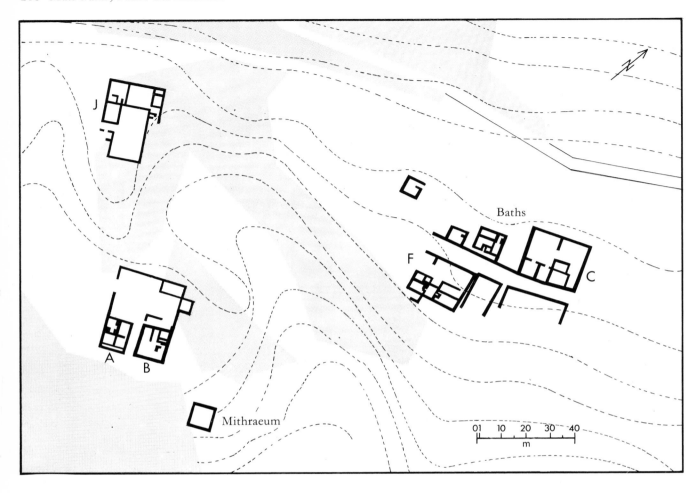

time when Noricum was not yet a province but only an affiliated client State.

At *Immurium* the road-station was not actually on the through road, but a little way off at a more suitable settlement area, doubtless linked to it by a field-path (the highways department was probably located at the fork). In the course of time a number of buildings had been put up. The complex A+B was there from the beginning: two small buildings (some 12 × 15 m) flanking an entrance-way leading to a large walled courtyard; this also had an entrance at the side. To judge from comparable examples of approach roads to large settlements, we have here a rest-

133 Plan of the Roman road-station of Immurium *at Moosham south of the Radstädter Tauern (Salzburg province). A/B and J were the actual resthouses, each with a large courtyard for accommodating vehicles and animals. C and F included living-quarters and workshops.*

house with accommodation for travellers and parking facilities for their vehicles and animals. The same applies to the partially excavated complex J, where on the south-east side further small rooms were no doubt aligned symmetrically with those that have survived. This would make it resemble still more closely a building up on the Little St Bernard pass (Ill. 134), which we must likewise assume to be a resthouse.

A road-station such as this, however, offered facilities over and above those provided by the resthouses themselves. In *Immurium*, lying at an altitude of 1100 m and with not too unfavourable a climate, further buildings were at all events added, and their function can be inferred from their structure and their contents. This applies in particular to the bath-house, a little self-contained building, which no Roman nor any who aspired to the Roman way of life would want to do without. That it could also be used by those in transit seems clear from the layout of the road station that has come down to us; when exactly it was built we do not know. Since the dwelling-houses E and G yielded finds from the late first century, the bath-house too will have been erected latest by then.

Building C accommodated workshops for processing metal, as tools and dross testify, and from Building F came a lead tag that was attached to the cord with which a bundle of three cloaks had been tied together, as the marking on it shows.[76] It is difficult to decide whether the weaving-mill itself was located in this house, or whether goods were merely assembled and stored there. Finally, mention should be made of a little sanctuary for the orientalizing god Mithras, whose cult spread through the Roman Empire from the second century on, mainly through the soldiers and traders.[77] Hence, to find a sanctuary in association with a road-station in the innermost Alpine region is not really all that surprising. The cemetery belonging to the place has also been discovered close by.

So *Immurium* shows up as a small stray settlement which, owing to its location on the through road, will have functioned as a sort of geographical focus for the surrounding farmsteads. Here the farmers and herdsmen brought sheep's wool or the finished textiles for re-sale, here they could acquire hardware and perhaps also jewellery, possibly in exchange for iron ore and other metals which they could readily come by in this mineral-rich area. Those who actually dwelt there enjoyed the luxury of a bath-house; whether they installed the alien god's sanctuary just for the benefit of travellers on their way through, or for themselves as well, is an open question. At all events, *Immurium* is, thanks to its having been so extensively laid

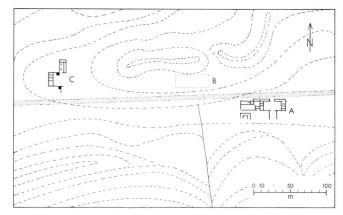

134 In *Alpia Graia* *is the name the Romans gave to the area of the Little St Bernard pass, over which ran a road from the Aosta valley to that of the Isère and on to the provincial capital of* Lugdunum/Lyon. *A = resthouse with inner courtyard; B = road check-point (?); C = sanctuary with annexes.*

bare by the archaeologists, an instructive example of how the romanization of even remote districts was accomplished in a very direct manner through the roads.

Along the roads, however, were to be found not only resthouses, catering for the comfort of the travellers, and road-stations the garrisoning *(beneficiarii)* of which was the responsibility of the military and which controlled the traffic, mostly in the immediate vicinity of the resthouses at particularly important places,[78] but also customs check-points, which the traders found less agreeable. In normal circumstances several imperial provinces were combined to form a single customs zone, at whose frontiers customs dues had to be paid. Such customs check-points were set up also in the Alpine region, for example at the frontier between Italia and Raetia or Italia and Noricum, but also where other provinces shared a common border. Thus an inscription recording the dedication of an altar to the goddess Diana by a customs inspector was found in the Zieltal above Partschins west of Merano:[79]

In h(onorem) d(omus) d(ivinae) sanct(ae) Dianae aram cum signo Aetetus Aug(ustorum) n(ostrorum) lib(ertus) p(rae)p(ositus) stat-(ioni) Maiens(i) XXXX Gall(iarum) dedic(avit) id(ibus) Aug(ustis) Praesent(e) cos(ule).

In honour of the divine (imperial) house this altar with her portrait was dedicated to Diana by Aetetus, imperial freedman, head of the customs station Maia, on 13 August, under the consulate of Praeses.

According to the given date the altar was put up in 217 or 246, when Raetia was part of the 'Gallic' customs area. It is usual to identify the customs station *Maia* with Meran-Obermais; it was to control the Via Claudia where it mounts the Adige valley and the route through the Passeiertal across the Jaufen pass. The duty payable here amounted to a fortieth part of the value of the goods, that is 2.5%, and was simply referred to as 'the Gallic fortieth' (*quadragesima [provinciarum] Galliarum*). The customs officers–like the tax collectors–were called *publicani* and operated on a State lease system. There is a place in the Western Alps which was known merely by the name of *Ad Publicanos* (At the Tax Collectors'), after the customs post on the frontier between Alpes Graiae and Gallia Narbonensis, namely Conflans at the confluence of the Isère and the Arly.

The debate over the location of Maia and the customs post has received fresh impetus in recent years.[80] For Partschins has yielded a second votive altar with a somewhat incomplete inscription, which in all probability is connected with a *beneficiarius*. This would seem to point to the existence of a road check-point in the Merano basin which, in view of its frontier location, is to be expected there. That the two stone monuments of Meran-Obermais were carried off to Partschins seems highly improbable. In this connection, the fact that the Töll gorge, through which the Adige forces its way opposite Partschins, formed the eastern boundary of Chur-Raetia and at least of the bishopric of Chur up until medieval times lends added weight to this inference.[81] Besides which the most recent investigations have shown that the Via Claudia–unlike the present-day highway–to the south of Merano ran along the western edge of the valley, dropped down into the valley somewhere near Marling and spanned the Adige at Algund by means of a stone bridge.[82] Then it avoided the Töll gorge by keeping to the northern slope of the now westward-curving Adige valley, until it once again followed the line of the modern road, presumably from Rabland (milestone!) onwards. In the light of these fresh findings a customs post at Meran-Obermais would appear to

135 Luxuriant locks and beard as well as the bundle of thunderbolts on his right shoulder characterize Jupiter, the supreme deity of the ancient Romans. As erstwhile weather-god he also commanded the awed veneration of those who journeyed over the passes; the native mountain-gods of the Alps soon merged in his person. This bust of Jupiter in sheet-silver comes from the shrine on the Little St Bernard pass: was it a cult-image or an unusually costly votive offering? 2nd-3rd century AD, *Ht 25 cm. Musée archéologique, Aosta.*

have served little purpose, particularly since in the second century the Brenner route was already fit for traffic over its entire length, thus rendering the Jaufen pass of no more than local importance. Even if *Maia* is in fact to be identified with Obermais (which yielded Roman finds), the corresponding customs post together with the road-station is far more likely to have been situated at Partschins. This, it is true, would mean that the border between Italia and Raetia from the Bolzano basin to the Merano basin followed the course of the Adige or even ran on the heights northeast of it.[83] This contention, besides conforming with the aforementioned bishopric border, is supported by the fact that similar conditions prevailed in the early Middle Ages: between Bolzano and Merano the Adige itself formed the boundary between the Lombards in the South and the Bavarians in the North. All this goes to show how flimsy are the foundations on which the pinpointing and interpretation rest when we have to rely on received inscriptions alone, and are not rescued by archaeology with excavations either planned or fortuitously revealing.

Even after the traveller had traversed valley after valley along dusty roads, crossed raging torrents on dizzily high bridges–mostly made of wood,–groped his way past deep abysses, and maybe even was let off lightly by the avaricious customs officials, he was still in danger of falling into the hands of highway robbers. Two inscriptions from Nyon on the Lake of Geneva record the fight put up by an official against the robbery menace (*praefectus arcendis latrocinis*). Direct proof is provided by a gravestone from Adjovscina on the road between Aquileia and *Emona/Ljubljana*, set up for Antonius Valentinus, a legionary officer who was killed by robbers while crossing the Julian Alps.[84] Was the traveller spared this, too, it was only right and proper that up on the pass he should make an appropriate offering to the gods, in gratitude, relief and the full expectation of a ŋo less propitious descent. The largest and most famous pass sanctuary was situated on the Great St Bernard, the most high-lying temple precinct in the whole of the Roman Empire (p. 159f.). Owing to the custom of dedicating small bronze tablets bearing a short inscription of a personal nature (Ill. 92) to *Iupiter Poeninus*, we get a good idea of the kind of person who made use of the pass. It was mainly soldiers, from the simple legionary to officers of all grades, belonging to the troops in the North, as well as traders of all sorts including slave-dealers.

There was also a small sanctuary on the Little St Bernard close to the resthouse, and one on the Julier (p. 159). Here the offerings consisted mostly of coins; as far as we are concerned, however, the travellers remain anonymous.

Road maps and guide books

For the purpose of planning major journeys, it was advisable not only for people to avail themselves of information by word of mouth from those more widely travelled, but also to make use of road maps. One such, in the form of a copy of the twelfth or thirteenth century, has been preserved. The National Library in Vienna treasures it as one of its most precious possessions; it is named the *Tabula Peutingeriana* (Ills 136–137), after the Augsburg humanist Konrad Peutinger, who at one time owned it.[85]

Users of present-day road maps will at first be perplexed by it, though puzzlement is likely to give way before long to the joys of discovery. The point is that the ancient cartographer was faced with a major difficulty: he had to set out the entire Roman Empire from Spain to the Euphrates, from Scotland to North Africa, on a single map, which needed to be both wieldy and detailed. And since the Romans scarcely knew books of the kind we are familiar with today and did not fancy folding maps, the poor cartographer had to resort to the method used at the time for documents and entire books: he had to make the Roman Empire fit on to a roll of parchment having the convenient width of not more than 35 cm. Hence it became nearly 7 m long. It is easy to see that the result bears little comparison with a modern map. All the coastlines and mountain ranges are distorted, misplaced, wrongly co-ordinated.

136 Section of the Tabula Peutingeriana, the medieval copy of a Roman road map in scroll form. That it dates so far back can be accounted for by the fact that the Brenner route, which was opened in the second century AD as a direct link between Italy and the North Alpine foreland, was evidently added without any notice being taken of earlier connections. As a result the Roman village of Epfach, the important spot where the road crosses the Lech, is marked twice over, both as Abodiaco *and as* Avodiaco.

137 Redrawn version of the section of the Tabula Peutingeriana (Ill. 136) incorporating the Alpine crossing from Verona to Augsburg over the Brenner. Also to be seen are on the right the Radstädter Tauern with the road-station of Immurium *at Moosham, on the left the Splügen pass with the route from Como to Chur. Being unimportant for road traffic, the Mediterranean and the Adriatic appear as narrow ribbons of water.*

ARMADAVSI. M V

Samuloceuis. XXV · Canabione · Clarenna · XXII · Ad lunam · XX · Aquilea · Opie · VII · Septemiaci · VII · Iosodica · XI · Mediatis · VIII · Iemaco · VII · Birciani · XVIII · Abr
XVIII · Augusta uindelicu · Pontone · F.2 · XXIIII · Tauoie · XVIII · Cambiduno · Escone · XVIII · Abodiaco · XIII · Urusa · XII · Britanatio · VII · Isin
XVIII · Viaca · XX · Rapis · XVIII · Adnous · Auodiaco · Couetaeas · XX · Tarteno · XX · Scarbia · XVIII · Vetonna · XVIII · Matreio · XX · Vepiteno · XXXVI · Sublabione · XXII · Pon
Vemania · Lapidaria · XVIII · Sumuaureu · X · Cruessedo · XX · Clauenna · XVIII · con.O · Bergomum · XX · Teuteris · XXXVI · Brixia · XXX
TRVMPLI · XXX · Medatanum · OTR ASPA · R O
ISVBRES · Zaumellium · XXVI · Ticeno · Laude pompeta · XXVI · Acerras · XVIII · Cremona · Britia · XX
Littas · XII · Lambrum · Quadrata · VII · Ad padum · XX · XX · Placentia · XV · Fla rentia · X · Fidenti
bria · Catulaemagus · Gilia · VIII · Pradu · Rigonu
na · XVI · comeli magus · Ambro
MACRA · Fluentia · Pistoris · VI · Vestidia · Hellana · VIII · Ad solaria · VIII · Florentia Tuscorom
SSAGAVRI · Luca · XII · Ad marris · VIII · In portu · IIII · Arnom · H
foro Clodi · Valuata · XVII · Aque Populanie ·
Ad taberna frigida · Pisis · VIII · Piscinas · VIII · Velins · Vadis Volateris · Aquis volaternis · T · XXIIII · Ad sertum · V
fossis papi rianis · turrita · Ad fines · X · Populonio · XII · Manliana · VIII · Saleborna · XII · umbro

Tricatva · XVII · Sublueo · XXXVI · Hyppone Regio · V · ubus flumen · 2
R XV · Ad uilam Seruilianam · XXX · O · XXV · Vico Iohani · XVIII · V
O Castulum Estatiunum · VI · Ad lapidem Baimi · Thibili · VII · Caprania
Ad cerriena · Ad rubras · VI · Galaupala · fonte fortuuno · IIII · Magri · IIII · Rustei · VIII · Ad pisirus
Zyrnas maseli · Ad calhalis · d german · X · E · Rugiata · T
aquis Herculis · VI · Mesar fila · XVIII · Ad piscinam · XXVIII · Gemellas · XXVIII · Tuabodeos ·

RHOMALLYH   QLV

teo·xvIII   Teleseo· III   Aruscha·xxvIII   Regino·   xvIIII   Sorniodino·   Narnii IIIo·   vIII   Arcizie·vII   Yana
                                    A·   Castelli Soladari·   Ditha·   Blaboriei·co·xII   Eleg·xvII   Dponte tces·   Sib
·n·xIII   Bediuo·   xvI   A?   Alesia   tinago·   Tartantone·xvIIII   lactatis·vxvIIII   Tergolape·vIIII   veteranis·xI   Totasbone·xII   Ornoi na·vIIII   Gabromagu·xv
inte·   Artbrige·xvI   tinvo·   xvIIII   Cucille·vxvII   vocario·xvIIII   Ant·   xvI   Inalpe·vIIII   Ad silanes·   in murro·
Cicutis·   Sarnis·xvIIII   ·xvIIII   H·   Tilabinte·   xxvII   Donte sonti·   H·frigido·
CIA   bentiro·vIII   vERONA   Mediacum·   Licenna·   xL   Aquite·Ad·   donte timani·xIIII
·n·xIII   ·xxxIIII   vicetia·xxvIII   Opiterrio·   H·   Concordia·xxx
   be   Toriaco·   ·xxvII   Patauis·xxx   Anno·
                  Auerona·Hostilia·   villa Passus·   Ad perciam·   H·
A   Manrva·   xxvIII   Amno·   Mino mediaco·
   H?   anno·   ·xxvIIII   Hostilia·   Mino mediaco·vI
Tannetum·xI   Corone·fossu
Satemum·   lepidoregio·   Gotina·   Ab hostilia·   per padum·   Hadriani
              xvII   vIII   Foro Li·   Vocum·   lecx fk·   H·iscx·   Silarum·   Radriam·
                        ·vIII   Bononia·   ·IIII   ·xvI   Claterna·vII   Silarum·H·xxvII   foro cornel·vI   Sinnum
Berxxiha·   ·vIIII   ·xvII
·xIIII   Vmbro·H·   ·x   Ad roglandem·   ·xII   Ad exreos·   ·vIIII   Ad novas·   Clufio·   ·vIIII   Pirusio·
·ha·   ·vI   Vmbro·H·xvI   Ad Mensulas·xvII   Manhana·   ·vIIII   ·vIIII   Pallia·H·
·S·   H·Albinia·   Cuccosa·   Saturnia·   ·xvII
Cosa·   cb·   ·vIII   Ar·menta·H·
Telamone·III   Albinia·H·vIIII   xv Port·Hercol·   Ad novas·   ·III
hre Hercul·
Armoniacum·H·   ·xv   ·xv   Tuniha·   ·xxvII
odiana·   L·   ·xxv   Begetti·   Amaggara·   ·xvII   Ad aquas·   C·
·xII   Ad molas·vI   Validce·v   Thacora·v   Sicca vexia·   ·v   Simitu colonia   Bulla R
              vico Valerian·   ·vIII   Ad turrala·   ·xvI   Sibus·   ·vIIII
·esi·   III   Vatari·   ·xxv   Flauia marci·   ·xv   Vasampus·   ·xII   Mova·   Tiuesie   ·xvIII
Ad mercurium·   Ad aquas castris·   ·vII   ·xv   ·xI   Ad mercurui·
Badias·   ·xxv   Ad Medias·   ·xxvIIII   Ad maiores·xvII   Vbiha Castellu·   xv   Theleste·c·
                                 Ad palmam·

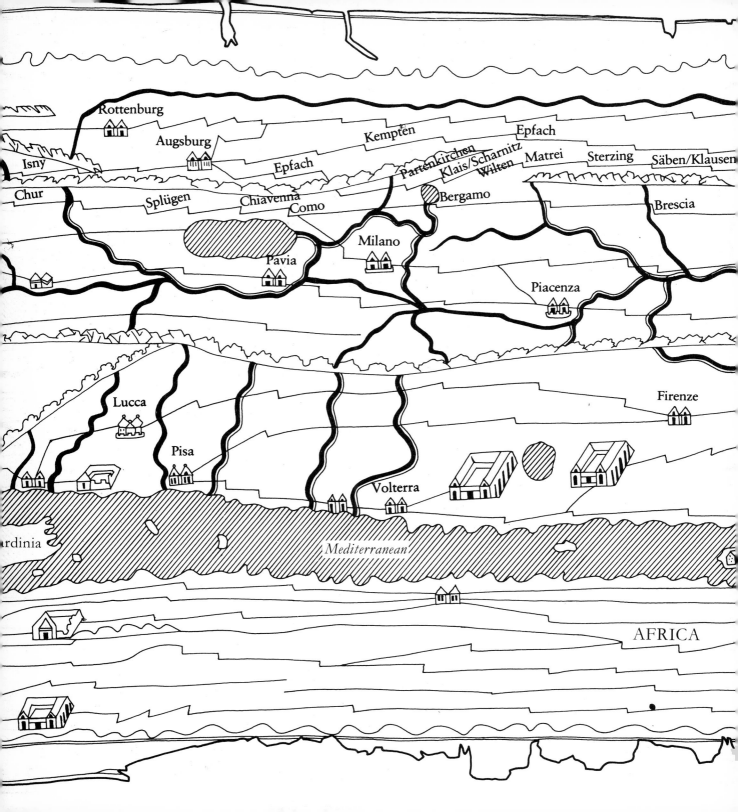

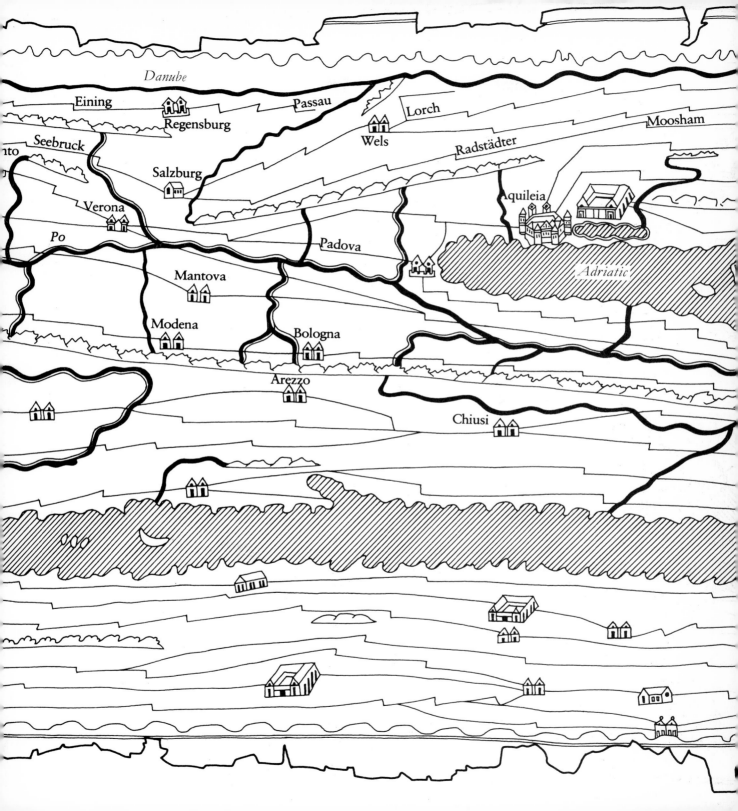

Danube

Eining

Regensburg

Passau

Lorch

Moosham

Wels

Radstädter

Seebruck

nto

Salzburg

Aquileia

Verona

Po

Padova

Adriatic

Mantova

Modena

Bologna

Arezzo

Chiusi

But in one respect it is correct: the schematic representation of the roads with intersections, stations. stated distances and place-names. Admittedly, the distances between places are out of proportion, being altered to suit requirements, but as the mileage figures were added, this did not matter to the user.

By way of illustration, a section covering the central Alpine area around the Brenner route is reproduced here. In the redrawn version several modern place-names have been added. Many stations round which no town or village grew up later can only be approximately located, though the distances marked on the map are of some help. Thus the station of *Scarbia* will have been situated between Innsbruck–Wilten and Partenkirchen in the vicinity of Mittenwald, where in early medieval times the 'in der Scharnitz' monastery was founded (p. 230). Excavations carried out there did not, it is true, disclose many traces of Roman material (some dispersed potsherds, two coins, no ruined walls of any kind), but the station cannot have lain far away.

The original map appears to have posed certain problems for the medieval copyist, as a result of which he introduced a number of palpable errors in the spelling of place-names (for instance, *Tarteno* instead of the correct *Partano*). Above all, there was the danger that, where the distances marked in miles were concerned, he might have been unable to read something clearly, relying instead on his own discretion. When dealing with Roman numerals, it was quite easy to introduce errors such as mistaking a 'V' for a 'II' on a hastily written original. At all events, the fact that there are undoubted copying errors adds greatly to the attraction of Roman road research. For should someone be determined to prove that a road followed a route quite other than that which had previously been supposed, it is possible for him to manipulate at will a number of place-names and all the distances. The mountain areas are admittedly subject to certain limitations in this respect, but the Alpine foreland provides many opportunities for engaging in this popular leisure-time activity.[86]

Fortunately, it is not the *Tabula Peutingeriana* alone that has come down to us, but also a corresponding traveller's guide-book made up of tables, for which no map has survived, namely the *Antonini Augusti itineraria provinciarum et maritimum*, the Guide-book of Antoninus Augustus for

Journeys through the Provinces and across the Sea, the original version of which probably appeared at the beginning of the third century AD. It lists only the names of inhabited places and resthouses and gives the distances in miles, adding occasional explanatory comments. A comparison with the *Tabula Peuteringeriana* shows the close connection between the two documents–which is hardly surprising, seeing that each records the fully developed road system of the Roman Empire. And just as there are variations in the spelling and the handling of names, so too the recorded distances do not always agree. Comparison of the particulars given for the Brenner route will help to make this clearer.

ANTONINI ITINERARIA	TABULA PEUTINGERIANA
Augusta Vindelicum	Augusta Vindelicum...
XXXVI	Ad Novas...
Abuzaco	Avodiaco...
XXX	Coveliacas XX
Parthano	Tarteno XI
XXX	Scarbia XVIIII
Veldidena	Vetonina XVIII
XXXVI	Matreio XX
Vipiteno XXXII	Vepiteno XXXV
Sublavione XXIIII	Sublabione XIII
Endidae XXIIII	Ponte Drusi XL
Tridento	Tredente

There is yet a third work deriving from antiquity which provides information on the Roman long-distance road network–the *Itinerarium Burdigalense* or *Hierosolymitanum*, bearing the date 333. It describes the route of a pilgrimage to Jerusalem, running from *Burdigale*/Bordeaux via *Arelate*/Arles and the Mont-Genèvre pass (referred to as *Matronam*) to *Segusio*/Susa and *Mediolanum*/Milan, from there on along the land-route to Constantinople.

Germanic peoples on Roman roads

The enemies of Rome who stormed across the Alps naturally possessed no road maps, but even so they found their way to Italy where they hoped to find rich booty. They left behind them death and destruction along the highways; hastily hidden hoards of coins indicate the affected areas. The first large-scale evidence of this was provided by the invasion of the Marcomanni in the year 170 (Ill. 22).[87] They forced their way from the northeast across the Alps into northern Italy; the rich finds of Ostriach and Gummern in the Drau valley above Villach may well be connected with this. That these same invaders also struck south from the Bohemian basin directly into Raetia and west Noricum is evidenced by the destruction wrought in Linz, Salzburg and the Wimsbach estate near Wels in a subsidiary valley. The route to the South is further indicated by the rich finds from the Veitlbruch by the Untersberg near Salzburg, those of Spital am Pyhrn and Althofen north of Klagenfurt, as well as the destruction of the *villa* of Katsch on the Mur. These places accurately mark the two pass routes in Noricum of the second century: the one from Salzburg across the Radstädter Tauern to *Virunum*, the other from where the Enns flows into the Danube, over the Pyhrn (945 m) and the Hohentauern (1245 m) likewise to *Virunum*.

In the West, the Alamanni similarly followed the convenient Roman roads. Though in the first half of the third century they were content to conquer the Northwest Alpine foreland, in 273 and 288 they stormed, not only across the Western Alps but also through the Alpine Rhine valley into northern Italy.[88] Several hoards of coins line this route, in which connection attention should be drawn in particular to the fact that a rich find from Vättis between the Tamina gorge and the Kunkels pass points to the use of this short-cut, and another from Malvaglia in the Blenio valley is only to be explained by presupposing an incursion over the Lukmanier pass or through the Lugnez via the Diesrut and Greina passes. But not all the named routes were developed as highways in Roman times, though certainly kept open as muletracks. To conclude from this that the Alamanni had shunned the better-guarded highways over the Splügen, Julier or Septimer passes would, in view of the small number of known finds, be assuming too much.

At all events, the Romans had by now recognized the importance of guarding the Alpine passes.[89] In late antiquity the forts of Bregenz, Schaan and Chur protected the Rhine road, and those at *Foetibus*/Füssen and *Veldidena*/Innsbruck-Wilten were meant to block the Reschen and Brenner routes. That this was ultimately not possible we know. During the migration period the armies of the Germanic peoples crossed the Alps wherever and whenever they wished. Above all, the approach route in the southeast of the Alpine range across the Birnbaumer Wald *(Ad pirum)* could never be made absolutely secure. Here the Goths and the Lombards would also break through, to establish themselves in Italy.

Disintegration in the early Middle Ages

With the crumbling of the Roman Empire the Roman road system disintegrated. There was no longer any military need to maintain it, no long-distance commerce, and the native population of the Alpine region was now, as ever, content to use a narrow pathway along which it was possible to proceed on foot or with a pack animal. Were a bridge to be carried away by flood-water, they lacked the means, the men and the technical knowledge that were needed to rebuild it in its original form; in future they had to make do with a rickety structure of planks. Should a section of road be buried by a landslip, either the rubble was shovelled aside or a fresh track simply made across it. Had the road slid several metres down the slope, effective repairs were scarcely possible. The resthouses stood empty and soon became derelict. That once upon a time hot water for bathing had been obtainable at such establishments was now no more than a curious notion that lived on in the memory of the mountain folk. Many a section of road built up by the Romans had in fact to be abandoned since its maintenance would have made too great demands on the technical resources of this time. A case in point was the Isarco gorge north of Bolzano, which was not re-opened for through traffic until the fourteenth century. In short, where communications were concerned, the early Middle Ages found themselves back in the pre-Roman stage from the technical and geographical point of view. Travellers, traders and invading armies still followed as far as possible the line of the Roman roads, and the former Via Claudia across the Reschen became once more the principal connecting link over the Central Alps, but the old mule-tracks–even those the Romans had not improved–assumed renewed importance.

There was no longer any question of a regulated road traffic, and safety on the roads was at a low pitch. When, in Severin's day, some of the last Roman soldiers in Passau set out in person for Italy with a view to collecting some pay, they were murdered by roving 'barbarians' before they had got very far; their bodies were found washed up on a bank of the Inn.[90] About this time, in the late fifth century, the Franks, too, frequently invaded Italy, and it was only under the Ostrogoth king Theodoric that conditions in the Alpine region were once again stabilized. Not until, in the first half of the sixth century, the Franks had extended their dominion right up to the edge of the Alps, even adding Inner Alpine Raetia to their territory, were the roads opened up again for organized traffic.

Only then was a journey such as that undertaken by Venantius Fortunatus reasonably safe. As a young man of about twenty-five, he set out on foot in the year 565 from Ravenna to visit the grave of St Martin at Tours. He was a compulsive writer, as a result of which we possess a fairly detailed account of his journey: a summary in the preface to his *Carmina* and 59 lines of verse in his *Vita Sancti Martini*, wherein his progress, only in the reverse direction, is described.[91] His journey led him from Aquileia over the Plöcken pass and the Gailbergsattel to *Aguntum* in the Lienz basin, then through the Pustertal across the Brenner and the Seefelder Saddle on to Augsburg. This was not strictly one of the most important routes, but if someone wished to travel from the north Adriatic to Augsburg and thence farther to the Northwest, it was in fact the shortest and most convenient way. Thus Venantius Fortunatus must have had a pretty good knowledge of its nature. That he had to swim across the rivers in the Alpine region and in the northern foreland, as he states, throws a vivid light on the condition of the roads and bridges.

Once the Lombards were established in Italy (568) and took part in the Central European power game, businessmen once more crossed the Alps in increasing numbers. The South regained its importance as supplier of exotic goods and source of artistic inspiration.[92] Envoys travelled to and fro, conferences alternated with skirmishing or war. But even monarchs themselves crossed the Alps

on friendly missions, as witness the Lombard king Authari who in 589 rode to Regensburg incognito with a few attendants in order to reassure himself that his prospective wife, the Bavarian duke's daughter Theudelinde, came up to his expectations.[93] When, on his return journey, he bade farewell to his Bavarian retinue at the frontier (at that time probably north of the Brenner), ostensibly satisfied with his intended, he gave vent to his feelings by rearing up on his horse, thrusting his battle-axe into a tree trunk and crying out 'Such blows does Authari deal!'

There is reason to believe that the custom, revived in early medieval times, of depositing or implanting spears on passes and heights as votive offerings to a mountain god or other deity[94] is a symptom of the predominantly warlike atmosphere that then prevailed. But as yet we know too little about the background to these sacrifices, who made them and which objects were favoured at any particular time (p. 164). Of historical importance, all the same, is a spearhead from the Lukmanier, dated in the sixth century on account of its shape, because it proves that this pass was already (or rather, again) used at this time.[95] The only instance of a votive offering on a pass, so providing evidence of its having been crossed, of fifth-century date is a coin of the Vandal king Geiserich on the Julier (p. 159). But it merely serves to show how circumspectly the archaeologist must tread when seeking to interpret a find that is determined by a number of different factors. This little coin in no way reflects the entire extent of the coming and going over the Alps.

We learn, for example, from literary sources that the Ostrogoths, the Byzantines and subsequently the Lombards sought to protect the Alpine crossings against the Franks in the north by fortifying them. A fort of this kind, dating to the first half of the fifth century, was excavated at Invillino,[96] a few kilometres west of Tolmezzo, where the road from the Tagliamento valley branches off northwards to the Plöcken pass. The Castel Grande of Bellinzona, too, played an important role as early as this as a blocking fort in the valley of the Ticino.[97]

Warrior graves of Germanic type with weapons, belts and other accoutrements are encountered mainly at strategically placed sites, which suggests a kind of guard post at control points. This would seem to account for a 'Frankish' warrior-grave of sixth-century date in Tamins at the confluence of the Vorderrhein and the Hinterrhein, as well as for a 'Lombardic' warrior grave in Civezzano (Ill. 81) northeast of Trento in the Val Sugana, which links the Piave and Adige valleys.[98]

Single finds of the sixth and seventh centuries at exposed places, even when the exact settlement structure is not known, may likewise be regarded as indications of such guard posts: Frankish-Alamannic ones on the 'Tummihügel'[99] above Chur (Ill. 41) at the entrance to the Schanfigg, Lombardic ones on the 'Rocca' of Rivoli high above the Adige in the Verona defile.

The monasteries and the road network

In addition to military guard posts, however, there were monasteries that were incorporated in increasing numbers in a sort of control system. Situated on the main roads, they offered the traveller shelter and assistance in case of need, as well as serving as a spiritual focus for the surrounding neighbourhood. Yet, in these early days in particular, strong political motives lay behind the founding of monasteries, which was normally undertaken by the nobility, the duke or the monarch (so that the new community should possess sufficient property and other sources of income to provide a livelihood),–even if only to keep a check on who exactly passed through and what their business was.

The first monastic foundation of the early Middle Ages in the Alpine region of which we have a record is St-Maurice d'Agaune in the lower Valais,[100] a royal monastery founded in 515 and belonging to the Burgundian ruling house. This place had previously been occupied by

Roman buildings whose purpose has not been ascertained, as well as a cemetery with early Christian burials; but it is precisely at this spot, it should be noted, that the road from Martigny to the Lake of Geneva could be sealed off,

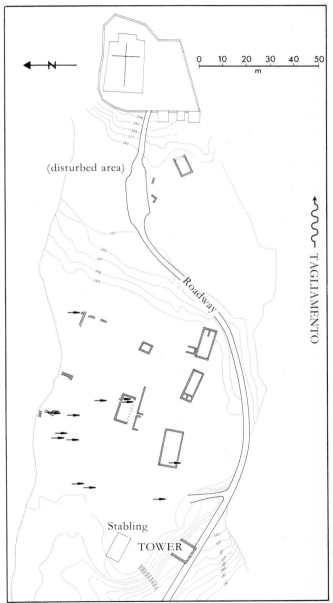

138 Countless arrowheads and spearheads were found during excavations at the fort on the island-like hill of Invillino in Friuli (Ill. 56). A survey shows evidence of bombardment from the north, that is from the direction of the level valley; to the south the Tagliamento flows below the hill's abrupt flank. The houses of the 5th/6th century that have been marked-in convey only an incomplete picture of the settlement, because on the north side in particular the rock continues down to below ground level and therefore scarcely any of the foundation walls remain.

since here there is only a narrow passage between the Rhône and the valley's steep face. The monks are unlikely to have had such intentions, but a few stone houses and a walled church were regarded by the king as adequate defence in case of emergency.

The eighth century saw a positive spate of monastic foundations in the Alpine region. The initiative came from the North, from the Merovingian-Carolingian empire of the Franks and also from Bavaria. The patron saints are almost in all cases St Peter and St Martin, both closely linked with Rome and/or the Frankish empire. Among the oldest monasteries on the northern fringe of the Alps are St Gallen and those on the island of Reichenau in the Lake of Constance, dating from the beginning of the eighth century. Operated as they are on the Columbanic-Benedictine principle, they represent rather the idea of the *locus amoenus*, the solitary and delightful spot for a monastic institution. The monasteries in the Inner Alpine region are a different matter: here the connection with the long-distance road network is unmistakable.[101] The oldest of these (*c.* 720) would seem to be Disentis,[102] where the road forks at the foot of the Oberalp and Lukmanier; the spearhead from the latter, referred to above, indicates that this pass had some significance as early as the sixth century. Pfäfers (735/40)[103] lies high above the Rhine valley at the entrance to the Vättisertal, the short-cut to the South across the Kunkels pass. The 'in der Scharnitz' monastery at Klais near Mittenwald, where precise excavation work was recently carried out,[104] was founded on 29 June 763 on the Roman road from Partenkirchen to the Brenner (functionally, it probably served as successor to the late-Roman road-station *Scarbia*), but had moved to Schlehdorf on the Kochelsee by 772. For, despite liberal donations from the Bavarian high nobility, the sources of subsistence–forestry and agriculture at an altitude of nearly 1000 m, and the modest revenue derived from the outlays of travellers and pilgrims–did not suffice. The monastery of Innichen, lying back in the Pustertal, founded six years later, was better placed because it was, like Kremsmünster on the northern fringe of the mountains, maintained as a base for the Slavic mission and therefore itself received support.[105]

Of the further monastic foundations in Graubünden from before 800, only Mustair (earlier fitted out as a hos-pice)[106] between the Ofen pass and the Vinschgau has survived. On the other hand, Mistail at Tiefencastel, situated near the road to Chur–to be reached from the Julier or Septimer passes via Lenzerheide (1549 m) or by way of the trying route along the Albula via Thusis–was soon abandoned[107] (allegedly on account of the unseemly behaviour of the nuns). These days the church of St Peter, standing isolated above the Albula gorge, counts as one of those places in Switzerland where grand scenery coupled with a monument steeped in history make an impressive combination.

The favourable location of the monasteries not only benefited the merchants but also the pilgrims, who crossed the Alps in ever-increasing numbers. Rome, as focal point of the Church, became the goal of many of the faithful from the North. The extent of the dangers that beset those undertaking such journeys is indicated by a legend surrounding St Corbinian, one of the missionary bishops in Bavaria, who twice travelled to Rome at the beginning of the eighth century. Here is a rendering of a late-nineteenth-century version of it,[108] as taught to Bavarian schoolchildren:

At the time when St Corbinian was spreading the Christian gospel in our Bavarian land, it still looked anything but inviting. Great forests and bogs and impenetrable undergrowth covered large tracts of it. The aurochs trampled down the bushes, the boar burrowed among the roots of century-old oaks, and wolf and bear went about their sinister business.

A journey to Rome was then still a perilous undertaking. But St Corbinian was unafraid; imbued with divine faith, he embarked on the journey to that city.

One night he sought refuge in a wild mountain district. He and his companions went to sleep, and all around them was still. Suddenly a shaggy bear sprang from his hiding-place and pounced upon the saint's horse. Its death-throes awakened the attendants, and when they went to investigate they found Corbinian's packhorse torn to pieces by the fierce animal's claws. Horrified, they bewailed to the man of God what had happened. But he said to Anserich, one of his travelling companions: 'Take this whip, and go and chastise the growler for the harm he has done.' When the man hesitated, Corbinian repeated: 'Go, and fear nothing! When you have punished the bear, place on his back the saddle which the horse wore and hold him ready for continuing the journey.' Anserich plucked up courage, chastised the bear, and lo and behold! the bloodthirsty creature patiently endures the blows, accepts the saddle and performs the horse's tasks for the entire journey.

That there were bears about at that time, which might imperil a lone traveller, should not come as a surprise; for the last bear in the Central Alps was dispatched in 1904, the last Bavarian one, on the other hand, in 1835. It is more to the point to note–and this tallies with what we know about medieval travel–that the saintly man did not ride but merely took along a packhorse, to carry his baggage.

In those early days not only did pilgrims, priests and bishops journey to Rome, but tradition has it that popes, too, crossed the Alps, much in the manner of Corbinian. One of the most momentous undertakings was the journey of Pope Zacharias to the Frankish royal palace at Ponthion on the Marne in 754, in order to enlist Pepin's help against the Lombards. That he travelled via the Great St Bernard, the shortest route to the Northwest, is not expressly stated but seems highly probable.

Once the Franks had conquered the Lombardic kingdom in 774, transalpine traffic increased still further; for connections with the now enlarged Frankish empire had to be soundly based. And when, for instance, we learn that the monastery of St Denis near Paris was granted estates in the Veltlin, contact between it and its possessions–whereby traffic was augmented by messengers, delegations and tours of inspection–must surely be assumed. Likewise, St Martin's in Tours owned wealthy properties on Lake Garda and in the Valcamonica.[109]

The most convincing testimony for the widespread communications of this period (Harun-al-Rashid sent a delegation to Charlemagne in Aix-la-Chapelle!) in the Alpine region is provided by the rich treasure of Ruschein near Ilanz[110] on the Vorderrhein. It was found at the foot of the Grüneck ruin, close to the old road. Here the road forks: one can proceed either straight on to the Disentis monastery and south over the Lukmanier pass, or directly into the Lugnez and over the Diesrut and Greina passes into the Blenio valley, a route which is known from as early as the Bronze Age. The find comprised not only 123 coins but also some gold ornaments, together with two small lumps of melted-down gold. Its implications are open to question: on the one hand, the contents hardly suggest the merchandise of a commercial traveller who feared a

139 Ruschein at Ilanz lies where two important routes from the Vorderrhein valley to the South fork, one running through the Lugnez across the high Diesrut and Greina passes, the other–longer but more convenient–across the Lukmanier pass. In 1904, during road-works below the Grüneck ruin, a cache was discovered comprising 70 gold and 53 silver coins, as well as ear-rings with inlaid gems forming crosses on the display side, five pendants from the necklace and two small lumps of gold. The coins are predominantly Lombardic and Frankish. The five foreign issues merit special attention: three pennies of the Anglo-Saxon kings Offa of Mercia and Egbert of Kent (second and third coins in the second row), as do two dirhems of the caliphs al-Mahdi and Harun-al-Rashid (second and third coins of the bottom row). End of the 8th century AD. *L of the ear-rings 5 and 5.3 cm. Rätisches Museum, Chur.*

sudden hold-up; on the other hand, there is no evidence at this time (the latest coin was struck in 790) of any major hostilities in Graubünden that might explain why this costly treasure should have been hidden by someone residing there. (Incidentally, a similar problem of interpretation applies to a destructive fire around 800 in the Castel Grande at Bellinzona.[111]) Whilst the gold ornaments probably derive from northern Italy, the coins indicate more wide-ranging connections. Among them were Lombardic coins dating from the time before the conquest by the Franks, gold coins of Charlemagne which were in circulation in northern Italy in 774–781, Frankish silver coins from the empire (the earliest still minted by Pepin III) and some new issues from northern Italy. Yet all of them had become obsolete on account of changes in the coinage system, so that at the time they were buried they possessed no more than the intrinsic value of the metal. This applied even more to the foreign coins, for who in Central and Southern Europe would have accepted by way of payment a penny of King Egbert of Kent or a dirhem of the caliph Harun-al-Rashid from North Africa, without first testing them for weight and metal content?

Throwing light on this period, when the Carolingian ruling house extended the road links to Italy, is a further discovery, which the Graubünden Archaeological Service made as recently as 1978.[112] While investigations were being carried out at a chapel in Domat/Ems, halfway between Chur and the confluence of the Vorderrhein and the Hinterrhein, it was found that not only was a tiny monastery originally attached to the chapel but that underlying the whole was an earlier structure which with its distinctive architecture and precise execution suggested a specific building style. It had been destroyed in a fire which, on the evidence of two coins of Charlemagne minted in northern Italy, occurred after 774. Since the building had apparently only been in existence for a few years, a possible explanation is that it served as a kind of resthouse for travellers engaged in official Frankish business, if not actually for the emperor himself. As the bishop resided in Chur and at the same time held temporal sway over Chur-Raetia until 806, it is highly probable that the Franks had no desire to make claims on the autonomy-seeking and ill-tempered churchman. But since, from 806 on, a Frankish count in Chur determined political affairs,

the road-station at Domat/Ems lost its strategic significance, and a little monastery was built which at least offered pilgrims en route a place where they could break their journey; the nobility lodged with the count in Chur and brought him the latest news of the empire.

Pilgrims and hospices

Because the majority of those who crossed the Alps were pilgrims on their way to or from Rome, the small and large monasteries and the hospices built for that very purpose increasingly took over the role which the Roman *mansiones* and *mutationes*, the resthouses, had formerly played. But initially the hospices were still located in the valleys or at the foot of the high passes. Thus there was a monastic unit in Splügen, where travellers could put up, and a hospice is known to have existed in the first half of the ninth century at San Gaudenzio near Casaccia at the foot of the Septimer and Maloja passes. What we have been able to discover about the early medieval traffic system[113] has not measured up to our knowledge of conditions in Roman times, with the result that we know but little about the distances that separated these simple refuges, the cost of maintaining them and the kind of people who frequented them. The legend of Corbinian's journey to Rome describes conditions which will have changed little during the ensuing two or three centuries: the traveller had to rely on his own initiative and had usually to spend the night in the open. The levy imposed by the Saracens on monasteries (for example, Disentis and St-Maurice) and hospices (for example, Bourg-St-Pierre at the northern approach to the Great St Bernard) in the first half of the tenth century appears to have constituted an additional hazard and burden where crossing the Alps was concerned.

Yet major politics were directed towards securing the routes to the South. Even King Canute took a hand in them. In Rome in 1027 he negotiated with Emperor Henry II and the Burgundian king Rudolf III. He complained of arbitrariness and chicanery, about which his subjects had informed him. In a letter to the English clergy he summarizes the outcome of his negotiations:[114]

I therefore spoke with the emperor and the lord pope and the princes who were present, concerning the needs of all the people of my whole kingdom, whether English or Danes, that they might be granted more equitable law and greater security on their way to Rome, and that they should not be hindered by so many barriers on the way and so oppressed by unjust tolls; and the emperor consented to my demands; and King Rudolf, who chiefly had dominion over those barriers, and all the princes confirmed by edicts that my men, whether merchants or others travelling for the sake of prayer, should go to and return from Rome in safety with firm peace and just law, free from hindrances by barriers and toll-gatherers.

It is evident that it was principally the route over the Great St Bernard pass that he had in mind. And there, indeed, the first hospice in the Central Alps that we know of was built high up on the pass by Bernard of Menthon some time in the second half of the eleventh century. So from this time on the venerable hospice has graced the Great St Bernard, a combination of the age-old pass sanctuary of tradition and the Roman road-station *In summo Poenino*. The earliest description of it, from the year 1125, in conjunction with investigations into the constructional history of the present-day hospice, allows us to reconstruct the oldest of the buildings.[115] It measured 18.0 × 13.5 m and had two storeys. On the ground floor were two entrances leading to a corridor, a pilgrims' rest-room with stove, and the kitchen which at the same time served as a refectory for the monks. The upper storey contained their bedroom, living room and chapel (with bell-tower). The stone walls were thick enough to defy the harshest weather.

Monks are still to be found there, but since the road tunnel was built, only two categories of tourists use the pass. Firstly, there are those—probably the lesser number—who on a trip through the Alps do not want to miss the experience of driving over a high Alpine pass; secondly, there are those anxious to see the St Bernard dogs, which are depicted nowadays on picture postcards with the legendary brandy cask round their necks, whereas they are actually only to be seen confined to narrow pens which are out of bounds unless one pays an entrance fee. Nothing better illustrates the transition from a life-saving institution to a tourist attraction than the hospice on the Great St Bernard pass.

The two old hospices on the Lukmanier are wholly submerged. They lie some 60 m beneath the water when the

reservoir north of the summit of the pass is filled up to the top of the dam. The archives tell us that the first hospice was founded on 28 January 1374. But that was the date on which it came legally into existence, it being dependent for its subsistence on the estates up on the pass and farther down in the Blenio valley. Actual construction can scarcely have begun before June of that year. The excavations

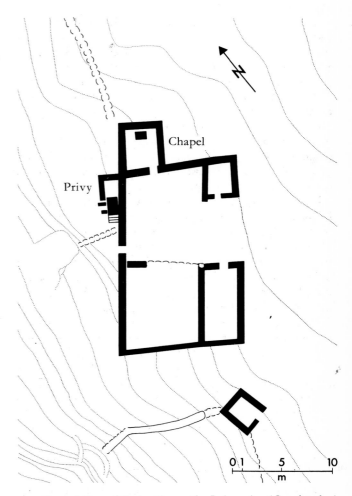

140 Ground-plan of the hospice on the Lukmanier (Graubünden) built in 1374. The living-quarters and workrooms as well as the little chapel are grouped round a large rest-room with fireplace.

which have been carried out by the Raetian Museum of Chur have exposed it, thereby preserving at least documentary evidence.[116]

The cement walls, between 0.6 and 1 m thick, enclosed an area of 17.5 × 10.1 m. This was divided into a large main room with a wide entrance (probably intended also for horses) containing a sunken hearth, adjoining which was a smaller room of like width, which may have served as a bedroom. On either side of the entrance ramp was a considerably smaller room, one of which was possibly used as a stable, the other as a workshop. At the northern corner were two extensions, one a tiny chapel with altar (dedicated to the Virgin Mary), which was reached from the main room, and a lavatory the door of which, understandably, did not lead into the main room but could only be reached up a few steps along the outer wall facing the mountainside.

Whether the building had an upper storey and how many monks performed their religious duties here is not known, for the height of the walls left standing nowhere exceeded 2 m, parts of them having been carted away when the later hospice was built slightly higher up in the sixteenth/seventeenth century. Glass fragments do, however, point to windows with bull's-eye panes. Altogether, the archaeology of medieval Switzerland has benefited greatly from the large amount of material found at this place. Its time-span, between 1374 and the sixteenth/seventeenth century, offers valuable points of reference for the dating of other find complexes for which received information is inadequate. Admittedly, piecing it together presents certain problems. For instance, no less than 35 knives were found, almost exclusively in the main room and in front of the outer wall to the northwest. It is hard to believe that they were all accidentally lost or thrown away as useless, any more than that the fragments of clay, steatite and glass, metal objects or tools meant nothing. For their quantities and distribution correspond in every way with the conditions one expects to find at early settlement sites. Yet the fragments of rock-crystal bearing marks of blows, which were picked up by the kilo, suggest that the pious brothers had a side-occupation: in the towns in the Po plain, where flint is lacking, rock-crystal was very welcome for making fire with tinder. Large quantities of iron dross in the area of the workshop indicate that they were engaged in other handicrafting operations, though smelting must have taken place elsewhere.

The hospice of the Virgin Mary on the Lukmanier was probably preceded by modest refuges of some kind or another, which the herdsmen of the upper pastures also used to shelter in. This is indicated by several finds which must date from before 1374. For a hospice of this kind receiving ecclesiastical or monastic support would only be installed if the traffic had grown so much, that looking after inexperienced mountain travellers and pilgrims up on the pass itself came to be a necessity and a Christian duty. The founding of the Disentis monastery in the Vorderrhein valley only makes sense if a more or less regular traffic over the Lukmanier pass is envisaged (p. 226). Latest investigations at the hospice on the St Gotthard have brought to light a pre-Romanesque structure which is older than the Chapel of the Saints consecrated in 1226.[117] Thus the St Gotthard already possessed a local significance as a link with the Ursenertal and Andermatt prior to the opening-up of the Schöllenen gorge by the Zähringers, though it was this latter development that turned the St Gotthard into one of the most important passes of medieval times. Simple as these refuges of the High Middle Ages may have been, every traveller overtaken by darkness, exhaustion or bad weather was glad to have a roof over his head and a fire to warm himself at.

Emperor Henry IV, we may be sure, would have been only too glad had he been able to spend the night at one of the aforementioned hospices. But because, for political reasons, the passes between the Aosta valley and the Brenner were barred to him, he had to choose the Mont-Cenis pass for his 'journey to Canossa'. It was in January 1077 that he crossed the pass with his trusty companions. The monk Lambert of Hersfeld gives us a convincing account of the undertaking:[118]

At the foot of the grim mountains the king hired some natives who were familiar with the region and were used to the sheer rock-faces of the Alps, so that they should lead his contingent past the steep mountainsides and through the piles of snow and in every possible manner make the way easier for those that followed. Once the summit had been reached under their guidance, there appeared to be no possibility of proceeding on the farther side. For the mountainside was precipitous and slippery on account of the icy cold and no means of climbing down presented itself. Thereupon the men tried with all their might to overcome the obstacle, and before long they were crawling on hands and knees and supporting themselves on the shoulders of the guides or, when their feet slipped, falling and rolling down, until at last, after risking life and limb, they reached the plain. The Queen and the women in her retinue laid the guides on ox-hides from the tents they had with them, and dragged them

141 Not until the middle of June do the swathes of snow retreat across the Great St Bernard pass, and weeks later bitter winds may still festoon with icicles the railings of the hospice where until the advent of the motorcar travellers sought refuge and warmth.

down on these. All manner of devices were used in order to bring some of the horses down, while others were pulled along with their legs tied, and many of these perished in the process: most of those that survived were in a pitiful state, few came through fit and unscathed.

From post-chaise to railway

A decisive improvement in traffic conditions[119] took place in the thirteenth and fourteenth centuries, when not only the St Gotthard was opened-up to long-distance traffic but on the initiative of wholesale merchants a number of good roads were constructed: through Heinrich Kunter in the Isarco defile north of Bolzano, through Jacob von Castelmur over the Septimer pass (above a Roman forerunner?); then, in the seventeenth century, through Jodokus Stockalper from Brig, over the Simplon pass. The peak period for road construction was, however, the first half of the nineteenth century. The routing of most of the pass roads dates from that time–if we except the constructional work of recent years. Improvements to the Simplon in 1801–1805 were carried out in the interests of Napoleon's military requirements. These passes were followed soon after by Mont-Cenis, St Gotthard, Splügen, Arlberg and even the Stilfser Joch, at 2757 m still the second highest Alpine road, which was meant to establish a link between Tyrol and Lombardy–at that time likewise part of Austria.

Thereby the requirements for a regular mail-coach service were for the first time met. For instance, the express coach across the St Gotthard from Altdorf on the Lake of Lucerne (departure time 8.30) to Bellinzona (arrival time 24.00) took only 15½ hours. After a brief halt, it continued its journey in the small hours, and the passenger would arrive in Milan at 12.30. Prior to that, such journeys could only be undertaken on horseback, and even then it was considered wise to join forces with larger parties. As early as 1627 people were advised to avail themselves of the 'Milan messenger', who accompanied the traveller from Lindau to Milan (where they called him the 'Corriere de Lindo'). One would set off from Lindau on Monday afternoon by ship for Fussach, ride from there to Feldkirch, then spend the second night in Chur. The journey through the Via Mala to Splügen called for particularly reliable horses. In the morning came the climb up to the pass, man and beast refreshing themselves in the hospice with Veltlin wine in which bread had been dunked. After spending the night in Chiavenna, a ship was boarded in Novate which was due in Como after a twenty-hour voyage across the lake. Milan was reached early on Sunday morning, after a ride through the night. It had taken the exhausted traveller five and a half days to complete what was a trying journey, for even crossing the Lake of Como was seldom a relaxation; frequently storms or turbulent winds would lead the ship into trouble (circumstances so graphically described where the Lake of Lucerne was concerned in the saga of William Tell). Those travelling on their own, moreover, ran the risk of being robbed. Instructions as to equipment to be carried at that time never omitted to mention the need for weapons; a couple of pistols were earnestly recommended.

Far quicker was the mounted postal service of Thurn and Taxis, which in the summer took only ten and a half days from Brussels to Rome (in winter 12 days), a total distance of 1570 km. This was of course only possible with a smoothly functioning system which always had horses and riders at hand and avoided halts.

All the same, most goods were still conveyed by carriers with their horses; to a certain extent–as, say, over the Great St Bernard pass–well into this century. An exhaustive study by the Salzburg historian Hans Klein[120] clearly demonstrates what the pack-animal traffic across the Tauern involved. It was not the utility articles of the little man that were carried, but valuable commodities which were highly prized at their ultimate destination: salt from Hallein went to Friuli, wine from Friuli and the slopes of the Julian Alps found ready takers at the princely archiepiscopal Salzburg.

A remarkable fact is that even at this late stage there was still no genuine long-distance commerce, the carrier himself took the risk: men such as those Carinthian farmers who, above all in autumn and early winter when the harvest had been garnered, crossed the mountains with their animals. Apart from simple peasants, however, who set off with one or two horses, there were also what could almost be described as large-scale contractors who entered the lists with thirty or more horses and a corresponding number of servants. So as to minimize the danger, the tendency was to form long caravans when approaching the passes. The commemorative stones record accidents incurred by plunging down the mountainside, by falling rocks, avalanches or a sudden spell of extreme cold with blizzards lasting several days and nights, but these do no more than hint at the actual perils. For the poor Carinthian farmers it was only a small, yet essential, subsidiary source of income; for the clients in the South and in the North, on the other hand, it meant a welcome gain entailing virtually no risk.

But no sooner had the roads been improved to a reasonable extent, than the days of mail carried on horseback and by coach were over. It was, however, not from the motor-car, grinding up the old mountain roads, that competition first came, but from an unexpected quarter, namely the railways. These needed completely re-aligned routes for sharp curves and steep inclines were out of the question. A new era in the opening-up of the Alps to traffic had dawned. The two earliest Alpine railways (Semmering 1854 and Brenner 1867) managed to surmount the lowest of the north/west passes without a tunnel, or with only a short one, after winding their way up in a series of loops. The tunnels that could not be avoided in dealing with steep slopes or spurs of rock were hewn out in the traditional manner by hand or blasted with gunpowder, as had been done earlier in the case of the Napoleonic Simplon road, where it took eighteen months' work to bore tunnels 180 m long in the Gondo gorge (operating from four separate places).

Railway building in the Alps was revolutionized by Alfred Nobel's invention of dynamite in 1867. This made it comparatively simple to construct tunnels beneath even the higher passes, provided the ascents from the valleys could be conveniently dealt with. As early as 1871 the 13½ km-long stretch of railway beneath the Col-de-Fréjus was opened (south of the corresponding road over the Mont-Cenis); the Arlberg tunnel (10¼ km) followed in 1882, and in the same year the Gotthard tunnel, which, nearly 15 km in length, is still the second longest of all the Alpine tunnels. Finally, the Lötschberg tunnel (14.61 km) was completed in 1913; in conjunction with the Simplon tunnel (opened in 1906 and with a length of 19.8 km the longest Alpine tunnel to date), it offers the fastest route from Milan to northern Switzerland and on into the Rhineland. The shortest route is still the Gotthard line, but the many turns and twists prevent the train from attaining a high speed. Hence plans have been afoot for several years now to build a much longer 'basic tunnel' which at its highest point will be far below the present depth of 1150 m. Of late, a 'basic tunnel' for the Brenner, too, has been suggested, but it seems that this presents more political difficulties than practical problems. At all events, we may assume that the desire for quicker trans-alpine railway links will mean that more such projects will be mooted.

The first transalpine flight and
the prohibition of motor-cars in Graubünden

It was less the craving for speed than the titillating sensation of embarking on a pioneering venture, that determined an event which took place on 23 September 1910. In 1903 the Wright brothers had developed the navigable powered flying-machine in America, yet the first flight by aeroplane across the main ridge of the Alps was made no more than seven years later. But it ended in tragedy. Jorge Chávez, a 27-year-old Peruvian (the airport in Lima is named after him) had sensibly chosen a promising route, namely from Brig to Domodossola via the Simplon—a relatively low pass offering good opportunities for take-off and landing in wide valleys not too far away on either side. The plane took off successfully in the Valais; gaining height between the mountains was no problem and the Simplon pass was sooned cleared, but the landing at Domodossola was—as landings still tend to be to this day—the most difficult stage of the flight. As the aircraft, with its young pilot crouching beneath the wings, approached, while the Italians and the jostling reporters gathered below yelled enthusiastically, came disaster: the plane stalled, went into a spin and, when only a few metres from the ground, crashed. Helpers rushed to the scene and pulled the pilot from the wreckage, but he soon succumbed to his injuries. All the world's newspapers acclaimed this pioneering achievement and lamented the tragic outcome.

The Museo della Fondazione Galetti in Domodossola commemorates this event: fragments of the aeroplane, pieces of equipment and the pilot's clothing (flecked with blood!), press cuttings, old photographs of take-off and descent—for the visitor who wishes to learn about the archaeology of the Toce valley, an unexpected leap forward into the twentieth century, into the archaeology of air travel. The old, somewhat dilapidated palace with its large approach stairway, the high, dark rooms, the faded curtains provides a unique setting, adding immediacy to the sharing of an experience, the grief coupled with pride over the fate of the young pilot from an alien country. In Peru, too, the memory of this daring feat lives on. When, a few years ago, the Italian president paid a visit there, he presented his host with some objects from the Domodossola museum, regarding them as valuable gifts. And those who pass through Domodossola on an Alpine tour—well away as it is these days from the beaten track—should spend a few hours there and ponder with what rapidity technical advance has taken place in our time. Between that 23 September 1910 and today, when the giant jets wing across the Alps in a matter of minutes at a height of many thousands of metres, lie some 70-odd years.

All the same, this technical advance was not welcomed everywhere. When, at exactly the same time, the motor-car began to take possession of the Alps, the canton of Graubünden came to a noteworthy decision on 11 May 1911: it refused to permit the use on its roads of these tearing, roaring and dust-raising monsters, which were a danger to pedestrians, made horses shy and ran over chickens. After 12 years, however, the canton authorities came to realize that this prohibition was doing them considerable harm economically, since the flourishing trade was going to neighbouring cantons and lands. Even so, when on 24 June 1923 it was decided to exempt one or two roads as a trial, the majority in favour was only 2356 votes (11,422 against 9066). These were the main through roads and the motorist had to pay a toll. As the consequences did not actually prove to be as serious as had been feared, the restriction was lifted in June 1925. The motor-car had finally won.

But there were exceptions; for, where circumstances allow, man resorts to something that was available to him from the outset—his own ingenuity. In August 1976, there was erected on the Monte Moro pass (2868 m), which leads from the Italian Anzasca valley across into the Swiss Saas-Fee, a stone monument in memory of smugglers who had lost their lives while engaged in their dangerous occupation; the donor was found to be a mysterious 'Committee from the Anzasca Valley'. A favourite smugglers' track ran over the pass, along which, while it still paid off, tons of cigarettes used to be carried to Italy (these days it is disposable cigarette-lighters, which are heavily taxed). Then, not a few of these lawbreakers laden with 30 to 40 kg of cigarettes would from time to time topple over the edge or be swept away by an avalanche. At the dedication ceremony three clergymen from the Anzasca valley conducted the mass for the dead.[121]

Those of us who cross the Alps in our tin boxes or in a heated railway compartment forget all too readily that even today the traffic strategists and motorway planners have not yet got the better of the mountains. Whenever the Brenner, say, is closed to traffic through avalanches, this represents an enormous trading loss running into millions on both sides of the Alps. And nobody any longer gives a thought to the far greater difficulties the travellers, merchants, carriers, soldiers and pilgrims had to contend with a mere 150 years ago.

142   The elegant design of this bronze flagon from the Dürrnberg above Hallein (Salzburg province) testifies to the bronze-working expertise of the craftsman responsible for it. The body of the vessel was fashioned from a single piece of sheet-metal without recourse to rivetting; nor are there any signs of welding, moulds having been used for the embossing. The base alone was separately attached. The religious concepts that underlie the figural ornamentation of the cast handle, which is rivetted on, are difficult to determine. At the lower end is a human head encircled by tendrils, at the upper end a monster with a human head in its mouth. On the part that extends above the neck stand two long-tailed fabulous beasts in the process of devouring another creature–ultimately an orientalizing motif. Everything points to this show-piece having been crafted on the Dürrnberg itself. 400–350 BC. Ht 45.8 cm. Museum Carolino Augusteum, Salzburg.

VI The Basics of Living – Husbandry, Mining, Commerce

Little fear of large animals

Man, regarded on the biological level as an all-consumer, relies mainly on plants and meat for his sustenance. At the very first find-spots in the Alpine region archaeologists discovered animal bones, the remains and refuse from meals. Represented among this material were all animals of the chase that were acclimatized to the surroundings. The largest of the animals hunted was the elephant, which at that time still inhabited the shores of the Mediterranean. It provided enough meat to assuage the hunger of an entire tribe for several days. Since it was not possible to set aside a reserve supply and the meat itself only kept for a few days in a cool place, all those present stuffed their bellies full; for no one knew in advance when there would be another such feast. Often, when there were no smaller creatures around, they had to make do with mussels, berries, mushrooms and honey. The hunters are unlikely to have bearded the large animals, but driven or lured them into prepared pits and towards precipices, over which they then plunged, thus falling an easy prey to their pursuers, who used simple wooden spears and hatchets with sharp-edged stones attached for the kill. Stone implements were useful above all for cutting-up the carcase, scraping the inner side of the hide and splitting the bones in order to extract the marrow. These needed to be specially shaped with sharp cutting edges, achieved by skilful chipping (Ill. 3); for this purpose, freshly obtained flint was best. Where this was not readily available (the nodules are only found embedded in limestone or chalk), less easily worked material had to be resorted to.

Towards the end of the Old Stone Age, when the final Ice Age was over, hunting methods had already reached an advanced stage. Among the weapons were spears with stone or bone heads, the bow and arrow, as well as harpoons for spearing fish.[1] It is to be assumed that snares and lime-twigs were also used, even though no archaeological evidence to this effect exists. Pictorial representations indicate that wild horse (Ill. 87), primitive forms of cattle and reindeer were among the most sought-after animals of the chase. In the Central Alps hunters ventured up to above 2000 m during the short summer season, tracking species of wild animal to which they were particularly partial.[2] At places where they stopped over for longer periods they also left behind them utensils for preparing hides and for sewing, for felling trees and removing the bark.

Corn, cattle and pottery

For many decades archaeologists defined the Late Stone Age as a period when both agriculture and stock-breeding began at the same time as the first pottery was made. Recent observations, however, make it seem more likely that, not only in the Near East but also in Central Europe including the Alpine region, these changes took place at different times in the cultural history of man. For one thing, botanical-archaeological investigations in the south German foreland and in the mountain interior have shown that the pollen from the earliest corn (to be distinguished from the wild varieties by its size) and the weeds peculiar to cornfields can be dated in the first half of the fifth millennium, that is to say several centuries before the earliest known dwelling-places containing earthenware vessels.[3] Knowledge of how to cultivate corn and generate high-yielding varieties spread northwestwards from the Near East. In particular, the original einkorn and millet, dwarf wheat and barley have been identified. Agriculture, even in its primitive form, implies that the people in question were to a certain extent sedentary, and this enabled them to engage in and develop the domestication of animals.

We cannot tell precisely when the keeping of livestock and stock-breeding, in comparison with the cultivation of corn, were introduced in Central Europe, because the differing circumstances in which the finds were made render the relationship between local occurrences very difficult to determine. Whereas it is in marshland that the pollen grains of corn are almost exclusively conserved, and dating is by scientific observation of the strata, the animal bones come from dwelling-places chronologically classi-

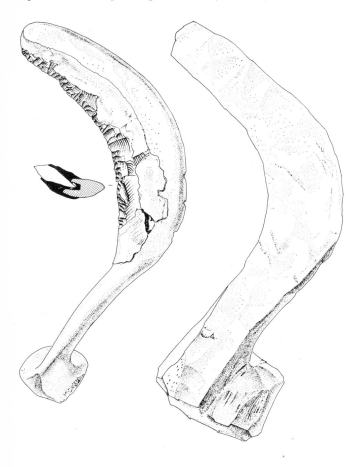

143 The sickle is inseparable from the harvesting of corn. Prior to the development of bronze sickles, an achievement of the 16th century BC which only made slow progress into the agriculturally backward Alpine region, little flint blades set into a shaped wooden matrix with birch tar served the purpose just as well. With these the corn was severed just below the ears. This meant that after a time the blades acquired a 'shine', so that flints that had been used in this way are often easily recognizable. Two finds from the 'lake-dwellings' of Fiavè (Trento province) provide evidence of the timeless appearance of such sickles and of their construction. Right, the wooden 'rough'; left, a finished sickle with the blades inserted. 2nd millennium BC. L of the 'rough' 34 cm. Museo di scienze naturali, Trento.

fied by the implements and pottery they contain. The importance to the economy of keeping domestic animals is obvious. Man was no longer dependent for his subsistence on the chase with all its uncertainties, for the livestock was always available as 'living reserves of food', not to mention the milk which sheep, goats and cows provided him with. Other animals to be domesticated were pigs and dogs, the latter not only as faithful companions and herders of livestock, but also for their meat. No sooner had the domestication of animals been introduced, than hunting was all but abandoned; the percentage of wild-animal bones in the settlements from the Late Stone Age onwards seldom exceeds 10%. All the more remarkable, therefore, is the lake-shore settlement–alas, only partially excavated–at Polling near Weilheim (Upper Bavaria), which registered a proportion of some 86% wild animals to 14% domestic (calculated, not on the number of bones but on the minimum number of individual animals), even though it dates from the end of the Late Stone Age.[4] Taking into account other observations and the extensive inventory of stone tools, one can only surmise that the people living there (only seasonally?) specialized in tanning and therefore did not conform to the overall culture-pattern of the time, that they exchanged their products for those of neighbouring settlements and were thereby relieved of other activities, such as agriculture.

A good general picture of one of the farming economies in the Alpine region is afforded by the provisional analysis of the animal and plant finds from the Bronze Age settlement of Fiavè above Lake Garda (pp. 74ff.).[5] This was situated in a little depression with a lake and areas of marshland, surrounded by steep-sided mountains. Agriculture and stock-breeding enabled the inhabitants to produce all the food they themselves needed. Emmer, which was particularly suited to this location, was the principal variety of corn. Wheat and legumes were also cultivated, possibly already in rotation as winter feed for the livestock. In addition, hay was obtained from the meadows, which could be used as pasture already in early spring. In summer, the herds were driven up into the mountain pastures, cattle not far away, sheep and goats to considerable altitudes. Of the animal bones, those of sheep and goat, with 51.9%, form the main component, the ratio being 3:1 to 4:1 (their respective bones are seldom distinguishable). At least 50% of these animals were slaughtered in their first or second year, above all the males, less of whom were needed for breeding purposes. Cattle account for 23.5% of the bones. Almost a fifth of them were slaughtered as calves less than six months old. This suggests a calculated decimation prior to the arrival of winter with its feeding

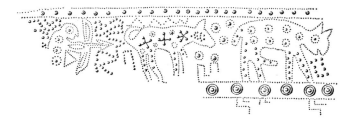

144 Although hunting is more often represented than are agricultural activities in the art of all ages, analysis of animal bones from the settlements has shown that since the Late Stone Age the chase no longer played an appreciable role in man's subsistence. Already at this early stage therefore hunting became progressively a sporting amusement of those who by virtue of their social position could afford the time to indulge in it. Certain animals, what is more, appear to have been regarded as important for religious ceremonies. Both these factors help to explain the frequency of hunting scenes on the works of 'situla art' of the 6th and 5th centuries BC. The bronze vessels in particular were objects upon which attention was focussed on official occasions for they contained either alcoholic beverages or a nourishing meat broth.

problems. Swine, representing 6.5%, scarcely count; the climate and surroundings (predominantly conifers) most likely did not suit them. Only a quarter of their total number reached the age of two. Deer, chamois and other wild animals are represented by only a few bones, as are fish and birds. So the diet of the herdsmen and farmers of Fiavè was, insofar as meat was concerned, quite definitely weighted in favour of that of domestic animals, doubtless supplemented by milk and cheese. By virtue of their size and weight, cattle were clearly the most important animals for the economy. Agriculture appears to have played a subordinate role, no doubt serving mainly to provide winter feed for the cattle. Taking the Fiavè basin as a whole, the maximum area of cultivated land is reckoned to have been 17.5% of the usable ground around the settlement.

Of a proper mountain-pasture economy[6] we have only indirect evidence.[7] In the Alpine region, high-altitude sites containing offerings are few and scattered where the Late Stone Age is concerned, but there are many dating from the Bronze Age. Some of them came to light on tracks across passes, and so it cannot be deduced that the herdsmen lived there for long periods at a time. Yet other finds so closely comply with the conditions at mountain-pasture economies of later date, as regards altitude and surroundings, that we can be sure there was some connection:[8] the offerings are such as herdsmen made to mountain-, weather- and fertility gods.[9] Notable examples of periodically visited Bronze Age settlement sites in caves or rock shelters at such high altitudes were discovered in the Simmental (canton Bern) during the organized search for finds of the Old Stone Age.[10] In marked contrast to the decidedly unrewarding upland huts of the Middle Ages,[11] they even yielded sherds of pottery. No corresponding stables or pens for the livestock appear to have been identified, though decaying walls were demolished time after time over the centuries for as long as upland stock-farming was carried on in the vicinity. Summer grazing on mountain pastures augmented the usable land of a settler-community without the need to do much clearing; for large open areas are often to be found below the general tree-level. During the Bronze Age the climate, being warm and dry, was particularly favourable, and this is borne out by the large quantities of high-altitude finds from this period.

Whether or not the deterioration in the climate around the eighth and seventh centuries BC[12] had an adverse effect on the upland pasture economy cannot be determined on purely archaeological grounds. For the fact that the high-altitude finds almost wholly cease at precisely this time and do not increase again until the last two centuries BC cannot be advanced as a valid argument: the votive offerings in the rivers and lakes on the plain show exactly the same tendency.[13] So here it is primarily a change in religious attitude that is indicated.[14] If we apply an especially strict yardstick, the signs mentioned above cannot be said to provide irrefutable proof of pre-medieval mountain husbandry.[15] But seeing that all other explanations are even less satisfactory–a point we shall not go into further–it seems reasonable to suppose that, at least from the Early Bronze Age on, when man began to make extensive use of food and other resources in the mountain areas, there will also have been high-altitude stock-farming of some kind.

The economic independence of small communities was limited where they had to rely on raw materials of foreign origin, such as metal. All other articles of daily use were produced on the spot or at least within the confines of the local valley unit,[16] above all the immense quantities of pottery that were used in the course of a year and were continually being broken. The potters were probably not yet specialized craftsmen but just specially deft women (and also men?), some of whom would perhaps be freed from time to time from work in the fields or herding livestock.[17] They shaped the vessels from lumps of clay and fired them in conveniently constructed kilns.[18] Suitable clay was no doubt available in the vicinity; it would be cleaned and washed in a pit, then mixed with sand, grit or some other appropriate material, so as to ensure that the vessels did not crack or become misshapen when drying out. Woodworking also reached a high standard.[19] The properties of the various types of wood were precisely understood and suitable ones were selected for the required purpose: making axe-hafts and wooden hammers, sickles and beaters, bowls and scoops. 'When choosing particular varieties', account was taken of 'resistance to pressure, cracking and bending, of a tendency to shrink and resistance to weathering. For the making of artefacts the most plentiful types of wood, such as oak, ash, beech, sycamore, hard-fruit and yew were employed. Ash is characterized

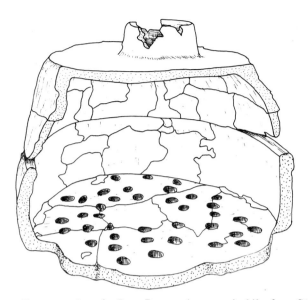

145   Reconstruction of a Late Bronze Age potter's kiln from Sévrier (Dép. Haute-Savoie). Beneath the perforated base plate was a fire compartment for providing the necessary heat. The heating chamber was divided into two, which made it easy to charge it with clay vessels, and shows that the pottery industry was already well developed. Early first millennium BC. Ht approx. 60 cm.

by its grainy strength, hard-fruit by the ease with which its outer surface can be worked, and yew by its extreme pliability.'[20] For the working of wood serviceable tools are needed; the preparation of the many hundreds of posts and poles for the houses and foundations of Fiavè (Ills 33 and 34) alone entailed an enormous amount of labour, using tools that had to be sharpened time after time. Whilst the by no means primitive stone implements met the requirements of the Stone Age, it was when he came to know copper and how to work it that man made the technical advance which was to prove decisive.

Wealth from the earth

When Georg Bauer, a Saxon who adopted the name of Georg Agricola in the manner of the humanists, published his comprehensive work *De re metallica libri XII* in 1556, people were still wholly ignorant of the fact that early man had with the aid of implements of stone and wood made the world about him suit his needs. How people could have led a truly human life before the discovery and working of metal was thus incomprehensible to Agricola:[21]

If people do not have the use of metals, every opportunity of protecting and prolonging their well-being and of leading a life comparable to our own culture is lacking. For, did metals not exist, men would lead the most horrible and wretched life among wild animals; they would resort to acorns and berries, would grub up shrubs and roots and eat them, would scoop out with their nails burrows in which to sleep by night, would roam all day in the forests and fields in the manner of wild animals. As this is quite unworthy of man's intelligence, the finest and best of Nature's gifts, is there anyone who would be so foolish as to deny that, for food and clothing, metals are essential and that they serve to preserve human life?

To those who lived at the time of the transition from the Stone Age to the Bronze Age events must have seemed far less dramatic. It took decades, indeed centuries, for man to master the new raw material. At that time not many people lived in the Alpine region, and the brief life-span that was granted to most of them adversely affected the handing-down of experience and knowledge.[22]

At the outset there were enterprising men who had learned in the Balkans how to smelt copper and sought worthwhile sources of the ore in Central Europe.[23] They knew that they could expect to find these only in the mountains, and undertook expeditions into the areas bordering the Alps. The Grauwacken zone, which stretches from Salzburg well into North Tyrol, yielded ore-bearing rock. Here copper is present in narrow veins, tectonically formed fissures, containing sulphurous copper pyrites.[24] Where the veins come to the surface they either appear as shallow humps in the rock-face (since they consist of harder stone than the surrounding rock), or betray their presence by the somewhat different plant growth they support (on account of the slight sulphur content). Most thoroughly researched is the ancient copper-mine in the Mitterberg district above Mühlbach west of Bischofshofen.[25] In the nineteenth century modern miners came across traces of the old props and galleries, and the Salzburg ancient historians soon interested themselves in the problems the early mines posed. Georg Kyrle and Olivier

Klose produced the first serviceable summary,[26] on which Karl Zschocke and Ernst Preuschen based their major work;[27] in recent years Clemens Eibner has investigated the ore-treating system there.[28] Today only the knowledgeable visitor can tell which was the entrance to the

146 *Freehand drawing of the Bronze Age mine at Mitterberg (Salzburg province) based on the results of excavations in and around 1900. Latest research has indicated certain modifications, making further methods of mine-working probable, but this drawing by J. Pirchl remains unequalled for clarity.*

ancient mine, where to look for the adits and the holes for the pit props. They are concentrated around the 'Mitterberger Hauptgang' (Mitterberg main vein) which runs in an easterly direction from the Arthur-Haus (1502 m) between the impressive rock-walls of the Hochkönig (2941 m) and the north face the Hochkeil (1783 m).

Mining at the Mitterberg began as early as the Early Bronze Age, reached its peak in the Late Bronze Age, and appears to have almost ceased by the Early Iron Age. This time-span of some 1000 years the archaeologist has arrived at by studying the finds in the galleries, the ore-washing areas and the associated settlements. The miners operated

147 Store of 250 ring-ingots and 62 fragments, together weighing 56.3 kg, found in 1970 on a steep hillside at Piding-Mauthausen near Reichenhall (Upper Bavaria). It was in this and like forms that copper, less frequently also bronze, was traded and used as primitive money. 18th–17th century BC. Diam. of ingots approx. 14 cm. Städtisches Museum, Reichenhall.

by digging tunnels, which followed the copper-bearing veins down to considerable depths. Where these veins were interrupted or displaced by faults in the rock, experienced men made narrow side-tunnels so as to locate the place where the vein continued. Bronze pickaxes and stones mallets with wooden hafts served as tools, but they were not used until the rock had been rendered friable through fire and quenching (cf. Hannibal's method of route-making, p. 207). The veins of copper ore were often many metres high, so that the miner had to go in for tall galleries or large chambers. Then carpenters built platforms of wooden beams, on which would be lit the fires for heating the rock above. The most recent investigations have established that a method without firing was also used, when the rock was slaty and so could be split by hewing alone, or when the tunnel lay-out did not allow a sufficient supply of air for extracting the smoke. Where necessary, the tunnels were lined with, or at least supported by wooden beams, whilst beams with treads cut into them helped the men to cope with particularly steep sections. The deepest levels of ancient mine-workings were found to be some 100 m below the present-day surface— convincing evidence of the expertise and fearlessness of the early miners.

What the carriers brought out from the galleries was, however, by no means pure copper, for the ore was closely amalgamated with the basic rock. So the recovery process involved considerable expenditure of time and money.[29] Heavy stone hammers were used to break up the rock into fragments the size of nuts or sometimes even pinheads, so that the particles of ore could be separated out. In order to extract the very last grain of copper the rock was in certain cases crushed by means of a heavy hand-mill having an artificially roughened upper surface. The resulting powder would then be sluiced through wooden boxes, in which the grains of copper sank to the bottom faster than the grit, and were there caught up in cloths or hides spread out for the purpose—a process similar to that used at all periods for the panning of gold from rivers.

The further processing of the concentrated ore took place down in the valley, where the climatic conditions were more favourable and adequate supplies of wood were at hand. First, the ore with such particles as still adhered to it was mixed with charcoal and brought to red heat, so as to remove the unwanted sulphur content. It was then transferred to the smelting furnaces, which in their primitive form were nothing more than pits in which the roasted ore and charcoal were arranged in layers.

Anyhow, an ample supply of air was needed in order to ensure a sufficiently high temperature (copper melts at about 1083°C). Where the air-currents ascending a hillside were inadequate, it was necessary to use bellows made of animal hide. This simple process, which could be speeded up by the addition of certain minerals, caused the fused metal to accumulate at the bottom of the pit, whilst the extraneous matter (principally slack containing iron which at that time was not turned to account, and traces of rock), having a lesser specific gravity, settled on top. Most likely such a smelting process had to be repeated several times, before anything like pure copper was produced. Getting rid of the iron component appears to have presented a particular problem at the Mitterberg. Initially, the product took the shape of 'cakes' of cast metal, which was the way they were naturally formed in the pit furnaces. They weighed from one to several kilograms and were not very handy for transporting over long distances. So it soon became the custom to cast the copper in more manageable standard shapes, be it as rings or slightly curved rods of about 200 g, or as axeheads weighing up to 3.7 kg (Ill. 160). These objects counted to a certain extent as 'money'.

The Mitterberg area was by no means the only one in the Alpine region that early man discovered and exploited. Maybe it was actually the most important but in those days, when the transportation of materials was difficult and costly, several smaller sources of copper appear to have been considered worth working. Most thoroughly investigated are those on the Kelchalpe at Kitzbühel,[30] which have acquired a certain reputation on account of the notched staves found there–little sticks with incisions[31] which presumably served as signs of ownership and were used as tallies.[32] In East Tyrol, proof of copper-mining well into the Late Iron Age is provided by the burial-grounds of the well-to-do inhabitants of Welzelach and Zedlach,[33] and in Switzerland and the Southern Alps, too, there are indications that copper was mined in a small way.[34] Scientific analyses of individual mines aimed at ascertaining the respective origin of raw copper have, despite the endeavours of Heinz Neuninger and Richard Pittioni, not been altogether successful.[35] For we still have insufficient information as to the extent to which the artisans were able, and indeed wished to improve the process of

casting and working copper and bronze, through the addition of small amounts of other ores.[36]

Mining of copper declined with the introduction of iron in the eighth century BC. Iron deposits do occur in the Alpine region, but the limonite and granular ore of the surrounding areas were much easier to reclaim since they did not call for underground mining.[37] So iron extraction in the mountains was usually restricted to the working of small deposits to satisfy local requirements. The ores of the Eastern Alps from Styria across Carinthia to Slovenia were alone of importance; it was to them that this area owed its economic and cultural upswing in the Iron Age. The Magdalensberg at Klagenfurt, the capital of the Norican kingdom, was as early as the second century BC a tar-

148 A small store found in a Late Bronze Age house at Cunter-Caschligns (Graubünden) included a rarity in the form of a bronze mould in two parts and an axe-head possibly cast in it. Second from the right is the rough casting, obtained from the mould, before being hammered out into its finished shape. 13th century BC. L of mould 23.8 cm. Rätisches Museum, Chur.

149 Clearly to be seen on the inner side of the round bronze bottle from the Dürrnberg above Hallein (Salzburg province) (Ill. 11) are not only the marks made by the embossing hammer but also the preparatory lines incised with a pair of dividers. They served as an aid in obtaining a regular curvature and concentric embossed ribs. 400–350 BC. Approx. actual size. Keltenmuseum, Hallein.

get for Roman merchants, who acquired the sought-after Norican iron there. For, as a result of an exceptional composition of the outcropping ores, its foundrymen had been able to experiment and gain experience, and so produce an iron that was but little inferior in quality to present-day steel.[38]

Of less economic significance were the lead workings in Carinthia, which were exploited from the Late Bronze Age on.[39] In pre-Roman times lead was only used for a few crafts (as, for example, filling the inverted rims of bronze buckets[40] or in the production of certain bronze alloys[41]) and as a substance possessing magical properties (pp. 180 f.).[42]

Silver-mining played no part in pre-Roman times, for it was in the last three centuries BC that silver jewellery first appeared in any appreciable quantities. The Romans were familiar with the deposits in Carinthia, which often have non-ferrous metals (lead, zinc, copper) in association and thus demand a corresponding experience of smelting.[43] In the Western Alps, too, small and readily accessible veins may have been worth working,[44] although it appears that already before the second century BC the famous Spanish silver-mines had supplied the Celts in France–and so of course the Romans to an even greater extent.

We must not assume that the mining of gold took place even at such important deposits as those round Rauris in the Tauern, even in Roman times.[45] It was much easier to obtain this metal from the rivers,[46] and tests of the gold finds from the Dürrnberg at Hallein have shown that no Central European mountain-gold was used, at most a limited amount of placer gold carried down by the river Salzach from the Inner Alpine regions.[47] Strabo[48] records that in the days of the historian Polybius, between about 147 and 132 BC, a vein of gold was discovered by the 'Norican Tauriscans' in the vicinity of Aquileia, which had soon drawn Roman merchants there too, thereby lowering the price of gold in Italy by a third. It was said to have lain only two feet below the surface and been nowhere more than 15 feet high. Here there was likewise no need for underground workings. The suggestion of Hermann Vetters[49] and Jaroslav Šašel[50] that this story relates to the Julian Alps is not very convincing on geological grounds, as veins of gold are not found in limestone rock. Here as always it is necessary to keep in mind the Inner Alpine region with its primeval rock formation. Indeed, it is to be doubted whether the inhabitants of the Alps in pre-Roman times had mastered the complicated processes by which gold was separated chemically from the rock that clung to it,[51] unless it could be prised out of thick veins. River gold, on the other hand, needed no further treatment or refining prior to being fashioned into jewellery or coins.

Metal-founders, smiths, turners and glaziers

At the outset copper was still very costly, and craftsmen did a lot of probing to make themselves familiar with the new material.[52] The earliest stage, during which the copper was hammered out into the desired shape of, say, a pin or an axe-head, ended when the casting process had been mastered. Pure copper, it is true, was very difficult to cast but resourceful people–made aware no doubt of natural pollution in some of the depots–hit upon the idea of remedying this by alloying it with other metals. Whilst arsenic or antimony was used initially,[53] tin soon proved to be the most suitable material,[53] for it did not cost too much either. The Alpine region obtained it from Spain or from Cornwall. For bronze, an alloy of copper and tin, a proportion of some 10% of the latter proved most satisfactory for most purposes. If the bronze contained more than 7% of tin, it was certainly hard to hammer cold, but further working of the cast raw product was still quite possible.[54]

There were various methods of casting. For simple objects produced in series (such as axes, swords and knives) the craftsman made moulds of stone, bronze or clay. These could be used many times over. Complicated articles, particularly those with plastic ornamentation, called for the 'lost wax' technique of casting. This entailed modelling the desired object in wax and then surrounding it with a mantle of clay, in which were drilled the casting aperture and others for expelling the air. When heated over the fire in the hearth the clay mantle hardened, the wax melted and ran out. Molten bronze from a little clay crucible[55] was then poured in to occupy the spaces thus left. After it had cooled down, the craftsman smashed the

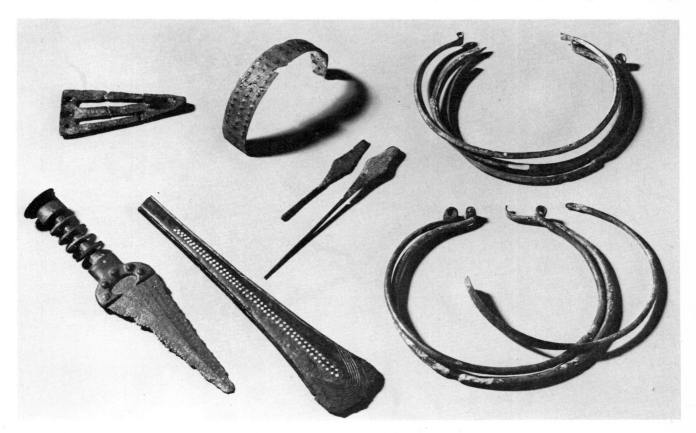

outer shell and smoothed the rough outer surface of the now exposed casting. In many instances this, whether implement or piece of jewellery, was only roughly shaped when cast, to be finished subsequently by hammering out certain parts or applying ornamentation.

On account of the thinness of the walls, it was not possible in pre-Roman times to produce bronze vessels by casting; they had to be hammered into shape.[56] A sheet of unwrought metal would be beaten out, during which process continual heating over a fire kept it in a malleable state. When it had been cut to the right shape (say for a bucket or a bowl), a chasing hammer was used to achieve the required curvature. Handles and feet would usually be riveted on; soldering with tin only came in gradually during the Iron Age.[57] For ornamentation a graver was employed, sometimes also a pair of compasses.

150 The first bronze-workers had already taken over the technique of inlay from the Balkans. The finds from the Early Bronze Age graves at Thun-Strättlingen (canton Bern) included a long-bladed axe ornamented in a special manner. A narrow strip of copper let into the blade is adorned with square gold nails which on account of their high silver content stand out against the ruddier copper. Such a decorated axe, of doubtful practical use, could only have belonged to a person of high rank. 17th century BC. L of axe-blade still 13.8 cm. Historisches Museum, Bern.

Iron called for a totally different treatment. The temperature of 1400° C required for casting was not attainable until recent times. So forging while the metal was in a red-hot state remained the only possibility. This presented no difficulty where large and simple objects were concerned,

151 *Belt-buckle from Riaz (canton Fribourg) with inlay decoration. Thin silver threads have been hammered into incised grooves, providing a colour contrast with the iron. The prominent motif of the cross attests the faith in the protective power of this Christian symbol on the part of the warrior who wore this belt. 6th century* AD. *L 9.4 cm. Service archéologique cantonal, Fribourg.*

152 *Implements for agriculture and stock-breeding, as well as for catching fish, from Swiss settlements of the Late Iron Age. 3rd–1st century* BC. *Various scales.*

but jewellery made up of many small pieces and articles of complicated design (chains, say) could not be fashioned from iron until the Late Iron Age. That bronze was regarded as a prized metal, particularly for personal adornment, well into the early Middle Ages is not only because of its hue, which many may have found unusually attractive, and its lustre, but also because of the readiness with which it lends itself to the casting process. The appearance of both these metals could be enhanced by additional ornamentation. From the fourth century BC the art of enamelling–filling little indentations on bronze rings or fibulae with molten coloured glass–was mastered. Damascening, that is, inserting inlays of gold or silver threads in iron, did not reach its peak until the early Middle Ages, although the technique as such was known since the Early Bronze Age. A further important invention that aided the metalworker remains to be mentioned: the lathe, which can be traced back to the sixth century BC in Central Europe, if only indirectly through the grooves on articles given an extra finish (for instance on arm-rings or the indentations for jewellery inserts).[58] They were also used in woodworking, for making bowls, jugs and the feet of pieces of furniture.

As from the seventh century BC, that is to say the Early Iron Age, Slovenia was a glass-making centre.[59] The prime product was the little glass bowls that copied metal

patterns; only a very few exemplars found their way northward as costly gifts: three to Hallstatt, one to the 'princely seat' on the Hellbrunner Berg between Hallein and Salzburg.[60] Slovenian women often wore hundreds of glass beads as adornment, and not infrequently the men did too; with their many shapes and colours, they presented a pleasing sight. Thanks to their small size these beads were handy for trading in and as presents, but it is highly probable that at important places elsewhere, say on the Dürrnberg at Hallein, an experienced and much-travelled man might be found who knew the secret of fashioning glass objects (a process requiring appreciably lower temperatures than did the manufacture of the glass itself, and at this stage of course none of the raw materials). Especially precious pieces are recognizable by their provenance, for example two 'face beads' in a young woman's grave of the fourth century BC at St-Sulpice on the Lake of Geneva, which came from Carthage. A bead with intricately constructed eyes, from the same grave, is likewise a rarity in Central Europe. However, one example of this type of bead was found in England, a few have appeared in France (Marne), several in Italy and Slovenia, many north and east of the Black Sea, and some even in eastern China.[61]

Salt–the white gold

While the metal riches of the Alps constituted an important foundation for all the crafts and for the economic flowering of this region from the Bronze Age on, that unspectacular substance, salt, was no less indispensable. To

it Hallstatt in the Salzkammergut and Hallein south of Salzburg owed their immense wealth during the Iron Age, as the great number of finds goes to show. Research into the salt-mines there is best described in two works by Othmar Schauberger,[62] himself a salt-mining engineer. Fritz Eckhart Barth has carried out investigations at Hallstatt for several years past;[63] systematic research in the mines at Hallein is, however, unfortunately not being supported by the current management. According to our present state of knowledge[64] salt-mining at Hallstatt began between 1000 and 800 BC and continued up until Roman times. What is remarkable, though, is that the oldest finds from the large cemetery in the valley high up above the lake date from as late as the eighth century BC,[65] so that the miners must have buried their dead for at least a hundred years at some other place. The datings from the Dürrnberg above Hallein show a somewhat lesser discrepancy. The earliest radiocarbon date obtained for the mine is 720 ± 80 BC.[66] Here mining ceased already before Roman times, for the traces of settlement then become so sparse, that the few people living there would have barely sufficed to keep the mines going.[67]

A mine such as this calls for organized working and above all readiness to back it up. At Hallstatt, as in Hallein, the miner had first to hack his way through 30–65 m of moraine and leached clay in his tunnel, before he got to the 'Haselgebirge', a mixture of salt, gypsum, clay and other comparatively soft sediments. It contains 40–70% of salt. Occasionally it is interspersed with bands of pure salt (named 'Kerngebirge'), which the miner naturally was anxious to follow up. In narrow tunnels the man with the pickaxe worked his way forward, while the haulier carried the resulting bits into the open in a leather sack; long pine

153 Implements for wood-, leather- and textile-working from the prolific find-spot of La Tène in Marin-Epagnier (canton Neuchâtel). 3rd–1st century BC. Various scales.

154 Leather sack from the Hallstatt (Upper Austria) salt-mine. The ingenious design makes emptying easy: the miner strapped the sack to his right shoulder and strung the wooden club over the other. When he let go of the club the sack tipped backwards to the right. Probably 7th–5th century BC. Ht 72 cm. Hallstatt Museum.

torches provided the necessary lighting. On Othmar Schauberger's reckoning, the monthly rate of progress was about 1 metre, which tests with implements copied from those used at the time have recently corfirmed.[68] In the summer, when the sun shone upon the tunnel entrances, it will have been scarcely possible to carry on with the work, owing to ventilation problems. For at Hallstatt the deepest point at which traces of prehistoric mining occur is 330 m below the surface; even in the Dürrnberg it is 200 m. The material found takes the form of implements along with their wooden hafts, sundry other pieces of wood and pine torches, remnants of fabric,[69] leather and hide, whetstones, leather pouches and even human excrement.[70] The salt preserved organic matter, too, and although the pressures that cause the mountain structure to warp blocked up the tunnels again after a few decades, the miner of medieval times and later had no difficulty in recognizing a prehistoric mine-working when he chanced upon one. Viewing them with a mixture of dread and awe, he would dub these places 'heathens' work'.

There can be no doubt about the dangerous nature of the work below ground at all times. A tunnel might collapse and cut off the miner's retreat; water might burst in from above and drown him. A horn from Hallstatt is a clear sign that an immediate warning signal to the miners was needed when danger threatened.[71] Three mummified corpses were actually found, but unfortunately none of them was taken sufficient care of and all were lost to posterity and research. One came to light in Hallstatt in 1734, two in the Dürrnberg in 1573 and 1616 respectively.[72] A graphic report on the latter two by Franz Dückher von Haslau appeared in his *Saltzburgischen Chronica* of 1666.[73]

But living conditions on the surface, too, will have been far from pleasant. Apart from the fact that at Hallstatt, situated as it is at the foot of the Dachstein, the winters are long (the Dürrnberg on the border of the Alps, with the settlement area at an altitude of 700–850 m, is somewhat more favourably situated), conditions from the point of view of hygiene were very bad. At all events, remnants of fabric found in the mine bore many signs of clothes-lice,[74] and the miners suffered severely from worms,[75] which must have seriously impaired their working capacity. The inhabitants of the Dürrnberg certainly had a shockingly low expectation of life (pp. 111 f.).

An idea of the overall performance, taking into consideration the rate of progress mentioned above, can be obtained from the minimum length of the tunnels as indicated by the finds from the 'heathens' work'–4100 m for

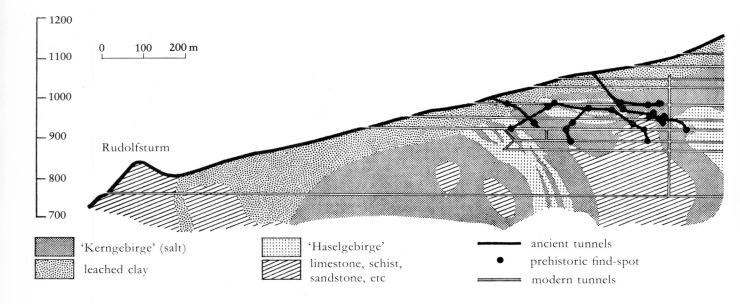

'Kerngebirge' (salt)

leached clay

'Haselgebirge'

limestone, schist, sandstone, etc

——— ancient tunnels

• prehistoric find-spot

=== modern tunnels

Hallstatt, 4350 m for the Dürrnberg. The actual distances were no doubt greater since firstly, the tunnel-endings so far traced were chance discoveries; secondly, the tunnels will not have run in a straight line but have followed bands of particularly pure salt with all their winding and faulting; thirdly, large operating chambers will have been constructed at suitable places. Apart from the hewers and hauliers, carpenters were needed as well for finishing the tunnels, also smiths for the manufacture and maintenance of the implements, as well as men who selected and prepared suitably shaped timber for the pickaxe handles which were in such heavy demand. If in fact operations were limited to the colder time of the year, it is probable that some sort of seasonal distribution of work was instituted, whereby in the summer not only did the people engage in agriculture but reserves of clothing made of fabric and hide, implements and wooden handles were stock-piled. In addition, potters would be hard at work, as would bronze-casters and wood-carvers. To what extent these activities were limited to specialist craftsmen we do not know, though we have from the Dürrnberg a turntable base from a potter's wheel, on which from about 450 BC thousands of vessels had been turned over a period of several centuries[76]–certainly the property of one particular man or a workshop possessing special aptitudes in that direction. Likewise the smiths and bronze-casters will have been men with many years' experience and correspondingly equipped. On the other hand there are indications both at Hallstatt and on the Dürrnberg that people from far away went there (and also died there!). How far this was a question of seasonal workers or of contingents under obligation to do several years' service, to what extent they

155 Idealized section through the Hallstatt salt-mine, showing the opened-up galleries of the ancient miners.

156 Optimum tool shapes, testifying to the great expertise of the salt-mining people. One method of working was for one miner to hold a pick and for a second man to hammer it in with a mallet. So as to minimize the effect of the recoil the cross-section of the wooden pick-handle was pared down in a particular way (right, original finds; outer left, reconstruction for a modern trial working). L of pick-handles approx. 50–60 cm.

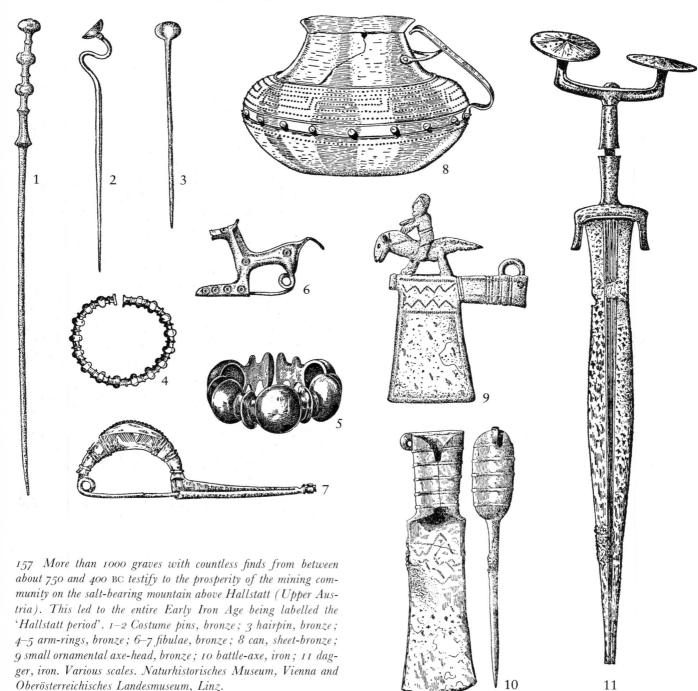

157   More than 1000 graves with countless finds from between about 750 and 400 BC testify to the prosperity of the mining community on the salt-bearing mountain above Hallstatt (Upper Austria). This led to the entire Early Iron Age being labelled the 'Hallstatt period'. 1–2 Costume pins, bronze; 3 hairpin, bronze; 4–5 arm-rings, bronze; 6–7 fibulae, bronze; 8 can, sheet-bronze; 9 small ornamental axe-head, bronze; 10 battle-axe, iron; 11 dagger, iron. Various scales. Naturhistorisches Museum, Vienna and Oberösterreichisches Landesmuseum, Linz.

were accompanied by women and children, what their social status was when they got there–these are questions to which the archaeologist can give no unequivocal answers.[77]

Neither Hallstatt not Hallein furnish any clear evidence as to whether and, if so, how the salt extracted from the mountain was subsequently processed.[78] The almost pure high-grade salt required no further refining, and the customer could–should he feel so inclined–remove minor impurities himself. For the most part, however, this was unnecessary; for the salt was very little used for seasoning, but much in demand as a means of conserving perishable foods, principally meat. Pure-white salt, such we are accustomed to (natural sea-salt, for instance, is grey) was not needed for this purpose since the impurities settled in the brine.

It is estimated that the Dürrnberg mine, when operating normally, produced and distributed at least 2000 kg of salt annually. This is difficult to relate to present-day consumption. Yet it is reckoned that even in early times a family will have used several kilograms: meat and fish were kept in a 10–20% solution of salt-brine so as to make sure of a sufficient supply of albumen throughout the winter. In his textbook on agriculture, Cato[79] refers to one bushel of salt (= 8.7 litres or 10.4 kg) for each member of the household. As late as the nineteenth century the peasants in the mountains were still living in much the same way:[80] 'An-average household slaughtered, generally shortly before Christmas, one head of cattle and two pigs for its own use. The meat was cut up into small pieces of one to two kilograms... which, made to keep by means of pickling and smoking, had usually to last the household for three-quarters of a year.' According to this, the salt-mines at Hallein and Hallstatt can between them have scarcely supplied more than 1000 families–a number that seems low for the northern Alpine foreland including Bohemia and Moravia, seeing that Georg Kossack[81] specifies 445 find-spots from the Early Iron Age (700–450 BC; predominantly burial mounds) for southern Bavaria alone. Admittedly, not all the relevant settlements will necessarily have been inhabited simultaneously, but this rough calculation may nevertheless give some idea of the value of salt in Central Europe and the prosperity that it brought to the mining communities of Hallstatt and Hallein.

158 View, facing West, across the Salzach valley, with Hallein in the foreground. Behind it is the Dürrnberg, 300 m higher, which takes the form of a plateau with numerous wooded knolls. Rising up beyond is the Hoher Zinken with the Hahnreinkopf backed by the snow-covered Hoher Göll. The photograph was taken many years ago, for the monastery on the Georgenberg, the sheltered settlement area at the approach to the Dürrnberg, and the late Romanic tower of the parish church no longer exist, having been destroyed in the second World War and replaced by modern buildings.

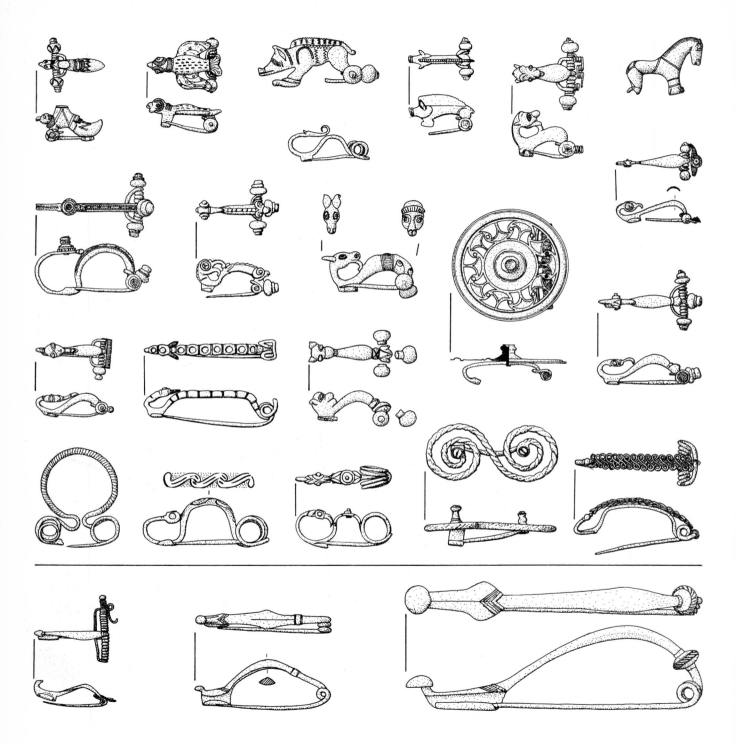

159 So much wealth did the salt-mining community on the Dürrn-berg above Hallein (Salzburg province) amass, that it attracted the most accomplished craftsmen to the area. In particular the fibulae which men, women and children used to fasten or merely to adorn their attire (though basically nothing more than safety-pins) pre-sented the bronze-caster with a great many opportunities to exercise his artistic ingenuity. The bottom row are types associated with the Inner and South Alpine regions; they lack ornamentation and show little variety. 450–350 BC. 2:3. Keltenmuseum, Hallein.

160 Metal was traded in various standard forms before stamped coins were introduced. A Late Bronze Age find from Schiers-Mon-tagna (Graubünden) contained among other things lumps of cast metal left over from copper working (bottom) as well as ingots in the shape of double axe-heads, from which the casting seams had not been smoothed away (top). The iron ingot, weighing 4.15 kg, with long hammered-out pointed ends from Splügen, a type familiar to us through many finds in Central Europe and dating from the Late Iron Age, falls into the category of votive offerings found up on the passes. L of iron ingot 68 cm. Rätisches Museum, Chur.

Precious money

Money existed long before coins came into use. Here it is proposed to accept Paul Einzig's[82] definition of 'money' as a unit or article which effectively fulfils its aim of possess-ing outward uniformity, is used in a broader context for calculating or as a method of making payments and is also widely accepted as such, and is then distributed once more in the same capacity. This definition does not postulate that such 'money' is always available everywhere and to everyone to a like extent, that it circulates in every busi-ness transaction as a tangible object, and that it must be made of metal. Besides which, the material, form and weight may alter in the course of centuries and undergo regional changes. (Currencies using cattle, sheep, woollen blankets or corn sacks as units cannot, understandably, be traced archaeologically.)

The earliest money to be identified in the Alpine region takes the form of ring- and bar-ingots, which are concent-rated in the Alpine foreland by the Salzach, Saalach and Inn, but spread all the way to central Germany, Bohemia, Moravia and Slovakia.[83] For a long time archaeologists assumed on this account that the Mitterberg copper was traded in this form and had swept, so to speak, into the

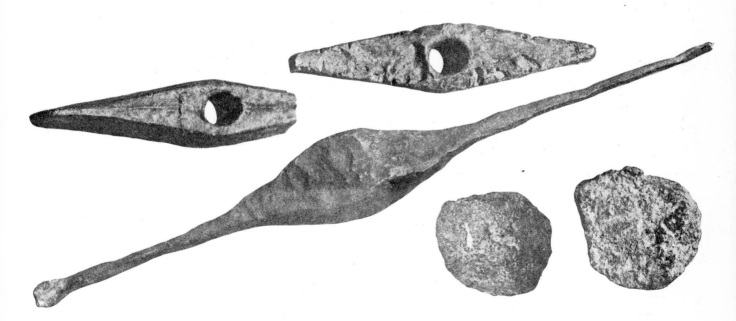

countries beyond the mountains, at first like a torrent, then more and more slowly. This interpretation can no longer be upheld since metal analyses have shown that these ingots are by no means all made of the same copper; on the contrary, numerous samples are available which certainly do not consist of Mitterberg copper.[84] Consequently we must draw the obvious conclusion that within a relatively small region north of the Salzburg copper belt the ingots functioned as money. Bigger businesses used them as units of accounting and liked to make payments with them. So the copper from other sources that they received by way of barter was re-cast in this form, provided it could not be fashioned directly into useful articles. The assumption, supported by only a few datable finds, that the average weight of the ingots had become less in the course of two or three centuries and thus indicated a kind of inflation,[85] needs careful checking against economic models. Simply attributing the decrease in the precious metal content of the coins to the state of the economy in Celtic and Roman times does not account for their complicated composition.

In the course of the Middle Bronze Age, from about 1500 BC on, this area rapidly ceased to function as a primitive money-based economy. To start with, it is by no means clear whether the economic system changed–if so, why,–whether copper was no longer hoarded but immediately marketed, whether the religious concepts that led to the deposition of many of the finds of ingots underwent a transformation. Possibly the many hoards of the Middle Bronze Age, which contain intentionally smashed bronze implements, should be treated as an indication of what was to become a very rudimentary monetary system.[86] In the Late Bronze Age we find–in far fewer quantities, it is true–flat, round 'cakes' of cast copper or bronze, which in their standardized form perhaps carried on the function of the ring- and bar-ingots (Ill. 160, bottom).[87] There are at the same time indications that in the Alpine region various forms of axe-heads served as money. This is particularly likely in the case of the large double axes in which the casting seam has not been removed (Ill. 160, top).[88] In the Late Iron Age, on the other hand, one once again finds ingots (now of course made of iron, the more valuable metal) which could not be confused with utensils. One kind is shaped like a double pyramid with long or short

extensions at either end (Ill. 160, centre), the other kind is a flat casting resembling a sword.[89] The standardized form it assumes over wide tracts of Central Europe[90] shows it to have been a unit of currency which was universally recognized there. Who established the norm and made sure that it was adhered to is a question that still awaits an answer.

The situation where coins are concerned is clear. These were commissioned by the ruler of the day, by powerful families or officials appointed for the purpose. An effigy or a corresponding inscription determined their function as authorized tender, whose value was guaranteed. The coins of the Greek colony of *Massilia*/Marseille, founded about 600 BC, and its daughter towns on the neighbouring Mediterranean coast scarcely penetrated the Alpine region; those who accepted them first carefully tested their metal content. The Celts in Gaul and north of the Alps had, as mercenaries in the Mediterranean area, got to know coins and received them by way of payment. When, from the second century BC on, the Celtic economy and social structure had developed correspondingly, the minting of coins began in the North as well.[91] Serving as patterns were coins of the Greek colonies in the West and above all those of the Macedonian kingdom under Philip II and Alexander the Great, and later also Roman ones. The technique used was the same: the planchet, a little cast minting blank of the chosen metal, would be stamped out between two dies. Minting-places can be identified by the presence of planchets or by the clay plate needed for casting them, in which little round impressions had been made with the finger prior to firing. Fragments of these from the end of the Iron Age have been found at such important places as Karlstein near Reichenhall and the Dürrnberg above Hallein.[92]

Nevertheless, the Alpine region had no money-based economy in the modern sense even as late as the first century BC. The coins of precious metal were far too costly to

161 Distribution map of Early and Middle Bronze Age ring-ingots made of pure copper or copper alloy. The area of concentration at the edge of the Alps is where these ingots were cast, delivered, accepted and stored as a sort of standard currency. In the case of single pieces outside this area it was only the pure metal content that counted.

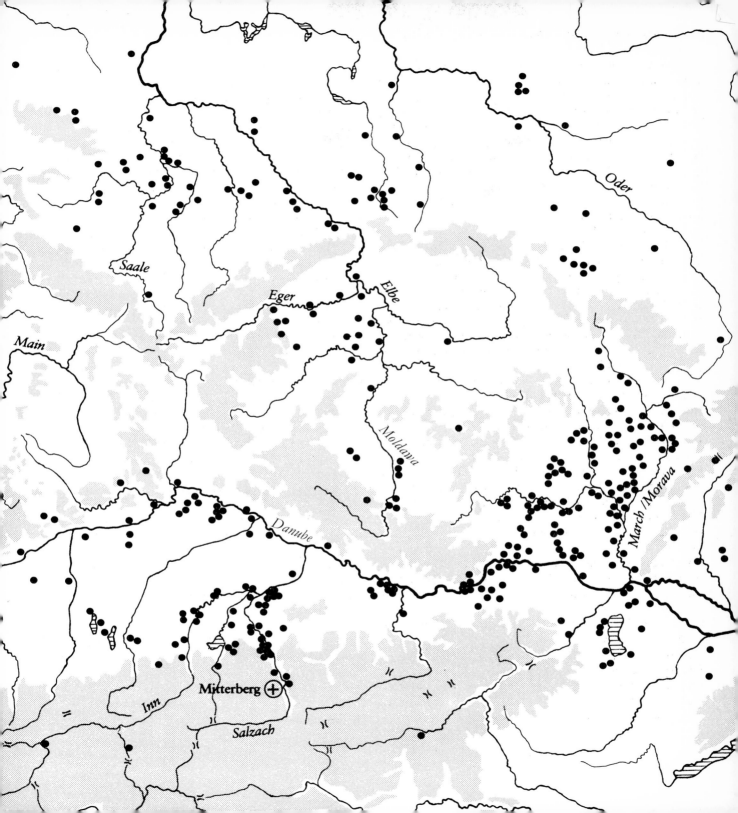

be introduced as daily tender; all the same, a few particularly worn exemplars show that it was not just a case of valuable pieces that everybody immediately concealed in a money-box. It was the Romans who first brought in small change, such as could be used also by ordinary businesses. This explains why lost coins first became more numerous in settlements in Roman times. Before that, finds of valuable Roman coins are more or less confined to hoards or votive offerings.[93] This gives rise to the suspicion that the Celts and the Alpine folk had, before they themselves accepted and minted coins as a practical means of payment, melted down foreign coins in order to obtain the silver they contained. The sudden proliferation of silver jewellery (it applied to the entire Celtic realm as far as the Balkans) from the third century BC seems therefore to have been due not only to supplies from Spanish and Romanian silver-mines but also to the melting-down of Greek and Roman silver coins, which reached the North less through trading than through pay or tribute money.

Delicacies in luxury dishes, mash in stone pots

The most important centre for trading with the Romans was, from the second century BC on, the town on the Magdalensberg at Klagenfurt (pp. 89 f.). The Norican iron, and also zinc and lead, acted as a magnet for the merchants from the South. They did a big wholesale trade above all in the products of the metalworkers. Some idea of the extent of this can be gained from inscriptions scratched on the walls of cellars and workshops.[94] One cellar bears the following jottings:

Sineros from Aquileia buys 110 bowls of 15 pounds (about 4.8 kg).
On intercalary day (= 24 February) buy 255 anvils.
Rullus dinner plates 170.

   In another cellar is scribbled:

Hooks 560, rings 575.

Wherever wholesale trade flourished, bankers were soon on the scene, as this inscription indicates:

From 1 May money loaned until 29 June.

The moneys, having been counted out, were kept in pouches, sealed with a little bone peg on which was

scratched the name of the responsible person.[95] That only Roman and Greek names but no indigenous ones appeared here tells us who, even including the lowly, had control of the accounting. Naturally, there is among the finds no lack of styluses, sealing stamps, calculating stones, weights,[96] nor of the lead markers that were affixed at the larger goods depots.

These markers bore the name of the manufacturer, the artisan, the quantity and the amount of remuneration paid.[97] This system was universally adopted. We have examples not only from the towns of *Brigantium*/Bregenz and *Cambodunum*/Kempten, as well as from the settlement on the Auerberg at Schongau,[98] but also from the road-station of *Immurium*/Moosham below the Radstädter Tauern (p. 217).[99] This latter states that a female slave Ategenta in the service of a certain Catto made three cloaks. As her pay is not entered, the weaving-mill may have been at the place itself. These little lead seals had the advantage that, after the account was settled, they could be rubbed smooth again and written on anew.

Thanks to the large number of inscriptions and their appraisal by the epigrapher Rudolf Egger, the excavations on the Magdalensberg provide a particularly rich fund of material for studying the daily life and economic conditions at a large settlement. For example, names scratched into table ware[100] show that—as in the case of the military in the forts on the Danube—here, too, a canteen service was provided, which must have been of special advantage to the traders and their employees who spent a lot of their time on the Magdalensberg without their families. Scientific tests[101] and scrutiny of the inscriptions on the containers used for transporting foodstuffs provide information about diet. Among the animal bones found, which mainly represent leavings from meals, the types that were domesticated since the Late Stone Age naturally predominate: 40.8% sheep or goat, 30.3% pig and 25% cattle. These percentages are based on the minimum number of individuals; taking the size of the animals into account, cattle were the most important source of meat and milk. As food, wild game scarcely played any role: only red deer, roe deer, wild boar and hare enhanced the fare to any extent worth mentioning (a proportion of about 1:15 as against domestic animals). Rare and shy animals are represented by only a few bones: aurochs, bison, ibex, elk,

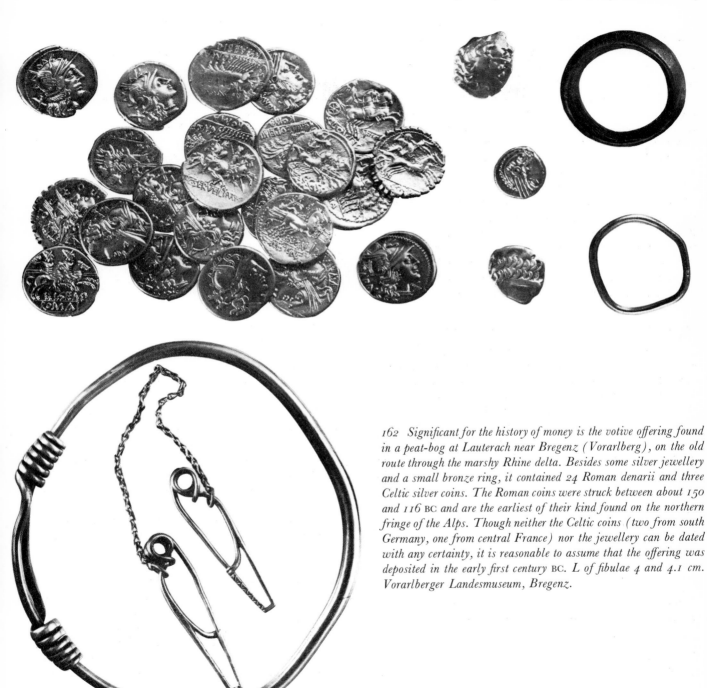

162 *Significant for the history of money is the votive offering found in a peat-bog at Lauterach near Bregenz (Vorarlberg), on the old route through the marshy Rhine delta. Besides some silver jewellery and a small bronze ring, it contained 24 Roman denarii and three Celtic silver coins. The Roman coins were struck between about 150 and 116 BC and are the earliest of their kind found on the northern fringe of the Alps. Though neither the Celtic coins (two from south Germany, one from central France) nor the jewellery can be dated with any certainty, it is reasonable to assume that the offering was deposited in the early first century BC. L of fibulae 4 and 4.1 cm. Vorarlberger Landesmuseum, Bregenz.*

163 Gravestone of the artisan Nammonius Mussa and his wife Kalandina, as well as a certain Saturnius whose relationship to them is not known. The nature of the man's craft is evident from the way he is portrayed. The small hammer is clearly an embossing tool–so Nammonius had been a bronze- or goldsmith. The pincers, moreover, are scarcely appropriate for a blacksmith even if they do not resemble those used for extracting the clay crucibles containing the molten bronze from the kiln. The woman wears Norican garb with head-dress, neck-ring, two fibulae and mantle; one hand is laid affectionately on her husband's shoulder. Found in Kalsdorf near Graz (Styria). First half of the 2nd century AD. Ht 1.06 m. Steiermärkisches Landesmuseum Joanneum, Graz.

fox and brown bear. Where birds are concerned, chickens were the most convenient to keep; apart from ducks and geese, the only others were species now more or less extinct: mountain fowl, heathcock, hazel-hen, Alpine snow-hen and common raven.

From the South, merchants imported specialities which the Romans did not wish to deny themselves:[102] oil, *garum* (concentrated fish sauce), preserved grapes and fruit, figs, oysters and various kinds of conserved fish. The earthenware amphora was the preferred vessel for conveying these commodities. The potters from Italy or nearby Istria stamped their products before firing, the contents being later specified by means of incised or painted letters and signs. The following inscription on the neck of an amphora[103] exemplifies the complete schema:

Ve(nuculae) d(efrutum) t(esta) LXXIIX p(ondo) CLIV.
Wine grapes preserved in juice, net weight of the amphora 78 pounds (= 23.4 kg), content 154 pounds (= 46.2 kg).

The merchants frequently formed themselves into corporate bodies with a view to minimizing the risks of long-distance trading. As a result, many became very rich, for the vast Roman Empire constituted a single large market with low customs duties (p. 220), favouring the exchange of goods. Even the most exorbitant demands were met, provided one paid a high enough price.

The provision of essential food supplies, above all corn and livestock for slaughtering, was the responsibility of the farming estates, the *villae rusticae* (pp. 101 ff.). Three basic works from the first century BC and the first century AD show how much attention the Romans paid to agriculture.[104] Work on the farming estates was attended to by managers, tenants and slaves. For economic reasons a limit was set to the size of individual undertakings (it varied from 2 to 5 km^2 in well researched districts),[105] though of course a landed proprietor could own several such estates–even in widely separated parts of the country.[106] Detailed information regarding the conditions of ownership, the yields, the number of people employed, etc. are unfortunately largely unavailable for the provinces, since the written sources are lacking.

The Roman custom of frequently recording on tombstones a man's trade, or actually representing it pictorially, gives us an insight into his essentially specialized craft

(p. 136). If we add to that the many tools that were found in the towns and *villae rusticae*, then–taking into account also what folklore teaches us–the techniques can be reconstructed in some detail.[107] It was only now that certain crafts gained in importance. This applies most clearly to the work of architects and masons; for the invention of mortar and burnt bricks and roof tiles fundamentally altered the method of construction and outward appearance of public and private buildings. Thin-walled glass vessels, from little scent bottles to wine jugs, attest the art of the glazier. Luxury ware of hard-baked clay, often with plastic decoration, the so-called *terra sigillata*, was manufactured at a few places only and widely distributed.[108] Crockery-menders carried out repairs.[109] Artists worked in stone or bronze; life-size statues adorned public squares and temple precincts (Ill. 83).

Intensification of long-distance commerce made increasing demands on the road system and its carrying capacity. This source of earnings afforded a supplementary income in the Alpine region in particular; for it was not only during the perilous winter months that there was a call for guides who were intimately acquainted with the locality and the weather. It was necessary to hold in readiness pack-animals for negotiating the steep slopes, as well as horses used to mountain work for the State courier service and for officials on their journeys. Pack-mule traffic on the unmade tracks had as before to be handled by the native inhabitants.

Under the Romans, exploitation of the mineral wealth of the Alpine region does not appear to have been intensified. With the exception of the unsurpassed Norican iron, the output of metal was as hitherto just enough to satisfy regional requirements; for the large, profitable gold and silver mines in other parts of the Empire were more convenient sources. All the same, from the third century AD a typically Alpine product won for itself a certain market north of the Alps, namely vessels made of steatite, or soapstone.[110] This substance occurs chiefly in the South Alpine valleys of Switzerland and can, in its pristine state, be easily worked.[111] The craftsman produced simple forms on his lathe:[112] bowls, dishes, beakers and buckets. They served as heat-proof cooking utensils, almost up until our own times in fact. It was modern industry that put an end to this traditional craft. The technical limitations of the process did not allow much variation in the forms, so that these too scarcely changed down the ages. For this reason late Roman/early medieval steatite vessels are only to be

164 Laves (local name for steatite) from the Southern Alps, supplemented and replaced earthenware on the North Alpine border, too, in late Roman times. As the soft stone was worked on a lathe, the shapes are conical and the ornamentation is confined to horizontal ribbing. The drawings are of vessels found in graves at Bonaduz (Graubünden). 4th–5th century AD. Diam. of large bowl 20 cm. Rätisches Museum, Chur.

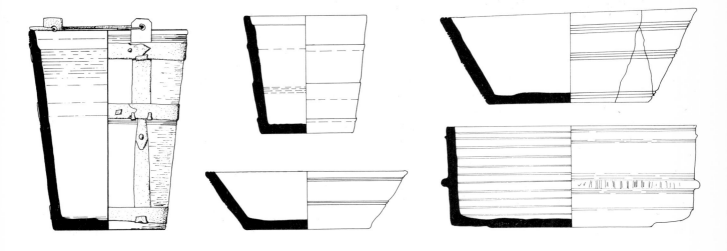

distinguished in rare instances from later ones, which renders it harder to date pieces found singly or at places containing little or no material that can be separated by stratification. Investigations at the hill settlement of Carschlingg at Castiel[113] near Chur have shown that here—and doubtless also for some distance around—vessels of steatite and of wood almost wholly replaced the pottery which in the difficult times from the fourth to the seventh century had to be imported and was therefore that much dearer.[114]

Poor farmers, well-filled treasuries

Many decades before the official end of the Roman Empire in 476 the economic and social conditions in the provinces and in the Alpine region had deteriorated fundamentally. The constant incursions of the Teutons since the third century had disrupted the overall supply system; the *villae rusticae* were nearly all given up. The wealthy retreated to the South. Those who remained entrenched themselves on heights and behind walls, if they didn't actually creep into caves (p. 104). The soldiery alone still received payment and occasionally also in the customary manner the produce of the South. Thus units of the 3rd Italic Legion (with headquarters in *Castra Regina*/Regensburg?) were stationed in *Teriolis*/Zirl near Innsbruck and *Foetibus*/Füssen, for the purpose of keeping going and controlling transalpine traffic on the Via Claudia and the Brenner route. In the Notitia Dignitatum, the register of troops and appointments of late antiquity, its function is described as *transvectioni specierum*—the provision of spiceries (this old-fashioned word hits the nail on the head exactly; in France a grocery is still known as an épicerie), that is, costly commodities such as delicatessen, herbs, spices and olive oil.[115]

But before long this came to an end too. In the fifth century a kind of militia took over the frontier defence along the Danube down-river from *Quintanis*/Künzing; the Raetian Alpine foreland was relinquished *de facto*. In the 'life' of St Severin are described the conditions that prevailed at the time in the small forts along the Danube and in the East Alpine area.[116] Every community of settlers had to fend for itself and was often a day's journey from its nearest neighbour. Outside the walls lay the fields and pastures which—unless the harvest failed or the Teutons drove away the cattle—assured them of their subsistence. In an emergency the State, or rather the Church, was just able to arrange for the delivery of corn or clothing; on one occasion a consignment from southern Noricum was even got across the mountains in mid-winter.[117] Apart from the farmers, who were involved in the family business, there appears also to have been a large group of *pauperes*, poor people without possessions who were virtually dependent on alms and whatever surpluses were available for distribution. This was effected by applying the tithe in the form of produce since money no longer played any role in this economy, being only needed or of advantage in special cases.[118] The soldiers, for example, had still to rely on it to some extent because they could not participate in the general production of foodstuffs (this is evidenced by the story of the soldiers from Passau who were killed on their way to the South to collect their pay: p. 227). Severin had probably to pay cash for the oil which the inhabitants of *Lauriacum*, accustomed to the life-style of the South, did not wish to do without; for the merchants of Italy, on their way back, did not in the prevailing conditions want to burden themselves with bartered goods, preferring instead a full purse.

In these circumstances, since everything depended on ensuring the essential means of subsistence, handicrafts degenerated as well. Raw materials and specialist craftsmen were lacking, as were customers. Only blacksmiths will have been at work making implements for daily use and for agricultural purposes. Lime-burners,[119] brickmakers and masons had drifted away, or were paid for special tasks only, such as church-building.[120] The lean times had, however, also eliminated many injustices, among them slavery.[121] Christian teaching did not allow a baptised person to become a slave, and the people of Noricum were relieved when they themselves were not carried off by the Teutons, who repeatedly invaded the country.

Conditions in the West Alpine region present a different picture.[122] Here the transition from the late-Roman State to a number of Germanic kingdoms took place without any interruption. Life in the towns went on as before; in 443 the Burgundians were quartered in Sapaudia (initially the capital was Geneva), the land divided up between them and the resident provincial population in accordance with a fixed code[123] (as, incidentally, was also the case with the Lombards in Italy a century later). The main features of the situation at this stage were large farming estates and long-distance communications with the Mediterranean and across it to places farther east. Slavery, too, was kept going as an institution; for, as late as the sixth century unfree craftsmen in the service of a master are mentioned in the *leges Burgundionum*.[124] Even where they were allowed to make things partly *in publico*, that is to say for the general market, they were in the first place still dependent upon the raw materials their master or current employer put at their disposal; secondly, it was the master's responsibility to see that all business was conducted in the right manner. The legal aspect of what seems to us a complicated arrangement is far from clear.

The economy here was even more closely bound up with Roman tradition than in the East, producing as it did corn, wine and a certain quantity of vegetables near the house. Stock-farming was not carried on systematically, at all events not with the aim of breeding powerful oxen and horses to pull large-bladed ploughs. It was the Germanic-style economy, which did not make so marked a distinction between cultivated land and the wooded parts used for keeping livestock, that brought about a change which once again ensured an adequate subsistence level for the people, and indeed a certain surplus. This benefited the king and the nobility, whereby the crafts in their turn profited, in that enough persons were free to engage in activities that were not wholly concerned with food production. Hence the tradition of craftsmanship in Western Europe

165 This most beautiful and costly goblet of early medieval times was donated by the Bavarian duke Tassilo III to the Kremsmünster monastery (Upper Austria), which was consecrated in 777. It is of embossed copper and covered all over with a polymorphic ornamentation enhanced by gilding, silver damascene and niello. Representations of animals in the Germanic style and medallions on Byzantine lines appear side by side. The most likely place of origin is the episcopal town of Salzburg, possibly the Mondsee monastery. The proud donor had himself and wife, daughter of a Lombard king, perpetuated on the base: Tassilo dux fortis/Liutpirc virga regalis = *Tassilo, valiant duke/Liutpirc, of royal blood. Ht 25.5 cm. Kremsmünster Foundation.*

as a whole, including the Western Alps, did not die out, even though the widespread economic decline in the fifth century had its effects.

Yet the prerequisites for a monetary economy in the Roman sense were still lacking.[125] The Frankish kings, it is true, and before long also the local 'coin-masters', struck gold coins modelled on East Roman ones (just as the Celts had, seven centuries earlier, based theirs on Greek proto-types), but these valuable pieces were intended in the first place as portrayals of the ruler, as propaganda (East Rome regarded it as a sacrilegious effront when Theudebert I in 540 had his name put on coins!), and as theoretical units in accountancy. They were used in the several codes of laws[126] for assessing penalties, but their use for cash payments even by the wealthy was restricted. The early medieval economy was so structured that goods which an agricultural undertaking could not itself produce were usually acquired through barter. It was under Charlemagne that the introduction of a silver currency with a low nominal value first became expedient and feasible. From then on small change was once again available in reasonable quantities, enabling business transactions to be concluded more easily and quickly.

Little is known about actual living standards in the early Middle Ages. Early medieval archaeology continues to devote far too much of its time to individual objects and reconstructions of apparel and to tracking down historically transmitted data relating to the finds from countless graves. By contrast, very few settlements have been investigated and evaluated (pp. 105 ff.)[127]–they do, admittedly, nearly always lie beneath present-day centres of villages and towns, and are therefore largely inaccessible or destroyed. Likewise, our information about salt-production in Reichenhall (Upper Bavaria) derives solely from literary sources; the cemetery of well-to-do people in the vicinity tells us relatively little that is pertinent (p. 142).

The Church concerned itself in various ways, and to an extent that it is difficult to estimate, with the economic system of the early Middle Ages. On the one hand, gifts caused great treasuries of precious metal to accumulate in the churches and monasteries, and this material was to a large extent fashioned into art-objects, thereby keeping the memory of the donor alive. On the other hand Christianity had to take part of the responsibility for ensuring

that, from the eighth century on, virtually no offerings were placed in the graves even in territories under Germanic influence (those of the Burgundians, Alamanni, Bajuvarii and Lombards), thus aiding the general public.

The view that tomb-robbing became prevalent as early as the sixth century has likewise been expressed in this connection.[128] The tempering of the Germanic concept of the after-life through Christianity at a time of metal shortage,[129] the argument runs, had brought about a legitimization–albeit subjective (for the Church was against it)–of the plundering of graves.

Yet the true causes lie deeper; for systematic robbing of cemeteries, which meant contravening the tabu of the grave, could only occur in times of great upheaval. Such, much like the Early Bronze Age, was the early medieval period, when as a result of the merging of ancient and Germanic traditions, coupled with the growing power of Christianity, a new world emerged: the 'Occident'. In most departments of life new values replaced the old, and many people could no longer find their way about. Only against this background was it possible to contemplate compensating for the shortage of metal–connected in other respects with the revolutionary changes taking place–by grave-robbing, an activity subject to dire penalties.

What we see here in the early Middle Ages, namely the close interweaving of economic, political, social and religious developments, can be assumed to have taken place also in pre-Roman times, before the use of writing. But how far the activities of those days were interdependent it is even harder to judge, since we have to fall back on indirect evidence. Much of this must remain hypothetical, and there is certainly more than one possible solution to most of the problems. At all events, it would be wrong, in describing life in prehistoric times, to pick on only one of the determining factors or to deal with it out of context. Analytical investigation down the ages clarifies developments and changes; that is why I have in this book discussed the various aspects of life in sequence. But one can, at any chosen point of time, take a snapshot which shows life in its entirety; the cross-references and a number of deliberate repetitions serve this end. It is the task of archaeology as an historical science to unite these two ways of looking at things and through purposeful research to make the pictures as sharp and bright as possible.

Notes

Abbreviations

ANRW   Aufstieg und Niedergang der römischen Welt (Berlin/New York 1972ff.)

ArchA   Archaeologia Austriaca (Vienna)

ArchKorrbl   Archäologisches Korrespondenzblatt (Mainz)

Atti CSDIR   Atti del Centro studi e documentazione sull'Italia romana (Milan)

AS   Archäologie der Schweiz. Mitteilungsblatt der Schweizerischen Gesellschaft für Ur- und Frühgeschichte (Basel)

BCSP   Bollettino del Centro Camuno di Studi preistorici (Capo di Ponte)

BerRGK   Bericht der Römisch-Germanischen Kommission (Frankfurt)

BPI   Bulletino di paletnologia italiana (Rome)

BVbl   Bayerische Vorgeschichtsblätter (Munich)

CIL   Corpus Inscriptionum Latinarum

Dessau   H. Dessau, Inscriptiones Latinae selectae (Berlin 1892–1916)

HelvA   Helvetia Archaeologica (Basel)

JbRGZM   Jahrbuch des Römisch-Germanischen Zentralmuseums (Mainz)

JbSGU   Jahrbuch der Schweizerischen Gesellschaft für Ur- und Frühgeschichte (Basel)

MAGW   Mitteilungen der Anthropologischen Gesellschaft Wien

MblSGU   Mitteilungsblatt der Schweizerischen Gesellschaft für Ur- und Frühgeschichte (Basel) (continuation = AS)

ÖJh   Jahreshefte des Österreichischen Archäologischen Instituts (Vienna)

PrAlp   Preistoria Alpina. Rivista annuale della sezione di paletnologia del Museo Tridentino di Scienze Naturali (Trento)

PrFr   La préhistoire française, Vols I (ed. H. de Lumley) and II (ed. J. Guilaine) (Paris 1976)

RE   Realencyklopädie der classischen Altertumswissenschaft

UFAS   Ur- und frühgeschichtliche Archäologie der Schweiz, Vols I–VI (Basel 1968–1979)

WPZ   Wiener Prähistorische Zeitschrift

ZSAK   Zeitschrift für Schweizerische Archäologie und Kunstgeschichte (Zurich)

I A Million Years of History in Review

1 H. de Lumley and L. Barral (eds), Sites paléolithiques de la région de Nice et Grottes de Grimaldi. *IXᵉ Congrès intern. sc. préhist. et protohist. Nice 1976, Livret-guide de l'excursion* B 1 (Nice 1976).

2 Cf. latterly W.–D. Langbein, *Die Brenztalkultur. Geologisches Alter und archäologische Bedeutung* (Frankfurt/Bern 1976); review of this by H. Müller-Beck, *Fundber. Baden–Württ.* 4, 1978, 420–423.

3 H. de Lumley et al., La grotte du Vallonnet, Roquebrune-Cap-Martin (Alpes-Maritimes). *Bull. Mus. d'Anthr. Préhist. Monaco* 10, 1963, 5–20. Summary and assessment of the situation to date: H. de Lumley and L. Barral (Note 1) 93–103.

4 Since there are still certain uncertainties over bringing into line botanical/zoological, geological, climatic and archaeological systems of chronology, a discussion of slightly deviant datings would be superfluous.

5 R. Grahmann and H. Müller-Beck, *Urgeschichte der Menschheit* (3rd edn Stuttgart 1967) 163. Contains a brief introduction on the 'History of the Origins of Man': 55–167.

6 H. de Lumley, Les fouilles de Terra Amata à Nice (Alpes-Maritimes). Premiers résultats. *Bull. Mus. d'Anthr. Préhist. Monaco* 13, 1966, 29–51; H. de Lumley and L. Barral (Note 1) 15–49.

7 F. Zorzi and A. Pasa, Il deposito quaternario di Villa di Quinzano presso Verona. *BPI* N.S. 8, 1944–45, 15–66 with Ills 10–15; L. Barfield, *Northern Italy before Rome* (London 1971) 20 Ill. 4.

8 E. Bächler, *Das Drachenloch ob Vättis im Taminatal* (Sankt Gallen 1921).

9 Survey with further bibliographical references in H. Müller-Beck, Das Altpaläolithikum. *UFAS* I, 89–106.

10 A. Bocquet, *Catalogue des collections préhistoriques et protohistoriques* (Grenoble 1969) 12.

11 A. Bocquet and M. Malenfant, Un gisement prémousterien près de Vinay (Isère). *Travaux Lab. Géol. Grenoble* 42, 1966, 77–82; A. Bocquet (Note 10) Pl. 1, 1–3.

12 W. Gräf and W. Modrijan (eds), *Höhlenforschung in der Steiermark* (Graz 1972).

13 M. Mottl, Das Protoaurignacien der Repolusthöhle bei Peggau, Steiermark. *ArchA* 5, 1960, 6–17: id., Die Repolusthöhle bei

Peggau (Steiermark) und ihre eiszeitlichen Bewohner. *ArchA* 8, 1951, 1–78. – O. Abel and G. Kyrle, *Die Drachenhöhle bei Mixnitz* (Vienna 1931).

14 M. Mottl, Die paläolithischen Funde aus der Salzofenhöhle im Toten Gebirge. *ArchA* 5, 1950, 24–34; K. Ehrenberg, Die paläontologische, prähistorische und paläo ethnologische Bedeutung der Salzofenhöhle im Lichte der letzten Forschungen. *Quartär* 6, 1953, 19–58; id., Die urzeitlichen Fundstellen und Funde in der Salzofenhöhle, Steiermark. *ArchA* 25, 1959, 8–24.

15 M. Mottl, Was ist nun eigentlich das 'alpine Paläolithikum'? *Quartär* 26, 1975, 33–52.

16 H. de Lumley and L. Barral (Note 1); P. Graziosi, *I Balzi Rossi* (5th edn Bordighera 1976).

17 J. Biegert, Herkunft und Werden des Menschen. *UFAS* I, 69–88.

18 A literary source for the year AD 563 (Gregory of Tours, *Decem Libri historiarum* IV 31) records a great landslide in the Valais at Saint-Maurice d'Agaune. It caused the Rhône to dam up to such a height that a huge wave of flood-water, on bursting out, caused serious damage to the harbour at Geneva at the farther end of the lake. Even milestones were torn away from the Roman road, these being subsequently found buried deep in an old bed of the Rhône at Yvorne (canton of Vaud): E. Mottas, *AS* 3, 1980, 154 ff.

19 H. Adler and M. Menke, Das Abri von Unken an der Saalach, ein spätpaläolithischer Fundplatz der Alpenregion. *Germania* 56, 1978, 1–23.

20 So far only preliminary reports have appeared; Colbricon on the Passo Rolle: *PrAlp* 7, 1971, 342–344; 8, 1972, 107–149. 260; 9, 1973, 227–229; 11, 1975, 201–235. 322; 12, 1976, 227. – Reiterjoch: *PrAlp* 12, 1976, 229. – Valle del Vajolet (some 1900 m): *PrAlp* 12, 1976, 235. – Fontana de la Teia in the Monte Baldo (Verona) (some 2000 m): *PrAlp* 12, 1976, 243–244. – Plan de Frea: *PrAlp* 14, 1978, 233–237. – This and several other new find-spots have now been treated in a comprehensive manner by R. Lunz, *Archäologie Südtirols* (Bruneck 1981) 6–8 and 40–61.

21 C. Corrain, G. Graziati and P. Leonardi, La sepoltura epipaleolitica nel riparo di Vatte di Zambana (Trento). *PrAlp* 12, 1976, 175–212.

22 S. Nauli, *JbSGU* 59, 1976, 221.

23 W. Buttler, *Der Donauländische und der westische Kulturkreis der jüngeren Steinzeit* (Berlin/Leipzig 1938) Pls 15–16; H. Quitta, Zur Frage der ältesten Bandkeramik in Mitteleuropa. *Prähist. Zeitschr.* 38, 1960, 1–38 and 153–188.

24 *UFAS* II, 79 (map). – Cf. S. Piggott, *Ancient Europe* (Edinburgh 1965) 57 Ill. 26.

25 *PrFr* II, 255–259.

26 Corn-pollen grains have been attested at a height of 1250 m on the Col Luitel near Grenoble, dated between 2700 and 2500 BC: *PrFr* II, 71 after S. Wegmüller, Neuere palynologische Ergebnisse aus den Westalpen. *Ber. Dt. Botan. Ges.* 85, 1972,

75–77. A comparison of the remains of wild and domesticated animals in more than ten settlements in the Alpine region has shown at most a figure of 16.3% of the former: L. Chaix, Les premiers élevages préhistoriques dans les Alpes occidentales. *Bull. d'Études préhist. Alpines* 8–9, 1976–77 (= L'Homme et la montagne. *Actes du 11ᵉ colloque anthropol. de langue franç.*, Aosta 1976) 67–76.

27 *PrFr* II, 292–294.

28 V. v. Gonzenbach, *Die Cortaillodkultur in der Schweiz* (Basel 1949); *UFAS* II, 47–66. Additionally C. F. W. Higham, Die Cortaillod-Kultur – ein Beitrag zur urgeschichtlichen Wirtschaftskunde, *ZSAK* 26, 1969, 1–7.

29 R. Pittioni, Italien, urgeschichtliche Kulturen. *Realencyklopädie d. class. Altertumswiss.* Suppl. XI (Stuttgart 1962) 177–182; G. Guerreschi, *La Lagozza di Besnate e il Neolitico superiore padano* (Como 1967).

30 The only survey to date is P. Biagi, Raffronti tra l'Paspetto ligure e l'aspetto padano della cultura dei vasi a bocca quadrata. In: *Atti XV riunione scient. Ist. Ital. Preist. e Protost. Verona – Trento 1972* (Florence 1973) 95–110 with distribution map Ills 6–8.

31 *UFAS* II, 122 Ill. 4.

32 M. Itten, *Die Horgener Kultur* (Basel 1970).

33 For instance H. Müller-Karpe, *Handbuch der Vorgeschichte 3: Kupferzeit* (Munich 1974) 13.

34 An informed survey full of ideas: H.-J. Hundt, Die Rohstoffquellen des europäischen Nordens und ihr Einfluss auf die Entwicklung des nordischen Stils. *Bonner Jahrb.* 178, 1978, 125–162.

35 Formulated for example by P. Anderson, *Passages from Antiquity to Feudalism* (London 3rd edn 1977) 80: 'inventions by individuals can remain isolated for centuries, so long as the social relations have not emerged which alone can set them to work as a collective technology.' With contrary emphasis G. Duby, *The early growth of the European economy. Warriors and peasants from the seventh to the twelfth century* (London 1974) 17: 'For we should be wrong in thinking that a human society feeds on what the surrounding land is best suited to produce. Society is a prisoner of practices passed on from generation to generation and altered only with difficulty. Consequently it endeavours to overcome the limitations of soil and climate in order to procure at all costs foodstuffs that its customs and rites ordain.'

36 H. Schickler, Aufnahme und Ablehnung der Metallurgie bei frühbronzezeitlichen Kulturen Europas. *Germania* 46, 1968, 11–19; Chr. Strahm, Der Übergang vom Neolithikum zur Frühbronzezeit in der Schweiz. *PrAlp* 10, 1974, 21–42.

37 J. Coles, *Archaeology by Experiment.* (London 1973) 19.

38 R. Peroni, *L'età del bronzo nella penisola italiana* I (Florence 1971) 93.

39 K. Gerhardt, *Die Glockenbecherleute in Mittel- und Westdeutschland* (Stuttgart 1953); additionally his contribution to the work mentioned in Note 40 (147–164).

40 The results of research to date summarized: *Glockenbecher-Symposion Oberried 1974* (Bussum/Haarlem 1976).

41 W. Witter, Über Metallgewinnung bei den Etruskern. *BerRGK* 32, 1942, 1–19; R. Peroni (Note 38) 234ff. – id. *Die älteste Erzgewinnung im nordisch-germanischen Lebenskreis* 1. *Die Ausbeutung der mitteldeutschen Lagerstätten in der frühen Metallzeit* (Leipzig 1938); H. Otto and W. Witter, *Handbuch der ältesten vorgeschichtlichen Metallurgie in Mitteleuropa* (Leipzig 1952).

42 R. Peroni (Note 38) 79ff.; H.-J. Hundt, Donauländische Einflüsse in der älteren Bronzezeit Oberitaliens. *PrAlp* 10, 1974, 143–178.

43 M. Lichardus-Itten, Die frühe und mittlere Bronzezeit im alpinen Raum. *UFAS* III, 41–54.

44 A useful compilation for Switzerland: R. Wyss, Die Eroberung der Alpen durch den Bronzezeitmenschen. *ZSAK* 28, 1971, 130–145.

45 Lothar Sperber has worked this out in a hitherto unpublished Munich dissertation of 1978.

46 L. Pauli, *Studien zur Golasecca-Kultur* (Heidelberg 1971) 15–52; the most recent mapping of the find-spots by M. Primas in: *Età del ferro a Como.* Exhibition catalogue Como (1978) 55 Ill 1.

47 L. Pauli (Note 46) 48–52; from the linguistic angle G. Devoto, Pour l'histoire de l'indoeuropéanisation de l'Italie septentrionale: Quelques étymologies lépontiques. *Revue de Philologie* 3. Ser. 36, 1962, 197ff.; K. H. Schmidt, *Glotta* 43, 1965, 163; M. Lejeune, *Lepontica* (Paris 1971).

48 L. Pauli (Note 46); M. Primas, *Die südschweizerischen Grabfunde der älteren Eisenzeit und ihre Chronologie* (Basel 1970); W. E. Stöckli, *Chronologie der jüngeren Eisenzeit im Tessin* (Basel 1975); *Età del ferro a Como.* Exhibition catalogue Como (1978); F. Rittatore Vonwiller, La civiltà del ferro in Lombardia, Piemonte, Liguria. In: *Popoli e civiltà dell'Italia antica* 4 (Rome 1975) 223–356.

49 The best overview is still provided by the map 'L'Italia centro-settentrionale dal X al III secolo a. C.' in: *Mostra dell'Etruria padana e della città di Spina.* Exhibition catalogue Bologna (1960).

50 G. Fogolari, La protostoria delle Venezie. In: *Popoli e civiltà dell'Italia antica* 4 (Rome 1975) 61–222.

51 The second most important find-spot, Padua, has in recent years been further spotlighted through a travelling exhibition: *Padua preromana.* Exhibition catalogue Padua (1976): abridged edition: *Padova vor den Römern. Venetien und die Veneter in der Vorzeit.* Exhibition catalogue Munich (1977).

52 Still most informative is the Exhibition catalogue of 1960 (Note 49).

53 Distribution map after R. Lunz, *Studien zur End-Bronzezeit und älteren Eisenzeit im Südalpenraum* (Florence 1974) Pl. 90B; R. Perini, *Studi Trentini di scienze storiche,* 2. sez. 55, 1976, 151 Ill. 1; E. Vonbank, *HelvA* 9, 1978, 135; with addenda.

54 L. Pauli (Chapter V, Note 12).

55 W. Witter (Note 41).

56 Pliny, *Nat. Hist.* XXXVI 2.

57 G. Smolla, Der 'Klimasturz' um 800 v. Chr. und seine Bedeutung für die Kulturentwicklung in Südwestdeutschland. In: *Festschr. für P. Goessler* (Stuttgart 1954) 168–186; rightly very critical of his all too direct deductions: G. Kossack, *BVbl* 21, 1956, 380ff.

58 H.-J. Hundt, *Mitt. Österr. Arbeitsgemeinschaft f. Ur- u. Frühgesch.* 24, 1973, 101; L. Pauli, Der Goldene Steig. Wirtschaftsgeographisch-archäologische Untersuchungen im östlichen Mitteleuropa. In: *Studien zur vor- und frühgeschichtlichen Archäologie (Festschr. für J. Werner)* (Munich 1974) 131f.

59 See the map with the sites of Hallstatt salt production in S. Piggott, *Ancient Europe* (Edinburgh 1965) 170 Ill. 94.

60 G. v. Merhart, 'Introduction' in the no longer issued volume 'Die Hallstattkultur' of the handbook on the prehistory of Germany (probably written 1937), first printed in: G. v. Merhart, *Hallstatt und Italien. Gesammelte Aufsätze zur frühen Eisenzeit in Italien und Mitteleuropa* (Mainz 1969) 1–6. – *Die Hallstattkultur.* Exhibition catalogue Steyr (1980); E. Lessing, *Hallstatt. Bilder aus der Frühzeit Europas* (Vienna/Munich 1980).

61 Mapped by W. Kimmig in: *Reallexikon der Germanischen Altertumskunde* (2nd edn) 2, 392f. Ills 84–85.

62 R. Lunz, *Studien zur End-Bronzezeit und älteren Eisenzeit im Südalpenraum* (Florence 1974) Pl. 81A (multi-headed pins); 82A (double-bossed bow fibulae); with notable spreading to the northwest also Pl. 81B (East Alpine animal-head fibulae; on their regularly overlooked presence in the Upper Palatinate cf. W. Kersten, *Prähist. Zeitschr.* 24, 1933, 134).

63 Chapter VI Note 77.

64 L. Pauli, *Der Dürrnberg bei Hallein* 3 (Munich 1978) 486ff.; F. Moosleitner, L. Pauli and E. Penninger, *Der Dürrnberg bei Hallein* 2 (Munich 1974) Pl. 210, 2–6.

65 J.-C. Courtois, *Revue Arch. de l'Est et du Centre-Est* 12, 1961, 292 Ill. 107.

66 Loc. cit. 194 Ill. 71, 2; G. Chapotat, Le char processionel de la Côte-Saint-André (Isère). *Gallia* 20, 1962, 33–78.

67 P. v. Eles, L'età del ferro nelle Alpi occidentali francesi. *Rhodania* 14, 1967–68.

68 See Note 48.

69 Osm. Menghin, Zur Historisierung der Urgeschichte Tirols. *Tiroler Heimat* 25, 1961, 5–39; R. Lunz (Note 62); M. A. Fugazzola, Contributo allo studio del 'Gruppo di Melaun-Fritzens'. *Annali dell'Univ. di Ferrara* N.S. Sez. XV, tomo II, 1 (Ferrara 1971).

70 Now clearly summarized by B. Frei, Osm. Menghin, E. Meyer and E. Risch, Der heutige Stand der Räterforschung in geschichtlicher, sprachlicher und archäologischer Sicht (Chur 1971 = Offprint of four essays from *JbSGU* 55, 1970, 119–147).

71 Still the best introductory work M. Pallottino, *The Etruscans* (London 1975).

72 Attempt at a synthesis: L. Pauli (Note 64) 443–485.

73 Indispensable as ever L. Contzen, *Die Wanderungen der Kelten, historisch-kritisch dargelegt* (1861, reprinted Wiesbaden 1968).
74 Most important account of the Celtic migrations in Italy and the siege of Rome: Livy V 33ff.
75 *I Galli e l'Italia.* Exhibition catalogue Rome (1978).
76 H. P. Uenze in: *Studien zur vor- und frühgeschichtlichen Archäologie (Festschr. für J. Werner)* (Munich 1974) 111f. Ill. 9; id., *Vor- und Frühgeschichte im Landkreis Schwabmünchen* (Kallmünz 1971) 42.
77 Cf. the papers from the Congress 'Kelti v Sloveniji' (The Celts in Slovenia): *Arheol. Vestnik* 17, 1966, 139–424.
78 H. Müller-Karpe, Zeugnisse der Taurisker in Kärnten. *Carinthia* I 141, 1951, 594–677.
79 H. Vetters, Zur ältesten Geschichte der Ostalpenländer. *ÖJh* 46, 1961–63, 201–228; G. Dobesch, *Die Kelten in Österreich nach den ältesten Berichten der Antike. Das norische Königreich und seine Beziehungen zu Rom im 2. Jahrhundert v. Chr.* (Cologne/Vienna 1979); id., Die Botschaft des Senats an die Alpenkelten im Jahr 183 v. Chr. *Schild von Steier* 15–16, 1978–79 *(Festschr. für W. Modrijan)* 75–78.
80 W. Schmid, H. Aigner and W. Modrijan, *Noreia. Forschungen – Funde – Fragen* (Graz 1973).
81 R. Loose, Kimbern am Brenner. Ein Beitrag zur Diskussion des Alpenübergangs der Kimbern 102/101 v. Chr. *Chiron* 2, 1972, 231–252 puts the case for the route through Noricum, down the Pustertal and into the Isarco/Adige valley. – On the general situation E. Demongeot, L'invasion des Cimbres – Teutons – Ambrons et les Romains. *Latomus* 37, 1978, 910–938.
82 J. Werner, Die Bedeutung des Städtewesens für die Kulturentwicklung des frühen Keltentums. *Die Welt als Geschichte* 5, 1939, 380–390; reprinted in: J. Werner, *Spätes Keltentum zwischen Rom und Germanien* (Munich 1979) 1–20. – V. Kruta and M. Szabó, *Die Kelten* (Freiburg 1978) 81ff. – J. R. Collis, Urban Structure in the Pre-Roman Iron Age. In: B. C. Burnham and J. Kingsbury (eds), *Space, Hierarchy and Society* (Oxford 1979) 129–136.
83 Caesar's own war commentary *(Commentarii de bello Gallico)* besides being taught in Latin classes by virtue of its admirable style, is also a unique document which archaeologists find indispensable for reconstructing late Celtic history and culture.
84 For somewhat later times cf. Note 96.
85 Strabo IV 205.
86 Cassius Dio LIII 25 records that Terentius Varro had no great difficulty in dealing with the Salassi, as they only attacked in small gangs. They had then to pay a tribute, which his soldiers were detailed to collect. On this pretext he sent them to the settlements, where 'all young personnel' were taken prisoner and sold in *Eporedia* in accordance with the conditions laid down. Strabo IV 205, on the other hand, speaks of 36,000 people and 8,000 able-bodied men, 'all' of whom were sold into slavery. By the analogy of Cassius Dio and on grammatical grounds 'all' can only refer to the 8,000 men, these being included in the 36,000 people – a figure which in any case seems excessively high for the Aosta valley. So the figures and the other particulars given in the regional literary sources, which would suggest the stamping out of virtually the entire tribe, are surely exaggerated. N. Bartolomasi, *Valsusa antica* 1 (Pinerolo 1975) 88f. for instance maintains that 44,000 warriors (among them 8,000 'youths') were enslaved.
87 Latterly dealt with by F. Fischer, P. Silius Nerva. Zur Vorgeschichte des Alpenfeldzugs 15 v. Chr. *Germania* 54, 1976, 37–76 and B. Overbeck, *ANRW* II 5, 665–668.
88 Tacitus, *Ann.* XV 32. – J. Prieur, *La province romaine des Alpes Cottiennes* (Villeurbanne 1968); C. Letta, La dinastia dei Cozii et la romanizzazione delle Alpi occidentali. *Athenaeum* N.S. 54, 1976, 37–76.
89 *Carmina* IV 14, 8–16. Tranl. C. E. Bennett 13th edn (London/Cambridge, Mass. 1967)
90 H.-J. Kellner, Zur römischen Verwaltung in den Zentralalpen. *BVbl* 39, 1974, 92–104; id., Zur Geschichte der Alpes Graiae et Poeninae. *Atti CSDIR* 7, 1975–76, 379–389.
91 J. Prieur, L'histoire des régions alpestres (Alpes Maritimes, Cottiennes, Graies et Pennines) sous le haut-empire romain (Ier–IIIe siècle après J.C.). In: *ANRW* II 5, 630–656. – F. Benoit, *Cimiez. La ville antique (Monuments – Histoire)* (Paris 1977).
92 *CIL* XII 113. – J. Prieur, *La Savoie antique* (Grenoble 1977) 96ff.
93 J. Formigé, *Le Trophée des Alpes (La Turbie)* (Paris 1949); N. Lamboglia, *Le Trophée d'Auguste à La Turbie* (3rd edn Bordighera 1964).
94 *Nat. Hist.* III 316–317. – *CIL* V 7817.
95 Regarding a neither geographically nor historically convincing attempt by J. Šašel to locate the *Ambisontes* in the Julian Alps, in the riverine district of the Isonzo (today Soča) (Zur Erklärung der Inschrift am Tropäum Alpium. *Živa Antika* 22, 1972, 135–144; adopted by P. Petru, *ANRW* II 6, 475ff.), cf. N. Heger, Salzburg in römischer Zeit. *Jahresschr. Salzburger Mus. C.A.* 19, 1973, 165 Note 24.
96 B. Galsterer-Kröll, Zum ius Latii in den keltischen Provinzen des Imperium Romanum. *Chiron* 3, 1973, 277–306.
97 *CIL* XVI 98.
98 Finally summarizing the wars of the Marcomanni: H. W. Böhme, Archäologische Zeugnisse zur Geschichte der Markomannenkriege (166–180 n. Chr.). *JbRGZM* 22, 1975, 153–217. Also important where the East Alpine region is concerned R. Noll, Zur Vorgeschichte der Markomannenkriege. *ArchA* 14, 1954, 43–67.
99 A drive up the Danube from Vienna as far as Lower Bavaria as postulated by H. W. Böhme (Note 98) 165 Ill. 3 conflicts with all the geographical aspects and the habitual behaviour of such warrior hordes, who sought to carry off as much booty as pos-

sible following the most direct route. – A record of the many signs of destruction in the Raetian-Norican frontier district is provided by S. Rieckhoff-Pauli (Regensburg); a notable treasure is that of 52 gold coins, the latest of which date from 164/165, found 1978 in Augsburg (briefly mentioned in: *Zeitschr. Hist. Ver. Schwaben* 73, 1979, 47 and *Castra Regina – Regensburg zur Römerzeit*. Exhibition Guide Regensburg [1979] 72). The doubts expressed in A. Lippold, Regensburg 179 n. Chr. – Die Gründung des Lagers der Legio III Italica. In: D. Albrecht (ed.), *Zwei Jahrtausende Regensburg. Vortragsreihe der Universität zum Stadtjubiläum 1979* (Regensburg 1979) 21–35 go to show the difficulties encountered by an ancient historian who wishes to be adequately conversant with the archaeological material and methods.

100 L. Pauli (Note 58) 115–139.

101 H.-J. Kellner, *Die Römer in Bayern* (4th edn Munich 1978) 131–155; Ph. Filtzinger, D. Planck and B. Cämmerer (eds), *Die Römer in Baden-Württemberg* (Stuttgart/Aalen 1976) 84–95.

102 W. Alzinger, *Aguntum und Lavant. Führer durch die römerzeitlichen Ruinen Osttirols* (3rd edn Vienna 1974) 14; S. Karwiese, *Der Ager Aguntinus. Eine Bezirkskunde des ältesten Osttirol* (Lienz 1975) 22f.

103 Comprehensively on this H.-J. Kellner, *Jahrb. Hist. Ver. Liechtenstein* 64, 1964, 74–82.

104 J. Garbsch, *Der spätrömische Donau–Iller–Rhein-Limes* (Stuttgart 1970).

105 The definitive publication is still awaited; meanwhile preliminary reports: J. Garbsch, *Spätrömische Schatzfunde aus Kastell Vemania. Vorbericht über die Kampagnen 1966–1968. Fundber. aus Schwaben* N.F. 19, 1971, 207–229; id., *Damenschmuck in der Kaserne. Kölner Römer-Illustrierte* 2, 1975, 134.

106 E. Howald and E. Meyer, *Die römische Schweiz* (Zurich 1940) No. 370; *JbSGU* 57, 1972–73, 345–347.

107 J. Werner, Spätrömische Befestigung auf dem Schlossberg in Füssen (Allgäu). *Germania* 34, 1956, 243–248.

108 No adequate excavations yet, but coins and some characteristic finds of the fourth century. Brief summary so far: A. Hild, Brigantium und seine Vorzeit. *Jahrb. Vorarlberger Landesmuseumsver.* 1952, 28–43; the coins in B. Overbeck, *Geschichte des Alpenrheintals in römischer Zeit auf Grund der archäologischen Zeugnisse*. Part 2: Die *Fundmünzen* (Munich 1973) 22–69.

109 It was always assumed that the late Roman fort lay on the mountain spur 'Hof', where today stand the cathedral and other episcopal buildings. The most recent excavations of the Graubünden Archaeological Service have now yielded architectural remains and finds: *JbSGU* 60, 1977, 142, 146f.

110 E. Ettlinger, Die Kleinfunde aus dem spätrömischen Kastell Schaan. *Jahrb. Hist. Ver. Liechtenstein* 59, 1959, 229–299; D. Beck, Das Kastell Schaan. Loc. cit. 57, 1957, 233–272.

111 A. Wotschitzky, Veldidena. *ÖJh* 41, 1954, Suppl. 1–42 and 44, 1957, Suppl. 5–70. A clear reconstruction in H.-J. Kellner (Note 101) 180.

112 Mentioned in the *Notitia dignitatum* Occ. XXXV 11.22.31, but unfortunately not traced so far by excavation. Cf. E. Walde, Die Grabungen in der Kirche St Martin in Martinsbühel. *BVbl* 40, 1975, 108.

113 J. Werner (ed.), *Der Lorenzberg bei Epfach. Die spätrömischen und frühmittelalterlichen Anlagen* (Munich 1969).

114 Excavated by Helmut Bender of the Kommission zur archäologischen Erforschung des spätrömischen Raetien der Bayer. Akademie der Wissenschaften. Short preliminary reports in: *Jahrb. Bayer. Akad. d. Wiss.* (since 1974) and in: *Das archäologische Jahr in Bayern 1980* (Stuttgart 1981) 146–147; and H. Bender, H. Tremel and B. Overbeck, Auswertung römischer Fundmünzen durch Datenverarbeitung. Demonstration an Hand der Grabung Wessling-Frauenwiese. *BVbl* 43, 1978, 115–146 with Suppl. 1 (Stand 1978).

115 H. Vetters, Die villa rustica von Wimsbach. *Jahrb. Oberösterr. Musealver.* 97, 1952, 87–109; abbrev. version: Ein in der Spätantike befestigtes Bauernhaus in Oberösterreich. In: Frühmittelalterliche Kunst in den Alpenländern. *Actes du IIIᵉ Congrès intern. pour l'étude du Haut Moyen Age 1951* (Olten/Lausanne 1954) 9–15. – D. Paunier, Un refuge du Bas-Empire au Mont-Musiège (Haute-Savoie). *Mus. Helveticum* 35, 1978, 295–306.

116 J. Garbsch, *Der Moosberg bei Murnau* (Munich 1966).

117 J. Boessneck in: J. Werner (ed.), *Studien zu Abodiacum-Epfach* (Munich 1964) 219f.; J. Garbsch, *Kölner Römer-Illustrierte* 2 (1975) 134.

118 E. Keller, Germanische Truppenstationen an der Nordgrenze des spätrömischen Raetiens. *ArchKorrbl* 7, 1977, 63–73.

119 J. Werner, Beiträge zur Archäologie des Attila-Reiches. *Abhandl. Bayer. Akad. d. Wiss.* N.F. 38 (Munich 1956); Otto J. Maenchen-Helfen, *The World of the Huns – Studies in their History and Culture* (Berkeley 1973).

120 J. Šašel, Antiqui Barbari. Zur Besiedlungsgeschichte Ostnoricums und Pannoniens im 5. und 6. Jahrhundert nach den Schriftquellen. In: J. Werner and E. Ewig (eds), *Von der Spätantike zum Frühmittelalter* (Sigmaringen 1979) 125–139.

121 R. Christlein, *Die Alamannen* (Stuttgart/Aalen 1978) 31ff.

122 *De gubernatione* V 25. 38–45.

123 On the difficulties of assessing received tradition: H.-J. Hundt, Die Rohstoffquellen des europäischen Nordens und ihr Einfluss auf die Entwicklung des nordischen Stils. *Bonner Jahrb.* 178, 1978, 125–162.

124 In late antiquity, instead of the nominative form *Quintanae, Batavae, Boidurum, Lauriacum*, etc. the locative became the undeclinable designation of a place. This applies not only to the road maps and troop registers but also to the Vita S. Severini, where the grammatical usage is evident. *Lauriacum* appears in the bowdlerized form *Blaboriciano* in the Tabula Peutingeriana (Ills 136–137). – Cf. additionally K. Zangemeister, Erstarrte Flexion von Ortsnamen im Latein. *Rhein. Mus. f. Phil.* 57, 1902, 168ff.

125 V. Bierbrauer, Zur ostgotischen Geschichte in Italien. *Studi* *medievali* (Spoleto) 3. Ser. 14, 1973, 1–37; an advance offprint of the chapter 'Historische Voraussetzungen' in his work: *Die ostgotischen Grab- und Schatzfunde in Italien* (Spoleto 1975) 16–52.

126 V. Bierbrauer, Zum Vorkommen ostgotischer Bügelfibeln in Raetia II. *BVbl* 36, 1971, 160ff.

127 Var. XII 4, 362.

128 A recent summary by O. P. Clavadetscher, Churrätien im Übergang von der Spätantike zum Mittelalter nach den Schriftquellen. In: J. Werner and E. Ewig (Note 120) 159–178; E. Meyer-Marthaler, *Rätien im Frühmittelalter* (Zurich 1948).

129 K. F. Stroheker, Studien zu den historisch-geographischen Grundlagen des Nibelungenliedes. *Dt. Vierteljahresschr. f. Lit. u. Geisteswiss.* 32, 1958, 216–240; M. Beck, Bemerkungen zur Geschichte des ersten Burgunderreiches. *Schweiz. Zeitschr. f. Gesch.* 13, 1964, 433–457; O. Perrin, *Les Burgondes. Leur histoire, des origines à la fin du premier Royaume* (534) (Neuchâtel 1968).

130 G. Löhlein, *Die Alpen- und Italienpolitik der Merowinger im 6. Jahrhundert* (Erlangen 1932); H. Büttner, Die Alpenpolitik der Franken im 6. und 7. Jahrhundert. *Hist. Jahrb.* 79, 1960, 62–88.

131 J. Werner, *Die Langobarden in Pannonien* (Munich 1962).

132 G. Barni, *I Langobardi in Italia* (Novara 1974); M. Brozzi, *Il ducato Longobardo del Friuli* (Cividale 1975); C. G. Menis, *Storia del Friuli dalle origini alla caduta dello stato patriacale (1420)* (Udine 1974).

133 The most recent work by C. Simonett, Geschichte der Stadt Chur, Part 1: Von den Anfängen bis ca. 1400. *Jahrb. Hist. Ant. Ges. Graubünden 104, 1974* (Chur 1976) contains several hypotheses that are presented all too confidently as fact.

134 G. Schneider-Schnekenburger, *Churrätien im Frühmittelalter auf Grund der archäologischen Funde* (Munich 1980); a short summary in: J. Werner and E. Ewig, (Note 120) 179–191. From the viewpoint of the linguistic researcher: S. Sonderegger, Die Siedlungsverhältnisse Churrätiens im Lichte der Namenforschung. Loc. cit. 219–254.

135 H. Schwab, Burgunder und Langobarden. *UFAS* VI, 21–38; J. Werner, Die romanische Trachtprovinz Nordburgund im 6. und 7. Jahrhundert. In: J. Werner and E. Ewig (Note 120) 447–465.

136 R. Egger, Der Alpenraum im Zeitalter des Übergangs von der Antike zum Mittelalter. In: *Die Alpen in der europäischen Geschichte des Mittelalters* (2nd edn Sigmaringen 1976) 15–28; H. Vetters, Die Kontinuität von der Antike zum Mittelalter im Ostalpenraum. Loc. cit. 29–48; F. Miltner, Zum Kontinuitätsproblem römischer Siedlung in den Ostalpen. *Der Schlern* 24, 1950, 389–392; Th. Ulbert, Zur Siedlungskontinuität im südöstlichen Alpenraum (vom 2. bis 6. Jahrhundert n. Chr.). In: J. Werner and E. Ewig (Note 120) 141–157.

137 Chapter III Notes 127–128.

138 Regional summaries recently by P. Petru and Th. Ulbert, *Vranje pri Sevnici* (Vranje near Sevnica). *Frühchristliche Kirchenanlagen auf dem Ajdovski gradec* (Ljubljana 1975) 56ff. with numerous critical notes, also by H. R. Sennhauser, Spätantike und frühmittelalterliche Kirchen Churrätiens. In: J. Werner and E. Ewig (Note 120) 193–218; id., Kirchen und Klöster. *UFAS* VI, 138–148.

139 H. Koller, Die Klöster Severins von Norikum. *Schild von Steier* 15–16, 1978–79 *(Festschr. für W. Modrijan)* 201–207.

140 J.-M. Theurillat, L'Abbaye de St-Maurice d'Agaune (515–830). *Vallesia* 9, 1954, 1–128. The excavations have really only taken in the early churches; in addition various reports of L. Blondel in the same periodical between 1948 and 1957.

141 F. Prinz, *Frühes Mönchtum im Frankenreich. Kultur und Gesellschaft in Gallein, den Rheinlanden und Bayern am Beispiel der monastischen Entwicklung (4.–8. Jahrhundert)* (Munich 1965).

142 There are no archaeological finds from this early period. The cemeteries of the 'Karantanisch–Köttlacher Kultur' do not begin until the Carolingian period: p. 144f.

143 G. Rohlfs, *Rätoromanisch* (Munich 1975); A Dami, Die Rätoromanen. *Jahrb. Vorarlberger Landesmuseumsver.* 106, 1962, 3–36; K. Finsterwalder, Romanische Vulgärsprache in Rätien und Norikum von der römischen Kaiserzeit bis zur Karolingerepoche, Historische Belege und sprachliche Folgerungen. In: *Festschr. für K. Pivec* (Innsbruck 1966) 33–64; F. Schürr, Die Alpenromanen. In: *Die Alpen in der europäischen Geschichte des Mittelalters* (2nd edn Sigmaringen 1976) 201–229.

144 H. Kreis, Die Walser, *Ein Stück Siedlungsgeschichte der Zentralalpen* (Bern 1958).

145 L. White, *Medieval Technology and Social Change* (3rd edn Oxford 1966) 1ff.: Stirrup, Mounted Shock Combat, Feudalism, and Chivalry.

146 Detailed assessment in terms of the history of costume, sociology and geographical transference by H. Vierck, in: H.-J. Hässler (ed.), *Studien zur Sachsenforschung 2* (Hanover 1980) 466ff.

147 K. Bosl, Die ersten siebenhundert Jahre deutsch–bayerischer Geschichte Südtirols. *Zeitschr. Bayer. Landesgesch.* 42, 1979, 15–30.

148 P. Kirn, *Aus der Frühzeit des Nationalgefühls* (Leipzig 1943) 39; F. Schürr (Note 143) 206; I. Reiffenstein in: M. Spindler (ed.), *Handbuch der bayerischen Geschichte* I (2nd edn Munich 1981) 613.

149 E. Schwarz, Walchen- und Parschalkennamen im alten Norikum. *Zeitschr. f. Ortsnamenforsch.* 1, 1925, 91–99; id., Baiern und Walchen. *Zeitschr. f. bayer. Landesgesch.* 33, 1970, 857–938.

150 E. Keller, Grabfunde der jüngeren Merowingerzeit aus Garmisch-Partenkirchen (Oberbayern). *ArchKorrbl* 3, 1973, 447–454.

151 L. Plank, Die Bodenfunde des frühen Mittelalters aus Nordtirol. *Veröff. Mus. Ferdinandeum* Innsbruck 44, 1964, 99–210.

152 M. v. Chlingensperg-Berg, *Das Gräberfeld von Reichenhall in Oberbayern* (Reichenhall 1890); M. Menke, Bad Reichenhall im frühen Mittelalter. In: *Führer zu vor- und frühgeschichtlichen Denkmälern* 19 (Mainz 1971) 150–160.

153 Cf. the map in L. Pauli, *Der Dürrnberg bei Hallein* 3 (Munich 1978) 493 Ill. 53.

154 Th. v. Grienberger, Die Ortsnamen des Indiculus Arnonis und der Breves Notitiae Salzburgenses in ihrer Ableitung und Bedeutung herausgestellt. *Mitt. Ges. Salzburger Landeskde.* 26, 1886, 1–76.

155 Baiernzeit in Oberösterreich. Exhibition catalogue Linz (1977).

156 O. P. Clavadetscher, Die Einführung der Grafschaftsverfassung in Räten und die Klageschrift Bischof Victors III. *Zeitschr. Savigny-Stiftung f. Rechtsgesch.*, kan. Abt. 39, 1953, 46–111.

157 For the paragraphs that follow literary references will be omitted almost entirely since no special studies are drawn upon here. Of value is the omnibus volume 'Die Alpen in der europäischen Geschichte des Mittelalters'. *Vorträge und Forschungen* 10 (2nd edn Sigmaringen 1976), likewise 'Schwaben und Schweiz im frühen und hohen Mittelalter'. Loc. cit. 15 (1972). Besides these enough historical summaries for every district are available.

158 K. Lechner, *Die Babenberger (976–1246).* (Vienna/Cologne/Graz 1976).

159 K. Schwarz, Die Birg bei Hohenschäftlarn – eine Burganlage der karolingisch-ottonischen Zeit. In: *Führer zu vor- und frühgeschichtlichen Denkmälern* 18 (Mainz 1971) 222–238.

160 B. Luppi, *I Saraceni in Provenza, in Liguria e nelle Alpi occidentali* (Bordighera 1973).

II From Wattle Hut to Palace – How the People Lived

1 Chapter I, Note 3.

2 Chapter I, Note 6.

3 A Springer, *Die Salzversorgung der Eingeborenen Afrikas vor der neuzeitlichen Kolonisation* (Jena 1918) 16.

4 H. de Lumley, Une cabane de chasseurs acheuléen dans la grotte du Lazaret à Nice. *Archaeologia* 28, 1969, 26–33; H. de Lumley et al., Une cabane acheuléenne dans la grotte du Lazaret (Nice). *Mém. Soc. Préhist. Franç.* 7 (1969); H. de Lumley et al., Grotte du Lazaret. In: Sites paléolithiques de la région de Nice et grottes de Grimaldi. *IXe Congrès Union intern. sciences préhist. et protohist. Nice 1976, Livret-Guide de l'excursion* B 1 (Nice 1976) 53–74.

5 Chapter I, Note 20.

6 Clear house reconstructions are to be found in W. Buttler, *Der Donauländische und der westische Kulturkreis der jüngeren Steinzeit* (Berlin/Leipzig 1938). The largest house (50 m × 10 m) of the Bandkeramik people so far found in south Germany was recently excavated at Lengfeld-Dantschermühle (Lower Bavaria): *Ausgrabungen und Neufunde in Niederbayern 1973–1976. Führungsblatt zur Ausstellung in Straubing.* (1978/79). Cf. also R. A. Maier, *Jahresber. Bayer. Bodendenkmalpfl.* 5, 1964, 26 Ill. 11 and 144 Ill. 102.

7 Chapter VI, Note 3.

8 *Das Pfahlbauproblem* (Basel 1954). A good survey of the 'pile-dwellings' problem including the latest research findings is provided by the publications '125 Jahre Pfahlbauforschung' (*AS* 2/1, 1979) and 'Zürcher Seeufersiedlungen – Von der Pfahlbau-Romantik zur modernen archäologischen Forschung (*HelvA* 12, 1981, 1–276 = fasc. 45–48).

9 *UFAS* II, 166 Ill. 13; 168 Ill. 15; also contains bibliographical data on the preliminary reports.

10 Chr. Strahm, Pfahlbauten – Neue Gedanken zu einem alten Problem. *Arch. Inf.* 1, 1972, 55–62; id., Les fouilles d'Yverdon. *JbSGU* 57, 1972–73, 7–16.

11 H. Schwab, *ArchKorrbl* 2, 1972, 292f.; H. Schwab and R. Müller, *Die Vergangenheit des Seelandes in neuem Licht – Über die Wasserstände der Juraseen* (Freiburg i. Ü. 1973). The chronological data given there of the greatest fluctuations need to be checked even more carefully; cf. in the first place L. Berger and M. Joos, Zur Wasserführung der Zihl bei der Station La Tène. In: *Festschrift W. Drack* (Stäfa 1977) 68–76.

12 Preliminary reports: R. Perini, *PrAlp* 7, 1971, 283–322; 8, 1972, 199–253; 11, 1975, 25–64; in addition id., Die Pfahlbauten im Torfmoor von Fiavè (Trentino/Oberitalien). *MblSGU* 7 (27) 1976, 2–12; id., L'abitato palafitticolo di Fiavè nel periodo del bronzo medio III^c. *Studi Trentini di Scienze Stor.* 55, 1976, 13–76.

13 R. Battaglia, La palafitta del Lago di Ledro nel Trentino. *Mem. Mus. Stor. Nat. Venezia Tridentina* (Trento) 7, 1943, 1–63; id., Presentazione della pianta topografica della palafitta di Ledro nel Trentino. In: *Atti I^e Convegno preist. italo-svizzero Locarno – Varese – Como 1947* (Como 1949) 47–53; J. Rageth, Der Lago di Ledro im Trentino und seine Beziehungen zu den alpinen und mitteleuropäischen Kulturen. *BerRGK* 55, 1974, 73–259.

14 Recommended as a guide: M. Ferrari, G. Scrinzi and G. Tomasi, *Das Ledrotal und seine Pfahlbauten* (Trento 1973).

15 For an overview see R. Munro, *Les stations lacustres d'Europe aux Ages de la Pierre et du Bronze* (Paris 1908). The finds and findings have been adequately published only in rare instances, as for example K. Willvonseder, Die jungsteinzeitlichen und bronzezeitlichen Pfahlbauten des Attersees in Oberösterreich. *Mitt. Prähist. Komm.* 11–12 (Vienna 1963–68). The new underwater archaeology has given fresh impetus to the systematic search for 'pile-dwellings'. Cf. for example J. Offenberger, Die österreichischen Pfahlbauten. Ein Arbeitsbericht. *Jahrb. Oberösterr. Musealver.* 121, 1976, 105–138; K. Czech, Pfahlbausuche und Lokalisierung der Pfahlbauten im Attersee, *Fundber. aus Österreich* 15, 1976, 29ff.; 16, 1977, 83ff. and 17, 1978, 9ff.

16 H. Schwab and R. Müller (Note 11) 50f.

17 Ibid. 51. Der Dolch: *JbSGU* 52, 1965, 95ff. Ill. 1.

18 Savognin (Graubünden) 'Padnal': J. Rageth, *JbSGU* 61, 1978, 183 Ills 18–19.

19 M. Primas, Archäologische Untersuchungen in Tamins GR: die spätneolithische Station 'Crestis'. *JbSGU* 62, 1979, 13–27.

20 M. Hell, Eine neolithische Muldensiedlung bei Maxglan. *Jahrb. f. Altertumskde.* 3, 1909, 209f.

21 R. Wyss, Siedlungswesen und Verkehrswege. *UFAS* III, 103–122.

22 Cf. J. Rageth, *AS* 2, 1979, 83 for the findings at Savognin 'Padnal'.

23 *UFAS* II, 172 Ill. 23.

24 E. Schmid, Zwei Tonlampen von Twann mit gelbglänzendem Bodenbelag. *MblSGU* 8 (32), 1977, 21–23.

25 After W. Lucke and O.-H. Frey, *Die Situla in Providence (Rhode Island)* (Berlin 1962) Pl. 67.

26 W. Burkart, *Crestaulta, eine bronzezeitliche Hügelsiedlung bei Surin im Lugnez* (Basel 1946).

27 Unpublished. The many little preliminary reports of *JbSGU* 33, 1947, 47 to 54, 1968/69, 118 form the basis of the short account in *UFAS* III, 114–116 with Ill. 12.

28 Detailed preliminary reports: J. Rageth, Die bronzezeitliche Siedlung auf dem Padnal bei Savognin (Oberhalbstein GR). *JbSGU* 59, 1976, 123–179; 60, 1977, 43–101; 61, 1978, 7–63; 62, 1979, 29–76; 63, 1980, 21–75; 64, 1981, 27–71 The latest situation: Neue Beobachtungen zu den Grabungen auf dem Padnal by Savognin. *AS* 2, 1979, 81–87.

29 First report: A. Gredig, Die ur- und frühgeschichtliche Siedlung am Tummihügel bei Maladers. *AS* 2, 1979, 69–74.

30 A quite similar situation in Scharans 'Spundas': *AS* 2, 1979, 88 Ills 1–2.

31 Chapter I Note 48.

32 M. Hell, Hausformen der Hallstattzeit aus Salzburg-Liefering. *ArchA* 1, 1948, 57–71.

33 F. Moosleitner and E. Penninger, Ein keltischer Blockwandbau vom Dürrnberg bei Hallein. *Mitt. Ges. Salzburger Landeskde.* 105, 1965, 47–87. Loosely associated with this finding the farmstead of the open-air museum on the Dürrnberg was reconstructed in 1980.

34 Chapter V Note 17.

35 Ch. Lagrand and J.-P. Thalmann, *Les habitats protohistoriques du Pègue (Drôme): Le Sondage N° 8 (1957–1971)* (Grenoble 1973); J.-J. Hatt, Les fouilles du Pègue (Drôme) de 1957 à 1975. *Gallia* 34, 1976, 31–56 and 35, 1977, 39–58; Ch. Lagrand, *Le Pègue-Drôme: Guide des Collections Préhistoriques et Protohistoriques* (Le Pègue 1978).

36 J.-C. Courtois, *Les habitats protohistoriques de Sainte-Colombe près d'Orpierre (Hautes-Alpes)* (Grenoble 1975).

37 B. Frei, Die ausgrabungen auf der Mottata bei Ramosch im Unterengadin. *JbSGU* 47, 1958–59, 34–43.

38 H. Miltner, *Die Illyrer-Siedlung Vill* (Innsbruck 1944).

39 R. Perini, Risultati dello scavo in una capanna dell'orizzonte retico nei Montesei di Serso (Pergine Valsugana – Trento). *Studi Trentini Scienze Nat.* Sez. B 42, 1965, 148–183 (= *Rendiconti Soc. Cult. Tridentina* 3, 1965, 32–67); id., 2000 anni di vita sui Montesei di Serso. Exhibition catalogue Pergine/Trento (1978), 52–85.

40 R. Perini, La casa retica in epoca protostorica. *Studi Trentini Scienze Nat.* Sez. B 44, 1967, 279–297 (= *Rendiconti Soc. Cult. Tridentina* 5, 1967–69, 38–56).

41 Still the most thorough investigation: A. zur Lippe, *Ein vorgeschichtlicher Weiler auf dem Burgberg von Stans bei Schwaz (Tiroler Unterinntal)* (Innsbruck 1960).

42 Chapter I Note 82.

43 Ultimate summary: W. Krämer, Zwanzig Jahre Ausgrabungen in Manching – 1955 bis 1974. In: *Ausgrabungen in Deutschland.* Exhibition catalogue Mainz (1975) Part 1, 287–297; id., Das keltische Oppidum bei Manching. In: *Vor- und frühgeschichtliche Archäologie in Bayern* (Munich 1972) 119–129.

44 F. Benoit, *Entremont. Capitale celto-ligure des Salyens de Provence* (2nd edn Gap 1969) based on numerous preliminary reports from *Gallia* 5, 1947.

45 Latest hints *Gallia* 33, 1975, 554f.; 35, 1977, 490f.

46 *JbSGU* 43, 1953, 85.

47 H. P. Uenze and J. Katzameyer, *Vor- und Frühgeschichte in den Landkreisen Bad Tölz und Miesbach* (Kallmünz 1971) 111–116 No. 51; H. P. Uenze, Oppidum 'Fentbach-Schanze'. In: Führer zu vor- und frühgesch. Denkmälern 18 (Mainz 1971) 199–206.

48 M. Hell and H. v. Koblitz, Die prähistorischen Funde vom Rainberge in Salzburg. Beitrag II in: G. Kyrle, *Urgeschichte des Kronlandes Salzburg* (Vienna 1918); M. Hell, Neue Funde vom Rainberg in Salzburg. *WPZ* 10, 1923, 17–22.

49 Cf. *Mitt. Ges. f. Salzburger Landeskde.* 101, 1961 (= *Festschr. für M. Hell*) 82 under the key word 'Biberg'. A first summary now by F. Moosleitner, Das Saalfeldener Becken in vor- und frühschichtlicher Zeit. In: F. Kowall, *50 Jahre Diabas-Tagbau in Saalfelden 1927–1977* (Vienna 1977) 27–53, partic. 44ff.

50 Chapter I Note 155 (M. Menke). For coin minting on the Dürrnberg and in Karlstein cf. Chapter VI Note 92.

51 The first twelve progressively augmented excavation reports appeared regularly in *Carinthia* I 139, 1949, 145–176 to 159, 1969, 283–422. From excavation report 13 (1973) and 14 (1977) they have been issued as a separate series by the Verlag des Geschichtsvereins für Kärnten (Klagenfurt). Short summaries nevertheless continue to appear in the regional journal (most recent G. Piccottini, Die Ausgrabungen auf dem Magdalensberg 1978–1980. *Carinthia* I 170, 1980, 7–40). Individual groups of finds (pottery, lamps and coins) are published as the current situation demands in the 'Archäologischen Forschungen zu den Grabungen auf dem Magdalensberg' (*Kärntner Museumsschriften*, Klagenfurt). Equally important are the 'Naturkundlichen Forschungen zu den Grabungen auf dem Magdalensberg' with animal-bone diagnoses and metallurgical tests. So far a comprehensive overview has only been attempted by A. Obermayer, *Kelten und Römer am Magdalensberg* (Vienna 1971). Invaluable as an introduction and aid to viewing of the excavations is G. Piccottini and H. Vetters, *Führer durch die Ausgrabungen auf dem Magdalensberg* (Klagenfurt 1978), which brings up to date the new issue of

the old Guide by R. Egger that appeared in its twentieth printing in 1977. – The excavation is one of the tourist attractions of Carinthia with a wide road leading to it. In 1978 the Carinthian county government replaced the dilapidated wooden barracks of the excavation personnel with stone buildings – an indication of the durability of simple wooden houses (not log-huts!) from the Stone Age.

52 G. Alföldy, *Noricum* (London 1974) 259f.; G. Winkler, *ANRW* II 6, 201f. Note 98. Opinions differ as to whether this unit was recruited within the home country, or from other Alpine areas as well. At all events *Vintium*/Vence in the Alpes maritimae yielded a partially preserved inscription for a *miles c(o)hor(tis) (al)pinorum qui (...)t in Pannunia (CIL* XII 15).

53 *ANRW* II 6, 302–354.

54 H. Vetters, Taurisker oder Noriker, Noreia oder Virunum! In: *Festschrift für R. Pittioni* 2 (Vienna/Horn 1976) 242–250.

55 N. Heger, Salzburg in römischer Zeit. *Jahresschr. Salzburger Mus. C.A.* 19, 1973, 99f.

56 G. Zahlhaas, Die Fresken des römischen Thermengebäudes von Schwangau. *BVbl* 43, 1978, 101–113; colour photographs: id., *Antike Welt* 9/4, 1978, 13–23.

57 H. Kenner, Wandmalereien aus AA/15f. *Carinthia* I 156, 1966, 435–447; G. Piccottini and H. Vetters, *Die Ausgrabungen auf dem Magdalensberg 1969–1972* (Klagenfurt 1973) 209–284.

58 W. Drack, *Die römischen Wandmalereien der Schweiz* (Basel 1950): id., *ArchKorrbl* 4, 1974, 365f.

59 G. Luraschi, Comum oppidum. Premessa allo studio delle strutture amministrative romane. *Rivista Arch. Como* 152–155, 1970–73, 207–394; G. Tibiletti, Per la storia di Comum nel I sec. a. C. Loc. cit. 159, 1977, 137–149.

60 They have not yet been completed. First information from the excavator: Der Auerberg. Ergebnisse und Probleme der neuen Ausgrabungen 1968–1974. In: *Ausgrabungen in Deutschland.* Exhibition catalogue Mainz (1975) Part 1, 409–433. I am much indebted to Günter Ulbert for information about the latest developments.

61 On the telling influences regarding comparable constructions in pre-Roman times cf. L. Pauli, Blockwandhäuser am Hallstätter Salzberg? *ArchKorrbl* 9, 1979, 81–86.

62 P. Barocelli, *Ricerche e studi sui monumenti romani della Val d'Aosta* (Aosta 1934); id., *Forma Italiae, Regio XI Transpadana 1. Augusta Praetoria* (Rome 1948); A. Zanotto, *Aoste. Histoire – Antiquités – Objets d'art* (Aosta 1967).

63 W. Drack, Zur Wasserbeschaffung für römische Einzelsiedlungen gezeigt an schweizerischen Beispielen. In: *Provincialia (Festschr. für R. Laur-Belart)* (Basel 1968) 249–268; on the difficulties cf. the case of Wulfingen near Winterthur (canton Zurich): *JbSGU* 59, 1976, 269.

64 A tunnel at least 306 m long for the water conduit to *Cemelenum*/Nice-Cimiez: *Gallia* 31, 1973, 566f. Ill. 35.

65 W. Haberey, *Die römischen Wasserleitungen nach Köln* (Düsseldorf 1971).

66 O. Steubinger, Die römischen Wasserleitungen von Nîmes und Arles. *Zeitschr. f. Gesch. d. Architektur* 1909, 236–304; E. Espérandieu, *Le Pont du Gard* (3rd edn 1968).

67 P. Barocelli, *Ricerche* (Note 62) 59–62.

68 Guide: P.-A. Février, *Forum Iulii (Fréjus)* (Bordighera 1963).

69 Not. dign. Occ. XXXV 32. There were probably also bases for lake as well as river navigation in Vienne and Arles (France), Yverdon (Switzerland), Como (Italy) and Enns-Lorch (Austria): XLII 9. 14. 15; XXXIV 43. For Como now comprehensively G. Luraschi, Il 'praefectus classis cum curis civitatis' nel quadro politico ed amministrativo del Basso Impero. *Rivista Arch. Como* 159, 1977, 151–184.

70 G. Kaenel, Aménagements d'une promenade archéologique à Vidy-Lausanne VD. *MblSGU* 7 (28), 1976, 5–12; id., Lousonna. La promenade archéologique de Vidy (Lausanne 1977).

71 W. Alzinger, *Aguntum und Lavant. Führer durch die römerzeitlichen Ruinen Osttirols* (3rd edn Vienna 1974); S. Karwiese, *Der Ager Aguntinus. Eine Bezirkskunde des ältesten Osttirol* (Lienz 1975).

72 W. Alzinger, Aguntum 1976. *Pro Austria Romana* 27, 1977, 12–15 with Suppl.; id., Ein Stadtplanfund in Aguntum. *Antike Welt* 8/1, 1977, 37–41.

73 An up-to-date conspectus of the Roman history of the place is lacking. In the first place excavation reports and reviews: L. Closuit and G. Spagnoli, *Inventaire des trouvailles romaines d'Octodurus (Martigny)* (Bern 1976); F. Wiblé, Un nouveau sanctuaire gallo-romain découvert a Martigny (VS). In: *Festschrift W. Drack* (Stäfa 1977) 89–94; reports nearly every year by F. Wiblé since 1975/76 in the periodicals *Annales Valaisannes* and *JbSGU*; several articles on Martigny are published in fasc. 39/40 of *HelvA* (10, 1979, 95–194); a critical review of them: F. Wiblé, *JbSGU* 64, 1981, 291–293. – Now available a guide from the excavator himself: F. Wiblé, *Forum Claudii Vallensium. La Ville romaine de Martigny* (Martigny 1981).

74 A. Defuns and J. R. Lengler, Die Bergung der römischen Wandmalereien von Chur-Welschdörfli. *AS* 2, 1979, 103–108. I am grateful to Christian Zindel for a lucid report.

75 A. Dumoulin, *Guide archéologique de Vaison-la-Romaine* (Vaison-la-Romaine 1976)

76 G. Th. Schwarz, Römische Villa und Gräberfeld bei Roveredo im Misox GR. *Ur-Schweiz* 29, 1965, 38–46; cf. also the overall plan of Katsch: W. Schmid (Note 80) 90 Ill. 50.

77 Chapter VI Note 105.

78 W. Drack, Die Gutshöfe. *UFAS* V, 49–72.

79 M. Hell, *Mitt. Ges. f. Salzburger Landeskde.* 108, 1968, 341ff.; N. Heger, Salzburg in römischer Zeit. *Jahresschr. Salzburger Museum C.A.* 19, 1973, 52.

80 W. Schmid, Siedelung und Gräberfeld von Chatissa-Katsch in Obersteiermark. *ÖJh* 25, 1929, Beibl. 97–148.

81 See Note 95. Volker Bierbrauer is still engaged in collating the finds and findings.

82 W. Modrijan, *Der römische Landsitz von Löffelbach* (3rd edn Graz 1971).

83 V. v. Gonzenbach, *Die römischen Mosaiken der Schweiz* (Basel 1961); id., *Die römischen Mosaiken von Orbe* (Basel 1974); W. Drack, *Der römische Gutshof bei Seeb* (Basel 1974) 17 Ills 14–15. – Mérande b. Arbin (Savoie): J. Lancha, *Gallia* 32, 1974, 63–83.

84 N. Heger (Note 79) 50ff. – Comparable at all events is the *villa* of Graz-Thalerhof inadequately excavated during the unfavourable years 1937–39: W. Modrijan, *Römerzeitliche Villen und Landhäuser in der Steiermark* (Graz 1969) 14ff.

85 *Carmina* 31. English translation by F. W. Cornish (17th edn Harvard/London 1976).

86 The excavations are very sketchily published. Essential information contained in the little guide-book of M. Mirabella Roberti, *Sirmione – Grotte des Catullus* (1974).

87 G. Tosi, Problemi tecnico-stilistici e cronologia della villa romana di Sirmione. In: *Venetia, Studi miscellanei di archeologia delle Venezie* 3 (Padua 1975) 73–142.

88 Chapter VI Note 107.

89 For instance the Söhlehöhle at Götzis in Vorarlberg (L. Franz and A. R. Neumann, *Lexikon ur- und frühgeschichtlicher Fundstätten Österreichs* [Vienna/Bonn 1965] 180), the 'Hohle Stein' at Calfreisen near Chur (*JbSGU* 22, 1930, 94) and the Tgilväderlishöhle at Felsberg in Graubünden (*JbSGU* 18, 1926, 124–127; 20, 1928, 104). The materials are discussed by B. Overbeck, *Geschichte des Alpenrheintals in römischer Zeit* 1 (Munich 1982).

90 Chapter VI Note 119.

91 Chapter I Note 114; H. Bemder, *BVbl* 43, 1978, 120.

92 J. Garbsch, *Der Moosberg bei Murnau* (Munich 1966).

93 Christian Zindel, Vorbemerkungen zur spätrömischen-frühmittelalterlichen Anlage von Castiel/Carschlingg. *AS* 2, 1979, 109–112. Also: *JbSGU* 60, 1977, 145f.; 61, 1978, 177–179. 197–199; 62, 1979, 138–141; Christian Zindel, Jürg Rageth and Silvio Nauli deserve my special thanks for providing a variety of information.

94 Der Negauer Helm von Castiel/Carschlingg. *AS* 2, 1979, 94–96.

95 Thesis submitted for the certificate of habilitation, Munich 1977; I have to extend my grateful thanks to Volker Bierbrauer for generously giving me permission to turn his findings to account here. Preliminary reports: G. Fingerlin, J. Garbsch and J. Werner, Die Ausgrabungen im langobardischen Kastell Ibligo-Invillino (Friaul). Vorbericht über die Kampagnen 1962, 1963 und 1965. *Germania* 46, 1968, 73–110 (also published in Italian in: *Aquileia Nostra* 39, 1968, 57–136); V. Bierbrauer, Gli scavi a Ibligo-Invillino, Friuli. Campagne degli anni 1972–1973 sul colle di Zuca. *Aquileia Nostra* 44, 1973, 85–126.

96 *Bell. got.* II 28.

97 *Hist. Lang.* IV 37.

98 Cassiodorus, *Var.* III 48 (dated 507/511) *Est enim in mediis campis tumulus saxeus in rotunditate consurgens, qui proceris lateribus, silvis erasus, totus mons quasi una turris efficitur... castrum paene in mundo singulare, tenens claustra provinciae* – 'a fort practically unique in the whole world, which holds in its hand the key to our province.' Here the meaning of *claustra*, already in the Latin something concrete and transmitted, is particularly clear: bolt, bar, key; barrier, cage; narrow passage; fortified frontier. In late antiquity the frontier fortification in the Southeast Alps against the Balkans was called *Claustra Alpium Iuliarum;* hence now the compilation of sources *Claustra Alpium Iuliarum 1. Fontes* (Ljubljana 1971). Incidentally *Verruca* also possessed a little church from the beginning of the sixth century with floor mosaic (unpublished).

99 C. Carducci, Un insediamento 'barbarico' presso il santuario di Belmonte nel Canavese. *Atti CSDIR* 7, 1975–76, 89–104.

100 R. Egger, Der Ulrichsberg – Ein heiliger Berg Kärntens. *Carinthia* I 140, 1950, (100 continued) 29–78; also available under the same title as a separate publication (2nd edn Klagenfurt 1976).

101 The excavation reports: *ÖJh* 17, 1914, 17ff. Introduction: R. Egger, *Teurnia. Die römischen und frühchristlichen Altertümer Oberkärntens* (7th edn Klagenfurt 1973).

102 F. Miltner, *ÖJh* 38, 1950, Beibl. 37ff.; 40, 1953, Beibl. 15ff.; 41, 1954, Beibl. 43ff.; 43, 1956–58, Beibl. 89ff. Also: id., Bemerkungen zur Geschichte von Lavant in Osttirol. *Carinthia* I 143, 1953 (= *Festschr. für R. Egger* 2) 843–853 (426–436). – The last excavations and assessments: W. Alzinger, *ÖJh* 47, 1964–65, Grabungen 1966, 64ff.; 49, 1968–71, Grabungen 1969, 54; id. (Note 71); S. Karwiese (Note 71) 50. – A critical commentary on the interpretation of the 'Celtic temple' and the fortification from 'late antiquity': H. Wiesflecker, Aguntum – St Andrä – Luenzia – Patriarchesdorf. In: *Alpenregion und Österreich. Festschr. für H. Kramer* (Innsbruck 1976) 171–191; likewise S. Karwiese, Lavant. Ein Schwerpunkt in der Frühgeschichte Osttirols. *Osttiroler Heimatbl.* 41, 1973, fasc. 7–10.

103 Compiled with all literary sources by H. R. Sennhauser, Der Profanbau. *UFAS* VI, 149–164.

104 M.-L. Boscardin and W. Meyer, *Burgenforschung in Graubünden* (Olten 1977) 51–171; also H. R. Sennhauser (Note 103) 159ff.

105 Leges Alamannorum: MGH LL 3 and 5, 1; Leges Alamannorum, K. A. Eckhardt (ed.) (Göttingen 1958 and 1962).

106 Only published in summarized form by W. U. Guyan, *Erforschte Vergangenheit* 2: *Schaffhauser Frühgeschichte* (Schaffhausen 1971) 187–212 with map pp. 202/3; additionally H. R. Sennhauser (Note 103) 158f.

107 H. Dannheimer, Die frühmittelalterliche Siedlung bei Kirchheim (Ldkr. München, Oberbayern). Vorbericht über die Untersuchung im Jahre 1970. *Germania* 51, 1973, 152–169. New rescue excavations 1980 exceed in extent and results everything previously known in southern Germany. Preliminary report by R. Christlein in: *Das archäologische Jahr in Bayern 1980* (Stuttgart 1981) 162f.

III The Living and the Dead – The Individual and the Community

1 R. Peroni, *L'età del bronzo nella peninsola Italiana 1* (Florence 1971) 111ff.

2 *UFAS* III, 150f.

3 M. Primas, *Die südschweizerischen Grabfunde der älteren Eisenzeit und ihre Chronologie* (Basel 1970); L. Pauli, *Studien zur Golasecca-Kultur* (Heidelberg 1971) 124.

4 W. Krämer, Das Ende der Mittellatènefriedhöfe und die Grabfunde der Spätlatènezeit in Südbayern. *Germania* 30, 1952, 330–337.

5 So too still D. Kahlke, *Die Bestattungssitten des Donauländischen Kulturkreises der jüngeren Steinzeit*. Part I: *Linienbandkeramik* (Berlin 1954) 121f.

6 R. Andree, Ethnologische Betrachtungen über Hockerbestattung. *Archiv f. Anthr.* N. F. 6, 1907, 282–307; J. Banner, A magyarországi zsugorított temetkezések. Die in Ungarn gefundenen Hockergräber. *Dolgozatok Szeged* 3, 1927, 1–122; J. v. Trauwitz-Hellwig, *Totenverehrung, Totenabwehr und Vorgeschichte* (Munich 1935).

7 L. Pauli, *Keltischer Volksglaube, Amulette und Sonderbestattungen am Dürrnberg bei Hallein und im eisenzeitlichen Mitteleuropa* (Munich 1975) 174f. – A summary of crouched burials in Roman crematorial cemeteries in S. Martin–Kilcher, *Das römische Gräberfeld von Courroux im Berner Jura* (Solothurn 1976) 108ff. with Note 22.

8 I. Schwidetzky, Sonderbestattungen und ihre paläodemographische Bedeutung. *Homo* 16, 1965, 230–247; H. J. Sell, *Der schlimme Tod bei den Völkern Indonesiens* (s'Gravenhage 1955) 9–18; L. Pauli (Note 7) 154–160.

9 N. Kyll, Die Bestattung des Toten mit dem Gesicht nach unten. *Trierer Zeitschr.* 27, 1964, 168–185; L. Pauli (Note 7) 175f. 189. M. Mackensen, *Das römische Gräberfeld auf der Keckwiese in Kempten 1* (Kallmünz 1978) 149f.

10 L. Pauli, Ungewöhnliche Grabfunde aus frühgeschichtlicher Zeit: Archäologische Analyse und anthropologischer Befund. *Homo* 29, 1978, 44–53.

11 L. Pauli (Note 7) 136f.

12 G. Kurth, *Die Bevölkerungsgeschichte des Menschen. Handbuch der Biologie IX* (Frankfurt/M. 1965) 496–507 (*Die Zuwachsraten*); Gy. Acsády and J. Nemeskéri, *History of Human Life Span and Mortality* (Budapest 1970).

13 F. Rittatore Vonwiller, *Sibrium* 1, 1953–54, 7–48; 3, 1956–57, 21–35.

14 I. Schwidetzky, Anthropologie der Dürrnberger Bevölkerung. In: L. Pauli, *Der Dürrnberg bei Hallein 3* (Munich 1978) 541–581.

15 E. Conradin, Das späthalstattische Urnengräberfeld Tamins – Unterm Dorf in Graubünden. *JbSGU* 61, 1978, 65–155.

16 R. Kaufmann, Die Hallstattzeitlichen Leichenbrände von Tamins GR, Unterm Dorf (Grabungen 1964 und 1966). Loc. cit., 157–161.

17 *Nat. Hist.* VII 72: *hominem prius quam genito dente cremari mos gentium non est* – To cremate a person before he has any teeth goes against the custom of the people.

18 M. Mackensen, *Das römische Gräberfeld auf der Keckwiese in Kempten 1* (Kallmünz 1978) 142–149 (51 inhumed new-born babies and infants up to the age of some six months).

19 This doubtless applies also to the cremation cemetery of Courroux: B. Kaufmann in: S. Martin-Kilcher (Note 7) 221f. Tab. 3 A–C: about 39% children and adolescents as well as a general life-expectation of 26.5 years).

20 J. A. Brunner, *Die frühmittelalterliche Bevölkerung von Bonaduz* (Chur 1972) 40: for men 36.8, for women 34.5 years.

21 Warning of an overestimation has lately been sounded by G. Kurth and O. Röhrer-Ertl, *ArchA* 61–62, 1977, 15 on the strength that specifically childbed deaths first rose so steeply in germ-laden nineteenth-century hospitals. This conflicts markedly with G. Kurth (Note 12) 505f. who then still maintained 'that the life-expectation among younger women was appreciably diminished through death in childbed'.

22 J. Szilágy, Zur Frage der durchschnittlichen Lebensdauer in der römischen Kaiserzeit. In: H.-J. Diesner, R. Günther and G. Schrot (eds), *Sozialökonomische Verhältnisse im Alten Orient und im Klassischen Altertum* (Berlin 1961) 285–289 on the strength of age recordings on the grave-stones; corroborated also by the findings at Courroux: B. Kaufmann (Note 19) 219: 39.5 to 36.3 years.

23 Some of the graves in the caves of the Balzi Rossi just at the border with France (partly housed in the little museum at the place itself) can be confidently dated in the Old Stone Age: F. Lacorre and L. Barral, *Rivista di Studi Liguri* 14, 1948, 5–38; O. Tschumi, *Urgeschichte der Schweiz 1* (Frauenfeld 1949) 516–519; P. Graziosi, *I Balzi Rossi* (5th edn Bordighera 1976) 36ff. Ills 15–17; 46ff. Ills 22. 25. 26; 56f. Ill. 28.

24 *PrFr* II, 294.

25 Find report: *JbSGU* 54, 1968–69, 112f. More detailed: R. Wyss, Ein jungsteinzeitliches Hockergräberfeld mit Kollektivbestattungen bei Lenzburg, Kt. Aargau. *Germania* 45, 1967, 20–34; W. Scheffrahn, Paläodemographische Beobachtungen an den Neolithikern von Lenzburg, Kt. Aargau. Loc. cit. 34–42.

26 R. Wyss, *UFAS* II, 155 (map).

27 O.-J. Bocksberger, Dalles anthropomorphes, tombes en ciste et vases campaniformes découverts à Sion. *BCSP* 3, 1967, 69–95; M.-R. Sauter, A. Gallay and L. Chaix, Le Néolithique du niveau inférieur du Petit-Chasseur à Sion. *JbSGU* 56, 1971, 17–76; O.-J. Bocksberger, Nouvelles recherches au Petit-Chasseur à Sion (Valais, Suisse). Loc. cit. 77–99. – Last comprehensive assessment: A. Gallay, Fouilles archéologiques du Petit-Chasseur (Sion, Valais), Rapport d'activité 1973: fouille du dolmen M XI. *BCSP* 12, 1975, 103–113. The first detailed publications of individual component complexes: O.-J. Bocksberger, *Le dolmen M VI. Le site préhistorique du Petit-Chasseur (Sion, Valais)* (Lausanne 1976): id., Horizon supérieur secteur occidental et tombes bronze ancien (Lausanne 1978).

28 *JbSGU* 56, 1971, 90 Ill. 16. – The scarcity of further pictorial representations or finds in Central Europe during the Bronze Age and the Iron Age leaves the question of the actual construction and the eastern connections open. Cf. J. Werner, Bogenfragmente aus Carnuntum und von der unteren Wolga. *Eurasia Sept. Ant.* 7, 1932, 33–58 and O. Maenchen-Helfen, *The world of the Huns* (Berkeley 1973) 222ff.

29 Chapter I Note 39.

30 K. Spindler, Eine kupferne Doppelspirale aus Font. *JbSGU* 59, 1971, 104–114.

31 Cf. Chapter I Note 40.

32 M. Ladurner-Parthanes, Bericht über die Aufdeckung einer alten Grabstätte in Gratsch bei Meran. *Der Schlern* 31, 1957, 39f.; L. Oberrauch-Gries, Die Seelensteine von Clavanz und Ager. *Der Schlern* 45, 1971, 105f. (= L. Oberrauch, *Kleine Schriften zur Urgeschichte Südtirols* [Bolzano 1978] 120ff.); R. Lunz, *Urgeschichte des Raumes Algund–Gratsch–Tirol* (Bolzano 1976) 27ff.

33 G. A. Colini, Il sepolcreto di Remedello Sotto nel Bresciano e il periodo eneolitico in Italia. *BPI* 24, 1898, 1–47; 88–110; 206–260; 280–295; 25, 1899, 1–27; 218–295; 26, 1900, 57–101; 202–267; 27, 1901, 73–132; 28, 1902, 5–43; M. O. Acanfora, Fontanella Mantovana e la cultura di Remedello. *BPI* 63, 1956, 321–385; L. Barfield, *Northern Italy before Rome* (London 1971) 55ff.

34 M. Primas, Untersuchungen zu den Bestattungssitten der ausgehenden Kupfer- und der frühen Bronzezeit. *BerRGK* 58, 1977, 56ff. (Switzerland and northern Italy).

35 R. Perini, I depositi preistorici di Romagnano-Loc (Trento). *PrAlp* 7, 1971, 7ff. 6off. (Grab 1969); id., La necropoli di Romagnano-Loc II e IV. Le tombe all'inizio dell'età del bronzo nella regione Sudalpina Centro-orientale. *PrAlp* 11, 1975, 295–315; M. Capitanio, I resti scheletrici umani riferibili agli inizi dell'Età del Bronzo, finora ritrovate a Loc di Romagnano (Trento). *PrAlp* 9, 1973, 7–43.

36 H. Müller-Karpe, *Handbuch der Vorgeschichte* 3 (Munich 1974) 71 (pithos burial).

37 The range extends from the many perforated stag's teeth from the Late Stone Age skull burials in the Great Ofnet cave in the Ries, Bavarian Suebia (*Jahresber. Bayer. Bodendenkmalpfl.* 4, 1963, 114 Ill. 64) to present-day costume jewellery (*Jagd und Trachtenschmuck*, Exhibition catalogue Munich [1978–79] with many examples). Yet there appear to have been certain times of intensification which remain to be investigated and recorded.

38 R. A. Maier, Ein Gräberfeld der Frühen Bronzezeit bei Raisting im Ammertal. In: Ausgrabungen in Bayern. '*Bayerland*' special issue (1967) 1–4; id., Rinderbackzähne und Rinderkiefer

in Frühbronzezeitgräbern von Raisting am Ammersee. *Germania* 50, 1972, 229ff.; plan: 230 Ill. 1.

39 W. Ruckdeschel, *Die frühbronzezeitlichen Gräber Südbayerns* (Bonn 1978).

40 Cf. Note 34.

41 *UFAS* III, 41ff., Ills 1, 5, 7 with the maps on pp. 51 and 53; K. Spindler, Die frühbronzezeitlichen Flügelnadeln. *JbSGU* 57, 1972–73, 17–83.

42 E. Vogt, Die Gliederung der schweizerischen Frühbronzezeit. In: *Festschrift für O. Tschumi* (Frauenfeld 1948) 53–69.

43 For instance Dürrnberg grave 80/2: F. Moosleitner, L. Pauli and E. Penninger, *Der Dürrnberg bei Hallein* 2 (Munich 1974) 46f. with Pl. 197.

44 M. Primas (Note 3) 82–85.

45 *Nat. Hist.* VII 187.

46 W. Burkart, Die Grabstätten der Crestaulta-Siedler. *Ur-Schweiz* 12, 1948, 5–9; id., Die bronzezeitliche Teilnekropole am Cresta petschna. Loc. cit. 13, 1949, 35–39; *UFAS* III, 46ff. Ill. 7; J. Bill, Grab 4 der Nekropole Cresta Petschna im Lugnez. *AS* 2, 1979, 75–77. The corresponding settlement: Chapter II Note 26.

47 Within the context of a Munich dissertation concluded 1978. He reported on it the following year in a lecture at Nördlingen.

48 In: *Studien zur Golasecca-Kultur* (Heidelberg 1971) 15–47 I still saw no possibility of proving that these seemingly 'older' groupings were indeed so. The case has been further argued since; more and more people are coming round to the opinion that the oldest graves date from as early as the Bronze Age C and are to be connected with a West/Inner Alpine category of burial custom. Cf. for instance R. de Marinis, Le spade di Monza della tarda età del bronzo. *Sibrium* 10, 1970, 99–107; id., Nuovi dati sulle spade della tarda età del Bronzo nell'Italia settentrionale. *PrAlp* 8, 1972, 73–105; M. Primas, Funde der späten Bronzezeit aus den Eisenzeitnekropolen des Kantons Tessin. *ZSAK* 29, 1972, 5–18; G. Vannacci Lunazzi, Appunti sui rispostigli dell' età del bronzo in Lombardia. In: *Contributi dell'istituto di Archeologia (Univ. Catt. Milano)* 4, 1974, 5–30; M. Primas, Zur Interpretation weiträumig verbreiteter Kulturelemente in Norditalien und dem alpinen Gebiet während der Jungbronzezeit. *Jahresber. Inst. f. Vorgesch. Frankfurt/M.* 1975, 46–56. – My own view on this: Just so long as only the old finds can go on being discussed, a final clarification of the situation is scarcely to be expected; naturally there have at all times been contacts between the Inner Alpine region and the Po plain.

49 See Note 13.

50 M. Primas (Note 3); W. E. Stöckli, *Chronologie der jüngeren Eisenzeit im Tessin* (Basel 1975).

51 M. Hell, Steinkistengräber der Hallstattzeit von Uttendorf im Pinzgau. *Jahresschr. Salzburger Mus. C. A.* 8, 1962, 53–64. For some years past F. Moosleitner has, in view of the plans to build over it, investigated the whole area; by 1979 the number of graves had risen to some 200 and the finds show close associations with Slovenia and northern Italy. Meanwhile preliminary reports: F. Moosleitner, Hallstattzeitliche Grabfunde aus Uttendorf im Pinzgau (Österreich). *ArchKorrbl.* 7, 1977, 115–119; id., Der Inneralpine Raum in der Hallstattzeit. In: *Die Hallstattkultur. Symposium Steyr 1980* (Linz 1981) 205–226. – I am grateful to Fritz Moosleitner for information not only about this cemetery but also all manner of questions concerning the Salzburg district.

52 A. Lippert, *Das Gräberfeld von Welzelach (Osttirol). Eine Bergwerksnekropole der späten Hallstattzeit* (Bonn 1972).

53 R. Lunz, *Studien zur End-Bronzezeit und älteren Eisenzeit im Südalpenraum* (Florence 1974) 275–286 with Pls 46–62; id., *Urgeschichte des Oberpustertales* (Bolzano 1977) 61–101.

54 R. Peroni, *Studi di cronologia hallstattiana* (Rome 1973) 58–62; R. Lunz, *Studien zur End-Bronzezeit und älteren Eisenzeit im Südalpenraum* (Florence 1974) 253–274 with Pls 11–35; brief summary: G. Bermond Montanari, *Pfatten* (Bolzano 1961).

55 See Note 15.

56 Chapter I Note 61.

57 *Carmina* IV 4, 17–22. Transl. C.E. Bennett (13th edn London/Cambridge, Mass. 1967). – On the 'halberd-axes' still used as weapons in the first century BC in the Inner Alpine area J. Nothdurfter, *Die Eisenfunde von Sanzeno* (Mainz 1979) 82ff. with Ill. 19 (distribution map).

58 Cf. M. Čižmář, *Panátky Arch*, 69, 1978, 142 with an example from Celtic Bohemia. – Additionally L. Pauli, *Der Dürrnberg bei Hallein* 3 (Munich 1978) 391f. with a reference to a man with amputated shank: F. Moosleitner, L. Pauli and E. Penninger, *Der Dürrnberg bei Hallein* 2 (Munich 1974) Pls 184 and 203.

59 K. Kromer, *Das Gräberfeld von Hallstatt* (Florence 1958); id., Gedanken über den sozialen Aufbau der Bevölkerung auf dem Salzberg bei Hallstatt, Oberösterreich. *ArchA* 24, 1958, 39–58.

60 R. Andree, *Die Metalle bei den Naturvölkern mit Berücksichtigung prähistorischer Verhältnisse* (Leipzig 1884) 40f. 85; A. Kollautz, *Saeculum* 5, 1954, 151ff. (on the Avars); M. Eliade, *Schmiede und Alchemisten* (Stuttgart 1960); R. Forbes, *Studies in Ancient Technology* 8 (Leiden 1960) 52–102: *The evolution of the smith, his social and sacred status;* B. Davidson, *Old Africa rediscovered* (London 1959) 71f.; E. Haberland, Eisen und Schmiede in Nordost-Afrika. In: *Beiträge zur Völkerforschung, H. Damm zum 65. Geb.* (Leipzig 1961) 191–210; O. Bischofsberger, *Paideuma* 15, 1969, 54–63; R. Wente-Lukas, loc. cit. 18, 1972, 129–143.

61 S. Nebehay, Das Latènezeitliche Gräberfeld von der kleinen Hutweide bei Au am Leithagebirge, p. B. Bruck a. d. Leitha, NÖ. (Vienna 1973) 14–16 with Pls 9, 2–4 and 13, 1–6; M. Taus, Ein spätlatènezeitliches Schmied-Grab aus St Georgen am Steinfeld, p. B. St Pölten, NÖ. *ArchA* 34, 1965, 13–16.

62 J. M. de Navarro, A Doctor's Grave of the Middle La Tène Period from Bavaria. *Proc. Prehist. Soc.* 21, 1955, 231–248; W. Torbrügge and H. P. Uenze, *Bilder zur Vorgeschichte Bayerns* (Constance 1968) 203ff. with Ills 185 and 187.

63 Here only the latest works: L. Károlyi, Die vor- und frühgeschichtlichen Trepanationen in Europa 1: Deutschland. *Homo* 15, 1964, 200–218; id., Daten über das europäische Vorkommen der vor- und frühgeschichtlichen Trepanation. Loc. cit. 14, 1963, 231–237; id., Das Trepanationsproblem. Beitrag zur Paläanthropologie und Paläopathologie. Loc. cit. 19, 1968, 90–93; K. Kunter, Die Schädeltrepanation in vor- und frühgeschichtlicher Zeit und bei den aussereuropäischen Völkern. *Ber. Oberhess. Ges. F. Natur- u. Heilkunde* N. F. naturkdl. Abt. 37, 1970, 149–159; J. Nemeskéri and R. Busch, Rekonstruktionsuntersuchungen an zwei neolithischen trepanierten Schädeln aus Börnecke, Kr. Wernigerode. *Nachr. aus Niedersachsens Urgesch.* 45, 1976, 1–29.

64 *Das römerzeitliche Gräberfeld von Salurn* (Innsbruck 1963).

65 *Tessiner Gräberfelder* (Basel 1941). An Italian translation of this out-of-print work has now appeared: *Necropoli romane nelle terre dell' attaule Canton Ticino* (Bellinzona 1978).

66 P. Donati et al., *Locarno – La necropoli romana di Solduno* (Bellinzona 1979).

67 M. Mackensen (Note 18).

68 General: J. M. C. Toynbee, *Death and Burial in the Roman World* (London 1971); R. Reece (ed.), *Burial in the Roman World* (London 1977).

69 Chapter I Note 76.

70 H. Menzel, Lampen im römischen Totenkult. In: *Festschrift Röm.-Germ. Zentralmus.* 3 (Mainz 1952) 131–138.

71 East Alpine women's costume provides a classical example. The female portraits on the grave-stones are frequently shown with neck-rings and necklaces as well as arm-rings (Ill. 163), whereas they are almost entirely lacking in the graves: J. Garbsch, *Die norisch-pannonische Frauentracht im 1. und 2. Jahrhundert* (Munich 1965) 12. 116f. Where the reasons for this type of burial rite lay is obscure, for the fibulae as dress fastenings besides the belts were clearly always placed in the grave, be it a cremation or an inhumation.

72 Juvenal, *Sat.* III 171ff.; J. Carcopino, *Daily Life in Ancient Rome* (8th edn Harmondsworth 1981) 155.

73 J. Bürgi, Eine römische Holzstatue aus Eschenz TG. *AS* 1, 1978, 14–22.

74 J. Garbsch (Note 71).

75 H. Geist and G. Pfohl, *Römische Grabinschriften* (2nd edn Munich 1976): a rather careless record containing several errors (for instance *Brixia* is identified as Brixen instead of Brescia); E. Meyer, Menschliches auf römischen Grabsteinen. *JbSGU* 36, 1945, 106–112; a well-founded and clearly documented compilation: A. Obermayer, *Römersteine zwischen Inn und Salzach* (Freilassing 1974); indispensable for Switzerland: E. Howald and E. Meyer, *Die römische Schweiz* (Zurich 1940); in addition recently G. Walser, *Römische Inschriften in der Schweiz, für den Schulunterricht ausgewählt, photographiert und erklärt.* 3 vols (Bern 1979/80). In the case of the examples that follow only the original editions are given, except where I follow specific translations, above all in verse form.

76 *CIL* XII 118.

77 *CIL* XII 122.

78 *CIL* V 4990.

79 Paulus Diaconus, *Hist. Lang.* III 23 records an enormous flood in northern Italy, such as had not been experienced 'since the time of Noah'. A thunderstorm in August 589 caused great devastation in the Adige valley at Verona: men and animals lost their lives, roads were destroyed, fields were strewn with boulders, part of the town wall collapsed. At the church of San Zeno on the outskirts of the town the water 'had risen as far as the upper windows'.

80 H. Geist and G. Pfohl (Note 75) No. 550.

81 Op. cit. No. 555.

82 Dessau 8202.

83 Dessau 8207b.

84 A. Obermayer (Note 75) 125f.

85 *CIL* 2473; 2472; J. Prieur, *La Savoie antique* (Grenoble 1977) 143ff.

86 H. Geist and G. Pfohl (Note 75) passim.

87 *CIL* III 4720: R. Egger, *Teurnia* (7th edn Klagenfurt 1973) 85.

88 F. Vollmer, *Inscriptiones Baiuvariae Romanae* (Munich 1915) No. 108 *(People from Trier)*. 135 *(Dealers in purple or dyers)*. 144 *(Dealers in pottery and hardware)*.

89 R. Egger, Aus römischen Grabinschriften 2. Weidwerk in Gebiete von Iuvavum-Salzburg. *Sitzungsber. Österr. Akad. d. Wiss., phil.-hist.* Kl. 252, 3 (Vienna 1967) 17–26; N. Heger, Salzburg in römischer Zeit. *Jahresschr. Salzburger Mus. C. A.* 9, 1973, 131 with Ill. 56.

90 Cf. Chapter II Note 52.

91 F. Mottas, Un nouveau notable de la Colonie Equestre. *AS* 1, 1978, 134–137. A similar inscription had already been found earlier: *CIL* XIII 5010 = E. Howald and E. Meyer (Note 75) No. 140.

92 Chapter V Note 84.

93 *CIL* V 6513 (Novara in Piedmont, through a former governor in Britain; cf. the honorary inscription *CIL* V 6514).

94 F. Wiblé, *AS* 1, 1978, 33 (Martigny in the Valais).

95 Concerning his pecuniary circumstances: R. Duncan-Jones, *The Economy of the Roman Empire. Quantative Studies* (2nd edn Cambridge 1977) 17ff. Cf. Chapter VI Note 106.

96 Epistulae I 8; IV 13; VII 18. Together with *CIL* V 5262.

97 W. Langhammer, *Die rechtliche und soziale Stellung der Magistratus municipales und der Decuriones in der Übergangsphase der Städte von sich verwaltenden Gemeinden zu Vollzugsorganen des spätantiken Zwangsstaates* (Wiesbaden 1973).

98 G. Alföldy, Ein römischer Grabaltar aus Frauenchiemsee. *BVbl* 31, 1966, 80–84.

99 A summary also of the most recent excavations: W. Czysz and

E. Keller. *Bedaium. Seebruck zur Römerzeit* (Seebruck 1978).

100 For some examples of town councillors from *Aguntum* (East Tyrol) and *Teurnia* (Carinthia) who died north of the Alps and most likely ultimately dwelt there, see H.-J. Kellner, *Die Römer in Bayern* (4th edn Munich 1978) 128.

101 A lucid introduction: H. W. Böhme, *Römische Beamtenkarrieren* (Stuttgart/Aalen 1977). – For the military sphere: A. v. Domaszewski, *Die Rangordnung des römischen Heeres* (2nd edn Cologne/Graz 1967); G. Webster, *The Roman Imperial Army* (2nd edn London 1974); P. Conolly, *Die römische Armee* (Hamburg 1976; with scrupulously exact drawings of the arms and the tactical formations); H. Ubl, Die römische Legion. In: *Vindobona – Die Römer im Wiener Raum.* Exhibition catalogue Vienna (1977/78) 24–43.

102 A. Stein, *Der römische Ritterstand* (Munich 1927); H. G. Pflaum, *Les carrières procuratiennes équestres sous le Haut-Empire Romain* (Paris 1960–61). – Two comprehensive studies from the British angle: E. Birley, Noricum, Britain and the Roman Army. In: *Beiträge zur älteren europäischen Kulturgeschichte. Festschrift f. R. Egger* 1 (Klagenfurt 1952) 175–188; id., Raetien, Britannien und das römische Heer. *BVbl* 45, 1980, 77–89.

103 For Raetia and Noricum recent summaries are available: G. Winkler: Die Statthalter der römischen Provinz Raetien unter dem Prinzipat. *BVbl* 36, 1971, 50–101; corrections to these: H. Chantraine, *BVbl* 38, 193, 111–115; additions thereto once more by Winkler op. cit. 116–120. – G. Winkler, Die Reichsbeamten von Noricum und ihr Personal bis zum Ende der römischen Herrschaft. *Sitzungsber. Österr. Akad. d. Wiss., phil.-hist. Kl.* 261, 2 (Vienna 1969), among them C. Baebius Atticus (33ff.) and Cl. Paternus Clementianus (43ff.)

104 *CIL* V 1838/9

105 U. Laffi, Sull'organizzazione amminstritava dell'area alpina nell'età Giulio-Claudia. *Atti CSDIR* 7, 1975–76, 391–418, partic. 397ff.; now more fully id., Zur Geschichte Vindeliciens unmittelbar nach der römischen Eroberung. *BVbl* 43, 1978, 19–24.

106 Now comprehensively B. Dobson, *Die primipilares. Entwicklung und Bedeutung, Laufbahnen und Persönlichkeiten einer römischen Offiziersranges* Cologne/Graz 1978).

107 G. Winkler, *BVbl* 36, 1971, 62ff.

108 *CIL* III 5211–5213.

109 K. Kraft, Familie und Laufbahn des Claudius Paternus Clementianus. In: J. Werner (ed.), *Studien zu Abodiacum-Epfach* (Munich 1964) 71–74 with Ill. I (marble bust from Hohenstein in Carinthia); H. W. Böhme (Note 100) 30–35 with Ills 11–14.

110 *CIL* XII 103; J. Prieur, *La Savoie antique* (Grenoble 1977) 133ff.

111 A. Hild, *Jahrb. Vorarlberger Landesmuseumsver.* 1952, 35, after C. v. Schwerzenbach and Dr Jacobs, loc. cit. 47, 1911, 78ff., who completed the few letters and words that have remained: . . . mu . . . cum . . . desiste m . . . Teucris.

112 For instance Salurn in the Adige valley (Note 64).

113 *UFAS* VI, 14. – The evaluation of this most important Inner Alpine cemetery constitutes the key topic of the work by Gudrun Schneider-Schnekenburger, *Churrätien im Frühmittelalter auf Grund der Archäologischen Funde* (Munich 1980).

114 P. Eggenberger, W. Stöckli and Chr. Jörg, *HelvA* 6, 1975, 22–26.

115 Chr. Bonnet, *Genava* N. S. 24, 1976, 262f.; *JbSGU* 61, 1978, 217f.

116 H. Lehner, Die Ausgrabungen in der Kirche Biel-Mett BE. *AS* 1, 1978, 149–154.

117 H.-M. v. Kaenel, Das spätrömische Grab mit reichen Beigaben in der Kirche von Biel-Mett. *AS* 1, 1978, 138–148.

118 Moosbrugger, Gräber frühmittelalterlicher Kirchenstifter? *JbSGU* 45, 1956, 69–75; F. Stein, *Adelsgräber des 8. Jahrhunderts in Deutschland* (Berlin 1967). The numerous finds of recent years, above all those referred to in what follows, fill out the picture materially.

119 W. Drack, Ein Adeligengrab des 7. Jahrhunderts in Bülach. *HelvA* 1. 1971, 16–22.

120 *JbSGU* 49, 1962, 94–96; W; Drack and R. Moosbrugger-Leu, Die frühmittelalterliche Kirche von Tuggen (Kt. Schwyz). *ZSAK* 20, 1960, 176–207.

121 *UFAS* VI, 60 Ill. 10, 4; 65 Ill. 16.

122 H.-G. Bandi, *Jahrb. Hist. Mus. Bern* 34, 1954, 166–172; *UFAS* VI, 60 Ill. 10, 1; 61, Ill. 11.

123 *JbSGU* 57, 1972–73, 392–398; G. Schneider-Schnekenburger (Note 113) 67 Ill. 10.

124 *UFAS* VI, 137 Ill. 5, 2; *JbSGU* 56, 1971, 252f.; G. Schneider-Schnekenburger (Note 113) 53 Ill. 5.

125 *UFAS* VI, 33ff. with Ills 38–42; *JbSGU* 61, 1978, 224ff. Ills 73–77.

126 L. Plank, *Veröff. Mus. Ferdinandeum Innsbruck* 44, 1964, 195–204; Tomb I and II.

127 G. Piccottini, *Das spätantike Gräberfeld von Teurnia – St Peter in Holz* (Klagenfurt 1976) – Now investigating and reporting on the conditions on the North Alpine side is R. Christlein, Das Gräberfeld auf dem Ziegelfeld bei Lauriacum-Lorch und die Vita Severini. *Ostbayer. Grenzmarken* 20, 1978, 144–152.

128 According to the latest report the graves meanwhile number 123: F. Glaser, Acht Jahre Grabung in Teurnia 1971–1978. *Carinthia* I 168, 1978, 51–66.

129 G. Schneider-Schnekenburger (note 113) 63; W. Sulser and H. Claussen, *St Stephan in Chur. Frühchristliche Grabkammer und Friedhofskirche* (Zurich 1978) 64.

130 G. Schneider-Schnekenburger (Note 113). Pl. 24, 1–5.

131 J. Werner, *Die Langobarden in Pannonien* (Munich 1962).

132 V. Stare, *Kranj – Nekropola iz časa preseljevanja ljudstev* (Ljubljana 1980).

33 J. Kastelic and B. Škerlj, *Slovanska Nekropola na Bledu* (Ljubljana 1950); J. Kastelic, *Slovanska Nekropola na Bledu* (Ljubljana 1960); A. Valič, *Staroslovansko grobišče na Blejskem gradu* (Izkopavanje 1960) J. Korošec, *Staroslovenska grobišča v severni Sloveniji* (Celje 1947).

134 F. Wieser, Das langobardische Fürstengrab und Reihengräberfeld von Civezzano (Innsbruck 1887 = offprint from *Zeitschr. d. Ferdinandeuns* III. Series 30); L. Franz, Die Germanenfunde von Civezzano im Tiroler Landesmuseum Innsbruck. *Veröff. Mus. Ferdinandeum Innsbruck* 19, 1939, 298–344.

135 M. v. Chlingensperg-Berg, *Das Gräberfeld von Reichenhall in Oberbayern* (Reichenhall 1890).

136 P. Reinecke, *Bayer. Vorgeschichtsfr.* 4, 1924, 35; on the Roman estate R. Christlein, *BVbl* 28, 1963, 30–57.

137 M. Menke, Bad Reichenhall im frühen Mittelalter. In: *Führer zu vor- und frühgesch. Denkm.* 19 (Mainz 1971) 150–160.

138 R. Christlein, *Das alamannische Reihengräberfeld von Marktoberdorf im Allgäu* (Kallmünz 1966) 79 Ill. 25.

139 A quite characteristic form for the east Alamannic-Bajuvarian area are for example the belt-ends embellished with human faces found between the Iller, Suebian-Frankish Jura and the Salzach. Two exemplars occurred well outside this area, one at Brescia and the other at the Danube dog-leg in Hungary; these could have really been taken so far afield only by a Teuton from the territory in question; distribution map in O. v. Hessen, Un ritrovamento bavaro del VII secolo di Brescia. *Commentari dell'ateneo di Brescia* 1964, 178 Ill. 3. Recently also H. Dannheimer in: *Führer zu vor- u. frühgesch. Denkm.* 18 (Mainz 1971) 95 with a few more farther to the West.

140 The amply illustrated and lucid analyses and descriptions of R. Christlein, *Die Alamannen* (Stuttgart/Aalen 1978) 63–82 and M. Martin, *Die Schweiz im Frühmittelalter* (Bern 1975) 42–65 can-allowing for regional particularities–be applied to the Bajuvarian and Langobardian territory, also in somewhat modified form to that of the Burgundians.

141 R. Christlein, Besitzabstufungen zur Merowingerzeit im Spiegel reicher Grabfunde aus West- und Süddeutschland. *JbRGZM* 20, 1973, 147–180.

142 J. Werner, Zur mitteldeutschen Skelettgruppe Hassleben-Leuna. In: *Festschr. für W. Schlesinger* (Cologne/Vienna 1973) 1–30.

143 R. Roeren, Zur Archäologie und Geschichte Südwestdeutschlands im 3. bis 5. Jahrhundert n. Chr. *JbRGZM* 7, 1960, 214–266, partic. 226–228; Chr. Pescheck, *Die germanischen Bodenfunde der römischen Kaiserzeit in Mainfranken* (Munich 1978) 15–19.

144 H. W. Böhme, *Germanische Grabfunde des 4. bis 5. Jahrhunderts zwischen unterer Elbe und Loire* (Munich 1974) 190.

145 Op. cit. 165 and 190.

146 J. Werner, Kriegergräber aus der ersten Hälfte des 5. Jahrhunderts zwischen Schelde und Weser. *Bonner Jahrb.* 158, 1958, 372–413.

147 J. Werner, Zur Entstehung der Reihengräberzivilisation. *Arch. Geographica* 1, 1950, 23–32 (reprint with postscripts in: F.

Petri [ed.], Sprache und Bevölkerungsstruktur im Frankenreich [Darmstadt 1973] 283–325).

148 This differentiated viewpoint appears to be asserting itself gradually: M. Martin, Bemerkungen zu den frühmittelalterlichen Gürtelbeschlägen der Westschweiz. *ZSAK* 28, 1971, 29–57; id., Die Romanen. *UFAS* VI, 11–20; H. Schwab, Die Burgunder. *UFAS* VI, 21–31; J. Werner, Die romanische Trachtprovinz Nordburgund im 6. und 7. Jahrhundert. In: J. Werner and E. Ewig (eds), *Von der Spätantike zum frühen Mittelalter* (Sigmaringen 1979) 447–465.

149 M. Martin, Die Ansiedlung der Burgunder in der Sapaudia. *MblSGU* 7 (28), 1976, 17 (map); Chr. Simon, La déformation crânienne artificielle de la nécropole de Sézegnin GE. *AS* 1, 1979, 186–188 with distribution maps, detailed for the Burgundian region between the Saône and the edge of the Alps. – In general also: J. Werner, *Beiträge zur Archäologie des Attila-Reiches* (Munich 1956) 96ff. 129 with Pls 69 and 73; id., Neue Daten zur Verbreitung der artifiziellen Schädeldeformation im 1. Jahrtausend n. Chr. *Germania* 36, 1958, 162–164; continued by K. Gerhardt, *BVbl* 38, 1973, 99f.; now supplemented by a child's skull: E.-M. Winkler, *Fundber. aus Österreich* 17, 1978, 197–209.

150 M.-R. Sauter and P; Moeschler, Caractères dentaires mongoloides chez les Burgondes de la Suisse occidentale (Saint-Prex, VD). *Archiv des Sciences* 13, 1960, 387–426.

151 P. Eggenberger, W. Stöckli and Chr. Jörg, La découverte en l'Abbaye de Saint-Maurice d'une épitaphe dédiée au moine Rusticus. *HelvA* 6 (21), 1975, 22–32.

152 J. Werner on the bone and reliquary buckles of the sixth century, in: J. Werner (ed.), *Die Ausgrabungen in St Ulrich und Afra in Augsburg 1961–1968* (Munich 1977) 275–351.

153 R. Cheneveau, Le cimetière paléo-chrétien de Sancta Maria de Olivo à Beaulieu-sur-Mer. *Mém. Inst. Préhist. et Arch. Alpes-Maritimes* 8, 1963–64.

154 S. Gagnière, Les sépultures à inhumation du IIIᵉ au XIIIᵉ siècle de notre ère dans la basse Vallée du Rhône. Essai de chronologie typologique. *Cahiers rhodaniens* 12, 1965, 53–110.

155 H. Dolenz, Die Gräberfelder von Judendorf bei Villach. Neues aus Alt-Villach. *Jahresber. Mus. Villach* 6, 1969, 7–92. Larger compilations: H. Dolenz and H. Mitscha-Märheim, Frühmittelalterliche Bodenfunde aus Kärnten. *Carinthia* I 150, 1960, 727–750; W. Modrijan, Die Frühmittelalterfunde (8. bis 11. Jhdt.) der Steiermark. *Schild von Steier* 11, 1963, 45–84.

156 P. Petru, V. Sribar and V. Stare, *Der Karantanisch-Köttlacher Kulturkreis. Frühmittelalterlicher Schmuck.* Exhibition catalogue Graz (1975).

157 V. Sribar and V. Stare, Das Verhältnis der Steiermark zu den übrigen Regionen der Karantanisch-Köttlacher Kultur. *Schild von Steier* 15–16, 1978–79, 209–225 with a distribution map of the pertinent finds.

158 J. Giesler, *Die 'Köttlacher Kultur'. Archäologie der karolingisch-ottonischen Zeit im Ostalpenraum (8.–10. Jahrhundert)* (Thesis Munich 1978). Published to date a small extract prior to completion of the work: Zu einer Gruppe mittelalterlicher Emailscheibenfibeln. *Zeitschr. f. Arch. d. Mittelalters* 6, 1978, 57–72.

159 See Note 133.

IV Religion and Art

1 *RE* 2. R. I A, 565ff. 'religio'.

2 W. Torbrügge, *Prehistoric European Art* (New York/London 1968); H. Müller-Karpe, Das vorgeschichtliche Europa. *Kunst der Welt* (Baden-Baden 1968); P. Graziosi, *L'arte preistorica in Italia* (Florence 1973).

3 E. Bächler, *Das Drachenloch ob Vättis im Taminatal* (Sankt Gallen 1921).

4 K. Hörmann, Die Petershöhle bei Velden in Mittelfranken, eine altpaläolithische Station. *Abhandl. Naturhist. Ges. Nürnberg* 34 (Nuremberg 1933); S. Brodar, Zur Frage der Höhlenbärenjagd und des Höhlenbärenkultes in den paläolithischen Fundstellen Jugoslawiens. *Quartär* 9, 1957, 147–159; L. Vértes, Die Rolle des Höhlenbären im ungarischen Paläolithikum. Loc. cit. 10–11, 1958–59, 151–169 and M. Malez, Das Paläolithikum der Veternicahöhle und der Bärenkult. Loc. cit. 171–188; G. Freund, *Jahresber. Bayer. Bodendenkmalpfl.* 4, 1963, 78.

5 Representing various points of view: O. Tschumi, *Urgeschichte der Schweiz* I (Frauenfeld 1949) 434ff. (sacrificial cult); H.-G. Bandi, Zur Frage eines Bären- oder Opferkultes im ausgehenden Altpaläolithikum der alpinen Zone. In: *Helvetia Antiqua (Festschr. für E. Vogt)* (Zurich 1966) 1–8 (almost dismissive); H. Müller-Beck, Das Altpaläolithikum. *UFAS* I, 89–106 (non-committal inclined to be positive).

6 E. Bächler, *Das Wildenmannsloch am Selun* (Sankt Gallen 1934).

7 E. Bächler, *Das alpine Paläolithikum der Schweiz im Wildkirchli, Drachenloch und Wildenmannsloch* (Basel 1940). As well O. Menghin, WPZ 29, 1942, 121ff. and W. Schmidt, *Anthropos* 35–36, 1940–41, 426–429.

8 H.-G. Bandi, Das Jungpaläolithikum. *UFAS* I, 107–122 (115ff.: miniature art).

9 A pebble with the head of a bull scratched on it from Riparo Tagliente at Grezzana (prov. Verona): L. Barfield, *Northern Italy before Rome* (London 1971) 29 Ill. 7.

10 Reproduced in every relevant book; on the find-spot itself now F. Felgenhauer, Willendorf in der Wachau. *Mitt. Prähist. Komm. Wien* 8–9 (1956–59).

11 H. Müller-Karpe, *Handbuch der Vorgeschichte* I (Munich 1966) Pl. 225 A 7. – P. Graziosi, *I Balzi Rossi* (5th edn Bordighera 1976) 36 Ill. 18; on the still debated find-circumstances H. Breuil, Renseignements inédits sur les circonstances des Baoussé Roussé. *Archivio per l'Anthr. e l'Etnol.* 58. 1928, 281ff.

12 O. Tschumi (Note 5) 697 Ill. 270; R. Wyss, *UFAS* II, 151 Ill. 16.

13 So far only brief reports in *PrAlp* 8, 1972, 269–274; 9, 1973,

245f.; 11, 1975, 332; 12, 1976, 229ff. – Summary of the most important 'art objects' in: *L'arte preistorica nell'Italia settentrionale*. Exhibition catalogue Verona (1978) 78ff. with Ills 11–14. – Measurements (from left to right: 14.0; 10.2; 6.1; 13.1 cm.

14 D. Srejović, *Europe's First Monumental Sculpture: New Discoveries at Lepenski Vir* (London 1972).

15 W. Krämer, Prähistorische Opferplätze. In: *Helvetia Antiqua (Festschr. für E. Vogt)* (Zurich 1966) 111–122.

16 M. v. Chlingensperg-Berg, Der Knochenhügel am Langacker und die vorgeschichtlichen Herdstellen am Eisenbichel bei Reichenhall in Oberbayern. *MAGW* 34, 1904, 53ff.; A. von den Driesch, Tierknochen aus Karlstein, Ldkr. Berchtesgadener Land. *BVbl* 44, 1979, 153f.: bones from the bone-mound. There were only a limited number available for analysis. Among the burnt bones cattle were most amply represented (principally head and feet!), with also sheep and goat, but not pig. The unburnt bones 'look like ordinary remains of slaughter' and in composition correspond more or less to the spectrum encountered at settlements. What conclusions can be drawn from this as to the ceremonies practised there, also as to the choice of particular animals and parts of the body, will only become apparent when other find-spots have been investigated.

17 K. Meuli, Griechische Opferbräuche. In: *Phyllobolia für P. v. d. Mühll* (Basel 1946) 185–288, partic. 201–209.

18 R. A. Maier, Brandopferplätze um Schongau in Oberbayern. *Germania* 47, 1969, 173–176.

19 K. M. Mayr, Vorgeschichtliche Siedlungfunde auf der Hochfläche des Schlern. *Der Schlern* 20, 1946, 9–12; R. Lunz, *Archäologie Südtirols* (Bruneck 1981) 147ff.; P. Mayr, Die neuen Funde vom Schlern und die alpine Retardierung. *Der Schlern* 46, 1972, 4ff.

20 C. F. Capello, Una stipe votiva d'età romana sul monte Genevris (Alpi Cozie), *Rivista Ingauna e Intemelia* 7, 1941, 96–137.

21 Note 18.

22 M. Hell, *MAGW* 56, 1926, 334. – A few years ago the find-spot was levelled and obliterated; a rescue operation by Gerhard Pohl showed that already in ancient times everything had been filled-in, so that no stratification sequence of the extensive material any longer existed. Whereupon a large number of packing-cases filled with haphazardly excavated sherds was taken to the Keltenmuseum Hallein; they still await sorting and collating.

23 W. Krämer, Ein frühkaiserzeitlicher Brandopferplatz auf dem Auerberg im bayerischen Alpenvorland. *JbRGZM* 13, 1966, 60–66.

24 M. Menke, Brandopferplatz auf der Kastelliernekropole von Pula, Istrien. *Germania* 48, 1970, 115–123.

25 This fortunate discovery was made only recently by R. Wyss, La statue celte de Villeneuve. *HelvA* 10, 1979, 58–67. The statue, 1.25 m high, had been found many years ago on the northern edge of the Rhône delta in the Lake of Geneva; in a deep fissure at arm-level one Celtic and two Massiliote silver coins were discovered when restoration was being carried out.

26 *Bibl. Hist.* V 27.

27 J. Maringer, Flussopfer und Flussverehrung in vorgeschichtlicher Zeit. *Germania* 52, 1974, 309–318.

28 J. Heierli, Die Bronzezeitliche Quellfassung von St. Moritz. *Anz. Schweiz. Altertumskde.* N. F. 9, 1907, 265–278; treated anew by A. Zürcher, Funde der Bronzezeit aus St. Moritz. *HelvA* 3/9, 1972, 21–28; *UFAS* III, 153f. Ill. 11.

29 *Führer zu vor- u. frühgesch. Denkmälern* 19 (Mainz 1971) 142.

30 The best survey by G. Fogolari in: *Popoli e Civiltà dell'Italia antica* 4 (Rome 1974) 184ff. Also E. de Lotto, *Una divinità sanante a Làgole (Calalzo di Cadore)* (Belluno 1961); C. B. Pascal, *The Cults of Cisalpine Gaul* (Brussels 1964) 140ff.

31 M. Lejeune, *Revue des études anciennes* 54, 1952, 51–82; *Latomus* 12, 1953, 3–13; loc. cit. 13, 1954, 118–123; *Revue des études latines* 32, 1954, 120–138; E. Vetter, Die neuen venetischen Inschriften von Làgole. *Carinthia* I 143, 1953 (= *Festschr. f. R. Egger 2*) 619–632 (123–136). – Now clearly summarized by G. B. Pellegrini and A. L. Prosdocimi, *La lingua venetica* 1 (Padua 1967) 469–567; the excerpts with Latin transliterations that follow are theirs.

32 K. Lukan, *Alpenwanderungen in die Vorzeit* (Vienna/Munich 1965) 90 with Ill. 52; E. Vetter, Die vorrömischen Felsinschriften von Steinberg in Nordtirol. *Anz. Österr. Akad. d Wiss., phil.-hist. Kl.* 94, 1957, 384–398; A. L. Prosdocimi, Note di epigrafia retica. In: *Studien zur Namenkunde und Sprachgeographie (Festschr. für K. Finsterwalder)* (Innsbruck 1971) 15–46.

33 G. Kaltenhauser, Die urzeitliche Zisterne von Telfes im Stubai. *Veröff. Tiroler Landesmus. Ferdinandeum* 58, 1978, 67–119.

34 Vor- und frühgeschichtliche Flussfunde. Zur Ordnung und Bestimmung einer Denkmälergruppe. *BerRGK* 51–52, 1970–71, 1–146.

35 Cf. for instance W. Torbrügge (Note 34) 59 Table 10; 64; 74 Table 13; 119ff. – M. Hell, Bronzenadeln als Weihegaben in salzburgischen Mooren. *Germania* 31, 1953, 50–54.

36 M. Hell, Über ältere Funde von Steinbeilen in Salzburg. *WPZ* 6, 1919, 63–66.

37 E. Penninger, Bronzebeile aus der Salzach und Saalach. *Mitt. Ges. Salzburger Landeskde.* 106, 1966, 13–15; F. Moosleitner, L. Pauli and E. Penninger, *Der Dürrnberg bei Hallein 2* (Munich 1974) 96 Ill. 1, 1–2.

38 G. Kyrle, *Urgeschichte des Kronlandes Salzburg* (Vienna 1918) 1 No. 3; O. Menghin, *Die vorgeschichtlichen Funde Vorarlbergs* (Baden b. Wien 1937) 18 No. 30; 51 Ill. 28; E. F. Mayer, *Die Äxte und Beile in Österreich* (Munich 1977) 177 No. 882.

39 J. Naue, *Prähist. Bl.* 16, 1904, 17ff. (at Cremona); *Not. Scavi* 1909, 275 Ill. 1 (from the estuary of the Adda) and 2 (at Brancere; in the vicinity a Roman helmet: loc. cit. 312).

40 J.-P. Millotte, *Le Jura et les Plaines de Saône aux âges des métaux* (Paris 1963) 350 No. 482. The armour has vanished, the circumstances under which it was discovered are derived from old reports. Millotte argues convincingly that they lie hidden among the pieces whose find-spot is given as 'Grenoble' or 'Naples', for they tally with the old descriptions: G. v. Merhart, Panzer-Studie. In: *Origines. Raccolta di scritti in onore di G. Baserga* (Como 1954) 33–61 with Pl. 1, 1.3 (reprinted in: *Hallstatt und Italien* [Mainz 1969] 149ff. 152 Ill. 1, 1.3). – That also the pieces of bronze armour from Fillinges in Savoy ought certainly not to be construed as 'merchant's depot' (thus G. v. Merhart) but as votive offerings is scarcely to be doubted, in view of the supraregional situation regarding shields and helmets of this time and is further confirmed by the scanty received information about the find-circumstances; according to this the armour was found on a burnt layer up to 30 cm thick extending over some 10 m² : Costa de Beauregard, Les cuirasses celtiques de Fillinges. *Revue arch.* 1901, 308ff.; W. Deonna, Les cuirasses Hallstattiennes de Fillinges au Musée d'Art et d'Histoire de Genève. *Préhistoire* 3, 1934, 93–143.

41 W. Torbrügge (Note 34) 49 Table 6.

41 P. Post, Der kupferne Spangenhelm. *BerRGK* 34, 1951–53, 126ff. Nos 5 and 13; M. Martin, *Die Schweiz im Frühmittelalter* (Bern 1975) 47 Ill. 32.

43 H. Schwab and R. Müller, *Die Vergangenheit des Seelandes in neuem Licht* (Freiburg i. Ü. 1973) 117 Ills 151–152; further examples from Switzerland: *JbSGU* 41, 1951, 135 with Pl. 21,2 (Lake of Biel); 42, 1952, 104 with Pl. 17,2 (Zihl); 47, 1958–59, 209 with Pl. 26 (Hasensee bei Uesslingen TG). There are also a lot of examples from Germany.

44 W. Torbrügge (Note 34) Beilage 24,2; J. Kneidinger, Der Greiner Strudel als urgeschichtliche Fundstätte. *MAGW* 72, 1942, 278–290.

45 N. Heger, Ein etruskischer Bronzeeimer aus der Salzach. *BVbl* 38, 1973, 52ff. Latterly a grave find from Lower Austria: Die Kelten in Mitteleuropa. Exhibition catalogue Hallein (1980) No. 50.

46 Here two examples only: a simple spring with no structuring at Kiesen (Bern): *JbSGU* 62, 1979, 144 and the sulphur spring of Bergfall in the remote Elsental, which drains into the Pustertal: R. Lunz, *Ur- und Frühgeschichte Südtirols* (Bolzano 1973) 181.

47 This association was underrated by W. Torbrügge (Note 34) 56; he seeks to explain the ingots of both the Iron Age and the Bronze Age 'largely... as loss in transport'.

48 O. Menghin, Eisenbarren aus Vorarlberg. *WPZ* 2, 1915, 133f.; R. Pittioni, *Urgeschichte des Österreichischen Raumes* (Vienna 1954) 741 Ill. 516. – *UFAS* IV, 106 Ill. 1, 1–2.

49 R. A. Maier, Frühbronzezeitliches Ösenhalsring-Opfer aus dem bayerischen Inn-Oberland. *Germania* 54, 1976, 200–202; at the outlet of the clear brook into a small marshy stream; particularly large and heavy with additional wire embellishments.

50 E. Vouga, *Les Helvètes à la Tène* (Neuchâtel 1885); P. Vouga, *La Tène. Monographie de la Station* (Leipzig 1923); K. Raddatz, Zur Deutung der Funde von La Tène. *Offa* 11, 1952, 24–28; R. Wyss, Die Funde aus der alten Zihl und ihre Deutung. *Germania* 33, 1955, 349–354; R. Pittioni, Zur Interpretation der Station La Tène. In: *Provincialia (Festschr. für R. Belart)* (Basel 1968) 615–618; R. Wyss *UFAS* IV, 178–182.

51 H. Schwab, Entdeckung einer keltischen Brücke an der Zihl und ihre Bedeutung für La Tène. *ArchKorrbl* 2, 1972, 289–294.

52 In this connection reference should be made to the Bronze Age station of Peschiera at the outlet of the Mincio from Lake Garda. According to its unfortunately never adequately published yield of finds (though the photographic archive of the Deutsche Archäologisches Institut in Rome offers an overview) the pins are represented in marked numbers. The fact that many of them are cast in a decidedly careless and faulty manner has led H.-J. Hundt, *PrAlp* 10, 1974, 160 to offer by way of 'explanation of this phenomenon that a proportion of the perforated sphereheaded pins found in the north Italian lakes was not intended for daily use but that these were produced as votive objects and were submerged in the water as offerings.' This attractive hypothesis would in that case apply not only to the Early Bronze Age round-headed pins but also to all other types up until the Late Bronze Age; a closer analysis of the pins is desirable.

53 Only W. Torbrügge (Note 34) 55f. with Table 8 and 72ff., through a consideration of the rough distribution on the strength of the date and nature of the objects, came to a like conclusion.

54 W. Torbrügge (Note 34) 67–69 with many examples.

55 For three centuries treasure-hunters had already rummaged among the find-strata before regulated excavations at last took place: short reports practically every year in *Notizie degli Scavi* 1883, 7 until 1894, 33–47. A brief summary by P. Barocelli, *Ricerche e studi sui monumenti romani della Val d'Aosta* (Aosta 1934) 53–59; the most important inscriptions also in M.-R. Sauter, *Préhistoire du Valais* (Sion 1950) 71–77.

56 *CIL* V 6865ff.: E. Howald and E. Meyer, *Die römische Schweiz* (Zurich 1941) No. 72ff.

57 English version based on E. Howald and E. Meyer (Note 56), No. 86.

58 F. E. Koenig, Der Julierpass in römischer Zeit. *JbSGU* 62, 1979, 77–99 with the earlier literature.

59 Here just a few examples: from the Radstädter Tauern (N. Heger, Salzburg in römischer Zeit. *Jahresschr. Salzburger Mus. C. A.* 9, 1973, 209 No. 82), from the 'Wallisgässli' on the Sanetsch at Gsteig in the canton of Bern (*JbSGU* 25, 1923, 99) and from the Kaiseregg at Plaffeien in the canton of Fribourg (*JbSGU* 59, 1976, 264). On the coins in the vicinity of the Gotthard massif P. Roubik, Ein Römischer Münzfund aus Uri. *HelvA* 10, 1979, 68ff.

60 M. Hell, Der Bronzedolch von der Glocknerstrasse. *ArchA* 10, 1952, 41–44.

61 G. Kyrle, *MAGW* 42, 1912, 203f.; id., *Urgeschichte des Kronlandes Salzburg* (Vienna 1918) 31f. Ills 12–15 and 16, 1–6. – E. F. Mayer, *Die Äxte und Beile in Österreich* (Munich 1977) No. 473, 1353–55 with Pl. 124A.

62 M. Hell, Ein Passfund der Urnenfelderzeit aus dem Gau Salzburg. *WPZ* 26, 1939, 148–156.

63 R. Wyss, Die Eroberung der Alpen durch den Bronzezeitmenschen. *ZSAK* 28, 1971, 130–145; Höhenfunde aus dem Fürstentum Liechtenstein. *HelvA* 9, 1978, 137–144. – E. Vonbank, Höhenfunde aus Vorarlberg und Liechtenstein. *ArchA* 40, 1966, 80–92.

64 E. F. Mayer, Bronzezeitliche Passfunde im Alpenraum. *Jahresber. Inst. Vorgesch. Univ. Frankfurt 1978–79,* 179–187; V. Bianco Peroni, Bronzene Gewässer- und Höhenfunde aus Italien. Loc. Cit. 321–335.

65 Knife: F. Rittatore Vonwiller, *Sibrium* 8, 1964–65, 45ff. Ills 1 and 3; ingot: *JbSGU* 46, 1957, 116 Ill. 46; sword: *JbSGU* 42, 1952, 78f. Pl. 11, Ill. 2.

66 R. Wyss, Ein neuer Schwerttyp aus dem hochalpinen Raum, *JbSGU* 47, 1958–59, 52–56.–A summary entitled 'latènezeitliche Höhen-, Pass- und Passwegfunde' is to be found in R. Wyss, *Der Schatzfund von Erstfeld* (Zurich 1975) 59 and 68. Though in the case of most of the spearheads represented there–to judge by what I have seen depicted–an early medieval dating is more likely. Cf. p. 161. Note 74.

67 The credit of having ascertained this goes to F. Fischer, *Der Trichtinger Ring und seine Probleme* (Heidenheim 1978) 24ff. with the List 35f., although he–in my opinion unjustifiably in this context–would like to 'exercise discretion when using the term "acultic", which comes to people's lips so glibly these days' (31).

68 O. Klose, Ein Halsring der la Tènezeit. *Jahrb. f. Altertumskde.* 6, 1912, 1–4; P. Jacobsthal, *Early Celtic Art* (Oxford 1944) No. 49; F. Moosleitner, Der goldene Halsring von der Maschlalm. *Salzburger Museumsbl.* 39, 1978, 13–16.

69 P. Jacobsthal (Note 68) No. 85; P. v. Eles, L'età del ferro nelle alpi occidentali francesi. *Cahiers rhodaniens* 14, 1967–68, 205 Pl. 15, 2.

70 *UFAS* IV, 64 Ill. 5.

71 R. Wyss, *Der Schatzfund von Erstfeld* (Zurich 1975). – Critical comments on the opinions there expressed concerning the region of origin of the rings (supposedly Italy) and the nature of the finds (supposedly concealed by a trader) voiced by M. Lenerz-de Wilde, *Germania* 56, 1978, 610–613 and K. Spindler, *Fundber. aus Baden-Württemberg* 4, 1979, 436–438, without of course being able to go into all the associated questions.

72 Worth looking at is the fine painting in P. Connolly, *Hannibal and the Enemies of Rome* (London 1977) 34/35, even though Hannibal is unlikely to have taken this route. Cf. also in this connection pp. 233ff. with Note 47.

73 M. Hell, Skarabäus-Amulett vom Sonnblickgletscher. *Alpenland* (Vienna) 35/5, 1967, 22; W. Haid, *Der Anschnitt* 20/2, 1968, 20f.; F. Moosleitner (Note 68) 15f. Ills 5–6.

74 W. Schmid, Römische Goldfunde in den Steiner Alpen. *Jahrb. f. Altertumskde.* 4, 1910, 110 Ill. 27; J. Garbsch, *Die norisch-pennonische Frauentracht im 1. und 2. Jahrhundert* (Munich 1956) 26.

79. 202 No. 442 (one example each in the Kunsthistorisches Museum Vienna and in the Narodni muzej Ljubljana); fibula in New York: E. Ettlinger, *Die römischen Fibeln in der Schweiz* (Bern 1973) 64.

75 *Churrätien im Frühmittelalter auf Grund der archäologischen Funde* (Munich 1980) 115 Ill. 29; 213. – Pfeilspitze vom Passweg über den Julier: *JbSGU* 49, 1962, 92f. Ill. 50.

76 P. 156. Distribution map in J. Werner, *BerRGK* 42, 1961, 320 Ill. 8; the find-circumstances described in P. Post (Note 42).

77 W. Lucke and O.-H. Frey, *Die Situla in Providence (Rhode Island). Ein Beitrag zur Situlenkunst des Osthallstattkreises* (Berlin 1962); *Situlenkunst zwischen Po und Donau.* Exhibition catalogue Vienna (1962); J. Kastelic, *Situlenkunst. Meisterschöpfungen prähistorischer Bronzearbeit* (Vienna/Munich 1964); O.-H. Frey, *Die Entstehung der Situlenkunst. Studien zur figürlich verzierten Toreutik von Este* (Berlin 1969); id., Figürlich verzierte Bronzeblecharbeiten aus Hallstatt und dem Südostalpengebiet. In: *Krieger und Salzherren.* Exhibition catalogue Mainz (1970) 82–95.

78 G. Kossack, *Gräberfelder der Hallstattzeit an Main und Fränkischer Saale* (Kallmünz 1970) 155ff. connects the situla art–analogous to Etruscan tomb paintings–all too closely with an elaborate cult of the dead, even if his idea, that 'actual cult practices and their material manifestation in the graves had been supplanted by the pictorial record', definitely deserves further examination, taking regional traditions into consideration. That such communal practices, at which maybe the bronze buckets were used as cooking vessels, may have been engaged in not only on the death of high-ranking persons is indicated by the manifold mends, which imply both intense and frequent application of heat (L. Pauli, *Der Dürrnberg bei Hallein* 3 [Munich 1978] 81ff.).

79 In addition to the named works (Note 77) O.-H. Frey, Eine figürlich verzierte Ziste in Treviso. *Germania* 44, 1966, 66–73.

80 This view in now also shared by A. Eibner, Darstellungsinhalte in der Kunst der Hallstattzeit. In: *Die Hallstattkultur. Symposium Steyr 1980* (Linz 1981) 261–284. Nevertheless there are still those who believe it to be mainly a question of superficial depictions of the 'aristocratic life'. Cf., say, O.-H. Frey, Situlenkunst. In: E. Lessing, *Hallstatt – Bilder aus der Frühzeit Europas* (Vienna/Munich 1980) 126–134; K. Kromer, Das Situlenfest. In: *Zbornik posvečen Stanetu Gabrovcu ob šestdesetletnici.* Situla 20–21 (Ljubljana 1980).–Regarding the ritual deposition of ploughs in north German bogs cf. G. Kunwald in: H. Jankuhn (ed.), Vorgeschichtliche Heiligtümer und Opferplätze in Mittel- und Nordeuropa. *Abhandl. Akad. d. Wiss. Göttingen* 44, 1966, 66–73.

81 E. di Filippo, Rapporti iconografici di alcuni monumenti dell'arte delle situle. In: *Venetia. Studi miscellanei di Arch. delle Venezie* 1 (Padua 1967) 97–200; J. Boardman, A Southern View of Situla Art. In: *The European Community in Later Prehistory. Studies in Honour of C. F. C. Hawkes* (London 1971) 121–140; O.-H. Frey, Der Ostalpenraum und die antike Welt in der frühen Eisenzeit. *Germania* 44, 1966, 48–66.

82 W. Schmid, Die Fürstengräber von Klein Glein in der Steiermark. *Prähist. Zeitschr.* 24, 1933, 219–282; H. Müller-Karpe (Note 2) 144ff. Ills 94–98; hunting with bow and arrows is particularly striking (Ill. 144); it is not otherwise shown any longer. – As ever R. Pittioni, *ArchA* 48, 1970, 4f. and 59–60, 1976, 479f. (backed by D. Ahrens, Zur Situlenkunst der ersten Hälfte des fünften Jahrhunderts v. Chr. *ÖJh* 48, 1966–67, Beibl. 231–250) disputes the early dating of these finds and the associated ones of Sesto Calende on the Lago Maggiore, without taking into account the consequences where the absolute chronology of the relevant grave inventories are concerned.

83 M. Louis and G. Isetti, *Les gravures préhistoriques du Mont-Bego* (2nd edn Bordighera 1964); Vallée des Merveilles, *IXᵉ Congrès intern. Sc. préhist. et protohist. Nice 1976, Livret-Guide de l'excursion* C 1 (Nice 1976).

84 J. T. Ozols, Die Felsbilder von Mont-Bego. In: *IXᵉ Congrès Union intern. Sc. préhist. et protohist. Nice 1976, Colloque XXVII* (Nice 1976) 37; J. Cabagno, Étude des visages et costumes taurins rituels dans la région du Mont Bégo. *Loc. cit.* 74–77; J. T. Ozols, Die Felsbilder des Mont Bego. *Antike Welt* 9/3, 1978, 45–48.

85 Such a 'basic orientation imbedded in the farmers' springtime custom' is defended by R. Pittioni, *RE* Suppl. IX (1962) 219ff. *(Italien, urgeschichtliche Kulturen)*.

86 For instance *CIL* IV 1882. 2210. 2360. 2375.

87 A perusal of *BCSP* published since 1966 will suffice to back up this statement.

88 E. Suess, *Rock Carvings in the Valcamonica* (Milan 1954); E. Anati, *Civiltà preistorica della Valcamonica* (Milan 1964); *Arte preistorica della Valcamonica*. Exhibition catalogue (Milan 1974); E. Anati, *Evolution and Style in Camunian Rock Art* (Capo di Ponte 1976).

89 E. Anati, *Metodi di relevamento e di analisi dell'arte rupestre* (2nd edn Capo di Ponte 1976).

90 E. Anati, *I massi di Cemmo* (2nd and Capo di Ponte 1968).

91 E. Schumacher, Die Felsbilder des Val Camonica und ihre Beziehungen zur Situlenkunst. *JbRGZM* 13, 1966, 37–43.

92 The neighbouring Valtellina will serve as a comparison: E. Anati, *Arte preistorica in Valtellina* (3nd edn Capo di Ponte 1968).

93 *Felsbilder in Österreich* (Linz 1972).

94 Chr. Zindel, Felszeichnungen auf Carschenna, Gemeinde Sils im Domleschg. *Ur-Schweiz* 32, 1968, 1–5; *JbSGU* 54, 1968–69, 171f.

95 A. Gallay, S. Favre and A. Blain, Stèles et roches gravées des alpes suisses. In: *IXᵉ Congrès (Note 84)* Colloque XXVII, 52–58; Corboud, La roche gravée de St-Leonhard VS. *AS* 1, 1978, 3–13. – A few examples from the adjacent Western Alps: Actes de la IIᵉᵐᵉ Rencontre-débat internationale sur l'art rupestre dans les Alpes. *Bull. d'Études Préhist. Alpine* 10, 1978, 43-151; also 5–10.

96 S. Gagnière and J. Granier, Nouvelles stèles anthropomorphes chalcolithiques de la vallée de la Durance. *Bull. Soc. Préhist. Franç.* 64, 1967, 699–706; *PrFr* II, 213 with Ill. 2,1. – The group continues with some interruption in Liguria: A. C. Ambrosi, *Corpus delle statue-stele lunigianesi* (Bordighera 1972).

97 M. O. Acanfora, Le statue antropomorfe dell'Alto Adige. *Cultura Atesina* 6, 1952, 2–32; H. Fink and K. M. Mayr, Der Menhir von Tötschling bei Brixen. *Der Schlern* 30, 1956, 42f.

98 Note 92.

99 Some examples: K. M. Mayr, Schalensteine in Südtirol. *Der Schlern* 20, 1946, 237–239. 309–312. 344; 21, 1947, 268–271; F. Haller, Die Schalensteine am Pfitschersee in Sprons. *Der Schlern* 22, 1948, 464f.; J. Viertler, Die Schalensteine bei Göriach ob Velden am Wörthersee. *Carinthia* I 168, 1978, 73–80; H. Suter, Über einige Schalensteine in den Kantonen Waadt, Wallis und Graubünden. *Ur-Schweiz* 31, 1967, 4–14.

100 M. v. Hepperger, Zum Rätsel der Schalensteine. *Der Schlern* 22, 1948, 110f.

101 A. Huber, Mittelalterliche und neuzeitliche Schalen- oder Lichtsteine in Kärnten. *Carinthia* I 168, 1978, 81–96.

102 H. Liniger and H. Schilt, Der astronomisch geortete Schalenstein ob Tüscherz (Biel). *JbSGU* 59, 1976, 215–219 with references to more such attempts.

103 W. Schmid, *Der Kultwagen von Strettweg* (Leipzig 1934): W. Modrijan, Der Kultwagen von Strettweg. *Jahrb. f. prähist. u. ethnograph. Kunst* 24, 1974–77, 91–97.

104 In the Alpine region for instance in Como (*Sibrium* 3, 1956–57, Pl. 19), Sesto Calende on the Lago Maggiore (*Sibrium* 1, 1953–54, 67ff.) and La Côte-Saint-André in Savoy (Chapter I Note 66).

105 A. A. Barb, Zur Deutung der sogennanten Deichselwagen und verwandter Geräte. *MAGW* 73–77, 1943–47, 139–151; A. Haberland, Ein Kannenwagen als Festtrankbehälter. *MAGW* 80, 1950, 78–85.

106 G. Kossack, Studien zum Symbolgut der Urnenfelder- und Hallstattzeit Mitteleuropas (Berlin 1954).

107 E. Sprockhoff, Nordische Bronzezeit und frühes Griechentum. *JbRGZM* 1, 1954, 28–110.

108 L. Pauli, *Der Dürrnberg bei Hallein* 3 (Munich 1978) 455ff.

109 J. Whatmough, Rhetia, the Venetic Goddess of Healing. *Journal Royal Anthr. Inst. Edinburgh* 53, 1922, 212–229; A. A. Barb, Noreia und Rehtia. *Carinthia* I 143, 1953 (= *Festschr. für R. Egger* 1) 204–219 (159–174); R. Battaglia, Riti, culti e divinità delle genti paleovenete. *Boll. Mus. Civ. Padova* 46, 1955, 1–50; G. Fogolari in: *Popoli e civiltà dell'Italia antica* 4 (Rome 1975) 176ff.; Osm. Menghin, *JbSGU* 55, 1970, 142.

110 G. B. Pellegrini and A. L. Prosdocimi, *La lingua venetica* 1 (Padua 1967) 464–468 (Ca 4).

111 G. Fogolari (Note 109) Pls 69–70; *Situlenkunst zwischen Po und Donau*. Exhibition catalogue Vienna (1962) No. 62.

112 Somewhat too hasty with his parallels is H. Kenner, Zu namenlosen Göttern der Austria Romana: Reitia. *Schild von Steier* 15–16, 1978–79, 109f.

113 Cf. for instance Augst BL: *UFAS* V, 134 Ills 17–18; the partly rebuilt Capitolium of *Brixia*/Brescia: B. Andreae, *Römische Kunst* (Freiburg/Basel/Vienna 2nd edn 1974) 552f. – today it contains the Civico Museo Romano.

114 A mine of information is E. Stemplinger, *Antiker Volksglaube* (Stuttgart 1948), though here only the literary sources are discussed. – Light is thrown on certain aspects chiefly from the archaeological angle by L. Pauli, *Keltischer Volksglaube. Amulette und Sonderbestattungen am Dürrnberg bei Hallein und im eisenzeitlichen Mitteleuropa* (Munich 1975). – For more recent material the various key-words in the *Handwörterbuch des deutschen Aberglaubens* (Berlin/Leipzig) are useful.

115 J. Lentz-ter Vrugt, *Mors immatura* (Groningen 1960).

116 Abundant material is provided by L. Hansmann and L. Kriss-Rettenbeck, *Amulett und Talisman. Erscheinungsform und Geschichte* (Munich 1966); in addition: *Jagd- und Trachtenschmuck*. Exhibition catalogue Munich (1978/79).

117 F. Moosleitner, L. Pauli and E. Penninger (Note 37) 34ff. Ill. 1: Pls 138–139.

118 A widespread phenomenon in the folklore of South Tyrol were for instance the 'Nörggelen', the spirits of small children, often depicted as dwarflike, who would do all kinds of harm to people.

119 L. Schmidt, *Heiliges Blei in Amuletten, Votiven und anderen Gegenständen des Volksglaubens in Europa und im Orient* (Vienna 1958).

120 Fittingly exemplified by M. Mackensen, *Das römische Gräberfeld auf der Keckwiese in Kempten* 1 (Kallmünz 1978) 42ff. 156ff.

121 Cf. for instance the reconstructed door from the *villa* at Anchettes in the Valais: *Musée archéologique du Valais*, Sion (1976) Ill. 20.

122 R. Christlein, *Die Alamannen* (Stuttgart/Aalen 1978) 77–82. This applies also to the Anglo-Saxons, as is demonstrated in the very important work by A. L. Meaney, *Anglo-Saxon Amulets and Curing Stones* (Oxford 1981).

123 L. Pauli, Heidnisches und Christliches im frühmittelalterlichen Bayern. *BVbl* 43, 1978, 147–157.

124 This is rightly pointed out by M. Martin, *UFAS* VI, 18

125 H. Schwab, *UFAS* VI, 27f.

126 R. Egger, Zu einem Fluchtäfelchen aus Blei. In: W. Krämer, *Cambodunumforschungen 1953-I* (Kallmünz 1957) 72–75.

127 A. Audollent, *Defixionum tabellae* (Paris 1904) 295f. No. 222.

128 H. Thaller, Ein Heiligtum bei Mautern a. d. Donau. *Öjh* 37, 1948, Beibl. 185–194.

129 R. Egger, Liebeszauber. *ÖJh* 37, 1948, 112–120.

130 H. Nesselhauf, Beschriftetes Bleitäfelchen aus einer raetischen Villa. *Germania* 38, 1960, 76–80.

131 Several additions by U. Schillinger-Häfele, *BerRGK* 58, 1977, 565 No. 225.

132 F. Cumont, *Die orientalischen Religionen im römischen Heidentum* (Stuttgart 1959).

133 R. Gordon, Mithraism and Roman Society. Social Factors in the Explanation of Religious Change in the Roman Empire. *Journ. of Religion and Religions* 1973, 92–122.

134 F. Cumont, *Die Mysterien des Mithra* (4th edn Stuttgart 1963); M. J. Vermaseren, *Mithras, Geschichte eines Kultes* (Stuttgart 1965) with further literature.

135 *UFAS* V, 141 Ill. 27.

136 M. P. Speidel, *The Religion of Jupiter Dolichenus in the Roman Army* (London 1978).

137 R. Noll, *Das Inventar des Dolichenusheiligtums von Mauer an der Url (Noricum)* (Vienna 1980).

138 A compilation of archaeological evidence in P. F. Barton, *Frühzeit des Christentums in Österreich und Südostmitteleuropa bis 788* (Vienna/Cologne/Graz 1975) 98.

139 *UFAS* V, 144 Ill. 30.

140 P. F. Barton (Note 138) 55 with Pl. 2 top. – The 'Good Shepherd' is a motif that appears in Hellenistic-Roman art already before Christianity (on this N. Himmelmann, *Bonner Jahrb.* 179, 1979, 788–795).

141 Lamps: J. Werner (ed.), *Der Lorenzberg bei Epfach. Die spätrömischen und frühmittelalterlichen Anlagen* (Munich 1969) Pl. 31, 19; H. Deringer, *Römische Lampen aus Lauriacum* (Linz 1965) Pl. 7, 347; *Flavia Solva* (Styria): *CIL* III 12012 104 b. – Toothpicks: *UFAS* V, 143 Ill. 29.

142 Rightly interpreted as an indication of the generally Christian orientation of everyday life by J. Engemann, Anmerkungen zu spätantiken Geräten des Alltagslebens mit christlichen Bildern, Symbolen und Inschriften. *Jahrb. f. Antike u. Christentum* 15, 1972, 154–173.

143 R. Laur-Belart, Der spätrömische Silberschatz von Kaiseraugst/Aargau (3rd edn Augst 1967). A comprehensive publication is in preparation.

144 Cf. the compilation for Switzerland in R. Moosbrugger-Leu, *Die Schweiz zur Merowingerzeit* (Bern 1971) 59 and M. Martin (Note 42) 15. For the East K. Reindel Bistumsorganisation im Alpen-Donau-Raum in der Spätantike und im Frühmittelalter, *Mitt. Inst. Österr. Geschichtsforsch.* 72, 1964, 277–310.

145 P. F. Barton (Note 138) 102.

146 *Vita Severini* 12,2.

147 Chapter III Note 115.

148 Chapter III Notes 116–117.

149 *JbSGU* 54, 1968–69, 155–163.

150 *Gallia* 31, 1973, 530f.

151 Chapter III Notes 127–128.

152 Two new examples: *JbSGU* 59, 1976, 253 (Hinwil ZH) and 261f. (Maur ZH).

153 An urgent warning has recently been sounded by M. Martin in: J. Werner and E. Ewig (eds), *Von der Spätantike zum Frühmittelalter* (Sigmaringen 1979) 436ff. against regarding the topographical connections between Roman *villa* and early medieval church or churchyard only from the viewpoint of 'continuity of ruins', maintaining that – at least for western Switzerland – there was in many cases a continuity of the population. But even in such cases one must surely assume that the decimated population of late antiquity and subsequently the Germanic immigrants administered or cultivated the still surviving clearings round the *villae*. The sparse open areas (as early as Roman times only representing about one third of the entire extent of an establishment) scarcely sufficed for urgently needed corn and vegetable cultivation (cf. G. Duby, *The early growth of the European economy. Warriors and peasants from the seventh to the twelfth century* [London 1974] 21–30). Thereby, however, the case for the unusable space among the ruins gains weight once more.

154 *UFAS* VI, 134f. Ill. 2, No. 8.

155 *UFAS* VI, 136 Ills 3–4, our Ill. 114 after *Ur-Schweiz* 33, 1969, 76 Ill. 19.

156 *Gallia* 31, 1973, 542; 33, 1975, 554f.

157 Summaries: H. R. Sennhauser, Kirchen und Klöster. *UFAS* VI, 138–148; id., Spätantike und frühmittelalterliche Kirchen Churrätiens. In: J. Werner and E. Ewig (Note 153) 193–218; P. Petru and Th. Ulbert, *Vranje pri Sevnici – Vranje bei Sevnica. Frühchristliche Kirchenanlagen auf dem Ajdovski gradec* (Ljubljana 1975) 65ff. with Ills 17–21; G. C. Menis, *La basilica paleocristiana nelle diocesi settentrionali della metropoli d'Aquileia (Città del Vaticano 1958)*; F. Oswald, L. Schäfer and H. R. Sennhauser, *Vorromanische Kirchenbauten* (Munich 1966ff.).

158 Clearly set out by Th. Ulbert (Note 157) 63 and 65; the church in *Ibligo*/Invillino, too, was a baptismal church, as the font indicates, though the bishop naturally resided in the *municipium Iulium Carnicum*/Zuglio, only a few kilometres away.

159 A comprehensive summary: M. Weidemann, Reliquie und Eulogie. Zur Begriffsbestimmung geweihter Gegenstände in der fränkischen Kirchenlehre des 6. Jahrhunderts. In: J. Werner (ed.), *Die Ausgrabungen in St Ulrich und Afra in Augsburg 1961–1968* (Munich 1977) 353–373.

160 H. Buschhausen, *Die spätrömischen Metallscrinia und frühchristlichen Reliquiare* 1. Catalogue (Vienna 1971); now additionally R. Noll, Ein Reliquiar aus Sanzeno im Nonsberg und das frühe Christentum im Trentino. *Anz. Österr. Akad. d. Wiss., phil.-hist. Kl.* 109, 1972, 320–337.

161 The most precious pieces in Switzerland: *UFAS* VI, 176ff. Ills 27. 29. 31–33. 38a. 40. – The findings in the cathedral of Chur and in the church of St Laurence at Paspels (Graubünden) show most clearly how relics and their receptacles were collected and could accumulate: Chr. Caminada, Der Hochaltar der Kathedrale von Chur. *ZSAK* 7, 1945, 23–38; W. Sulser et al., Die Kirche St Lorenz bei Papels. Loc. cit. 23, 1963–64, 61–90. The Paspels findings show, moreover, that plain wooden boxes satisfied modest demands and limited means.

162 Literature devoted to interpreting this is vast. The essentials are to be found in R. Egger, *Teurnia* (7th edn 1973) 28ff. and P. F. Barton (Note 138) 149–159.

163 Chapter I Note 141.

164 Chapter I Note 139.

165 Chapter I Note 140.

166 W. Müller, Die Christianisierung der Alemannen. In: W. Hübener (ed.), *Die Alemannen in der Frühzeit* (Freiburg 1974) 169–183; R. Christlein, *Die Alamannen* (Stuttgart/Aalen 1978) 112–121.

167 A balanced account taking into consideration the difficult time-strata and theological trends of 'Christianity' is presented by H. Wolfram, Die Christianisierung der Bayern. In: *Bayernzeit in Oberösterreich*. Exhibition catalogue Linz (1977) 177–188.

168 E. Zöllner, Der bairische Adel und die Gründung von Innichen. *Mitt. Inst. Österr. Geschichtsforsch.* 68, 1960, 362–387.

169 Die Anfänge des Klosters Kremsmünster. *Symposion* 1977. *Ergänzungsbd. d. Mitt. Oberösterr. Landesarchiv* 2 (Linz 1978).

170 Since 1978 Volker Bierbrauer (now Bonn), Georg Kossack and Günter Ulbert (Munich) have in collaboration with Johannes Nothdurfter (Sterzing) been carrying out excavations in Säben in order to clarify further the late Roman-early medieval history of this highly important place. Cf. for the present H. Nothdurfter, Der Burgberg von Säben in vor- und frühgeschichtlicher Zeit. Topographie und Stand der archäologischen Forschung. *Der Schlern* 51, 1977, 25–42.

171 P. Anderson, Passages from Antiquity to Feudalism (London 1974) 117f.

V Mule-tracks, Passes and Resthouses – The Traffic over the Alps

1 *JbSGU* 15, 1923, 97.

2 R. Nierhaus, *Studien zur Römerzeit in Gallien, Germanien und Hispanien* (Bühl 1977) 28f.

3 O. Brandstätter, *Südtiroler Verkehrswege in alter und neuer Zeit* (= offprint from *Reimmichls Volkskalender*, Bolzano 1970) 162; *Vom Saumpfad zur Autobahn*. Exhibition catalogue Munich (1978) Nos. 105–106.

4 H. Büttner in: *Die Alpen in der europäischen Geschichte des Mittelalters* (2nd edn Sigmaringen 1976) 108–110. – Some Roman coins from saddlebacks nearby prove that other paths were well known: P. Roubik, Ein römischer Münzfund aus Uri *HelvA* 10, 1979, 68–75.

5 A. Planta, *Alte Wege durch Die Rofla und die Viamala* (Chur 1980) with a supplement in *Bündner Monatsbl.* 1980, 186–188.

6 O. Brandstätter (Note 3) 165ff.

7 H. Büttner, Zur frühen Geschichte der Abtei Pfäfers. *Zeitschr. Schweiz. Kirchengesch.* 53, 1959, 1–17. – At Vättis itself a hoard of coins from year 270: B. Overbeck, *Geschichte des Alpenrheintals in römischer Zeit auf Grund der archäologische Zeugnisse*. Part 2: *Die Fundmünzen* (Munich 1973) No. 60.

8 See Note 17.

9 Facsimile reproduction Lindau 1977, 305f.

10 Chapter I Note 20

11 Chapter II Note 26. – It should be noted that in recent years Vrin itself earned the keen attention of historians, geographers and folklorists. The results in the first place throw light on the agricultural situation and secondly confirm that traffic across the passes played a by no means insignificant role: 'Today's connection of Vrin with the outer Lugnez and in particular with the Vorderrhein valley was not always so predominant. Formerly close ties with the South were maintained across the then more important, though never rebuilt Diesrut-Greina route. They were forged by the cattle-sales by the Vrin farmers to the Ticino and Lombardy. The 'Oechsli'-trade flourished up until the last century and also marked out an emigration route that led many Vrin people to Milan.' R. Kruker, Inneralpine Transportprobleme und kulturelle Lösungsmuster. Alltagsstrukturen und einfache Techniken. *Schweiz. Zeitschr. f. Gesch.* 29, 1979, 109ff.: 'Zum Beispiel Vrin: Verkehrs- und Transportprobleme einer Berggemeinde'.

12 L. Pauli, Die Golasecca-Kultur und Mitteleuropa. Ein Beitrag zur Geschichte des Handels über die Alpen. *Hamburger Beitr. z. Arch.* 1, fasc. 1, 1971.

13 Chapter IV Note 55.

14 A find-spot map of the Late Stone Age and the Bronze Age now in E. Anati et al., *BCSP* 13–14, 1976, 203 Ill. 121.

15 P. Barocelli, *BPI* 57, 1938, 130. – Distributed by J. D. Cowen, *BerRGK* 36, 1955, 73ff. with map C.

16 L. Pauli (Note 12) 65 map 4.

17 H. Schwab, Châtillon-sur-Glâne. Ein Fürstensitz der Hallstattzeit bei Freiburg im Üechtland. *Germania* 53, 1975, 79–84; id., Un oppidum de l'époque de Hallstatt près de Fribourg en Suisse. *MblSGU* 7, 1976, 2–13; D. Ramseyer, Châtillon-sur-Glâne– un centre commercial du premier âge fer en Suisse. *Archéologia* 146, 1980, 64–71. The excavations are still in progress.

18 The Romans are already said to have toyed with the idea of establishing a Rhône–Saône–Moselle–Rhine link by means of a canal: Tacitus, *Ann.* XIII 53.

19 Good summaries in D. Ellmers, Keltischer Schiffbau. *JbRGZM* 16, 1969, 73–122; id., Vor- und frühgeschichtliche Schiffahrt am Nordrand der Alpen. *HelvA* 5, 1974, 94–104; J. Reitinger, Das goldene Miniaturschiffchen vom Dürrnberg bei Hallein. *Mitt. Ges. f. Salzburger Landeskde.* 115, 1975, 383–405.

20 Navigation on the Adige and the Inn (until the nineteenth century) called for good organization, above all for the purpose of installing and maintaining the important tow-paths; on this briefly O. Brandstätter (Note 3) 167f. In more detail: E. Neweklowsky, *Die Schiffahrt und Flösserei im Raume der oberen Donau* 1–3 (Linz 1952–1964); a condensed version: id., Die Salzschiffahrt im Raume der oberen Donau. *Der Anschnitt* 14, 1962, Sonderheft.

21 R. Lunz, *Ur- und Frühgeschichte Südtirols* (Bolzano 1973) map on end-paper; in addition the map 'L'italia centrosettentrionale dal X al III secolo a.C.' in: *Mostra dell'Etruria Padana e della città di Spina.* Exhibition catalogue Bologna (1960) vol. 2. – Important as supplement for farther to the West: P. Donati, Sull'uso dei valichi alpini dal Gottardo al Bernina in epoca preromana. *Quaderni ticinesi di numism. e ant. class.* 1979, 131–142.

22 P. 29 with Note 76.

23 Cf. the map of 1960 referred to in Note 21. – The long-awaited correction now by P. Cassola Guida, l'area orientale della civiltà paleoveneta. In: *Este e la civiltà paleoveneta a cento anni delle prime scoperte. Atti del' XI Convegno di Studi etruschi ed italici, Este/Padova 1976* (Florence 1980) 107–122.

24 Cf. for instance the spread of the works of situla art and its imitations (Ill. 97); in conjunction L. Pauli, *Der Dürrnberg bei Hallein* 3 (Munich 1978) 269–273, 489. – Now a summing-up by A. Siegfried-Weiss, Der Ostalpenraum in der Hallstattzeit und seine Beziehungen zum Mittelmeergebiet. *Hamburger Beitr. z. Arch.* 6, 1979, 1–221.

25 L. Pauli (Note 24) 468 Ill. 52; id., Der Goldene Steig, Wirtschaftsgeographisch-archäologische Untersuchungen im östlichen Mitteleuropa. In: *Studien zur vor- und frühgeschichtlichen Archäologie (Festschr. für J. Werner)* (Munich 1974) 115–139.

26 Chapter IV Notes 68 and 73.

27 Chapter IV Note 103.

28 Chapter IV Note 82; on the yield of finds (only 4 instead of 5 hills) now K. Dobiat, Bemerkungen zu den 'fünf' Fürstengräbern von Kleinklein in der Steiermark. *Schild von Steier* 15–16, 1978–79, 57–66.; id., *Das Hallstattzeitliche Gräberfeld von Kleinklein und seine Keramik* (Graz 1980) confirms the importance of this route by arguing that even the Drau gorges west of Maribor are very difficult to negotiate.

29 W. Modrijan, *Frauenberg bei Leibnitz. Die frühgeschichtlichen Ruinen und das Heimatmuseum* (Leibnitz 1955); id., *Vorzeit an der Mur* (Graz 1974) 34ff.; latest excavation findings in E. Hudeczek, Kelten auf dem Frauenberg. *Steiermärkisches Landesmus. Joanneum* 2/1979.

30 N. Negroni Catacchio, Le vie dell'ambra, i passi alpini orientali e l'alto Adriatico. In: *Aquileia e l'arco alpino orientale* (Udine 1976) 21–57. – Worth reading for its generally valid comments on the problems of road-routing: F. Freising, *Die Bernsteinstrasse aus der Sicht der Strassentrassierung* (Bonn–Bad Godesberg 1977).

31 R. Joffroy, *Le trésor de Vix* (Paris 1962) 48–62. Reproduced in every major work on prehistoric or Celtic archaeology and art.

32 Strabo IV 207, V 214, VII 314.

33 H. Zürn, Eine hallstattzeitliche Stele von Hirschlanden, Kr. Leonberg (Württemberg). *Germania* 42, 1964, 27–36; id., An Anthropomorphic Hallstatt Stele from Germany. *Antiquity* 38, 1964, 224–226.

34 Châtillon: D. Ramseyer, *Archéologia* 146, 1980, 69 Ill. 18. – Martigny: unpublished (communication from F. Wiblé).

35 W. Drack, *JbSGU* 54, 1968–69, 16 Ills 3, 37 (captions interchanged!).

36 E. Conradin, *JbSGU* 61, 1978, 93 Ill. 27; distribution map in R. Lunz, *Studien zur End-Bronzezeit und älteren Eisenzeit im Südalpenraum* (Florence 1974) Pl. 81,1.

37 W. Krämer, Fremder Frauenschmuck aus Manching. *Germania* 39, 1961, 305–322.

38 L. Pauli (Note 24) 309ff. 492ff.

39 L. Stauffer, M. Magetti and Chr. Marro, Formenwandel und Produktion der alpinen Laugener Keramik. *AS* 2, 1979, 130–137.

40 A. Crivelli, Presentazione dal ripostiglio di un fonditore di bronzi dell'epoca del ferro scoperto ad Arbedo (Svizzera). *Rivista di Studi Liguri* 12, 1946, 59–79; M. Primas, Zum eisenzeitlichen Depotfund von Arbedo (Kt. Tessin). *Germania* 50, 1972, 76–93.

41 S. Ricci, *Riv. Arch. Como* 51–52, 1906, 43ff.

42 L. Pauli, *Studien zur Golasecca-Kultur* (Heidelberg 1971) 83 Ill. 34; O.-H. Frey, Fibeln vom westhallstättischen Typus aus dem Gebiet südlich der Alpen. Zum Problem der keltischen Wanderung. In: *Oblatio. Racolta di studi in onore di A. Calderini* (Como 1971) 355–386, partic. 374f.

43 R. Winkler, Der Bronzen-Depotfund von Obervintl. In: *Beiträge zur Vorgeschichte des westlichen Pustertals* (Innsbruck 1950) 3–60.

44 *Ab urbe condita* V 34. Transl. B. O. Foster (6th edn London/Cambridge, Mass. 1969).

45 *Universal History* III 47–60.

46 *Ab urbe condita* XXI 31–38. Transl. B. O. Foster (6th edn London/Cambridge, Mass. 1969).

47 A well-founded calculation by E. Meyer, Hannibals Alpenübergang. *Mus. Helveticum* 15, 1958, 227–241; 21, 1964, 99–102. He shows that Livy, unlike Polybius, had embroidered his account with details added obviously by himself. This also includes the march through the valley of the *Druentia*/Durance. On these grounds the case for the Mont-Genèvre would be nullified; Hannibal should have crossed the Col du Clapier. – Cf. also H. Lieb and R. Wüthrich, *Lexicon topographicum der römischen und frühmittelalterlichen Schweiz 1. Römische Zeit, Süd- und Ostschweiz* (Bonn 1967) 149–159 with similar conclusion.

48 Thus J. Prieur, *La Savoie antique* (Grenoble 1977) 57ff.

49 Thus P. Connolly, *Hannibal and the Enemies of Rome* (London 1977) 44ff. But cf. Note 47.

50 G. Hanke (Note 4) 231–233.

51 Chapter I Note 81.

52 *CIL* V 8002 (Feltre); 8003 (Rabland).

53 A. de Bon et al., *La Via Claudia Augusta Altinate* (Venice 1938). Without giving any reasons this claim is disputed by W. Dondio, *Der Schlern* 47, 1973, 98 Note 2. – The course north of the Reschen pass has been explored by A. Planta, Neues von der Via Claudia. *Mus. Ferdinandeum Innsbruck* 60, 1980, 155–187.

54 R. Nierhaus, Die Westgrenze von Noricum und die Routenführung der Via Claudia Augusta. In: *Ur- und Frühgeschichte als historische Wissenschaft (Festschr. für E. Wahle)* (Heidelberg 1950) 177–188; reprinted in R. Nierhaus (Note 2) 23–30.

55 A. Planta, Zum römischen Weg über den Grossen St Bernhard. *HelvA* 10, 1979, 15–30.

56 R. Nierhaus (Note 2) 30.

57 N. Heger, Salzburg in römischer Zeit. *Jahresschr. Salzburger Mus.* C.A. 19. 1973, 61f.

58 H. Erb and G. Th. Schwarz, *Die San Bernardinoroute von der Luzisteig bis in die Mesolcina in ur- und frühgeschichtlicher Zeit* (Chur 1969); in connection with this the justified criticism of A. Planta, Unumgängliche Fragen zur römischen St Bernadinroute. *Bündner Monatsblatt* 1975, 32–44.

59 *BVbl* 21, 1956, 289 with Pl. 35.

60 R. Noll, *Griechische und lateinische Inschriften der Wiener Antikensammlung* (Vienna 1962) 92f. 119ff. (= *CIL* III 5732–36; 4649–52; 4641–45); G. Winkler, Die römischen Meilensteine von Ivenca. *Arheol. Vestnik* 23, 1972, 417ff. As many as seven, admittedly badly preserved milestones of the third/fourth century at one and the same place come from the northern approach to the Radstädter Tauern: N. Heger, Die römischen Meilensteine von Hüttau. *Jahresschr. Salzburger Mus.* C.A. 23–24, 1977–78, 127–134.

61 R. Knussert, Zu den Römerstrassen im Raum südlich von Kempten. *BVbl* 28, 1963, 152–164.

62 H. Bender, *Römische Strassen und Strassenstationen* (Stuttgart 1975) 7.

63 *CIL* V 2116.

64 *CIL* XII 107.

65 *CIL* V 1862–64.

66 *CIL* III 5715 and 11835.

67 A. Maiuri, *Die Altertümer der Phlegräischen Felder* (3rd edn Rome 1958) 14ff. ('Crypta Neapolitana'); 147ff. (Tunnel in the mountain of Cumae) and 158ff. ('Grotto of Cocceius'), at present several hundred metres long. But these exceptions are undoubtedly due to the special geological conditions at the Bay of Naples, the tufa there being very easy to work and hollow out.

68 K. Lukan, *Alpenwanderungen in die Vorzeit* (Vienna/Munich 1965) 104 with Ill. 57; L. Casson, *Travel in the Ancient World* (London 1974) Ill. 40. Surprisingly the distance between the ruts in the rock here measures 144 cm, a width which exceeds all others that have been ascertained for pass routes in antiquity or medieval times (cf. A. Planta [Note 55] 16: 107/108 cm for the Roman period, even a mere 99 cm for the Middle Ages; 107 cm for the Roman Brenner pass road at Franzensfeste/Fortezza: R. Lunz, *Archäologie Südtirols* [Bruneck 1981] 306). Yet the milestone hewn into the rock-face does in fact testify to the Roman origin of this passage, just as on the French side of the approach to the Mont-Genèvre at the 'Porte de Bons' near Oisans a comparable arrangement and the same track-width of 144 cm is manifest (J. Prieur, *ANRW* II 5, 641). In the flat land, too, there are equally wide tracks (W. Drack, *Der römische Gutshof bei Seeb* [4th edn Basel 1974] 20: 148 cm = 5 Roman feet), as also evidence from early modern times of a track-width of 105 cm (F. Moosleitner, Auffindung einer Geleisestrasse bei Pfarrwerfen. *Pro Austria Romana* 29, 1979, 22 : corduroy road in a marsh radiocarbon-dated in the post-1650 period). Possibly an elucidation of all available dates may show that in the plain at all times vehicles with wider tracks were used, in the mountains ones with a narrower gauge, which could cope better with narrow roads and sharp bends. This would naturally affect the organization of trade and travel; for changing vehicles or switching of loads at specific points calls for a costly system.

69 A. Planta, Die römische Julierroute. *HelvA* 7/25, 1976, 16–25; id., Zum Römerweg zwischen Maloja und Sils. Loc cit. 10/37, 1979, 42–46.

70 H. Bulle, Geleisestrassen des Altertums. *Sitzungsber. Bayer. Akad. d. Wiss., phil.-hist. Kl.* 1947, 2.

71 Cf. the discussion of H. Bulle's work by R. Nierhaus, *Gnomon* 22, 1950, 268–273; reprint: R. Nierhaus (Note 2) 221–226.

72 Suetonius, *Caesar* 56. In those days he wrote a grammatical work called 'de Analogia', about which Aulus Gellius, *Noctes Articae* 1 10 has left us the remarkable sentence 'You should steer clear, as it were a reef, of every seldom heard and unfamiliar word.' – In the same chapter we read that Caesar was 24 days en route from Rome to southern Spain. However, the journey across the Alps to Gaul began in northern Italy, so it could scarcely have occupied more than four to seven days. Had the work been preserved, it would provide further evidence of Caesar's creative ability.

73 M. Hell, Keltische Hufeisen aus Salzburg. *ArchA* 7, 1950, 92–95; additions to this in *ArchA* 12, 1953, 44–49 and 25, 1959, 111–117. A new find (1978) from the Dürrnberg above Hallein in a late Celtic settlement corroborates Hell's view afresh.

74 The last comprehensive works: H. Bender, *Archäologische Untersuchungen zur Ausgrabung Augst-Kurzenbettli. Ein Beitrag zur Erforschung der römischen Rasthäuser* (Freuenfeld 1975) 125–135; id., *Römische Strassen und Strassenstationen* (Stuttgart 1975); id., *Römischer Reiseverkehr, Cursus publicus und Privatreisen* (Stuttgart 1978).

75 R. Fleischer, Immurium-Moosham. *ÖJh* 47, 1964–65, Beibl. 105–208; 48, 1966–67, Beibl. 165–230; 49, 1968, Beibl. 177–228; id., *RE* Suppl. XI (1968) 845–849.

76 Chapter VI Note 99.

77 N. Heger, Nachlese zu den Funden aus dem Mithraeum von Moosham im Lungau (Immurium) nebst Rekonstruktion des Kultbildes. *Jahresschr. Salzburger Mus.* C.A. 23–24, 1977–78, 119–126. – Cf. also Chapter V Notes 133–134.

78 J. Fitz, Beneficiarier in Noricum. *Schild von Steier* 15–16, 1978–79, 79–81 expresses the opinion that these check-points were only located in the vicinity of the towns and forts as well as on the major roads near the frontiers, and had an operational radius of 50–70 km. A closer range is postulated by H. Bender, *Römische Strassen und Strassenstationen* (Stuttgart 1975) 19–22.

79 *CIL* V 5090.

80 W. Dondio, Stand und Problematik der Römerstrassenforschung in Südtirol. *Der Schlern* (47, 1973, 98–108; R. Lunz, *Urgeschichte des Raumes Algund – Gratsch – Tirol* (Bolzano 1976) 69–95; id., *Archäologie Südtirols* (Bruneck 1981) 277–282.

81 F. Huter in: *Die Alpen in der europäischen Geschichte des Mittelalters* (2nd edn Sigmaringen 1976) 249. 255.

82 W. Dondio (Note 80) Pls 3–4; R. Lunz (Note 80) 92ff. Ills 131–132.

83 Cf. by contrast the outdated frontier course in R. Nierhaus (Note 2) 27 Ill. 2 and in H.-J. Kellner, *BVbl* 39, 1974, Beilage III with Noricum's unmotivated encroachment southwestwards across the mouth of the Isarco.

84 L. Flam-Zuckermann, A propos d'une inscription de Suisse (*CIL*, XIII 5010) : étude du phénomène du brigandage dans l'Empire romain. *Latomus* 29, 1970, 451–473; the second inscription: Chapter III Note 91. – Grave-stone of Ajdovščina: *Inscriptiones Italiae* X 4, 339.

85 *Codex Vindobonensis* 324. Complete facsimile edition in original format (Graz 1976) with a brief commentary by E. Weber. Previously mainly used was the edition of K. Miller (Ravensburg 1887 and Stuttgart 1916, reprinted 1962).

86 Among many containing much untenable matter there is finally A. Adam, Römische Reisewege und Stationsnamen im südöstlichen Deutschland. *Beitr. z. Namenforsch.* N.F. 11, 1976, 1–59.

87 H. W. Böhme, Archäologische Zeugnisse zur Geschichte der Markomannenkriege. *JbRGZM* 22, 1975, 175 Ill. 7 with a map of the coin hoards and traces of destruction: Cf. p. 41f. with Note 99.

88 B. Overbeck, Alamanneneinfälle in Raetien 270 und 288 n. Chr. *Jahrb. f. Numismatik u. Geldgesch.* 20, 1970, 81–150.

89 T. Tomasevic, Die militärischen Befestigungen im Alpengebiet. *Atti CSDIR* 7, 1975–76, 619–623. On the line of fortification in the Julian Alps with the new excavation results on the pass across the Birnbaumer Wald: *Claustra Alpium Iuliarum* I: *Fontes* (Ljubljana 1971) and Th. Ulbert (ed.), *AD PIRUM (Hrušica). Spätrömische Passbefestigung in den Julischen Alpen* (Munich 1981).

90 Eugippius, *Vita Severini* 20, 1–2.

91 *Carminum epistularum expositionum praefatio* 84, p. 2 ; *Vita S. Martini* IV 630–688.

92 J. Werner, Fernhandel und Naturalwirtschaft im östlichen Merowingerreich nach archäologischen und numismatischen Zeugnissen. *BerRGK* 42, 1961, 307–346.

93 Paulus Diaconus, *Hist. Lang.* III 30.

94 Chapter IV Note 74.

95 *UFAS* VI, 45 Ill. 6. – The founding of the Disentis monastery (probably in the early eighth century) above the Vorderrhein on the ascent to the Lukmanier through the Medeltal first became needful and expedient when an appreciable traffic crossed the pass.

96 Chapter II Note 95.

97 W. Meyer, *Das Castel Grande in Bellinzona* (Olten 1976).

98 Tamins: Chapter III Note 130; Civezzano: Chapter III Note 134.

99 'Tummihügel': A. Gredig, Die ur- und frühgeschichtliche Siedlung am Tummihügel bei Maladers. *AS* 2, 1979, 69–74 (in 1979 sherds of impressed pottery of Alamannic-Frankish provenance came to light, knowledge of which I owe to Arthur Gredig). – 'Rocca di Rivoli': L. H. Barfield, Excavations on the Rocca di Rivoli (Verona 1963). *Mem. Mus. Civ. Storia Nat. Verona* 14, 1966, 79 Ill. 38 (Lombardic belt-mounting); 83 Ill. 40, 1 (early medieval arrowhead with spiral shaft, known from several cemeteries of this time); other finds too could belong to the early rather than the high Middle Ages, though on this no clear decision can be reached.

100 Chapter I Note 140; a last brief report about excavations in *HelvA* 6/21, 1975, 22–32.

101 With emphasis on the historical rather than the geographical-routing aspect: W. Störmer, Fernstrasse und Kloster. Zur Verkehrs- und Herrschaftsstruktur des westlichen Altbayern im frühen Mittelalter. *Zeitschr. Bayer. Landesgesch.* 29, 1966, 299–343 (above all on Benediktbeuren and Schäftlarn); id., Engen und Pässe in den mittleren Ostalpen und ihre Sicherung im frühen Mittelalter. In: Beiträge zur Landeskunde Bayerns und der Alpenländer (Festschr. für H. Fehn). *Mitt. Geogr. Ges. München* 53, 1968, 91–107.

102 I. Müller, Die Anfänge von Disentis. *Jahresber. Hist. – Ant. Ges. Graubünden* 61, 1931, 75ff.; id., *Disentiser Klostergeschichte 700–1512* (Einsiedeln 1942); id., *Geschichte der Abtei Disentis von den Anfängen bis zur Gegenwart* (Zurich 1971). The old road ran from Disentis not – as now – through the gorge of the Medel Rhine but directly south, crossing the Vorderrhein by way of a steep descent and ascent, and then climbed up to Mompé/Medel. This explains the seemingly remote situation of the little church of Santa Gada with its interesting tenth-century paintings (best reached on foot along a path through the meadows–first collecting the key at the local vicarage): N. Curti and I. Müller, St. Agatha bei Disentis. *ZSAK* 3, 1941, 41–49.

103 H. Büttner, Zur frühen Geschichte der Abtei Pfäfers. *Zeitschr. Schweiz. Kirchengesch.* 53, 1959, 1–17.

104 W. Sage, Das frühmittelalterliche Kloster in der Scharnitz. Die Ausgrabungen auf dem 'Kirchfeld' zu Klais, Gemeinde Krün, Landkreis Garmisch-Partenkirchen, in den Jahren 1968–1972. *Beitr. z. Altbayer. Kirchengesch.* 31, 1977, 11–133.

105 Chapter IV Notes 168–169.

106 H. Büttner and I. Müller, Das Kloster Müstair im Früh- und Hochmittelalter. *Zeitschr. Schweiz. Kirchengesch.* 50, 1956, 12–84.

107 E. Poeschel, *Die Kunstdenkmäler des Kantons Graubünden* 2 (Basel 1937) 266ff. with literature; E Maurer, *ZSAK* 7, 1945, 108–114 (excavation 1943); *JbSGU* 54, 1968–69, 155; 56, 1971,

233 (new excavations); I. Müller, Zur churrätischen Kirchengeschichte im Frühmittelalter. *Jahresber. Hist.-Ant. Ges. Graubünden* 99, 1969, 93ff.

108 A. Frietinger and H. Heindl (eds), *Weiss und Blau. Erzählungen, Sagen, Geschichtsbilder, Schilderungen* (Munich 1893) 10f.

109 H. Büttner, *Schweiz. Zeitschr. f. Gesch.* 3, 1953, 576; in general P. Darmstädter, *Das Reichsgut in der Lombardei und Piemont* (Strassburg 1896).

110 F. Jecklin, Der langobardisch-karolingische Münzfund bei Ilanz. *Mitt. Bayer. Numism. Ges.* 25, 1906–07, 28–93; H. H. Völckers, Karolingische Münzfunde der Frühzeit (751–800). *Abhand. Akad. d. Wiss. Göttingen, phil.-hist. Kl.*, 3. series 61 (Göttingen 1965) 73–79; E. Bernareggi, I tremissi longobardi e carolingi del ripostiglio di Ilanz nei Grigioni. *Quaderni ticinesi di numism. e ant. class.* 1977, 341–364.– On the second coin hoard (of 1811), buried about AD 900, now B. Overbeck and K. Bierbrauer, Der Schatzfund von Ilanz 1811. *AS* 2, 1979, 119–125.

111 W. Meyer, *Das Castel Grande in Bellinzona* (Olten 1976) 20ff.; 108 with Note 8.

112 A. Carigiet, Die Ausgrabung der karolingischen Kirche St. Peter in Domat/Ems. *AS* 2, 1979, 113–118.

113 For a restricted area O. P. Clavadetscher, Verkehrsorganisation in Rätien zur Karolingerzeit. *Schweiz. Zeitschr. f. Gesch.* 5, 1955, 1–30.

114 F. N. Stenton, Anglo-Saxon England. In: *English Historical Documents* I (2nd edn London/New York 1979) 477.

115 L. Blondel, L'Hospice du Grand St-Bernard, Étude archéologique. *Vallesia* 2, 1947, 19–44.

116 H. Erb and M.-L. Boscardin, *Das spätmittelalterliche Marienhospiz auf der Lukmanier-Passhöhe* (Chur 1974).

117 P. Donati, *JbSGU* 61, 1978, 212–214; Airolo – Cappella del San Gottardo. In P. Donati (ed.), *Monumenti ticinese – Indagini archeologiche.* Exhibition catalogue Bellinzona (1980) 3–8.

118 G. Hanke (ed.), *Die grossen Alpenpässe. Reiseberichte aus neun Jahrhunderten* (Munich 1967) 244f.

119 A comprehensive history of traffic from late medieval to recent times is still lacking; an overall impression was conveyed by the exhibition 'Vom Saumpfad zur Autobahn' shown in various places, in conjunction with the exhibition catalogue Munich 1978.

120 H. Klein, Der Saumhandel über die Tauern. *Mitt. Ges. Salzburger Landeskde.* 90, 1950, 37–114.

121 dpa report in the *Süddeutsche Zeitung* Munich.

VI The Basics of Living– Husbandry, Mining, Commerce

1 H.–G. Bandi, Das Jungpaläolithikum. *UFAS* I, 107–122.

2 Chapter I Note 20.

3 G. Kossack and H. Schmeidel, Vorneolithischer Getreideanbau im bayerischen Alpenvorland. *Jahresber. Bayer. Bodendenkmalpfl.* 15–16, 1974–75, 7–23.

4 R. a. Maier, Jäger und Gerber in der Neolithstation Polling im Alpenvorland. Loc. cit. 24–32.

5 M. R. Jarman, The Fauna and Economy of Fiavè. *PrAlp* 11, 1974, 65–73.

6 Key word 'Alm-(Alp)wirtschaft' in: *Reallexikon der Germanischen Altertumskunde*, 2nd edn, Vol. 1, 181–189. – N. Grass and F. Maier-Böttcher, Die Almwirtschaft in der Urzeit und im Mittelalter. In: H. Beck et al. (eds), Untersuchungen zur eisenzeitlichen Flur in Mitteleuropa und ihre Nutzung. *Abhandl. Akad. d. Wiss. Göttingen, phil.-hist. Kl.*, 3. Series 115, part II (Göttingen 1980) 229–286.

7 Bronze Age cow-dung in the 1800 m-high mining area of the Kelchalm at Kitzbühel (North Tyrol) provides concrete evidence of the presence of cattle, but not of mountain pasturage (Almwirtschaft) in the stricter sense. This would appear to be an exceptional case, namely of herding animals in order to keep the miners who worked up there supplied: W. Amschler, Die Haustierreste von der Kelchalpe bei Kitzebühel. *Mitt. Prähist. Komm. Wien* 3 (1939) 96–120.

8 R. Pittioni, Urzeitliche 'Almwirtschaft'. *Mitt. Geogr. Ges. (Wien)* 74, 1931, 108ff.; id., Stand und Aufgaben der Urgeschichtlichen Forschung im Oberetsch. *Beih. z. Jahrb. f. Gesch., Kultur u. Kunst* 6 (Bolzano 1940) 34–38. The pointed counter-arguments brought by O. Menghin, *WPZ* 27, 1940, 227f. have all meanwhile been refuted as far as the relevant archaeological and historical sources go (cf. in this respect above all *Reallexikon der Germanischen Altertumskunde*, 2nd edn, vol. 1, 183f. and for the history of the settlements in the side valleys of South Tyrol R. Lunz. *Ur- und Frühgeschichte Südtirols* [Bolzano 1973] as well as id., Ur- und frühgeschichtliche Siedlungsspuren im Passeier. *Der Schlern* 48, 1974, 410–414).

9 In this sense also assessed by R. Wyss, Die Eroberung der Alpen durch den Bronzezeitmenschen. *ZSAK* 28, 1971, 130–145.

10 R. Wyss (Note 9) 131 after find-reports in *JbSGU* 22, 1930, 112f.; 24, 1932, 113; 26, 1934, 28. Zernez (Graubünden): loc. cit. 24, 1932, 115–118; 25, 1933, 133.

11 W. Geiser (ed.), *Bergeten ob Braunwald – ein archäologischer Beitrag zur Geschichte des alpinen Hirtentums* (Basel 1973) 8of. Ills 8–9. – A detailed study from a neighbouring district, and more recent: P. Hugger, *Hirtenleben und Hirtenkultur im Waadtländer Jura* (Basel 1972).

12 Chapter I Note 57.

13 W. Torbrügge, Vor- und frühgeschichtliche Flussfunde. Zur Ordnung und Bestimmung einer Denkmälergruppe. *BerRGK* 51–52, 1970–71, 1–146; partic. 47ff.: *Zur periodischen Gliederung.*

14 This association is confirmed by the hesitation – not first formulated there – on the part of R. Wyss (Note 9) 140 to equate the scarcity of high-altitude finds with a decline in mountain pasturage; he has however discarded his doubts meanwhile:

HelvA 9, 1978, 143. – On the early medieval spears on mountain pastures and passes in Graubünden cf. p. 164.

15 Still sceptical is E. Meyer, Die Wüstungen als Zeugen des mittelalterlichen Alpwesens. *Schweiz. Zeitschr. f. Gesch.* 29, 1979, 257 – admittedly without his knowing of the detailed essay of R. Wyss (Note 9). For the Eastern Alps mention should be made of the very recently investigated settlement site of Basso sul Campetto at Recoaro Terme in the Veneto, which lies at an altitude of some 1300 m. It yielded only stone tools, a few sherds and a late Roman coin. The stone tools belong in the Bronze Age and it is at present impossible to tell whether this place was still visited in the Iron Age; at all events the sherds and coin attest renewed use in late antiquity. The primitive nature of the tools and the assortment of animal bones (nearly all sheep/goat, some wild game, virtually no cattle) indicate that this was a seasonal settlement of shepherds and goatherds. P. Visonà, *PrAlp* 12, 1976, 242–243.

16 Providing also an insight into the early historical circumstances: W. Hirschberg and A. Janata, *Technologie und Ergologie in der Völkerkunde* (Mannheim 1966).

17 Very graphic: N. David and H. David-Hennig, Zur Herstellung und Lebensdauer von Keramik. Untersuchungen zu den sozialen, kulturellen und ökonomischen Strukturen am Beispiel der Ful aus der Sicht des Prähistorikers. *BVbl* 36, 1971, 289–317.

18 After *PrFr* II, 492, Ill. 6, 1.

19 An example from the Late Stone Age: H. Müller-Beck, *Seeberg, Burgäschisee-Sud 5. Holzgeräte und Holzbearbeitung* (Bern 1965). For the early Middle Ages: P. Paulsen and H. Schach-Dörges, *Holzhandwerk der Alamannen* (Stuttgart 1972).

20 M. Stotzer, F. H. Schweingruber and M. Sebek, Prähistorisches Holzhandwerk. *MblSGU* 7, 1976, 13–23.

21 Georg Agricola, *Vom Berg- und Hüttenwesen* (3rd edn Düsseldorf; pocketbook edn Munich 1977) 11f.

22 G. Kurth, Die Bevölkerungsgeschichte des Menschen. Eine Kombination aus biologischer Kapazität und humaner Leistungsfähigkeit. *Handbuch der Biologie* IX (Frankfurt 1965) 461–562.

23 A clear summary by: H.-J. Hundt, Donauländische Einflüsse in der frühen Bronzezeit Norditaliens. *PrAlp* 10, 1974, 143–178.

24 J. Bernhard, Die Mitterberger Kupferkieslagerstätte, Erzführung und Tektonik. *Jahrb. Geol. Bundesanstalt (Wien)* 109, 1966, 3ff.

25 J. Pirchl, Geschichte des Mitterberger Kupferbergbaues neuer und alter Zeit. *ArchA* 43, 1968, 18–91.

26 G. Kyrle, *Urgeschichte des Kronlandes Salzburg* (Vienna 1918): contribution by O. Klose; followed by L. Franz, *Vorgeschichtliches Leben in den Alpen* (Vienna 1929) 23–62.

27 *Das urzeitliche Bergbaugebiet von Mühlback-Bischofshofen, Salzburg* (Vienna 1932); on this in turn is based the description of R. Pittioni, *Urgeschichte des österreichischen Raumes* (Vienna 1954) 523–528.

28 Preliminary reports: *Der Anschnitt* 22/5, 1970, 12–19; 24/2, 1972, 3–15; 26/2, 1974, 14–22. Finally a summary: Zum Stammbaum einer urzeitlichen Kupfererzaufbereitung. *Berg- und hüttenmännische Monatshefte* 124, 1979, 157–161. Additionally an unpublished paper 1978 in Goslar: 'Neue Ergebnisse zum Kupfererzbergbau in Österreich'.

29 Agricola (Note 21) 239–309 devotes his eighth book, the longest, to describing 'the means by which the ore is picked out, pounded, roasted, crushed, ground to a powder, sieved, washed, roasted in a roasting oven and burnt'. The copious illustrations above all provide a picture of the manifold methods of 'washing', in order to separate out metal-rich material from the barren rock.

30 Three reports from R. Pittioni and E. Preuschen: Untersuchungen im Bergbaugebiet der Kelchalpe bei Kitzbühel, Tirol. *Mitt. Prähist. Komm. Wien* 3, 1–3 (1937) and 5, 2–3 (1947); *ArchA* 15, 1954, 7–97.

31 The embittered argument about their age and their bearing on the dating of the Inner Alpine alphabets has now simmered down for want of actual inducement. Cf. in this connection R. Pittioni, Zur Frage der Herkunft der Runen und ihrer Verankerung in der Kultur der europäischen Bronzezeit. *Beitr. z. Gesch. d. dt. Sprache* 65, 1942, 373–384; F. Altheim and E. Trautmann, *Kimbern und Runen – Untersuchungen zur Ursprungsfrage der Runen* (Berlin 1942) 48–53; R. Pittioni, Kelchalpenhölzer und Runen. *Nachr. Akad. d. Wiss. Göttingen, phil.-hist. Kl.* 1944, 87–92; F. Altheim, Runenforschung und Val Camonica. *La Nouvelle Clio* 1–2, 1949–50, 166–185; R. Pittioni, loc. cit. 385–387 with a 'closing comment' by Altheim.

32 C. Eibner in his paper read at Goslar (Note 28) based on earlier sources. Cf. also the 'Beigla', which served to define the grazing areas: *Liechtensteinisches Landesmuseum Vaduz – Wegleitung* (Vaduz 1975) 65.

33 Cf. p. 124. On mining E. Preuschen and R. Pittioni, Osttiroler Bergbaufragen. *Carinthia* I 143, 1953 (= *Festschr. für R. Egger* 2) 575–585 (64–74); find-spots in North Tyrol apart from the Kelchalpe: E. Preuschen and R. Pittioni, Neue Beiträge zur Topographie des urzeitlichen Bergbaues auf Kupfererz in den österreichischen Alpen. *ArchA* 18, 1955, 45–79; R. Pittioni, Neue Schmelzplätze im Bergbaugebiet Jochberg bei Kitzbühel, Tirol. In: *Studia Palaeometallurgica in honorem E. Preuschen. ArchA Beiheft* 3 (Vienna 1958) 41–45; id., Beiträge zur Kenntnis des urzeitlichen Kupferbergbauwesens um Jochberg und Kitzbühel. *ArchA* 59–60, 1976, 243–264.

34 A distribution map of the most important (certainly not all) of the copper deposits by M. Primas, Frühe Metallverarbeitung und -verwendung im alpinen und zirkumalpinen Bereich. In: *IXᵉ Congrès Union intern. sciences préhist. et protohist. Nice 1976*, Colloque XXIII (1976) 111 map 1. – Individual investigations in the South: E. Preuschen, Der urzeitliche Kupferbergbau von Vetriolo (Trento). *Der Anschnitt* 14/2, 1962, 3–7; id., Estrazione miniera dell'età del bronzo nel Trentino. *PrAlp* 9, 1978, 113–150 (= Bronzezeitlicher Kupferbergbau im Trentino. *Der Anschnitt* 20/1, 1968, 3–15); copper dross is also mentioned in *PrAlp* 8, 1972, 258–260. 262; 9, 1973, 254f.

35 Discussion about the method and purpose of metal examination by spectroscopic analysis has in recent years yielded to a pragmatic approach, though this has not helped to answer basic questions relating to the geological, metallurgical, physiographical and archaeological aspects. Cf. S. Junghans, E. Sangmeister and M. Schröder, *Metallanalysen kupferzeitlicher und frühbronzezeitlicher Bodenfunde aus Europa* (Berlin 1960); id., *Kupfer und Bronze in der frühen Metallzeit Europas. Die Materialgruppen beim Stand von 12 000 Analysen* (Berlin 1968). – A. Hartmann, *Prähistorische Goldfunde aus Europa* (Berlin 1970); also supplement for the Iron Age: id., *Ergebnisse spektralanalytischer Untersuchung späthallstatt- und latènezeitlicher Goldfunde vom Dürrnberg, aus südwestdeutschland, Frankreich und der Schweiz.* In: L. Pauli, *Der Dürrnberg bei Hallein* 3 (Munich 1978) 601–617 and H. Neuninger and R. Pittioni, Bemerkungen über zwei Methoden der spektralanalytischen Untersuchung urzeitlicher Kupfer- und Bronzegeräte. *ArchA* 31, 1962, 96–102; H. Neuninger, Zur Frage der Koordinierung verschiedener spektralanalytischer Untersuchungsmethoden in der Urgeschichtsforschung. Loc. cit. 103–107.

36 Circumspectly advanced by C. Eibner, Legierung oder Lagerstätte? In: Festschrift für R. Pittioni 2. *ArchA Beiheft* 14 (Vienna/Horn 1976) 43–57.

37 Brief references in L. Pauli (Note 35) 404.

38 W. Modrijan, Die Erforschung des vor- und frühgeschichtlichen Berg- und Hüttenwesens und die Steiermark. In: *Der Bergmann – Der Hüttenmann* (exhibition catalogue Graz 1968) 41–87; H. Straube, B. Tarmann and E. Plöckinger, *Erzreduktionsversuche in Rennöfen norischer Bauart* (Klagenfurt 1964). – Studies on the history of iron-working in the Alps: H. Malzacher et al., *Ergebnisse und Folgerungen aus den gemeinsamen Untersuchungen deutscher und österreichischer Archäologen und Eisenhüttenleute zur Frage der frühgeschichtlichen Eisenverhüttung in Kärnten* (Düsseldorf 1964); G. Sperl, *Über die Typologie urzeitlicher, frühgeschichtlicher und mittelalterlicher Eisenhüttenschlacken* (Vienna 1980); H. Malzacher, Der norische Stahl. *Carinthia* I 160, 1970, 611–622. On steel now fully O. Schaber, H. Müller and I. Lehnert, Metallkundliche Untersuchungen zur Frühgeschichte der Metallurgie. *Arch. u. Naturwiss.* 1, 1977, 221–269.

39 W. Modrijan (Note 38) 72.

40 L. Pauli (Note 37) 406 with further literature.

41 Ibid. 349.

42 L. Schmidt, *Heiliges Blei in Amuletten, Votiven und anderen Gegenständen des Volksglaubens in Europa und im Orient* (Vienna 1958).

43 H. Wiessner, *Geschichte des Kärntner Bergbaues* 1. *Edelmetalle* (Klagenfurt 1950); R. Kerschagl, *Silber. Die metallischen Rohstoffe, ihre Lagerungsverhältnisse und ihre wirtschaftliche Bedeutung* 13 (Stuttgart 1961).

44 This might explain the remoteness of the West Alpine settlement of Sainte-Colombe: p. 86f.

45 N. Heger, Salzburg in römischer Zeit. *Jahresschr. Salzburger Mus. C. A.* 19, 1973, 132.

46 E. Preuschen, Die Salzburger Schwemmlandlagerstätten. *Berg- und hüttenmännische Monatshefte* 86, 1936, 36–45; W. Freh, Oberösterreichs Flussgold. *Oberösterr. Heimatbl.* 4, 1950, 17–32.

47 A. Hartmann in: L. Pauli (note 37) 603ff.

48 *Geogr.* IV 6, 12,

49 Zur ältesten Geschichte der Ostalpenländer. *ÖJh* 46, 1961–63, 209–228.

50 Miniera aurifera nelle Alpi orientali. *Aquileia Nostra* 45–46, 1974–75, 147–152.

51 F. Freise, *Geschichte der Bergbau- und Hüttentechnik* 1. *Das Altertum* (Berlin 1908, reprinted Wiesbaden 1971) 103f.; R. Forbes, *Studies in Ancient Technology* 8 (Leiden 1964) 175f.

52 Cf. Note 23.

53 K. Spindler, Zur Herstellung der Zinnbronze in der frühen Metallurgie Europas. *Acta Praehist. et. Arch.* 2, 1971, 199–253.

54 A. Mutz, Arbeitstechnische Unterscheidungen an frühmittelalterlichen Bronzegefässen aus Südbayern. *BVbl* 31, 1966, 134–141.

55 A smelting furnace with crucibles: G. Piccottini and H. Vetters, *Führer durch die Ausgrabungen auf dem Magdalensberg* (Klagenfurt 1978) 92 Ill. 27. – A detailed description of the technique: M. Martin, Römische Bronzegiesser in Augst BL. *AS* 1, 1978, 112–120.

56 Exact description of the operations in M. Seeberger, *Der Kupferschmied. Sterbendes Handwerk* 21 (Basel 1969).

57 H. Hirschhuber, Helm, Flasche und Situla aus dem Fürstengrab. Bemerkungen zu ihrer Restaurierung und Beobachtungen zur vorgeschichtlichen Toreutik. In: E. Penninger, *Der Dürrnberg bei Hallein* 1 (Munich 1972) 97–119.

58 A. Rieth and K. Langenbacher, *Die Entwicklung der Drehbank* (Stuttgart/Cologne 1954); A. Mutz, *Die Kunst des Metalldrehens bei den Römern. Interpretationen antiker Arbeitsverfahren auf Grund von Werkspuren* (Basel/Stuttgart 1972). Some Iron Age examples in L. Pauli (Note 37) 402f.

59 Th. E. Haevernick, Zu den Glasperlen in Slowenien. In: *Opuscula J. Kastelic sexagenario dicata. Situla* 14–15, 1974, 61–65.

60 Th. E. Haevernick. *JbRGZM* 5, 1958, 8–17; K. Kromer, *Das Gräberfeld von Hallstatt* (Florence 1959) Pl. 216; F. Moosleitner, Ein Hallstattzeitlicher 'Fürstensitz' am Hellbrunnerberg bei Salzburg. *Germania* 57, 1979, 70 Ill. 14, 1.

61 Th. E. Haevernick, Funde aus fernen Ländern. *HelvA* 10, 1979, 50–57; id., Gesichtsperlen. *Madrider Mitt.* 18, 1977, 152–231; id., Perlen mit zusammengesetzten Augen. *Prähist. Zeitschr.* 47, 1972, 78–93.

62 O. Schauberger, *Ein Rekonstruktionsversuch der prähistorischen Grubenbaue im Hallstätter Salzberg* (Horn/Vienna 1960); id., *Die vorgeschichtlichen Grubenbaue im Salzberg Dürrnberg/Hallein* (Horn/

Vienna 1968); id., Neue Aufschlüsse im 'Heidengebirge' von Hallstatt und Dürrnberg/Hallein. *MAGW* 106, 1976, 154–160.

63 F. E. Barth, Neuentdeckte Schrämspuren im Heidengebirge des Salzberges zu Hallstatt, OÖ. *MAGW* 100, 1970, 153–156; id., Die Erforschung des prähistorischen Salzbergwerkes in Hallstatt. *Oberösterreich* 22, 1972, 16–20; id., Ein prähistorischer Salzbarren aus dem Salzbergwerk Hallstatt. *Ann. Naturhist. Mus. Wien* 80, 1976, 819–821; id., Abbauversuche im Salzbergwerk Hallstatt. *Der Anschnitt* 28/1, 1976, 25–29.

64 F. E. Barth, H. Felber and O. Schauberger, Radiokohlenstoffdatierung der prähistorischen Baue in den Salzbergwerken Hallstatt und Dürrnberg-Hallein. *MAGW* 105, 1975, 45–52.

65 F. E. Barth, Salzbergwerk und Gräberfeld von Hallstatt. In: *Krieger und Salzherren.* Exhibition catalogue Mainz (1970) 40–52.

66 L. Pauli (Note 37) 487.

67 N. Heger (Note 45) 132.

68 See Note 63.

69 H.-J. Hundt, Vorgeschichtliche Gewebe aus dem Hallstätter Salzberg. *JbRGZM* 6, 1959, 66–100; 7, 1960, 126–150; 14, 1967, 38–67. A summary: id., Gewebefunde aus Hallstatt. Webkunst und Tracht in der Hallstattzeit. In: *Krieger und Salzherren.* Exhibition catalogue Mainz (1970) 53–71. – Id., Neunzehn Textilreste aus dem Dürrnberg in Hallein. *JbRGZM* 8, 1961, 7–25; id., Die Textilreste aus den Gräbern vom Dürrnberg. In: F. Moosleitner, L. Pauli and E. Penninger, *Der Dürrnberg bei Hallein* 2 (Munich 1974) 135–142.

70 F. Morton, Die Auffindung eines vorgeschichtlichen Bos brachyceros-Hornes mit Bergmannsexkrementen im Hallstätter Salzbergwerk. *Kali, verwandte Salze und Erdöl* 35, 1941, 134–135.

71 F. E. Barth, Ein prähistorisches Signalhorn aus dem Salzbergwerk in Hallstatt. *MAGW* 100, 1970, 157.

72 H. Klein, Der Fundort des 'Mannes im Salz'. *Mitt. Ges. Salzburger Landeskde.* 101, 1961, 139–141.

73 E. Penninger and G. Stadler, *Hallein – Ursprung und Geschichte der Salinenstadt* (Salzburg 1970) 241.

74 H.-J. Hundt, *JbRGZM* 7, 1960, 148.

75 H. Aspöck et al., Parasitäre Erkrankungen des Verdauungstraktes bei prähistorischen Bergleuten von Hallstatt und Hallein (Österreich). *MAGW* 103, 1973, 41–47.

76 F. Moosleitner, Eine Unterlagsplatte für eine Töpferscheibe vom Dürrnberg bei Hallein, Land Salzburg. *ArchA* 56, 1974, 13–20.

77 O.-H. Frey, Hallstatt und die Hallstattkultur. *Mitt. Österr. Arbeitsgem. Ur- u. Frühgesch.* 22, 1971, 110–114; I. Kilian-Dirlmeier, Beobachtungen zur Struktur des Gräberfeldes von Hallstatt. Loc. cit. 71–72; L. Pauli (Note 37) 492ff.

78 Whether in the late La Tène period brine was actually evaporated on the 'Dammwiese' above Hallstatt, farther up in the Salzberg valley, can scarcely be ascertained from the few definite findings and reports: F. Morton, Das Problem der Dammwiese. *Heimatgaue* (Linz) 1930, 240–259; id., *Hallstatt und die Hallstattzeit*

(Hallstatt 1953) 99–103. – Currently G. Weisberger of the Deutsches Bergbau-Museum (Bochum) is inclined to postulate that natural and artificial brine was being evaporated at Hallstatt even after the early Hallstatt period. This most recent opinion is based on some water reservoirs built of timbers (see Chapter II, Note 61); these are, however, also known at places where there is no salt production. It is hoped that further investigations will settle this question: G. Weisberger, Noch einmal zu den Blockwandbauten am Hallstätter Salzberg. *ArchKorrbl* 11, 1981, 119–125.

79 *De agri cultura* 58.

80 M. Ladurner-Parthanes, Feiertage und Essensbräuche im Burggrafenamt vor 1900. *Der Schlern* 48, 1974, 186–196. With clarity also P. Rachbauer, Essen und Trinken vor 1200. In: *Nibelungenlied*. Exhibition catalogue Hohenems (1979) 135–143.

81 *Südbayern während der Hallstattzeit* (Berlin 1959).

82 *Primitive Money* (2nd edn Oxford 1966) 309ff.

83 Distribution map of ring-ingots after H.-J. Hundt, *PrAlp* 10, 1974, 148 Ill. 6. Finally the bar-ingots in O. Kleemann, Eine neue Verbreitungskarte der Spangenbarren. *ArchA* 14, 1954, 68–77, supplemented for the hoard-finds on the Middle Danube by E. Schubert, *Germania* 44, 1966, 280 Ill. 1.

84 H.-J. Hundt (Note 83) 146f.

85 F. Moosleitner, Ein Sparrenbarrendepot aus Obereching an der Salzach, Salzburg. *ArchA* 53, 1973, 40.

86 M. Primas, *Jahresber. Inst. Vorgesch. Univ. Frankfurt a. M.* 1977, 171.

87 Some further examples: from the Mittersee at Elixhausen (Salzburg): L. Franz, *Wirtschaftsformen der Vorzeit* (2nd edn Brno 1943) Ill. 23; Feldkirch (Vorarlberg): A. Hild, Ein Verwahrfund aus Feldkirch, Vorarlberg. *ArchA* 1, 1948, 88–90.

88 E. F. Mayer, Die Äxte und Beile in Österreich. *Prähist. Bronzefunde* IX 9 (Munich 1977) 14f. 256f.

89 E. g. the Limmat in Zurich: *UFAS* IV, 106 Ill. 1, 1.

90 The final stage of the spread of the double-pyramid-shaped ingots can be seen by studying two maps in conjunction: W. Kimmig, *Germania* 49, 1971, Pl. 7,1 and *PrFr* II, 240 Ill. 2 top. The find from the Splügen pass (Ill. 161) offers an important addition at the southern edge of the distribution area.

91 K. Pink, *Einführung in die keltische Münzkunde mit besonderer Berücksichtigung Österreichs* (3rd edn Vienna 1974); B. Overbeck, *Die Welt der Kelten im Spiegel der Münzen* (Munich in preparation); R. Göbl, *Typologie und Chronologie keltischer Münzprägung in Noricum* (Vienna 1973); G. Dembski, Die keltischen Fundmünzen aus Österreich. *Numism. Zeitschr.* 87–88, 1972, 37ff.; A. Pautasso, *Le monete preromane dell'Italia settentrionale* (Milan 1966); H.-J. Kellner, Zur Goldprägung der Helvetier. In: *Provincialia (Festschr. für R. Laur-Belart)* (Basel 1968) 588–602.

92 M. Menke, Schrötlingsformen für keltisches Silbergeld aus Karlstein, Ldkr. Berchtesgaden (Oberbayern). *Germania* 46, 1968, 27–35.

93 Besides Lauterach (Ill. 162) a find from a bog at Bruggen (canton St Gallen) should be mentioned: J. Heierli, *Anz. Schweiz. Altertumskde.* N. F. 5, 1903–04, 247f.; H.-M. v. Kaenel, Der Münzschatzfund von Bruggen – Sankt Gallen. *Schweiz. Num. Rundschau* 60, 1981, 41–63.

94 R. Egger, Die Stadt auf dem Magdalensberg, ein Grosshandelsplatz. Die ältesten Aufzeichnungen des Metallwarenhandels auf dem Boden Österreichs. *Denkschr. Österr. Akad. d. Wiss., phil.-hist. Kl.* 79 (Vienna 1961); G. Piccottini and H. Vetters, *Führer durch die Ausgrabungen auf dem Magdalensberg* (Klagenfurt 1978) 45.

95 For instance R. Egger, *Carinthia* I 159, 1969, 396ff. Ills 64–66.

96 A large, egg-shaped stone weighing 52.5 kg (= 1000 Gallic ounces of 52.8 g) seems to indicate a weighing-machine: R. Egger, Ein Gewicht nack keltischem Mass. *Carinthia* I 156, 1966, 478–481 with Ill. 134.

97 In the end R. Egger came to the conclusion that these were marks for identifying items of clothing that were used in some sort of cleaning and dyeing establishments employing cutters and menders (Fünf Bleietiketten und eine Gussform. Die neuesten Magdalensbergfunde. *Anz. Österr. Akad. d. Wiss., phil.-hist. Kl.* 104, 1967, 195–210; *Carinthia* I 159, 1969, 401–403). The new find from the little road-station of *Immurium* (Note 99) again supports the old interpretation, for it seems highly improbable that there would have been such an establishment with a regular clientele up there.

98 R. Egger, Epigraphische Nachlese 1. Bleietiketten aus dem rätischen Alpenvorland. *ÖJh* 46, 1961–63, 185–197.

99 E. Weber, Ein Bleietikett aus Immurium – Moosham. *ÖJh* 49, 1968–71, Beibl. 229–234.

100 R. Egger, Inschriften auf Ess- und Trinkgeschirr vom Magdalensberg. In: *Provincialia (Festschr. für R. Laur-Belart)* (Basel 1968) 269–277.

101 M. Hornberger, *Gesamtbeurteilung der Tierknochenfunde aus der Stadt auf dem Magdalensberg in Kärnten (1948–1966)* (Klagenfurt 1970); H. L. Werneck, *Pflanzenreste aus der Stadt auf dem Magdalensberg bei Klagenfurt in Kärnten* (Klagenfurt 1969).

102 R. Egger, Der Lebensmittelimport aus Italien auf dem Magdalensberg. *Carinthia* I 159, 1969, 410–416.

103 H. Vetters and G. Piccottini, *Die Ausgrabungen auf dem Magdalensberg 1969–1972* (Klagenfurt 1973) 307 No. 24. The complement d(ulce) would also be a possibility.

104 H. Gummerus, Der römische Gutsbetrieb als wirtschaftlicher Organismus nach den Werken des Cato, Varro und Columella. *Klio* Beiheft 5 (Wiesbaden 1906, reprinted Aalen 1963); H. Dohr, *Die italischen Gutshöfe in den Schriften Catos und Varros* (Diss. Colegne 1965).

105 Cf. for instance W. Drack, Die Gutshöfe. *UFAS* V, 49; W. Czysz, *Der römische Gutshof in München-Denning und die römerzeitliche Besiedlung der Münchner Schotterebene* (Kallmünz 1974) 40f.; id., Situationstypen römischer Gutshöfe im Nördlinger Ries. *Zeitschr.*

Hist. Ver. Schwaben 72, 1978, 70–94; S. Martin-Kilcher, *Das römische Gräberfeld von Courroux im Berner Jura* (Basel 1976) 139ff.; id., *Die Funde aus dem römischen Gutshof von Laufen-Müschhag* (Bern 1980) 113ff.

106 Thus Pliny the Younger possessed a whole range of *villae* around Como and around *Tifernum-Tiberinum* in Umbria. Letters IX 7 to those on the Lake of Como: 'On its shores several country houses belong to me. Two of them give me particular pleasure. . .' Cf. also Chapter III Note 95.

107 Clearly summarized by A. Mutz, Römisches Schmiedehandwerk. *Augster Museumhefte* 1 (Augst 1976); W. Gaitzsch, *Eiserne römische Werkzeuge* (Oxford 1980). Regarding the general status of the craftsmen A. Burford, *Craftsmen in Greek and Roman Society* (London 1972).

108 On the first workshops in Arezzo (central Italy): H. Comfort et al., *Terra sigillata – La ceramica a rilievo ellenistica e romana* (Rome n.d. = offprint from Enciclopedia dell'arte antica classica e orientale); H. Dragendorff and C. Watzinger, *Arretinische Reliefkeramik* (Reutlingen 1948). – From early in the first century AD new workshops in the south of France supplied western Central Europe: B. Pferdehirt, *Die römischen Terra-Sigillata-Töpfereien in Südgallien* (Stuttgart 1978). They were followed by those in central France: J. A. Stanfield and G. Simpson, *Central Gaulish Potters* (London 1958). – Between 160 and 170 at the latest the potteries in Rheinzabern (Palatinate) were started up and promptly controlled the market, while also supplying the Western Alpine territory to the south; on the most recent excavations H. G. Rau, Die römische Töpferei in Rheinzabern. *Mitt. Hist. Ver. Pfalz* 75, 1977, 47–73 and *Terra Sigillata in Rheinzabern* (Museum catalogue Rheinzabern n.d. [1977?]). – Only a few years later branch installations were set up near the edge of the Alps on the Inn, whose products were traded to the Southeast: H.-J. Kellner, *Die Sigillatatöpfereien von Westerndorf und Pfaffenhofen* (Stuttgart 1973); the last distribution map for the Pfaffenhofen wares in D. Gabler, *Acta Arch. Hung.* 30, 1978, 97 Ill. 18. – On small works of recent times, which met a local demand, E. Ettlinger and K. Roth-Rubi, *Helvetische Reliefsigillaten und die Rolle der Werkstatt Bern-Enge* (Bern 1979) 23–25.

109 S. and M. Martin, Geflicktes Geschirr aus dem römischen Augst. In: *Festschrift E. Schmid* (= *Regio Basiliensis* 18/1, Basel 1977) 148–171.

110 There is as yet no distribution map; the boundary can only be marked out roughly by means of individual find-spots. Cologne: M. Riedel, Drei bemerkenswerte Gefässfunde aus dem römischen Hafengelände in Köln. *ArchKorrbl* 6, 1976, 321–324; Trier: R. Schindler, *Führer durch das Landesmuseum Trier* (Trier 1977) Ill. 240; Enns: *Fundber. aus Österreich* 15, 1976, 283 Ill. 21; H. Ubl, Das erste Lavezgefäss aus Lauriacum. *Mitt. Museumsver. 'Lauriacum' Enns* N. F. 15, 1977, 7–10; E. M. Ruprechtsberger, Ein Lavezgefäss aus Lauriacum. *ArchKorrbl* 11, 1981, 145–147. The area where it was in regular use was of course much smaller.

The situation in the Western Alps, however, calls for further investigation. There appear to be places where deposits of steatite occur. I am indebted to W. Dehn (Marburg) for information on residue from steatite-turning that was found at Chambéry and points to a workshop there. Indeed there are some steatite vessels in the Annecy museum, found in the Roman town of *Boutae* not far away.

111 E. A. Gessler, Die Lavezstein-Industrie. *Anz. Schweiz. Altertumskde.* N. F. 38, 1936, 108–116; O. Lurati, *L'ultimo laveggiaio di Val Malenco* (Basel 1970); A. Mutz, Die Technologie der alten Lavezdreherei. *Schweiz. Archiv f. Volkskde.* 73, 1977, 42–62.

112 The earliest dateable vessels from early Roman times are not as yet turned but shaped by hand: G. Graeser, Ein hochalpiner gallorömischer Siedlungsfund im Binntal (Wallis). In: *Provincialia (Festschrift für R. Laur-Belart)* (Basel 1968) 345f.

113 Chr. Zindel, *AS* 2, 1979, 111.

114 This still applies extensively to medieval castles: M.-L. Boscardin and W. Meyer, *Burgenforschung in Graubünden* (Olten 1977) 97ff.

115 *Not. Dign. Occ.* XXXV 21–22.

116 On the problem of interpretation cf. F. Lotter in: J. Werner and E. Ewig (eds), *Von der Spätantike zum frühen Mittelalter* (Sigmaringen 1979) 63–72.

117 *Vita Severini* 29, 1. According to the legend, the men who carried the loads *collo suo*–on their own backs–owe their safe arrival at their destination solely to a bear which 'for a distance of 200 miles' laid the course after they had been snowed-in on the pass.

118 F. Lotter (Note 116) 71f. likewise only cites the two examples mentioned here, but none the less claims 'a money economy that continued to function until 476'.

119 For the relevant costs cf. W. Sölter, *Römische Kalkbrenner im Rheinland* (Düsseldorf 1970).

120 In Invillino the houses were built of wood, the church alone having cemented walls (pp. 124ff.). – In the Edict of the Lombard king Rothari issued 645, the 'Masters from Como' are moreover referred to for the first time as master-builders and stone-cutters, whose capabilities were in demand south as well as north of the Alps up until the Baroque period.

121 F. Lotter (Note 116) 70.

122 A stimulating overview for western Central Europe in G. Duby, *The early growth of the European economy. Warriors and peasants from the seventh to the twelfth century* (London 1974).

123 C. Schott, *UFAS* VI, 209.

124 J. Werner (ed.), *Die Ausgrabungen in St Ulrich und Afra in Augsburg 1961–1968* (Munich 1977) 333–337; id., in: J. Werner and E. Ewig (Note 116) 463f.

125 G. Duby, *Warriors and peasants* (Note 122) 61ff.

126 Lex Baiuvariorum: MGH LL I 5; K. Beyerle, *Lex Baiuvariorum. Lichtdruckwiedergabe der Ingolstädter Handschrift des bayerischen Volksrechts mit Transkription*, Textnoten, Übersetzung, Einführung, Literaturübersicht und Glossar (Munich 1926); B. Krusch, *Die Lex Baiuvariorum* (Berlin 1924). – Leges Alamannorum: MGH LL 3 and 5, 1; Leges Alamannorum, edited by K. A. Eckhardt (Göttingen 1958 and 1962). – Leges Langobardorum: MGH LL 4; F. Beyerle, *Die Gesetze der Langobarden* (Weimar 1947); Leges Langobardorum 643–866, edited by F. Beyerle (Witzenhausen 1962); Edictum Rotharis Regis, translated into italian by M. Boroli in: B. Barni, *I Longobardi in Italia* (Novara 1974) 393–444.

127 One of the few assessments: A. von den Driesch, *Viehhaltung*

und Jagd auf der mittelalterlichen Burg Schiedberg bei Sagogn in Graubünden (Chur 1973).

128 H. Roth, Bemerkungen zur Totenberaubung während der Merowingerzeit. *ArchKorrbl* 7, 1977, 287–290; id., Archäologische Beobachtungen zum Grabfrevel im Merowingerreich. In: H. Jankuhn, H. Nehlsen and H. Roth (eds), *Zum Grabfrevel in vor- und frühgeschichtlicher Zeit. Abhandl. Akad. d. Wiss. Göttingen, phil.-hist. Kl.* 3. Series 113 (Göttingen 1978) 73f.

129 G. Duby, *Warriors and peasants* (Note 122) 13–17.

Sources of illustrations

Half-title After *Arte Preistorica della Valcamonica.* Exhibition catalogue Milan (1974) No. VII–17a;

1 Mario Broggi, Triesen (Liechtenstein); **2** After G. Nangeroni, Atti *CSDIR* 7, 1975–76, 24 Ill. 9; **3** After H. de Lumley in: *Sites paléolithiques de la région de Nice et Grottes de Grimaldi* (Nice 1976) 101 Ill. 49; **4** Historisches Museum, Bern; **5** After Chr. Strahm, *PrAlp* 10, 1974, 34 Ill. 13; **6** After A. Gallay in: *Glockenbecher-Symposion Oberried 1974* (Bussum/Haarlem 1976) 299 Ill. 15, 1; **7** After K. Spindler, Die frühbronzezeitlichen Flügelnadeln. *JbSGU* 57, 1972–73, 17ff. with Ills 1ff.; **8** Service archéologique cantonal, Fribourg; **9** Design Ludwig Pauli (cf. Chapter I Note 53); **10** Naturhistorisches Museum, Vienna; **11** Bayer. Landesamt für Denkmalpflege, Abt. Bodendenkmalpflege, Munich (L. Römmelt); **12** Historisches Museum, Bern; **13** Schweizerisches Landesmuseum, Zurich; **14** Hubert Häusler, Munich; **15** Adaptation Günther Sturm, Munich; **16** Landesmuseum für Kärnten, Klagenfurt; **17** Staatliche Münzsammlung, Munich; **18** Robert Berger, Cologne; **19** After B. Andreae, Romische Kunst (Freiburg/Basel/Vienna 1973) Ill. 891; **20** Hubert Häusler, Munich; **21** Hubert Häusler, Munich; **22**

Design Ludwig Pauli based on H. W. Böhme, *JbRGZM* 222, 1975, 163 Ill. 2; **23** Bayer. Landesamt für Denkmalpflege, Abt. Bodendenkmalpflege, Munich; **24** Ludwig Pauli; **25** Foto Anderson, Rome; **26** Bayer. Landesamt für Denkmalpflege, Abt. Bodendenkmalpflege, Munich; **27** Militärflugdienst Dübendorf (canton Zurich); **28–29** Foto Marburg; **30** After C. Carducci, *Atti CSDIR* 7, 1975–76, 101 Ill. 17; **31** Rudolf Degen, Zurich; **32** Kantonale Denkmalpflege, Zurich; **33–34** Renato Perini, Trento; **35–37** Layout Jürg Rageth, Chur; **38** After W. Lucke and O.-H. Frey, *Die Situla in Providence (Rhode Island)* (Berlin 1962) Pl. 67; **39** Historisches Museum, Bern; **40** After E. Anati, *Civiltà preistorica della Valcamonica* (Milan 1964) 212 Ills 156–157; **41** Hubert Häusler, Munich; **42–43** Adaptation Günther Sturm, Munich; **44** Design Ludwig Pauli; drawing Günther Sturm, Munich; **45** After R. Perini, *2000 anni di vita sui Montesei di Serso*, Exhibition catalogue Pergine/Trento (1978) 53; **46** Salzburger Museum Carolino Augusteum; **47** Landesmuseum für Kärnten, Klagenfurt; **48** Salzburger Museum Carolino Augusteum; **49–50** Hubert Häusler, Munich; **51** After a frequently reproduced plan, finally in W. Schleiermacher, *Cambodunum-Kempten, eine Römerstadt im Allgäu* (Bonn 1972), Ill. 2; **52** Robert Berger, Cologne; **53–54** Layout

Günther Sturm, Munich; **55** Adaptation Günther Sturm, Munich; **56** Hubert Häusler, Munich; **57** Adaptation Günther Sturm, Munich; **58** Rätisches Museum, Chur; **59** Based on I. Schwidetzky in: L. Pauli, Der Dürrnberg bei Hallein III (Munich 1978) 566 Ill. 1; **60** Rätisches Museum, Chur/Archäologischer Dienst Graubünden, Chur; **61** After D.-J. Bocksberger, *JbSGU* 56, 1971, 87 Ill. 12; **62** After A. Gallay, *BCSP* 12, 1975, 111 Ill. 42; **63** After E. Anati, *Civiltà preistorica della Valcamonica* (Milan 1964) 135 Ill. 87; **64** After R. Perini, *PrAlp* 11, 1975, 296 Ill. 1; **65** Bayer. Landesamt für Denkmalpflege, Abt. Bodendenkmalpflege, Munich; **66** Schweizerisches Landesmuseum, Zurich; **67** Service archéologique cantonal, Fribourg; **68** Fritz Moosleitner, Salzburg; **69** Steiermärkisches Landesmuseum Joanneum, Graz; **70** Design Ludwig Pauli; **71** Keltenmuseum, Hallein (Alfons Coreth, Salzburg); **72** After G. v. Merhart in: Festschrift des Römisch-Germanischen Zentralmuseums in Mainz (Mainz 1952) Pl. 26; **73** Naturhistorisches Museum, Vienna; **74** Drawing Römisch-Germanisches Zentralmuseum, Mainz; **75** Historisches Museum, Bern; **76** Steiermärkisches Landesmuseum Joanneum, Graz; **77** Landesmuseum für Kärnten, Klagenfurt; **78** Rätisches Museum, Chur/Archäologischer Dienst Graubünden, Chur; **79** After E. Keller,

ArchKorrbl 3, 1973, 447ff. Ills 2–3; **80** Historisches Museum, Bern; **81** After F. Wieser, *Das langobardische Fürstengrab und Reihengräberfeld von Civezzano* (Innsbruck 1887) Pl. I; **82** Werner Stöckli, Moudon (Foto Fibbi-Aeppli, Moudon); **83** Kunsthistorisches Museum, Vienna; **84** After O. Tschumi, *Urgeschichte der Schweiz* 1 (Frauenfeld 1949) 513 Ill. 205, 2; **85** After H. Müller-Karpe, *Handbuch der Vorgeschichte* 1 (Munich 1966) Pl. 225 A 7; **86** After *PrAlp* 8, 1972, 273 Ills 25–26 and 9, 1973, 245f. Ills 2–3; **87** Historisches Museum, Bern; **88** Schweizerisches Landesmuseum, Zurich, in conjunction with R. Wyss, Fruchtbarkeits-, Bitt- und Dankopfer um Gutenberg. *HelvA* 9, 1978, 151ff.; **89** After A. Zürcher, HelvA 3/9, 1972, 23; **90** After G. B. Pellegrini and A. L. Prosdocimi, *La lingua venetica* 1. *Le iscrizioni* (Padua 1967): Ca 14; **91** Ludwig Pauli; **92** Schweizerisches Landesmuseum, Zurich; **93** Rätisches Museum, Chur; **94** Schweizerisches Landesmuseum, Zurich; **95** After W. Lucke and O.-H. Frey, *Die Situla in Providence (Rhode Island)* (Berlin 1962) Pl. 73; **96** After W. Schmid, *Prähist. Zeitschr.* 24, 1933, 268 Ill. 45b; **97** Design Ludwig Pauli, based on O.-H. Frey, *Germania* 44, 1966, 51 Ill. 3 and 55 Ill. 5; **98** After E. Anati, *Evoluzione e stile nell'arte rupestre Camuna* (Capo di Ponte 1975) 74 Ill. 61; **99** Centro Camuno di Studi Preistorici, Capo di Ponte; **100** After *Arte preistoica del-*

la Valcamonica. Exhibition catalogue Milan (1974) No. XI–15; **101** Rätisches Museum, Chur; **102** Foto Fürbeck, Graz; **103** After *Arte preistorica della Valcamonica.* Exhibition catalogue Milan (1974) No. X–7; **104** Prähistorische Staatssammlung, Munich; **105** After A. Crivelli, *Riv. Arch. Como* 159, 1977, 27 Ill. 9; **106** Ludwig Pauli; **107** Vorarlberger Landesmuseum, Bregenz; **108** Kurt W. Zeller, Salzburg; **109** Prähistorische Staatssammlung, Munich; **110** Service archéologique cantonal, Fribourg; **111** After E. Egger in: W. Krämer, *Cambodunumforschungen 1953–I* (Kallmünz 1957) 73 Ill. 8; **112** Reinhold Leitner, Sterzing; **113** Service archéologique cantonal, Fribourg; **114** After *UrSchweiz* 33, 1969, 76 Ill. 19; **115** Volker Bierbrauer, Munich; **116** Volker Bierbrauer, Munich; adaptation Günther Sturm, Munich; **117** Musée Valère, Sion; **118** Schweizerisches Landesmuseum, Zurich; **119** Landesmuseum für Kärnten, Klagenfurt; **120** Landesdenkmalamt Bozen (H. Walder); **121** Hubert Häusler, Munich; **122** Walter Drack, Zurich; **123** Design Ludwig Pauli; **124** Service archéologique cantonal, Fribourg; **125** Römisch-Germanisches Zentralmuseum, Mainz; **126** Schweizerisches Landesmuseum, Zurich; **127–130** Ludwig Pauli; **131** Erwin Keller, Munich; **132** Landesmuseum für Kärnten, Klagenfurt; **133** From

the facsimile edition of the 'Tabula Peutingeriana', Codex vindobonensis 324 of the Akademische Druck- und Verlangsanstalt, Graz 1976; **134** Design Ludwig Pauli; **135** Adaptation H. Holzbauer, Munich, in: H. Bender, *Römische Strassen und Strassenstationen* (Stuttgart 1975) 55 Ill. 26; **136** Adaptation H. Holzbauer, Munich, in: H. Bender (as **132**) Ill. 25; **137** Soprintendenza alle Antichità, Aosta; **138** Design Volker Bierbrauer, Munich; adaptation Günther Sturm, Munich; **139** Rätisches Museum, Chur; **140** Adaptation Günther Sturm, Munich; **141** Sabine Rieckhoff-Pauli, Regensburg; **142** Römisch-Germanisches Zentralmuseum, Mainz; **143** After R. Perini, *PrAlp* 8, 1972, 253 Ill. 31, 500–501; **144** After W. Lucke and O.-H. Frey, *Die Situla in Providence (Rhode Island)* (Berlin 1962) Pl. 76 and W. Schmid, *Prähist. Zeitschr.* 24, 1933, Pl. I; **145** After *PrFr* II, 492 Ill. 6, 1; **146** After G. Kyrle, *Urgeschichte des Kronlandes Salzburg* (Vienna 1918) supplement II, 2 Ill. 1; **147** Bayer, Landesamt für Denkmalpflege, Abt. Bodendenkmalpflege, Munich; **148** Rätisches Museum, Chur; **149** Bayer, Landesamt für Denkmalpflege, Munich (L. Römmelt); **150** Historisches Museum, Bern; **151** Service archéologique cantonal, Fribourg; **152** Based on an original model by R. Wyss, Technik, Wirtschaft, Handel und

Kriegswesen der Eisenzeit. In: *UFAS* IV, 126 Ill. 22; **153** As 149, 120 Ill. 14; **154** Naturhistorisches Museum, Vienna; **155** After F. E. Barth in: *Krieger und Salzherren.* Exhibition catalogue Mainz (1970) 46 Ill. 2; **156** Models Fritz Eckhart Barth, Vienna; **157** After K. Kromer, *Das Gräberfeld von Hallstatt* (Florence 1959); **158** Reproduced from an old postcard; **159** Ludwig Pauli; **160** Rätisches Museum, Chur; **161** After H.-J. Hundt, *PrAlp* 10, 1974, 148 Ill. 6; **162** Based on a photo in the Vorarlberger Landesmuseum, Bregenz (Toni Schneiders, Lindau); **163** Steiermärkisches Landesmuseum Joanneum, Graz; **164** Models Gudrun Schneider, Markdorf; **165** Bundesdenkmalamt, Vienna

Where 're-drawings' are concerned details of the original appear in the publications named in the Notes.

Bibliographical references for some of the illustrations

18 Important as an introduction to the question of publicly erected statues: *Die Bildnisse des Augustus. Herrscherbild und Politik im kaiserlichen Rom.* Exhibition catalogue Munich/Berlin (1978/79).

29 A. Alföldi, Die Goldkanne von Saint-Maurice. *ZSAK* 10, 1948, 1–27.
75 R. Wyss, Das Schwert des Korisios. Zur Entdeckung einer griechischen Inschrift. *Jahrb. Hist. Mus. Bern* 34, 1954, 201–222.
91 L. Pauli, Ein latènezeitliches Steinrelief aus Bormio am Stilfser Joch. *Germania* 51, 1973, 85–120; abridged version with further contributions by F. Rittatore Vonwiller and M. Sordi: *Rivista Arch. Como* 152–155, 1970–73, 91ff. 113ff. 125ff.
102 W. Schmid, *Der Kultwagen von Strettweg* (Leipzig 1934); W. Modrijan, Der Kultwagen von Strettweg. *Jahrb. f. prähist. u. ethnograph. Kunst* 24, 1974–77, 91–97.
105 W. Burkart and J. Whatmough, Die Schnabelkanne von Castaneda. *Anz. f. Schweiz. Altertumskunde* N. F. 40, 1938, 119–123.
137 *Not. Scavi* 1924, 391; C. Carducci, Un busto argenteo di Giove nel Museo di Aosta. *Boll. d'Arte* 31, 1937–38, 73–80.
142 H.-J. Hundt, Die Bronzeschnabelkanne aus Grab 112. Bericht über ihre Restaurierung und die Technik ihrer Herstellung. In: F. Moosleitner, L. Pauli and E. Penninger, *Der Dürrnberg bei Hallein* 2 (Munich 1974) 125–132.
165 G. Haseloff, *Der Tassilokelch* (Munich 1951); id., Zum Stand der Forschung über den Tassilokelch. In: *Baiernzeit in Oberösterreich.* Exhibition catalogue Linz (1977) 221–236.

Index of place-names

Index of place-names

(I) = illustration; (M) = map
Where archaeological cultures have derived their names from a find-spot in the Alpine region, this is indicated in the first instance, otherwise only by way of direct reference.

Austria

Aguntum (East Tyrol) 38, 40, 43, 54, 97, 106, 228
Albing (Lower Austria) 41, 132
Althofen (Carinthia) 227
Arlberg, pass (North Tyrol, Vorarlberg) 211, 235, 236
Attersee (Upper Austria) 17, 74
Au. a. L. (Lower Austria) 127
Bad Deutsch Altenburg (Lower Austria) see *Carnuntum*
Bad Ischl (Upper Austria) *Kienbachklamm* 170
Bischofshofen see *Mitterberg*
Bregenz (Vorarlberg) 40, 48, 57, 97, 137, 178 (I), 211, 227, 262
Brenner see under Italy
Carnuntum (Lower Austria) 59, 60, 238
Dölsach (East Tyrol) see *Aguntum*
Donawitz, Stadt Leoben (Styria) 129 (I)
Drachenhöhle near Mixnitz (Styria) 12
Dürrnberg see Hallein
Ehrwald (North Tyrol) 211
Enns (Upper Austria) see *Lauriacum*
Felber Tauern (Salzburg, East Tyrol) 202
Feldkirch (Vorarlberg) 235
Flavia Solva near Leibnitz (Styria) 40, 92, 202
Fritzens (North Tyrol) 27
Frög (Carinthia) 26
Fussach (Vorarlberg) 235
Gailbergsattel (Carinthia) 202, 228
Graz (Styria) 54
Grein (Upper Austria) 156
Gummern (Carinthia) 227
Hallein (Salzburg) 24, 25, 26 (I), 27, 31, 84 (I), 85, 85 (I), 86, 89, 92 (I), 111, 112, 112 (I), 125 (I), 152, 166 (M), 170, 180 (I), 201, 203 (I), 204, 236, 238 (I), 247 (I), 248, 253-60
Hallstatt (Upper Austria) 24, 25, 26, 28, 29, 31, 83, 126, 127 (I), 152, 165, 166 (M), 201, 202, 253-9
Hochkönig (Salzburg) 244
Hochtor, pass at the Grossglockner (Salzburg, Carinthia) 160, 202
Hohenstein (Carinthia) 136
Hohentauern, pass (Styria) 227
Hölzelsau (North Tyrol) 175 (I)

Immurium (Salzburg) 182, 217, 218 (I), 219, 262
Innsbruck (North Tyrol) 62, 209
Innsbruck-Vill (North Tyrol) 87
Innsbruck-Wilten (North Tyrol) *Veldidena* 48, 57, 211, 226, 227
Iselsberg, pass (East Tyrol, Carinthia) 202
Judenburg (Styria) 202
Kalsdorf (Styria) 264 (I)
Karnburg (Carinthia) 60
Katsch a. d. Mur (Styria) 101, 227
Katschberg, pass (Salzburg, Carinthia) 202, 209
Kitzbühel (North Tyrol) *Kelchalpe* 245
Klagenfurt (Carinthia) 133 (I)
Kleinklein (Styria) 26, 123 (I), 164
Köttlach (Lower Austria) 146
Kremsmünster (Upper Austria) 59, 146, 189, 230, 267 (I)
Kuchl (Salzburg) 50, 57
Kuffarn (Lower Austria) 166 (M)
Kufstein (North Tyrol) 193
Lauriacum/Lorch (Upper Austria) 41, 42 (M), 50, 57, 91, 132, 183, 266
Lausnitzhöhe, pass (Salzburg, Carinthia) 209, 217
Lauterach (Vorarlberg) 263 (I)
Lavant (East Tyrol) 97, 106, 186
Leibnitz (Styria) 202; see also *Flavia Solva*
Lienz (East Tyrol) 38, 40, 97, 135, 202; see also *Aguntum*
Linz (Upper Austria) 57, 227
Löffelbach (Styria) 40, 98 (I), 101, 102
Loig (Salzburg) 101
Lustenau (Vorarlberg) 156
Magdalensberg (Carinthia) 30, 33, 34 (I), 89, 90 (I), 91, 92, 93, 147 (I), 170, 176, 246, 262
Mallnitzer Tauern (Salzburg, Carinthia) 202
Maria Saal (Carinthia) 217 (I)
Maschlalm near Rauris (Salzburg) 160, 202
Matrei (North Tyrol) 166 (M)
Mauer a. d. Url (Lower Austria) 183
Mautern (Lower Austria) 182
Mitterberg near Bischofshofen (Salzburg) 19, 24, 243 (I)-245, 259, 261 (M)
Mondsee (Upper Austria) 17, 74, 267
Moosham by the Radstädter Tauern (Salzburg) see *Immurium*
Mühlbach see *Mitterberg*
Noreia (Styria?) 31
Ostriach (Carinthia) 227
Pass Lueg (Salzburg) 126 (I), 159, 193, 215
Pass Luftenstein (Salzburg) 159

Petronell (Lower Austria) see *Carnuntum*
Pfaffenhofen (North Tyrol) 140
Plöcken see under Italy
Pyhrn, pass (Upper Austria, Styria) 227
Radl, pass (Styria, Carinthia) 202
Radstädter Tauern (Salzburg) 58, 202, 217, 218, 225 (M), 227
Rauris (Salzburg) 161, 202, 248; see also *Maschlalm*
Rauriser Tauern (Salzburg, Carinthia) 202
Reisach (Carinthia) 133
Repolusthöhle near Mixnitz (Styria) 12
Reutte (North Tyrol) 211
Saalfelden (Salzburg) *Biberg* 88 (I), 89
Salzburg 19, 40, 41, 50, 57, 58, 63, 64, 77, 82, 83 (I), 85, 89, 92 (I), 101, 131, 133, 134, 175, 189, 193, 196, 213, 227, 236, 250, 267
Salzofenhöhle in the Toten Gebirge (Styria) 12
St Georgen a. St. (Lower Austria) 127
St Peter in Holz (Carinthia) see *Teurnia*
Schwechat (Lower Austria) 211
Seefeld (North Tyrol) 211
Semmering, pass (Lower Austria, Styria) 236
Spital am Pyhrn (Upper Austria) 170 *(Höll)* 227
Steinberg on the Achensee (North Tyrol) 155, 175
Strasswalchen (Salzburg) 57
Strettweg (Styria) 26, 172, 173 (I), 174 (I), 202
Tauern 161, 209, 236
Telfes in the Stubai (North Tyrol) 155
Teurnia (Carinthia) 40, 50, 53, 54, 106, 140, 141, 186, 188, 191 (I), 209
Traunsee (Upper Austria) 74
Turracher Höhe, pass (Salzburg, Carinthia) 202
Ulrichsberg (Carinthia) 60, 106
Untersberg near Salzburg 91, 202
Uttendorf (Salzburg) 24, 122 (I), 122
Vienna 9, 40, 57, 131, 211
Villach (Carinthia) 22, 145, 202
Virunum near Klagenfurt (Carinthia) 40, 41, 54, 90, 91, 92, 131, 135, 136, 217 (I), 227
Volders (North Tyrol) 122
Warmbad Villach (Carinthia) 215
Wels (Upper Austria) 48, 91
Welzelach (East Tyrol) 24, 122, 166 (M), 205 (I 144 bottom), 245
Willendorf (Lower Austria) 149
Wimsbach (Upper Austria) 48, 227
Zedlach (East Tyrol) 24, 245
Zirl (North Tyrol) 48, 57, 211, 266

France

Aime-en-Tarentaise (Savoie) 36, 88, 131, 137, 186, 212
Aix-en-Provence (Bouches-du-Rhône) 31
Aix-les-Bains (Savoie) 132
Antibes (Alpes-Maritimes) 27, 133
Arles (Bouches-du-Rhône) 60, 98, 226
Beaulieu-sur-Mer (Alpes-Maritimes) 144
Bourg-St-Maurice (Savoie) 212
Briançon (Hautes-Alpes) 161
Brigantio near Aime (Savoie) 131
Chanoz-Curson (Drôme) 12
Chassey (Saône-et-Loire) 15
Chavignières-Avançon (Hautes-Alpes) 26
Cimiez see Nice
Col Bayard (Hautes-Alpes) 208
Col du Clapier (Savoie, Piedmont) 208
Col de la Forclaz du Prarion (Haute-Savoie) 36
Col de Fréjus (Savoie, Piedmont) 236
Col de Manse (Hautes-Alpes) 208
Conflans (Savoie) 220
Die (Drôme) 45 (I), 133
Entremont (Bouches-du-Rhône) 88
Fillinges (Haute-Savoie) 126 (I)
Fontaine (Isère) 113
Fréjus (Var) 53, 61, 96, 97, 107, 186
Gap (Hautes-Alpes) 208
Grenoble (Isère) 12, 62, 185, 208
Grotte du Vallonnet see Roquebrune – Cap Martin
La Balme (Isère) 113
Lac de Paladru (Isère) 74
Lac du Bourget (Isère) 74
La Côte-Saint-André (Isère) 26
La Turbie (Alpes-Maritimes) 37 (I)
Le Pègue (Drôme) 27, 86, 88
Lérins, island (Alpes-Maritimes) 53, 188
Les Plagnes near Chamonix (Savoie) 36
Little St Bernard (Savoie, Valle d'Aosta) 32, 37, 62, 93, 159, 195, 209, 212, 213, 214, 219 (I), 220 (I), 221
Luxeuil (Haute-Saône) 53, 188
Lyon (Rhône) 32, 34 (I), 52, 132, 133
Marseille (Bouches-du-Rhône) 27, 30, 60, 188, 197, 199, 260
Mont Bégo (Alpes-Maritimes) 165, 167, 168, 170
Mont-Blanc tunnel (Haute-Savoie, Valle d'Aosta)
Mont-Cenis, pass (Savoie, Piedmont) 61, 207, 234, 235, 236
Mont-Genèvre, pass (Hautes-Alpes, Piedmont) 33, 40, 161, 208, 209, 226

Narbonne (Aude) 30
Nice/Nizza (Alpes-Maritimes) 10, 27, 30, 36, 64, 69
Nîmes (Gard) 98
Orange (Vaucluse) 31, 98
Pallon (Hautes-Alpes) 160, 161
Pont du Gard near Remoulins (Gard) 95
Roquebrune – Cap-Martin (Alpes-Maritimes) 10, 11 (I), 67
Saint-Dalmas-de-Tende (Alpes-Maritimes) 10
Sainte-Colombe near Orpierre (Hautes-Alpes) 86
Sévrier (Haute-Savoie) 242 (I)
Vaison-la-Romaine (Vaucluse) 98
Vallée des Merveilles see *Mont Bégo*
Véria (Jura) 156
Vézeronce (Isère) 156
Vienne (Isère) 153, 155
Vinay (Isère) 12
Vix (Cote-d'Or) 203

Germany

Auerberg near Schongau (Upper Bavaria, Bav. Suebia) 88, 93, 152, 181 (I), 262
Augsburg (Bav. Suebia) 36, 40, 41, 48, 57, 61, 133, 134, 183, 208, 209, 213, 216 (I), 226, 228
Bad Reichenhall (Upper Bavaria) 31, 58, 82, 89, 141, 151, 152, 268
Constance, Lake of (Baden-Württemberg, Bavaria) 17
Damasia see Auerberg
Eggstädt (Upper Bavaria) 132f
Eining (Lower Bavaria) 40
Epfach (Bav. Suebia) *Abodiacum* 48, 57, 136, 137, 221
Fentbach (Upper Bavaria) 89
Freiburg i. B. (south Baden) 63
Füssen (Allgäu) 48, 57, 88, 209, 227, 266
Garmisch-Partenkirchen (Upper Bavaria) see Partenkirchen
Hirschlanden (north Württemberg) 203
Immenstadt (Allgäu) 211
Irschenberg (Upper Bavaria) 89
Isny (Allgäu) *Vemania* 45, 46, 48, 211
Karlstein (Upper Bavaria) 89, 260
Kempten (Allgäu) *Cambodunum* 40, 44 (I), 57, 92, 96 (I), 130, 178, 181, 182, 183, 262
Klais near Mittenwald (Upper Bavaria) see also Scharnitz 215, 216 (I), 230
Künzing (Lower Bavaria) 50, 266
Laufen (Upper Bavaria) 156
Lechfeld near Augsburg (Bav. Suebia) 61
Lindau (Allgäu) 235
Mainz (Rheinland-Palatinate) 38

Manching (Upper Bavaria) 88, 204
Marzoll (Upper Bavaria) 141
Mauer (north Baden) 10
Mittenwald (Upper Bavaria) 215, 226, 230
Moosberg near Murnau (Upper Bavaria) 48, 49 (I), 103
Munich (Upper Bavaria) 128, 213
Partenkirchen (Upper Bavaria) 57, 58, 141 (I), 211, 226, 230
Passau (Lower Bavaria) 50, 228, 266
Peiting (Upper Bavaria) 182
Piding-Mauthausen (Upper Bavaria) 244 (I)
Polling (Upper Bavaria) 240
Raisting (Upper Bavaria) 118 (I), 120
Regensburg (Upper Palatinate) 40, 41, 42 (M), 43, 62, 158, 228, 266
Reichenau (south Baden) 57, 189, 230
Rosenheim (Upper Bavaria) 156
Sachsenkam (Upper Bavaria) 59
Seebruck (Upper Bavaria) 134
Sonthofen (Allgäu) 211
Schäftlarn (Upper Bavaria) 61
Scharnitz, monastery in der (Upper Bavaria) 216 (I), 226, 230
Schlehdorf (Upper Bavaria) 230
Schwangau (Allgäu) 91
Unteruhldingen (south Baden) 71
Vemania see Isny
Walchensee (Upper Bavaria) 57
Wessling (Upper Bavaria) 48, 103

Hungary

Sopron 211

Italy

Albenga (Liguria) 53, 186
Algund (South Tyrol) 220
Altino/*Altinum* (Veneto) 134
Aosta (Valle d'Aosta) 17, 32 (I), 37, 39 (I), 40, 91, 93, 95 (I), 107, 113, 195 (I), 197, 198, 199, 208, 210 (I), 213, 214 (I), 215, 219 (I)
Aquileia (Venezia Giulia) 30, 41, 42 (M), 48, 89, 189, 203, 228, 248
Asiago (Veneto) 54
Bagnolo, Gde Malegno, Valcamonica (Lombardy) 167 (I)
Balzi Rossi near Ventimiglia (Liguria) 12, 149 (I)
Bellagio (Lombardy) 9 (M)
Belluno (Veneto) 166 (M)
Bobbio (Emilia-Romagna) 53
Bologna (Emilia-Romagna) 22, 27, 53, 130, 164, 165 (I 96 top), 166 (M)
Bolzano (South Tyrol) 57, 64, 151, 194, 204, 209, 221
Bormio (Lombardy) 157 (I)
Brenner, pass (North Tyrol, South Tyrol) 31, 40, 43, 57, 194, 201, 209,

211, 216 (I), 226, 228, 230, 234, 236–238
Brescia (Lombardy) 33, 36, 116, 133, 168
Brixen/Bressanone (South Tyrol) 62
Calalzo (Veneto) Lagole 152, 155 (I)
Canegrate (Lombardy) 22, 111, 122
Canossa (Emilia-Romagna) 61
Capo di Ponte, Valcamonica (Lombardy) 168, 169 (I)
Cemmo, Valcamonica (Lombardy) 4 (I), 168
Chiavenna (Lombardy) 193, 235
Civezzano (Trentino) 58, 141, 144 (I), 229
Cividale (Friuli) 52
Col du Clapier see under France
Col de Fréjus see under France
Col S. Angelo (Veneto) 202
Como (Lombardy) 9 (I), 22, 92, 107, 134, 166 (M), 193, 197, 198, 204, 205, 212, 221, 235
Concordia Sagittaria (Veneto) 133
Cremona (Lombardy) 30, 212 (I)
Cuorgne (Piedmont) 104
Défilé de Pierre-Taillée (Valle d'Aosta) 195 (I), 214 (I)
Derby (Valle d'Aosta) 213
Diémoz (Valle d'Aosta) 212
Domodossola (Piedmont) 237
Donnaz (Valle d'Aosta) 215
Eppan (South Tyrol) 166 (M)
Este (Veneto) 22, 27, 164, 166 (M), 176, 202
Exilles (Piedmont) 29
Feltre (Veneto) 209
Ferrara (Emilia-Romagna) 31
Fiavè (Trentino) 17, 71, 73 (I), 74, 240 (I), 240ff
Golasecca (Lombardy) 22, 27, 29, 120
Grado (Venezia Giulia) 189
Gratsch (South Tyrol) 116
Great St Bernard (Valais, Valle d'Aosta) 27, 28, 31, 33, 54, 61, 62, 64, 65 (I), 93, 157, 158 (I), 159, 183, 197, 199, 201, 204, 205, 208, 209, 221, 231, 232, 233, 235 (I), 236
Grimaldi see *Balzi Rossi*
Imola (Emilia-Romagna) 183
Innichen (South Tyrol) 59, 146, 189, 230
Invillino (Friuli) 53, 101, 104, 105 (I), 106, 107, 186, 187 (I), 188 (I), 229 (I)
Ivrea (Piedmont) 32
Jaufen, pass (South Tyrol) 194, 220
Jochgrimm (South Tyrol) 14
Klausen (South Tyrol) 58, 192 (I), 194
Kreuzbergsattel (South Tyrol) 202
Kunter gorge near Bolzano (South Tyrol) 201, 209, 235
La Chalp at the Monte Genevris (Piedmont) 152
Lago di Ledro (Trentino) 17, 74, 75 (I), 76 (I)

Làgole see Calalzo
Lagozza, Gde Besnate (Lombardy) 15
Laugen (South Tyrol) 22, 23 (M)
Lecco (Lombardy) 9 (M)
Little St Bernard see under France
Lodi (Lombardy) 212 (I)
Magenta (Lombardy) 64
Mantua/Mantova (Lombardy) 27, 64
Marling (South Tyrol) 220
Martignano (Trentino) 149, 150 (I)
Melaun (South Tyrol) 26, 27
Menaggio (Lombardy) 9 (M), 204
Merano (South Tyrol) 116, 194, 209, 219, 220
Milan (Lombardy) 22, 40, 43, 53, 63, 64, 122, 133, 212, 221, 226, 235, 236
Modena (Emilia-Romagna) 27, 30
Mont-Blanc tunnel see under France
Mont-Cenis see under France
Montebelluna (Veneto) 176
Monte Moro, pass (Valais, Piedmont) 236
Montesei di Serso (Trentino) 87 (I)
Mont-Genèvre see under France
Niederrasen (South Tyrol) 122
Novara (Piedmont) 53, 212
Novate (Lombardy) 236
Nus (Valle d'Aosta) 212
Obervintl (South Tyrol) 205
Oderzo (Veneto) 41, 42 (M)
Padua/Padova (Veneto) 202, 205
Parma (Emilia-Romagna) 27, 30
Partschins (South Tyrol) 219f
Pavia (Lombardy) 52, 56, 212
Pergine (Trentino) 126 (I)
Pfatten (South Tyrol) 122
Piacenza (Emilia-Romagna) 27, 30, 43, 212
Plöcken, pass (Carinthia, Friuli) 40, 53, 135, 184, 202, 209, 212, 228
Polada (Lombardy) 110
Pondel (Valle d'Aosta) 95 (I), 95
Quart (Valle d'Aosta) 212
Quarto Cagnino (Lombardy) 212 (I)
Quinto Romano (Lombardy) 212 (I)
Quinzano, Gde Verona (Veneto) 11
Rabland (South Tyrol) 209, 220
Ravenna (Emilia-Romagna) 30, 55, 228
Reiterjoch (South Tyrol) 14
Remedello (Lombardy) 116
Reschen(scheideck) (North Tyrol, South Tyrol) 40, 61, 208, 209, 227
Rimini (Emilia-Romagna) 30
Ritten above Bolzano (South Tyrol) 194
Riva (Trentino) 131
Rivoli (Veneto) 82, 229
Romagnano (Trentino) 117 (I), 118
Rubico, River (Marche) 32
Runaz (Valle d'Aosta) 213
Säben (South Tyrol) 57, 189, 192 (I)
Salurn (South Tyrol) 130
Sanzeno (Trentino) 78, 79 (I), 166 (M)
Schlern (South Tyrol) 151

Sellajoch (South Tyrol) 14
Senigallia (Marche) 30
Sette Comuni (Veneto) 54
Settimo Milanese (Lombardy) 212 (I)
Sirmione (Lombardy) 101, 102, 102 (I)
Solferino (Lombardy) 64
Spina (Emilia-Romagna) 27
Splügen see under Switzerland
Sterzing/Vipiteno (South Tyrol) 58, 184 (I), 189
Stilfser Joch (South Tyrol, Lombardy) 157 (I), 235
Susa (Piedmont) 29, 33, 33 (I), 36, 40, 92, 177 (I), 208, 227
Trento (Trentino) 54, 58, 61, 62, 63, 104, 107, 141, 149, 209
Treviso (Veneto) 211
Turin/Torino (Piedmont) 62, 63, 64, 205
Tyrol, castle (South Tyrol) 62, 63
Udine (Friuli) 202
Valcamonica (Lombardy) 4 (I), 33, 36, 80 (I), 116 (I), 167, 168, 169 (I), 170, 231
Vatte di Zambana (Trentino) 14
Venice/Venezia (Veneto) 47 (I), 134
Ventimiglia see *Balzi Rossi*
Vercelli (Piedmont) 212
Verona (Veneto) 11, 50, 62, 63, 91, 98, 99 (I), 102, 132, 209, 221
Villar Focchiardo (Piedmont) 61 (I)
Viverone (Piedmont) 194
Zuglio (Friuli) 135, 184, 212
Zurla, Valcamonica (Lombardy) 171 (I)

Jugoslavia

Bled (Slovenia) 141, 146
Celje (Slovenia) 40, 135, 211
Hrušica/Birnbaumer Wald, pass (Slovenia) 227
Ivenca (Slovenia) 211
Kranj (Slovenia) 141
Ljubljana 9, 26
Pula (Istria) 152
Ptuj (Slovenia) 183, 184
Škocjan (Slovenia) 126 (I)
Split (Dalmatia) 46
Vače (Slovenia) 25 (I), 163 (I), 166 (M)

Liechtenstein

Balzers, *Gutenberg* 153 (I)
Schaan 48, 227

Monaco

Monaco 10, 36, 37

Switzerland

Aigle (Vaud) 194
Alpnach (Obwalden) 98 (I)
Altdorf (Uri) 235
Andermatt (Uri) 194, 205, 234
Arbedo (Ticino) 119 (I), 124 (I), 204
Ardon (Valais) 185
Augst (Baselland) 38, 57, 208
Auvernier (Neuchâtel) 71, 73
Avenches (Vaud) 38, 43, 183
Bad Ragaz (St Gallen) 194
Basel 38
Bellinzona (Ticino) 106, 204, 228, 232, 235
Bern 11, 63, 160
Berschis (St Gallen) 106
Berslingen (Schaffhausen) 106f, 107 (I)
Biel-Mett (Bern) 139, 185
Bonaduz (Graubünden) 52, 112, 113 (I), 138, 139 (I), 140, 265 (I)
Bourg-Saint-Pierre (Valais) 213 (I), 232
Brig (Valais) 237
Brugg (Aargau) 62: see also Windisch
Bülach (Zurich) 140
Carschenna near Sils (Graubünden) 170, 172 (I)
Casaccia (Graubünden) 193, 215, 232
Castaneda (Graubünden) 160 (I)
Castiel (Graubünden) 103, 140, 266
Cazis (Graubünden) 79, 80, 82
Châtillon-sur-Glâne (Fribourg) 86, 196, 199, 201 (I), 203, 204
Chiasso (Ticino) 9 (I)
Chilchli, Simmental (Bern) 11
Chillon (Vaud) 194
Chur (Graubünden) 11, 48, 52, 57, 80, 81 (I), 82, 98, 103, 106, 107, 140, 186, 188, 194, 196, 197, 221, 227, 232, 235
Col des Mosses (Vaud) 194, 195, 199
Cornans (Fribourg) 156
Cortaillod (Neuchâtel) 15
Crestaulta, Gde Lumbrein (Graubünden) 20, 79, 80, 81, 121, 122, 197, 198 (I)
Cunter/Caschligns (Graubünden) 246 (I)
Daversco-Soragno (Ticino) 108 (I)
Davos (Graubünden) 160, 196
Diesrut, pass (Graubünden) 197, 227, 231
Disentis (Graubünden) 61, 106, 230, 232, 234, 236
Domat/Ems (Graubünden) 232
Drachenloch see Vättis
Egolzwil (Lucerne) 71
Erstfeld (Uri) 29 (I), 160, 161 (I), 205
Felsberg (Graubünden) 160 (I)
Flüela, pass (Graubünden) 196
Freiburg im Üechtland/Fribourg 63

Geneva 31, 36, 38, 52, 53, 61, 63, 88, 107, 139, 156, 185, 194, 199, 221
Giubiasco (Ticino) 176 (I)
Gondo (Valais) 194, 236
Göschenen (Uri) 194
Grächwil, Gde Meikirch (Bern) 28 (I)
Great St Bernard see under Italy
Greina pass (Graubünden, Ticino) 197, 227, 231
Habsburg (Aargau) 62
Horgen (Zurich) 17
Ilanz see Ruschein
Illnau (Zurich) 204
Irgenhausen (Zurich) 51 (I)
Julier, pass (Graubünden) 40, 80, 159, 197, 209, 215, 221, 227, 228
Kaiseraugst (Aargau) 184
Kunkels pass (Graubünden) 141, 194, 227, 230
La Porta im Bergell (Graubünden) 193
La Tène, Gde Marin-Epagnier (Neuchâtel) 25, 28, 29, 82, 125, 156, 205 (I), 252 (I)
Lausanne (Vaud) 97
Lenzburg (Aargau) 113
Lötschberg tunnel (Bern, Valais) 236
Lukmanier, pass (Graubünden, Ticino) 227, 228, 230, 231, 233, 233 (I), 234
Lumbrein see *Crestaulta*
Maladers (Graubünden) *Tummihügel* 81, 81 (I), 82, 229
Maloja, pass (Graubünden) 193, 197, 209, 215, 232
Malvaglia (Ticino) 227
Martigny (Valais) 36, 40, 92, 97, 157, 184, 197, 199, 204, 230
Mesocco (Graubünden) 14, 106
Mistail, Gde Alvaschein (Graubünden) 230
Monte Moro, pass see under Italy
Morgarten (Schwyz) 63
Murtensee (Vaud, Fribourg) 77
Müstair (Graubünden) 56 (I), 196, 230
Neuchâtel, Lake (Neuchâtel, Vaud, Bern, Fribourg) 25, 77
Nyon (Vaud) 38, 133, 221
Oberalppass (Graubünden) 230
Ofenpass (Graubünden) 196
Orbe (Vaud) 101
Pfäfers (St Gallen) 189, 196, 230
Plaffeien (Fribourg) 121 (I)
Port (Bern) 128 (I)
Ramosch (Graubünden) 87
Rhäzüns (Graubünden) 140
Riaz (Fribourg) 182 (I), 185 (I), 250 (I)
Riva San Vitale (Ticino) 53, 186
Robenhausen (Zurich) 79
Ruschein (Graubünden) 231, 231 (I)

Saas-Fee (Valais) 237
Sagens/Sagogn (Graubünden) 106
Saint-Maurice d'Agaune (Valais) 53, 59 (I), 61, 139, 144, 145 (I), 188, 189, 229, 232
Saint-Sulpice (Vaud) 250
San Bernardino, pass (Graubünden) 194, 197, 209
St Gallen 11, 189, 230
St Gotthard (Uri, Ticino) 63, 161, 194, 205, 234, 235, 236
St Moritz (Graubünden) 152, 154 (I), 193
Sargans (St Gallen) 40
Savognin (Graubünden) 80
Schalunen (Bern) 160
Schiers (Graubünden) 140, 259 (I)
Schnurenloch, Simmental (Bern) 11
Schöllenen gorge (Uri) 161 (I), 194, 205, 234
Scuol (Graubünden) 166 (M)
Seeb (Zurich) 40, 68 (I), 100 (I), 101
Seeberg-Burgäschi (Bern) 149
Septimer, pass (Graubünden) 197, 209, 227, 232, 235
Simplon, pass (Valais) 194, 235, 236, 237
Sion (Valais) 19, 19 (I), 54, 57, 113, 114 (I), 115 (I), 116, 170, 189 (I)
Solduno (Ticino) 130
Solothurn 183
Spiez (Bern) 80 (I), 140, 151 (I)
Splügen, pass and village (Graubünden, Lombardy) 40, 160, 160 (I), 193, 197, 224, 232, 235, 259 (I)
Stabio (Ticino) 108 (I), 140, 143 (I), 190 (I)
Strela pass (Graubünden) 196
Tamins (Graubünden) 112, 122, 141, 194, 204, 229
Thayngen (Schaffhausen) 149 (I)
Thun (Bern) 249 (I)
Thusis (Graubünden) 106
Trins (Graubünden) 106
Trun (Graubünden) 106
Tuggen (Schwyz) 140
Ursins (Vaud) 186f (I)
Vättis (St Gallen) 11, 148, 196, 227
Via Mala (Graubünden) 194, 197, 235
Vinelz (Bern) 16 (I), 18 (I)
Vrin (Graubünden) 197
Vuadens (Fribourg) 21 (I)
Walensee (Glarus, St Gallen) 57
Wildenmannlisloch in the Churfirsten 148
Wildkirchli by the Säntis (St Gallen) 11
Windisch (Aargau) 36
Winterthur (Zurich) 46
Yverdon (Vaud) 71, 73, 92
Zernez (Graubünden) 196
Zurich 40, 57, 204